The Mahābhārata

Book 4 *The Book of Virāṭa*

Book 5 *The Book of the Effort*

The

The University of Chicago Press   Chicago and London

Mahābhārata

Translated and
Edited by
J. A. B. van Buitenen

4 *The Book of Virāṭa*

5 *The Book of the Effort*

The University of Chicago Press, Chicago 60637
The University of Chicago Press, Ltd., London

93 92 91 90 89 88 87 86 85   10 9 8 7 6 5 4 3 2

Library of Congress Cataloging in Publication Data
Mahābhārata. English.
The Mahābhārata.
Includes bibliographical references.
CONTENTS: v. 1. The book of the beginning. v. 2. The book of the assembly hall. The book of the forest. v. 3. The book of Virāṭa. The book of the effort.
I. Buitenen, Johannes Adrianus Bernardus van, tr.
PK3633.A2B8   294.5'923   72-97802
ISBN 0-226-84650-4 (cloth)
0-226-84665-2 (paper)

The relief sculpture on the title page, dating from the second half of the fifth century A.D., depicts Nara and Nārāyaṇa in Viṣṇu temple, Deogarh, U.P., India. Photo by courtesy of Pramod Chandra.

The publication of this work has been assisted by a subvention from the Institute of Traditional Science, Haven O'More, Director.

Contents

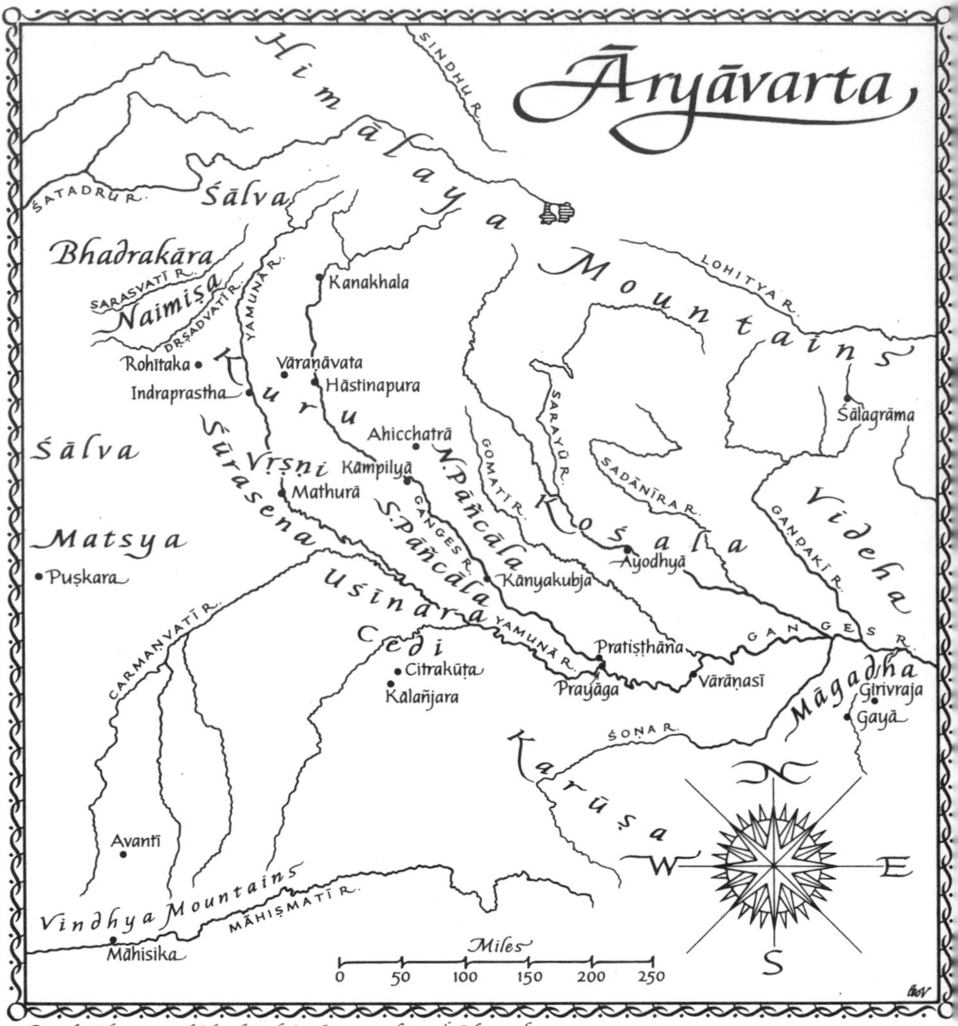

Based on "The Historical Atlas of South Asia", courtesy of Joseph Schwartzberg, Department of Geography, The University of Minnesota

Preface

The present volume carries the translation of the *Mahābhārata* well beyond the first third of the text but not yet up to the mid-way point; that happy marker will be reached somewhere in the middle of the *Droṇaparvan* in the next volume.

At this point it is becoming possible to be more specific about the contents of future volumes. Volume IV will comprise *MBh.* 6 and 7, the books of *Bhīṣma* and *Droṇa*; Volume V *MBh.* 8–11, the books of *Karṇa*, *Śalya*, the *Night Attack*, and the *Women*; Volume VI *MBh.* 12, the book of the *Peace*; Volume VII *MBh.* 13–18, the books of *Instructions*, the *Horse Sacrifice*, the *Hermitage*, the *Clubs*, the *Great Journey*, and the *Ascent to Heaven*. The sizes of the Volumes will vary, the most massive being Volume VI, if indeed it is decided to incorporate the entire *Śāntiparvan* within a single volume.

It is more difficult to be precise about dates of publication. It is clear that the pace of publishing three volumes within a period of six years cannot be kept up. Moreover, this pace is only apparent, since the work for Volume I, which saw the light of day in 1973, was started in late 1967, and the three volumes that have appeared so far represent the labor of nine years. I doubt whether it will be feasible to publish Volume IV before 1980. But by that time most of the work on Volume VI will have been done so that both Volume V and Volume VI can be expected by 1983, and Volume VII within a reasonable time thereafter.

Even then, more will need to be done. While I hope that work can be started sooner, if scholarly and financial support is forthcoming, there will remain the chores of indexing, thematic bibliographies, *addenda et corrigenda*, and other residual matters, which so far I have deliberately left for a later volume when the principal task, that of the translation itself, will have been completed.

While I am filled with hope that a great deal of the burden of such a volume will be lightened by the assistance of co-workers, I shall reserve for myself the more congenial obligation to sum up, in a concluding essay, what I have over the years been able to learn from the *Mahābhārata* about its being and its purposes. I have already learned from the *Mahābhārata* to cultivate the patience not to hurry that day.

Once more I have the pleasant duty to speak of my gratitude to my colleagues, students, reviewers, and publisher. While this enterprise, by the very nature of its complexity and time span, cannot really be shared, as a favorite book can be shared between people who have read it time and again, the interest of others in this venture of many years has been most encouraging to me. And I see the first signs of what is the ultimate satisfaction of the scholar: that his work is being used by others for purposes of study that lay beyond his scope, and indeed his competence.

Finally let me say a word of special thanks to Haven O'More, who has subsidized the publication. His kind of support is perhaps the purest form of philanthropy. His financial contributions do not in any material way benefit either me, or the University of Chicago Press, or himself. Only the reader profits from them, and that unwittingly, by the lower price of the book that he purchases. Thus, in a very immediate sense, Mr. O'More's support has not only helped the publication of the *Mahābhārata* but substantially increased its distribution.

Chicago, February 1977 J. A. B. van B.

The Mahābhārata

Translated

Book 4 *The Book of Virāṭa*

Introduction

The Pāṇḍavas' Masquerade

"The instants are joined together," remarks Bhīṣma sagely, "and so are the hours, days, fortnights, months, lunar houses, planets, seasons, and years: thus the wheel of time revolves with the divisions of time."[1] This observation is delivered on the occasion when the issue is raised whether the Pāṇḍavas have indeed completed the thirteen years of the exile which they had covenanted at the end of *The Book of the Assembly Hall.* It is not an easy matter to determine this, and the patriarch of the clan, grandsire of Pāṇḍavas and Kauravas alike, is called upon to give his authoritative decision.

"Because of an excess of time," he proceeds, "and the deviation of the luminaries, there are two additional months every five years." The ancient Indians observed a combined solar and lunar year—with the inevitable "deviation" of sun and moon—of 360 days, distributed over twelve months of 30 days each. This falls over 5 days short of the real year, which has 365 days, 5 hours, 48 minutes and 46 seconds. In order to bring every cycle of five years—a *yuga*—back into line, the *Jyotiṣa,* our oldest Indian source on astronomy,[2] adopts a complicated system whereby five years is equal to sixty-two months of $29\frac{16}{31}$ days each, the two additional months being intercalary. It is this system which Bhīṣma follows. He continues: "So I calculate that to thirteen years there are five additional months and 12 days." He comes to this conclusion by dividing the thirteen into two *yugas*

1. 4.47.1 ff.

2. *Jyotiṣa* = *Vedānga,* a comparatively late text (200 B.C.?) that purports to continue the *Vedánga* (Vedic Auxiliary) of the same name, whose purpose it was to aid in computing the proper dates of Vedic rituals.

of five years, which require four intercalary months, and one half *yuga*, requiring one more month, giving a total of five. This leaves a final half year to be accounted for. According to the *Jyotiṣa* rule this half year would require only 6 additional days, not 12 as Bhīṣma avers, but apparently he treats the last half year, beginning after the intercalary months inserted at midpoint in the *yuga*, i.e., after two and a half years, as already requiring the 12 days that the entire year needs.

It is interesting to note that the Pāṇḍavas do not seem to need these complicated calculations. While one might well have expected them to count the days until their hardships were over, there is no talk of it. Presumably with his superior wisdom, Yudhiṣṭhira merely had to glance at the stars as we look at the calendar.[3]

At the final game of dice it was stipulated that the loser would spend twelve years in the forest and a thirteenth year unrecognized in the open. If the loser *were* recognized, he would have to return to the forest for another twelve years.[4] It is a curious stipulation, which has led some scholars[5] to assume that this thirteenth year is not original and that *The Book of Virāṭa* is a later addition to the *Bhārata*. This may or may not be the case—we shall return to this question—but the matter is now of little interest. What is of interest is that there *is* this *Book*, and it must have been felt to function within the sequence of the *Mahābhārata*.

Whenever in ancient India the number twelve appears as a unit of time, one must irresistibly connect it with the twelve-month year. Countless are the passages in which the twelvefold nature of the year is stressed. It is therefore hard, if not impossible, not to assume that the twelve years are based on the twelve months and that the entire span is a sort of *grand year*. In *The Book of the Forest* Bhīma notes that in the *Veda* a month can stand for a year, and the group might as well adopt this convenient equation and leave the forest *now*.[6] Contrariwise, a year might well stand for a "month" of a "year" of twelve years.[7]

When we take this view, this thirteenth year becomes far more intriguing than if we simply regard the thirteen as a baker's dozen. It becomes the hinge between one completed term and the next one, with the liminality that in European folklore is associated with the Eleven Nights. In India, however, the New Year did not begin on the

3. The disguises of the thirteenth year are kept up till 4.65, when Yudhiṣṭhira is identified by Arjuna.

4. 2.67.8 ff.

5. Cf. below, "On the lateness of *The Book of Virāṭa*," p. 18.

6. 3.36.31 f.

7. If a *yuga* is a cycle of five years in the older reckoning, another well-known cycle, the sixty-year *Bṛhaspati*, or Jovian cycle, could similarly be regarded as a *yuga* of five grand years of twelve years each.

first of January; it began in the spring month of Phālguna. And there can be little doubt that then as today the transition from one year to another was observed by a peculiar celebration.

Today the celebration is the Holī festival, the Indian form of saturnalia, in which, in the words of one acute observer, "insubordinate libido inundate[s] all established hierarchies of age, sex, caste, wealth and power."[8] In classical India, as it is filtered through the Sanskrit texts,[9] it was the festival of Kāma, when a happy carnival promiscuity was, surely in the most satisfying fashion, supposed to contribute to the fertility of the year that was about to begin anew.

The licentious side of the masquerade of *The Book of Virāṭa* is understated, although it is there. But there are so many other elements in it that correspond to the temporary role reversals associated with the Spring and Holī festivals, that it is at least worthwhile, if not enlightening, to look upon it in that light.

The New Personae

The obligation to live unrecognized but in the open required that the Pāṇḍavas disguise themselves. Earlier Bhīma had justifiably voiced doubt about whether that was possible at all—"I see me disguised like Mount Meru!"[10] This must have occurred to other Indians, and as so often someone helpfully, if clumsily, has provided a sort of solution by invoking no other than the God Dharma himself appearing as a Yakṣa in the form of a crane, and letting the god bestow on them the boon that they will go unrecognized and their appearance will conform to the roles they adopt.[11]

In fact there is fortunately no evidence that their appearance was indeed changed, as was Nala's when he was changed into a hunchback.[12] They work hard at hanging on to their disguises, however intolerable that at one time becomes.[13] Even Arjuna, however preposterous and risqué his *masque*, still shows the scars of the bowstring on his wrists.[14]

8. McKim Marriott, "The Feast of Love," in Milton Singer, ed., *Krishna: Myths, Rites and Attitudes* (Honolulu, 1966), pp. 200 ff.

9. J. J. Meyer, *Trilogie altindischer Mächte und Feste der Vegetation* (Zürich–Leipzig, 1937), *I: Kāma.*

10. 3.36.27.

11. 3.298.18 f. As though this were still not enough, a later text tradition added a further boon from the Goddess Durgā in response to Yudhiṣṭhira's apocryphal *Durgāstava*: see below, p. 19.

12. 3.63.1 ff.

13. Notably at Draupadī's molestation: 4.15.

14. 4.2.21.

There is a distinct tone of hilarity in the first chapter of *Virāṭa*, when the Pāṇḍavas discuss what roles they will adopt. Here it is illuminating to quote at length McKim Marriott describing the Holī he experienced.

> Who was that "King of the Holī" riding backward on the donkey? It was an older boy of high caste, a famous bully, put there by his organized victims (but seeming to relish the prominence of his disgrace).
>
> Who was in that chorus singing so lustily in the potter's lane? Not just the resident caste fellows, but six washermen, a tailor, and three Brahmans joined each year for this day only in an idealistic musical company patterned on the friendship of the gods.
>
> Who were those transfigured "cowherds" heaping mud and dust on all the leading citizens? They were the water carrier, two young Brahman priests, and a barber's son, avid experts in the daily routines of purification.
>
> Whose household temple was festooned with goat's bones by unknown merrymakers? It was the temple of the Brahman widow who had constantly harrassed neighbors and kinsmen with actions at law.
>
> In front of whose house was a burlesque dirge being sung by a professional ascetic of the village? It was the house of a very much alive moneylender, notorious for his punctual collections and his insufficient charities.
>
> Who was it who had his head fondly anointed, not only with handfuls of the sublime red powders, but also with a gallon of diesel oil? It was the village landlord, and the anointer was his cousin and archrival, the policeman of Kishan Garhi.
>
> Who was it who was made to dance in the streets, fluting like Lord Krishna, with a garland of old shoes around his neck? It was I, the visiting anthropologist, who had asked far too many questions, and had always to receive respectful answers.[15]

"And what will you do, King Pāṇḍava?" asks Arjuna two thousand years earlier. "How will you pass through this misfortune that has befallen you?"

"Hear ye, scions of Kuru, what work I shall do!" Yudhiṣṭhira replies. "I shall be the Royal Dicing Master of the king!"

"Wolf-Belly," he continues, "what kind of a job will you play at?"

"I shall be a kitchen chef and wait on King Virāṭa. I'll make him curries! I am good in a kitchen."

"What shall Arjuna do?" asks Yudhiṣṭhira.

"Sire, I'll be a transvestite! I'll hang rings from my ears that sparkle like fire, and my head shall sport a braid!"

"Nakula, what will you do?"

"I shall be King Virāṭa's horse groom."

15. Marriott, p. 211 f.

"Sahadeva, how will you amuse yourself at Virāṭa's?"
"I shall be the cow teller of King Virāṭa. Don't worry, I'll do quite well!"[16]
"And what will Draupadī do?"
"I'll call myself a chambermaid with a skill in hairdressing."

These are remarkable choices of roles with the carnival spirit of insanity only mildly tempered by an Indian brand of rationalization. For Yudhiṣṭhira to wish to become the King's Own Master of Games requires a certain extent of humorous distance from his own fateful "flaw" which, as Draupadī and Bhīma have so relentlessly reminded him,[17] brought them all this misery. It is like a reformed drunk electing to become a bartender. But, and it is here that the Indian rationalization comes in, the sage Bṛhadaśva had bestowed on him the "heart of the dice," after telling him the story of Nala.[18] Not that Yudhiṣṭhira seems to have won a lot in his new role, for he is popular among the courtiers.[19]

Bhīma, who is not for nothing called a Wolf-Belly, and who according to his mother "always eats much" and should be accorded half the family's food,[20] chooses to cook the food that others eat—although there are no doubt leftovers.[21] Also he will act as king's wrestler and gladiator: he who killed only to preserve the safety and fortune of the family will wrestle wild animals for the entertainment of the ladies of the sérail.[22]

Arjuna, superman, diademed hero, left-handed archer, son of Indra, he, Jiṣṇu, Guḍākeśa, Vijaya, will become an effeminate dance teacher whom it is perfectly safe to let go among nubile daughters of the court. But of course, Citrasena the Gandharva himself had taught him while he was whiling away five years in Indra's heaven.[23]

Compared with those of their elder brother, the choices of the twins are pedestrian. Nakula chooses to become King Virāṭa's stable master, and Sahadeva the king's cow teller. These are typical *vaiśya* trades, which puts us in mind of the fact that the two younger brothers do not enjoy exactly the same status as the three older ones. It may be recalled that they were the sons of Pāṇḍu by his second and junior wife Mādrī, who herself was not, like Kuntī, won at a *svayaṃvara* (which in the epic seems to be a status symbol for highborn women), but merely purchased from her family.[24] She became the unwilling

16. 4.1.15–3.1 ff.
17. 3.28 ff.
18. 3.77.15 ff.
19. 4.12.1 ff.
20. 1.184.6.
21. 4.12.5.
22. 4.12.25; 18.1 ff.
23. 3.45.1 ff.
24. 1.105.1–5.

cause of her husband Pāṇḍu's death, and, as the first *satī* of record, followed him into death.[25] Cattle tending and horse training are obviously trades that Nakula and Sahadeva followed before in Yudhiṣṭhira's kingdom, and their choices are less *carnavalesque* than those of the others.

Of particular interest is Draupadī's choice. There was no social niche for a wellborn woman outside the bounds of the family as daughter, wife, and mother. Outside these family bounds she was literally and figuratively a loose woman. Characteristically Yudhiṣṭhira begins his question to Draupadī with: "Now this is our beloved wife, who is dearer to us than our lives, as a mother to be protected, as an elder sister to be honored."[26] It is with no regrets at all but pride that her seniormost husband declares that "she does not know the work that women do. From the day she was born the radiant woman has had knowledge but of garlands, perfumes, ornaments, and all manner of clothing."[27]

In Draupadī's case the skewness lies not so much in the choice of occupation, but in the self-imposed isolation from her husbands. She, the wife who had gone through everything with her husbands and in the process suffered grievous humiliation—still unavenged—and extreme hardships, the wife who easily could have waited out the exile in comfort at her father Drupada's court in Pāñcāla (as Subhadrā, Arjuna's wife, is still doing at Dvārakā),[28] who had let go of her children to stay with the Pāṇḍavas in the forest,[29] she must now pretend not even to know them. One imagines that she might well have declared herself to be the wife of one of her husbands—though that might have shown an unwanted partiality. But she is made to prefer a life apart.

The occupation she chooses is that of a lady's maid; in spite of Yudhiṣṭhira's opinion, she *does* discover in herself a talent for hairdressing. The word I have translated as "chambermaid" is in Sanskrit *sairaṃdhrī*. The word belongs to a group with the variations of *sairaṃdhra*, *sairiṃdha*, and *sairiṃdhra*, and appears to be a Sanskritization of a loan from a non-Aryan source. The fact that *sairiṃdha* is recorded makes the traditional derivation from **siram-dhra* unlikely in the extreme; this word could mean "plowholder" but is not attested. The *Sairaṃdhras/Sairiṃdhas/*

25. 1.116.
26. 4.3.12.
27. 4.3.13.
28. 3.23.44 f., where Kṛṣṇa takes Subhadrā and Abhimanyu to Dvārakā. In 3.23.47 Dhṛṣṭaketu of Cedi takes "his sister" to his city Śuktimatī; she is apparently "Kareṇuvatī of the Cedis," junior wife of Nakula in 1.90.87, otherwise unknown. Clearly there was an exodus of all wives except Draupadī.
29. 3.23.46, where Dhṛṣṭadyumna takes his sister Draupadī's sons to his city in Pāñcāla; they do not reappear till 5.1.6.

Sairiṃdhras are known as a people. Manu folds them into the caste system by making a Sairaṃdhra the son of a *dasyu* and an *ayogava* woman;[30] the latter is herself the issue of a *śūdra* father and a *vaiśya* mother.[31] That a *dasyu* is supposed to be the father indicates that the Sairaṃdhras, etc., were an aboriginal tribe, not necessarily of agriculturalists. My own inclination would be to connect the name with *śilindhra, silindhra* "mushroom," also a borrowed word in Sanskrit, so that the Sairindhras might be a tribe of mushroom gatherers or eaters, whose women, as so often with tribals, enjoyed a freedom unusual among caste women. As a tribal woman, Draupadī would not provoke incredulity and shock when asserting that she had five husbands, for certain northern tribes did practice polyandry.[32] These husbands, she says, are Gandharvas. Since she is not questioned about the remarkable fact that she, a low-born woman, hardly within the caste system, should be wedded to supernatural beings of great beauty and artistry, it is likely that these Gandharvas were understood as wandering minstrels with a fancy title.

That the Pāṇḍavas assume new names as part of their disguises is, of course, the most obvious precaution. The reasons behind the names are, however, by no means obvious. Yudhiṣṭhira calls himself Kanka, which is the name for a heron.[33] May that be in memory of the crane in which God Dharma manifested himself to Yudhiṣṭhira at the end of *The Book of the Forest?*[34] Bhīma's new name is Ballava, not a very common word for "cowherd." Arjuna goes under the name Bṛhannaḍā, which is a feminine; it is interesting to note that though Arjuna parades as a eunuch with at least the appearance of a man, he adopts a feminine name. Even if we do not know "what name Achilles bore among the women," we have Arjuna's. The name means "large reed," or "having a large reed"; it is likely to be a joke that he who condemns himself to an effeminate life is endowed with a large reed.

Nakula adopts the name of Granthika. This is a word for a narrator, a bard, who "knots" stories together—*granthi* is a word for "knot." But since Nakula's new calling is that of a horse groom, the name has probably to do with an ability to knot the harness of a

30. Manu 10.32 describes the *sairandhra* as being skilled in such services as *prasādhana* "beauty care," as living in servitude though not a slave, and as living by trapping.

31. Manu 10.12: the *āyogava* is born from a *kṣatriya* father and a *śudra* mother.

32. I am rather doubtful about this representation, but nothing else makes much more sense. Sairaṃdhrī's claim to five husbands would have been a giveaway otherwise.

33. The only real Kanka that the *MBh.* mentions is a Vṛṣṇi prince; cf. 1.1.173; 177.18.

34. 1.295.10 ff.

horse properly and securely.[35] The occupational reference of Sahadeva's name is the clearest of all: Tantipāla, which literally means "guardian, or holder, of the *tanti*," a rope to which calves are tied by means of shorter ropes, so that one can lead a row of them at once. Sairaṃdhrī functions as the name of Draupadī.

While it is not remarkable that the Pāṇḍavas go under assumed names it is intriguing that that is not enough: Yudhiṣṭhira also gives them a new set of *secret* names. It is well known that at the naming ceremony the Indian child received a public and a secret name, the latter one controlling his inner essence. It may be an extension of this custom that at the present "naming ceremony" a new secret name is added. It may also be further testimony that the Pāṇḍavas are "literally" not themselves any more. It may also be a simple recognition signal if they are to be called without others being the wiser. It is as such that the secret names function the only time they are used. When Draupadī is dragged to the cremation ground, she cries out: "Jaya, Jayanta, Vijaya, Jayatsena, Jayadbala, listen to me!"[36] and Bhīma pays immediate heed. All the names have to do with *jaya* "victory." And, secret or not, Vijaya is one of Arjuna's ten real names.[37]

Life at the Court of Virāṭa

The Matsyas (for Sanskrit likes to call a country by the name of its people) are a prosperous country west of the river Yamunā in what is at present the state of Rajasthan. It is famed today for its magnificent cattle, and so it was in Virāṭa's days. King Virāṭa is a cattle baron, and his cattle will be very much in evidence in this *Book*. Curiously we do not learn the name of his capital;[38] the only city named is Upaplavya, where the Pāṇḍavas set up headquarters in preparation for the war with the Kauravas. It is a strange omission: perhaps knowledge was too vague about even this close-by country, but more likely it is accidental that the capital is not referred to by name.

Virāṭa himself is sketched humorously. He is a gullible cattle baron, who not only is taken in completely by the Pāṇḍavas, but keeps offering his kingdom to them. He is not very bright: when a raiding party of Trigartas begins to rustle his cows, he goes at them with his entire force, without leaving any reserves in the city in case of a second raid. He is so proud of his son Uttara that when

35. He is also called Dāmagranthi "knotter of the girth," in 4.18.32.
36. 4.22.12 ff.
37. 4.39.8.
38. It is simply called "Virāṭa's city."

Yudhiṣṭhira keeps insisting that it must have been Bṛhannaḍā who defeated the Kauravas, not Uttara, he flies into a rage and throws the dice in Yudhiṣṭhira's face.[39]

He is married to Sudeṣṇā, by whom he has at least one daughter, Uttarā. Sudeṣṇā at first is unwilling to employ Draupadī as her maid, because she is afraid that Virāṭa will be infatuated with her.[40] There are probably co-wives, for the women's quarters seem to be well populated and provide an appreciative audience for Bhīma's gladiatorial fights with wild animals, which upset Draupadī greatly.[41]

Sudeṣṇā herself is the sister of Kīcaka, the marshal of King Virāṭa and a member of the *sūta* caste. Kīcaka is a powerful man in Matsya: he brags to Draupadī that he is the real power in the land,[42] and that there is substance to his boast is borne out by the fact that once the report of his death reaches Hāstinapura, a cattle raid is immediately proposed[43] and undertaken. His caste fellows, also called Kīcakas, or Upa-Kīcakas, form a powerful faction in the city, for after Kīcaka's killing they band together and prevail upon the king to have Draupadī burn with him.[44]

All the Pāṇḍavas have their proper place in Virāṭa's establishment. Yudhiṣṭhira is habitually in the Hall, where he gambles with king and courtiers. Bhīma works and sleeps in the kitchen, Arjuna lives in the sérail, and works in the dance pavilion, a loosely guarded structure apparently outside the women's quarters. Nakula and Sahadeva are out in the fields or the stables. Draupadī, of course, is by Sudeṣṇā.

In spite of their priest Dhaumya's dark warnings about the hazards of court life (one of the few occasions that the worthy *purohit* speaks up), which hardly seem to apply to Virāṭa's simple establishment, the Pāṇḍavas seem to be comfortable enough. But Draupadī is not. This princess of Pāñcāla is an extremely proud lady on whom the servitude of her husbands and herself grates painfully. Not only that, she has the misfortune to be noticed by Kīcaka, who, with a measure of collusion by Sudeṣṇā, keeps importuning her. This is the subject of *The Killing of Kīcaka*, the second of the Minor Books of *The Book of Virāṭa*.

The Killing of Kīcaka

It is one of the more curious features of the *Mahābhārata* that, in spite of the important role of Draupadī in the development of the

39. 4.63.35 ff.
40. 4.8.1 ff.
41. 4.18.1 ff.
42. 4.21.9.
43. 4.29.1 ff.
44. 4.22.1 ff.

narrative, so little stress is laid on the fact that she must have been an extremely desirable woman. It is as though the authors, once saddled with a polyandrous marriage, thereupon tried, and very successfully at that, to direct our attention away from its implications. The fruits of her marriage, the five Draupadeyas, are rather carefully kept out of our sight, and when the war breaks out, collectively eliminated.[45] Except when Yudhiṣṭhira is about to stake her,[46] no words of love are heard. It is not until *The Killing of Kīcaka* that she is actually held in a husband's arms.[47]

Yudhiṣṭhira muses (2.58.33 ff.): "She is not too short or too tall, not too black or too red, and her eyes are red with love. . . . Eyes like the petals of autumn lotuses, a fragrance as of autumn lotuses, a beauty that waits on autumn lotuses—the peer of the Goddess of fortune! . . . Last she lies down who was the first to wake up, who knows what was done or left undone, down to the cowherds and goatherds. Her sweaty lotuslike face shines like a lotus. Her waist shaped like an altar, hair long, eyes the color of copper—such is the woman . . . the beautiful Draupadī!" Upon which he gambles her away.

This expression of love is not only rare but unique. Were it not for the infatuation of other men one might forget that she is not only a very strong but also a very beautiful woman. When King Jayadratha of Sindhu sets eyes upon her in the forest he exclaims: "Whose is this woman of flawless limbs, if she is human at all? There is no point for me to marry now that I have seen this superbly beautiful lady! It is she I shall take and return to my kingdom! Go and find out, my friend, whose she is, who she is, and from where. Why has this woman of the lovely brow come to the thorny forest? Will this gem of the world with the comely curves, the perfect teeth, the long eyes, the slender waist, share my love today? Shall my desires be fulfilled by my obtaining this choicest of women?"[48]

Queen Sudeṣṇā, consort of Virāṭa, is equally impressed and not a little apprehensive: "Your heels are flat, your thighs are full . . . your hair is fine, your nipples are pretty, you are shapely, with full breasts and buttocks, you are endowed with every grace like a filly from Kashmir! Your eyelashes curl nicely, your lips are like *bimba* berries, your waist is slender, your throat lined like a conchshell, your veins are hidden, and your face is like the full moon." She continues: "I would lodge you on my own head, if I did not suspect that the king would go to you with all his heart! Look, all the women in the

45. 10.8.
46. 2.58.32 ff.
47. 4.20.36.
48. 3.248.12 ff.

palace and those in my quarters stare at you in fascination—what man would you not infatuate? Look at the trees that stand firm in my quarters, they are bending over to you—what man would you not infatuate? When King Virāṭa sees your superhuman body with the beautiful buttocks and hips, he will cast me aside and turn to you with his whole heart! For any man whom you, with your flawless limbs and long eyes, look at fondly will fall under the sway of love. Any man who looks at you, woman of the sweet smile and faultless body, will fall under the sway of the Love God. Just as a she-crab conceives for her own destruction, so would I, I think, destroy myself were I to give you lodging, sweet-smiling woman!"[49]

No wonder then that the king's marshal Kīcaka falls in love with her at first sight and asks his sister Sudeṣṇā:

> My pretty, who is this ravishing Goddess,
> Do tell me, who is she and whence, this lovely?
> She stirs up my spirits and sways my heart,
> I know of no medicine that could cure me![50]

And to Draupadī he exclaims:

> I will shed the wives whom I had before,
> Sweet-smiling wench, they shall be your slaves!
> I myself am your slave now, my comely woman,
> For you to command, my pretty, forever![51]

Draupadī, of course, rejects his advances wrathfully. Sudeṣṇā takes pity on her brother and arranges for the two to get together in Kīcaka's own quarters by ordering her to fetch some liquor from him on the occasion of a holiday. One suspects that this holiday, when a man can feel free to indulge his lust after plying the woman with liquor, was the "Carnival of Love," which, I think, has been one of the inspirations of *The Book of Virāṭa*.

Draupadī goes reluctantly, and to insure that she remain unharmed if the protection of her constancy were to fail, the Sun sends her an invisible bodyguard.[52] Once she is in his quarters, Kīcaka advances on her, but she throws him on the floor and runs for shelter to the men's hall, where Yudhiṣṭhira is gaming.[53] And before his very eyes, Kīcaka throws Draupadī on the floor and kicks her; whereupon in his turn the Rākṣasa bodyguard throws him on the floor. Yudhiṣṭhira pays no attention, and in fact sends her on her

49. 4.8.10 ff.
50. 4.13.7.
51. 4.13.12.
52. 4.14.19.
53. 4.15.6.

way, in order not to give away their identities.[54]

This scene is, of course, based upon that earlier humiliation of Draupadī in the hall of the Kauravas, where she was molested by Duḥśāsana before the eyes of her husbands who were reduced to powerless slaves.[55] The present version has Bhīma also present in the hall, white with fury but restrained by Yudhiṣṭhira,[56] as before, at the Kauravas', Arjuna had restrained him.[57] But this element seems to be secondary, since later on Bhīma is blissfully asleep and has to be told by Draupadī what had happened.[58]

That Kīcaka must die—as also Duḥśāsana, her earlier molester—is clear enough. It is interesting, but really predictable, that she chooses Bhīma for her instrument, not Yudhiṣṭhira, who has witnessed it all, not even Arjuna, who, as an inmate of the seraglio, might have been more accessible. It is to Bhīma she turns for real protection: "It was you who saved me from the ghastly Jaṭāsura, likewise you defeated Jayadratha with your brothers. Kill this villain too, who despises me!"[59] Bhīma tells her to send Kīcaka to the dance pavilion for an assignation. There, in a scene surely meant to be hilarious, Kīcaka begins to stroke the champion amorously and finds an ignominious death.[60]

The resulting uproar among Kīcaka's caste fellows and their destruction by Bhīma makes King Virāṭa apprehensive and he tells Sudeṣṇā to dismiss Draupadī. She begs for thirteen days' delay:[61] we have come close to the end of the term, and whatever festival there was is almost over.

The Cattle Raid

While the Pāṇḍavas and Draupadī are in hiding in Matsya, Duryodhana's spies keep combing the kingdoms, but to no avail. At Hāstinapura the Kauravas argue whether their enemies are dead or alive, and while the younger generation would prefer to think of them as dead, the older generation of Bhīṣma, Droṇa, and Kṛpa holds out no such hope.[62] When news arrives that Kīcaka has fallen, the visiting Trigarta king, Suśarman, proposes a cattle raid in Matsya. Duryodhana falls in with the suggestion and devises a battle plan

54. 4.15.32 ff.
55. 2.61.40 ff.
56. 4.15.11 ff.
57. 2.61.7 ff.
58. 4.17 ff.
59. 4.20.30 f.
60. 4.21.42 ff.
61. 4.23.28.
62. 4.26 ff.

that calls for two waves of invaders: Suśarman and his Trigartas will go in first, and Duryodhana and his Kauravas will follow a day later.[63] Although he wisely does not say so, Duryodhana's hope is that Virāṭa will engage the Trigartas with his whole force, leaving safe and easy pickings for Duryodhana. If we assume that *The Book of Virāṭa* is relatively late and presumes a knowledge of the war that is to follow, it is tempting to connect this perhaps suicidal mission in which the Trigartas are to safeguard Duryodhana with the episode of the Sworn Warriors in the great war, when the Trigarta brothers take an oath to fight Arjuna, an oath so suicidal that they perform their own obsequies beforehand.[64]

Virāṭa indeed engages the Trigartas with his entire army, to which he also conscripts the Pāṇḍavas, except the effeminate Arjuna. At this point all pretense at disguise is really being given up. For Yudhiṣṭhira, heretofore posing as the brahmin Kanka, to mount a war chariot is a clear sign of the end of the masquerade. When Virāṭa is temporarily captured by the enemy and Yudhiṣṭhira sends off Bhīma to free him, he still cautions him not to use his superhuman strength,[65] but it is only a matter of hours now. For Duryodhana has started the second wave and the city of Matsya has no one to field against that raiding party but the young son of the king, Uttara. This Uttara is a comic figure, a braggart who claims to equal Arjuna—if only he had a charioteer. Draupadī resents the claim and points out that Bṛhannaḍā, the dancing teacher, had often driven for Arjuna—which happens to be news to Arjuna himself. Bṛhannaḍā is fetched, clowns with his weapons to the squealing delight of his young things, and drives off, after giving the girls his solemn promise to bring back the mighty Kauravas' clothes for their dolls.[66] Obviously the burlesque is not over yet.

Uttara, on seeing the banners of the Kauravas, panics and refuses to fight. He jumps off the chariot and Arjuna, his braid streaming in the wind and his skirts flapping about him, pursues him. It is intriguing to look upon this scene as a reversal of the scene at the beginning of the *Bhagavadgītā*.[67] There, facing the Kaurava army, with "teachers, fathers, sons, grandsires, uncles, fathers-in-law, grandsons, brothers-in-law and other relations,"[68] Arjuna loses his nerve like Uttara. And just as Arjuna's charioteer Kṛṣṇa tries to put

63. 4.29.24.
64. 7.16.
65. 4.32.18 ff.
66. 4.35.23 ff.
67. Georges Dumézil, *Mythe et épopée* (Paris, 1968), 1: 93 f., quite correctly stresses this resemblance. I am not sure whether the scene is a "réplique comique" to the *BhG.*, or further building by the *Gītā* on this episode.
68. 6.23 (= *BhG.*1).34.

the man back into Arjuna, so Uttara's charioteer berates Uttara. "Don't become a eunuch, Pārtha!" cries Kṛṣṇa, "it does not fit you!"[69] "If you are unable to fight the enemy," says Arjuna (masquerading as a eunuch) to Uttara, "come and drive the horses while I fight them!"[70]

Arjuna retrieves the weapons that are still hanging in the *śamī* tree, binds up his braid, puts on a turban, and shows himself as he really is. He identifies himself and the others to Uttara. The masquerade is over, the Kauravas recognize him. Duryodhana refuses to give up the kingdom, and this refusal starts the mock battle, as it will start the real war.

The battle that ensues is like a *fantasia*, a staged battle of northwest African warriors on horseback, which has all the trappings of a real battle, except that no blood flows—or at least very little, and none of it important. The first to flee is Karṇa.[71] This supposedly great warrior, the sworn enemy of Arjuna, was put to flight before, when the Kauravas were embattled with the Gandharvas during *The Cattle Expedition*.[72] Karṇa's flight in the two contexts seems to be related to his refusal to fight as long as Bhīṣma is leading the army and to his withdrawal from battle as a result of this Achilles-like grudge.[73]

The theatrical aspect of Arjuna's grandstanding is pointed up by the arrival of Gods and ancient kings who watch and applaud like delighted spectators.[74] Kṛpa is dismounted and carried off. Droṇa is engaged, but only after the teacher gives his permission by shooting the first arrow.[75] Aśvatthāman relieves his father and is worn down. Karṇa returns but must once more leave the battlefield, and so on. Then the Kauravas regroup, attack Arjuna but are driven off. Bhīṣma attacks Arjuna amid loud applause, but in the end must give way. Finally Duryodhana himself is eliminated.

Arjuna blows the victory blast on his conch, and all the Kauravas fall stunned to earth in a mock death, except for Bhīṣma, though he is incapacitated.[76] This last detail seems to me quite telling. When we agree that Arjuna's battle is in fact a preview of the great war in which all the Kauravas die, Bhīṣma's lone retention of his consciousness, while all the others are stunned into a swoon, must parallel Bhīṣma's lone survival, though incapacitated on his bed of arrows, after the real war.[77] If this is so, *The Book of Virāṭa* must be

69. *klaibyaṃ mā gamaḥ Pārtha na tat tvayy upapadyate*, 6.24 (= *BhG*.2).3.
70. 4.36.43.
71. 4.49.23.
72. 3.230.31.
73. 5.165.9 ff.
74. 4.51.
75. 4.43.15 ff.; cf. Yudhiṣṭhira's request for permission to fight, in 6.41.
76. 4.61.14.
77. 6.95.

quite a late component of the *Mahābhārata*.

The battle over, Arjuna tells Uttara to send word to the city and claim victory in his own name.

The Wedding

Upon returning victoriously to his city after the defeat of the Trigartas, Virāṭa is disquieted by Uttara's solo expedition against the Kauravas.[78] Then his son's victory is announced, and the king exults. He flies into a rage, however, when Yudhiṣṭhira suggests that it must have been the doing of Bṛhannaḍā, whom Virāṭa only knows as a eunuch. Insulted, he flings the dice in Yudhiṣṭhira's face—a fitting end to the latter's career as a gambler. Yudhiṣṭhira catches his blood before it hits the floor, for to shed blood on Virāṭa's land would make it a battlefield.[79] Uttara is announced, enters and is aghast at Yudhiṣṭhira's bloody nose. When the bleeding stops, Bṛhannaḍā enters. Uttara declares that the victory was not his, but was achieved by the son of a God.

Two days later the Pāṇḍavas absolve themselves from their thirteen-year vow with a ritual bath, and in all the splendor of their white robes and jewelry, like young brahmins who have returned from their *brahmacarya* at the feet of their teacher,[80] seat themselves on thrones in Virāṭa's hall. Arjuna introduces the real Yudhiṣṭhira, Bhīma, himself, Nakula, Sahadeva, and Draupadī. King Virāṭa effusively apologizes for any slight to the brothers.

Soon, as a good father, he is concerned about the virtue of his daughter Uttarā, in whose company Arjuna, obviously very much a man, had been living as the eunuch Bṛhannaḍā, and offers her in marriage to Arjuna. Arjuna declines her for himself, but accepts her for his son, so her reputation will be intact. It would indeed be hard to imagine that an Indian father would allow his own son to marry a young woman of whose lapse of honor he knew, so to say, at first hand.

The Pāṇḍavas settle in the city of Upaplavya, the wedding is celebrated with Kṛṣṇa and other Vṛṣṇis, the kings of the Kāśis and Śibis, and Drupada and his sons present as guests. With Virāṭa they offer Yudhiṣṭhira a total, so far, of four *akṣauhiṇīs*, vast armies, to aid him in a war of which no mention is made but which is simply taken for granted.

78. 4.63.9 ff.
79. 4.63.53.
80. The *samāvartana* ritual; recent comments on this ritual are to be found in J. C. Heesterman, "Samāvartana," in *Pratidānam* (= Festschrift Kuiper) (The Hague, 1969).

On the Lateness of The Book of Virāṭa

Addressing himself to the origin and development of the *Mahābhārata* in *The Great Epic of India*, E. Washburn Hopkins writes:

> Having already given an example of two of the late features in the pseudo-epic [i.e. the three quarters of additions overlaying the original *Bhārata*], I would now point to some of the characteristic marks of the later poem in other regards. Midway in the development of the epic stands the intrusion of the fourth book [*The Book of Virāṭa*], where to fill out an extra year, not recognized in the early epic, the heroes live at court in various disguises. Here the worship of Durgā is prominent, who is known by her Purāṇic title, *mahiṣāsuranāśinī*, iv, 6, 15, "whose grace gives victory," ib. 30 (though after the intrusion of the hymn nothing is further heard of her). The Durgā here depicted bears a kheṭaka (as she does when the same hymn is repeated in vi, 32, 7), iv, 6, 4. This word for spear, amid innumerable passages describing arms, is unknown in the epic except in connection with Durgā, but it is found in the post-epical literature. It stands in the same historical position as does the epithet just mentioned. In those cases we have general evidence of the lateness of the book as well as of the hymn to Durgā. Matter and meter go hand in hand.
>
> A very striking example is given further in the show of arms which are described in this book. Although Arjuna is still a young man, yet, when the exhibitor comes to show his bow Gāṇḍīva, he says "and this is the world-renowned bow of the son of Pṛthā, which he carried for five-and-sixty years," iv, 43, 1–6. Nothing could be plainer than this passage. The exhibition of arms was composed when the later poet had in mind the actual number of years the hero carried the bow according to the epic story. He forgot that he was composing a scene which was to fit into the hero's young manhood and not into the end of his life. In iv, 71, 15 Arjuna is recognized as still a "dark-featured youth," and some time after this scene it is expressly stated that it was even then only thirty-three years since the time Arjuna got the bow, v, 52, 10 (referring to the Khāṇḍava episode, i, 225).[81]

I have quoted this passage at length, because it gives an opportunity to consider the problems of some of Hopkins' conclusions.

Every student of Sanskrit literature is familiar with the ubiquitous problem of interpolation, by which new elements inserted into a pre-existing text expand, embroider, correct, justify, or otherwise alter it. The traditional attitude is one of scorn toward interpolations: something historically valuable has been cheapened by the alteration and should be restored to its original integrity. Often enough it proves possible to isolate specific interpolations, which are then thrown away.

81. *The Great Epic of India* (New York, 1901), pp. 382 f.; additions in brackets mine; footnotes omitted.

To this somewhat cavalier historical method there has been a recent reaction which goes to the other extreme. The text is such as we have it, and we should accept the text in its entirety.[82]

It is to an early proponent of the latter view that Hopkins is reacting (to my mind overreacting) in the chapter under discussion. Rather foolhardily, Joseph Dahlmann had argued that the entire *Mahābhārata* is simultaneous and is from its inception both epic and *Dharmaśāstra.*[83] Others now would probably refine this by saying not that it is simultaneous, but that it is contemporaneous.

My own position is between these two extremes, but before enlarging on it let me address Hopkins' specific points. First of all, I have no difficulty accepting the historical lateness of *The Book of Virāṭa*, though I think a better argument can be made for that. It may, or it may not, be the case that the "earlier" (=older) epic does not recognize the thirteenth year, but one should like specific references. Even if they could be adduced, what would one do with them? If they speak of the twelve years of forest exile, this does not prove the absence of the thirteenth year. I should like to believe that there is *organic* growth in the *Mahābhārata*, in the sense that an interpolation was not extraneous to the text but was attracted, even at times provoked, by an incident in the "original": the starting point of *Virāṭa* may have been the unexplained fact that in the beginning of *Mahābhārata* 5, *The Book of the Effort*, the Pāṇḍavas find themselves headquartered at Upaplavya in Matsya. What took them *there*, instead of, for example, Pāñcāla, or Mathurā?

The very specific references that Hopkins adduces pose another problem: his evidence is as poor as the texts he used, that is, the Calcutta and Bombay editions. The critical edition, which, in spite of the strictures that have been directed at it, we have no choice but to follow on pain of random eclecticism,[84] notes after *MBh.* 4.5:

> After adhy. 5, Dn $D_{3.5\text{-}7.9.11.12}$ T_2 ins[ert] an additional adhy. given in App. I (no. 4.C,D,E,F,G), one of the versions of what is popularly known as the Durgāstava; cf. v.1. 29, 30. All reference to Durgā is missing in K B $D_{1.3}$ and in S (except the composite MS. T_2).[85]

Here then there is a problem within a problem: there can be occasions when a particular text portion (*Virāṭa*) *appears* to be an interpolation *in toto*, because of a secondary interpolation *in parte* (*Durgāstava*).

82. I return to this issue in detail below, p. 142 ff.
83. *Das Mahābhārata als Epos und Rechtsbuch* (Berlin, 1895).
84. See below, p. 152.
85. In the code of the critical edition, K represents the Kashmir recension, B the Bengal one, D the Devanāgarī one, S the southern one; in other words, the *Durgāstava* is missing in all recensions.

In his second example, Hopkins abbreviates his quotation, which runs cr. ed. 4.38.39 cd–41 (below, p. 87). In this passage the history of the Gāṇḍīva bow is given: Brahmā held it (*adhārayat*) for a thousand years, Prajāpati for 503 years, Indra for 85, Soma for 500, Varuṇa for 100, Arjuna for 65. Of course, this account assumes prior knowledge of the duration of Arjuna's life span; but does this prove that after the entire story was over, someone sat down, counted Arjuna's years, and wrote the whole *Virāṭaparvan* just to incorporate these lines? Is it not far more likely that they constitute a secondary insertion?

In spite of obvious difficulties, the attempt of Hopkins and other scholars to analyze the various layers that have gone into the epic as we now have it remains laudable. But it is not enough to cut out "later" portions and leave them lying in limbo; for often the interpolation is at least as interesting as the "original" into which it "intruded" itself. No one would have liked to lose *The Story of Śakuntalā* or *The Story of Yayāti*, although they are extraneous to *The Book of the Beginning*. Such text portions have two histories, their own history as separate texts, and their subsequent history as parts of another text. For it is not sufficient to decide *what* was interpolated; it is necessary to ask *why* it was interpolated.

While I have much sympathy for those who argue that a text like the *Mahābhārata* should not be cut up in pieces but should be viewed as a work that, whatever its various origins, functioned as a whole, I do think that a middle position can be taken. It is only *after* we have learned to discern what disparate parts have gone into the making of the *Mahābhārata* that we are allowed the question *why* these parts were felt to be compatible so that the text as a whole made sense.[86]

Thus, if *The Book of Virāṭa* is a later appendix to *The Book of the Forest*, as so many Sanskrit texts grew by their appendices, the question still remains, why *this* appendix?

Virāṭa unmistakably injects a frivolous element into the *Mahābhārata*, at least in its early parts. I myself would like to think that this *Book* is inspired by the frivolities with which the change from one year to the next is celebrated: there are the masquerade and the reversal of roles on the part of the Pāṇḍavas and Draupadī, during the period when they are "nameless," which ends with Arjuna triumphantly roaring out his ten names.[87] There is also the merrymaking licentiousness of Kīcaka, lusting after Draupadī. And it is then, with the onset of the month Phālguna and the new year it introduces,[88] that we have the grand Eroica of Arjuna, who is

86. See below, p. 153 ff.

87. 4.39.

88. *ŚatBr.* 6.2.2.18; *Kauṣītaki Br.* 5.1. More precisely, the Indian year starts with the night of the full moon of the second Phālguna month, which is also the first day of spring.

Phalguna:[89] in a deliberate phantasy the hero alone outshines the Kauravas, just as in the real war the Pāṇḍavas outfight the Kauravas, who outnumber them. Thus *Virāṭa* is an Indian January's Janus, looking back on what went before, the exile and the molestation of Draupadī, and forward to the war that is to follow. And, with *The Wedding, The Book of Virāṭa* looks even farther ahead: for from the union of Abhimanyu and Uttarā a child will grow, to be almost killed in the womb by a final act of barbarity,[90] but to be born as Parikṣit, with whom a new age in the history of the Kauravas begins.

This *Book of Virāṭa* constitutes a midpoint in the epic itself, when according to the letter of the covenant the old order should have been restored. Instead, war is chosen and a new part of the epic begins.

I find it hard to look upon this *Book* as just an intrusion. Certainly, it is not "needed" by the course of events, and it is likely that an earlier form of the *Bhārata* did without it. It is an addition, no doubt, but in the sense that an embellishment is an addition, pointing up a particular beauty of the wearer.

89. There is no doubt some connection, though it is difficult to be precise. Compare *ŚatBr*. 2.1.2.11: "The Phālgunīs are the *nakṣatras* named Arjuna, this being his obscure name, and the Phālgunīs are also called Ārjunīs."
90. 10.12–16.

Contents

4(45) *The Book of Virāṭa*

4.1–12 (B. 1–13; C. 1–372)
1 (1; 1). Yudhiṣṭhira returns to his hermitage and gives the fire-drilling woods back to the brahmin. Now that the twelve years of forest exile are over, he asks Arjuna to suggest a place to live during their thirteenth year of concealment (1–5). Arjuna names several countries from among which Yudhiṣṭhira should choose (5–10). He chooses the Matsya kingdom of Virāṭa and asks what disguise each will wear (10–15). He himself will be a games-master to the king (15–20).
2 (2; 28). Bhīma will be cook and gladiator (1–5). Yudhiṣṭhira praises Arjuna: what will he do? (5–20). Arjuna will be an effeminate eunuch and music and dance teacher to the king's women, under the name of Bṛhannaḍā (20–25).
3 (3; 60). Nakula will be the horse groom Granthika (1) and Sahadeva a cattle tender by the name of Tantipāla (1–10). Yudhiṣṭhira questions Draupadī (10–15). She will be a lady's maid (15).
4 (4; 83). Yudhiṣṭhira makes arrangements for his retainers (1–5). Dhaumya recounts the hazards of court life (5–40). He performs the rites for a safe journey (45).
5 (5; 141). The Pāṇḍavas travel through Śūrasena to Matsya and present themselves in that country as hunters (1). Draupadī wants to rest outside the city, but

Yudhiṣṭhira tells Arjuna to carry her and presses on (1–5). Before entering the city they unstring their bows, pack their weapons, and Nakula ties them up in a śāmī *tree; They hang a decomposing corpse by their weapons (saying it is their mother) to keep people away (5–25). They enter the city; Yudhiṣṭhira gives them secret names (25–30).*

6 (7; 214). Yudhiṣṭhira presents himself to Virāṭa as the brahmin Kanka (1–5). Upon the king's questions he states that he is Yudhiṣṭhira's former master of games, and wishes to be so employed by Virāṭa. The king complies (5–15).

7 (8; 231). Bhīma arrives with spoon, ladle and sword; the king is amazed (1–5). He states he was Yudhiṣṭhira's former cook Ballava and is looking for work; Virāṭa engages him (5–10).

8 (9; 244). Draupadī arrives as a chamber maid, and is observed by Virāṭa's wife Sudeṣṇā, who praises her beauty (1–10). Draupadī describes herself as Satyabhāmā's and Draupadī's former maid (15). Sudeṣṇā says she would employ her but fears that she may infatuate Virāṭa; Draupadī protests that she is already married to five Gandharvas; the queen engages her (15–30).

9 (10; 280). Sahadeva appears before Virāṭa and seeks service as Yudhiṣṭhira's former cow teller, Tantipāla (1–10). Virāṭa engages him (10–15).

10 (11; 296). Arjuna is disguised in a woman's dress and jewelry; Virāṭa queries him (1–5). The king offers him the kingdom (5). Arjuna, using the name Bṛhannaḍā, offers his services as a dance master, and Virāṭa engages him (5–10).

11 (12; 312). Nakula is observed inspecting Virāṭa's horses; the king is impressed. Nakula identifies himself as Yudhiṣṭhira's horse handler Granthika (1–5). Virāṭa engages him (5–10).

12 (13; 325). Yudhiṣṭhira is a popular court gambler; he shares his winnings with his brothers (1–5). Bhīma sells leftover foodstuffs, Arjuna sells secondhand ladies' clothing, Sahadeva provides his brothers with dairy products, Nakula shares his earnings as a horse groom, while Draupadī looks after them all (5–10). At the Feast of Brahmā wrestlers converge on the city. One champion challenges them all (10–15). Virāṭa orders Bhīma to take him on, and Bhīma defeats him and others (15–25). He is also made to fight lions in the harem (25). All the brothers give Virāṭa great satisfaction (25–30).

Janamejaya said:
4.1.1 How did my great-grandfathers live in the city of Virāṭa in
concealment, in fear of Duryodhana?
Vaiśaṃpāyana said:
When Yudhiṣṭhira, that first of the bearers of the Law, had
obtained those boons from Dharma in that fashion, he returned to
the hermitage, and told it all to the brahmins. And after relating all
to the brahmins, Yudhiṣṭhira handed the drilling woods to that
brahmin.
Thereupon the high-minded King Yudhiṣṭhira, the son of Dharma,
O Bhārata, gathered all his younger brothers together, and said to
5 them, "We have these twelve years lived outside our kingdom, and
now the thirteenth year has come, a hard year that will be difficult
to live out. All right then! Arjuna Kaunteya, choose a dwelling place
away from here where we can lodge for all the coming nights without
being discovered by our enemies."
Arjuna said:
Lord of the people! By virtue of the boon granted by Dharma
himself we shall roam unrecognized by men, bull of the Bharatas. But
I shall name some lovely and secluded kingdoms where we might
dwell—approve one or the other of them. There are lovely countrysides
which are rich in food, around the land of the Kurus: Pāñcāla, Cedi,
Matsya, Śūrasena, Paṭaccara, Dāśārṇa, Navarāṣṭra, Malla, Śālva,
10 Yugaṃdhara. Which one among these appeals to you, king, to live
in? Where shall we dwell this last year, Indra of kings?
Yudhiṣṭhira said:
Indeed, strong-armed prince, it is precisely as the blessed lord,*
the sovereign of all creatures, has said, and not otherwise. Of a
certainty we must look for a lovely, holy, and pleasant place to live,
unthreatened from anywhere, after all of us have taken counsel
together. The powerful Matsya king Virāṭa will protect the Pāṇḍavas.
He is law-minded, liberal, old, and very rich. This year we shall take
jobs, and amuse ourselves in the city of Virāṭa, Bhārata friend!
15 Let each of us speak up, scions of Kuru, and say what kind of work
he will be able to do!
Arjuna said:
God among men, what kind of work will you yourself do in the
kingdom of King Virāṭa that amuses you, good man? You are a mild

* = Dharma.

man, liberal, law-minded, and you put your strength in your truth. What will you do, King Pāṇḍava, pressed by this emergency? You do not know the ordinary labors of common people, king. How will you pass through this misadventure that has befallen you?

Yudhiṣṭhira said:

Hear ye, scions of Kuru, what work I shall do! When I come to
20 King Virāṭa, that bull among men, I shall be the Royal Dicing Master
of the great-spirited king, and pose as a brahmin by the name of Kanka, one who knows the dice and is an ardent gambler. I shall roll out the fascinating dice, those made of beryl and gold and ivory, the phosphorescent nuts, and the black and red dice! If he questions me, I shall tell the king that at one time I was a bosom friend of Yudhiṣṭhira's. So here I have told you how I shall amuse myself.

Wolf-Belly! What kind of job will you play at?

Bhīma said:

2.1 I think I shall be a kitchen chef, giving my name as Ballava, and
wait on King Virāṭa. I'll make him curries! I am good in a kitchen. I'll defeat the masters who had made creations for him before, and curry favor with him! I shall fetch the largest piles of firewood, and when he sees how hard I work, the king will be pleased. If I have mighty elephants to tame, king, or powerful bulls, I shall subdue those
5 too. Whatever professional fighters are set on me, I'll strike down in
the contests, and the king's favor will increase. Still, I won't kill those fighters at all, just down them so they won't die. Anyone asks and I'll tell him I was cook, cow butcher, curry maker, and pugilist to Yudhiṣṭhira, lord of the people. I'll go about protecting myself by myself, and that is the way I promise I shall enjoy myself!

Yudhiṣṭhira said:

Now he, choicest of men, whom the Fire God once encountered in
the guise of a brahmin when he wished to burn down the Khāṇḍava
10 Forest, he who was seconded by the Dāśārha!* That powerful,
strong-armed, unvanquished scion of Kuru, Dhanaṃjaya Kaunteya, what job shall he take? He faced the conflagration, and satiated the Fire. On a single chariot he defeated Indra, killed snakes and Rākṣasas, and proved the greatest of contestants—what shall Arjuna do? The sun is greatest of heat-givers, the brahmin first among the bipeds, the cobra chief of the snakes, the fire foremost of fiery substances, the thunderbolt choicest of weapons, the humped bull master of bovines, the ocean lord of the ponds, the monsoon vastest of rain-clouds, Dhṛtarāṣṭra greatest of the Snakes, Airāvata mightiest of the elephants, the son dearest of loved ones, the wife friendliest of friends
15 —Wolf-Belly, I tell you, whoever is greatest in his class, so great is

* = Kṛṣṇa.

the youth Guḍākeśa, the greatest of bowmen!

Not the lesser of Indra, O Bhārata, nor of Vāsudeva, what will he do, this Gāṇḍiva bowman of the white horses, this Terrifier? Five years he sojourned in the dwelling of the Thousand-Eyed God,* and, in a luminous God-shape, obtained celestial missiles. I think he is the twelfth Rudra, the thirteenth of the Ādityas! His arms are smooth, long, callused by string glances, both the right and the left, like the withers of draught-oxen.

Yea, of mountains the Himālaya, of rivers the Ocean, of the thirty
20 Gods Śakra, of the Vasus the offering Fire, of game the tiger, of birds
the Garuḍa—so of the war-girt is Arjuna: what will he do?

Arjuna said:

Sire, I am a transvestite, I'll vow, for these big string-scarred arms
are hard to hide! I'll hang rings from my ears that sparkle like fire,
and my head shall sport a braid, king! I shall be Bṛhannaḍā. Listen,
I'll be a woman, and tell sweet little tales and tell them again and
amuse the king and the other folk in the seraglio. I myself shall teach
the women in the palace of King Virāṭa to sing, king, and to dance in
25 many ways, and to make music in still others! I shall have much to
say about the ascendancy of creatures as a result of their feats, and
thus, Kaunteya, cover myself, by sheer wizardry! "I was at
Yudhiṣṭhira's place, a maid of Draupadī's; I lived in!" so I'll tell the
king if he asks me, Bhārata. In this artful way, not unlike Nala, I
shall amuse myself pleasantly, Indra of kings, in Virāṭa's palace.

Yudhiṣṭhira said:

3.1 Nakula my boy, delicate, brave, handsome and used to comforts, what job will you do?

Nakula said:

I shall be King Virāṭa's groom and call myself Granthika. I like that kind of work. I am good at training horses and curing them. I have always liked horses as you have, king of the Kurus. If people question me in the city of Virāṭa, I shall tell them how I amuse myself!

Yudhiṣṭhira said:

5 Sahadeva, how will you amuse yourself at Virāṭa's? At what job will you work, my boy, while in hiding?

Sahadeva said:

I shall be the cow teller of King Virāṭa. I am a tender and milker, and good at counting cows. I shall be called by the name of Tantipāla, remember. Don't worry, I'll do quite well. You yourself always used me at the time with the cows, and at yours I learned a good job, lord of the people. I can tell the tell-tale signs, ways and

* = Indra.

10 luck marks all very well, and more yet, king. I know even what bulls
are well-favored, by the smell of whose piss barren cows get with
calf. That is what I will do, for it always gives me pleasure. No one
will find me out, and you'll be pleased, king!

Yudhiṣṭhira said:

Now this our beloved wife, who is dearer to us than our lives, as a
mother to be protected, as an elder sister to be honored. What kind
of work shall Kṛṣṇā Draupadī perform, for she does not know how
to do the work that women do? Delicate, young, a famous princess,
15 devoted to her husbands and a lady, how shall she perform? From
the time she was born the radiant woman has had knowledge but of
garlands, perfumes, ornaments, and all manner of clothing.

Draupadī said:

Bhārata, there are in this world maidservants who serve as
chambermaids and live under no one's protection. No other women
go about like this, in the verdict of the people. I'll call myself
Sairaṃdhrī, a chambermaid with a skill in hairdressing. If you ask
me, I shall say I am my own mistress. I'll wait on Sudeṣṇā, the king's
famous wife. She'll look after me when I get there, don't be so
worried.

Yudhiṣṭhira said:

You speak well, Kṛṣṇā, like a woman born to family. You do not
recognize wickedness. Good! You have made a vow to be a good
woman.

Yudhiṣṭhira said:

4.1 You have stated what kinds of work you will do, and as far as I
understand it, I approve decidedly. Our family priest shall keep the
agnihotras in Drupada's palace, together with the cooks and the
kitchen chefs. Indrasena and the other drivers in my judgment should
take the empty chariots and ride quickly to Dvāravatī. All the serving
women of Draupadī must go to Pāñcāla, with the cooks and the
5 kitchen chefs. And they all must say, "We do not know where the
Pāṇḍavas are, for they dispersed us and all of them have left the
Dvaita Forest."

Dhaumya said:

Affection allows friends to speak even about matters that are well known; therefore I too shall speak: listen to my argument. Let me describe to you, princes, the life at a king's court, how a servant doing his work does not come to harm at a court. Hard is the life in a king's palace, even for one who has known it, Kauravyas, and so it will be for you, worthy of high honor, when you live there a full year, unhonored and unknown.

When shown the door, take the door, and put no trust in kings.

Seek out the seat that no one claims. One should live at a court without mounting the other's wagon, palanquin, stool, elephant, and chariot, thinking one is his favorite. If malicious persons are suspicious when you sit where you sit, do not sit down there again, and you'll survive at the court. Never offer advice to a king when he does not ask for it; sit in silence and compliment him at the right time. For kings are disenchanted with people who demur, and equally despise a councilor who argues wrongly. A sagacious man shall on no account strike up friendships with the wives of kings, the men that serve in the women's quarters, and ill-wishers the king hates. A courtier should perform even the most insignificant tasks with the king's foreknowledge, and if he conducts himself in that way, he will never face ruin from his king.

One should always serve a king as diligently as the fire, or the Gods; for if he is served mendaciously, the king is sure to do harm. One should follow the directions the king lays down, and avoid negligence, pride and anger. Whenever the king asks for advice, the courtier should describe what is profitable and pleasant, but more of the profitable than the pleasant. One should be amenable to the king in all conversations, and never hold up to him what is both unpleasant and unprofitable. A wise man should serve thinking that he is out of favor, and do warily and zealously what is profitable and pleasant. As long as he does not serve those whom the king dislikes, does not congregate with his ill-wishers, and does not stray from his rank, he survives at court.

The wise man will sit at the king's right or left, for the space behind him is reserved for the armed bodyguard; and a grand seat in front of the king is at all times forbidden. One should make no mention at all in his presence of prosperity, for even from the poor that would be most offensive. Do not disclose to people any lies the king speaks, and do not talk to a man who is out of favor. Nor should one proudly think, "I am a brave man, I am an astute man," for only by complying with the king does one become favored and comfortable. Having found rare power and favor from the king, the courtier should concentrate on what profits and pleases his master. What man respected by the wise would even in thought wish harm to one whose anger is most hurtful and whose grace most fruitful? He should not purse his lips, nor speak with great emphasis; and he should sneeze, break wind, and clear his throat quite softly.

When there are occasions for laughter, he should not be too merry and laugh like a madman, but also not act too solemnly lest he be taken as ponderous. Rather should he display a gentle and gracious smile. If he does not rejoice at a gain, and does not wince at a slight, and is always alert, he survives at court. If one is a sagacious adviser

who always satisfies the king or his son, he will enjoy good fortune
for a long time. A favorite adviser who has fallen out of favor for
good reasons, yet does not blame the king, will regain his privileges.
He who lives off the king or dwells in his realm should wisely speak
35 of his virtues when he is present and when he is not. For an adviser
who pesters the king too forcefully for benefits will not keep his rank
long, and he risks his life. Keeping at all times his own good in view
he will not contradict the king, or best him ever on the playing fields.
If one is at all times fit, brave, strong, faithful as a shadow, true-
spoken, gentle, and reserved, he survives at the court. If one jumps
forward when another is being given an errand, saying, "But I, what
may I do?" he survives at the court. If one does not hesitate when
ordered about in heat or cold, night or day, he survives at the court.
40 If one lives away from one's houses and forgets one's dear ones, and
seeks comfort with discomfort, he survives at the court.

He should not wear the same clothes as the king, nor laugh too
loud in his presence, nor give advice too often: so does one become a
favorite of the king. While entrusted with a mission he should not
take bribes, for by taking bribes he earns jail or death. Whatever the
king gives him, conveyance, clothes, ornaments, and so forth, he
should always use, and thus become a greater favorite. If you wish
to cultivate these habits this year, sons, you will regain your land,
and live as you please.

Yudhiṣṭhira said:

45 We stand instructed, hail to thee! No one but you will talk like
this, except mother Kuntī and the sagacious Vidura. Now pray do
at once what need be done for us to overcome suffering, to make our
departure and to triumph.

Vaiśaṃpāyana said:

After these words of the king, that good brahmin Dhaumya performed all the rites that are laid down to ensure good departure. He kindled the fires for them and offered into them with spells for the attainment of fortune and growth, and for the conquest of the world. They circumambulated the fire and the brahmin ascetics, then the six strode forth, with Yājñasenī at their head.

Vaiśaṃpāyana said:

5.1 Swords girt, wrist and finger guards tied on, other weapons and
quivers ready, the heroes traveled to the river Kālindī.* Going on
foot the powerful archers followed the southern bank, spending nights
in hill and forest fastnesses, and shooting game. North of Daśārṇa
and South of Pāñcāla the Pāṇḍavas passed through Yakṛlloma and
Śūrasena; and, calling themselves hunters, they entered the kingdom

* = Yamunā

of Matsya from the wilderness. When they reached that countryside, Kṛṣṇā said to the king, "Look, there are foot tracks here and acres planted in various crops. It is clear that Virāṭa's capital is still at some distance. Let us spend the rest of the night here. I am mightily tired."

Yudhiṣṭhira said:

Dhanaṃjaya Bhārata! Lift up Pāñcālī and carry her. We shall sleep in the capital, and be rid of the forest!

Vaiśaṃpāyana said:

Like the king of the elephants Arjuna swiftly took Draupadī and set her down when they came close to the city. On reaching the capital Kaunteya said to Arjuna, "Where shall we hang up our weapons, before we go into the city? We shall no doubt cause consternation among the people if we enter the city armed, friend. For we have promised that as soon as just one of us were found out, we would go back to the forest for another twelve years."

Arjuna said:

There is a big *śāmī* tree on a hilltop close to the cremation field, with formidable branches making it hard to climb, Indra among men. And there is not a person to be seen here, king. This tree has grown in a patch of forest off roads infested with game and beasts of prey. Let us hang up our weapons in this tree, and go on to the city, Bhārata, and enjoy ourselves there as we please!

Vaiśaṃpāyana said:

After he had said this to the law-spirited King Yudhiṣṭhira, he began to lay down his weapons there, bull of the Bharatas. The Pārtha, the scion of Kuru, unstrung and made harmless his bow Gāṇḍīva, that noble, roaring bow, slayer of rivals, with which he, standing alone on his chariot, had defeated Gods, men, and Snakes, and conquered prosperous countrysides. Enemy-burner Yudhiṣṭhira loosened the unbreakable string from the bow with which the hero had protected the Field of the Kurus. Lord Bhīmasena took down the string loop from the bow with which he had vanquished the Pāñcālas in battle, and alone had withstood many rivals during the conquest of the world, at the twang of which, like the bursting asunder of a mountain or a thunderbolt, enemies were accustomed to run away in battle, and with which he had manhandled King Saindhava,* O prince sans blame. The Pāṇḍava champion who roared in battle** undid the string of the bow with which he had conquered the West, and heroic Sahadeva unstrung the bow with which the dextrous prince had won the South.

They lay down their long yellow swords, costly quivers, and razor-sharp arrows with the bows. Nakula of his own accord climbed up

* = Jayadratha.
** = Nakula.

the tree and put the bows there. He tied them very tightly with
25 strong nooses to branches which he thought were strong enough
and afforded room enough, and where he saw the rain would not
enter. Along with the weapons the Pāṇḍavas tied up the body of a
dead man, so that people would henceforth shun that *śamī* tree from
afar, knowing by the putrid stench that there was a corpse tied up
there. "This is our 180-year-old mother," they said to cowherds and
shepherds who questioned them while they were stringing the body
up in the tree; "this is a family Law of ours, practiced by our
ancestors."

Then the enemy-burning, enemy-crushing Pārthas went to the
30 city. Yudhiṣṭhira gave them secret names: Jaya, Jayanta, Vijaya,
Jayatsena, and Jayadbala. Thereupon, according to the promises they
had made, they entered the great city to live their thirteenth year
in that kingdom undiscovered.

Vaiśaṃpāyana said:

6.1 On his way to King Virāṭa, enthroned
In his hall, the king first fastened his dice,
The golden and beryl-colored, beneath
His armpit, and drew his cloak around,

On his way then went that famous king,
Kuru's scion, to the famed lord of the land,
The puissant king received by all princes,
Unapproachable like a venomous snake,

In power and beauty a bull among men,
Grand, like an Immortal in fiery luster,
A sun surrounded by masses of clouds,
A fire obscured by its ashes—a hero.

And beholding that Pāṇḍava fallen on him
As the moon amidst clouds, the king of Virāṭa
Put to his councilors, brahmins and bards
And commoners, all who sat in assembly,
This question, "Who is it that's meeting me here,
Setting eyes on this hall for the first time yet?

"A man superb, he will not be a brahmin—
I think he must be a king of the earth!
No servant has he, nor earrings or chariot,
But close by he blazes like Indra himself!

"From the marks on his body I can make out
That he is a king whose head was anointed.
He strides in my presence with no concern,

Rutting elephant to a lotus pond!"

Yudhiṣṭhira, bull among men, approached
And spoke to Virāṭa, who was thus reflecting,
"Great king, pray know that a brahmin has come
For a living from you, having lost all his wealth.

"I wish to live here, O prince without blame,
In your habitation, and act on your wishes."
The king at once bade Yudhiṣṭhira welcome
And said to him, "Pray, accept our reception!

"I greet you with pleasure, my son. Now tell,
From what king's realm have you journeyed here?
And quote in truth both your name and your line,
And whatever craft you are wont to pursue."

Yudhiṣṭhira said:
10 At one time I was Yudhiṣṭhira's friend,
A brahmin of Vyāghrapada's line,
A gamester clever at rolling the dice—
I am known by the name of Kanka, Virāṭa.

Virāṭa said:
I will grant you forsooth what boon you desire,
For I am your servitor. Govern the Matsyas!
Shrewd gamesters have always been dear to my heart,
And you, God-like, deserve a kingdom!

Yudhiṣṭhira said:
If the ultimate quarrel arises, King Matsya,
I will suffer nothing from anyone lower.
No one I defeat shall keep his riches:
May this be my boon from your grace, my lord!

Virāṭa said:
I shall slay the unslayable, if he offends you,
And banish the brahmins from my realm.
Hear ye, my assembled countrymen,
That Kanka is lord of the realm like me!

As my friend you shall ride on the same conveyance,
Have plentiful clothing and food and drink.
You may always look both inside and outside,
My door shall always be opened for you.

15 When gaunt, workless men come appealing to you,
You may promise them things on my behalf.
I shall give what you promised, no doubt of that,

You'll have nothing to fear in my presence at all.

Vaiśaṃpāyana said:
Having gained an audience, and his boon,
From King Virāṭa, the bull among men
And hero dwelt happily there, fully honored,
And no one was there who found out his design.

Vaiśaṃpāyana said:
7.1 Then another man came, blazing with luster,
Of terrible strength, with a lion's light step;
He held in his hand a spoon and a ladle,
And an unsheathed black-iron sword that was spotless.

Disguised as a cook he illumined this world
With his peerless effulgence like the sun.
He was dressed in black, of Himālayan firmness,
And approaching the king of the Matsyas he stood.

When he saw him arrive the curious king
Said to the countrymen there assembled,
"This youth, this bull among men, who is he,
Like a lion high-shouldered, of beauty surpassing?

"Such a man I have never before beheld.
He's a sun, I cannot guess his full measure!
Though deeply reflecting I cannot in truth
Fathom the mind of this bull among men."

5 The Pāṇḍava now came up to Virāṭa.
The spirited man looked sad as he spoke.
Said he, "Great king, I am Ballava the cook,
Engage me, I cook most excellent curries!"

Virāṭa said:
Pride-giver, I cannot believe you a cook,
For you mirror the God of the Thousand Eyes.
With your beauty and luster and majesty
You shine, my friend, as the best among men!

Bhīma said:
Great king, I am but your servant and cook,
I know, most of all, exceptional sauces,
Which the King Yudhiṣṭhira long ago
Used to savor too, all of them, O king!

In strength no man is the equal of me—
A veteran wrestler I have always been:
I fight with lions and elephants,
I shall give you much pleasure, prince sans blame!

Virāṭa said:

I shall give you your wish in the kitchen forsooth,
And so you will work there, as you say you can.
Yet I do not think such work does suit you,
You deserve the entire sea-rimmed world!

10 "But let it be done the way you desire,
You shall be the chief cook in my kitchens.
Be at my appointment the overseer
Of the men who formerly suited me there.

Vaiśaṃpāyana said:

And so was Bhīma placed in the kitchen;
He became most dear to the King Virāṭa.
And, king, while he dwelt there no single person
Nor any one servant did find him out.

Vaiśaṃpāyana said:

8.1 Then black-eyed Kṛṣṇā braided her perfect, curly-tipped locks, hid
them at her right side, and wrapped herself in one long, black, very
dirty robe. And having thus assumed the guise of a chambermaid,
she walked about as though in trouble. Seeing her darting about,
men and women hurried to her and asked, "Who are you, and what
is your purpose?" Thereupon, great king, she told them, "I have
come as a chambermaid. I want to work for anyone who wishes
5 to feed me." Because of her beauty, her dress, and her gentle speech,
they did not believe that she was a serving woman who had come
for food.

But Virāṭa's wife, a princess of Kekaya, who was very highly
regarded, saw Drupada's daughter while she was looking down from
the palace balcony. And seeing her in her circumstances, without a
protector, and dressed in one piece of clothing, she summoned her
and said, "Good woman, who are you, and what is your purpose?"
Thereupon, great king, she told her, "I have come as a Śairaṃdhrī
chambermaid. I want to work for anyone who wishes to feed me."

Sudeṣṇā said:

The people you mention are not as beautiful as you, radiant
woman—so beautiful are only they who order many slaves and slave
10 women who are maids! Your heels are flat, your thighs are full, you
are deep in the three places, high in the six, red in the five red spots,
and your voice halts like a wild goose's. Your hair is fine, your
nipples are pretty, you are shapely, with full breasts and buttocks,
you are endowed with every grace like a filly from Kashmir! Your
eyelashes curl nicely, your lips are like *bimba* berries, your waist is
slender, your throat lined like a conch shell, your veins are hidden,
and your face is like the full moon! Tell me who you are, my dear,
since you are not a serving woman at all. Are you a Yakṣī, a

Goddess, a Gandharvī, or Apsarā? Alambuṣā, Miśrakeśī, Puṇḍarīkā, Mālinī, Indrāṇī, Vāruṇī, or the Maker's consort, the Placer's, or Prajāpati's? Who of the Goddesses are you, my lovely, who are famed among the Gods?

Draupadī said:

15 I am not a Goddess, nor a Gandharvī, Āsurī, or Rākṣasī. I am a servant, a chambermaid, I tell you the truth! I know how to dress hair, and I grind ointment oils well. I can weave the most beautiful and colorful garlands. I have pleased Satyabhāmā, Kṛṣṇa's favorite queen, and Kṛṣṇā, the wife of the Pāṇḍavas, the unique beauty of the Kurus. I go hither and yon, earning a very fine keep, and as long as I get fine clothes I am happy. The queen herself used to call me her garland girl! And here, Queen Sudeṣṇā, I have come to your house.

Sudeṣṇā said:

20 I would lodge you on my own head, if I did not suspect that the king would go to you with all his heart! Look, all the women in the palace and those in my quarters stare at you in fascination—what man would you not infatuate? Look at the trees that stand firm in my quarters, they are bending over to you—what man would you not infatuate? When King Virāṭa sees your superhuman body with the beautiful buttocks and hips, he will cast me aside and turn to you with his whole heart! For any man at whom you, with your flawless limbs and long eyes, look fondly will fall under the sway of
25 love. Any man who looks at you, woman of the sweet smile and faultless body, will fall under the sway of the Love God. Just as a she-crab conceives for her own destruction, so would I, I think, destroy myself were I to give you lodging, sweet-smiling woman!

Draupadī said:

Neither Virāṭa nor any one man can have me at all! Five young Gandharvas are my husbands, radiant queen, the sons of a mettlesome king of the Gandharvas, and the Gandharvas always protect me—I am trifled with on pain of death! My Gandharva husbands allow me to lodge with one who does not serve me
30 leftovers or have me wash his feet. Any man who covets me like any commoner's woman enters another body that very same night. No one can make me stray, woman, for my irascible Gandharvas are stronger than I!

Sudeṣṇā said:

If that is so, I shall give you lodging, my joy, as you wish! And you shall in no way touch other's feet or leftovers.

Vaiśaṃpāyana said:

Thus was Kṛṣṇā comforted by Virāṭa's wife, and no one there knew who she really was, Janamejaya.

Vaiśaṃpāyana said:

9.1 Sahadeva, too, having assumed a perfect cowherd's disguise and adopted the appropriate manner of speech, went up to Virāṭa. Seeing him coming, that bull among men who spread splendor, the king approached and asked the scion of Kuru, "Whose son are you, whence are you, and what, son, do you seek to do? Tell me the truth, bull among men, for I have never set eyes on you before."

When he got to the king, the enemy-burner
Spoke up in a voice that roared like the rains:
"A Vaiśya am I, named Ariṣṭanemi,
I have been cow teller of the bulls of the Kurus.

5 "I'd like to live with you, chief of the people,
For I no longer know the lionlike Pārthas.
No other trade do I have to live by,
And no master but you attracts me, sire."

Virāṭa said:

You must be a brahmin, perchance a baron:
You look like a lord of the sea-fellied earth.
Enemy-plougher, do tell me the truth:
No commoner's trade is fitting for you!

From what king's realm have you traveled to here?
And what kind of craft would you really do?
And would you forever settle with us?
Do tell me what wages you will demand.

Sahadeva said:

King Yudhiṣṭhira, who was the eldest of Pāṇḍu's five sons, had
herds of eight hundred, a thousand, a hundred thousand, ten
thousand, twelve thousand, and twenty thousand cows. I was his
10 cow counter; they know me as Tantipāla. Not a count was beyond
me within ten leagues, past, present, or future. My talents were well
known to that great-spirited prince; yes, the Kuru king Yudhiṣṭhira
was well pleased with me.

For my cows do multiply quickly and never
Does any pest descend on them:
Such various trades are part of my skill,
And such are the trades that have stayed with me.

King, I know how to single out bulls by the mere smell of whose piss even barren cows calve!

Virāṭa said:

A hundred thousand cows do I own

Divided by colors according to virtue.
I give you the cattle along with the herdsmen,
My cattle will now all be in your care

Vaiśaṃpāyana said:
15 So, unknown to the king, O lord of your people,
That master of men dwelled happily there.
There were none who found out who he really was,
And the king paid him out the wages he wanted.

Vaiśaṃpāyana said:
10.1 Then one more man appeared, a large man who bore
The adornment of woman and beauty supreme,
Wearing earrings the size of ramparts and walls
And long bright conch shells set into gold.

The big-armed man with an elephant's power
Had combed out his long and plentiful hair;
And shaking the earth as he strode he now
Approached Virāṭa enthroned in his hall.

Upon seeing him come to the floor of the hall,
That enemy-churner who hid in his guise
And shone about him with splendor superb,
That son of great Indra of elephant power,

The king queried all who were sitting about him:
"From whence has he come, a stranger to me?"
But none of the men pretended to know him,
And the king gave voice to his wonderment.

5 "A handsome man, completely endowed,
A swarthy youth like an elephant leader,
Who is wearing bright conches set into gold,
And sporting a braid and a pair of earrings!

"Thick-haired and crested, but wrongly attired
You must be a bowman with arrows and mail.
On a chariot of racers ascended you shall
Ride about as a match for my sons, or myself!

"An old man now, I want to retire—
Take instant charge of all my Matsyas.
No man of your stature resembles an eunuch
In any which way, so it seems to me!"

Arjuna said:
I sing and I dance and make fine music,

I am good at the dance and a master of song.
Pray give me to Uttarā, sire, to serve her,
I shall be the dance master of your queen.

The reason I have this form – what profit
Is there in recounting it but great pain?
Bṛhannaḍā, sire, is my name, deserted
By father and mother as son and daughter.

Virāṭa said:
10 All right, Bṛhannaḍā, I'll give you your wish:
Teach my daughter to dance and the damsels like her.
Still I think this trade is not equal to you,
You deserve the entire sea-fellied earth!

Vaiśampāyana said:
The king of the Matsyas tried Bṛhannaḍā
In dancing and music and other arts;
And on learning for sure he was not a man
He allowed him to go to the princess's quarters.

And Lord Dhanaṃjaya taught the daughter
Of King Virāṭa music and song
As well as her friends and her maids-in-waiting,
And the Pāṇḍava soon had enamoured them.

So in his disguise Dhanaṃjaya dwelled there
In control of himself and doing them favors;
And none of the people there found him out,
Neither those in the house nor those outside.

Vaiśaṃpāyana said:
11.1 Then another lordly Pāṇḍava came
To the King Virāṭa, who was viewing his horses;
The people saw him appear as he came
Like the orb of the sun from behind the clouds.

He inspected the horses hither and yon,
And the king of the Matsyas watched him inspecting.
Said the enemy-scourge to the people about him,
"From whence has this Godlike man arrived?

"He is thoroughly checking these horses of mine,
He is certain to be an expert horseman.
Let him quickly be fetched and brought to my presence,
For the hero appears an Immortal to me."

The enemy-slayer now spoke to the king,

"Be victory thine, and good fortune, O king!
I have wide renown as a handler of horses,
I shall be your expert charioteer."

Virāṭa said:

5 I'll give you my mounts, a dwelling and wages,
And you must become my charioteer.
Whence are you, and whose? And why have you come?
Pray tell me the trade that is vested in you.

Nakula said:

King Yudhiṣṭhira, the eldest of the five sons of Pāṇḍu, formerly employed me in his stables, enemy-plougher. I know the nature of horses, how to train them all, how to control the vicious ones, and how to cure them of everything.

No horse of mine will ever be shy,
Not a mare malicious, let alone the stallions.
The people—and so did the Pāṇḍava
Yudhiṣṭhira—call me Granthika.

Virāṭa said:

Whatever I have of horses and mounts
Shall henceforth all be under your care,
And the handlers of horses I already have,
And the charioteers, shall be under you.

10 And tell me, Godlike man, your desire:
What wages are you expecting from me?
The grooming of horses is surely beneath you,
For to me you appear no less than a king.

This appearance of you with the gracious mien
Is as pleasing to me as Yudhiṣṭhira's.
But how can the Pāṇḍava find any pleasure
As he lives in the woods bereft of his servants?

Vaiśaṃpāyana said:

The youth who resembled a ranking Gandharva
Was joyfully honored by King Virāṭa.
The others inside did in no way know him,
As he made himself there agreeable.

So did the Pāṇḍavas settle in Matsya
According to promise—their sight bore fruit.
Very warily living a life of concealment
But in grief, these kings of sea-fellied earth.

Janamejaya said:

12.1 While the Pāṇḍavas were thus living in the city of the Matsyas, what did the powerful men do thereafter, brahmin?

Vaiśaṃpāyana said:

Listen to what these scions of Kuru did, while living thus in concealment and winning the favor of the king. Yudhiṣṭhira as the royal gamester became the favorite of the courtiers as well as of Virāṭa and his sons, lord of your people. The Pāṇḍava, who knew the heart of the dice, played as he pleased at dicing with them as
5 with so many birds tied to a string. The King Dharma, tiger among men, without Virāṭa's knowledge distributed the wealth that he won to his brothers as they deserved it. Bhīmasena sold for Yudhiṣṭhira the meats and various dishes that the Matsya passed up. Arjuna sold the worn clothes he obtained in the serail and passed the proceeds on to all his brothers. Sahadeva Pāṇḍava, wearing his cowherd's disguise, gave the Pāṇḍavas curds, milk, and ghee. Nakula too shared his earnings from horse grooming, which the satisfied king gave him,
10 with the Pāṇḍavas. The wretched Kṛṣṇā looked after all the brothers, and the radiant woman saw to it that she went unrecognized. And so, complementing each other and looking to Kṛṣṇā, the great warriors lived in concealment, king of men.

In the fourth month there took place in Matsya a very grand festival of Brahmā, richly celebrated, which the people held in great esteem. Wrestlers gathered there by the thousands from all countries, O king, gigantic and powerful men like Kālakhañja Asuras. Glorying in their might, and of surpassing strength, with the shoulders, hips, and necks of lions, quite clean and in fine spirits, they all were welcomed by the king; many a time had they won
15 their bouts before that prince in his arena. There was one big man among them who challenged all the wrestlers; and not a single one dared approach him as he pranced about the ring.

When all the wrestlers had lost heart and spirit, the king of the Matsyas ordered his cook to grapple with the wrestler. At his urging, Bhīma made up his mind with difficulty, for he could not publicly defy the king. Then the tigerlike man with the loose step of a tiger entered the great ring and brought happiness to Virāṭa. The Kaunteya, to the delight of the people, fastened his girdle, and thereupon Bhīma challenged the wrestler, who was the like of Vṛtra.
20 They both had extraordinary staying power, both had ruthless strength and stood as large as two rutting sixty-year-old elephants. Enemy-killer Bhīma plucked at the bellowing wrestler and pulled him with his arms, roaring himself, as a tiger attacks an elephant. The big-armed strongman lifted him up and spun him around, to the huge astonishment of the wrestlers and the Matsyas. Strong-armed Wolf-Belly swung the wrestler around a hundred times, till he lost nerve and wits, and then trampled him on the ground.

The wrestler, world-famous Jīmūta, lay beaten, and Virāṭa and

25 his family were greatly delighted. From sheer pleasure the great-
minded king showered largess on Ballava in the arena, as though he
were Vaiśravaṇa himself. After Bhīma had beaten very many wrestlers
and strongmen in the same way, he earned the highest favor from the
Matsya king. When no man was to be found who was a match for
him, the king had him fight with tigers, lions, and elephants. Again
Virāṭa had the Wolf-Belly wrestle in the midst of the women in the
serail with crazed and powerful lions.

Terrifier Arjuna, too, gave satisfaction to Virāṭa and all the women
30 of the serail with his songs and fine dancing. Nakula pleased the king,
O best of kings, with the trained and swift horses that had been
collected there. And upon seeing Sahadeva's well-trained bulls,
O lord, the king was pleased to give him much treasure as a reward.
So the bulls among men lived there concealed, doing their chores
for King Virāṭa.

4(46) The Killing of Kīcaka

4.13–23 (B. 14–24; C. 373–860)
13 (14; 373). After ten months Kīcaka, marshal of Virāṭa and brother of Queen Sudeṣṇā, falls in love with Draupadī and tells Sudeṣṇā (1–5). He proposes to Draupadī and she, being another's wife, indignantly rejects him (10–20).
14 (15; 431). Kīcaka enlists Sudeṣṇā's help: she will send Draupadī to him on a holiday to fetch liquor (1–5). Sudeṣṇā orders Draupadī to go to Kīcaka; she at first refuses, then goes with a goblet (5–15). She prays to the Sun, who sends her an invisible Rākṣasa as a body guard (15–20).
15 (16; 452). Kīcaka welcomes Draupadī and importunes her (1–5). He caresses her and she flees to the men's hall, where Yudhiṣṭhira is sitting. Kīcaka grabs her by the hair, throws her on the floor and kicks her; the Rākṣasa pushes him to the floor (5–10). Bhīma, also present, is enraged but checked by Yudhiṣṭhira (10). Draupadī complains to Virāṭa and berates her husbands without giving them away (15–25). Virāṭa pays no attention, but the courtiers praise her conduct; Yudhiṣṭhira sends her off, implying the time is not ripe for revenge (30–35). Draupadī undoes her hair and runs

to Sudeṣṇā, who is riled at her maid's treatment (35–40).
16 (17; 503). Draupadī bathes. In the night she searches out Bhīma and embraces him as he sleeps (1–10). He wakes up and questions her (10–15).
17 (18; 523). Draupadī complains bitterly about Yudhiṣṭhira, recalling his erstwhile fortune, while now he is reduced to servitude (1–25).
18 (19; 557). Draupadī mentions how afraid she is when Bhīma fights wild animals. Once she fainted and the other women mocked her (1–5). Arjuna, once the hero, is now incapacitated and a servant (5–20). So are Sahadeva and Nakula (20–35).
19 (20; 604). Draupadī complains about her own lot as a servant and shows Bhīma her callused hands (1–20). She weeps (20–30).
20 (21; 641). Bhīma tries to comfort her with examples of other self-sacrificing heroines (1–10). Draupadī tells how she has been fending off Kīcaka and how he has humiliated her (10–30). He must die, or else she will take poison (30–35).
21 (22; 694). Bhīma promises so. Draupadī should arrange to meet Kīcaka in the dance pavilion, where there is a couch. Bhīma will be there (1–5). In the morning Kīcaka prances before Draupadī and offers her money and slaves (5–10). Draupadī assents to an assignation but demands that it be kept a complete secret. He agrees; they will meet at night in the dance pavilion (10–15). Kīcaka wears through the day (15–20). Draupadī tells Bhīma in the kitchen and urges him on; Bhīma swears he will kill Kīcaka. He waits for the other in the dance pavilion (20–35). Kīcaka arrives and strokes the figure on the couch (35–45). Bhīma rises and they wrestle (45–50). When Kīcaka begins to tire, Bhīma crushes him mercilessly and, holding him by his hair, roars out. He pushes Kīcaka's extremities into his trunk, shows the mangled body to Draupadī, and leaves (50–60). Draupadī calls the guards and triumphantly declares that her Gandharva husbands have killed him (60–65).
22 (23; 793). Kīcaka's kinsmen mourn him and carry him outside to cremate him. One calls for Draupadī's death: she should burn with Kīcaka (1–5). They ask Virāṭa's leave and he grants it; they tie Draupadī up and carry her to the cremation ground (5–10). Draupadī cries out to the Pāṇḍavas by their secret names. Bhīma

hears her, rushes out, seizes a tree and storms at the Kīcakas (10–20). They let go of Draupadī and flee back to the city; Bhīma kills 105 of them and comforts Draupadī (25–30).
23 (24; 829). The people, alarmed, tell Virāṭa of the danger from the Gandharvas (1–5). Virāṭa orders the cremation of the Kīcakas and tells Sudeṣṇā to order Draupadī to leave, to prevent further reprisals from the Gandharvas (5–10). Kṛṣṇā, on her return to the city, panics the citizens; she praises Bhīma (10–15). At the dance pavilion, where Arjuna is teaching, the girls come out and congratulate Draupadī, who snaps at Arjuna (15–20). Sudeṣṇā tells Draupadī to leave; she asks for thirteen days' delay (20–25).

Vaiśaṃpāyana said:
13.1 While the Pārthas were dwelling in the city of the Matsya, these great warriors in incognito, ten months passed by. But Yajñasena's daughter, so worthy of being served herself, O Janamejaya, lord of the people, lived quite uncomfortably obeying Sudeṣṇā. Then Virāṭa's marshal saw the lotus-faced Daughter of Pāñcāla serving in Sudeṣṇā's house. And no sooner had Kīcaka seen her going about like a child of a God, a Goddess herself, than he was hit by the arrows of Love,
5 and he desired her. Burned by the fires of lust, the marshal approached Sudeṣṇā and laughingly said:

"I have never before beheld this beauty
Here in the palace of King Virāṭa.
This radiant maid intoxicates me
With her loveliness like a grog with its smell!

"My pretty, who is this ravishing Goddess,
Do tell me, who is she and whence, this lovely?
She stirs up my spirits and sways my heart,
I know of no medicine now that could cure me.

"Aho! Your beautiful lass attracts me,
That incomparably pretty serving wench.
But surely her serving you is not fitting—
Command me and all that I command!

"Let her shed luster on my grand house
With its plentiful elephants, horses and chariots,
With its opulent wealth, rich in liquors and viands,
That charms with its gold and varied adornment."

10 Then Kīcaka, after consulting Sudeṣṇā,
Approached the child of a king of men,
And he spoke in soothing manner to Kṛṣṇā—
A jackal addressing a lioness:

"Your shape and your age are superb, my pretty,
But kept by themselves are of no avail
Like a beautiful garland that is not being worn:
Though radiant you be, you shine not, my pretty.

"I will shed the wives whom I had before,
Sweet-smiling wench, they shall be your slaves!
I myself am your slave now, my comely woman,
For you to command forever, my pretty."

Draupadī said:

Son of a sūta, you have designs on me whom you should not covet,
an ugly, contemptible chamber maid, who dresses hair! I am the wife
of another, good fortune to you! and your proposals are beneath you.
15 Wives are dear to the creatures—think of the Law! You should never
set your mind in any way on the wife of another. For it is the life
rule of good men to avoid the forbidden. Indeed, a man of evil soul,
who in his folly covets wrongly, finds despicable disgrace and gets
into very great danger. Don't rejoice, son of a *sūta,* lest you forfeit
your life this very day, by desiring me who am unattainable and
protected by heroes. You cannot have me: my husbands are
Gandharvas, and they will strike you down in wrath. Come, enough
of this, don't seek your perdition. You want to walk a road that is
impassable to men. You want to act like a witless child on a river
bank wanting to walk across to the other side.

20 You may dig into earth, or fly up in the sky,
You may flee to the farther shore of the ocean,
But yet you will never escape from them,
For my men are ferocious children of Gods!

Do you, Kīcaka, covet me now as though
You were sick and yearned for the night of your death?
Do you want me, indeed, as a baby abed
On the lap of his mother holds out for the moon?

Vaiśaṃpāyana said:

14.1 Having been spurned by the princess, Kīcaka said to Sudeṣṇā, for
he was overcome by an unbridled and dreadful lust, "Kaikeyī, see to
it that I get together with the chamber maid. I must have her, or
I shall give up my life!" After listening many a time to his wailing,

Virāṭa's spirited queen took pity on him. While keeping her own end
in view and reflecting on his end, as well as on Kṛṣṇā's indignation,
5 Sudeṣṇā said to the *sūta*, "Have some liquor and dishes prepared for
the holiday. That day I shall send her to you to get me some liquor.
Try and comfort her as you please, when I have sent her off and she
is under no restraint in private—if indeed she be comforted enough
to make love."

Kīcaka went home and at his sister's suggestion had liquor fit for
a king fetched, that had been well-strained. He had his skilled cooks
prepare an excellent dish of goat and lamb meat, a platter of many
and various kinds of venison, and a fine array of food and drink. This
done, Queen Sudeṣṇā, who had been quietly informed by Kīcaka,
dispatched her chamber maid to Kīcaka's house.

Sudeṣṇā said:

10 You up and go to Kīcaka's house, maid. Get me something to
drink, pretty, my thirst is killing me.

Draupadī said:

I won't go to that man's place, princess! You know, my queen,
how shameless he is! I shall not, flawless and flushed mistress, be
promiscuous in your house and betray my husbands. Madam, you
know the agreement we had when I entered service in your house,
good lady. Fair-tressed lady, Kīcaka is a fool emboldened by lust.
When he sees me, he will insult me. I am not going there, comely
15 lady. You have many other serving women who obey you, princess.
Send somebody else, good luck to thee, for he is sure to insult me!

Sudeṣṇā said:

He will do you no harm, when I myself have sent you.

Vaiśaṃpāyana said:

With these words she handed her a golden goblet with a lid on it.
Weeping and filled with suspicions, Draupadī put her trust in fate and
started for Kīcaka's house to fetch liquor.

Draupadī said:

If it be true that I do not recognize any other man but the
Pāṇḍus, then by this truth Kīcaka must not overpower me when I
get there!

Vaiśaṃpāyana said:

The woman worshiped the Sun for a moment. Sun heard everything
from the thin-waisted woman and consigned an invisible Rākṣasa to
20 her protection. And the Rākṣasa did not under any circumstances
leave the side of the blameless maid.

When the *sūta* saw Kṛṣṇā approach like a trembling doe, he rose
happily, as one who wants to cross a river and finds a ferry.

Kīcaka said:

15.1 Welcome, my fair-tressed lovely, my night has joyously dawned into day. You have come as my mistress, now make me happy! Let them fetch golden garlands, shells, and earrings made of gold, silken robes, and furs. I have a beautiful bed all spread for you. Come with me and drink honey-mead!

Draupadī said:

The queen has sent me to you to fetch liquor. "Bring me quickly something to drink," she says, "I am thirsty."

Kīcaka said:

5 Some other maid will bring the queen the well-strained liquor.

Vaiśaṃpāyana said:

The *sūta*'s son caressed her right hand; she shook at Kīcaka's touch
and threw him on the floor. She ran for shelter to the hall where King
Yudhiṣṭhira was sitting, and Kīcaka grabbed the flying woman by the
hair. And while the king looked on, he threw her on the floor and
kicked her with his foot. But the Rākṣasa whom the Sun had assigned
to her pushed Kīcaka away with the speed of the wind, Bhārata. Hit
by the Rākṣasa's force he fell on the floor; he whirled and lay
10 motionless like a tree whose roots have been cut. Bhīmasena and
Yudhiṣṭhira, who were sitting there, saw Kṛṣṇā and could not bear
her being kicked by Kīcaka. High-minded Bhīma, ready to kill the evil
Kīcaka off, ground his teeth in fury; but the King Dharma squeezed
his thumb with his own, O king, and restrained Bhīma out of fear
that they would betray themselves. Weeping, the full-hipped woman
clung to the hall door and, ignoring her dejected husbands, Drupada's
daughter said to the Matsya king, guarding her disguise and Law-
conforming pledge, while blazing with dreadful eyes—

Draupadī said:

15 Me, the proud wife of men whose enemy that walks the earth dare
not sleep, me a *sūta*'s son has kicked with his foot. Me, the proud wife
of men who give and do not beg, brahminic and true-spoken, me a
sūta's son has kicked with his foot. Me, the proud wife of men the
sound of whose war drums and bow strings is heard ceaselessly, me
a *sūta*'s son has kicked with his foot. Me, the proud wife of
resplendent, restrained, powerful, and prideful men, me a *sūta*'s son
has kicked with his foot. Me, the proud wife of men who could kill
off this entire world but are tied in the noose of the Law, me a *sūta*'s
20 son has kicked with his foot! Where on earth are the great warriors
roaming in disguise, they who were the refuge of those who sought
shelter? How can those powerful, boundlessly august men like
castrates suffer that their beloved and faithful wife is kicked by a
sūta's son? Where has their intransigence gone, where their virility
and splendor, if they choose not to defend their wife who is being
kicked by a blackguard? What am I to do with Virāṭa here who sees
the Law violated, an innocent woman kicked, and allows it? King,
you do not act like a king at all in the matter of Kīcaka, for your Law

25 is the Law of the Dasyus and does not shine in the assembly! Neither Kīcaka nor the Matsya abide in any way by their own Law. I don't blame you, King Virāṭa, in the assembly of the people, but it is not right that I am struck in your presence, Matsya! Let the courtiers bear witness to the crime of Kīcaka.

Virāṭa said:

You two quarreled out of my sight, and I don't know what it is all about. If I don't know the truth of the matter, how can I act sanely?

Vaiśaṃpāyana said:

Thereupon the courtiers learned the facts and gave praise to Kṛṣṇā: "Well done!" they said and condemned Kīcaka.

The courtiers said:

The man who has this long-eyed and fine-limbed woman for his wife has gained all and need never worry!

Vaiśaṃpāyana said:

30 The courtiers watched and applauded Kṛṣṇā there in this fashion, but the sweat of rage stuck to Yudhiṣṭhira's forehead. Then the Kauravya said to his beloved queen, the daughter of a king, "Don't tarry, maid, go to the house of Sudeṣṇā. The wives of heroes suffer indignities when they comply with their husbands; but in spite of the indignities, they win their husbands' worlds with obedience. I think your husbands do not regard this as the time of wrath; that is why the sunlike Gandharvas do not rush to your help. You have no notion of time, maid, you flutter about like a dancing wench. You disrupt the Matsyas who are dicing in the king's hall! Go, maid, the Gandharvas shall make you happy."

Draupadī said:

35 I follow the Law in the cause of men who are all too considerate! Any one may kick those whose eldest is a gambler!

Vaiśaṃpāyana said:

With these words the full-hipped Kṛṣṇā undid her hair and, with eyes bloodred from rage, ran to Sudeṣṇā's house. When she had stopped crying her face shone like the orb of the moon in the sky when it has shed streaks of clouds.

Sudeṣṇā said:

Who has beaten you, my pretty, why do you cry, woman with the lovely hips? Who shall suffer for it today, my dear, who has displeased you?

Draupadī said:

Kīcaka kicked me when I went to get liquor for you, while the king in the hall looked on as though we were alone!

Sudeṣṇā said:

40 I'll have Kīcaka killed, if you want, fair-tressed woman, for being crazed by his lust and having designs on you who are unattainable!

Draupadī said:

Surely others will kill him, whom he has wronged. I'm quite sure that he will die this very day!

Vaiśaṃpāyana said:

16.1 Having been kicked by that son of a *sūta* the flushed princess Kṛṣṇā burned with rage and planned the death of the marshal. Drupada's daughter, slim-waisted Kṛṣṇā, went to her room, where she washed up thoroughly. After she had washed her body and her clothes with water, she pondered tearfully on how to resolve her grievance: "What shall I do? Where should I go? How do I succeed?" And while she was thinking, she thought of Bhīma, "No one but Bhīma will now carry out what I want in my heart."

5 In the night Kṛṣṇā rose; the spirited woman left her bed and
rushed out, seeking her protector in a greatly troubled frame of
mind. The bright-smiling Pāñcālī approached Bhīmasena as an all-
white, three-year-old heifer that was born in the forest approaches a
bull, or an elephant cow a large male elephant. As a creeper clings
to a mighty flowering *śāla* tree on the bank of the river Gomatī, the
blameless woman embraced him and woke him up, as the female of
the king of animals wakes up a lion in a dense forest. Speaking
sweetly as a well-struck lute gives voice to the Gāndhāra note, the
innocent Pāñcālī said to Bhīmasena, "Get up, get up! How can you
lie as if dead, Bhīmasena? For that evil-doer who molested the wife
10 of one not dead shall not live! How can you enjoy sleeping as long
as that most evil marshal, my enemy, lives after perpetrating his
crime?"

Awakened by the princess, the Kauravya got up from his bed, and
sat down on a cushioned couch, appearing large as a raincloud. He
said to the princess, his beloved queen, "Why have you come to me
as though in a hurry? Your color is not normal, you look wan and
pale. Tell me everything completely so I will know, whether pleasant
or unpleasant, hateful or agreeable. Tell me everything exactly—I
15 will know what to do next. You can trust me in all matters, Kṛṣṇā,
and in adversity I shall save you again and again. Say quickly what
you want to have done and then go to bed again before others
wake up."

Draupadī said:

17.1 What pity doesn't a woman deserve who has Yudhiṣṭhira for her husband? You know all my troubles, so why do you ask me? It burns me, Bhārata, that an usher dragged me in the hall, in the middle of the assembly, calling me a slave! What woman like me, the daughter of a king, mark you, would want to live after experiencing such grief, except for Draupadī? And who would be able to bear being molested a second time, at the hands of the wicked Saindhava, when living in the forest? Now, before the eyes of the Matsya king, while that gamester looked on, I was kicked by Kīcaka—what woman like me would care to live after that? Don't you know, Bhārata Kaunteya, the many grievances that plague me? What point is there for me to live? This Kīcaka of the most evil heart, marshal and brother-in-law of King Virāṭa, O tiger among men, this blackguard constantly accosts me while I am living in the king's palace in the disguise of a chambermaid. "Become my wife," he says! Killer of your rivals, because I have been propositioned by a man who deserves to die, my heart is bursting like a fruit that has ripened with time.

Revile your eldest brother the gambler—it is his doing that I have gotten into this never-ending trouble! For who but a gambler would give up his kingdom, all property and himself, and gamble for a forest life? If he had wagered property worth a thousand *niṣkas* morning and evening for many years, he would never have exhausted his gold ore, gold bars, clothes, wagons, teams, sheep and goats, and herds of horses and mules. Under the name of a dicing match he was toppled from his fortune, and now sits silently like one dumb, brooding on his affairs. He who had ten thousand lotus-dotted, gold-caparisoned elephants to follow him where he went, now lives by gambling. A hundred thousand boundlessly splendid men waited on Mahārāja Yudhiṣṭhira in Indraprastha. A hundred thousand slave girls in the kitchen always fed, with platter in hand, his guests day and night. Thousands of *niṣkas* has that most generous man given away, and now he is covered with utter disaster on account of his dicing. Many bards and minstrels in fine voice, with earrings of polished gems, attended on him morning and evening. A thousand seers always sat in this hall, men of learning and austerity, and all had their wants seen to. Happily he supported all the blind, old, and unprotected and destitute in the kingdom; Yudhiṣṭhira was never mean. And now he has earned hell as a waiter of the Matsya. Yudhiṣṭhira calls himself Kanka, gamesmaster in the king's hall! He to whom at the time that he lived in Indraprastha all kings brought tribute now seeks wages from others. He who held all the kings on earth in his power now is helplessly in the power of others. Having illumined the whole earth with his brilliance like a sun, he is now the floor gambler of King Virāṭa. Pāṇḍava, looks at the Pāṇḍava: he on whom kings and seers waited in his hall now sits below another. Who does not grieve when he sees the undeserving, wise, and law-spirited Yudhiṣṭhira serve a king for his living? Bhārata, look at the Bhārata whom the entire earth obeyed in his hall—now he sits below another! Bhīma, don't you see how I am oppressed with many sorrows, in the midst of an ocean of grief?

Draupadī said:

18.1 This is my great grief, Bhārata, which I will relate to you. Do not
take me wrongly; I speak out of sorrow. When you are fighting with
tigers, buffalo, and lions in the inner court and that Kaikeya woman
watches you, I become faint. Getting up to look at me and noticing
that I seem to have taken faint, the Kaikeya woman of flawless limbs
will tell her women, "I think our brightly smiling maid has been
sleeping with the cook and out of love grieves over him when he is
made to fight with powerful creatures. Our chambermaid is quite
5 pretty, and Ballava is a most handsome man. A woman's heart is
hard to fathom, but I think they suit each other. The maid always
worries over him because they sleep together happily—and both of
them have been living in the king's palace for the same length of
time." She always makes me conspicuous with such words, and
when she sees my anger, she suspects me with you. When she talks
like that I feel very bad, and, drowning in my sorrow over Yudhiṣṭhira,
I cannot bear to live.

Sole chariot rider, he defeated Gods, men and Snakes, he who is
10 now the youthful dancing master of the daughters of King Virāṭa! The
Pārtha of measureless soul who satisfied the Fire God in the Khāṇḍava
lives now in the serail, fire hidden in a pit. Dhanaṃjaya, that bull
among men of whom the enemies always lived in fear, wears a
disguise that is despised by the world. At the sound of his bowstring
and palms the enemies trembled—to his pretty songs do women now
happily attend. A diadem resplendent like the sun sparkled on his
head—now Dhanaṃjaya has braided his hair in tresses. He, the
great-spirited man who possessed all celestial weapons, treasury of
15 all sciences, now wears earrings. Thousands of kings of matchless
prowess could not pass beyond him as the ocean does not pass
beyond the floodline—now he is the youthful dancing master of King
Virāṭa, hiding behind his disguise, the servant of girls. At the sound
of whose chariot the earth trembled, Bhīma, with mountains and
forests, standing and moving creatures, the lordly man at whose
birth Kuntī shed all grief, he now makes me suffer, Bhīmasena, your
younger brother. When I see him come, adorned with golden jewelry
20 and earrings, with conch shell in hand, my heart sinks. My heart
sinks, Bhīma, when I see Arjuna of the terrible bow with his hair
braided into a tress and surrounded by young girls. When I see the
Pārtha of the godlike appearance encircled by girls like a rutting
elephant by its cows, and in the service of the Matsya Virāṭa, his
paymaster, with his musical instruments all around him, I don't
know which way to turn.

Surely the Lady does not know to what straits Dhanaṃjaya has come or how deep the fool gambler Ajātaśatru Kauravya has sunk. When I see Sahadeva, the youngest, a master of warriors, going about

25 the cattle as a cowherd, I grow pale, Bhārata. I cannot find anything
that Sahadeva has done wrong, strong-armed Bhīma, however much
I think about his doings, which could have earned this man, whose
valor is his truth, such misery. I burn, best of the Bhāratas, when I
see your dear brother who looks like a bull among the cattle, try to
find favor with the Matsya. Zealous, wearing his red outfit, he leads
the cowherds and greets Virāṭa humbly, and it gives me a fever. For
the Lady always praises the brave Sahadeva to me for his high birth,
behavior, and character: "He is restrained by modesty, and gentle-
spoken, I love him, daughter of Yajñasena—you must watch over
30 him in the woods, even at night." Seeing him now preoccupied with
cows and sheltered at night by calf hides, our Sahadeva, the best of
warriors, how can I go on living, Pāṇḍava?

Nakula, always endowed with the three virtues of beauty,
swordsmanship, and intelligence, is Virāṭa's groom—look how the
times have changed! Crowds of onlookers turn out for Dāmagranthi
when he trains the horses in speed, while the great king watches.
I have seen him wait on the illustrious Virāṭa, the radiant king of the
Matsyas, showing off his horses. How can you think I am happy,
enemy-burning Pārtha, when I am plagued with hundreds of sorrows
35 on account of Yudhiṣṭhira? I suffer under even worse grievances,
Bhārata Kaunteya: I shall tell you, listen. What could be more
grievous than that all kinds of sufferings dry up my body, while you
are alive?

Draupadī said:

19.1 Because of that gamester I run about in the royal palace in the
guise of a chambermaid, cleaning up after Sudeṣṇā. I am a princess,
enemy-burner, but look at my sorry degradation! I am sitting out my
time as a sick person sits out all his miseries. Indeed, as they say,
fickle is the luck of man's affairs, his triumphs and defeats, and it is
with this thought that I wait for the resurgence of my husbands.
I wait, knowing that what causes a man to triumph also causes his
5 defeat. Men, so I have heard, first give, then beg; kill, then are
killed; fell, and are felled by their foes. Nothing is too heavy a burden
for fate, and there is no bypassing fate; and so I am waiting for fate
to descend. Reflecting that where there has been water before there
will be water again, I hope for our luck to turn, and await our
resurgence. As they say, if one's affairs come to nothing, however
well conducted, he should try to make his luck return, if he is wise.

Ask me, wretched woman that I am, what my real purpose is in
10 telling you this. Or don't ask, I'll tell you anyway! I, the queen of the
sons of Pāṇḍu and the daughter of Drupada, have come to this pass—
what woman but me would care to go on living? The sorrow that

has set upon me, Bhārata, enemy-tamer, disgraces all the Kurus,
Pāñcālas and Pāṇḍaveyas. What woman, slayer of enemy heroes,
could bear to be so miserable after having been elevated by her many
brothers, fathers-in-law, and sons? Surely I must have offended the
Placer as a child, and his disfavor, bull of the Bharatas, has brought
me misfortune. Pāṇḍava, look at my pallor, such as never visited me
15 before in the worst misery. Bhīma Pārtha, you know how happy I
have been; now I have been reduced to servitude, and helpless I find
no peace.

It cannot be but fate, I am sure, that Dhanaṃjaya Pārtha of the
fearful bow and strong arms sits there like a fire that has burned out.
Man cannot fathom the course of the creatures, Pārtha. I know the
downfall of all of you was beyond imagining. I whose face you
watched, you who are the likes of Indra, now watch the face of other
women inferior to myself, Pāṇḍava. Look at my circumstances which
20 I did not deserve. I on whose word earth waited to her boundaries
of oceans—I now timidly wait on the word of a Sudeṣṇā! I who had
servants before and behind me now run before and behind a Sudeṣṇā!
Listen to this insufferable grievance of mine, Kaunteya. Never before
had I ground make-up paste, even for my own body—except for
Kuntī and now, bless you, I am grinding sandalwood paste! Look at
my hands, Kaunteya; they certainly didn't look like that before.

Vaiśaṃpāyana said:

And with these words she showed him both her callused hands.

Draupadī said:

I was never afraid of either Kuntī or any one of you, but now I
25 stand as a scared serving wench before Virāṭa: "What shall the great
king say to me? Did I prepare the unguent well?" For it happens the
Matsya does not like the sandalwood as ground by others.

Vaiśaṃpāyana said:

Flushed, Kṛṣṇā wept softly while she enumerated her grievances
to Bhīmasena, watching his face. Sighing again and again she said
in a tear-choked voice, grating Bhīmasena's heart, "My offense to
the Gods cannot have been trifling, if I go on living in my misfortune
while I should die." Then the Wolf-Belly, slayer of enemy heroes, put
the swollen and callused hands of the shivering woman on his face
30 and sobbed. The valiant Kaunteya took her hands and, shedding a
tear in utter misery, said—

Bhīmasena said:

20.1 A plague on the strength of my arms and Phalguna's Gāṇḍīva, if
the hands that once were rosy have now become callused! I would
have wrought a great slaughter in Virāṭa's hall, if the King Dharma
had not stopped me with a glance. Catching his hint I stayed, radiant

woman. Our fall from the kingdom and my failure to murder the Kurus, Suyodhana, Karṇa, and Śakuni Saubala, and to cut off the head of the evil Duḥśāsana still burn me, fair Kṛṣṇā, like a thorn that is stuck in the heart. Don't destroy the Law, full-hipped Kṛṣṇā; abandon your wrath, sagacious woman. If King Yudhiṣṭhira were to hear this censure from you, fair woman, he would completely do away with himself, and so would Dhanaṃjaya, thin-waisted and full-hipped Kṛṣṇā, and the twins as well. And when they have gone to the other world, I shall not be able to survive myself.

Sukanyā, the daughter of Śaryāti, followed into the forest the Bhārgava Cyavana, who had become an anthill, in order to appease him. Indrasena Nāḍāyanī, of whose beauty you may have heard, followed her decrepit, one-thousand-year-old husband. You may have heard how Janaka's daughter, Sītā of Videha, followed her husband when he dwelled in the great forest. Rāma's beloved and fair-hipped queen was subdued by a Rākṣasa, and though she suffered she still followed no one but Rāma. Lopāmudrā likewise, O timid woman, while endowed with youth and beauty, gave up all her more than human comforts and followed Agastya. Just as these beautiful and faithful women have become famous, so you too, fair Kṛṣṇā, shall prevail with all your virtues. Don't grieve, bear this short time that is left, just a month and a half. When the thirteenth year is full you shall be a king's queen!

Draupadī said:

The tears that I shed in my sorrow, Bhīma, welled up because I cannot control my suffering, not to censure the king. The time has come, mighty Bhīmasena, for Kīcaka to be rid of his life; stand ready at once! Kaikeyī suspects I surpass her in beauty, Bhīma, and worries constantly that the king may come to me. Knowing her state of mind and seeing things in a false light himself, the wicked Kīcaka constantly propositions me. He has made me angry, Bhīma, but again and again, controlling my anger, I have told the love-besotted man, "Watch out for yourself, Kīcaka! I am the beloved wife of five Gandharvas, and those unassailable and violent champions may kill you!" But the evil Kīcaka replied to me, "I am afraid of no Gandharvas, sweet-smiling chambermaid. I'll kill a hundred or a thousand Gandharvas arrayed for battle, give me a chance, timid girl!" When he said that, I told the lovesick *suta* again, "You are no match for the glorious Gandharvas. I have always lived by the Law, Kīcaka, I am of good family and character. I don't want anyone killed; that is why you are alive, Kīcaka!" But the villain laughed out loud; he has not stayed on the path of the strict nor cultivated the Law. His soul is evil, his nature is evil, he is under the sway of his lust and passion. That boorish and corrupt man may have been rejected repeatedly, but at every encounter he strikes, so that I am ready to give up my

life. While you all strive for Law, a great Law is perishing: while
you keep up the covenant, your wife will be no more. But when you
guard your wife, offspring is protected, and when offspring is safe,
the self is safe. I have heard the brahmins propound the four classes
and life-stages, and never is there a Law for the baron but the
extirpation of his foes.

While the King Dharma looked on, and in your full sight too,
30 mighty Bhīmasena, a Kīcaka kicked me! It was you who saved me
from that ghastly Jaṭāsura, likewise you defeated Jayadratha with
your brothers. Kill this villain too, who despises me. Because he is
the king's favorite he pesters me, Bhārata! Break the love-crazed churl
as a pot on a stone, for he is the cause of my many woes, Bhārata.
If tomorrow the sun rises on him alive, I'll mix poison and drink it,
lest I fall victim to Kīcaka! It is better for me to die, right in front
of you, Bhīmasena!

Vaiśaṃpāyana said:

Clinging to Bhīma's chest, Kṛṣṇā began to cry. And Bhīma
embraced her and comforted her soothingly, while he thought of
Kīcaka and licked the corners of his mouth.

Bhīmasena said:

21.1 I shall do what you ask, my dear timid woman—today I shall
butcher Kīcaka and his kin. Make a tryst with that man for tomorrow
evening and shed your sorrow and grief, sweet-smiling Yājñasenī!
That dance pavilion that the Matsya king has had built—the girls
dance there by day, and at night they go home. There is a couch
there, timid Kṛṣṇā, well constructed with sturdy legs. There I shall
5 show him his predeceased grandfathers! Take care that people don't
see you when you make your tryst with him, my pretty, and see to
it he is there.

Vaiśaṃpāyana said:

So they talked and wretchedly shed a tear and bore with their
hearts the abominable remainder of that night. When the night had
passed, Kīcaka rose at dawn, went to the royal palace, and said to
Draupadī, "I threw you down and kicked you in the hall before the
king's eyes, and you found no rescue when someone stronger than
he manhandled you. The rumor among the Matsyas is that he is king
only in name, for I myself, the marshal of the army, am the king of
10 the Matsyas! Be happy, timid girl, I shall be your slave. I shall give
you a hundred *niṣkas* at once, full-hipped woman. I'll give you a
hundred slave women and another hundred male slaves, and a
chariot yoked with she-mules: let us tryst, timid woman!"

Draupadī said:

First accept one condition I have, Kīcaka: neither friend nor
brother must know that you are visiting me, for I am afraid that

the glorious Gandharvas may find out. Give me your promise, then
I am yours.

Kīcaka said:

I'll do as you tell me, full-hipped woman. I'll come alone to your
15 empty bedroom, my dear, to lie with you of the plantain thighs, madly
in love, so that your splendiferous Gandharvas do not find you out!

Draupadī said:

There is that dance pavilion that the Matsya king has had built.
The girls dance there by day, and at night they go home. Go there
when it is dark, and the Gandharvas won't notice it. Thus we will
avoid mistakes, no doubt of that.

Vaiśaṃpāyana said:

For Kṛṣṇā who was talking with Kīcaka about the affair the half
day became like a whole month, king. Mightily awash with joy,
Kīcaka went home—the fool did not realize that death had come in
20 the form of a chambermaid. Being beyond measure fond of perfumes,
ornaments, and garlands, he quickly prettified himself under the spell
of love. Time passed slowly while he did his work and thought about
his long-eyed woman. There was a bright luster about him who was
soon to lose all light, as there is about an oil lamp at the hour of its
extinction when it is about to burn up its wick. Love-crazed Kīcaka,
dupe of his trust, hardly noticed the day pass while he thought about
their meeting.

Thereupon Draupadī went to Bhīma in the kitchen, and the
25 beautiful woman approached her Kauravya husband. Finely tressed
Kṛṣṇā said to him, "I have made an assignation with Kīcaka in the
dance pavilion as you told me, enemy-burner. Kīcaka will come
tonight alone to the empty dance pavilion—butcher Kīcaka, my
strong-armed man! When that love-emboldened son of a *sūta* Kīcaka
comes to the pavilion, Kaunteya, rid him of his life, Pāṇḍava! His
insolence makes this *sūta*'s son despise Gandharvas! Pull him out,
best of fighters, as an elephant pulls out a reed, and wipe away the
tears of my misery, Bhārata. Bless you, make yourself and your
lineage proud!"

Bhīmasena said:

30 Welcome, woman of the lovely hips, now that you bring me good
news, for I don't want anyone to accompany him, fair lady. I take
the same pleasure in being told by you about the assignation with
Kīcaka, fair-skinned Kṛṣṇā, as I took in killing Hiḍimba. I swear to
you by my brothers and the Law that I'll kill Kīcaka as the Lord
of the Gods killed Vṛtra. Whether in public or in hiding I'll crush
Kīcaka; and if the Matsyas find out, I'll surely kill them too. Then
I'll kill Duryodhana and recover the earth—and let Kuntī's son
Yudhiṣṭhira wait on the Matsya as he pleases!

Draupadī said:
35 Strike down Kīcaka in secret, hero, keep your word!
Bhīmasena said:
I shall do today as you tell me, timid woman, unseen in the murky
night, blameless Kṛṣṇā. I shall crush the head of that evil Kīcaka,
who covets the unattainable, as an elephant tramples a wood apple.
Vaiśaṃpāyana said:
Bhīma was the first to get there, and he sat down hidden in the
night; and he waited for Kīcaka as an invisible lion for a deer.
Kīcaka, who had adorned himself to his fancy, arrived at the
appointed time in the dance pavilion, expecting to meet the Pāñcāla
40 princess. With his mind on the tryst he entered the room. And when
he had entered the large chamber, which was covered by dense
darkness, the villain came upon Bhīma of boundless luster, who had
arrived earlier and was sitting on the side. The *sūta* stroked the man
on the couch, who was to be his death and who seethed with rage
over Kṛṣṇā's molestation. Love-crazed Kīcaka came closer and, his
heart churning with pleasure, said smilingly, "I have brought you
infinite riches of many kinds, intending it all for you, and have come
45 to you hurriedly. The women in the house suddenly have begun to
sing my praises, 'No man is as gorgeous and handsome as you!'"
Bhīmasena said:
How fortunate you are handsome, how fortunate you vaunt
yourself! But never before have you been caressed like this.
Vaiśaṃpāyana said:
With these words strong-armed Bhīma Kaunteya of terrible power
jumped up and laughed at the vile man. Bhīma grasped him by his
chapleted and scented hair. Kīcaka, himself quite strong, freed his
hair from his powerful grasp and quickly seized the Pāṇḍava by the
arms. They began to wrestle, those furious lionlike men, as two
50 mighty bull elephants in spring over a cow. When Bhīma was fading
a little and staggered from sheer rage, the powerful Kīcaka threw
him on the floor on his knees. Brought down by the brawny Kīcaka,
Bhīma flew rapidly up like a snake that is hit with a stick. Drunk
with their strength, the mighty *sūta* and Pāṇḍava competed in
wrestling in the desolate pavilion at the dead of night. That fine
building shook again and again, and the raging men roared at each
other powerfully. Bhīma hit strong Kīcaka on his chest with the flat
55 of his hands, but Kīcaka, blazing with fury, did not miss a step. After
enduring for a while the other's unendurable impact on the wrestling
ground, the *sūta* began to fail in strength under the pressure of
Bhīma's blows. Knowing that he was fading, the mighty Bhīmasena
clutched him quickly to his chest and squeezed him till he fainted.
Panting, the rage-possessed Wolf-Belly, that greatest of victors, grabbed

Kīcaka painfully by the hair. Holding Kīcaka the powerful Bhīma
roared out like a tiger that is hungry for meat and has caught a large
deer. He pushed his feet, hands, head, and neck all into his trunk,
as the Pināka bowman once did with the beast.
60 When Kīcaka had been rendered one mangled ball of flesh, mighty
Bhīmasena showed him to Kṛṣṇā. And the resplendent joy of the
Pāṇḍavas said to Draupadī, "Look, princess of Pāñcāla, what has
become of your lover!" Having killed Kīcaka and quenched his rage,
he took leave from Kṛṣṇā Draupadī and hurried back to the kitchen.
Now that Draupadī, choicest of women, had had Kīcaka killed, she
rejoiced and felt no longer vexed. She told the hall guards, "Kīcaka
here lies killed at the hands of my Gandharva husbands, for he lusted
65 madly after another's wife. Come and look at him!" Upon hearing her
words the guards of the dance pavilion hastily crowded in by the
thousands, carrying torches. They went into the building and saw
Kīcaka felled and lifeless and splashed with blood. "Where is his neck,
where are his feet, where his hands and head?" they wondered, and
concluded that he had been killed by a Gandharva.

Vaiśaṃpāyana said:
22.1 In time all Kīcaka's kinsmen gathered there and, on seeing him,
surrounded him and wept. Their hair stood on end, and they shivered
when they saw Kīcaka with all his limbs mangled, like a tortoise
pulled up on dry land, crushed by Bhīmasena as a Dānava by Indra.
They began to carry him outside, wanting to perform the funerary
rites. Then the gathered *sūta*'s sons saw Kṛṣṇā of the flawless limbs
5 standing not too far away where she was leaning on a pillar. While
the *sūtas* crowded together, an Upakīcaka said to them, "Let us kill
at once this whore for whom Kīcaka has been killed! Or rather, let
us not kill her here but burn her with her lover. Let the *sūta*'s son
have his pleasure, even though dead!"
They said to Virāṭa, "Kīcaka has been killed for this woman. Let
her burn with him now; give us permission!" Knowing that the
sūtas had the upper hand, the king approved that the chambermaid
be burned with the *sūta*'s son, O lord of your people. The Kīcakas
made for the lotus-eyed Kṛṣṇā, who stood trembling, and grabbed her
10 hard while she swooned away. They lifted up the slim-waisted woman,
tied her, and all carried her to the burning field. But while the
blameless Kṛṣṇā was being carried off by the *sūta*'s sons, O king, she
began to scream for her protectors, for she had protectors.
Draupadī said:
Jaya, Jayanta, Vijaya, Jayatsena, Jayadbala, listen to me! The
sūta's sons are taking me away. Glorious and impetuous Gandharvas,
the terrifying clang of whose bows and palms is heard in grand

battles like the crackle of lightning, and the thunder of whose chariots is mighty, listen to me, the *sūta*'s sons are taking me away!"

Vaiśaṃpāyana said:

15 As soon as Bhīma heard the piteous plaints of Kṛṣṇā, he jumped
from his bed without hesitation.

Bhīmasena said:

I hear what you are saying, chambermaid. Therefore you have nothing to fear, fearful woman, from those sons of *sūtas*!

Vaiśaṃpāyana said:

The strong-armed man, in a murderous rage, stretched his body
and made it swell. He adjusted his clothing, burst out the door, and
went outside. Bhīmasena hastily tore a tree from the ramparts and
stormed to the burning field where the Kīcakas had gone.
Brandishing the tree, which was ten spans long, with trunk and
branches and all, the strongman ran to the *sūtas* like Death wielding
20 his staff. Banyan, *aśvattha*, and *kiṃśuka* trees fell on the ground from
the impact of his thighs and lay in piles.

When they saw the Gandharva storming at them like an angry
lion, all the *sūtas* trembled and shook with fear and despair. The
Upakīcakas, watching the Gandharva come like Death when they
were about to burn their eldest brother, said to one another, shaking
with fear and despair, "There is a mighty Gandharva coming,
furiously brandishing a tree. Quick, set the chambermaid free, we
are in great danger!" And seeing that tree swung by Bhīmasena,
they let go of Draupadī and fled toward the city.

25 When Bhīmasena saw them in full flight, as the Thunderbolt-
wielder sees the Dānavas, he sent a hundred and five of them to
Yama's realm. Then the strong-armed men freed Kṛṣṇā and
comforted her, O lord of your people, and the unassailable, strong-
armed Wolf-Belly said to Draupadī of Pāñcāla, who was wretched,
her face streaming with tears, "There they lie slaughtered, timid
woman, they who molested you in your innocence. Go on to the
city, Kṛṣṇā, you have nothing to fear. I'll go to Virāṭa's kitchen by
a different road."

Thus, O Bhārata, a hundred and five lay killed like a big forest
that has been cut and its trees scattered. Those hundred and five
Kīcakas were dead, king, as was the marshal before them, in all a
30 hundred and six of them. And when the men and women had
gathered and saw that great miracle, they were completely astounded,
Bhārata, and found nothing to say.

Vaiśaṃpāyana said:

23.1 When they saw the *sūtas* slain, they went and told the king, "Sire,
more than a hundred sons of *sūtas* have been killed by Gandharvas.

The *sūtas* are like the mighty crown of a mountain that has been rent
and scattered by a thunderbolt! That chambermaid has been set free
and is returning to your house. Now your entire city is in danger,
sire! For the chambermaid is so beautiful, the Gandharvas are
powerful, and men, no doubt, have a pleasurable propensity to
5 copulation. Lay down at once a policy by which this city of yours
does not meet its destruction in the guise of a chambermaid, king!"

Virāṭa, master of armies, listened to their words and replied, "Let
the obsequies be performed for these *sūtas*. All the Kīcakas are at
once to be cremated in one single, well-kindled fire with jewels and
incense all around." And the king said to his queen Sudeṣṇā, for he
had become terrified, "When the chambermaid comes back, tell her
in my name, 'Go away, chambermaid, bless you, go anywhere you
please, full-hipped woman, for the king fears defeat at the hands of
10 the Gandharvas!' I cannot myself tell her that, for she is protected by
Gandharvas, but women are inoffensive, and that is why I ask you
to tell her."

Kṛṣṇā now, rescued from danger with the *sūta*'s sons annihilated,
and set free by Bhīmasena, went back to the city, like a young but
spirited doe that had been terrified by a tiger, after washing her limbs
and both pieces of clothing with water. When men saw her, O king,
they fled in all ten directions, and in terror of the Gandharvas some
shut their eyes. Then, sire, the princess of Pāñcāla saw Bhīmasena
standing at the kitchen door like a large rutting elephant.
15 Wonderstruck she said softly in secret language, "Homage to the
Gandharva king who has set me free!"

Bhīmasena said:

The men that wander here at a woman's beck and call now, having
but heard her word, wander without debts!

Vaiśaṃpāyana said:

Then she saw strong-armed Dhanaṃjaya in the dance pavilion
where he was teaching the daughters of King Virāṭa to dance. The
girls came out of the pavilion with Arjuna and saw Kṛṣṇā come, who
had been molested in her innocence.

The girls said:

How lucky that you have been freed, chambermaid, how lucky
that you have come back! How lucky again that the *sūtas* who
molested you, an innocent woman, have been killed off!

Bṛhannaḍā said:

20 How have you been set free, chambermaid, how did the villains
get killed? I want to hear from you everything that happened!

The chambermaid said:

Bṛhannaḍā, what business do you have with a chambermaid? You
always live comfortably in the girls' quarters, my pretty. You do not

find the sorrows that chambermaids reap, so you question me, wretch, as a joke!

Bṛhannaḍā said:

Bṛhannaḍā too, reduced to bestiality, finds misery beyond measure, my pretty. You do not know her, child!

Vaiśaṃpāyana said:

Thereupon Draupadī entered the royal palace with the girls and,
25 not being wont to retreat, went to Sudeṣṇā. In Virāṭa's name the princess said to her, "Chambermaid, go at once wherever you want to go. The king, bless you, fears defeat at the hands of the Gandharvas. Besides, girl with the lovely brows, you are young, and peerless on earth in beauty!"

The chambermaid said:

Let the king excuse me for just thirteen days more. Then, no doubt, the Gandharvas will have done what they set out to do. And then they will take me away and do you favors. They surely will bestow felicity on the king and his kinsmen.

4(47) The Cattle Raid

4.24–62 (B. 25–67; C. 861–2159)

24 (25; 861). The land of the Matsya is pleased to be rid of the Kīcakas (1). Duryodhana's spies searching for the Pāṇḍavas return unsuccessful to Hāstinapura and report to Duryodhana that the Pāṇḍavas have disappeared (1–15). They also report that Kīcaka of Matsya has been overthrown (15–20).

25 (26; 883). Duryodhana, disappointed, is about to send out his spies again, when Karṇa suggests he employ better ones (1–10). Duḥśāsana supports Karṇa, but expresses the opinion that the Pāṇḍavas may well be dead (10–15).

26 (27; 902). Droṇa, however, doubts that the Pāṇḍavas, sustained by their mutual loyalty, could have perished; a new search should be made (1–10).

27 (28; 912). Bhīṣma now raises his voice: he agrees with Droṇa that the Pāṇḍavas are alive. There is one sure way to find them: they will be living in a country which, thanks to their virtues, is prospering in every respect (1–20). But he doubts they can be found at all (25).

28 (29; 947). Kṛpa agrees with Bhīṣma: the Pāṇḍavas will inevitably reemerge; therefore the Kauravas should

secure their allies and levy an army (1–10).
29 (30; 971). The Trigarta king Suśarman, previously vanquished by Kīcaka of Matsya, happens to be visiting in Hāstinapura and proposes that with Kīcaka out of the way Virāṭa is powerless and vulnerable to an invasion and cattle raid: Kauravas and Trigartas should band together (1–10). Karṇa supports Suśarman's idea of launching an expedition with the consent of the elders (10–15). Duryodhana agrees: Suśarman and his Trigartas should make a sneak attack on Matsya, with the Kaurava forces following up one day later (20–25). Suśarman agrees, marches out and raids cattle (25).
30 (31; 1000). At this point the Pāṇḍavas' covenant of the thirteen years has expired. Suśarman raids Virāṭa's cattle, and the chief herdsman reports to Virāṭa (1–5). The king marshals his troops, including those of his brother Śatānīka and the latter's son Madirāśva (5–10). A description of the armor of the combatants is given (10–15). Virāṭa orders the Pāṇḍavas (except Arjuna) armed and mounted (15–25). Virāṭa rides out to counter the Trigartas (25–30).
31 (32; 1036). The Matsyas engage the Trigartas (1–10). Various Matsya heroes penetrate the enemy's rank. Virāṭa pushes on to Suśarman and fights him on his chariot (15–20).
32 (33–34; 1067). At nightfall both sides withdraw, but when the moon rises, fighting resumes. Suśarman and his brother attack Virāṭa, kill his horses and capture him (1–5). The Matsyas give way. Yudhiṣṭhira urges Bhīma to free Virāṭa, but not to show his superhuman strength (5–20). Together the Pāṇḍavas return to the battle, dispatching many hundreds (20–25). Yudhiṣṭhira attacks Suśarman, who puts up a fight; Bhīma kills Suśarman's horses, Suśarman's guards flee, and Virāṭa jumps from the chariot. Bhīma captures Suśarman (25–35). Virāṭa rewards his liberators, and wishes to anoint Yudhiṣṭhira to the kingdom. Yudhiṣṭhira advises him to send messengers to proclaim victory in the city (35–50).
33 (35; 1149). Meanwhile Duryodhana invades Matsya and drives off 60,000 head of cattle (1–5). The herd overseer hurries to the city, enters the palace and exhorts Virāṭa's son Uttara to attack the Kauravas (5–20).
34 (36; 1171). Uttara explains that he has no

charioteer, otherwise he would rout the Kauravas all by himself; he brags, comparing himself to Arjuna (1–5). Draupadī resents this and tells Uttara that Bṛhannaḍā has been Arjuna's charioteer. Bṛhannaḍā is fetched by Uttara's sister (5–15).

35 (37; 1195). Uttara's sister asks Bṛhannaḍā to drive for Uttara (1–5). Uttara too asks him (10–15). Arjuna clowns before the girls; then they ride out. The girls ask Arjuna to bring back clothes for their dolls, and he promises to do so (15–25).

36 (38; 1230). Soon the Kaurava army appears and Uttara panics, despairing of attacking these powerful enemies (1–10). Arjuna drives on as Uttara whines (10–15). Arjuna berates him: he will be the laughing stock of the town after his bragging (15–20). Uttara does not care and jumps from the chariot, and Arjuna, with his skirt flapping, pursues him on foot. The enemy soldiers laugh (20–25). But the Kauravas think that the charioteer may be Arjuna. Uttara tries to buy Arjuna off, but the latter tells him that, if he cannot fight, he can at least drive; he forces the prince back on the chariot (40–45).

37 (39; 1285). The Kauravas tremble at the sight of Arjuna; bad portents appear, indicating that Arjuna is matchless (1–10). Karṇa and Duryodhana protest (10–15).

38 (41–43; 1311). Arjuna reaches the sāmī *tree where the weapons are hidden. He tells Uttara to get them (1–5). Uttara protests: there is a polluting corpse there (5–10). Finally he climbs the tree and unwraps the packs (10–15). Uttara asks whose weapons they are and describes them (20–35). Arjuna gives the history of Gāṇḍīva (35–40) and identifies the other weapons (40–55).*

39 (44; 1367). In response to Uttara's question where the Pāṇḍavas themselves are, Arjuna identifies himself and the others (1–5). Uttara asks for Arjuna's ten names and their significance; Arjuna tells him (5–20). Uttara salutes him and expresses affection (20).

40 (45; 1394). Arjuna announces his intention of attacking all the Kauravas and recovering the cattle; Uttara is no longer afraid. But how, he asks, did Arjuna become a eunuch? Arjuna replies that he is not really a castrate; he merely kept a vow of chastity (1–10).

Uttara calls himself a great charioteer. Arjuna assumes his proper appearance (10–25).
41 (46; 1436). Arjuna rides out, reassuring Uttara, who is frightened by the sound of Arjuna's conch and by his standard (1–15). Droṇa recognizes Arjuna by the signs; the Kauravas must stand firm (15–20).
42 (47; 1471). Duryodhana states that the thirteenth year is not over yet, so the Pāṇḍavas have to go back to the forest. He worries about the fate of the Trigartas and stresses his duty to fight instead of standing idle (1–15). Droṇa is partial to Arjuna, he says, because he is his teacher; actually, one should ignore pundits (15–30).
43 (48; 1507). Karṇa boasts that he is at least Arjuna's equal, and will kill him (1–20).
44 (49; 1530). Kṛpa scoffs. He lists Arjuna's feats—what has Karṇa done? It is folly to fight Arjuna (1–20).
45 (50; 1554). Aśvatthāman joins in: Karṇa talks a brave fight (1–10). Arjuna has not forgiven Draupadī's molestation and the deceitful dicing game (10–20). Aśvatthāman opposes the idea of fighting (25).
46 (51; 1583). Bhīṣma, however, thinks that they should fight, and that Droṇa and Aśvatthāman, who are both brahmins and warriors, should forgive Karṇa (1–10). They do so. Droṇa asks Bhīṣma about the time expired (10–15).
47 (52; 1606). Bhīṣma starts calculating. Thirteen years include five intercalary months and twelve days. The Pāṇḍavas have indeed carried out the covenant (1–5). Being true to the Law, they will not give up now. The Kauravas should prepare for war (5–10). Duryodhana refuses to give back the kingdom (15). Bhīṣma proposes a battle plan (15).
48 (53; 1630). Arjuna approaches and Droṇa recognizes his standard (1–5). Arjuna tells Uttara to drive so he can scout out Duryodhana (10–15). Duryodhana understands the maneuver and orders an attack on Arjuna's rear (16–20). Arjuna blows his conch and at the sound the raided cows lift their tails and turn around (20).
49 (54; 1660). Arjuna tries to push through to Duryodhana and Karṇa (1–5). Vikarṇa attacks him, but Arjuna shoots down his standard, and Vikarṇa flees. Śatruṃtapa and many others fall (5–15). Karṇa's brother Saṃgrāmajit is decapitated; Karṇa attacks

Arjuna, but is hit with many arrows and takes to flight (15–20).

50 (55; 1696). Arjuna directs Uttara toward Kṛpa and Droṇa. He will not strike Droṇa first (1–5). Close by Droṇa is his son Aśvatthāman. Duryodhana's appearance is described (5–10). Karṇa and Bhīṣma are also there (15–20). Uttara drives to Kṛpa (20).

51 (56; 1759). Indra and other Gods arrive to watch the power of their weapons handled by Arjuna. Many ancient kings also appear (1–10). The presence of the Gods is spectacular (10–15).

52 (57; 1779). Arjuna and Kṛpa engage in a great duel of arrow volleys (1–5). Arjuna shoots Kṛpa's horses, which rear so that Kṛpa loses his footing; Arjuna holds off. Arjuna then cuts Kṛpa's bow in two and blows off his armor without hurting him (5–20). He splits a second bow and hits his chest. Kṛpa throws his club, which is stopped by Arjuna. Kṛpa is quickly carried away (10–25).

53 (58; 1823). Arjuna tells Uttara to drive to Droṇa, whom he praises (1–5). Droṇa drives up and blows his conch (5–10). Arjuna salutes Droṇa and tries to placate him. Droṇa shoots (10–15). The two duel with bow and arrow in heroic fashion (15–60). Indra applauds Arjuna. Aśvatthāman joins the duel so that Droṇa can withdraw (60–65).

54 (59; 1901). They fight until Aśvatthāman's horses are weary. He cuts Arjuna's bowstring, to the Gods' applause. Arjuna restrings his bow (1–10). Arjuna, whose quivers are inexhaustible, waits out Aśvatthāman. Karṇa now attacks and Arjuna turns his attention to him (10–15).

55 (60; 1923). Arjuna taunts Karṇa to prove his boasts; he will avenge Draupadī (1–5). Karṇa accepts the challenge with insults; Arjuna replies that Karṇa fled after his own brother's death (5–10). They duel. Arjuna cuts the other's quiver strap; Karṇa wounds Arjuna's hand. Finally Arjuna shoots Karṇa's horses and wounds him in the chest. Karṇa leaves the battlefield and Arjuna reviles him (10–25).

56 (61; 1950). Arjuna directs Uttara to Bhīṣma, whom he will now attack. He recites his own feats to reassure Uttara (1–15). Attacked, Bhīṣma holds his ground. Duḥśāsana, Vikarṇa, Duḥsaha, and Viviṃśati rally to

Bhīṣma. Uttara is wounded by Duḥśāsana, whom Arjuna then puts to flight. Vikarṇa, Duḥsaha, and Viviṃśati are likewise eliminated (15–25).

57 (62; 1998). All the Kauravas now converge on Arjuna and he fells many in a great massacre (1–15).

58 (63; 2021). Duryodhana attacks, with many others returning to the battle. Sorely pressed, Arjuna manages to keep himself covered (1–5). He counterattacks and drives his opponents to flight (5–10).

59 (64; 2035). Bhīṣma himself now attacks, blowing his conch. He hits Arjuna's standard; the other cuts down his umbrella, and hits his standard and horses (1–5). The arrows volley back and forth, as the Kauravas cheer Bhīṣma (10–20). Both duelists receive applause. Arjuna splits Bhīṣma's bow; he takes another. More arrows fly. The battle sways back and forth (20–25). The Gods watch and Citrasena praises Arjuna. Indra rains flowers on both (25–35). Finally Arjuna hits Bhīṣma in the chest and his charioteer drives him off (40).

60 (65; 2086). Duryodhana attacks and is struck in the forehead. He furiously presses on, joined by Vikarṇa (1–5). Arjuna kills Vikarṇa's elephant and hits Duryodhana, who flees (5–15). Arjuna challenges him to return to battle (15).

61 (66; 2105). Stung, Duryodhana turns about and is followed by Karṇa, Bhīṣma, Droṇa, Kṛpa, Viviṃśati, and Duḥśāsana. They surround Arjuna (1–5). Arjuna blows his conch and the sound stuns all to unconsciousness. He tells Uttara to collect the warrior's clothes, except Bhīṣma's. He does so. Bhīṣma alone is still conscious and shoots a few last arrows; he is incapacitated by Arjuna (5–15). Arjuna withdraws. When Duryodhana comes to, he berates Bhīṣma, who laughingly tells him to go home. The Kauravas all now retreat (15–20). Arjuna sends arrows after them, shooting off Duryodhana's crown. He blows his conch in triumph, and orders Uttara to return to the city (20–25).

62 (67; 2136). Straggling Kaurava soldiers appear, and Arjuna sends them off (1–5). Arjuna tells Uttara to give the herdsmen time to collect the cattle and to rest the horses. Then, Arjuna says, Uttara is to have victory proclaimed in his own name (1–10).

Vaiśaṃpāyana said:
24.1 The slaying of Kīcaka and his younger brothers, O lord of your
people, made the folk recall how hateful they had been, and they
were astonished. In city and countryside everywhere the gossip went,
"The mettlesome Kīcaka was the king's favorite because of his
bravery, but he was a bully with men and an evil-minded woman
chaser. And now, to be sure, the Gandharvas have killed the wicked
man!" Thus the people in region after region gossiped about the
unassailable Kīcaka, who in his day had scattered enemy armies.
5 The spies abroad who were in the Dhārtarāṣṭra's employ had been
searching many villages, kingdoms, and towns, while carrying out the
country-by-country inspection to which they had been assigned; and
at last they returned with anxiety to the City of the Elephant. There
they saw the King Kauravya, who was the son of Dhṛtarāṣṭra, along
with Droṇa, Karṇa, Kṛpa, and the great-spirited Bhīṣma. They said
to Duryodhana, who was seated in the middle of the assembly hall,
in the company of his brothers and the Trigarta warriors, "Indra
among men! We have been making the greatest of efforts to find
10 those Pāṇḍavas in that vast wilderness. The forest is empty of people,
but teeming with game; it is wooded with many kinds of trees and
creepers, with plentiful canopies of lianas, and full of tree clumps of
many sorts. But we have not found out where the Pārthas of
steadfast bravery may have gone. Everywhere and in every way have
we searched for their trail, on high mountain peaks and in many
countrysides, in populous regions and mountain hamlets and towns.
Indra of men, in many directions have we searched, but we have not
found the Pāṇḍavas. They have disappeared totally, good luck to
thee, bull among men!

"While we were looking for the trail of the warriors, O best of
warriors, Indra of men, we followed for some time their charioteers,
15 and in our search we tracked them down expertly and made certain
they had reached Dvāravatī without the Pārthas, enemy-burner.
The Pāṇḍavas are not there, king, nor their faithful Kṛṣṇā; they have
vanished completely. We don't know where the great-spirited men
have gone and are living, nor do we have any tidings of the Pāṇḍavas
and the work they are doing. Instruct us, Indra among men, lord of
your people! What are we to do next again in the search for the
Pāṇḍavas?

"But now examine our pleasanter message, which is to your benefit
and bodes well. The very man who vanquished the Trigartas with a
large army, the great-spirited Kīcaka, the charioteer of King Matsya,
20 lies fallen and killed in the night by unseen Gandharvas, King
Bhārata! He the villain himself, as well as his brothers, unvanquished
lord! Having heard the happy news of the downfall of your enemies,

you can be contented, Kauravya. Take measures for the future."

Vaiśaṃpāyana said:

25.1 When King Duryodhana heard their words, he remained sunk in
thought for a long while, then replied to the men in the hall, "Indeed,
it is very hard to probe the course of events to the end. Therefore all
of you must find out where the Pāṇḍavas may have gone. There is
little time left, indeed most is gone, of their life in concealment in this
thirteenth year. When the Pāṇḍavas complete the rest of this year,
they will have accomplished the covenant, devoted as they are to the
5 vow of truth. Like gliding princes of Snakes, like poisonous serpents,
they will all surely be sorely enraged at the Kauravas. But, if they
are discovered before the time is up, they will once more return to
the forest, controlling their anger and wearing their wretched
disguises. Therefore seek to discover them quickly, so that our
kingdom may be for a long time completely stable, without discord,
undistracted, and without rivals!"
Thereupon Karṇa said, "Bhārata, have other and shrewder men
go, clever and faithful agents. Let them travel in disguise to
prosperous and populous regions and there inquire at any gatherings,
10 among saints and mendicants, on trails, at sacred fords and various
mining areas, where people might find them out with well-guided
reasoning. Let different devoted and fully expert men in clever disguises
shrewdly search for the hiding Pāṇḍavas at rivers and bowers, fords,
villages and towns, in lovely hermitages, on mountains and in caves!"
Then the younger brother Duḥśāsana said to his elder brother,
who was amenable to his evil nature, "Let us look to what Karṇa
just said: let all our spies search hither and yon as ordered, these and
many others more, from country to country and in the proper
15 fashion. No trace has been found of the Pāṇḍavas' trail, residence,
and occupation. They are either most untowardly concealed, or have
gone across the ocean. Those self-styled champions may well have
been devoured in the vast forest by beasts of prey, or otherwise have
come to grief and perished for good. Therefore clear your mind of
everything else, joy of the Kurus, and do your task vigorously, if you
agree, king of men!"

Vaiśaṃpāyana said:

26.1 Thereupon spoke mighty Droṇa, who saw the truth of the matter,
"Such men do not perish, nor do they meet defeat, for they are
gallant, informed, sagacious, in control of their senses, conversant
with the Law, grateful, and loyal to the King Dharma, who, himself,
knows the truths of policy, Law, and Profit, wishes them well like
a father, abides by the Law, and rests on his truth—their eldest

brother who respects his elders. King, the brothers are devoted to
their great-spirited brother, Ajātaśatru, and that modest man himself
5 is devoted to his brothers. Why should the prudent Pārtha not have
at heart the well-being of his obedient brothers, great-spirited and
faithful? Therefore they must be waiting expectantly for their luck to
improve, for I see in my mind that they have not met their death.
Reflect sanely therefore and waste no time doing what the hour
dictates to find out where they are living. Pāṇḍu's sons, who hold
their own in all matters, brave and sinless men committed to
austerity, will surely be hard to find out. The pure-spirited and
virtuous Pārtha, true-spoken, prudent, and upright, who can be
10 called a mass of splendor, would blind a person's two eyes! Let us
act in that knowledge and once more search for them with the aid
of brahmins, spies, and holy men, and whoever else has the skill!"

Vaiśaṃpāyana said:

27.1 Then Bhīṣma Śāṃtanava, grandfather of the Bharatas, learned in
the Veda, knowledgeable about places and times, alert to the facts,
wise in all the Laws, raised his voice when the Teacher had finished
speaking. To the Bhāratas he addressed his words for their benefit,
words partial to the law-wise Yudhiṣṭhira and consistent with the
Law. Bhīṣma made his speech, which was difficult for the lax to
receive, but desirable to the strict and welcomed by the good.

"It is as the brahmin Droṇa, who knows all the facts of Profit, has
said: The Pāṇḍavas, who are endowed with all propitious marks,
5 cannot be dead! They have learning and manners, they follow good
vows, they are bent upon instruction by the old, and devoted to the
vow of truth. Since they know of covenants, and are keeping the
covenant, being pure in their vows, they cannot collapse while they
are carrying the yoke of the strict. The Pāṇḍavas are protected by the
Law and their own prowess, and my belief is that they have not yet
met their death.

"I shall expound my thoughts concerning the Pāṇḍavas, Bhārata,
albeit the policy of the prudent cannot be fathomed by others. What
is possible for us while we reflect on the Pāṇḍavas is to solve the
question with intelligence, not with hostility. I shall speak to it then;
10 listen. Son, a man who abides by the instruction of his elders and
practices the truth must give good counsel, and in no way evil. If
one is wise and wishes to give advice in the midst of the strict, he
must inevitably, in order to obtain Law, speak entirely according to
his lights. I do not think as the others do in this matter. In the town
or countryside where King Yudhiṣṭhira dwells there will be no people
who are discontented, jealous, offensive in speech, or envious.
Everyone will be avowed to his own Law. The sounds of the *brahman*

will be plentiful, the oblations will be completed, and the sacrifices
15 will be abundant and rich. There, no doubt, God Parjanya will rain
in the proper season, and the earth will bear rich crops and be free
from plagues. The rice will be fine, the fruit juicy, the garlands
fragrant, speech gentle, the wind pleasant to feel, visits agreeable,
and no fear will enter where King Yudhiṣṭhira lives. Cows will be
teeming, none of them lean or poor milk-givers; the milk, curds and
butter will be tasty and wholesome. Water will be salubrious and
foodstuffs delicious in the country where King Yudhiṣṭhira lives.
20 Taste, touch, smell, and sound will be full of virtue, and sight serene,
where King Yudhiṣṭhira lives. All things will have their proper virtues
in this thirteenth year in the country that shelters the Pāṇḍavas, my
son. The people there will be confident, contented, pure, and healthy,
affectionate to Gods, guests, and all creatures, liberal, vigorous, always
devoted to the Law, hostile to the impure, eager for the pure, always
sacrificing and holy in their vows, where King Yudhiṣṭhira lives. They
will be without falseness in their words, my son, of pure, beautiful,
and auspicious aspect, desirous of holy things, and of holy spirit,
where King Yudhiṣṭhira lives, and always follow agreeable vows.
25 "The law-spirited Pārtha, invisible, cannot in the end be found out
by brahmins, let alone by common people! In him are truth,
perseverance, liberality, complete serenity, firm patience, modesty,
fortune, fame, superb splendor, gentleness, and honesty. Therefore
I think that the sagacious man is there concealed under his disguise—
I cannot explain his sublime course otherwise. Think then upon what
act you deem beneficial and do it quickly, Kauravya, if you have
faith in me."

Vaiśaṃpāyana said:

28.1 Now Kṛpa Śāradvata spoke, "What the old man has said about the
Pāṇḍavas is fitting and apt, consistent with Law and Profit, agreeable,
and argued factually. Listen now to what I have to say in agreement
with Bhīṣma. Let us discover their trail and their present dwelling
place through holy men, and execute a policy which is now to our
profit. Son, if a man wishes to go on living he should not despise even
an ordinary enemy, let alone the Pāṇḍavas, who are expert with all
5 the weapons of war. Therefore, since the Pāṇḍavas are in disguise,
and are living in hiding until the time is up, you should make sure
of your own strength in your own kingdom and those of others.
When the time for resurgence has come for the Pāṇḍavas, those
great-spirited and powerful Pārthas, having accomplished their
covenant, will no doubt be full of vigor, for the Pāṇḍavas are
extremely energetic. Therefore lay down a force, a treasury, and a
policy, so that, when the time comes, we can properly treat with

10 them. I think, son, that you should ascertain your full strength
relative to all your allies, whether strong or weak. When we know
whether we are stronger, weaker, or on a par, we shall treat with
the others, happily or unhappily. We shall persuade the stronger
enemies with diplomacy, alienation, bribery, punishment, and tribute,
in the right manner, and persuade the weaker ones with force. Having
reassured our allies, we should levy an army easily, and with a
bountiful treasury and force you will attain to complete success. You
will battle other powerful enemies that attack, or the Pāṇḍavas, who
are lacking in forces and mounts. Having thus taken your decision
according to your own Law at the proper time, Indra among men,
you shall find happiness for a long time!"

Vaiśaṃpāyana said:

29.1 Then Suśarman, the king of the Trigartas, a leader of a flock of
chariots, who had been repeatedly defeated in the past by the
Matsyas allied with the Śālveyakas, and by Matsya's charioteer
Kīcaka, hastened to speak these opportune words. Having been
forcibly oppressed with his relatives by the powerful warrior, he
looked at Karṇa and said to Duryodhana, my lord, "The Matsya king
has over and over again oppressed my kingdom with his superior
5 might. The powerful Kīcaka used to be his marshal, a cruel,
intransigent, evil-spirited man, whose bravery was famed on earth.
The cruel villain has now been killed by Gandharvas, and with him
dead, king, I am convinced that Virāṭa will be left without pride,
recourse, and initiative. If you approve, prince sans blame, I think
that I, all the Kauravas, and the great-spirited Karṇa should mount
an expedition there. The happenings in my view demand urgent and
profitable action: march upon his kingdom with its opulent crops.
We shall plunder his jewels and various treasures, or we may take
10 his villages and realms and divide them. We might also reduce his
city by force and rob his many thousands of fine cattle. Joining forces
with the Kauravas and Trigartas, let us drive off his cows, lord of
your people, well attended by all! Or we can bridle his valor and,
having defeated his entire army, dictate peace and bring him under
our sway. After we have subjugated him, we shall dwell there
happily, and your army will no doubt swell accordingly!"

When he heard his words, Karṇa said to the king, "Suśarman has
15 spoken well and timely, and to our profit. Let us have our armored
forces yoke their mounts, array the ranks, and march out at once,
or whatever you think, prince sans blame. Let us mount an expedition
in any way that the sagacious eldest of the Kurus, who is grandfather
of us all, the Teacher Droṇa, and Kṛpa Śāradvata think best. Let us
quickly consult, and march and overpower the king! Why bother

with the Pāṇḍavas, who are lacking in possessions, forces, and valor?
Either they are totally lost, or have departed for Yama's realm. King,
let us attack the land of Virāṭa without apprehension, for we shall
take his cattle and manifold treasures."
20 King Duryodhana quickly accepted the advice of Karṇa Vaikartana
and himself immediately gave orders to Duḥśāsana, who always
waited on his command: "Consult at once with the elders and have
the army yoked. We shall go as ordered with all the Kauravas. The
great warrior King Suśarman shall go to his assigned part of the
country with his Trigartas and his complete force of troops and
mounts, but under cover at first, to the land of the Matsya. We shall
bring up the rear one day later and march together on the very rich
25 kingdom of the Matsya. Arriving suddenly at Virāṭa's city we should
immediately subdue the cowherds and take their ample wealth. We
shall divide our army into two and rob his hundreds of thousands of
glossy-coated and excellent cattle."

King Suśarman as agreed marched in a southwesterly direction and
on the seventh day of the warm fortnight began to rob cattle. A day
later all the Kauravas joined forces and on the eighth day robbed
the thousands of cowsheds.

Vaiśaṃpāyana said:
30.1 It was then, great king, that for the great-spirited and boundlessly
lustrous Pāṇḍavas, who had assumed disguises while they were living
in Virāṭa's fine city doing chores for the king, the time of the
covenant expired. Then, at the end of the thirteenth year, O Bhārata,
Suśarman robbed the ample cattle wealth swiftly. The herdsman
hastened with great speed to the city and, with his earrings on,
5 jumped from his chariot and saw the Matsya king, who was
surrounded by warlike champions wearing earrings and upper-arm
bracelets, together with his good councilors and the bull-like
Pāṇḍavas. He approached the great king seated in the hall, bowed
to Virāṭa, who caused his kingdom to prosper, and said, "The
Trigartas have defeated and overpowered us and our relatives in a
skirmish and are now driving off hundreds of thousands of your cows.
Look after them, Indra among men, lest your cattle be lost!"

When the king heard this, he had the army of the Matsyas yoked
with a great number of chariots, elephants, and horses; the
assemblage stirred with foot soldiers and pennants. At their various
positions the kings and princes put on their glistening and colorful
10 armor, well worth the honor they paid it. Virāṭa's favorite brother
Śatānīka donned a golden cuirass with an underlay of diamond-hard
iron. Madirāśva, Śatānīka's junior, put on a hard, solid-iron coat of
mail which was beautifully plated. The king of the Matsya himself
wore a well-nigh impenetrable armor with a hundred suns, a hundred

circles, a hundred dots, and a hundred eyes. On Sūryadatta's armor
a hundred lotuses and *saugandhikas* were embossed, and it was gold-
plated and bright as the sun. Śankha, Virāṭa's gallant eldest son, wore
15 a white, steel-based cuirass with a hundred eyes. The hundreds of
great warriors of divine aspect, all put on their armor and took up
their weapons, ready to give battle. The warriors yoked to each of
their bright and large, fully equipped chariots horses which were
harnessed in gold. On the divine chariot of the Matsya a majestic
standard of gold was raised, shining like the sun and moon, and the
baronial champions hoisted more standards of various design and
with gold ornamentation; each raised his own on his chariot.
Thereupon King Matsya said to his junior Śatānīka, "It is my
intention that Kanka, Ballava, the cowherd, and heroic Dāmagranthi
20 also should fight, no doubt of that. They too should be given chariots
with flags; they must wear on their bodies colorful cuirasses, both
hard and supple ones, and be issued weapons. They are men with
the bodies of champions, like the trunks of kings of elephants. I am
sure they have never refused to give battle."
Hearing the king's orders the quick-witted Śatānīka assigned
chariots to the Pārthas, O king, to Sahadeva, the king, Bhīma, and
Nakula. Charioteers, showing their loyalty to the king, quickly yoked
the chariots that had been assigned by the king of men. The colorful
cuirasses, both hard and supple, which Virāṭa had given to these men
of unsullied deeds, the enemy-burners put on their limbs and thus
25 were armored. Still in disguise, the impetuous and experienced fighters,
bull of the Kurus, all followed Virāṭa—those four heroic Pāṇḍava
brothers whose strength was their truth. Terrifying rutting elephants
with riven temples, well-tusked sixty-year-olds like gliding clouds,
well-mounted by expertly trained riders, followed behind the king like
moving mountains. His experienced Matsya followers, obedient and
cheerful, had 8,000 chariots, 1,000 elephants and 60,000 horses to
march with. That army of Virāṭa, O bull of the Bharatas, shone as
30 it marched, great king, and sought the trail of the cows. There
was a splendor about Virāṭa's fine army on the march, with its
ranks of heavily armed men and masses of elephants, horses, and
chariots.

Vaiśaṃpāyana said:

31.1 After marching forth from the city the warlike Matsyas, arrayed
in ranks and carrying weapons, made contact with the Trigartas when
the sun went down. The powerful Trigartas and Matsyas, furious and
battle-drunk, shouted at one another, greedy for cattle. The terrifying
rutting elephants were goaded with lances and hooks by the mounted
chieftains, who were expert riders. At the clash of these forces there
arose an ugly, hair-raising roar while the sun sank, as of the Gods

5 and Asuras. Dust arose from the ground, nothing could be discerned,
birds tumbled to the ground covered with dust. The sun disappeared
behind arrows shot back and forth, but the compact sky was lit up
as though by fireflies. The gold-backed bows of the archers, world-
famous heroes who shot right-handed and left, got tangled when they
fell. Chariots engaged chariots, foot soldiers other foot soldiers, riders
attacked riders, elephants elephants. They hit one another with
swords, three-bladed spears, missiles, javelins, and lances, while they
10 were raging in battle, O king. While these champions with arms like
bludgeons pressed their attack furiously, they were unable to turn
the enemy champions back. A severed head was seen with the upper
lip gashed, the fine nose intact, the hair shorn, bejeweled, covered
with dust and still wearing earrings. There were limbs of heroes cut
in pieces by arrows in the mêlée, looking like *śāla* trunks. The earth
was covered with many earringed heads like coils of snakes, still
sprinkled with sandal. Dampened by the spurting blood the dust
subsided, but the foul and grisly battle went on unbridled.
15 Śatānīka, killing a hundred, and Viśālākṣa, killing four hundred,
penetrated the grand Trigarta army. The great warriors pressed on
furiously, hair to hair and nail to nail. On seeing the chariot park of
the advancing Trigartas, Sūryadatta and Madirāśva brought up the
rear. Virāṭa, having felled five-hundred warriors in the fight, hundreds
of horses and five great champions, made his way variously among
the chariots, that herdsman of a flock of chariots, till he encountered
Suśarman of Trigarta on his golden chariot on the battlefield. The
two great-spirited and powerful kings struck out at each other,
20 roaring like two bulls in a cowpen. The chariot fighters circled each
other on their chariots, loosing arrows as nimbly as clouds let go of
their water streams. Impatiently and furiously they pursued each
other with their honed arrows, expertly carrying their swords,
javelins, and clubs. Then the king pierced Suśarman with ten arrows
and his four horses with five arrows each; but likewise battle-crazed
Suśarman hit the Matsya king most skillfully with fifty sharp shafts.
The armies of the Matsya king and Suśarman vanished in the dust-
laden evening and could not discern each other.

Vaiśaṃpāyana said:

32.1 When the world was bathed in darkness and dust, Bhārata, the
fighters withdrew for the nonce without breaking ranks. Then rose
the moon, dispelling the darkness, and washed clean the night,
gladdening the barons on the battlefield. With light restored the
battle resumed its ugly shape and the combatants had no regard for
one another. Suśarman of Trigarta and his younger brother rushed at
the king of the Matsyas from all sides with a host of chariots.

5 The brothers, bulls among barons, jumped from their chariots, each
wielding a bludgeon, and ran fiercely to the horses.

> And the raging forces of all of them
> Began to attack and to storm one another
> With bludgeons and swords and battle-axes
> And sharp-pointed arrows with fine copper blades.
>
> Suśarman, the overlord of Trigarta,
> With his troops churned up the Matsya's forces
> And masterfully dealt the Matsya defeat,
> Then stormed at Virāṭa of august might.

The two killed both the draft horses and the outriders and
captured alive the king of the Matsyas, who had lost his chariot.
Suśarman manhandled him as though he were a crying new bride,
had him mount his own chariot, and went on with his swift steeds.
10 When the chariotless Virāṭa, though himself a strong man, had
been captured, the Matsyas under the heavy pressure of the Trigartas
began to flee in terror. And with them frightened away, Kuntī's son
Yudhiṣṭhira said to the strong-armed Bhīmasena, "Suśarman Trigarta
has taken captive the king of the Matsyas. Set him free, strong-armed
champion, let him not fall in the hands of the enemy! We all have
happily stayed with him and been treated hospitably with all
comforts. Bhīmasena, you must acquit us of the debt we owe him
for our sojourn!"

Bhīmasena said:

I shall rescue him on your orders, king. Behold my great feat
15 when I battle the enemy! Stay here on the side with our brothers,
relying on the strength of your own arms, and witness my bravery
now! This tall tree with the sturdy trunk stands here like a club—I
shall uproot it and drive off the enemies!

Vaiśaṃpāyana said:

Yudhiṣṭhira, the King Dharma, said to his gallant brother who like
a mad elephant was eyeing the giant of the forest, "Don't commit
violence, Bhīma! Let that tree stand, Bhārata, lest the people, when
you do your superhuman feats with a tree, recognize you for Bhīma.
Get hold of some other, human weapon, a bow or spear, a sword or
20 battle-axe. Take a human weapon that will not be noticed by the
others and quickly free the king. The powerful twins will guard your
wheels, while you in battle formation protect the king of the Matsyas,
friend!"

Thereupon they all together goaded their horses, displaying divine
weapon spells, impatient with the Trigartas. Seeing that the Pāṇḍavas
were returning on their chariots, the mighty host of Virāṭa took

furious heart and fought a most wonderful battle. Kuntī's son
Yudhiṣṭhira struck down a thousand, while Bhīma showed seven
hundred fighters the way to the other world. Nakula too dispatched
25 seven hundred with his arrows, and the majestic Sahadeva three
hundred champions. As Yudhiṣṭhira had ordered, the bull among
men scattered and slew the vast army of the Trigartas, O bull
among men.

Then the great warrior King Yudhiṣṭhira made haste and rushed
at Suśarman, pelting him with his arrows. Suśarman in turn attacked
furiously and shot Yudhiṣṭhira with nine arrows, and his four horses
with four. Now Kuntī's fast-acting son the Wolf-Belly attacked
Suśarman and annihilated his horses, O king. He killed his two rear
guards with superbly directed arrows and fiercely tore the charioteer
30 from his seat. Suśarman's wheel guard, a famous champion named
Śoṇāśva, seeing the Trigarta king without a chariot, abandoned him
in terror. Virāṭa now jumped from Suśarman's chariot, grasped his
club and mightily assaulted the other—the old warrior, brandishing
his club, pursued him like a youth. Bhīma of terrible mien jumped
from his chariot—with his earrings still on—and caught the king of
Trigarta as a lion catches a small deer.

When the great Trigarta warrior had lost his chariot and was
captured, the entire force of Trigarta broke up, sick with fear. After
Suśarman's defeat all the mighty sons of Pāṇḍu turned the cattle
35 around and took back all the treasure. Endowed with strong arms but
restrained by modesty, those men of strict vows spent the night
happily in the vanguard of the army.

Virāṭa rewarded the great warrior sons of Kuntī, whose prowess
was superhuman, with wealth and honors.

Virāṭa said:

My jewels are yours as they are mine. Use them, all of you, as you
wish and please. I shall give you bejeweled girls and all manner of
treasures, and whatever else comes to your mind, uprooters of foes!
It is by your valor that I have been rescued today and am safe here;
therefore you are now all lords of the Matsyas.

Vaiśaṃpāyana said:

40 To the Matsya who had thus praised them, each of the Kauraveyas,
preceded by Yudhiṣṭhira, made his reply with folded hands, "We
welcome your entire word, lord of your people, but this alone restores
our faith: that you have been set free from your enemies today!"
Thereupon the Matsya king, pleased, again said to Yudhiṣṭhira, did
that strong-armed Virāṭa, that most excellent king, "Come, I shall
anoint you, you must be the king of us Matsyas! Whatever you have
in mind, uprooter of enemies, that I shall give you, for you deserve
everything from us! Vaiyāghrapadya, Indra among brahmins, take

jewels, cows, gold, gems, and pearls, and in every way be there
45 homage to thee! For it is because of you that I am alive today to see
my kingdom and myself. The enemy who did me violence is now in
my power!"

Yudhiṣṭhira replied again to the Matsya, "I welcome the kind
words you speak, Matsya! Be always disposed to gentleness and be
happy forever. Let messengers quickly go to your city, king, to bring
the happy news to your family, and let them proclaim your victory."
At his words the Matsya instructed his messengers, "Go to the city
and announce that I have triumphed in battle! Adorn the princes
and let them come here from the city, and let all musical instruments
50 come out and the courtesans in their finery!" And having gone that
same night they proclaimed in the city at sunrise the victory of Virāṭa.

Vaiśaṃpāyana said:

33.1 When the Matsya was marching to Trigarta to recover his cattle,
Duryodhana and his councillors invaded Virāṭa's territory. Bhīṣma,
Droṇa, Karṇa, the master of arms Kṛpa, Droṇa's son, Saubala, and
Lord Duḥśāsana, Viviṃśati, Vikarṇa, and the valiant Citrasena,
Durmukha, Duḥṣaha, and the other great warriors invaded the
Matsya country of King Virāṭa, captured the cow stations swiftly, and
5 forcibly plundered the cattle wealth. The Kurus drove off 60,000 cows,
encircling them with a large train of chariots. In the cowsheds rose
the loud outcry of the cowherds being killed by the warriors in the
terrifying encounter.

The overseer of the cattle in panic quickly mounted a chariot and
drove to the city in deep grief. Arriving at the city he went on to the
king's palace, jumped hurriedly from the chariot and entered to
report. He found there a prideful son of the Matsya's, Bhūmiṃjaya
by name, and he told him the entire story of the plunder of the cattle
10 of the kingdom: "The Kurus are driving off 60,000 cows! Rise up to
recover the cattle wealth, which is the prosperity of the kingdom.
Prince, if you have your well-being at heart, march quickly out in
person, for King Matsya has left you in charge of the empty country.
The king boasts of you in the midst of the assembly: 'My son takes
after me, he is a hero and the mainstay of the dynasty. He is an
expert with arrows and javelins, my son, and always a brave fighter.'
Make the words of the king come true and turn back the Kurus and
recover the cattle, best of the cattle-rich! Burn down their ranks with
15 the terrible fire of your golden-nocked shafts, smoothed at the joints,
from your bow. Break the ranks of the enemy like the chief of an
elephant herd. Sound forth the lute of your bow, with the loops as
its end blocks, the string as its cord, the back as its base, the arrows
as its notes; sound forth the singing lute of your bow in the midst

of the enemies. Let your silvery white horses be yoked to the chariot,
and let them raise your standard, the golden lion, my lord. The
golden-nocked, smooth-tipped arrows which you dexterously shoot
shall obfuscate the sun and half the lives of the kings! Having
vanquished all the Kurus in battle as the Thunderbolt-wielder
vanquished the Asuras, you shall earn great fame on returning to
20 the city. For you, the Matsya king's son, are our last resort. Let all
that dwell in the land find in you their recourse today!"

When he was so addressed amidst the womenfolk, the prince
applauded these confidence-inspiring words and made his reply.

Uttara said:

34.1 This very day I would follow the trail of the cows with my hard
bow, if some expert horseman were my charioteer. I don't know
what man could drive me. Look quickly for a charioteer who will
suit me as I ride out! My own charioteer was killed in that great
battle that lasted surely twenty-eight days if not a month. If I find
another driving expert, I shall swiftly ride out with my great standard
5 raised, plunge into the enemy army with its numerous elephants,
horses, and chariots, defeat the Kurus, who will be unmanned by the
majesty of my sword, and bring back the cattle! I shall sow panic in
the hearts of Duryodhana, Śāṃtanava, Karṇa Vaikartana, Kṛpa,
Droṇa and his son, and all the assembled great archers in the battle,
as the Thunderbolt-wielder did to the Dānavas, and in an instant
bring back the cows. Finding the country empty, the Kurus march
away with our cattle wealth, but what am I to do when I am not
there? The assembled Kurus shall today behold my prowess: "Is it
Arjuna the Pārtha himself who is beating us down?"

Vaiśaṃpāyana said:

10 When Uttara spoke like that amidst the women again and again,
the princess of Pāñcāla resented the mention he made of the Terrifier.
She approached him from among the womenfolk, and with a bashful
air the apparently humble woman said softly to him, "That handsome
youth like a mighty elephant, known as Bṛhannaḍā, has been the
charioteer of the Pārtha. He was the great-spirited man's pupil and
not his lesser with the bow. I have seen him before, hero, when I
served with the Pāṇḍavas. When Fire burned down the vast
15 Khāṇḍava forest, he drove Arjuna's fine horses. With him as his
charioteer the Pārtha defeated all creatures everywhere in the
Khāṇḍava Tract, for there is no driver like him. Your younger virgin
sister with the shapely hips, he will certainly carry out her orders,
hero! If he is your charioteer, then without a doubt you are sure to
return after defeating all the Kurus!"

At these words of the chambermaid Uttara spoke to his sister, "Go,
my girl of the flawless limbs, and fetch that Bṛhannaḍā." Dispatched

by her brother, she hastened to the dance pavilion where the
strong-armed Pāṇḍava lived hidden behind his disguise.

Vaiśaṃpāyana said:
35.1 When Bṛhannaḍā saw his friend the large-eyed daughter of the
king, he laughed and asked why she had come, O king. Approaching
the bull-like man the princess said to him, displaying her affections
amidst her friends, "The cattle of the kingdom are being driven off
by the Kurus, Bṛhannaḍā! My brother is going out to defeat them
with bow in hand. A short time ago his charioteer was killed in
battle, and there is no driver who is his equal to handle the chariot.
While he was busy looking for a charioteer, Bṛhannaḍā, the
chambermaid mentioned to him your expertise with horses. Do the
driving for my brother, please, Bṛhannaḍā, before the Kurus take
our cows too far away. If you don't do today what I am asking you
with affection, I'll give up my life!"
At these words of his full-hipped friend, the enemy-burner of
boundless luster approached the prince. And while he made haste
like a rutting elephant, the large-eyed girl followed him as a baby
10 elephant follows its mother. Seeing him at a distance the prince
addressed him, "With you as his charioteer, the Pārtha satisfied the
Fire God in the Khāṇḍava, with you Kuntī's son Dhanamjaya
conquered the entire earth. That is what the chambermaid told me,
for she has known the Pāṇḍavas. Drive my horses as well, Bṛhannaḍā,
while I battle with the Kurus to recover our wealth of cattle. At one
time you were the favorite charioteer of Arjuna, and with you as
his companion the bull of the Pāṇḍavas conquered the earth!"
Bṛhannaḍā replied to the prince, "What skill do I have in handling
15 a chariot in a pitched battle? If you want a song or a dance or some
piece of music, I can do that, bless you, but how would I drive a
chariot?"
Uttara said:
You shall be a songster and dancer again, Bṛhannaḍā, but first
you must get on my chariot and drive my fine horses!
Vaiśaṃpāyana said:
The enemy-tamer, who knew it all, jested merrily in front of
Uttarā.* He put on his coat of mail upside down, and the wide-eyed
maidens giggled when they saw him. Seeing his confusion, Uttara
20 himself tied the costly armor on Bṛhannaḍā. Himself wearing a
superb coat of mail which shone like the sun, and raising his lion
standard, he ordered the other to handle his chariot. Taking expensive
arrows and many glittering bows, the hero rode out with Bṛhannaḍā
as his driver.
Then Uttarā and her girl friends said to him, "Bṛhannaḍā, you

* = Uttara's sister.

must bring back to us bright clothes for our dolls, fine and colorful
clothes of all kinds, when you have beaten the Kurus in battle, led
by Bhīṣma and Droṇa!" The Pārtha, the joy of Pāṇḍu, replied to the
words of the girls, laughing in stentorian tones, like thunder or a
25 kettledrum, "If Uttara defeats those great warriors in battle, I'll bring
you back heavenly and beautiful clothes!" And with these words the
heroic Terrifier goaded the horses on toward the Kurus, who flew
flags and pennants of many kinds.

Vaiśaṃpāyana said:

36.1 Bhūmiṃjaya, the son of Virāṭa, rode out of the capital and said to
his charioteer, "Drive on to the Kurus! I shall defeat the Kurus, who
have joined ranks desirous of victory; I shall recover the cows
quickly and return to my city." Pāṇḍu's son thereupon urged on the
fine steeds, and under the urging of the lionlike man the wind-fast
horses in their golden harnesses carried the two men as though
scraping the sky.

They had not gone very far before the enemy-killing son of the
Matsya and Dhanaṃjaya espied the army of the powerful Kurus; and
5 he approached the Kurus close by a burning field. Their large army,
which roared like the ocean, appeared like a heavily wooded forest
crawling through space. The dust thrown up by their crawl was
clearly visible, blinding the creatures and reaching up to the sky,
O best of men.

When the son of Virāṭa saw that vast host teeming with elephants,
horses, and chariots, and protected by Karṇa, Duryodhana, Kṛpa,
Śāṃtanava, and the great sagacious archer Droṇa with his son, the
hair on his body bristled, and terror-stricken he said to the Pārtha,
"I cannot do battle with the army of the Kurus, with its multitude of
champions: it is most dreadful, unassailable even by the Gods, and it
stretches endlessly! I have no hopes of penetrating the Bhārata army
with its fearsome bows, masses of chariots, elephants, and horses,
10 and its innumerable foot soldiers and flags. For merely the sight of
the army on the battlefield makes my soul tremble! There are Droṇa,
Bhīṣma, Kṛpa, Karṇa, Viviṃśati, Aśvatthāman, Vikarṇa, Somadatta,
Bāhlika, and brave King Duryodhana, best of the chariot warriors,
all those brilliant archers experienced in warfare. Just the sight of the
Kurus, armed and in battle ranks, makes my hair stand on end!
I have lost all courage.

Vaiśaṃpāyana said:

But Arjuna did not change course while the braggart, who had
lost his bearings in his folly, looked on. The nitwit wailed before the
15 left-handed archer, "Father has marched on the Trigartas after
placing me in charge of an empty kingdom, and he has taken the

entire army along. I have no troops! I am all by myself, a child without experience; I won't be able to do battle with so many experienced armsmen. Turn around, Bṛhannaḍā!"

Arjuna said:

You are wretched with fear and add to the joy of your enemies! And the others haven't done a thing yet in the way of battle! You told me yourself to drive to the Kurus; well, I'll take you where their numerous battle flags are flying! I shall take you, my strong-armed hero, to the middle of the Kurus, who are murderous like vultures
20 greedy for food, were they to fight underground! To men and women you boasted of your manliness; still bragging you rode out, so why don't you want to fight? If you return home now without having captured those cows, all the men and women will laugh at you, hero. I too was praised by the chambermaid for my driving—I won't be able to go back to the city without recovering the cows. The chambermaid praised me, you ordered me, so why should I not fight all the Kurus? Be calm!

Uttara said:

So let the Kurus rob most of the wealth of the Matsya, let the men and the women laugh at me, Bṛhannaḍā!

Vaiśaṃpāyana said:

25 With these words the earringed coward jumped from the chariot and fled, stupidly abandoning his pride and throwing away his bow and arrows.

Bṛhannaḍā said:

Flight never was known to the ancient as the Law of the baron, It is better for you to die than to flee like a coward!

Vaiśaṃpāyana said:

Saying this Dhanaṃjaya Kaunteya leaped from that fine chariot and pursued the running prince; his long braid was trailing and his red skirts fluttering. Not knowing that it was Arjuna running there with the fluttering braid some of the soldiers burst out laughing at the spectacle. But on seeing him run nimbly the Kurus said: "Who
30 is that behind his disguise, as fire below its ashes? He has something of a man and something of a woman. He is built like Arjuna and wears the form of a eunuch. That is his head, his neck, his bludgeonlike arms, that is his stride, he is no one but Dhanaṃjaya! As Indra is among the Immortals, so is Dhanaṃjaya among men. Who on earth but Dhanaṃjaya would attack us alone? One son of Virāṭa was posted in the empty city and he, mind you, ventured out, not out of bravery but in childish folly. Surely that is Arjuna Pārtha running there hidden beneath his disguise. Uttara made him his
35 charioteer when he rode out of the city, but I take it, when he saw the flags, he ran away in terror. And now surely Dhanaṃjaya is

trying to catch the young prince." So were all the Kurus speculating
individually, but could not arrive at a final conclusion, when they
saw the Pāṇḍava concealed by his disguise, Bhārata.

Dhanaṃjaya meanwhile kept after Uttara and in a hundred paces
overtook him and quickly caught him by his hair. Virāṭa's son, caught
by Arjuna, began to wail as though in pain, wretchedly and at length:
"I'll give you a hundred *niṣkas* of pure gold and eight sparkling beryl
40 gems set in gold and a chariot with a golden standard, yoked with
well-grazed horses and ten rutting elephants—let me go, Bṛhannaḍā!"

Vaiśaṃpāyana said:

While Uttara was wailing mindlessly in this fashion, the tigerlike
man laughed and dragged him to the chariot. Then the Pārtha said to
the panic-stricken youth who had lost his mind, "If you are unable to
fight with the enemy, enemy-plougher, come and drive the horses
while I fight the enemy. Protected by the strength of my arms let us
attack the dread, unassailable host of chariots that is guarded by
heroic warriors, first of princes: you are a baron, enemy-killer!
45 I myself shall fight with the Kurus and win back your cattle. Be my
driver and penetrate the battle line of chariots, which is hard to
breach and assault, while I fight the Kurus."

Thus speaking, the unvanquished Terrifier reassured Uttara awhile,
bull of the Bharatas; then the Pārtha, greatest of fighters, forced the
witless, reluctant, and terror-stricken prince onto the chariot.

Vaiśaṃpāyana said:

37.1 Seeing the bull-like man standing on the chariot in the guise of a
eunuch and heading for the *śāmī* tree, after forcing Uttara onto the
chariot, the chief warriors of the Kurus, from Bhīṣma and Droṇa
onward, felt their hearts tremble out of fear of Dhanaṃjaya. Noticing
their loss of vigor as well as observing wondrous portents, the
Teacher Bhāradvāja, best of the bearers of arms, said, "Changeable
winds are blowing, harsh and grating, the sky is covered with an
5 ashen darkness, the clouds look rough-textured and are strange to
behold, our various weapons are falling from their sheaths! Jackals
are howling, grisly there on the burning horizon, the horses are
shedding tears, and the flags are fluttering in the stillness. With such
and so many portents seen, you must stand prepared, for a battle
will be forthcoming.

"Protect yourselves! Array the army! Expect a bloodbath! Watch
the cattle wealth! A hero has come, a great archer, the best of the
10 bearers of arms: it is the Pārtha no doubt, in the guise of a eunuch. It
is the valiant Pārtha, the enemy-killing left-handed archer. He will
not turn back without giving battle, were he to fight all the bands of
the Maruts. Hardened in the forest and trained by Vāsava, the

champion has become implacable and is going to do battle, no doubt of that. I don't see a fighter to match him, Kauravas! It is said that even the Great God was satisfied by the Pārtha in a duel!"

Karṇa said:

You always malign us with the virtues of Phalguna, but Arjuna isn't worth a fraction of me or Duryodhana!

Duryodhana said:

If he is the Pārtha, Rādheya, my task will be finished. Once recognized, they will have to wander once more for twelve years.
15 Or if that is another human in the guise of a eunuch, I shall cast him to the ground with sharp arrows!

Vaiśaṃpāyana said:

While the enemy-burner Dhārtarāṣṭra was speaking these words, Bhīṣma, Droṇa, Kṛpa, and Droṇa's son cheered his manly courage.

Vaiśaṃpāyana said:

38.1 Reaching the *śamī* tree, the Pārtha said to Virāṭa's son, whom he recognized as being quite delicate and not very experienced in combat, "On my orders fetch quickly my bows, for these ones of yours will not be able to stand my strength, to tolerate heavy pressure, to strike down an elephant, or to measure up to the full range of my arms, when I am about to vanquish our enemies here. Therefore make haste and climb this leafy *śamī* tree, Bhūmiṃjaya,
5 for in it are hidden the bows of the sons of Pāṇḍu, Yudhiṣṭhira, Bhīma, the Terrifier, and the Twins, as well as the standards, arrows, and the celestial armor of the champions. There is also the powerful bow Gāṇḍīva of the Pārtha, which by itself is worth a hundred thousand ordinary bows, assuring the well-being of the kingdom. It is supremely supple; it is as tall as a vine palm, matches any other weapon, and wreaks havoc among enemies; it is inlaid with gold, divine, smooth, long, and without blemishes. It can stand heavy pressure, and is terrifying and beautiful to the eyes. All the other bows are similarly powerful and tough."

Uttara said:

But I have heard them say that there is a body tied up in this
10 tree! I am a prince; how could I touch it with my hand? It is unbecoming for me, born a baron, a high prince who knows rituals and spells, to handle such a thing! Why would you make me as polluted as a cadaver-carrier, Bṛhannaḍā, and open to condemnation, as I would be if I touch a corpse?

Bṛhannaḍā said:

You shall be open to condemnation but unpolluted, Indra of kings! Have no fear: there are bows here, not corpses. Why would I force you, the heir of the king of the Matsyas, the spirited son of a dynasty, to do a condemned act, prince?

Vaiśaṃpāyana said:

At these words of the Pārtha the earringed son of Virāṭa jumped from the chariot and, against his inclination, climbed the *śāmī* tree. The enemy-killer Dhanaṃjaya ordered him from behind, where he stood on the chariot, "Remove the wrappings quickly!" The other loosened the wrappings all around and set eyes on Gāṇḍīva and four other bows. And from the bows, effulgent as the sun, there emanated while they were being unwrapped a divine luminescence as of planets on the ascendant. When Uttara saw the shapes of the bows, like stretched-out snakes, his hair stood on end and for a moment he felt terror. Touching the luminous and sturdy bows, O king, the son of Virāṭa said to Arjuna—

Uttara said:

Whose is this superb bow, worth a thousand millions, in which a hundred golden eyes are set? Whose is this superb bow with the smooth sides and easy grip, on the back of which glisten tusked elephants in gold? Whose is this superb bow, on whose back there are sixty fireflies in patterns made of the purest gold? Whose is this superb bow on which sparkle three golden suns with their rays, ablaze with splendor? And whose is this superb bow, on which there are golden locusts adorned with refined gold and encrusted with gems set in gold? These thousand feathered arrows with golden and silver nocks, encased in a golden quiver, whose are they? And these wide arrows with vulture feathers, whetted on stone, yellow like turmeric, finely tipped, made of copper and solid iron? This black quiver marked with five tigers and pig's ears, which holds ten arrows, whose is it? Whose are these broad, long, solid copper arrows, these seven hundred blood-thirsty shafts? And these arrows, well-fletched, with a shaftment like parrot feathers, with an upper shaft of copper and with golden nocks, honed on stone? Whose is this long and large sword with a frog in its back and a frog on its head, sheathed in a tiger-skin scabbard, with a gold-ornamented hilt? Whose is this divine, golden-hilted sword without the slightest blemish, with its fine sheath, black with bright color, and little bells? Whose is this stainless, golden-hilted Niṣadhan sword, sheathed in a cow-leather scabbard, unassailable and capable of any task? Whose is this sword with its golden grip, stuck in a sheath made of the skin of a five-clawed beast, of fine size and shape, yellow like the sky? And this heavy, well-tempered copper sword, completely without blemishes in its firelike sheath of refined gold? Tell me as it is the case at my bidding, Bṛhannaḍā. Seeing all this grand weaponry I have become greatly amazed!

Bṛhannaḍā said:

The first one of all the bows you are asking about is the Pārtha's

bow Gāṇḍīva, the uprooter of enemy armies, famed in the worlds.
Foremost of all weapons and adorned with fine gold, this Gāṇḍīva
was Arjuna's exquisite weapon. Measuring up to a hundred thousand
and assuring the success of the kingdom, this bow aided the Pārtha
in withstanding Gods and men in battle. Brahmā wielded it for a
thousand years, and it was worshiped by Gods, Dānavas, and
40 Gandharvas for years without end. After him Prajāpati held it for
503 years, Śakra for 85, King Soma for 500, and Varuṇa for a
hundred. The Pārtha of the white horses has it for 65 years, this
magnificent, large, and divine bow of great power. Honored among
Gods and mortals, it bears a superb beauty. That fine-sided, golden-
gripped bow is Bhīmasena's, with which the enemy-killing Pārtha
conquered the entire eastern world. The bow with the sparkling
fireflies and handsome grip is the great weapon of King Yudhiṣṭhira,
45 O son of Virāṭa. The one on which the luminous golden suns shine,
ablaze with splendor, is Nakula's weapon. The one with the beautiful
locusts decorated with gold is the bow of Mādrī's son Sahadeva.
These thousand fletched arrows like razor blades are Arjuna's, son
of Virāṭa, and they are like the venom of snakes. Flaming in battle
with splendor and speeding nimbly, they are inexhaustible, when the
hero shoots at the enemy in battle. These wide and long shafts
showing crescent moons are the honed arrows of Bhīma, which
50 slaughter the enemy. These golden-nocked, stone-whetted arrows
yellow like turmeric and this quiver marked with five tigers are
Nakula's, with which he subjugated the entire West in war; this was
the quiver of the sagacious son of Mādrī. These luminous-looking
arrows of solid copper, beautiful and effective, are the sagacious
Sahadeva's. And these sharp and wide copper arrows with their long
fletching, golden nocks and three joints are the king's.
This long sword, frog-backed and frog-crowned, was Arjuna's
55 tough weapon, capable of heavy burdens in war. This great sword in
a tiger-skin scabbard is Bhīmasena's—divine, capable of hard work,
and terrifying to the enemies. This fine-bladed, brightly sheathed,
golden-hilted sword is the superb weapon of the sage Kaurava, the
King Dharma. The one in the colorful lion-skin scabbard is Nakula's
tough, hard-working sword. The stainless sword in a cow-leather
sheath—know that it is the tough weapon of Sahadeva, capable of
heavy tasks.

Uttara said:

39.1 The golden-encrusted weapons of the great-spirited and swift-acting Pārthas sparkle resplendently. But where may Arjuna Pārtha himself be, and Yudhiṣṭhira Kauravya, Nakula, Sahadeva, and Bhīmasena Pāṇḍava? Since they lost the kingdom at dice, there has been no word ever of any one of the great-spirited destroyers of all their enemies. And where is Draupadī Pāñcālī, famed as a jewel among women? Kṛṣṇā followed them into the forest when they had been defeated at dice.

Arjuna said:

I am Arjuna Pārtha. The Court games master is Yudhiṣṭhira. Ballava is Bhīmasena, the curry cook of your father. Nakula is the groom, and Sahadeva is at the cowshed. And know that the chambermaid on whose account the Kīcakas were killed is Draupadī.

Uttara said:

I will believe all you say if you can quote the ten names of the Pārtha which I have heard mentioned before.

Arjuna said:

All right, I cite you my ten names: Arjuna, Phalguna, Jiṣṇu, the Diademed One, He of the White Horses, the Terrifier, Vijaya, Kṛṣṇa, the Left-handed Archer, and Dhanaṃjaya!

Uttara said:

Why are you called Vijaya, why are you the One of the White Horses, why the Diademed One, how did you come to be the Left-handed Archer? Why Arjuna, Phalguna, Jiṣṇu, Kṛṣṇa, the Terrifier, and Dhanaṃjaya? Tell me the truth, I have heard all the reasons for that hero's names!

Arjuna said:

They call me Dhanaṃjaya because I stand in the midst of booty after conquering all the countrysides and plundering their entire wealth. They know me as Vijaya because once I ride out to battle against war-crazed warriors I do not return before I have defeated them. While I fight in battle, white, golden-harnessed horses are yoked to my chariot, therefore I am He of the White Horses. I was born on the roofbeam of the Himālaya under the two constellations of Phālgunī in the firmament, therefore they know me as Phalguna. Once Śakra gave me, when I was fighting the bulls of the Dānavas, a diadem lustrous as the sun for my head, and so they call me the Diademed One. When I do battle I can in no way perpetrate a loathsome deed, and therefore I am known among Gods and men as the Terrifier. Both my hands are right hands when I draw the Gāṇḍīva, therefore they know me among Gods and men as the Left-handed Archer. My coloring is rare on this four-cornered earth, and I do white deeds, therefore I am known as Arjuna. I am hard to reach, hard to tame, a tamer myself, and the son of the Chastiser of Pāka, and thus I am famed as Jiṣṇu among Gods and men. My father gave me Kṛṣṇa for my last name, out of love for that little boy of the dazzling black complexion.

Vaiśaṃpāyana said:

Thereupon Virāṭa's son approached and saluted the Pārtha, "I am named Bhūmiṃjaya and also called Uttara. It is my good fortune to set eyes on you, Pārtha, be welcome, Dhanaṃjaya! Strong-armed, red-eyed, with arms like the trunks of kings of elephants, pray forgive me for what I said to you in my ignorance. Because of the wonderful and difficult deeds you have accomplished before, my fears have subsided and I feel the greatest love for you."

Uttara said:
40.1 Riding the wide chariot with me at the reins, hero, which of the
troops will you attack? At your orders I shall drive there!
Arjuna said:
I am pleased, tigerlike man, that you are without fear. I will harry
all of the enemy in battle, experienced warrior. Be steady, sagacious
friend, and watch me fight with the enemy and accomplish terrifying
exploits in the slaughter. Hurry and tie all these quivers to my chariot,
5 and bring that gold-ornamented sword. I shall battle with the Kurus
and recover your cattle. Under my protection the carriage of your
chariot shall become a fortress, with the destructiveness of my will,
the bulwarks and towers of my arms, thronged by the triple staff and
quivers, astir with numerous flags, with the angry catapult of my
bowstring, and the kettledrums of my tires! Manned by me, the
Gāṇḍīva bowman, this chariot shall be invincible in the encounter
with the troops of the enemy, son of Virāṭa; shed all fear!
Uttara said:
I am no longer afraid of them! I know that you are steadfast in
battle, no less even than Keśava or Indra himself. But there is one
thing that puzzles me when I think about it, and fool that I am, I
10 come to no conclusion at all. By what quirk of fate could a man of
such virile appearance and with all the marks of manhood become a
eunuch? I think of you, going about in the disguise of a eunuch, as
the Trident-wielder, as the match of the king of the Gandharvas,
or the God of the Hundred Sacrifices!
Arjuna said:
It is at the behest of my eldest brother that I observe for this year
a vow of chastity; I swear this is the truth. I am not a eunuch,
strong-armed man, but under another's orders and compliant with
the Law. Now, to be sure, I have fulfilled the vow and am released,
prince.
Uttara said:
It is the greatest satisfaction to me today that my surmise has not
proved wrong, for such splendid men are not eunuchs on earth.
15 I have found a battle companion and I can fight even with Immortals!
My heart is no more faint. What shall I do? Order me! I shall drive
your horses which breach the enemy chariots, for I have been trained

in chariot driving by an expert, bull among men. Know that I am as
trained in driving as Dāruka of Vāsudeva or Śakra's Mātali, bull-like
man. The horse that is yoked on the right of the pole, whose feet as
they touch the ground are a blur to the eyes, is the equal of Sugrīva.
That fine steed on the left of the pole, a beautiful animal, is, I think,
20 in speed the equal of Meghapuṣpa. The splendid horse with the golden
harness which is yoked to the left of the axle is, I think, faster than
Sainya, while the one on the right, supple and eager, is in my view
braver in speed than even Balāhaka. This chariot can hold you with
your bow in battle, and on this chariot you will be able to fight,
I am sure!

Vaiśaṃpāyana said:

The hero took the bracelets from his arms and put on bright
leather wrist guards, which would resound like drums. He tied up his
black, curly hair with a white turban, quickly corded Gāṇḍīva and
25 drew the bow. And when the bow was being drawn, it twanged aloud
with the sound of rock hitting rock. Earth shook, a violent wind blew
in the air, birds started in the sky, and mighty trees trembled. And
from the sound like the crackle of lightning, the Kurus knew that
Arjuna was drawing that best of bows with his arms on the chariot.

Vaiśaṃpāyana said:

41.1 Having made Uttara his charioteer and circumambulated the *śāmī*
tree, Dhanaṃjaya took all his weaponry and rode out. The warrior
took down the lion standard from the chariot, placed it at the feet of
the *śāmī*, and rode out with Uttara at the reins. Then he fastened
on his chariot his golden standard with the emblem of a monkey with
a lion's tail—divine wizardry wrought by Viśvakarman—and thought
5 of the grace of the Fire God. The latter, divining his thought, ordered
his beasts to the flag. The great warrior, the Terrifier Kaunteya of the
White Horses, riding the beautifully worked chariot with quivers and
the flag on top, with his sword girt, the wrist guards put on, and the
bow ready, set out in a northerly direction, crested by the chief of the
monkeys. The powerful enemy-crusher, relying on his strength, blew
his great and sonorous conch shell, which set the hair of the enemy
on end. The swift horses knelt on the ground and Uttara, terrified, sat
down on the box. Arjuna Kaunteya made the horses stand up,
restrained them with the reins, and embraced and reassured Uttara:
10 "Have no fear, high prince, you are a baron, enemy-burner! Why,
lion among men, do you sink down in the midst of the enemies? You
have heard the sound of conches before and the great roar of
kettledrums and the trumpeting elephants that stand arrayed in
battle ranks. Then why are you now frightened by the sound of this
conch and why do you look dejected and afraid like an ordinary
person?"

Uttara said:

Indeed I have heard the sound of conches and the great roar of kettledrums and the trumpeting of elephants that stand in arrayed battle ranks. But never before have I heard such a blast of a conch nor have I seen a flag like that! Never before have I heard anywhere such a twang of a bow, and from the blast of the conch, the twang of the bow, and the noise of the chariot, my mind is reeling badly. I have lost all sense of direction, and my heart seems to shiver. All of space is obscured for me by the flag, and my ears are deafened by the sound of Gāṇḍīva!

Arjuna said:

Stand aside on the chariot and plant your feet firmly, hold fast to the reins; I am going to blow the conch again!

Vaiśaṃpāyana said:

The earth shook under the blast of the conch, the roar of the chariot tires, and the twang of Gāṇḍīva.

Droṇa said:

The way the chariot thunders and the conch is sounded and the earth is shaking, that cannot but be the left-handed archer! Our weapons have lost their sparkle, the horses their spirits, and the well-lit fires their glow—this bodes no good. All the wild animals run from us toward the sun with grisly wailing, and crows alight on our standards—this bodes no good. The birds flying toward the left presage our great danger. There is a jackal running howling in the midst of the army, and it is escaping without a blow; it portends great danger. I see that your hairs are bristling in your pores, and your army is overwhelmed: no one wants to fight. All the warriors are almost entirely pale in their faces and dispirited. Let us drive off the cattle and stand our ground, armed and arrayed!

Vaiśaṃpāyana said:

42.1 King Duryodhana spoke to Bhīṣma, the tigerlike Droṇa, and the very great warrior Kṛpa, "I and Karṇa have told the teacher repeatedly, and I'll say it again, for I don't tire of saying it: when they were defeated, they were to live in the forest for twelve years and one year unrecognized in some countryside, for that was our stake. Now, their thirteenth year is not over yet, their year of concealment. And now the Terrifier has encountered us! So, the Terrifier has arrived before their exile was completed, and the Pāṇḍavas shall have to live for another twelve years in the forest! Either their greed made them forget, or confusion has seized us. Bhīṣma should know whether they are still short of time or past the designated period. However, if matters are in dispute, there is always room for doubt, for a matter may be thought to be one way and turn out to be another. We were hunting for Uttara and ready to fight the army of the Matsyas, so if

the Terrifier arrives, who would turn away? We have come here to
fight with the Matsyas in behalf of the Trigartas.
10 "From fear they sought refuge with us, and we gave them our
promise. We agreed with them that they were to seize the great
cattle wealth of the Matsyas first, in the afternoon of the seventh,
and we would do so at runrise on the eighth. Either they did not
find the cattle, or they may have been defeated, or they may have
deceived us and made common cause with the Matsyas, or the
Matsya has attacked them with his countrymen and is now marching
on us with his entire army to give battle. One great champion among
them has taken the lead and has come to defeat us here; or it may
15 be the Matsya himself. Whether it be the king of the Matsyas or the
Terrifier who is coming, we have made a covenant that we all
would fight.

"So why are our great warriors standing idle on their chariots,
our Bhīṣma, Droṇa, Kṛpa, Vikarṇa, and Droṇa's son? They are all
muddle-headed at this time, but there is nothing better to do than to
fight; we must pull ourselves together! If, to save our cattle, we have
to do battle with the thunderbolt-wielding God himself, or even with
Yama, who would flee to Hāstinapura? Who of the foot soldiers, when
their force has been hit by arrows and broken up in the dense forest,
would escape with his life were there doubt about the horsemen?
20 "Let us ignore the teacher and carry out a course of action. For he
knows the minds of others, hence he tries to intimidate us. I notice
that he has a special affection for Arjuna; that is why when he sees
the Terrifier come he praises him. Let us follow a course of action so
that the army is not routed outside their own country, in the vast
wilderness and in the summer. Let us carry out a course of action
so that the army does not stray in confusion and fall victim to the
enemy. Why praise the enemy when you hear the horses whinnying?
Horses always whinny, whether standing or trotting, the wind always
blows, Vāsava always rains, and we hear the sound of the thunder
25 often enough. What does that have to do with the Pārtha? Why
praise him? Unless it is out of love for them and pure hatred and
rancor toward us!

"Indeed, teachers are compassionate and wise, and they see where
things go wrong, but they should not be consulted at all when great
danger looms. It is when they tell their pretty tales in fine palaces,
assemblies, and lodges that pundits shine. It is when they perform
many marvels in the assembly of the people, in the clever fixing of
arrow to bow, that pundits shine. It is with the knowledge of others'
weaknesses, of human behavior, and errors in the preparation of food
30 that pundits shine. But ignore the pundits that mouth the praises of
the enemy, and rather carry out a course of action that overcomes

the enemy. Let them immediately start the cows on their way to our kingdom and put the army in battle formation. Let guard patrols be posted where we will fight the foe!"

Karṇa said:

43.1 I see that all you great lords are terrified and trembling, and stand
idle with no mind to fight! If that is the king of the Matsyas coming,
or the Terrifier, I'll hold him off as the floodline holds off the ocean.
When I shoot my flat-jointed arrows, they will not be unsure of their
aim like crawling serpents. The arrows I shoot sure-handedly, with
golden nocks and very sharp piles, shall cover the Pārtha as locusts
5 a tree. The bowstring, hard pressed by the nocked arrows, shall slap
both wrist guards with the sound of struck kettledrums. The Terrifier,
who has been of a single purpose for thirteen years and has learned
to love war, shall strike out at me, but the Kaunteya, like a virtuous
brahmin, shall be a worthy vessel to receive the floods of arrows
I shoot by the thousands!
Indeed, the great archer is famed in the three worlds but I, ye
chiefs of the Kurus, am in no way less than Arjuna! Today the sky
shall be covered as with fireflies hither and yon with the golden
10 arrows, fletched with vulture feathers, which I shall send off. By
killing Arjuna in battle today I shall repay to the Dhārtarāṣṭra the
long-standing debt which I promised him of old. The range of my
shafts that split asunder and fly off in all directions shall appear like
that of locusts in the sky. I shall plague the Pārtha, whose touch is
like that of Indra's bolt and whose splendor is like great Indra's, as
an elephant with firebrands. Like a great monsoon cloud with jets of
arrows preceded by the wind gusts raised by horses and roaring with
the thunder of masses of chariots, I shall douse the blazing fire of
the Pāṇḍava that burns the enemies fueled by swords, spears, and
15 arrows, scarcely to be overcome like fire itself. The arrows leaping
from my bow shall crawl like poisonous snakes to the Pārtha, like
serpents to an anthill. Relying on the power of the weapons I
obtained from Jāmadagnya, that best of seers, I would fight even
with Vāsava!
Let the monkey that stands on the top of Arjuna's standard this
very day tumble in the dust, screeching in terror, when I hit it with a
bear arrow. And the outcry of the creatures that dwell in the enemy's
flag shall reach up to heaven as they flee in all directions under my
pressure. Toppling the Terrifier from his chariot, I shall today pull
out, root and all, the thorn that has so long lain in Duryodhana's
20 heart. Today the Kauravas shall see the Pārtha with his horses dead,
his chariot gone, and his manliness spent, hissing like a snake. The
Kurus may go if they wish, and simply take their plunder, or stand

idle on their chariots while they watch my battle!

Kṛpa said:

44.1 Your bloody mind is always set on fighting, Rādheya. You don't know the nature of things, nor do you regard their aftermath. For when we study the texts we can think of many courses of action, but the ancient sages tell us that war is the worst course of all. War if suited to time and place will bring victory, while the same war out of time will yield no fruit. Bravery at the right time and place is enjoined for our well-being. It is by weighing the advantages of the effects that a decision should be reached, for the wise do not judge a chariot's capacity by the boast of its maker.

5 On reflection an encounter with the Pārtha is not to our advantage. Alone he rescued the Kurus, alone he sated the Fire God, alone he lived for five years in the aura of the *brahman.* Alone he lifted up Subhadrā and challenged Kṛṣṇa, to a chariot duel. In this very same forest the Black One won back Kṛṣṇā, who had been abducted. Alone he learned about weapons from Śakra for five years; he brought fame to the Kurus by defeating Sāṃyamanī. Alone the enemy-tamer defeated Citrasena, the king of the Gandharvas, nimbly in a fight, him and his invincible army. Likewise by himself he brought down in battle the Nivātakavaca and Kālakhañja Dānavas, whom even the deities were
10 unable to slay. What have you accomplished on your own, Karṇa? Name it! Have you, like every single one of them, brought kings under your sway? Even Indra is unable to battle with the Pārtha. He who hopes to fight with him had better take medicine. Without a moment's thought you want to stretch out your right hand and pull the fang from an angry poisonous snake with your forefinger! Or wandering alone in the forest, you want, without a hook, to mount a rogue elephant and ride it into the city! Smeared with butter and dressed in bark you want to walk right through a blazing fire fed
15 with butter, marrow, and fat. If one were to tie himself up and hang a big rock around his neck in order to swim across the ocean, what possible manliness would there be in that? Karṇa, if a very weak and inexperienced man wants to fight as strong and experienced a warrior as the Pārtha, he is out of his mind. We tricked him into these thirteen years, and now that he is free as a lion from a trap, he will not leave one of us alive.

In our ignorance we have stumbled on the Pārtha waiting in ambush as on a fire hidden in a pit. We are in extreme danger! We shall together fight the war-crazed Pārtha when he comes; let the
20 troops stand girt, arrayed, and armed! Droṇa, Duryodhana, Bhīṣma, yourself, and Droṇa's son and I shall all fight the Pārtha, Karṇa;

don't be so rash! On six chariots we can counter the resolute Pārtha, who is as eager as the Thunderbolt-wielder, if we join forces. With the troops arrayed and the great archers prepared, we shall fight Arjuna, as the Dānavas fight Vāsava.

Aśvatthāman said:
45.1 The cattle has not been won yet, nor has it crossed the boundary,
nor has it reached Hāstinapura, and already you are boasting, Karṇa!
Men do not talk of their bravery at all, though they may have won
a good many battles, obtained plentiful booty, and conquered enemy
country. Fire cooks speechlessly, the sun shines silently, and earth
carries quietly its many creatures, standing and moving. The sages
have laid down tasks for the four classes of society, by which they
5 prosper and by the doing of which they do not go wrong. The
brahmin should learn the Vedas and sacrifice for himself and for
others; the baron should rely on the bow and sacrifice, but not for
others. The commoner should acquire property and have the rites
of the *brahman* performed.
These lordly men had obtained this earth while acting according
to the scriptures, and they paid respect to their elders, however
corrupted. What baron would be contented with acquiring a kingdom
by so cruel a dicing, like a common man? What sensible man would
brag like a trapper, when he had gotten loot through trickery, acting
with deception? In what chariot duel have you vanquished
Dhanaṃjaya, Nakula, or Sahadeva; whose wealth you have robbed?
10 In what battle have you beaten Yudhiṣṭhira and Bhīma, strong of the
strong? In what war have you ever taken Indraprastha? Likewise,
where was the battle in which you won Kṛṣṇā? In her single garment
she was dragged into the hall, miscreant, when she was in her
month! Hungry for anything of value you have cut their mighty
root like a sandal tree. You had to order them to work, champion—
what did Vidura have to say about that?
Men, so we notice, have only the serenity of which they are
capable, and so do the other creatures, down to the worms and the
ants. The Pāṇḍava is incapable of forgiving the molestation of
Draupadī; Dhanaṃjaya has appeared to the Dhārtarāṣṭras' perdition.
15 Pretending to be wise, you like to say your piece again and again;
but Jiṣṇu will put an end to the feud and leave no survivors. Kuntī's
son Dhanaṃjaya is not afraid to fight Gods, or Gandharvas, or
Asuras, or Rākṣasas. Whomever he falls furiously upon in battle he
will storm and cut down like a tree under the impact of Garuḍa. He
bests you in valor; with the bow he is the equal of the king of the
Immortals, in battle the match of Vāsudeva. Who will not pay his
respects to the Pārtha? He will defeat divine armament with divine,

20 human with human—what man is equal to Arjuna? They who know
the Law know that a pupil is second only to a son, and it is for this
reason that the Pāṇḍava is dear to Droṇa. Fight the Pāṇḍava the
same way you gambled and took Indraprastha, the same way you
dragged Kṛṣṇā into the hall! This sagacious uncle of yours, so imbued
with the Law of the baronage, this cheating gamester Śakuni of
Gāndhāra, let him fight here! Gāṇḍīva shoots no dice, neither ace
nor deuce; Gāṇḍīva shoots arrows, blazing and honed! The terrifying
and fiercely burning shafts with vulture fletching shot from Gāṇḍīva
25 strike holes even in mountains! The Finisher, the Destroyer, Death,
and the Mare-headed Fire might leave some survivors, but not the
angry Dhanaṃjaya! Let the Teacher fight Dhanaṃjaya, if he wishes;
I shall not, for the Matsya is our business, if he comes tracking
the cows.

Bhīṣma said:
46.1 Droṇa sees it right, and Kṛpa sees it well, but Karṇa wants a proper
fight in accordance with the Law of the baronage. No man who
knows him can malign the Teacher; but it is my view, considering
time and place, that we should fight. What wise man who has five
sun-like armed rivals would not be bewildered at their ascendancy?
All men, even if they know the Law, are confused when their self-
interest is at stake; that is why I speak here, king, if it pleases you.
5 Karṇa spoke as he did to excite vigor; let the Teacher's son pardon
it, for a great task is at hand. You, the Teacher, and Kṛpa must forgive
everything, for this is no time for strife, when the Kaunteya is at
hand! You three have weapon sense as the sun has light. Just as the
spots cannot be removed from the moon, so is vested in you the
power of the brahmins and the weapon of the *brahman*. We may find
the four Vedas somewhere, and baronial power somewhere else, but
as far as I know we have never heard of the two combined in anyone
but the Teacher of the Bhāratas and his son. The weapon of the
10 *brahman* and the Vedas are not found together in anyone else. Let the
Teacher's son forgive; this is not the time for us to break up; let us
all fight in full concord with this son of the Chastiser of Pāka, who
has now come. Of the vices of power that the sages have described
a breach is the worst, so the wise know.

Aśvatthāman said:
Let the Teacher forgive, and let peace be restored here; for if the
guru was maligned, it was done in anger.

Vaiśaṃpāyana said:
Thereupon Duryodhana asked Droṇa's pardon, Bhārata, with
Karṇa, Bhīṣma, and the great-spirited Kṛpa.

Droṇa said:
I was appeased by the first words of Bhīṣma Śāṃtanava. Let us go

15 on from here and work out a plan to ensure that while Duryodhana
is engaged no evil strikes the soldiers either from rashness or folly.
Dhanaṃjaya would not have shown himself, if their exile were not
over, and he is not going to spare us without recovering the cattle.
Let us follow a course by which he does not embattle and defeat the
Dhārtarāṣṭras in any way. Gāngeya, remember the question that
Duryodhana has raised before, and pray answer truly!

Bhīṣma said:
47.1 The instants are joined together, and so are the hours, days,
fortnights, months, lunar houses, planets, seasons, and years: thus
the wheel of time revolves with the divisions of time. Because of an
excess of time and the deviation of the luminaries, there are two
additional months every five years. So I calculate that to thirteen
5 years there are five additional months and 12 days. Everything
promised has been carried out by them, and knowing this for certain
the Terrifier has now come. They are all great-spirited men, all experts
in Law and Profit: why should they whose king is Yudhiṣṭhira offend
the Law?

The Kaunteyas are not covetous, and they have accomplished a
difficult feat. Also, they do not just want the kingdom by hook or by
crook, for then these joys of the Kauravas would have tried to prevail
at that very time. No, tied by the noose of the Law, they have not
strayed from their baronial vow. If it was necessary to decide whether
to be called a liar or to meet their doom, the Pārthas would choose
10 death over being false. But now that the time has come, these bulls
among men will not give up what is coming to them, were it
protected by the Thunderbolt-wielder himself, for so heroic are the
Pāṇḍavas! We must counter in battle the greatest of all bearers of
arms. Therefore let every action be speedily taken that the strict of
the world consider as being honest, lest our profit passes over to the
others. For I have never seen in the event of a battle a successful
outcome completely assured, Kaurava, Indra of kings—but now
Dhanaṃjaya has come. When battle begins there is life and there is
death, victory and defeat, which inevitably fall to one or the other,
that is found to be wholly true. Therefore quickly carry out whatever
actions pertain to war, if consistent with the Law, for Dhanaṃjaya
has come!"

Duryodhana said:
15 I shall not give the kingdom away to the Pāṇḍavas, Grandfather!
Hurry and prepare for war!

Bhīṣma said:
Listen to my plan, if you please. Take one quarter of the army and
hurry back to the city. Another quarter force must take the cattle and
march. We shall counter the Pāṇḍava with the remaining half of the

army, or the Matsya if he comes back, or Indra himself! Let the Teacher stand in the center, Aśvatthāman on the left, and let the sagacious Kṛpa Śāradvata protect the right flank. The Sūta's son Karṇa in his armor should stand in the vanguard, and I myself shall stand behind the entire army in the rear as protection.

Vaiśaṃpāyana said:
48.1 When the battle ranks had thus been drawn up by the Kauraveya
warriors, Arjuna approached swiftly, with the roar of his chariot
resounding. They saw the flag, they heard the chariot thunder, and
the piercing twang of the violently vibrating Gāṇḍīva. Seeing all this,
Droṇa said, observing that the Gāṇḍīva warrior was coming, "That is
the flag of the Pārtha shining from afar, that is his monsoonlike
5 thunder, that is his monkey that is screeching. And that best of
warriors, standing on his chariot, driving off other chariots, is
drawing his great bow, lightning-like Gāṇḍīva! Two arrows strike at
my feet, two more whirr by my head: for having lived his forest
life, and having accomplished superhuman feats, the Pārtha now
makes his prostration at my feet and his queries at my ears!"
Arjuna said:
Charioteer! Drive the horses within arrow range of the army, until
I see where among the troops that foul Kaurava is. When I see that
insolent man, I'll ignore all the others and swoop down on his head;
10 then the rest will be defeated. There is Droṇa standing in position;
behind him is Droṇa's son. There stand Bhīṣma, Kṛpa, and Karṇa,
great archers all. But I don't see the king here; he is going with the
cattle, I suspect, turning south to save his life. Skirt the chariot force
and go where Suyodhana is; there I shall fight, son of Virāṭa, and
the battle won't be meatless! When I have defeated him, I shall take
the cows and return.
Vaiśaṃpāyana said:
At these words Virāṭa's sons with an effort reined in the horses
from where the bulls of the Kurus were waiting, and goaded the steeds
to where Duryodhana was going. But when the One of the White
Horses avoided the chariot line, Droṇa divined his plan and said,
15 "The Terrifier does not want to make a stand without the king! Let
us attack his rear while he tries the assault. For there is no one who
is able to fight this enraged man singly in battle, except the
Thousand-eyed God and Devakī's son Kṛṣṇa. What do we care about
the cattle and our vast wealth, when Duryodhana has like a boat
sunk in the water of the Pārtha?"
The Terrifier went on, proclaimed his name, and scattered the
enemy swiftly with his arrows that swarmed like locusts. The soldiers,
scattered by the torrents of shafts shot by the Pārtha, could no more
20 see the earth and the sky, for these were covered with arrows. Their

inner thoughts were set neither on battle nor on flight, and in their hearts they praised the swiftness of the Pārtha. Then he blew his conch shell, raising the enemy's hair; he drew his great bow and exhorted the creatures on his flag. At the sound of the conch, and the thunder of the chariot wheels, and the screeching of the inhuman creatures who dwelled in his flag, the cows waved their upright tails, and bellowing on all sides, turned back toward the south.

Vaiśaṃpāyana said:

49.1 Having routed the enemy force with his fury
And recovered the cattle, that greatest of archers
Stormed onward to face Duryodhana,
For Arjuna wanted to pleasure himself.

While the cows stampeded toward the Matsyas,
The Kaurava heroes thought that Kirīṭin
Had now gained his goal, and they quickly attacked
Him, storming to face Duryodhana.

On seeing the many and deeply arrayed
Attacking troops with their plentiful pennants,
The enemy-slayer addressed Vairāṭi
The son of the Matsya, and spoke this word:

"Make these white horses in golden bridles
Rush swiftly forward along this way,
And try to get them with all their speed
To rencounter this mass of lionlike warriors!

5 "That villainous son of a charioteer
Who wants to fight me on elephants,
Whom Duryodhana's favor has made bold,
Take me to him, O son of a king!"

The son of Virāṭa broke through the line
Of chariot warriors with his wind-fast
Large destriers harnessed in gold-studded thongs
And drove to the midst of the field the Pārtha.

Citrasena, Saṃgrāmajit, Śatrusaha
And Jaya, great warriors, rallied to Karṇa
And with their arrows and javelins
Encountered the onrushing Bhārata.

The champion of men with the flame of his bow
And the heat of his speeding arrows began
In fury to burn the hordes of chariots
Of those bulls of the Kurus, as fire burns a forest.

As the fearful battle began, Vikarṇa
The Kaurava hero attacked the Pārtha,
Who was Bhīma's junior, raining fierce torrents
Of shafts from his car on the eminent hero.

But he drew his taut-corded bow that was plated
With the finest gold, and routing Vikarṇa,
He felled the standard mast on his chariot,
And with standard broken the other fled fast.

Śatruṃtapa, not controlling his rage
On seeing the bane of the enemy troops
Accomplish his superhuman exploits,
Aimed at the Pārtha a tortoise-nail.

And hit by that eminent warrior king
He plunged in the flag-flying host of the Kurus.
He pierced Śatruṃtapa with five swift arrows,
And killed his charioteer with ten more.

Śatruṃtapa, hit by the Bhārata bull
With an arrow that went through his body armor,
Fell dead on the ground of the battlefield,
As a gale-snapped tree from a mountain top.

The warrior bull broke the warrior bulls,
The greater hero the heroes in battle;
They shook as in time great forests do
When trembling under the rage of the wind.

Young champions slain by the Pāṇḍava
Lay asleep on the ground in their finery,
Those givers of largess, of Indra-like valor,
Defeated in war by Vāsava's son,
Like full-grown Himālayan elephants,
Their bulk clad in armor of iron and gold.

The Gāṇḍīva bowman, hero of men,
Cutting down his foes on the battlefield,
Ran hither and thither in the mêlée,
A forest fire at the end of the summer.

As the wind in springtime adrift in the sky
Blows down and asunder the scattering leaves,
So the Diademed One did scatter his rivals
As the warrior prince ranged about on his chariot.

Cutting down the steeds of the driver of red steeds
Saṃgrāmajit, Vaikartana's brother,

He cheerfully then with but one arrow
Carried off his diadem-decked head.

His brother slain, the *sūta*'s son
Vaikartana now displayed his valor,
As an elephant king displays his tusks,
Or a tiger attacks a big buffalo.

With a dozen of antelope-dappled shafts
Vaikartana rushed at the Pāṇḍava;
With his arrows he hit all over their bodies
The horses and also the son of Virāṭa.

A grand elephant struck by an elephant,
He tore sharp bear arrows from his quiver;
He drew full circle the bow to his ear
And hit the *sūta*'s son with his shafts.

The enemy-crusher struck him in battle
In arms and thighs, in head and brow,
In the throat and in all the parts of the chariot
With lightning-like arrows shot from Gāṇḍiva.

Propelled by the arrows shot by the Pārtha,
An elephant beat by an elephant,
The fierce Vaikartana abandoned the vanguard
And fled as he burned with the Pāṇḍava's shots.

Vaiśaṃpāyana said:

50.1 When Rādheya had fled, others led by Duryodhana attacked the Pāṇḍava each with his own troops, and pelted him with arrows. Observing the many assaults of that army in battle array, which assailed him with arrows, the son of Virāṭa said: "Which of the troops do you want to attack with me as your charioteer on your bright chariot, Jiṣṇu? I shall drive wherever you tell me!"

Arjuna said:

That ill-fated, red-eyed warrior with the tiger skin whom you see there standing on his chariot with the dark azure standard, that is Kṛpa: take me to his chariot troops. I shall show that archer with the tough bow the swiftness of my arrows. The one with the beautiful golden water gourd on his flag is Droṇa the Teacher himself, first of all bearers of arms. Circumambulate him with a tranquil heart, hero, without opposing him, for that is the eternal Law. If Droṇa is the first to strike at my body, then I shall strike back at him, so he will not resent it.

The one not far from him who has a bow on his flag is the great warrior Aśvatthāman, the son of the Teacher. I have always

respected him, as have all bearers of arms: when you reach his
chariot, rein in again. The one in the chariot rank wearing a golden
coat of mail, who stands in the midst of a third fine army that is to be
reckoned with and who has the emblem of an elephant on a field of
gold, is Dhṛtarāṣṭra's son, the illustrious King Suyodhana. Bring the
chariot up before him who breaks enemy chariots, hero; he wreaks
havoc with his splendor and goes berserk in battle. He is regarded as
the fastest of Droṇa's pupils, but I shall show him aplenty what
fastness with arrows means!

15 Over there, the one who has a red elephant's girth in his device is
Karṇa Vaikartana, whom you already know. When you get to the
chariot of that wicked son of Rādhā, be on your guard; he always
seeks to rival me in battle. The one with the emblem of five stars on
dark azure, who stands heroically on his chariot, holding a large bow
in his gauntleted hand, on whose chariot waves the beautiful flag
bright with stars and sun, over whose head spreads a spotlessly white
umbrella, who stands in the front of that great line of chariots flying
20 many flags and pennants, like the sun in front of the clouds, and
whose cuirass is golden and shines like sun and moon, with a golden
helmet almost bringing a shiver to my heart—he is Bhīṣma
Śāmtanava, the grandfather of us all. He wears the royal fortune
and submits to Duryodhana's wishes. He should be approached last,
lest he put obstacles in my way. When I fight with him, hold the
horses carefully!

Vaiśaṃpāyana said:

The son of Virāṭa drove the left-handed archer with the greatest care to where Kṛpa was standing, who was about to engage Dhanaṃjaya, O king.

Vaiśaṃpāyana said:

51.1 The troops of the awesome Kuru archers appeared like slow-
moving rain clouds under a gentle wind at the end of the summer.
Close by stood the horses mounted by armed riders, and terrifying
elephants goaded with spikes and hooks.

Thereupon Indra arrived with the hosts of the Gods, riding on
Sudarśana, O king, in the company of the Viśve Devas, Aśvins, and
Maruts. Astir with Gods, Yakṣas, Gandharvas, and great Snakes, the
5 cloudless sky shone as with the planets. They had come to watch
the power of their weapons employed on humans, and the terrible
battle in the encounter of Bhīṣma and Arjuna. The sky-going, divine
chariot of the King of the Gods, capable of going anywhere it pleased
and adorned with all manner of gems, shone with a hundred times a
hundred thousand pillars made of gold and others made of precious
stones which upheld the edifice. The Thirty-three Gods were there

with Vāsava; so were the Gandharvas, Rākṣasas, Snakes, Ancestors,
and great Seers. Likewise King Vasumanas, Balākṣa, Supratardana,
10 Aṣṭaka, Śibi, Yayāti, Nahuṣa, Gaya, Manu, Kṣupa, Raghu, Bhānu,
Kṛśāśva, Sagara, and Śala were seen to shine on the chariot of the
King of the Gods.

With each at his appointed compass point, there shone the chariots
of Agni, Īśa, Soma, Varuṇa, Prajāpati, the Placer and Disposer,
Kubera, Yama, Alambuṣa, Ugrasena, and the Gandharva Tumburu.
All the hosts of the Gods, the Siddhas, and supreme Seers had come
to watch the battle of Arjuna and the Kurus. The holy fragrance of
divine garlands spread all over as of flowering woods at the
15 beginning of spring. The red and reddish umbrellas of the Gods who
were standing there were visible, and their robes, garlands, and fans.
All the dust of the earth subsided suffused with rays, and the wind
carrying divine perfumes caressed the warriors. The sky was
colorfully adorned and illumined by the gathering and waiting
chariots, which were lit up by all kinds of gems, manifold and
wondrous, which were brought by the eminent Gods.

Vaiśaṃpāyana said:

52.1 Meanwhile mettlesome Kṛpa, best of the bearers of arms, of great
bravery and prowess, advanced: the great warrior was eager to do
battle with Arjuna. The two powerful, sunlike warriors who were
about to fight appeared, as they took up their positions, like two
clouds in autumn. The Pārtha drew his superb weapon Gāṇḍīva,
famous throughout the world, and shot many iron arrows that could
cut into weak spots, but Kṛpa split the blood-thirsty shafts into
hundreds and thousands of pieces with hundreds of arrows, before
5 they reached him. Angered the Pārtha warrior exhibited artful
maneuvers and darkened the air with his arrows. The lordly Pārtha
of measureless soul put one vast shadow on the sky and covered
Kṛpa with hundreds of reeds. Hit by the sharp arrows like flame
crests, Kṛpa quickly aimed at the boundlessly lustrous and great-
spirited Pārtha a thousand of his own and roared out on the
battlefield.

Thereupon heroic Arjuna pierced Kṛpa's four horses rapidly with
four sharp, smoothed, golden-nocked, and superior arrows shot
from Gāṇḍīva. All the horses, hit with the sharp shafts like flaming
10 serpents, reared up violently, so that Kṛpa lost his balance. When
the scion of Kuru saw that Gautama had lost his footing, the killer
of enemy heroes refrained from striking him in order to preserve the
other's dignity. Gautama regained his balance and hit the left-handed
archer swiftly with ten heron-feathered shafts. Then the Pārtha cut
Kṛpa's bow into two with one honed bear arrow and tore it from his

hand. Next he blew off the other's cuirass with sharp arrows that
sought out weak spots, but the Pārtha did not hurt his body.
Denuded of his coat of mail, his body shone like that of a snake
15 which in time sheds its skin. With one bow split by the Pārtha,
Gautama took another and strung it—it seemed a miracle. But the
Kaunteya split that one too with a flat-jointed arrow. Likewise the
Pāṇḍava, slayer of enemy heroes, shattered many other bows of
Śāradvata as dexterously.

With his bows broken the majestic warrior seized a spear and sent
it off to Pāṇḍu's son like a blazing thunderbolt. With ten arrows
Arjuna cut up the gold-studded spear as it came streaking through
the sky like a big meteor, and it fell on the ground, broken in ten pieces
by the skillful Pārtha. Kṛpa, now between yokes with bow in hand,
20 nimbly stung the Pārtha with ten sharp bear arrows. Angrily the
resplendent Pārtha replied on that battlefield with thirteen stone-
whetted arrows with the splendor of fire: he powerfully hit the yoke
with one, killed the four horses with four, cut off the charioteer's
head with a sixth, struck the three bamboo poles with three, the two
axles with two, and split the standard with a twelfth bear arrow.
Then, laughingly, the Indra-like Phalguna hit Kṛpa in the chest with
a thirteenth arrow like a thunderbolt. His bows broken, chariot gone,
horses dead, charioteer killed, Kṛpa nimbly jumped down with a club
25 in his hand and hurled the club. But the heavy, well-studded club
that Kṛpa threw was stopped by Arjuna with arrows and came back
the other way. In an attempt to save the rancorous Śāradvata the
fighters pelted the Pārtha on the battlefield with showers of arrows.
Virāṭa's son turned the horses left and, executing a double circle, held
off the warriors. The bull-like men took the chariotless Kṛpa and
hastily carried him away from Kuntī's son Dhanaṃjaya.

Arjuna said:

53.1 Friend, bless you, drive me to Droṇa's array, there where a golden
altar like a blazing fire crest rises high on the golden standard pole,
adorned with pennants. Blood-red, large, and handsome horses, the
color of smooth coral, with copper-red mouths, pleasing to the eyes,
appear yoked to his superb chariot, trained to perfection. Majestic,
long-armed Bhāradvāja, endowed with strength and beauty, is famed
in all the worlds. In wisdom he is the equal of Uśanas, in policy the
match of Bṛhaspati; the four Vedas are lodged with him forever, as
5 are the observances of the Brahman, knowledge of all divine weapons
and how to retract them, friend, and the science of archery in its
entirety. Patience, self-control, truthfulness, mercy, uprightness, these
and many other virtues are found in the preeminent brahmin. I wish
to give battle to that lordly man, therefore drive fast and take me to
the Teacher!

Vaiśaṃpāyana said:

At these words of Arjuna, Virāṭa's son urged on the golden-harnessed horses toward Bhāradvāja's chariot. Droṇa drove up to meet the Pāṇḍava, best of chariot-warriors, who came storming at
10 him, as one crazed elephant at another. He blew his conch, which roared with the sound of a hundred drums and shook the entire army like a stormy sea. At the spectacle of the fine red horses commingling in battle with the horses that were as fast as thought and as white as wild geese, the men in the field were amazed. The vast host of the Bhāratas shuddered violently again and again when they saw in the vanguard those two gallant warriors, Droṇa and Pārtha, teacher and pupil, both undefeated, learned, spirited, and strong, clasp each other.

Thrilled with joy and laughing, the valiant Pārtha warrior
15 encountered Droṇa's chariot on his own chariot; Kaunteya, the strong-armed slayer of enemy heroes, saluted Droṇa and spoke in a spirit of conciliation with a gentle voice, "We have lived our spell in the forest and now seek requital. Pray do not be wroth with us, you who are forever invincible in battle. I shall not strike you ere you have struck, lord sans blame! Thus have I decided—you be pleased to act." Thereupon Droṇa sent him over twenty arrows, and the Pārtha splintered them dexterously before they reached him. Displaying his swift bowmanship, mighty Droṇa showered the Pārtha's chariot with a thousand arrows.

20 Thus began the battle of Bhāradvāja and the Diademed One, who loosed at each other blazing shafts on the field of battle. Both were famous for their feats, both the likes of the wind in speed, both acquainted with divine missiles, both of surpassing grandeur; and hurling nets of arrows they amazed the kings. All the warriors there assembled were astounded and applauded with cheers the two who were shooting it out: "Who but Phalguna can fight Droṇa? Grisly is the Law of the barons if he is to fight with his guru!" said the men who stood in the vanguard. From close by the two ferocious warriors
25 covered each other with volleys of arrows. Drawing wide his very large bow, which was gold-backed and irresistible, Bhāradvāja fiercely fought back at Arjuna. Spreading a net of stone-whetted, sunlike shafts over Arjuna's chariot, he darkened the light of the sun. The strong-armed warrior hit the Pārtha with honed and swift shafts as the monsoon cloud hits a mountain with rain. The bold and mighty Pāṇḍava, too, joyously took up his divine bow Gāṇḍīva, fast killer of foes, the supreme instrument of the Bhāratas, and dispatched many beautiful gold-studded arrows from his bow, frustrating Bhāradvāja's
30 shafts quickly—it seemed like a miracle. Going about on his chariot the handsome Dhanaṃjaya Pārtha displayed all his weapons in all directions at once. He decked the whole sky with one vast shadow with his arrows, so that Droṇa became invisible, as though shrouded

by fog. When he was covered with fine arrows, he had the appearance of a mountain with fires raging on it.

But seeing that his own chariot was covered with the Pārtha's arrows on the battlefield, Droṇa drew his handsome bow taut with the crackle of monsoon thunder. Stretching his terrifying bow till it looked like a circle of fire, Droṇa, who was wont to shine in assemblies, shattered all the arrows, and there was a loud burst as of burning bamboos. With his golden-nocked shafts that leaped from his superb bow, the man of measureless soul darkened the air and the light of the sun. Many creatures became visible in the sky to the sky-going, smoothed, golden-nocked arrows. As Droṇa's nocked arrows welled forth from his bow, it appeared as though there was one single continuous arrow in space. Thus, while shooting their golden-studded arrows, the two heroes seemed to cover the sky with firebrands. Their reeds, robed in the feathers of herons and peacocks, looked like rows of migrating geese in the autumn sky. The battle of the great-spirited Droṇa and Pāṇḍava became as ferocious and fearsome as that of Vṛtra and Vāsava. Like two elephants goring each other with the points of their tusks, they attacked each other with arrows from bows stretched to the utmost. The fierce warriors, shining in battle, continued discharging their divine missiles from side to side of the battlefield. Arjuna, foremost of victors, parried the stone-whetted arrows the eminent teacher shot with many arrows of his own. Showing his awesome side, Indra's son of awful puissance quickly darkened the sky with multitudinous shafts.

While Droṇa, the eminent teacher, best of the bearers of arms, began to play with the tigerlike, sharply resplendent Arjuna, who sought to kill him, with smoothed arrows, Phalguna warded off missile with missile and gave battle to Bhāradvāja, who was launching divine projectiles on the field of their duel. The encounter of that pair of irate, rancorous, lionlike men was as of Gods and Dānavas. With his own missile the Pāṇḍava devoured the Indra, Vāyu, and Agni missiles whenever Droṇa loosed them.

Thus these champion archers cast shadows on air with the showers of arrows they shot. When Arjuna set off his shafts and they struck people, the sound that was heard was that of thunderbolts striking mountains. Elephants, warriors, and horsemen, O lord of your people, looked like flowering *kiṃśuka* trees in their unguent of blood. With their braceleted arms, sparkling chariots, gold-glittering cuirasses, standards, and soldiers fallen under the barrage of the Pārtha's arrows, the troops were routed in the encounter of Droṇa and Arjuna. Waving their bows, which were capable of any load, the two heroes covered each other with arrows and suffered them. The applause of those who praised Droṇa filled the air: "Difficult is Droṇa's feat of battling Arjuna, that powerful router, unassailable and hard of fists, the vanquisher of Gods, Daityas, and Snakes, a grand warrior!"

At the sight of the Pārtha's indefatigability, skill, deftness, and far
range in the duel, Droṇa stood amazed. Now, O bull of the Bhāratas,
the intransigent Pārtha raised the divine bow Gāṇḍīva and drew it
with his arms on the battlefield. He shot a torrent of arrows like a
plague of locusts, and not even the wind could crawl through a hole
60 in them. Ceaselessly he affixed and shot and took aim again, and not
a pause could be detected. And while the horrifying exchange of fast
arrows so went on, the Pārtha shot off more arrows faster than fast.
The smoothed shafts fell by the hundreds and thousands at a time on
Droṇa's chariot. And as the Gāṇḍīva bowman bestrew Droṇa with
his arrows, there arose a wail of woe from the troops, O bull of the
Bhāratas.

Maghavat himself applauded the swift bowmanship of the Paṇḍava,
65 as did the Gandharvas and Apsarās gathered there. Then with a
mighty host of chariots the Teacher's son, herd-leader of chariots,
suddenly attempted to stop the Pāṇḍava. In his heart Aśvatthāman
applauded the feat of the great-spirited Pārtha, but he flew in a rage
with him. Overcome by fury he stormed at the Pārtha on the field of
battle, showering thousands of arrows like rain-rich Parjanya.
Turning the horses to Drauṇi's attack the Pārtha afforded Droṇa a
hole to slink away. And having a chance, the champion made off
with swift steeds, cut up by superior arrows, his armor and standard
broken.

Vaiśaṃpāyana said:

54.1 The Pārtha received Aśvatthāman, who came storming with the
speed of the wind and rained shafts like a cloud, with a massive
barrage of arrows. There was a great falling-to of the pair as of God
and Asura, as they spattered torrents of arrows like Vṛtra and
Vāsava. No sun shone, no wind blew, while the sky, filled with
arrows, was overcast on all sides. As they struck each other there
was a loud crackling and snapping, as of burning bamboos, O victor
5 of enemy cities. Arjuna exhausted all the other's horses, and
Aśvatthāman was so confused, king, that he could not make out
the directions.

Then, while the mighty Pārtha was roaming about, Droṇa's son detected a tiny opening in the other's defenses and cut through his bowstring with a razor-sharp barb. At the spectacle of his superhuman feat the Gods applauded him. Thereupon, retreating eight bow lengths, Droṇa's son hit the Pārtha in the chest with a heron-feathered shaft. The strong-armed Pārtha laughed aloud and powerfully corded Gāṇḍīva with a fresh string. Turning a half circle he engaged the

other, as one crazed elephant, leader of a herd, would engage another
10 crazed tusker. Then began, in the center of the battlefield, the great
and hair-raising encounter of the two unique champions on earth.
Filled with amazement, all the Kurus watched the two heroes battle
like two herd leaders locked in combat. The bull-like men hit each
other with arrows in the shape of poisonous snakes, which spat fire
like serpents.

The two divine quivers of the great-spirited Pāṇḍava were
inexhaustible; therefore the heroic Pārtha could bide his time on the
field of battle, immovable like a mountain. But the arrows of
Aśvatthāman, who was shooting fast, soon ran out; in that Arjuna
15 had the upper hand. Thereupon Karṇa drew his large bow in fury
and shot, and a loud wail arose. The Pārtha looked at where a bow
had been drawn, saw Rādhā's son there, and his wrath grew beyond
measure. Overcome by rage and lust to kill Karṇa, the bull of the
Kurus stared at him with wide open eyes. But when the Pārtha
turned away his face, the men hurriedly brought arrows by the
thousands to Droṇa's son, O king. Strong-armed Dhanaṃjaya, the
vanquisher of his rivals, ignored Droṇa's son and made a sudden
rush at Karṇa. Assailing him, the Kaunteya, who hoped for a chariot
duel, said with rage-reddened eyes—

Arjuna said:

55.1 Now is the time, Karṇa, to prove your frequent boasts in the
middle of the assembly that no one is your equal in war! You have
cast aside the whole Law and you have spoken bitter words, but I
think your ambition is hard to fulfill. Now make good what you have
bragged without taking any account of me, son of Rādhā; make it
good with me amidst the Kurus! You watched how evil men molested
the Princess of Pāñcāla in the assembly hall—now reap the entire
5 harvest of that! I suffered it before, since I was tied by the noose of
the Law, but now, Rādheya, watch the triumph of my wrath in
battle! Come, Karṇa, agree to fight with me, and let all the Kurus
and their troops be spectators.

Karṇa said:

Carry out with deeds, Pārtha, what you say with words, for it is
well known on earth that the deed surpasses the word. You suffered
disgrace before, only because you were impotent; that is the way I see
10 it, perceiving as I do your cowardice. If you suffered it before because
you were tied with the noose of the Law, you know you might as
well have been untied as tied. If so far you have carried out the stay
in the forest as promised, now you, self-styled expert on the Law,
wretchedly seek to break the covenant. If Śakra himself were to fight
in your cause, Pārtha, it would be of no concern to me, for I am

about to triumph! Son of Kuntī, your desire will be quickly fulfilled: you shall fight with me. Now witness my strength!

Arjuna said:

Just now you fled from battle with me; that is why you are alive, Rādheya, and why your brother is dead. What man but you would cause his brother's death, desert the battle, and then talk like this in the midst of honest men?

Vaiśaṃpāyana said:

15 Speaking thus to Karṇa, the undefeated Terrifier attacked him,
shooting armor-piercing arrows. Karṇa received the arrows, which
were like fire crests, with a mighty shower of shafts of his own, like
a raining cloud. Everywhere there flew up ghastly volleys of arrows.
Arjuna hit his horses and the leather guards on his arms one by one.
Relentlessly he cut through Karṇa's quiver strap with a smoothed,
sharp-piled arrow. Karṇa, taking other arrows from his quiver, hit
20 the Pāṇḍava in the hand, so that his grip weakened. Then the strong-
armed Pārtha broke Karṇa's bow; the other hurled a javelin at him,
but the Pārtha blew it apart with arrows. The many footmen of
Rādheya attacked, but the Pārtha dispatched them to Yama's realm
with arrows shot from Gāṇḍīva. Thereupon the Terrifier hit Karṇa's
horses with sharp and effective arrows shot from ear height, and they
fell dead on the ground. With another sharp and fiery shaft the
strong-armed, powerful Kaunteya hit Karṇa in the chest. The arrow
pierced his armor and struck flesh; and he was overwhelmed by
25 darkness and lost consciousness for a while. Then in great pain he
left the battlefield for the north, and Arjuna and the great warrior
Uttara reviled him.

Vaiśaṃpāyana said:

56.1 The Pārtha, having defeated Vaikartana, said to Virāṭa's son, "Take
me to the army where that golden palm is standing. There Bhīṣma
Śāmtanava with the aspect of an immortal, our grandfather, has
taken his stand on his chariot eager to do battle with me. I shall cut
his bowstring in a duel! You shall now see me hurl the divine missile
which streaks through the sky like the lightning in a thunderstorm.
The Kurus shall behold my gold-backed Gāṇḍīva, and all my foes here
5 assembled shall wonder, 'With which hand is he shooting, the right
or the left?' I shall cause to well forth an impassable river with waves
of blood, whirlpools of chariots, and crocodile-like elephants, which
will wash toward the hereafter. I shall with my smooth bear arrows
cut down the forest of the Kurus branching with hands, feet, heads,
backs, and arms. I shall blaze a hundred trails like fire in a forest,
when I with my bow vanquish alone the Kaurava army. You shall
see their whole host wounded and reeling like wheels.

"Stand unperturbed on the chariot through the rough and the
smooth; I shall cleave with my blades through a mountain which
reaches heaven. At Indra's behest I once slew the Paulomas and
10 Kālakhañjas by the hundreds and thousands. I obtained my firm grip
from Indra; my dexterity from Brahmā; my deep, fearsome, and
wondrous penetration from Prajāpati. Across the ocean I crushed
Hiraṇyapura after vanquishing 60,000 chariot warriors who wielded
terrible bows. I shall set afire with the glow of my missiles the forest
of the Kurus with the trees of their banners, the straw of their
footmen, and the prides of lions of their chariots. Alone I shall with
my smoothed arrows drive them out of the nests of their chariots,
as the Thunderbolt-wielder did to the Asuras. From Rudra I obtained
the Raudra, from Varuṇa the Vāruṇa, from Agni the Āgneya, from
Mātariśvan the Vāyavya, and from Śakra the thunderbolt missile and
15 others. Son of Virāṭa, let your fears disappear, I shall extirpate the
dread forest of the Dhārtarāṣṭras guarded by its lions of men!"

Thus reassured by the left-handed archer, Virāṭa's son plunged
into the terrifying chariot army of the sagacious Bhīṣma. But that
warrior of cruel deeds purposefully withstood strong-armed
Dhanaṃjaya when he attacked to vanquish his enemies. Then
Duḥśāsana, Vikarṇa, Duḥsaha, and Viviṃśati, in colorful garlands
and jewelry, experienced and spirited, rushed at the fearful bowman,
pulling the bowstrings with their arms, and tried to stop the Terrifier.
20 Duḥśāsana hit Virāṭa's son Uttara with a bear arrow and valiantly
struck Arjuna in the chest with another one. Jiṣṇu turned and cut his
gold-studded bow in two with a vulture-feathered shaft with a broad
blade, and then hit him in the chest with five arrows. Duḥśāsana
abandoned the fight and fled, pressed by the Pārtha's arrows.
Dhṛtarāṣṭras's son Vikarṇa then pelted Arjuna, killer of enemy heroes,
with sharp, straight-flying, vulture-fletched arrows, but the Kaunteya
hit him immediately in the forehead with a smooth shaft, and the
25 other fell wounded from the chariot. Now Duḥsaha and Visiṃśati
stormed at the Pārtha and showered him with sharp arrows in the
battle while they tried to save their brother. Dhanaṃjaya alertly hit
them, both at once, with honed, vulture-fletched arrows and killed
their horses. With their horses dead and their limbs wounded, the
footmen of both sons of Dhṛtarāṣṭra ran to them and led them away
on other chariots. The diademed Kaunteya, the unvanquished
Terrifier, attacked powerfully in all directions, wherever he found
a target.

Vaiśaṃpāyana said:

57.1 All the great warriors of the Kauravas now banded together and
determinedly counterattacked Arjuna, O Bhārata. The hero of

measureless soul covered the warriors everywhere with nets of arrows
as a fog covers mountains. With the large elephants trumpeting, the
horses whinnying, and the drums and conches thundering, the roar
was terrifying. Cutting through the bodies of men and horses, and
through iron armor, the multitudes of the Pārtha's arrows struck
5 home by the thousands. Rushing about and shooting his shafts, the
Pārtha shone on the battlefield like the bright midday sun in autumn.
Terrified, the chariot warriors leaped from their chariots, the riders
from horseback, and the footmen scurried on the ground. There was
a loud din as copper, silver, and iron cuirasses were struck by arrows.
The whole battlefield was covered with the bodies of the dead, and
with elephants, horses, and other animals whose lives had been taken
by the shafts. The ground was bestrewn with men that had fallen
from their chariot pits; and, bow in hand, Dhanaṃjaya seemed to
dance through the battle.
10 Hearing the twang of Gāṇḍīva like the crackle of lightning, all
creatures fled in terror from the grand battle. Heads were seen fallen
in the pitched fighting, still wearing their earrings and turbans,
garlanded with gold. Earth appeared as if covered with arrow-
churned limbs and bow-clutching arms with hands and bracelets. As
sharp shafts caused heads to drop on the ground, it was like a shower
of rocks, bull of the Bhāratas. Showing his grisly self, the Pārtha of
grisly might roamed about after having been held in check for
thirteen years, and the Pāṇḍava let loose on the Dhārtarāṣṭras the
15 fearsome fire of his wrath. Witnessing his prowess as he burned the
army, all the fighters became set on making peace before the
Dhārtarāṣṭra's* very eyes. Arjuna, greatest of victors, darted about
striking terror in the army and putting the great warriors to flight,
O Bhārata. He caused a ghastly river to flow, with billowing waves
of blood and the massing duckweed of bones, which was as though
fashioned by Time at the end of the Eon. The Pārtha created a great,
horrific stream with rafts of bows and arrows, mud of flesh and blood,
and islands of great chariots, gurgling with conches and drums, and
fiercely crimson. For as he took his arrows, nocked them, drew
Gāṇḍīva, and shot, no pause could be discerned.

Vaiśaṃpāyana said:

58.1 Then Duryodhana, Karṇa, Duḥśāsana, Viviṃśati, Droṇa and his
son, and the superior warrior Kṛpa returned in fury to the battle,
lusting to kill Dhanaṃjaya, while they drew their large and tough
bows. The monkey-bannered warrior went to meet them all on his
chariot, splendid as the sun, on which the standard was displayed.
Attempting to stop the heroic Dhanaṃjaya with their mighty missiles,

* = Duryodhana.

5 Kṛpa, Karṇa, and Droṇa, greatest of chariot fighters, sent off floods
of arrows like clouds in the rainy season and released showers of
shafts on the attacking Diademed Prince. Taking positions close by,
they determinedly and swiftly pelted him on the battlefield with many
feathered arrows. But while he was being bestrewn from all sides
with divine projectiles, not even a two-finger opening in his guard
was to be detected.
The Terrifier laughed aloud, and the great warrior affixed the divine
Indra missile to Gāṇḍīva, which shone like the sun. Burning like the
sun, the powerful, diadem-crowned Kaunteya covered all the Kurus
10 with his ray-like darts. Gāṇḍīva was like the lightning in a
thunderhead, like a fire on a mountain, and as long as the rainbow.
Just as lightning flickers in the sky when Parjanya rains, so the flying
Gāṇḍīva covered all ten regions. All the warriors became totally
terrified and desirous of peace and had no thought of their own but
to turn away from the battle, their minds deranged. So all the hosts,
broken, fled in all directions, O bull of the Bhāratas, without hope of
surviving.

Vaiśaṃpāyana said:

59.1 Thereupon Bhīṣma Śāṃtanava, majestic and unassailable, stormed
at Dhanaṃjaya, while the warriors were being slaughtered. Taking
up a superb bow adorned with gold and sharp-piled arrows that
struck wounds in weak spots, the tigerlike man, with a white parasol
held over his head, shone like a mountain at sunrise. Gāngeya blew
his conch, exhilarating the Dhārtarāṣṭras, circled toward the right,
5 and prepared to battle the Terrifier. When the Kaunteya, slayer of
enemy heroes, saw him come, he joyfully received him as a mountain
a rain cloud. Then the mighty Bhīṣma aimed eight arrows at the
Pārtha's standard, fast and hissing like snakes; and the blazing shafts,
striking the standard of Pāṇḍu's son, hit the monkey and the creatures
on top of the flag. But with a broad-bladed long bear arrow the
Pāṇḍava cut off Bhīṣma's umbrella, and it thudded to the ground.
Acting swiftly the Kaunteya hit the other's standard hard with
arrows, as well as the chariot's horses and the two side-horse drivers.
10 The battle of the two became fearsome and hair-raising, this battle
of Bhīṣma and the Pārtha as of Bali and Vāsava.* The bear arrows
of Bhīṣma and the Pāṇḍava, meeting each other in the sky during
their duel, glittered like fireflies in the rainy season. With the Pārtha
shooting his arrows with right and left hands Gāṇḍīva became like a
swinging wheel of fire, O king. He covered Bhīṣma with hundreds of
sharp shafts, like a rain cloud covering a mountain with water jets.
But Bhīṣma blew away that cloudburst of arrows like a stormy

* = Indra.

15 floodline with arrows of his own, and stopped Arjuna. The broken
shafts fell shattered in pieces around Phalguna's chariot.
Then a new shower of golden-nocked arrows rose swiftly from the
Pāṇḍava's chariot like a plague of locusts, and once more Bhīṣma
blew them asunder with hundreds of sharp shafts. All the Kurus
cried, "Bravo! Bravo! Bhīṣma is doing a difficult deed, fighting
Arjuna! The Pāṇḍava is strong, young, dexterous, and fast-acting—
who can withstand the impact of the Pārtha but Bhīṣma Śāṃtanava
and Devakī's son Kṛṣṇā, or that most eminent of teachers the
20 powerful Droṇa Bhāradvāja?" Fighting off missiles with missiles, the
two mighty, bull-like men played on, bewildering the eyes of all
creatures. The great-spirited pair ranged over the battlefield
employing the Prajāpati, Indra, the terrifying Agni, Kubera, Varuṇa,
Yama, and Vāyu projectiles.
Astounded, the observers watched them on the field and cried,
"Bravo, strong-armed Pārtha! Bravo, Bhīṣma! It is not for mere
humans, this grand encounter of mighty missiles that we are
watching in the duel of Bhīṣma and the Pārtha!" Thus went on the
battle of the pair, who knew how to handle all weapons. Then, with
25 a wide-bladed arrow, Jiṣṇu cut in two Bhīṣma's gold-studded bow. In
a twinkling of the eye, strong-armed Bhīṣma took another bow,
strung it, and wrathfully shot a great many arrows off at
Dhanaṃjaya. Splendid Arjuna, for his part, hurled many honed and
wondrous arrows at Bhīṣma, and Bhīṣma at the Pāṇḍava. While
the two, who knew how to employ all weapons, were ceaselessly
shooting, neither of the great-spirited pair could be seen to have the
advantage, king. Both the diadem-crowned Kaunteya warrior and
the champion Śāṃtanava filled the air with their arrows. Now the
Pāṇḍava surpassed Bhīṣma, then Bhīṣma the Pāṇḍava in that duel,
O king; it was a wonder in the world.
30 The valiant chariot guards of Bhīṣma killed by the Pāṇḍava lay
piled up before the Kaunteya's chariot. The nocked arrows of Him of
the White Horses that leaped from Gāṇḍīva flew to extirpate the
enemy. His white, golden-robed shafts winging up from his chariot
looked like rows of wild geese in the air. In the sky all the Gods with
Indra watched the divine weaponry that he massively and
marvelously shot. At the spectacle the majestic Gandharva Citrasena,
35 greatly delighted, said in praise to the king of the Gods, "Watch
these enemy-shattering arrows go as though linked in a chain, as
Jiṣṇu is shooting his divine weaponry! Humans would not believe
this, for it does not occur among them. How wonderful is the
encounter of the ancient great weapons! The hosts are unable to
face the Pāṇḍava, as they cannot face the midday sun blazing in the
sky. Both are famous for their feats, both are experienced in warfare,

both are equals in their exploits, both are irresistible in battle!" At his words the king of the Gods applauded the duel of the Pārtha and Bhīṣma with a divine rain of flowers, O Bhārata.

40 Then, laying on an arrow to counter the left-handed archer, who was open, Bhīṣma Śāṃtanava aimed at his left side. But the Terrifier laughed aloud and with a broad-bladed, vulture-fletched arrow cut the bow of the boundlessly lustrous Bhīṣma. Now Kuntī's son Dhanaṃjaya hit his striving, valiant foe with ten arrows in the chest. Wounded, the strong-armed, irresistible son of the Ganges held on to the chariot pole and stood in that position for a long time. Then the driver of the chariot horses, remembering his training, drove off to save the great warrior, who had lost consciousness.

Vaiśaṃpāyana said:

60.1 When Bhīṣma had left the battlefield
And taken to flight, Dhṛtarāṣṭra's son,
Great-spirited prince, roared out and raised
His standard and stormed at Arjuna.

While Dhanaṃjaya, terrible archer, was ranging
Heroically midst the host of his foes,
He drew to his ear full circle the bow
And shot an arrow into his forehead.

With that honed, gold-studded arrow stuck
In his brow, O king, that warrior prince
Of illustrious exploits shone as a lovely
One-peaked hill with a single bamboo.

From the wound of the hero rent by the arrow
There appeared a steady hot trickle of blood,
And beautifully rare as flowers of gold
It sparkled upon him a colorful garland.

5 Once hit by the arrow he flew in a rage;
With the thrust of the wrath Duryodhana roused
He took out arrows like poison and fire
And shot at the king, not at all downhearted.

The heroes of men, who were both Ājamīḍhas,
Embattled each other in that arena;
Duryodhana dreadful of splendor, the Pārtha,
And sole champion Pārtha, Duryodhana.

And, riding a great rutting elephant
Of mountainous bulk, now also Vikarṇa
With four brave guards of the tusker's legs
Assaulted Jiṣṇu, the son of Kuntī.

While the elephant fast bore down on him,
Dhanaṃjaya with a swift iron arrow
From his bow drawn wide to his ear full circle
Hit the beast in between its frontal knobs.

That kite-fletched shaft dispatched by the Pārtha
Penetrated the elephant down to its nock,
And cleft that beast like a towering peak
As the bolt shot by Indra a mountain range.

10 The elephant smarting from the arrow
In limbs atremble, in soul diseased,
Sank down and slowly fell to the earth—
A mountain top hit by a thunderbolt.

With that grand elephant felled to the ground
Vikarṇa in haste dismounted from it
And for eight hundred paces he went and ran
And climbed on Viviṃśati's chariot.

Having slain that elephant with that arrow,
A thunderbolt downing a peak or a cloud,
The Pārtha now with the same kind of arrow
Shot through the chest of Duryodhana.

There king and elephant lay pierced,
With Vikarṇa broken and the elephant guards;
And nudged by the shafts shot from Gāṇḍīva
The foremost of warriors ran off fast.

No sooner he saw the elephant killed
And observed that his fighters were all in flight
Than the Kaurava hero turned round the chariot
And ran from the field to where the Pārtha was not.

15 The Diademed One, who was minded to fight,
Addressed Duryodhana fearfully running,
And the quivered enemy-tamer spoke
To the shaft-struck foe who was spitting blood—

Arjuna said:

Giving up your fame and opulent glory
Why escape from the battle and flee for your life?
No, today they are no more playing the music
That sounded for him who was going to war.

Of Yudhiṣṭhira I am the faithful agent,
The third of the Pārthas and steadfast in war:
Therefore turn around and show your face,
Recall how kings act, Dhārtarāṣṭra!

In vain shall be your name on earth,
The name you once held, "Duryodhana."
You have no more Duryodhana in you,
Who leave the fight and take to flight!

And neither before you nor behind you
See I one to defend Duryodhana.
Now run from the battle, you Kaurava champion,
And save your dear life from the Pāṇḍava!

Vaiśaṃpāyana said:

61.1 Dhṛtarāṣṭra's son, now challenged to battle
By that great-spirited warrior prince,
Was goaded back by that hook of his words,
As a mad tusker by the hook of its driver.

A warrior stung with insults, and resentful,
By a greater warrior, he grew ferocious
And bravely turned his chariot around,
Like a cobra kicked with the flat of a foot.

But Karṇa, seeing him turning around,
Turned back and firmed up in his wounded limbs,
And to Duryodhana's right he came up
To attack that gold-crowned hero the Pārtha.

Śāṃtanava Bhīṣma also returned
And hurried his golden-harnessed horses
To protect Duryodhana from the rear
From the Pārtha, with bow strung and arms strong.

5 And Droṇa and Kṛpa, Viviṃśati
And Duḥśāsana hastened and turned about;
All hurriedly came with arrows and bows
At the ready to guard Duryodhana.

The Pārtha espying those selfsame armies
Returning alike unto rivers in spate,
Flew counter to them in impetuous fight
Like a goose to a cloud that is suddenly looming.

They encircled the Pārtha on every side,
Took up celestial weaponry
And attacking showered arrows upon him
As clouds pour rains on a mountain peak.

The Gāṇḍīva bowman countered with missiles
The missiles of those Kaurava bulls;

The foe-endurer then made to appear
The Bewilderment weapon, uncounterable.

He covered thereon all points of the compass
With honed, well-bladed and well-nocked shafts,
And the powerful man with the sound of Gāṇḍīva
Struck quivering fear in the minds of them.

With his hands he now seized the mighty conch
Of the fearsome sound and the noble call;
The Pārtha, the slayer of foes, made echo
The points of the compass, the sky and the earth.

And the Kaurava heroes were stupefied
By the sound of the conch shell the Pārtha blew;
They cast off their irresistible bows
And all became then set upon peace.

And when all were unconscious, Arjuna
Bethought himself of Uttarā's words.
To the son of the Matsya he said, "Go out
From the center as long as they're out of their wits.

"Go fetch the Teacher's and Kṛpa's white
And Karṇa's yellow and reddish robes,
And the blue ones of Droṇa's son and the king,
Go fetch their robes, thou hero of men!

"I believe that Bhīṣma is still by his wits:
He knows how to counter that weapon of mine.
Therefore keep his mounts to the left of thee,
For thus one should near those of unmuddled wits."

The son of Virāṭa gave over the reins
And leaped from the chariot on to the ground.
He took the robes of the eminent warriors
And quickly ascended his chariot again.

He thereupon ordered his four white steeds,
Did the son of Virāṭa, in harness of gold,
And passing the host of the standard-bearers
Drove Arjuna from the center field.

But when the hero of men went by,
Impetuous Bhīṣma shot him with arrows;
But he laid low the horses of Bhīṣma
And struck in his side with ten of his arrows.

Abandoning Bhīṣma on the battlefield
And killing his driver, the invincible bowman
Emerged from the midst of the chariot host
Like the thousand-rayed sun after shattering Rāhu.

Regaining his wits, the Kaurava hero,
Dhṛtarāṣṭra's son, saw Indra-like Pārtha
Who was standing alone, withdrawn from the battle,
And the Dhārtarāṣṭra hastened to speak.

20 "How could this man escape from you?
One should keep him in check, so he won't get away!"
And laughingly Bhīṣma replied to him:
"Where went your wits, where was your valor,

"That you stood there putting your faith in peace,
Casting off your arrows and beautiful bow?
Of no cruel deeds is the Terrifier able,
Nor is his mind set on deviltry.

"He would not shirk his Law if it lost him the world,
That is why we have not been slain in battle.
Return to the Kuru land, Kaurava hero,
Let the Pārtha return with the cows he has won!"

And when Duryodhana heard these words
Of the Grandfather, which were of profit to him,
He lost his desire for war, and, resentful,
The king sighed deep and made no reply.

Observing the wisdom of Bhīṣma's words
And the growing fire of Dhanaṃjaya,
They set their minds on traveling back
While careful to guard Duryodhana.

25 Dhanaṃjaya Pārtha, seeing depart
The Kaurava heroes, happy of heart
Drove after them so as to address them
And greatspiritedly to honor his gurus.

To Bhīṣma Śāṃtanava, ancient grandsire,
And Droṇa the Teacher he bowed with his head;
And Drauṇi and Kṛpa and all his elders
He greeted with colorful arrows too.

Of Duryodhana did the Pārtha shear off
With an arrow the finely bejeweled crown.
Having greeted the heroes to whom he owed homage
And filling the world with Gāṇḍīva's sound,

He suddenly sounded his conch Devadatta,
The hero, and shattered the minds of his foes.
And having defeated his enemies all
He shone with his flag which was netted with gold.

The Diademed One, on seeing the Kurus
Depart, said with joy to the son of the Matsya,
"Turn around thy horses, thy cows have been won.
The enemy's gone, go content to thy city!"

Vaiśaṃpāyana said:
62.1 After vanquishing the Kurus in battle, the bull-eyed hero herded
back the vast wealth of Virāṭa. When the sons of Dhṛtarāṣṭra had
all been crushed and gone, many soldiers of the Kurus came out of
the dense woods; with their hearts trembling from fear they
appeared from hither and yon. They were seen to stand there with
disheveled hair and folded hands, plagued with hunger, thirst, and
fatigue in an alien land, and out of their wits. They bowed and in
confusion said to the Pārtha, "What should we do?"
Arjuna said:
5 Go safely, be blessed. Have no fear at all. I have no wish to
slaughter the miserable, I want to assure you.
Vaiśaṃpāyana said:
Hearing his reassuring words the gathered fighters gladdened him
with benedictions that bestowed long life, fame, and glory; thereupon
the men from Kurukṣetra, broken and defeated, returned home.
Taking the road himself, Phalguna said, "Strong-armed and heroic
prince, wait till all the herds of cows and their herdsmen have been
collected. In the afternoon we shall go to the city of Virāṭa, after
10 resting the horses, and letting them drink and roll. Now you must
send cowherds to hurry to the city and tell the good news and
proclaim your victory."
Uttara then quickly gave orders to messengers: "At the bidding of
Arjuna himself proclaim my triumph!"

4(48) The Wedding

4.63–67 (B. 68–72; C. 2160–376)
63 (68; 2160). Virāṭa and the four Pāṇḍavas return victorious to the city where Virāṭa inquires about Uttara. Told that he has gone to counter the Kauravas, Virāṭa is disturbed and sends an army to relieve his son (1–10). Yudhiṣṭhira says that, with Bṛhannaḍā on

hand, Uttara cannot lose (15). Uttara's impending arrival is announced and Yudhiṣṭhira congratulates Virāṭa who sends out a gay welcoming party (15–25). Virāṭa calls for a game of dice, but Yudhiṣṭhira thinks he is too excited; moreover, gambling is evil (30–35). They do play while Virāṭa keeps extolling Uttara's success and Yudhiṣṭhira keeps stressing Bṛhannaḍā's role. Virāṭa becomes angry. When Yudhiṣṭhira insists that only Bṛhannaḍā could have defeated the Kauravas, Virāṭa throws the dice in his face (35–45). Yudhiṣṭhira's nose begins to bleed and he catches the blood in his hand; Draupadī then brings a golden water bowl to catch the blood (45). Uttara arrives at the palace and is announced along with Bṛhannaḍā. Virāṭa invites both in, but Yudhiṣṭhira has him let Bṛhannaḍā wait: he would be enraged at seeing his blood (45–50).

64 (69; 2241). Uttara enters and sees Yudhiṣṭhira bloodied; he asks who did it, and Virāṭa replies he did. Uttara begs him to placate Yudhiṣṭhira. Virāṭa apologizes—Yudhiṣṭhira had already forgiven him by preventing the blood from falling on the floor: a circumstance that would have been the ruin of the kingdom (1–5). When the bleeding has stopped Bṛhannaḍā is fetched in. Virāṭa praises Uttara's valor (5–15). Uttara protests that not he but a "son of a God" did it all, and recounts some incidents (15–25). Virāṭa asks where he is: he has vanished. The Pāṇḍavas still do not reveal their true identities. Arjuna presents the clothes he has plundered to Virāṭa's daughter (30–35).

65 (70; 2260). Two days later the Pāṇḍavas dress up in white robes and ornaments and take thrones in Virāṭa's hall. Virāṭa is surprised at their pretensions (1–5). Arjuna identifies Yudhiṣṭhira with great praise (5–10).

66 (71; 2289). Virāṭa asks after the others and Arjuna identifies them and himself (1–10). Uttara recounts Arjuna's exploits (10). Virāṭa is contrite for having hit Yudhiṣṭhira; he will give his daughter Uttarā in marriage to Arjuna. He relates how Bhīma set him free from captivity, and apologizes for any slight (15–20). Virāṭa is extremely pleased and gives Uttarā to Arjuna; he accepts her as bride of his son Abhimanyu (20–25).

67 (72; 2326). Questioned, Arjuna explains that he has

been in Uttarā's constant company for a year, while she was nubile, so that suspicions might well arise. Her marriage to his son will lay them to rest. Virāṭa accepts this (1–10). Yudhiṣṭhira approves and sends messengers to Kṛṣṇa, with whom Abhimanyu has been staying (10). Arjuna then goes to fetch his son. The king of the Kāśis and the king of Śibi arrive with an akṣauhiṇī *each in support of Yudhiṣṭhira's cause; so does Drupada. The Vṛṣṇis arrive in force with Abhimanyu and bring many presents (10–25). With much pomp the wedding is celebrated and the dowry presented. Yudhiṣṭhira bestows largess on the brahmins (25–35).*

Vaiśaṃpāyana said:

63.1 Virāṭa too, commanding an army, had won back his cattle wealth and joyfully entered his city with the other four Pāṇḍavas. After defeating the Trigartas in battle and recapturing all his cows, the great king, surrounded by his good fortune, gloried with the Pārthas. The hero, who heightened the joy of his friends, was seated on his throne, and all the ministers and brahmins waited on him. The Matsya king and his army returned their homage; then he dismissed the ministers and brahmins.

5 Then the army-commanding King Virāṭa of Matsya asked about Uttara. "Where has he gone?" he said. The women, maidens, and others who lived in the palace seraglio said cheerfully, "Our wealth of cattle had been robbed by the Kurus, and, furious, Bhūmiṃjaya has driven out, alone and audaciously, with Bṛhannaḍā to vanquish the six superior warriors who assailed us, Droṇa, Bhīṣma, Kṛpa, Karṇa, Duryodhana and Droṇa's son."

Virāṭa the king was deeply disturbed
On hearing his son on one chariot gone
With Bṛhannaḍā driving, his war-happy son,
And he spoke to his principal councilors,

10 "Indeed, the Kurus and the other kings of earth will not remain still when they hear that the Trigartas have been defeated. Therefore let my warriors, those that have not been wounded by the Trigartas, march out with a large force to save my son Uttara!"

He ordered his elephants, horses and chariots
And valiant footmen swiftly to march
In the cause of his son, and all were equipped
With various weapons and jewelry-decked.

And the army-commanding King Virāṭa of Matsya immediately gave orders to his four-membered army: "Quickly find out whether the prince is alive or not. With a eunuch along as his charioteer, I don't think he will live."

15 With a laugh King Dharma then said to Virāṭa,
Who was troubled and deeply disturbed by the Kurus:
"When Bṛhannaḍā is his charioteer,
Great king, no enemy'll take your cattle!

"For your son, well-served by that charioteer,
Is quite well able to vanquish in battle
All the gathered kings of the earth and the Kurus—
Gods, Asuras, Yakṣas, and Snakes as well!"

Then the swift-moving messengers Uttara had sent arrived at the city of Virāṭa and proclaimed his victory. The chief councilor then reported to the king the great triumph, the defeat of the Kurus, and the returning of Uttara: "All the cows have been recovered, the Kurus have been defeated, and Uttara is safe with his charioteer, enemy-burner!"

Kanka said:

20 By good fortune have the cows been recouped and the Kurus defeated; by good fortune is it that we hear that your son is alive, bull among kings! But I deem it no wonder that your son has vanquished the Kurus, for certain is he to triumph who is driven by Bṛhannaḍā.

Vaiśaṃpāyana said:

King Virāṭa was thrilled with excitement when he heard that his boundlessly august son had won the victory. He rewarded the messengers with robes and ordered his councilors, "Let my royal roads be decked with bunting and all the deities be worshipped with auspicious offerings! Let the princes, chief warriors, and well-adorned
25 courtesans, and all musical instruments go out to meet my son! Let my bell-ringer quickly mount a rutting elephant and proclaim my victory at all crossroads. Uttarā too, with a retinue of many maidens, must go and receive Bṛhannaḍā, wearing the costume and jewelry that betoken love."

And on hearing the orders of the great king
All people went carrying *svastikas*
And cymbals and drums and conch shells too,
And beautiful harlots in precious robes,

And bards as well and Magadhan minstrels
With all manner of musical instruments,
From the mighty Virāṭa's capital
To meet his endlessly valiant son.

After dispatching his army, maidens, and well-adorned courtesans,
the sagacious great king said cheerfully, "Fetch the dice,
30 chambermaid, and let the game begin, Kanka!" The Pāṇḍava looked
at him when he said this and replied, "One should not play, we have
heard, with an excited gambler. I should not properly play with you
now that you are so happy! But I will give you the pleasure; let it
begin if it pleases you."

Virāṭa said:

You won't save me my women, cattle, gold, and whatever else I own even without dicing!

Kanka said:

Why must you dice, Indra among kings? Many are the vices,
giver of pride, that lurk in gambling, and therefore one should shun
it. Haven't you seen or heard of Yudhiṣṭhira Pāṇḍava? He lost his
very large and prosperous kingdom, his brothers who were the likes
35 of the Thirty, he lost *everything* at dicing. Therefore I do not like to
play. But what do you think? If you want to, we shall play.

Vaiśaṃpāyana said:

While the dicing was going on, the Matsya said to the Pāṇḍava,
"Look how my son has defeated the grand Kurus in battle!"
Yudhiṣṭhira, the son of Dharma, replied to the king of the Matsyas,
"How could he have lost with Bṛhannaḍā driving him?" Angrily
King Matsya told the Pāṇḍava, "You praise a eunuch in the same
breath as my son, insolent brahmin! Don't you know what can be
said and what not? Surely you are showing contempt for me! Why
should he not defeat all of them with Bhīṣma and Droṇa at their
40 head? But for friendship's sake I'll forgive your mistake, brahmin;
only speak like that no more if you wish to live!"

Yudhiṣṭhira said:

Droṇa and Bhīṣma were there, and Droṇa's son, and Vaikartana, Kṛpa, and Duryodhana, great king, and all the other mighty warriors, or suppose the God of the Hundred Sacrifices himself were there in the midst of his bands of Maruts—who but Bṛhannaḍā could fight them all together?

Virāṭa said:

I have warned you repeatedly but you do not watch your language. If no one were restrained, nobody would observe the Law.

Vaiśaṃpāyana said:

In a fit of anger the king hit Yudhiṣṭhira in the face with a die,
45 shouting irately, "I will not have it!" So powerfully was Yudhiṣṭhira
struck that the blood streamed from his nose, and the Pārtha caught
it in his hand before it trickled to the floor. The Law-spirited man
looked askance at Draupadī who stood on the side; and she, obedient
to her husband's thoughts, divined his meaning. The blameless
woman filled up a golden bowl with water and caught in it the blood
that flowed from the Pārtha.

Then Uttara slowly made his joyous entrance into the city, decked
with fine perfumes and manifold garlands. While he was being
honored by the townspeople, women, and countryfolk, he approached
50 the palace gate and had himself announced to his father. The
gatekeeper entered at once and said to the king, "Uttara is standing
at the gate with Bṛhannaḍā." Happily the king of the Matsyas told
the steward, "Bring them both in immediately; I am longing to see
them!" But the Kuru king whispered in the steward's ear, "Let
Uttara alone enter; don't let Bṛhannaḍā in. He has sworn an oath,
strong-armed one, that if anyone inflicts a wound on my body or
makes blood appear outside of battle, he will surely die. If he sees
me bloodied, he will fly in a rage and not bear it; he would kill
Virāṭa here with his councillors, troops, and mounts!"

Vaiśaṃpāyana said:

64.1 Thereupon Bhūmiṃjaya, the eldest son of the king, entered. He saluted his father's feet, then saw the King Dharma. The innocent prince was sitting on the floor on the side, smeared with blood and distracted; and the chambermaid was attending to him. Hurriedly Uttara asked his father, "Who has beaten him, king, who has perpetrated this crime?"

Virāṭa said:

I have beaten this rogue, and less than he deserved! When I was praising you as a hero, he praised the eunuch!

Uttara said:

5 You have done wrong! Placate him at once, lest the fearsome brahmin poison burn you root and all!

Vaiśaṃpāyana said:

When Virāṭa, prosperer of his kingdom, heard the words of his son, he asked the Kaunteya—a fire hidden beneath ashes—for forgiveness. The Pāṇḍava replied to the pleading king, "I have already forgiven it, king, and I feel no anger. For if that blood from my nose had fallen on the ground, you would for a certainty have perished with your kingdom, great king. I do not blame you, Mahārāja, for hitting an innocent man; for cruelty comes quick to the powerful."

10 Then, when the bleeding had stopped, Bṛhannaḍā entered and, after saluting the king and Kanka he remained standing. After he had placated the Kauravya, the Matsya now began praising Uttara, returned from the battle, within the left-handed archer's hearing. "In you I have really an heir, joy of Kaikeyī! None of my sons are your match, or will be. How was your encounter with Karṇa, son, who when he moves does not miss a step in a thousand? How was your encounter with Bhīṣma, son, who has no equal in the entire

world of men, who is as imperturbable as the ocean and unbearable
like the fire of Doomsday? How was your encounter with Droṇa, son,
the brahmin teacher of the Vṛṣṇi heroes and the Pāṇḍavas, the
15 teacher of the entire baronage, first of all bearers of arms? How was
your encounter with him who is famed as Aśvatthāman, the
Teacher's son, champion among all bearers of arms? How was your
encounter with Kṛpa, son, at the sight of whom soldiers collapse in
war like merchants robbed of their goods? How was your encounter
with Duryodhana, son, the king's son, who could cleave a mountain
with his great arrows?

Uttara said:

It was not I who won back the cattle, nor I who defeated the
20 enemies: everything was done by one son of a God. When I ran
away in terror, that youth, that son of a God, stopped me, and he
stood in the pit of the chariot like the Thunderbolt-wielder himself!
He recovered the cows, he vanquished the Kurus, the feat was this
hero's, father, not mine. For with his arrows he put Śāradvata,
Droṇa, Droṇa's valiant son, the son of the *sūta*, and Bhīṣma to flight.
He broke Duryodhana in battle like a leader of an elephant herd,
and spoke to the mighty but panic-stricken prince, "I see no escape
25 at all for you in Hāstinapura! Make an effort to save your life, son
of the Kaurava! You shall not escape by running away, king; set
your mind on battle! When you triumph, you shall enjoy the earth,
or, dead, attain to heaven." The tigerlike man then returned, shooting
his boltlike arrows, while he stood surrounded by his councillors on
his chariot and hissing like a cobra. My hair stood on end, father,
and my thighs were paralyzed, when he blew apart with his arrows
that army that was massed like clouds. Then the mighty youth with
the lion build routed the chariot army, king, and laughingly took
away the robes of the Kurus. Alone that hero encircled the six
warriors, as an angry tiger grazing deer in the forest!

Virāṭa said:

30 Where is that strong-armed hero, that glorious son of a God, who
in battle won back my wealth, which had been plundered by the
Kurus? I wish to see the mighty man and pay him honor, for that
son of a hero has saved you and my cattle.

Uttara said:

That majestic son of a God disappeared, father, but I fancy he will
reappear tomorrow or the day after.

Vaiśaṃpāyana said:

While he was so being described, the Pāṇḍava remained concealed
behind his disguise; and Virāṭa did not know that Arjuna Pārtha
was living there. Thereupon the Pārtha, with the great-spirited
Virāṭa's permission, presented in person those captured robes to

35 Virāṭa's daughter. Beaming, Uttarā accepted those many robes, which
were precious and sheer, and she was delighted. The Kaunteya had
secretly worked out with Uttara a plan concerning their entire task
with respect to King Yudhiṣṭhira, and so he cheerfully carried it out,
that bull of the Bhāratas, together with the Matsya's son, O bull
among men.

Vaiśaṃpāyana said:

65.1 On the third day the five Pāṇḍava brothers, freshly bathed, dressed
in white, having fulfilled their vow according to the covenant, and
adorned with all their ornaments, placed Yudhiṣṭhira at their head;
and, radiant like lotus-spotted elephants, the great warriors went to
Virāṭa's hall and seated themselves on regal thrones, like fires on
their hearths, all brilliant like fire. While they were sitting there,
5 King Virāṭa came into the hall to attend to all his royal affairs. Seeing
the illustrious Pāṇḍavas blazing like fires, the Matsya said to Kanka,
who sat godlike, like the lord of the Thirty with the bands of the
Maruts, "I made you only my dicing master, mind you, just my
official gamester, so why are you seated in your finery on a regal
throne?"

When Arjuna heard Virāṭa's words, O king, he said smilingly to
make a joke of it, "Sire, this man is worthy to sit even on Indra's
throne! He is brahminic, learned, generous, wont to sacrifice, firm
in his vows—he is the bull of the Kurus, Yudhiṣṭhira, son of Kuntī!
10 His fame dwells on earth like the light of the rising sun, the rays of
his glory travel to all the regions, as do the rays of his splendor like
the risen sun's. While he lived in Kurukṣetra, sire, ten thousand
powerful elephants and thirty thousand golden-garlanded warriors
followed behind him on fine golden-harnessed horses. Eight hundred
bards always followed behind with earrings of polished gems and
sang his praises with Magadhan minstrels as the seers praise Śakra.
The Kurus always waited on him as so many servants, and so did
15 all the kings, king, as the Immortals on Kubera. At that time all the
lords of the earth paid tribute to him, great king, willy-nilly, like
subservient commoners. Eighty thousand *snātaka* brahmins lived off
this king of well-kept vows. My lord, he protected by the Law the
old, orphaned, crippled, and halt subjects like his sons. True to his
vows in Law, self-control, and ire, the king was full of favor,
brahminic, and true-spoken.

"The lordly Suyodhana suffers under his illustrious majesty, along
20 with his band, Karṇa and Saubala. There is no counting his virtues,
lord of men—the Pāṇḍava is always beholden to the Law and is free
of all cruelty. Thus is endowed the great King Pāṇḍava, bull among
kings: would such a king not deserve a throne worthy of kings?"

Virāṭa said:
66.1 If he is King Yudhiṣṭhira Kauravya, the son of Kuntī, who is his
brother Arjuna, who the strongman Bhīma, or Nakula and Sahadeva,
or the glorious Draupadī? The Pārthas have not been discovered
since they were defeated at dice.

Arjuna said:
The one who is called Ballava, your cook, O king of men, he is the
strong-armed Bhīma of terrible speed and prowess. In a rage he slew
demons on Mount Gandhamādana and plucked divine *saugandhika*
5 flowers for Kṛṣṇā. He is the Gandharva who slew the villainous
Kīcakas and killed tigers, bears, and boar in your seraglio. Your horse
groom is the enemy-burner Nakula, and the other of Mādrī's warlike
twins is your cow teller. Wearing the guise and the ornaments that
betoken love, handsome and glorious, these two bull-like men are
capable of overcoming many thousands of warriors. And this slim-
waisted, sweet-smiling chambermaid with eyes like lotus petals is
Draupadī, in whose cause the Kīcakas were killed. And I, great king,
am the Arjuna of whom you have doubtless heard, the son of Pṛthā,
10 younger brother of Bhīma and the elder of the twins. We have
dwelled happily in your domain for our term of concealment, like
infants in the womb!

Vaiśaṃpāyana said:
When Arjuna had revealed the five heroic Pāṇḍavas, Virāṭa's son
recounted Arjuna's gallantry, "It is he who in the midst of the
enemies, a lion among deer, ranged among the troops of warriors,
killing the best of them. With a single arrow he shot a large elephant,
and the beast in its golden caparison sank to the ground, embedding
its tusks in the battlefield. It was he who recovered the cattle and
vanquished the Kurus in battle; the sound of his conch has deafened
my ears!"
15 Upon hearing his words the majestic king of the Matsyas replied
to Uttara, aware he had given offense to Yudhiṣṭhira, "The time has
come, I think, for me to placate the Pāṇḍava. And I shall bestow
Uttarā on the Pārtha, if you agree."

Uttara said:
They deserve worship, veneration, and honor. I think the time has
come. Let homage be paid to the lordly Pāṇḍavas, who are worthy
of homage.

Virāṭa said:
I myself, indeed, when I was in the power of the enemies in the
battle, was rescued by Bhīmasena, and the cattle were recovered.
By the might of their arms we gained victory in battle, therefore let
us all with our councilors placate the bull of the Pāṇḍavas, Kuntī's
20 son Yudhiṣṭhira, and his brothers. Whatever we may have said in

our ignorance to the king of men, pray let him forgive it all, for the Pāṇḍava is Law-spirited!

Vaiśaṃpāyana said:

> Then Virāṭa rejoiced in the highest degree
> And concluded a covenant with the king;
> He offered his kingdom entire to him
> With staff and treasure and capital.

Thereupon the king of the Matsyas spoke to all the Pāṇḍavas, paying special honor to Dhanaṃjaya, "I am fortunate! Fortunate!"

He embraced and kissed on the head Yudhiṣṭhira, Bhīma, and the
twin sons of Mādrī and Pāṇḍu. Army-commander Virāṭa was not
sated with looking at them, and most contentedly he said to King
25 Yudhiṣṭhira, "How fortunate that you all have come out of the forest
unharmed; how fortunate that you have survived the dangers
unbeknownst to these villains! Let the Pārthas accept our entire
kingdom and what wealth we possess without hesitation. Let the
left-handed archer Dhanaṃjaya accept Uttarā, for that august
Pāṇḍava is a suitable husband for her."

At these words the King Dharma looked at Dhanaṃjaya, and at his brother's glance Arjuna spoke to the Matsya, "I accept your daughter, O king, but as my daughter-in-law, for our alliance is fitting, of eminent Matsya and Bhārata!"

Virāṭa said:

67.1 Why do you decline to accept, best of the Pāṇḍava, my daughter
whom I am giving you for a wife?

Arjuna said:

When I lived in the seraglio, I saw your daughter constantly in
public and private, and she trusted me as a father. I was dear to her
and respected as a dancer and experienced singer—your daughter
always thought of me as her teacher. Sire, for a full year I have
lodged with her while she was nubile, and suspicion on your part
5 and the people's, my lord, would not be out of place. Therefore, lord
of the earth, I beseech you for your daughter. I have been pure,
have remained master of my senses, and have been controlled, and
I have preserved her chastity. I do not see how suspicion could fall
on a daughter-in-law and daughter for my son and yourself; therefore
purity will be preserved. I abhor false accusations and suspicion of
hypocrisy, enemy-killer, therefore I accept your daughter Uttarā as
my daughter-in-law. My strong-armed son Abhimanyu is the nephew
of Vāsudeva himself. He is like the child of a God, the favorite of the
Discus-wielder, and, while still a child, is experienced with weapons,
lord of your people. He is a suitable son-in-law for you and husband
for your daughter!

Virāṭa said:
10 This is indeed appropriate for Kuntī's son Dhanaṃjaya, best of
the Kurus! The Pāṇḍava is constant in the Law and possessed of
wisdom. Let what you think ought to be done be done at once. All
my desires are richly fulfilled, if I am allied to Arjuna!

Vaiśaṃpāyana said:
When that Indra among kings spoke thus, Kuntī's son Yudhiṣṭhira approved the covenant of an alliance between the Matsya and the Pārtha. The Kaunteya and King Virāṭa thereupon sent messengers to all their friends and to Vāsudeva, Bhārata.

Then, the thirteenth year being complete, the five Pāṇḍavas all
15 went and settled in Virāṭa's city Upaplavya. While living there, the
Terrifier Pāṇḍava went to fetch Janārdana, Abhimanyu, and the
other Dāśārhas from Ānarta. The King of the Kāśis and the King of
Śibi, who were friendly to Yudhiṣṭhira, came together with two
grand-armies, O lord of the people. The powerful and puissant
Yajñasena came with a grand-army, and Draupadī's gallant sons
and the unvanquished Śikhaṇḍin, as well as the unassailable
Dhṛṣṭadyumna, best of all bearers of arms. And these commanders
of grand-armies were all sacrificers, too, who gave large stipends.
They all knew all weaponry and were all champions ready to risk
their lives.

When the Matsya, that best of all bearers of Law, saw them come,
20 he was pleased he had given his daughter to Abhimanyu. After the
kings had arrived from hither and yon, Vāsudeva, the plough-armed
Rāma garlanded with forest flowers, Kṛtavarman Hārdikya,
Yuyudhāna Sātyaki, Anādhṛṣṭi, Akrūra, Sāmba, and Niśaṭha came,
too, those enemy-killers, bringing Abhimanyu and his mother.
Indrasena and all the other servants arrived on their well-tended
chariots, after having stayed away for a whole year. With ten
thousand elephants, a hundred myriad horses, a full ten million
chariots, and a billion soldiers, the Vṛṣṇis, Andhakas, and august
Bhojas in their multitudes followed that tiger of Vṛṣṇis, resplendent
25 Vāsudeva. Kṛṣṇā gave the great-spirited Pāṇḍavas each a retinue of
many women, gems, and clothes.

Then the marriage alliance of the Matsya and the Pārtha took
place ceremonially. Conches, kettledrums, trumpets, and war drums,
collected by the Pārthas, sounded forth in the palace of the Matsya,
who was honored by the Pārthas. Songsters and storytellers, actors
and panegyrists sung their praises, as well as bards and Magadhan
minstrels. The great ladies of the Matsyas, with Sudeṣṇā at their
head, filed in, beauteous in all their limbs and wearing earrings of
30 polished gems. All the women were lovely and shapely and well-
adorned, but Kṛṣṇā surpassed them all in beauty, glory, and fortune.
They all surrounded Princess Uttarā in her finery, and waited upon

her with honors as on a daughter of Indra's. Dhanaṃjaya Kaunteya accepted for his and Subhadrā's son the flawless daughter of Virāṭa. The great King Yudhiṣṭhira, son of Kuntī, stood there bearing the beauty of Indra and accepted her as a daughter-in-law.

When the Pārtha had accepted her, paying honor to Janārdana,
he celebrated the wedding of the great-spirited son of Subhadrā.
35 The king gave him a dowry of seven thousand wind-fast horses,
two hundred fine elephants, and much wealth. After the wedding
Dharma's son Yudhiṣṭhira gave the brahmins the riches that Acyuta
had brought, thousands of cows, gems, all kinds of clothes, beautiful
ornaments, and wagons and beds. The city of the king of the Matsyas,
O bull of the Bharatas, crowded with happy and well-fed folk, shone
in the splendor of the grand festival.

The Mahābhārata

Translated

Book 5 *The Book of the Effort*

Introduction

In Outline

Like *Virāṭa*, *The Book of the Effort* takes its name from the first of the Minor Books it comprises, for these eleven Minor Books are all more or less directly concerned with the preparations for the great war. This "effort," in Sanskrit *udyoga*, may be understood both as a peace effort—so *The Book of Contents* in *The Book of the Beginning* interprets it—and as a war effort. It is to the latter meaning that the etymology of the word points: "the yoking up" of the horses, chariots, and elephants of the army in preparation for making an attack; also simply *yoga*, "the yoking."[1]

The structure of the *Effort* is quite simple: it is the narrative of the negotiations between the Pāṇḍavas, who demand their half kingdom back, and Duryodhana, who refuses. These negotiations are formally carried out by means of four embassies, each preceded by a great deal of internal consultation on both sides. Before the negotiations start, each side raises armies, the Pāṇḍavas seven, the Kauravas eleven, and thus both are able to negotiate from strength (Book 49).

Yudhiṣṭhira, as always in complete control of his brothers and allies, with the exception of Kṛṣṇa, begins with sending a Vedic brahmin, the house priest of his father-in-law King Drupada of Pāñcāla, to the Kauravas in order to find out what Duryodhana's attitude is. Before Duryodhana himself speaks up, his father Dhṛtarāṣṭra decides to send his bard Saṃjaya as envoy to Yudhiṣṭhira for the double purpose of making a courtesy call—after all, his nephews the Pāṇḍavas have been gone for thirteen years—and finding out what Yudhiṣṭhira's demands really are. While remaining a model of courtesy, the Pāṇḍava insists on his kingdom (Book 50).

1. E.g., 5.149.47.

Before he hears Saṃjaya's report, Dhṛtarāṣṭra spends a sleepless night, during which he is much edified with a sermon by his brother Vidura (Book 51) and the seer Sunatsujāta (Book 52).

In the consultations ensuing from Saṃjaya's report, Duryodhana is put under great family pressure, but remains adamant, refusing to allow as much as a "pinprick of land" to Yudhiṣṭhira (Book 53). Before his position has been officially reported, Kṛṣṇa betakes himself on a peace-seeking mission on behalf of both parties, but he fails to sway Duryodhana (Book 54). As a last resort Kṛṣṇa seeks to win over Karṇa by revealing his real parentage; his now-revealed mother Kuntī tries the same; both fail. Kṛṣṇa reports to Yudhiṣṭhira, who, with many misgivings, orders "the Yoke" (Book 55) and marches out (Book 56). Duryodhana installs Bhīṣma as marshal of his eleven armies (Book 57), and sends Ulūka with a declaration of war (Book 58). The entire *Book of the Effort* ends with a review of the principal warriors (Book 59), and a lengthy account by Bhīṣma of the bizarre and complex prehistory of one warrior, Śikhaṇḍin, whom he shall refuse to fight (Book 60), presaging the next Major Book, *The Book of Bhīṣma*.

Interwoven with this main narrative are other stories. If we regard the preachings of Vidura and Sanatsujāta, as well as the story of *Ambā*, as strictly speaking irrelevant to the action, these parts and the interlaced stories add up to 69 out of the 196 chapters, or roughly a third of the Book, outside the main text. As usual, a great deal of interest attaches to these parts.

The Protocol of Negotiations

The occurrence in this Book of no less than four embassies should give us some help in determining the conduct of diplomacy in ancient India. For here, as elsewhere, I assume that there was some degree of verisimilitude in the Mahābhārata's depictions of life. There is some, not much, textual evidence on the subject of the *dūta* "messenger, envoy" in *Dharmaśāstra* and *Arthaśāstra*, both of which texts are prescriptive. This material has been usefully gathered and studied by Ludo Rocher,[2] on whom I gratefully rely. It may be interesting to see how the epic describes embassies which supposedly took place in reality.

First, be it noted that all four embassies are officially sanctioned. The envoys come openly and are publicly heard. They are thus sharply distinguished from spies, with whom they are sometimes classified in the texts.[3] Of course, they may try some secret

2. Ludo Rocher, "The 'Ambassador' in Ancient India," *Indian Year Book of International Affairs* (Madras), 1958.

3. *Yājñavalkyasmṛti* 1.328; *Kamaṇḍakīnītisāra* 12.32.

subversion, as in the case of Kṛṣṇa with Karṇa,[4] but that too is aboveboard, since *bheda* "subversion, alienation of a potential enemy's allies" is an accepted part of Indian diplomacy.

The four envoys are all different kinds of men with different qualifications. The first envoy, from Yudhiṣṭhira to the Kauravas, is a brahmin of the highest Vedic purity, and King Drupada's house priest to boot. Dhṛtarāṣṭra's return envoy is his personal bard Saṃjaya. Kṛṣṇa comes on a personal peace mission, as a prince in his own right who is benevolently disposed to both parties. Duryodhana's envoy Ulūka, given the patronymic Kaitavya, "son of a gambler," appears to be a man of low status.

It would seem that the social status of one's envoy is part of one's message. For Drupada to send, in Yudhiṣṭhira's behalf, his own house priest, a Vedic brahmin of unimpeachable conduct and veracity, signals at once his high respect for the dynasty to which he is related maritally through his daughter Draupadī; the purity of Yudhiṣṭhira's case; and his own staunch support of it. The envoy's task is to address himself to Drupada's contemporaries, pointing out past wrongs done to the Pāṇḍavas and the imperative need to restore the kingdom to them.

In reply, Dhṛtaraṣṭra sends Saṃjaya, who is only a *sūta*, a class distinctly below that of Drupada's brahmin, which is a minus only partially offset by the plus that Saṃjaya is a well-regarded friend of the family.[5] It is noteworthy that he *could* have sent his brother Vidura, who is a much dearer friend of the Pāṇḍavas. He had sent Vidura years ago,[6] when the Pāṇḍavas emerged from their first exile and had won the alliance of Pāñcāla through their marriage with Draupadī: at that time Dhṛtarāṣṭra really wanted peace and ended up partitioning the kingdom.[7] Now that the partitioned kingdom is once more at issue, he sends, not the partisan Vidura, old guarantor of the partition, but his bard. Obviously Dhṛtarāṣṭra is not all that eager to surrender half the kingdom again. Since Dhṛtarāṣṭra's case has no merit, he can, through Saṃjaya, only appeal to Yudhiṣṭhira's renowned rectitude and the moral imperative of avoiding a family war.[8] Upon his return Saṃjaya is sufficiently outraged with his master to refuse him his report until morning, causing him a sleepless night.

Kṛṣṇa's embassy is, of course, *sui generis*. He comes, not so much as anyone's envoy as in the character of self-appointed mediator, supported by a troupe of divine seers,[9] eloquently presenting the

4. *The Temptation of Karṇa*, 5.138 ff.
5. So far, however, Saṃjaya has been little in evidence.
6. 1.192 ff.
7. 1.199.
8. 5.25.
9. 5.81.27 f.; 92.40 ff.

merits of Yudhiṣṭhira's case, thunderously elaborating upon the prowess of the Pāṇḍavas, balefully denouncing Duryodhana's villainy, and in the end not eschewing the subversion of Karṇa.

Duryodhana's contemptuous answer to Yudhiṣṭhira is to send Ulūka Kaitavya, the son of a gambler. Later books of the *Mahābhārata*[10] identify his father as Śakuni himself, the one who beat Yudhiṣṭhira at the dicing. It can only be called cynical for Duryodhana to convey his latest challenge through the mouth of the son of the very gambler who in Duryodhana's eyes had defeated Yudhiṣṭhira once and for all.[11]

The first and last of the envoys are strictly mouthpieces who convey the prince's message and have no power of discretion. They are examples of what the *Dharmaśāstra*[12] calls *saṃdiṣṭārtha* "an envoy whose purpose is to convey a message" and the *Arthaśāstra*[13] describes as *parimitārtha* "one whose purpose is circumscribed." Compared with them Saṃjaya has more discretion; Dhṛtarāṣṭra's final charge to him is:

> Whatever you think is opportune with them
> And profitable for the Bhāratas,
> That, Saṃjaya, say in the midst of the kings
> If it does not arouse them and lead to war.[14]

In this, Saṃjaya appears to approximate the *nisṛṣṭārtha*, the "authorized" envoy, who, "while expounding his king's affairs, has authority at his own responsibility to adapt his words to the circumstances."[15]

Still Saṃjaya is clearly not a plenipotentiary. For one thing, he is the messenger only of the older Kaurava generation, and has no mandate at all from Duryodhana, who is king *de facto*. His embassy is more in the nature of a courtesy call, and thus a useful, but quite preliminary step in a series of negotiations. The true plenipotentiary (and how could he fail to be?) is Kṛṣṇa. He offers to go in behalf of both parties: "I myself shall go to the assembly of the Kurus in the cause of both of you. If I make peace without hurting your cause, I shall gain very great merit, king, and the action will have great consequences" (5.70.80 f.). Yudhiṣṭhira demurs, but Kṛṣṇa insists. Yudhiṣṭhira gives him *carte blanche*: "You know us, you know the others, you know Profit, you know the words. Tell Suyodhana

10. E.g., 6.86.5; 7.146.32.
11. 2.53 ff.
12. *Mitākṣara* on *Yājñavalkyasmṛti* 1.328.
13. *ArthŚ.* 1.16.
14. 5.22.39.
15. Rocher, p. 5.

whatever redounds to our Profit, Kṛṣṇa. Whatever sound advice is consistent with the Law, you can give them that, Keśava, whether it be for peace, or war."[16] This is the ultimate mandate of an envoy, which makes *Manu* describe him thus: "Peace and the reverse are upon the envoy" (7.65).

In his mission Kṛṣṇa has the unanimous consent of Yudhiṣṭhira's councilors: Bhīmasena (5.72–75), Arjuna (76–77), Nakula (78), Sahadeva (79), and Draupadī (80), as a result of whose counsel Kṛṣṇa's mission fits the precept of Kauṭilya: it is *uddhṛtamantra* "with counsel fully resolved," the prerequisite to the sending of an envoy (*uddhṛtamantro dūtapraṇidhiḥ*, *ArthŚ*. 1.16). He thus has the *amātyasaṃpad* "the unanimity of the household councilors" (ibid.).

As ambassador plenipotentiary Kṛṣṇa is free to employ the usual means of diplomacy. As he himself reports (5.148.8 ff.): "First I used a conciliatory approach, hoping for a sense of brotherliness to prevail," no doubt referring to his appeal in 5.93. "When conciliatoriness failed, I tried alienation and recited your feats, human and divine"; compare 5.122. Kṛṣṇa seems successful in this approach, for Bhīṣma, Droṇa, and Dhṛtarāṣṭra now urge Duryodhana to heed Kṛṣṇa's advice (5.123–24), but he responds with intransigence. "Once more conciliatory, I mentioned gifts"; and finally, "Now I see no other course open but the fourth—punishment."

Thus Kṛṣṇa successively tries out the four diplomatic tactics (*upāya*) which *Manu* recognizes (7.109): *sāman* "conciliation"; *bheda* "subversion of allies"; *dāna* "bribery"; and *daṇḍa* "punishment."

Kṛṣṇa's diplomacy nevertheless fails to the point where Duryodhana actually plots to take Kṛṣṇa prisoner, thus violating the sanctity of an ambassador's person. "Malicious brute, with your vile band of friends," explodes Duryodhana's father Dhṛtarāṣṭra, "you are conspiring with evil henchmen to perpetrate a crime! A heinous, infamous crime, abhorrent to all decent people, such as only deluded defilers of their families like you could conceive!"[17] Kṛṣṇa calmly replies with a miracle: the host of the Gods and the host of the Pāṇḍavas spring *en miniature* from Kṛṣṇa's limbs.[18]

In a final effort Kṛṣṇa tempts Karṇa with all the riches of the earth if only he will assume the position of eldest son of Pāṇḍu, to which he is entitled by writ of the *Dharmaśāstra* as the premarital son of Pāṇḍu's wife Kuntī. Politely and with complete dignity Karṇa refuses the offer. But in the very act of making the offer, the circumstances and background of which are unknown to Yudhiṣṭhira and which are also not reported to him, Kṛṣṇa shows how heavily the issue of

16. 5.70.94.
17. 5.128.34.
18. 5.129.

"peace and the reverse" weighs upon him, and to what ends he is allowed to go to secure the former.

The Allies

Yudhiṣṭhira is joined by seven kings, while eleven join Duryodhana, each bringing an *akṣauhiṇī* "grand army." The patterns of these alliances make an interesting study.

Some of the aliances are predictable. Yudhiṣṭhira's first ally is, of course, his father-in-law Drupada, who has not only sound marital reasons to support the Pāṇḍavas, but also is motivated by that old feud with Droṇa, who had taken the Pāñcāla possessions on the left bank of the Ganges. Virāṭa of Matsya is also related by law—his daughter Uttarā has married into the Pāṇḍava family as the wife of Arjuna's son Abhimanyu.[19] By the same token one might have expected Śalya of the Madras to join the Pāṇḍavas, for he is the brother of Mādrī, the second wife of Pāṇḍu and the mother of the twins Nakula and Sahadeva.

But something goes wrong in this case. While Śalya is indeed on his way to Yudhiṣṭhira with an army, he finds on his itinerary well-appointed rest houses,[20] which he confidently assumes are provided by Yudhiṣṭhira's courtesy. When he discovers that Duryodhana had them built, he impulsively grants him a boon, and the Kaurava chooses Śalya's alliance for himself. Śalya remains a half-hearted ally, though, and readily accedes to Yudhiṣṭhira's request that, when his time comes to act as Karṇa's charioteer, Śalya demoralize the warrior so that his might is diminished.[21] This is the first hint of perfidy on Yudhiṣṭhira's part that we have met; it might be in part justified by the fact that Duryodhana won Śalya with some deception, but there it is.

Very complex is the case of the Vṛṣṇis. They are related by marriage to Arjuna, who abducted his wife Subhadrā from them, but among the Vṛṣṇis, family ties are not of the strongest. Nor do they have a great deal of unity. This collection of tribes or clans, which go under the most general name of Yādavas, do not constitute a monarchy, but an oligarchy that is hard to analyze. Their nonmonarchical structure may go all the way back to the curse that King Yayāti lay on his son Yadu, the progenitor of the Yādavas: "Your offspring shall have no share in the kingdom."[22] They are to be not *rājās*, but

19. 4.67.
20. *Sabhā*; I was wrong in asserting that the meaning of *sabhā* in 3.59.4 is unique to that *passus* (*Mahābhārata* II, 183, n. 56).
21. 5.18.23.
22. 1.79.7.

bhojas: not consecrated kings but "users"—not quite usurpers but *tyrannoi*.

At any rate, however their present state has come about, they are riven with factions: Kaṃsa overthrew Ugrasena and was killed by Kṛṣṇa, who restored Ugrasena.[23] Śisupāla of Cedi, though a Yādava, attacked Mathurā as Jarāsaṃdha of Magadha's marshal,[24] and for this he is eventually killed by Kṛṣṇa.[25] Eventually the Yādavas will kill off one another in *The Book of the Clubs*.[26] The various loyalties of the Yādavas are well illustrated by the alliances they contract: Yuyudhāna Sātyaki chooses to go with Yudhiṣṭhira,[27] Kṛtavarman Hārdikya with Duryodhana.[28] Balarāma Vāsudeva washes his hands of the entire conflict, wishing that Kṛṣṇa Vāsudeva would do the same.[29] Kṛṣṇa's loyalties are equally divided; but he, always an activist, divides himself up: his "Nārāyaṇas" go with Duryodhana; he himself, though as noncombatant, with the Pāṇḍavas, more precisely with Arjuna.[30] Of course, all manner of symbolism can be, and has been, superimposed on Kṛṣṇa's tilted neutrality, but the fact of it cannot be isolated from the fissiparous tendencies of the Yādavas in the *Mahābhārata*. Chapter 5.19 identifies the troops of Sātyaki as the Sātvatas, while those of Kṛtavarman are Bhojas and Andhakas. But elsewhere these names are used synonymously, and the *Mahābhārata* provides no hard evidence to sort them all out.

Nevertheless, the connection with the Yādavas is significant: it is their hereditary alignment with Cedi which seems to have brought Dhṛṣṭaketu of Cedi into Yudhiṣṭhira's camp; and the alignment of Cedi with Magadha brings Sahadeva-Jayatsena along. Both their fathers have been killed in Yudhiṣṭhira's rise to power: Sahadeva's father Jarāsaṃdha was eliminated to open up the position of *samrāj*,[31] Dhṛṣṭaketu's father Śiśupāla when he made his challenge at the Consecration;[32] both killings were the handiwork of Kṛṣṇa. Filial piety is perhaps too much to expect in ancient ruling houses, but a certain reluctance to choose Yudhiṣṭhira over Duryodhana would not have been surprising, if other forces were not at work. I think such forces are to be found in a traditional coalition that now has been restored after the Jarāṣaṃdha-Śiśupāla hegemony, which was broken

23. 5.126.36 ff.
24. 2.13.25; 44; in 2.42.6 Kṛṣṇa accuses Śiśupāla, his cousin, of razing Dvārakā.
25. 2.42.
26. *Mahābhārata*, Book 16.
27. 4.67; 5.3.
28. 5.7.29.
29. 5.7.21 ff.
30. 5.7.15 ff.
31. 2.13.
32. 2.37 ff.

by Kṛṣṇa in Yudhiṣṭhira's behalf. It is a coalition that stretches from Mathurā in the north to Magadha in the east, forming a practically continuous front on the right bank of the river Yamunā and, past the confluence of the two rivers, of the Ganges. Somewhere in this bond fits Uśīnara, whose king Śaibya Auśīnari[33] also joins Yudhiṣṭhira with a grand army. If Yudhiṣṭhira were restored to Indraprastha, we would have one grand defense line reaching from present-day Delhi to Patna on the right bank of the Ganges.

This line is backed by the Matsyas and Karūṣas southwest of Mathurā, and is now also supported by the Southern Pāñcālas across the Yamunā, but no longer across the Ganges. Thus we have a coalition of no less than six peoples whose domains, or at least spheres of influence, are contiguous: Sātvata-Vṛṣṇis, Matsyas, Uśīnaras, Cedi, Pāñcālas, and Magadha.

Distinctly outside this coalition of contiguous peoples is the Pāṇḍya, who is hard to place geographically, but in any case well to the south of the others. It is hard to make out whether he can be in any way connected with the well-known Pāṇḍya kingdom in the extreme south of the subcontinent.[34]

One thing is clear: there is no significant alliance with peoples on the left bank of the Ganges, until after its confluence with the Yamunā. It is also apparent that the coalition is a defensive one, facing not south or east, but north and west—toward the Kurus and their allies.

Kaurava influence stretches quite far into the northwest. There is a geographical grouping in this quarter similar to the coalition just described: Gāndhāra, northwest of the Panjāb; Kāmboja in the Panjāb; Sindhu-Suvīra down the river Indus; Śālva, Madra, and Trigarta between the Panjāb and the river Yamunā; and, straddling the Ganges, Kuruksetra itself; this is a continuous region that also happened to be the path of early Aryan settlement in India. Much farther east is Prāgjyotiṣa (Assam), whence Bhagadatta comes with his mountain tribes. Completely outside this picture is the region from which no less than three grand armies arrive, comprising Avanti and Mahiṣmatī, just north of the Vindhya range, and southwest of Yudhiṣṭhira's Yamunā River coalition.

This seems to be the general distribution of the two coalitions: one from the northwest pointing southeast as far as the left bank of the Ganges; and one stretching from farther south to the east lining the right bank of the Yamunā, with some assorted allies much farther

33. 4.67.16, where also the king of the Kāśis is mentioned as bringing an army; neither is mentioned in another listing in 5.19.

34. The Pāṇḍyas are first mentioned in an inscription of Aśoka.

south. The eastern edges are fuzzy: the Kāśis, from around Vārāṇasī, join Yudhiṣṭhira[35]—an old family connection since Vicitravīrya's wives were from Kāśi.[36] Their neighbors the Kosalas are mentioned now on Duryodhana's side,[37] then on Yudhiṣṭhira's.[38] There are two parties of Kekayas: the five Kekaya brothers, who apparently lost their land and are with Yudhiṣṭhira, and Kekaya troops with Duryodhana. Nevertheless the geographical cores of the two coalitions remain well-defined. And to my mind at least, if we consider the Kauravas the aggressors with their greater numbers, they suggest a continuing military push from the northwest to the southeast against a defense line that stretches down the rivers Yamunā and Ganges, the clash between the two forces occurring at the disputed bridgehead of Indraprastha on the right bank of the Yamunā.

The Number Eighteen

There is a peculiar fascination with the number eighteen in the *Mahābhārata* which in all likelihood is to be explained from within the context of the epic itself. Ancient Indian philosophers were fond of symbolic numbers: there are many inventories that come in threes and fives,[39] a few in fours,[40] twelves,[41] and sixteens,[42] and one in seventeen.[43] Eighteen, however, seems to be the exclusive property of the *Mahābhārata*. There are eighteen books, eighteen armies, eighteen days of battle, eighteen chapters of the *Bhagavadgītā*, and eventually, following the epic, eighteen Purāṇas.

This prevalence of eighteens can hardly be coincidental, and it is hard to escape the inference that there must have been a primordial, epically significant set of eighteen that was the starting point of the proliferation of other eighteens. Which one?

I do not think that the Eighteen Major Books were the starting point, for this division is fairly arbitrary compared with the much more precisely topical division in the hundred Minor Books, and it is unbalanced within itself: there is a Book of a thousand pages, and one of twenty. Nevertheless, an early division of the epic materials into eighteen broad topics—Beginning, Assembly Hall, Forest, etc.—

35. 4.67.16.
36. 1.96.
37. 6.47.15; 8.17.3; 37.2.
38. E.g., 7.22.47.
39. These are the numbers that occur most frequently in the *Upaniṣads*.
40. *Taittirīya Upanisad* 1.5; also: *varṇas*, *āśramas*, Vedas.
41. Twelves usually indicate year symbolism; also: *ādityas*.
42. There are sixteen priests at the Soma sacrifice.
43. Prajāpati, the God of the Vājapeya sacrifice, is seventeenfold.

is likely to have inspired the division of the *Bhagavadgītā*—or the further content appended to it (Rāmānuja rightly calls the last six chapters residual)[44]—into eighteen chapters. And the Eighteen Books surely occasioned the division of the Purāṇic material into Eighteen Grand Purāṇas (*mahāpurāṇāni*), a division at least as old as Al-Bīrūnī's recording of it. The listing is arbitrary, for there are many more Purāṇas, but eighteen had become an official epic-purāṇic number.

Rather, I think, the eighteens derive from a legendary, truly epic event that put the new number eighteen forever in the catalogue of numbers. The list offers a choice between the Eighteen-Day Battle and the War of the Eighteen Armies. In the annals of military history it is quite common to name wars, battles, and campaigns after the units of time they lasted (Thirty-Year War, Six-Day War, etc.), but the Eighteen-Day Battle does not seem to figure so much in the *Mahābhārata*.[45] More so do the Eighteen Armies; and my guess is that one dramatic event involving them, the massing of the eighteen armies for a war that spelt the end of an eon and gave pause to a civilization, proliferated all the other eighteens.

Perhaps the number eighteen, once firmly established, spawned other numbers in a tradition that had a staunchly decimal arithmetic. Having become a number for an important and complete event, a "round number," this eighteen, understood as 10 + 8, may well have inspired the completing of already round numbers with eight. Thus we have the round 108, as in the 108 *Upaniṣads*, the round 1008, as in the 1008 names of Viṣṇu. The custom is still alive in India today, where for instance gifts for religious purposes are oftentimes made with an 8 added to the 100, 1000, etc. It has spread as far as Japan where Buddhist shrines still ring in the New Year with 108 peals of the temple bell.

On Myth and Epic—1. Levels of Criticism

Over the last decades a remarkable number of studies have appeared dealing with the mythological content of the *Mahābhārata*. These studies do not necessarily address themselves to the readily identifiable myths that are scattered throughout the text, but to the epic itself as one titanic myth on its own; and they attempt once more to put holistic interpretations on the Epic. The historical dimension of the text, which after all is an event in history, is in the process forgotten, or rather, consciously cast aside. Madeleine Biardeau, for example, insists on the necessity of resisting any

44. Rāmānuja, *Gītābhāṣya*, on *Bhagavadgītā*, ch. 13.
45. So far the only mention is in 1.2.26.

"hypothèses d'ordre historique."[46] Georges Dumézil contrasts the comparativist like himself with "les spécialistes . . . plus disposés à faire crédit aux textes, à voir dans les scènes les plus fabuleuses des 'événements' réels simplement enjolivés."[47] The difficulty is that without events there is no epic left.

I have so far deliberately abstained from making general statements on the "origin and development" of the epic, apart from a few preliminary remarks at the outset of this work. I have abstained for two reasons: first, I have too often seen methodology harden into ideology and the scholar wind up talking to himself and his disciples about method and less and less about the materials; second, I wanted to let the text happen to me without encumbering myself with the theories of others before I myself had a sufficient grasp on it. Now that close to half of the text lies tractable before me and the reader, I have grown more confident of both my right to speak and my reader's to answer.

Nevertheless, it must have become clear that the verities of time and place are inescapable for me. Many of the peoples and older individuals of the text occur in the earlier Vedic literature without any mythological context, and I think of them as human. I find a palace-building Asura more plausible as a human than as a demon; a dicing match mandatory to a Vedic ritual more interesting as a narrative device than as a cosmic symbol; *The Book of Virāṭa* far more fetching as a year-long Holi festival than either as a silly interpolation[48] or as a mine of information in trifunctional characteristics;[49] the line-up of the Pāṇḍava and Kaurava allies much more enlightening as a geographical distribution of coalitions than as a symbolic polarity of North and South.[50]

This attitude can be summed up as a willingness to listen to what the text has to say in so many words before groping for what it is *not* saying in so many words. Sometimes, I confess, I come away from reading some of the holistic interpretations, from Dahlmann and Holtzmann onward, with a disconcerting uncertainty about whether we are talking of the same text. Perhaps I do not see the forest for the trees, but might I not rather be walking among the trees than overlooking a forest?

Personally I do not see any conflict in the end between the

46. Madeleine Biardeau, "Conférence de Madeleine Biardeau," *Annuaire* 7 [19]: 170. (Ecole pratique des hautes études, Ve section: Sciences religieuses.)

47. Georges Dumézil, *Mythe et épopée*, vol. 2 (Paris, 1971), p. 143.

48. So E. Washburn Hopkins in *The Great Epic of India*: cf. above, Introduction to *The Book of Virāṭa*, p. 18–21.

49. So Stig Wikander, "Nakula et Sahadeva," *Orientalia Suecana* 76 (1957); Dumézil, *Mythe et épopée* 1: 70 ff.

50. F. D. K. Bosch, *De Gouden Kiem* (Amsterdam, 1948), pp. 88 ff.

"comparativist" or "generalist," and the "specialist." Philology, that bane of the broader viewers, has long ago resolved this "conflict" by making a clear distinction between higher and lower textual criticism. Lower criticism establishes the text on the basis of the best possible evidence and explains it; higher criticism then may address itself to further questions of the influences that have worked on the text as received. While there is a distinction, there is also a continuity. But lower criticism must of necessity take precedence over higher criticism, for without the former the latter has no basis. Clearly one cannot compare one text with another text, or a set of them, before knowing what the texts are actually saying; if one does one may well lie, however well-intentionedly. Only when one has the lower truth of a text can a possible transcending truth be hoped for.

There is, to be sure, a fascinating, though resistible, seductiveness in assuming that the higher precedes the lower, that the lower is but an epiphenomenon of the higher, that the apparently real is but an island of consciousness floating upon the vast ocean of the unexpressed and unmanifest, that "Alles Vergängliche ist nur ein Gleichniss"—of something or other. It is also a peculiarly Indian fascination; the previous sentence can be rendered into Sanskrit: not only would it lose nothing in translation, it would gain from all the resonances of *māyā* in late Purāṇic literature. No doubt, Hindu symbolification of the epic started quite early and has become an overlying part of the text itself. This process went on in the *Purāṇas*, and this specious "continuity" between "epic" and *Purāṇas* can easily lead one to lay a Purāṇa–Hindū interpretation upon the *Bhārata*, if one resists all "hypothèses d'ordre historique."

I am the last to suggest that the analysis of and distinction between the old and the new is at any time easy or at all times possible; but I think it is necessary. It seems to me that those who from the outset decline to accept the historical dimension of the *Mahābhārata* impoverish their text. To this they will protest that it is, on the contrary, the historical critics who impoverish the received text. This issue is important.

The argument is that since the *Mahābhārata* is a myth, any historical analysis is specious, for myths are unhistorical. In pursuing an analytic course, Louis Dumont avers, "on 'explique' une difficulté en la décomposant au long d'une dimension temporelle imaginaire, en la transformant gratuitement en événement. Nous verrons ainsi une contradiction devenir un conflit."[51] Rather, asserts Biardeau, we should reject the position that the epic, or Hinduism itself, is an amalgam (*accrétion*), "la rencontre fortuite d'éléments, ainsi isolés

51. Louis Dumont, *La civilisation indienne et nous* (Paris, 1964), p. 33.

et reduits à leur signification originelle supposée."[52] It is of no real importance where the elements came from, for they are meaningful only "dans les structures idéologiques d'ensemble,"[53] for she maintains with Pouillon that symbols "n'ont pas une signification intrinsèque et invariable. Leur signification est d'abord de position."[54]

There is in this position a massive incidence of *petitio principii*. First, one may reply to Dumont, no one "explains" a problem by analyzing its history; at best one gives a historic perspective on it. Nor is the temporal dimension "imaginary": time is not something one invents. Nor by the same token is the treatment of a problem "gratuitously transformed into an event," if the problem is about an event. Nor, *pace* Biardeau, does an amalgam have to be a "fortuitous encounter," or elements "isolated," instead of singled out, and "reduced to their supposed original significance," instead of being placed in a reasonably traceable history of their varying significance in different places. And why should it be of no real importance where the elements came from? Their provenance could illumine why *they* were chosen, not others. Why, one may ask Pouillon, should they be meaningful only in "structures" instead of in their own right; why should these structures be "ideological"; and why should these elements be meaningful only in ideological structures of a "whole"? What whole?

The overriding question that is begged is, of course: Why treat the *Mahābhārata* as a myth at all? It is a circular argument: This epic is not, in Ezra Pound's phrase, a "poem containing history," but a "myth," which in this context apparently means "a poem containing symbols." Now symbols, according to Pouillon, have no unvarying meaning peculiar to them—their meaning is positional, not historical. Therefore a historical inquiry is pointless, since a history of something meaningless bestows no meaning on it. Therefore, since historical analysis is by definition meaningless, forget about all history. In fact, forget about the *Mahābhārata* as epic and as literature; treat it as a timeless verbified and versified Hinduism.

Fine, if one wants to do that, and if it can be done. So far it has not been done, and I honestly wonder why anyone would try. I doubt that even anyone embracing this faith would deny that at least half a millennium has gone into the making of the *Mahābhārata*. Did time stand still? Are we to attribute to these five centuries that saw the flowering of Buddhism and Jainism, the decline and rise of Brahmanism, the restructuring of society, the Dharma of Aśoka and

52. "Brahmanes et potiers," *Annuaire* 79 (1971–72): 55.
53. Ibid., p. 54.
54. J. Pouillon, "L'Analyse des mythes," *L'Homme* 6, 1 (1966), pp. 100–105, n. 1.

the Horse Sacrifice of Puṣyamitra, and the kingdom of the Greeks, a changeless immobility?

It is only on the basis of such an immense supposition that Biardeau can assume that myths found in the *Mahābhārata* have undergone no development at all, that all versions of them are simultaneous and must be interpreted in concert.[55] She has illustrated this method with particular reference to the myth of Rāma and Kārtavīrya, and we may take her lead there to explore whether her method of homogenization does in fact yield more meaning than the historical method.

The *Mahābhārata* frequently refers to the myth of a certain Rāma, the son of Jamadagni, who killed a King Arjuna Kārtavīrya, and eventually exterminated the *kṣatriyas*. This myth is enshrined in later Vaiṣṇavism, as that of an *avatāra* of the God Viṣṇu, who descended to earth in order to rid it of the *kṣatriyas* who had become oppressors —the myth of Paraśu-Rāma.

The *Mahābhārata* tells the story of Rāma and Kārtavīrya twice, once in 2, chapters 115–17, and once in 12, chapter 49. The first account, which we shall call Version A, reads as follows. King Kārtavīrya raids the hermitage of Rāma's brahmin father Jamadagni and steals the calf of his sacrificial cow. Rāma in retaliation cuts off the one thousand arms of Kārtavīrya. Thereupon Kārtavīrya's sons kill Jamadagni, and in revenge Rāma destroys all *kṣatriyas*.

The second account, Version B, has this. King Kārtavīrya is a pious emperor (*samrāj*). At the demand of the Fire God Kārtavīrya surrenders to him all the dwellings of the humans, and, in the course of the ensuing conflagration, the hermitage of a certain seer called Āpava is burned. Āpava lays a curse on Kārtavīrya to the effect that he will lose his thousand arms. Kārtavīrya's sons then steal the calf of Jamadagni's sacrificial cow. Rāma cuts off Kārtavīrya's arms, and the latter's sons shoot off Jamadagni's head. Thereupon Rāma destroys all *kṣatriyas*.

It is clear enough that both versions are parallel, but the variations are conspicuous. In Version A Kārtavīrya is a villain, in Version B he is a pious king, who becomes the victim of his generosity toward the Fire God. What are we to do with this one variation, if we hold both versions to be equivalent? To Biardeau the notion that the two versions are equivalent is "not incongruous, provided we stop looking for some historical value in the MhBh. and take it as primarily didactic in purpose."[56] What then is the moral of this didactic

55. This is the burden of her argument in "The Story of Kārtavīrya without Reconstruction," *Purana* 12 (1970): 2.
56. Ibid., p. 299.

excursion? That it is against the just order of things if *kṣatriyas* are either too generous or too niggardly with brahmins? This amounts to the lesson that excess offends the moral order.

It would seem to me that the historical method yields richer fruit. It starts, not from a belief that both versions are equivalent, but from the admission that while they treat the same story, the two versions are different. It is not easy to see how either one version can be derived from the other, but on the face of it the probabilities are that the villainy of Kārtavīrya is more central to the story than his generosity, if only to account for the fateful consequences of his actions. Both versions appear to lack something essential: the motivation of Kārtavīrya, whether he is presented as virtuous or villainous.

It is good method if we find two versions of a story that are difficult to reconcile in a satisfactory fashion to look for more evidence elsewhere. Are there other stories in which offspring of a Kṛtavīrya (for that is what *Kārtavīrya* means) are in bloody conflict with brahmins? There is one that I have found: the story of Aurva, in *Mahābhārata* 1.169, which we may call Version Y. In this account there is a King Kṛtavīrya, who was the patron of brahmins of the Bhṛgu clan whom he enriched with ample gifts. At Kṛtavīrya's death, his heirs—surely to be considered Kārtavīryas[57]—find themselves impoverished and seek their patrimonial wealth back from the Bhṛgus. Some of the brahmins share their riches, but most hide it away. Then a (Kārtavīrya) *kṣatriya* finds a cache of treasure, and in anger all Kṛtavīrya's heirs ransack the brahmins' hermitages and kill all the Bhṛgus "down to the children in the womb." One embryo, who was carried in his mother's thigh, survives. Upon his birth this child, Aurva, "willed the downfall of the entire world."[58] His ancestors appear and warn him off.[59] Thereupon Aurva deposits the fire of his wrath in the ocean.[60]

Here we have a story structurally the same as Versions A and B. A too generous King Kṛtavīrya who overextends his gifts to brahmins; his Kārtavīrya heirs who villainously rob the brahmins, ransack their hermitages, and kill them all; total extermination threatened by a son, which is precariously averted. Version Y provides a motivation for Kārtavīrya villainy: Kṛtavīrya's heirs tried unsuccessfully to reclaim their patrimony. Kṛtavīrya's generosity in Version Y is magnified in Version B in his gift of all human dwellings to the Fire God, the patron of all brahmins, and even further (in an addition that is found in the

57. Kārtavīrya is a patronymic of Kṛtavīrya.
58. 1.170.9.
59. 1.170.14.
60. 1.170.21.

Vulgate text of Version B, and dropped from the critical edition) in his gift of the earth to the brahmins.[61]

A comparison with Version Y clears up puzzling features of Versions A and B. We understand why Kārtavīrya has a thousand arms:[62] he represents the numerous heirs of Kṛtavīrya. We see why Kārtavīrya should paradoxically be a most generous patron of brahmins and yet perish: King Kṛtavīrya of Y and Kārtavīrya of B have coalesced. We realize why Rāma's slaughter should be so complete: in Y it was all Kārtavīryas against all Bhṛgus, and then, in Y, A, and B, the one son against all Kārtavīryas, indeed the "entire world."

Compared with Version Y, A and B have modifications: the original King Kṛtavīrya is lost and with him Kārtavīrya's motivation. The "downfall of the entire world" is now the extermination of all *kṣatriyas*. While the "downfall" is prevented, this extermination proceeds, though the feature of the "warning of the ancestors" persists. Kārtavīrya of A and B has become a thousand-armed individual paralleling the single brahmin combatant. There is a new generation of "sons" of Kārtavīrya to compensate for the loss of King Kṛtavīrya, which left only Kārtavīrya in the field. The whole massacred clan of Bhṛgu has become one killed Bhṛgu, namely Jamadagni.

There is one more specific crime, which is interesting in that it shows how a single narrative element can grow by association. The ransacking of brahmin hermitages, which probably always formed part of the story of assaults against brahmins, is dramatized by the stealing of the calf of a sacrificial cow. This cow is Jamadagni's in both A and B. Version B adds the further detail that the hermitage of a certain Āpava is burned. This Āpava is rather anomalous here. The name is that of the seer Vasiṣṭha, a seer not very likely to turn

61. The cr. ed. and the Vulgate (my references, like Biardeau's, are to the Citraśālā Press edition) diverge on this point. Cr. ed. 12.49.30 reads: "At this time Kṛtavīrya's son Arjuna, a Haihaya *kṣatriya*, burned all of earth in battle with the might of his arms and supreme dharma," while the Vulgate (12.49.35 f.) reads: "At this time Kṛtavīrya's son Arjuna, king of the Haihayas, having a thousand arms by the grace of Dattātreya, a powerful *cakravartin*, gave away to the brahmins at a Horse Sacrifice all of earth, having conquered it with the might of his arms, being a knower of the supreme *dharma*." Biardeau prefers "gave away" (*dadau*) of the Vulgate to cr. ed. "burned" (*dadāha*, marked doubtful). One may concede this (though it leaves cr. ed. *ajau* "in battle" dangling), but this change does not authenticate Vulgate vs. 36, in which Arjuna gives earth to the brahmins, for the sequel shows that he gave earth over to the Fire God. In my view the Vulgate version, saddled with a reading *dadau sarvāṃ pṛthivīm*, tried to make sense of it by anticipating Rāma's gift of the earth to Kaśyapa (Vulgate 12.49.68).

62. Standing for: "a mighty army of sons of Kṛtavīrya." This unique feature had of course later to be "explained:" so the Vulgate versions suddenly invoke as donor a sage Dattātreya who is, outside the context of Kārtavīrya's thousand arms, unknown to the *MBh*.

up in a context with Jamadagni, for the latter sage is a grandson of Viśvāmitra, who was Vasiṣṭha's bitter enemy. Āpava appears to be attracted to the story by the stealing of the sacrificial cow's calf: for Vasiṣṭha, again under the name Āpava,[63] had one legendary possession, his sacrificial milch cow coveted at different times by the Vasu Gods,[64] and by Viśvāmitra.[65] It is as though Āpava should make a courtesy appearance where a sacrificial cow is coveted and its calf abducted.[66]

The most important difference between Version Y and Versions A and B is, of course, that the latter tell Aurva's story about Rāma. The two have much in common: both are Bhṛgus, both are survivors of brahmin slaughter by Kārtavīryas, both vow wholesale destruction, both are warned by their ancestors. Henceforth the story will remain Rāma's, in so exclusive and dramatic a fashion, involving the eradication of *kṣatriyas* twenty-one times over, that it seems unlikely that if it had always been Rāma's story a soon-forgotten Aurva could have usurped it.

Am I, in analyzing and contrasting the three *Mahābhārata* versions of Kārtavīrya, "explaining away," in Dumont's sense, the problem of their variation "along an imaginary temporal dimension" and "transforming" the accounts "gratuitously into an event," so that "contradiction becomes conflict"? Apart from the fact that I am willing to entertain the notion that the account was about an event (real or imagined: excessive generosity of a king toward brahmins might well have incited resentments in his heirs on occasion, or could easily be imagined to have done so), I am not explaining anything away. On the contrary, I am adducing additional evidence about the myth, but evidence that shows that something has happened between Versions Y and B, and that something is *change*, all manner of interesting change. If we were to treat all variation of elements as simultaneous and the elements themselves as being without "une signification intrinsèque et invariable," and on top of that deny any narrative virtue to the myth but accept solely a "didactic purpose"

63. It is noteworthy that Āpava as a name of Vasiṣṭha occurs *only* in these two contexts of the *MBh.* and is, in spite of Vasiṣṭha's recurrence, otherwise unknown. In both contexts Āpava's cow is threatened (indirectly in 12.49). In 1.93 the cow is coveted by the Vasus, and its abduction leads to the curse of the Vasus and eventually to Bhīṣma's birth.

64. 1.93.

65. 1.165: here there is no curse, but another manifestation of power by the brahmin Vasiṣṭha, which causes Viśvāmitra to resolve to become a brahmin himself.

66. My construction is that the theft of the calf of Jamadagni's cow (Version A) was homologized to the theft of Āpava's cow, and Jamadagni thus temporarily replaced by Āpava in Version B. B needed a curse put on the otherwise pious Kārtavīrya to account for his downfall. Version A did not need a curse, for Kārtavīrya still was as wicked as the Kārtavīryas of Version Y.

for it, we impoverish our materials.[67] One may go farther and submit that treating the "ensemble" of the stories of Kārtavīrya as a "myth," and by ultimate extension the entire *Mahābhārata* as a "myth" whose purpose it merely is to "express certain abstract ideas through stories," is itself a myth-making that impoverishes.

And even if the *Mahābhārata*'s substance were one myth, its form is a text like any other text, and thus amenable to the dictates of lower textual criticism. We grant with total confidence that, while the *Mahābhārata* was being recorded in writing, any number of variants in its stories may have existed in the recitations of professional singers, but we do not know those variants. What we have is what we know. If by good luck we have several variants recorded, as in the case of Kārtavīrya, we can draw inferences from them, but that is higher criticism, over which lower criticism takes precedence, even when it declines accepting Rāma as a *proto-avatāra* of Viṣṇu.[68]

I have gone into such detail about the accounts of Kārtavīrya not to question one interpretation of a single group of stories, which cover perhaps 0.01 percent of the text, by a scholar whom I greatly respect, but to insist on the boundaries of criticism. For Biardeau uses (Vulgate) Version A to dispute the need for removing from the critical edition *any* text portions that an older text transmission ignores, e.g., Rāma as a benevolent Viṣṇu instead of a furious avenger.[69] In arguing this, she mixes two levels of criticism, to the detriment of both.

The objection frequently raised against the critical edition is that the principles and practices of textual criticism were developed for written texts, first of all the European Classics, and that they cannot apply with the same force and dependable results to a text like the *Mahābhārata*, which was oral literature and continues to be a living presence in Hinduism. There is a good deal of cogency to this objection, but it is not as compelling as some seem to think.

67. In reference to her assertion that the *MBh.* is "primarily didactic in purpose" (p. 299) Biardeau notes: "This in itself is open to question, but we shall not touch on the problem here, because any Indian mind is ready to accept that the MhBh. wants to express certain abstract ideas through stories. That is what I believe basically." The question remains open.

68. In (Vulgate) Version A, in vss. 3.115.11 ff., which are dropped from the cr. ed., Kārtavīrya threatens the Gods, even Indra, who is dallying with Śacī; whereupon the Gods, in Purāṇic manner, resort to Viṣṇu, who with Indra "plots for the destruction of Kārtavīrya" (ibid., 17). Even (Vulgate) Version B has nothing of the sort, but Biardeau believes that Āpava's curse parallels Viṣṇu's "decision" (p. 298 f.). Rāma, the actual killer, is nowhere in the *MBh.* explicitly identified with Viṣṇu; in my view the Paraśu-Rāma *avatāra* is a later Purāṇic example of Vaiṣṇava expansionism.

69. "It is indeed a fact that the passage corresponding to the heavenly part of the drama (3.115.9–19) does not occur in all MSS. But is this passage less 'authentic' than the rest and on what grounds? . . . Why not rather consider that this was an 'authentic' part of some versions, or, say, or a particular line of tradition? This idea is not incongruous, provided we stop looking for some historical value in the MhBh. and take it as primarily didactic in purpose" (p. 299).

First of all, be it accepted that once the *Mahābhārata* was recorded it ceased to be oral literature *only*: it began a new life of its own in its codices; it is that life, and nothing else, that textual criticism seeks to explore. It cannot be its task to grope for other oral literature that may have existed at the period of its writing, for we have no texts of it, with the exception of the oral literature embedded in the *Rāmāyaṇa*.[70] True enough, the simultaneous existence of parallel or diverging versions of stories also included in the *Mahābhārata* must have influenced the formation of the text as we now know it. The text itself provides ample evidence for that: the stories of Kārtavīrya above are eloquent testimony.

Second, the rejection of an *Urtext* of the *Mahābhārata*, which is implied in the objection, is accepted by all. Sukthankar himself rejected the existence of an archetypal text in so many words: "The *Mahābhārata* problem is a problem *sui generis*," he writes in his *Prolegomena*. "It is useless to think of reconstructing a fluid text in a literally original shape, on the basis of an archetype and a *stemma codicum*. What is then possible? Our objective can only be to reconstruct *the oldest form of the text which it is possible to reach*, on the basis of the manuscript material available [all italics his]."[71] It is a modest enough ambition, despite the enormous labor it has involved.

It is also a valid ambition. For every scholar who regards Hinduism not as a changless simultaneity of elements significant only "dans les structures idéologiques d'ensemble," but as a civilization that has known change over more than two millennia, is quite properly interested in the history of a text like the *Mahābhārata*, which laid the groundwork for Hinduism. The text of the critical edition takes us back to a text of about the sixth century A.D., fluid no doubt but, considering its size, of remarkable consistency;[72] while at present Sukthankar recognizes something like twelve more or less independent versions spread all over India.[73] The sixth-century text[74] and the ensuing versions permit the study of changing, or reaffirmed, interests, concerns, and emphases over a period of time and expanse of space. Thus the critical edition can be a valuable tool of scholars like

70. Where, of course, we have the same issue: oral tales have become manuscripts.

71. Sukthankar, "Prolegomena," *The Mahābhārata: Ādiparvan*, fascicle 7 (Poona, B.O.R.I., 1933), p. lxxxvi.

72. I can only point to the text of the cr. ed. that I have translated: there are not all that many inconsistencies left; they have not been weeded out, they have evaporated.

73. Sukthankar, p. lxxvii.

74. This is admittedly an arbitrary date, for as always it is *ante quem*. Much of the text contains the *ipsissima verba* of the recorders, whose dates are unknown, and part of it contains transmissional changes after this recording, but I think the sixth-century is a reasonable cut-off date, for considering the methods used in the critical edition, it is unlikely that additions from after this "date" survive in it.

Biardeau interested in Purāṇic Hinduism, and the rejection of it is detrimental to higher criticism of the Purāṇic portions of the *Mahābhārata* and of the *Purāṇas* alike.

Not all scholars are interested in Purāṇic Hinduism. Some are interested in the text as one of the few world epics, others in the restructuring of Vedic society, still others in population movements, the early history of Kṛṣṇaism, the sources of Śaivism, the beginnings of Indian philosophy, etc. For them the sixth-century text as the earliest one recoverable is an invaluable source of information, and its homogenization with later Purāṇic text is completely detrimental to, if not destructive of, what little evidence is left.

For what is the alternative? Hardly the whimsical monstrosity that Sylvain Lévi suggested while reviewing the first fascicles of the critical edition:[75] don't provide an edited text, simply reprint the Vulgate with all the variants collected at the bottom of the page, and let every reader compose his own text. This is a brief for guideless eclecticism, which would allow one to read into an old story, with its own relevance for its time, an interpretation drawn from later reworkings with their own relevance for their times; thus epigonic apocrypha could become the sources of their source.

When I here use the word *apocrypha*, I mean only "texts not included in the critical text constituted on the basis of the best available manuscript evidence," not in the sense of texts that are "inauthentic," whatever meaning that adjective could have when applied to the "*Mahābhārata* through the ages." While written stories can be dated, their date is always *ante quem*, and implies no judgment as to the "original date" of the story as story. This is too obvious to need any argument. What needs argument, and more than it has received, is why the critical edition could be vitiated by excluding stories that might in their substance be as old as, if not older than, the text as presented. This accusation is plainly illogical: inclusion and exclusion are dictated by evidence judiciously calibrated and weighed. While no doubt a great deal of ancient lore has been preserved in the *Mahābhārata*, this was by no means the *only* line of transmission. Exclusion of a story from the text merely means that before A.D. 600 the *Mahābhārata* was not the transmitter of that story. It does not make it disappear in a vanishing act; there will always be a "*Mahābhārata* through the ages."

It will not, however, do to "authenticate" as simultaneous to the *Mahābhārata* of A.D. 600 any and all stories that got attached to the text, however lately recorded. For example, I doubt that any scholar would hold that the charming tale of Vyāsa and Gaṇeśa is authentic

75. *Journal asiatique* 215 (1929): 345 ff.; 225 (1934): 281 ff.

even in a puranizing sense.[76] It relates how Vyāsa dictated to the elephant-headed God, patron of scribes, the text of the *Mahābhārata* so it would be written. To keep Gaṇeśa from nodding off during this lengthy and at times boring task, Vyāsa every now and then threw in an unusual construction or phrase, which made him sit up and take notice—and no doubt snicker at times. One hates to see the story go, until reminded that it is still there: it has *not* been eliminated from the history of Indian civilization. On the contrary, it has found its rightful place as the latter-day jest on the *Mahābhārata* which it is.

Nor will many scholars protest that certain cultist episodes are not yet there: Yudhiṣṭhira's prayer to Durgā[77] at the beginning of the *Virāṭaparvan*, for instance. This is now generally accepted as a later testimony to a Northern devotion. Tempers may begin to rise when it is found that, when Draupadī is being disrobed by Duḥśāsana, her sari is not miraculously replaced by Kṛṣṇa at her appeal,[78] but silently by her own modesty.[79] But beyond this point there is great confusion, worse confounded by stubborn refusals to accept that, indeed, some hallowed stories may well be meaningful derivatives from, and therefore later than, stories that are chronologically more securely embedded in the text.

If we wish to find a way of lending some order to the confusion, we had better look at the individual stories themselves, and see if we can relate their variants or cognates historically, substantially, or symbolically, as the cases dictate. For the *Mahābhārata* as a whole there are precious few guidelines: just those from its past, its present, and its future.

I wish to submit that the most satisfactory explanation of the *Mahābhārata* and the elements thereof is from within the text itself, its *present*. That it is a forbiddingly long present, five historically fateful centuries, must not deter us; nor should its extension into a still lengthier past or an indefinite future seduce us too soon. A present protracted so long will be fluid:[80] we must accept that stories and incidents in the *Mahābhārata* have sequels in the text itself. We must also expect that the text is not oblivious of its times, and that actual history may brush it.

The guidelines that its future may provide are in this case more easily dealt with than those of its past. The history of Indian writing provides us with a general picture of the *Mahābhārata*'s future: *The Book of the Contents* already puts it concisely before us:

76. *MBh.* (Vulgate) 1.1 (79).
77. *MBh.* (Vulgate) 4.6.1 ff.
78. *MBh.* (Vulgate) 2.67 f.
79. Cr. ed. 2.61.40 ff.
80. That is, the text was not necessarily fixed once and for all in the form in which it was first recorded.

"(99) *The Appendix of the Genealogy of Hari* [Harivaṃśa], and (100) the great, wondrous *Book of the Future* [Bhaviṣyapurāṇa],[81] among the Appendices" (1.2.69). The compiler anticipated, because he *knew*, the Purāṇic literature that took over after the *Mahābhārata*. What it took over from is from what it had become: an epic transformed into a work of religious and didactic purpose. The war is over in Book 11, the new Eon has set in, and the *Purāṇas* are the executor of a legacy which Pāṇini knew only as *war*. Henceforth the only war the *Purāṇas* acknowledge as still raging is between individual Gods and individual Demons, while the *Bhārata* war only bequeathes a number of still-to-be-resolved residual questions.[82] The epic is dead. There is really a new age in brahmin-oriented Indian civilization: the age of Hinduism. And like every new age it likes to interpret its past in the image of its present. Therefore the *Purāṇas* are partially irrelevant to the *Mahābhārata*. To make them wholly irrelevant is to deny the conclusion of the *Mahābhārata*; to make them wholly relevant is to kill the core of it.

The *Mahābhārata*'s past is even more complex a guide. By rough archaeological evidence the setting of most of the epic of the *Mahābhārata* is later than the founding of most of the important cities (ca. 1000 B.C.) but earlier than Magadhan dominance (ca. 300 B.C.). This is well within the Vedic period, but the surviving composition is by language and style not for the most part datable to much before 300 B.C. But by the principle that the past is rather more relevant to a present than its future, we are guided by the assumption that a good deal of ancient material will have to be taken into account.

On Myth and Epic – 2. The Mahābhārata's Present: King Porus

Is there any reflection of real South Asian history in the *Mahābhārata*? Is the epic in Pound's minimal definition a "poem containing history"? The answer now, from historians and structuralists alike, is a resounding *no*. There is, it has been pointed out often enough, no evidence to speak of that this Eighteen-Day Battle of the Eighteen Armies ever took place. The closest we can get to the individual personages of the *Mahābhārata* in literature outside it is to immediate precursors and immediate successors of that warring generation – a fact curious enough in itself, but unenlightening. There is recorded a Dhṛtarāṣṭra, son of Vicitravīrya, in *Kaṭhaka Saṃhitā* 10.6 and

81. While a *Bhaviṣyat-Purāṇa* is extant, there is nothing to show that it has any peculiar relation to the *MBh*. It is tempting to interpret *bhaviṣyapurāṇam* as a collective: "the *Purāṇas* of the future."

82. E.g., *Mārkaṇḍeya P.* 1.1 ff.

Śatapatha Brāhmaṇa 13.5.4.22, but if the sparse references deserve more credence (or more credulity) than those of the *Mahābhārata* (so Macdonell-Keith), he was not even a Bhārata. And there is recorded a Parikṣit, who at least was a Kuru (*Atharvaveda* 20.127.7–10), and in the epic is the son of Arjuna's son Abhimanyu, and the father of the Janamejaya to whom the *Mahābhārata* is recited. But even Parikṣit vanishes. Yājñavalkya is asked (*BĀUP* 3.31): "Where, O where have the Pārikṣitas gone?" and there is no real answer. However one may distrust any argument *e silentio*, this silence is deafening.

Obviously, the individual heroes and their warring are only kaleidoscopically illuminating of a dimly remembered past. Only the largest-scale events have some outline: notably, an epoch-making, disastrous war between a coalition of peoples pushing from the northwest to the southeast, meeting a rival coalition holding the right bank of the river Yamunā.

Nothing, then, but the dimmest reflection of little light upon the oldest past. No history; perhaps a glimmering of legend in King Śaṃtanu's double misalliance with the rivers Ganges and Yamunā; no "national myth" at all. And this is as much as anyone would be able to say about the period of the setting of the epic, the middle of the last millennium B.C., from the texts we have quoted.

Is there even *anything* historical to events or persons contemporary to the composition of the text, say after 400 B.C.? Not too much: Greeks are known, Rome is mentioned, Magadha is known as a power, an Ahura-worshiper is introduced as the builder of Yudhiṣṭhira's hall—it is little indeed. But in the end the *Mahābhārata* never disappoints: it assuredly knows of King Porus.

Writing in 1922 in the first volume of *The Cambridge History of India*, E. R. Bevan exclaimed: "And yet, if the Paurava was not a champion of nationalism, India may well reckon the proud and brave prince among her national heroes. Unhappily India has long since forgotten his name. We know of him only through the Greek books, which call him Porus. It would have seemed a strange fate to him, had any astrologer been able to predict it—to pass quickly out of the memory of his own people, and to be a familiar name for centuries in lands of which he had no conception, away to the West!"[83] Bevan's reference is, of course, to Poros, the Panjābī king who attempted to stop Alexander the Great from crossing the river Jhelum (Sanskrit *Vitastā*, Greek *Hydaspes*), when the conqueror entered India to secure the erstwhile Achaemenid satrapy of northwestern India. Poros lost a son in the battle, and, although he inflicted heavy losses on the Macedonian's army, was in the end defeated, as much by his

83. E. J. Rapson, ed., *The Cambridge History of India*, vol. 1 (Cambridge, 1922), p. 360.

own elephants as by the enemy, and later restored in his dominion when Alexander withdrew from India.[84]

It seems generally accepted that the Hellenized name Poros corresponds to the Sanskrit *Paurava*; only Vincent Smith appears to decline committing himself on this identification.[85] The Sanskrit nominative *Pauravaḥ* surely was locally pronounced in its Prakrit forms of *Poravo* or *Poro-o*. No other attested name fits the Greek transcription better, not even Pūru, which is suggested in *The Oxford History of India*.[86]

There are, nonetheless, some problems with this identification. When Bevan speaks of *the* Paurava king, he seems to take the name as derivative either from a location or a dynasty. No place of the name Paurava is known. On the other hand the Paurava dynasty is very well known; it takes its name from Pūru, son of Yayāti.[87] However, this dynasty, if we may judge by the heroes of the *Mahābhārata* who belonged to it, was located not in the Panjāb but in Kurukṣetra, well to the East, between the rivers Yamunā and Ganges. In the epic itself Paurava is an ancient name that is far less often used than the styles of Bhārata and Kaurava.[88] For the time being it appears to be more prudent simply to take Paurava as the personal name of the king who engaged Alexander.

Do we have to accept Bevan's opinion that India has forgotten him? Or is it possible to discover traces of this king in Sanskrit literature? Poros was not a local potentate but a substantial king who could muster 200 war elephants and 4,000 horses. He had designs on the powerful city of Taxila, which had welcomed Alexander and prompted his expedition against the Indian king; he had an important though reluctant ally in King Abisares of Kashmir. Such a king, had he been on the periphery of India, might well have left vestiges in the memory of the bards of the *Mahābhārata*, who loved to recite long lists of kings. The Paurava we are looking for should be simply named Paurava and located in northern Panjāb.

The extreme Northwest was for the epic authors a region of strange, barbaric, and mythical races. From there hailed, according to *Mahābhārata* 2.47–48, such tributaries to Yudhiṣṭhira's Royal Consecration as: "Other folk with two eyes, three eyes, or one in their

84. I base my references on Hans Schäfer's article "Poros" in Pauly-Wissowa, Realencyclopädie des classischen Altertumswissenschafts, vol. 43, p. 1226 f.

85. Vincent A. Smith, *Early History of India* (Oxford, 1904), p. 53, simply refers to "the king whom the Greeks called Poros." He is likewise noncommittal in A. V. Williams Jackson, ed., *History of India* (London, n.d.), p. 55.

86. Vincent A. Smith, *The Oxford History of India*, 3rd ed., part 1, revised by Sir Mortimer Wheeler and A. L. Basham (Oxford, 1958), p. 87.

87. *MBh*. 1.79–80.

88. S. Sörensen, *An Index to the Names in the Mahābhārata* (repr.; Belhi, Banarsidass, 1963), has just ten listings for the plural *Pauravas*.

foreheads, Bāhukas, Cannibals, one-footed tribes, Chinese, Huns, Scythians, Tukhāras, Kankas, Romaśas, Horned Men . . . Tanganas and Farther Tanganas (who) brought the gold called Pipīlaka, which is granted as a boon by the *pipīlaka* ants," etc. In the last line we have at last an Indian confirmation of the existence of those Indian ants, which, according to Herodotus,[89] dug up gold. Obviously any glimpses of a real Northwest with a Paurava in it are likely to be fleeting.

Nevertheless, it is indeed possible to identify in the *Mahābhārata* a King Paurava who answers this minimal description. In *Mahābhārata* 5.4.14, in a passage in which Drupada exhorts Yudhiṣṭhira to seek the alliance of various kings, he mentions Paurava as a *mahāratha*, and, if we judge by the context, this Paurava is to be found in the vicinity of Bactria (Bāhlīka is mentioned), Śakas, Pahlavas, Daradas, Kambojas, Western Anupakas (ibid. 15), the Panjab (*pancanada nṛpāḥ*), and the Pārvatīyas. These peoples cover Persia, Bactria, the Panjāb, the foothills of Kashmir, and the coastal area of the Indus basin.

This Paurava, furthermore, must be the same one who is defeated by Arjuna on his Conquest of the North (*MBh.* 2.24.13 ff.): *abhyagacchat Pauravaṃ; vijitya cāhave śūrān pārvatīyān . . . dhvajinyā puraṃ Pauravarakṣitaṃ* . . . (14). These Pārvatīyas clearly belong to the hills that lead up to Kashmir, as is indicated by the text (ibid. 15–16): *Pauravaṃ tu vijitya dasyūn parvatavāsinaḥ . . . tataḥ Kāśmīrakān vīrān . . . vyajayat* (16).

Arrian[90] reports that Poros was allied with a certain Abisares, a king of highland tribes in Rajauri and Bimber in Kashmir. The name *Abisarēs* certainly has Abhisāra behind it; the Abhisāras are known as a people bordering on Kashmir.[91] It is, however, probably incorrect to equate Abisares with Abhisāra. Just as Taxilēs is used as the title of Omphis,[92] king of Taxila, Abisares is more precisely the king of the location Abhisāra.

Now, it is at least remarkable that, in the same context of the Digvijaya in which Arjuna successively defeats Paurava and the heroes of Kashmir, the text goes on to read *abhisārīm tato ramyāṃ vijigye* "he thereupon conquered the lovely [city of] Abhisārī" (2.24.17). This places Paurava and Abhisārī in each other's vicinity, and the alliance of Poros and Abisares as recorded by the Greek

89. Herodotus, *History*, 3.102.

90. Arrian, *Indica*, 5.20.6.

91. H. H. Wilson, trans., *The Viṣṇu Purāṇa*, ed. F. Hall (London, 1888), notes *apud VP*. 2.3 (vol. 2, p. 174, n. 4): "Those are the inhabitants of the country bordering on Kashmir, South and West; known to the Greeks as the kingdom of Abisares."

92. This name is usually sanskritized as Ambhi, apparently on the basis of the *gaṇa* on Pāṇini 4.1.96; it has no other attestations.

historians comes as no surprise on the basis of their proximity as recorded by the *Mahābhārata.*

To sum up, the evidence from the second and fifth books of the *Mahābhārata* demonstrates that the composers of the *Mahābhārata* were to a degree familiar with a King Paurava in northeastern Panjāb and familiar with a town Abhisārī close to the location of this Paurava, but clearly independent of him, since it is separately subjugated. I believe we can be confident that we have identified the King Poros who encountered Alexander the Great by the river Jhelum.

Paurava, like the Abhisāras, was allied with Duryodhana.[93] In 5.167.19–20 it is predicted of him that "he shall burn up the Pāñcālas as fire burns up deadwood." It is for this reason, no doubt, that Paurava is given an Asura past in *The Book of the Partial Incarnations* (1.61.28): *Surabhaḥ . . . Pauravo nāma rajarṣiḥ sa babhūva nareṣv iha* "Surabha was born as the royal sage named Paurava here among men." That this must be the same as our Paurava from the Panjāb is clear from the company he keeps, which corresponds closely to his company in 5.4. Where Paurava is mentioned in 1.61.28 and 5.4.14, Bāhlīka is mentioned in 1.61.25 and 5.4.14; Muñjakeśa in 1.61.27 and 5.4.14; Ṛṣika in 1.61.30, and the Ṛṣikas in 5.4.15; and the Western Anūpaka in 1.61.31, and the Western Anūpakas in 5.4.15. This paralellism clearly suggests the currency of a list of kings of northwestern India in which Paurava had a fixed place.

We have so far taken for granted that the individual named Paurava of the *Mahābhārata* is identical with the Poros of the Greek records. However, Arrian[94] makes mention of a second Poros, who was quick to surrender to Alexander, before the Macedonian engaged the greater Poros. Arrian calls him a "hyparch of Indians." Strabo[95] makes him into a cousin (or nephew) of the first Poros. It seems therefore that we have to do here with a family, or, if you will, a dynasty, called Paurava. And this raises the question whether the *Mahābhārata* does not use Paurava as a title rather than a name. This cannot be decided on the scant evidence. But however this may be, it seems likely that in the Paurava of the Panjāb, to whom the *Mahābhārata* testifies, we should see a king of the stature that Alexander himself recognized when, upon his withdrawal, he left him in charge of his conquests in the Panjāb.

In any case the war books in the *Mahābhārata* know of one Paurava by just this name. In 6.57.20 it is reported that Paurava's

93. Cf. *MBh.* 8.51.8, where this company is Tukhāras, Yavanas, Khasas, Daradas, and Śakas, again pointing to the extreme Northwest.
94. Arrian, 5.21.6.
95. Strabo, *Geography*, 15.1.30.

heir Damana has been killed. In 6.111–112 Paurava and Dhṛṣṭaketu are embroiled in an evenly matched fight in which both lose their chariots; eventually Paurava's son Jayatsena lifts him on his own chariot and the duel remains undecided. Less evenly matched are Paurava and Abhimanyu, whom he attacks; after first bringing down Abhimanyu's standard, umbrella, and horses, he is in turn deprived of both charioteer and horses. Abhimanyu accosts Paurava on his chariot and grabs him by the hair. When Jayadratha, his neighbor from Sindhu, sees Paurava in trouble, he comes to his rescue. The critical edition has no record of Paurava's death, but the Bombay edition reports in 8.5.36 that he has been slain by Arjuna.

All in all, the *Mahābhārata* appears to treat this Paurava as a single individual, not a central figure to be sure, but not entirely without background.

The point of this *excursus* is that when one marginal king among the hosts of kings arrayed can be reasonably identified with a historical figure, we cannot close our eyes to the distinct possibility that other kings, for instance Jayadratha of Sindhu, might also be historical. This, of course, does not make the war a historical event; it only indicates that the epic also could function as a *Who's Who* of ambitious princes, and that the epic as war epic had not died a Purāṇic death in some quarters. As late as the twelfth century, Kalhaṇa, the chronicler of Kashmir, found it necessary to explain in his *Rājataranginī* why no king of Kashmir participated in the *Mahābhārata* war.[96] This intimates that at least in martial circles in India the epic was looked upon as an account of *history*.

On Myth and Epic – 3. Myths: Old and New

An Old Myth and Its Sequel

The first Minor Book (*MBh.* 5.49) of *The Book of the Effort* contains a most intriguing account of the "victory of Indra,"[97] which treats of Indra's victory over Vṛtra and Viśvarūpa in an unexpected way. The titanic struggle between Indra, the greatest god in the Ṛgvedic pantheon, and the dragon Vṛtra, which obstructs the breaking of the monsoon, is probably the single most important early Indian myth. This emphasis is quite intelligible, for Indian life depended (and depends) on the monsoon.

The nature of the myth is made unusually explicit. Let me quote from A. A. Macdonell's self-explanatory inventory of the texts, while

96. Cf. the passage in his *Rājataranginī* (ed. Viśva Bandhu, Hoshiarpur, 1963), 1.49–82), which ends *iti Kāśmīrako rājā vartamānaḥ sa śaiśave/sāhāyakāya samare na ninye Kuru-Pāṇḍavaiḥ.*

97. 5.9–18.

omitting his more than three dozen specific references from the *Ṛgveda*:

> Exhilarated by Soma and generally escorted by the Maruts he enters upon the fray with the chief demon of drought. . . . The conflict is terrible. Heaven and earth tremble when Indra strikes Vṛtra with his bolt, even Tvaṣṭṛ who forged the bolt trembles at Indra's anger. Indra shatters Vṛtra with his bolt. He strikes Vṛtra with his bolt on his back, strikes his face with his pointed weapon, and finds his vulnerable parts. He smote Vṛtra who had encompassed the waters or the dragon who lay around the waters; he overcame the dragon lying on the waters. He slew the dragon hidden in the waters and the sky, and smote Vṛtra, who enclosed the waters, like a tree with the bolt. . . . Indra being frequently described as slaying Vṛtra in the present or being invoked to do so, is regarded as constantly renewing the combat, which mythically represents the constant renewal of the natural phenomena. . . . He cleaves the mountains, making the streams flow or taking the cows, even with the sound of his bolt. When he had laid open the great mountains, he let loose the torrents and slew the Dānava, he set free the pent up springs, the udder of the mountain. He slew the Dānava, shattered the great mountain, broke open the well, set free the pent up waters. . . . Having slain Vṛtra, he opened the orifice of the waters which had been closed. His bolts are dispersed over ninety rivers. References to this conflict with Vṛtra and the release of the waters are extremely frequent in the *RV*. The changes on the myth are rung throughout the whole of one hymn.[98]

The *Mahābhārata* account of the battle of Indra and Vṛtra has lost all this rich texture: it is done within a few verses (5.10.30–35). But very rich are the prehistory and after-effects of the slaying. The story (Sanskrit has no word for "myth"; it uses *upākhyāna* "explanatory story") starts out with a vengeful Tvaṣṭar, the God Artificer, creating a three-faced son Viśvarūpa, the "omniform." Why Tvaṣṭar is aggrieved is not told, but his disaffectation may possibly relate to the story of Indra's obtaining the Soma either in the house of his father (*ṚV*. 3.68) or in that of Tvaṣṭar (4.18). Indra obtains there the Soma at birth, overcomes Tvaṣṭar, and upon stealing the Soma drinks deep (3.48). Or he seizes his father by the foot and shatters him (4.18). He is asked "Who has made your mother a widow?" (ibid.). It is clear enough, as Macdonell[99] points out, that Indra's father *is* Tvaṣṭar, whom he kills to obtain the Soma. The memory of an old feud about Tvaṣṭar, starting with parricide and the enormous guilt of

98. A. A. Macdonell, "Vedic Mythology," in G. Bühler, *Grundriss* (repr.; Varanasi, 1963), pp. 58 f.
99. Macdonell, p. 57; I base my references on his.

this sin, may account for Indra's crushing guilt after he has slain, though not Tvaṣṭar, still Tvaṣṭar's monstrous son Viśvarūpa. As to the latter: in the *Ṛgveda* Indra kills him in order to steal the cows he is guarding (11.8.8 f.).

Closer to the *Mahābhārata* story is that in *Taittirīya Saṃhitā* 2.4.12.1, more fully developed in *Śatapatha Brāhmaṇa* 1.6.3.1 ff.:

> Tvaṣṭar, now, had a son, three-headed, six-eyed; he had three mouths, and because he was so formed he was Viśvarūpa by name. One mouth of his drank Soma, one drank liquor, one he had for other eating. Indra hated him—he cut off his three heads. From the mouth that drank Soma a woodcock issued: it was brownish, for King Soma is brownish. From the mouth that drank liquor issued a sparrow, because it talks like a drunk. From the mouth for other eating issued a partridge, because it is most multicolored: there are spots like *ghee* drops here, like honey drops there dripped on their wings, and of such form was the food he ate with that mouth [and this detail gives us a satisfactory historical explanation of the birds—departing spirits—issuing from his mouths in the *Mahābhārata*, too].
>
> Tvaṣṭar was angry: "Has he killed my son?" He fetched Soma without giving to Indra; and as the Soma flowed without Indra, it was Indra-less. Indra thought, "They are barring me from the Soma!" As the stronger takes from the weaker, he, though uninvited, consumed the pure draught in the jar. Tvaṣṭar was angry: "Has he drunk down my Soma uninvited?" He himself polluted his sactifice, for he let the left-over pure Soma roll away, saying, "Grow as Indraśatru!"[100] When it reached the fire, or some say in between, it took on form. . . . As it took form rolling, it was Vṛtra;[101] as it was footless, it was a serpent.

Since Fire and Soma were combined in Vṛtra, Indra sought to extract these two from Vṛtra, promising them a share in the sacrifice,[102] and finally killed the demon.

Perhaps it was this element of bribery in Indra's extraction of Fire and Soma from Vṛtra that inspired the theme of treachery in the *Mahābhārata* account. Here indra labors under the guilt of two major crimes: that of brahmin murder for his killing Viśvarūpa, and of treachery for killing Vṛtra.

On the subject of Indra's treachery, the *Mahābhārata* account seems contradictory. The sequence is as follows:

100. This is the famous case of "fate by erroneous accent" (*Taittirīya Saṃhitā*, 2.4.12.1; Patañjali, *Mahābhāṣya*, 1.1.1.): Tvasṣṭar seals his son's fate of being killed by Indra by accenting the compound not as a *tatpuruṣa* as he intended (*indraśátru* "enemy of Indra") but as a *bahuvrīhi* (*índraśatru* "whose enemy is Indra").

101. Pseudo-etymology of Vṛtra as though from root *vṛt* "to roll"; the etymon *vṛ* is evidenced by the *Ṛgveda*.

102. Cf. the *MBh.* account 5.16.30 ff.

1. A vengeful Tvaṣṭar creates Vṛtra, whom he feeds with the *tejas* of his *tapas* until he is invincible (5.9.50 ff.).

2. Indra and the Gods in despair seek counsel from Viṣṇu, who suggests a "device": they should contract a truce with Vṛtra: "By virtue of my *tejas*, Indra will proceed and I shall enter his thunderbolt" (5.10.10 ff.).

3. Vṛtra is persuaded by Indra's faithfulness to his word, but lays down the following conditions (*samaya*): "I am not to be slain by Śakra and the Gods with matter dry or wet, rock or wood, thunderbolt or weapon, by day or by night" (5.10.30).

4. Indra sees his chance: "It is grisly twilight now, and 'neither day nor night.' . . . He saw foam there in the ocean: 'This is neither dry nor wet, nor is it a weapon.' . . . Quickly he threw the foam at him with the thunderbolt, and Viṣṇu entered the foam and destroyed Vṛtra" (5.10.34 ff.).

So it would seem that Indra did observe the conditions of the truce, unless one stipulates that he should not have used his *vajra*. This probably is the body of his crime: on the one hand, the tradition that Vṛtra was slain and that the deed was accomplished by Indra's thunderbolt was ineradicable; on the other hand there is the tradition now of a truce with Vṛtra under apparently ironclad conditions, which were violated by Indra; but the circumstances of the crime remain confusing. Nevertheless, Indra's sense of guilt is very evident.

How Tvaṣṭar's son Viśvarūpa came by his brahminhood is also not very clear. One might suppose that Tvaṣṭar himself was regarded as a brahmin at a later time when the Gods, too, had brahmins among them. In *Ṛgveda* 2.23.17 he is the father of Bṛhaspati; in 10.2.7 and 10.46.9 he is the father of the Bhṛgus. Perhaps Viśvarūpa's brahminhood is simply derived from the fact that he drinks the Soma, a privilege more and more reserved for the brahmin. But, as I suggested above, a tradition of Indra's parricide, though this myth seems suppressed, may have surrounded other killings of Indra with an aura of heinous guilt, which was interpreted as the guilt attached to brahminicide. The idea that this was indeed "brahmin-murder" apparently needed some bolstering: the *Nārāyaṇīya* section of the *Mokṣadharma* has provided it.

This section knows Viśvarūpa as a son of Tvaṣṭar and a sister's-son to the Asuras, meaning that his mother was an Asura herself, thus building a dubiety into the offspring. He "gave the sacrificial share publicly to the Gods, and secretly to the Asuras" (12.329.17). The Asuras protest to his mother about this unequal treatment. At his mother's demand he henceforth favors the Asuras, for which Indra rightfully kills him (ibid. 18–27). This variation does not contribute much to a clarification of Viśvarūpa's brahmin standing, but at least it tries to justify Indra's killing of a doubtful brahmin, who had been the Gods' *purohita.*

Georges Dumézil sees in this diffuse and confusing "myth" a much simpler truth than appears on the surface. Arguing as always within the framework of his Indo-European theology-sociology of the three functions (sacerdotal-legislative; martial; populist-fertile), he finds reflected in Indra's two crimes two of the three debilitating sins which the warrior risks committing against the three functions:[103] Indra sinned against the first function by killing a representative thereof, a brahmin; and against the second function by breaking a compact within the warrior bond. Since nothing of the sort is found in the *Veda,* Dumézil must leapfrog that body of evidence and rely on narratives in the epic and even *Purāṇa*[104] to support his hypothesis that such "ordered" sins are found in Indo-Aryan tradition, as they are, in his view, in other Indo-European traditions. I shall not pronounce on the merits of the Indo-European components of his case, since the theory is irrelevant to our understanding of the *Mahābhārata* until all other possibilities of explaining Indra's "guilt" from the *Mahābhārata* itself have been exhausted.

While they share fundamental underlying views and attitudes, Dumézil and Biardeau stand on the two sides of the Great Divide of the traditional periodization of Indian civilization into Vedic and post-Vedic: Biardeau to the south of it, as she takes the *Mahābhārata* to be part and parcel of a Hinduism stretching indefinitely futureward; Dumézil to the north of it, as he mines the epic for a treasure of reminiscences of not only a Vedic, but a pre-Vedic, Indo-Iranian, even Indo-European trifunctional inheritance. Neither in so doing shows great respect for, or even much interest in, the possible integrity of the *Mahābhārata* as unique product in the growth of Indian civilization; the text seems fated to be relevant to anything but itself.

In my view Dumézil's treatment of the epic is too early, Biardeau's too late. My view can no more be proved than theirs, but at least let me record it. With their insistence on the exclusively prototypal, or if you wish "symbolic," roles of the epic's protagonists, these two French scholars, themselves both individuals of a unique and admirable originality, offhandedly dismiss these persons as individuals: "Dans le *Mahābhārata,*" writes Dumézil, "les personnages, entièrement définis par leur fonction, ne présentent guère d'interêt psychologique: Yudhiṣṭhira, Bhīma, Arjuna, Dhṛtarāṣṭra, Bhīṣma sont tout d'une pièce, et l'on peut prédire à coup sûr ce que chacun fera en toute

103. Georges Dumézil, *Aspects de la fonction guerrière chez les Indo-Européens* (Paris, 1956), pp. 69–76; *Mythe et épopée* 1: 113 ff.

104. He relies heavily on *Mārkaṇḍeya P.* 1.1.1 ff.

nouvelle circonstance."[105] Biardeau, who at least accepts the periodization between Vedic and "classical Indian" (= Purāṇa-Hindū) societies, because she holds that a new motivation, that of renunciation, separates the two, must of necessity reject the *ṛta* of Dumézil as the basis of the *dharma* of the *Mahābhārata*.[106] Nevertheless she shares his attitude: "En abandonnant la comparison indo-européenne, il importe de ne pas abandonner ce qui fait la fecondité de sa [Dumézil's] méthode, à savoir que les personnages mythiques ne sont jamais réduits à eux-mêmes, mais représentent tout un complexe de notions, de valeurs, de types d'activité qui définit leur place unique dans un ensemble donné."[107] For both scholars, then, the roles of the heroes are fixed: for the one in an unchanged, though epically transposed, mythical trifunctional order of values; for the other in a changeless Hindū ethos of values.

In so doing they both decline to be distracted by the quirks of their types: the domestic side of Bhīma, for all his ferocity; the lone-ranger imagery of Arjuna on his philandering or heroic wanderings; Karṇa's emotional love for his foster-parents, for all his war-mongering; the underlying slyness of Dhṛtarāṣṭra's indecisions; the occasional perfidy of Yudhiṣṭhira, for all his rectitude.

Indra, though a God, also has his quirks. In his elderly years now, he is more a fugitive from his fixed station of warrior in the trifunctional order than a martial incumbent of it. I find it remarkable that just when he retires as warrior he becomes encumbered with unprecedented feelings of guilt. For Indra does not do battle any more; all his battles of the past have become enshrined in clichẹs of similes for the warriors who are battling *now*. The king of the Gods is getting on, and uses his guilt to retire. The compilers of *The Victory of Indra*, for their part, may well have used his mythological decline in order to impose a guilt on him to rationalize it. Only the most heinous crime of them all, the killing of a brahmin, can account for it. For such is indeed the burden of the sequel of this novel, if not factitious, "myth" of Indra's guilt: the story of Nahuṣa.

Nahuṣa's part in *The Victory of Indra* is grafted upon the somewhat mythical "myth" of Indra going underground under water out of a sense of guilt. The Gods and the world are now kingless and suffer. They appoint (the reason for his selection goes unexplained) a human king, Nahuṣa, as their new ruler. He rightly protests his lack of *tejas*, which here might be paraphrased "sufficient prestige." The Gods correct this lack by giving him the power of draining away and

105. *Mythe et épopée* 1: 602 f.; on p. 209 he calls them "*marionettes*."
106. "Etudes de mythologie hindoue," II, *Bulletin de l'Ecole française de l'Extrême-Orient* 55 (1969), pp. 98 ff.
107. Ibid., p. 97.

appropriating the *tejas* of any one God or other creature on whom Nahuṣa sets eye. The inevitable happens: Nahuṣa gets *hubris.*

He begins to covet Śacī, Indra's wife, because he feels that he should be Indra's successor in all respects. Faithful Śacī seeks refuge with the brahmin of the Gods, Bṛhaspati, who advises her to stall Nahuṣa until Indra has been found. Indra is found and exonerated by a scrifice to Viṣṇu; but since Nahuṣa with his power is invincible, Indra disappears again. At Bṛhaspati's advice, Śacī, no longer able to stall Nahuṣa, demands that he court her in a chariot drawn by, or carried by, brahmin seers: this is the ultimate chariot of state. Nahuṣa delightedly complies.

This is *hubris* unspeakable: Nahuṣa must now be brought down. The occasion of his downfall is his failure to answer correctly an erudite riddle: "The *mantras* that have been promulgated by Brahmā for the Sprinkling-of-the-Cows, are they authentic to you or not?"[108] Even worse, he has touched the head of the seer Agastya with his foot—a gross insult. Thus Nahuṣa stands condemned on three counts: he has despoiled the pure *brahman* of the Veda by denying the authenticity of certain *mantras*; he has touched Agastya's head with his foot; and he has made brahmin seers his beasts of burden. For this he shall be a boa constrictor for ten thousand years.

No one will accept that this story of the reign of the human king Nahuṣa over the Gods during Indra's temporary self-exile was organic to the myths of Indra's slayings of Viśvarūpa and Vṛtra; it is an innovation in the *Mahābhārata.* The moral of this innovative "myth" is that a *kṣatriya,* even if by a fluke raised to the sovereignty of the Gods, is subject to swift punishment if he forgets himself: Nahuṣa is ignominiously tumbled from his throne when he dares to humble a *brahmin,* and instantly turned into a boa constrictor—whereupon a most penitent Indra, after having sufficiently suffered for his own brahmin-killing, is restored to his well-worn throne by the placated brahmin Agastya. "Thus the scoundrel was cast from divine kingship," reports Agastya, "and now we [brahmins] thrive with good fortune, Śakra—that thorn of brahmindom is gone! Consort of Śacī, return to heaven and protect the worlds, with your senses mastered and your enemies slain, amidst the praises of the great seers!"[109]—and watch out, he might as well have said aloud, if their praise turns into condemnation.

Assuming that a new sequel may cast new light on an old myth, it is not hard for one reading *The Victory of Indra* to discern how myth might have been manipulated. There are enough older details to suggest continuity with Vedic exemplars, and thus authenticity. But

108. 5.17.9.
109. 5.17.16 ff.

the end result is, not the reaffirmation of Indra's destiny to kill Vṛtra in order to release the monsoon, but the affirmation of the manifest destiny of the brahmin to impose drastic penalty on anyone, however powerful, who wrongs him.

Indeed I think that this episode is didactic in purpose, homiletic even, with the apposite rhetoric of drawing on ancient scripture to make a novel point presumably intended by scripture. The question remains why it was felt that this made sense in the context of *The Effort*. The immediate context, lest we forget, is that Śalya, who has just chosen to ally himself with the wrong party, tells the story to Yudhiṣṭhira, who has recently returned from thirteen years of misery and must now fight. In this context, Yudhiṣṭhira clearly has not been at fault with the brahmins, like Indra and Nahuṣa, and yet has had his troubles, like Indra and Nahuṣa, while Śalya himself has good reason to be a little on the defensive and might want to make amends. It occurs to me to wonder, therefore, whether the story might be meant to introduce Yudhiṣṭhira's first attempt at perfidy—a sin he had, as it were, exonerated himself from in advance by his undeserved hardships. In any case, no sooner has Śalya finished reciting than Yudhiṣṭhira repeats his request to his father-in-law, the king of the Madras: "You will no doubt become Karṇa's charioteer: obscure his splendor by your praises of me!"[110]

It would seem to me, in conclusion, that there is no compelling need to account for the "crimes of Indra" as a heritage from Indo-European mythology; not because such a heritage might not exist, but because it distracts from the clear message of *The Victory of Indra*: it is a *māhātmya* of brahmin power, of which we have seen more examples: the story of *Vasiṣṭha*,[111], the story of *Aurva*,[112], the story of *Kārtavīrya*,[113] and other tales from *The Tour of the Sacred Fords*, foremost among them, the story of *Agastya*.[114]

New Myth: Mātali

While *The Victory of Indra* draws on vestigial Vedic myth to make a new point, the story of *Mātali*[115] exemplifies the "new myth," by which I mean a myth with no discoverable Vedic provenance and with a distinctively new outlook. One may question whether the word *myth* is at all applicable to this story. Indra's charioteer Mātali makes, with Nārada as his guide, a tour of netherworlds in order to find a bridegroom for his nubile daughter. After visiting Varuṇa, and with

110. First request 5.8.25; second 18.23.
111. 1.164 ff.
112. 1.169 ff.
113. 3.115 ff.
114. 3.94 ff.
115. 5.95 ff.

his leave, the travelers tour the World of the Waters, which is also the haunt of Rākṣasas and Bhūtas, the depository of the weapons of the Gods, and burial ground of those of the demons. They proceed to the World of the Elephants,[116] which includes the city of Pātāla, inhabited by Daityas and Dānavas, and which is also the jail of the Daityas, the hereafter of ascetic brahmins, the birthplace of great elephants, and the resting place of a mysterious egg that at the end of the world will explode.[117] They continue to the city of Hiraṇyapura, where the Dānavas are still active; the World of Garuḍas; Rasātala, the "seventh level," the domain of cows; and at last the city of the Snakes, Bhogavatī. All this time Mātali is looking for a bridegroom; it does not occur to him to look among humans.

In the World of the Snakes Mātali spies a handsome Snake, Sumukha, whom he chooses for his daughter. However, Sumukha has been earmarked for Garuḍa's next meal. Mātali persists and takes Sumukha to Indra, whom Viṣṇu is visiting. The latter tells Indra to go ahead and give Sumukha the Elixir of Immortality.[118] Indra is afraid of Garuḍa (no wonder, for he cannot encompass a single feather of Garuḍa's),[119] but when urged on he finally does so. Garuḍa is angry and threatens Indra.[120] Viṣṇu then berates Garuḍa and shows him his strength. The Fair-Winged Bird is properly chastised.[121] The moral of the story is that Duryodhana should not fight the Pāṇḍavas, who have Viṣṇu-Kṛṣṇa on their side.[122]

I call it a myth only because it involves somewhat divine beings. At that they are at best second-rank: Indra's charioteer Mātali; the semi-celestial, semi-terrestrian Nārada; archetypal elephants, Daityas and Dānavas, Garuḍas, and Snakes: denizens of a celestial *demimonde* appropriately shown its place by a more and more timid Indra and an ever more powerful Viṣṇu.

It is a *Purāṇa*-like myth, and, like the Purāṇas themselves, more easily described than defined: Purāṇic "myths" are usually short narratives that are replete with supernatural detail, not just about Great Gods, but their paraphernalia and palaces as well, and about vaguely or fully demoniac creatures and their netherworlds, with kathenotheistic glorifications of one Great God in his different aspects and incarnations, and kathenodemoniac villainy effortlessly put down

116. 5.97.1; the word is *nāgaloka*; while *nāga* ordinarily means "Snake" in the *MBh.*, I take it here as "elephant" (attested for the *MBh.*; cf. also *nāgapura* for Hāstinapura), since the world of the Snakes is described later (5.101), and elephants live in this world.

117. 5.97.17.

118. 5.102.24 f.

119. 1.29.20 f.

120. 5.103.3 ff.

121. 5.103.18 ff.

122. 5.103.31 ff.

with his little finger by that God, around whom paeans of praise incessantly burst forth—vignettes more than images, iconographic poses in words, concretizations of omnipresent power that can only be inventoried (endlessly) but never exhausted. In a word, Purāṇic "myths" are myths of adoration, in which human pride is instantly humbled, and humility itself becomes a yardstick of devotion.

Epic myth has a different character: it is frankly more manly. Perhaps, indeed, there is an inherent contradiction in the concept of "epic myth" if the epic is about humans. I believe there is great depth of feeling in the many discussions in the *Mahābhārata* of *daiva*, the fate that comes from the Gods, and *pauruṣa*, the courage of men.[123] Duryodhana's final taunt to Yudhiṣṭhira, "Show you are a man!"[124] is the essence of the *Mahābhārata* as epic. Indra's struggle with Vṛtra is an epic myth on the divine level; Arjuna's struggle with the Mountain Man is epic on a heroic level—the fight is not thrown before the match begins, as it would be in the *Purāṇas*.

The distinction I am groping for is perhaps best illustrated in two challenges to Śiva—the only two episodes about him in the *Mahābhārata* so far. One is the book of *The Mountain Man*;[125] the other the story of *The Five Indras*.[126] In *The Mountain Man* the hero Arjuna is storming heaven and finds his way barred by a man of the mountains, Śiva; there is an issue: who had the right to shoot the boar? Arjuna fights, and goes on fighting until he is reduced to his bare fists. He loses, of course, but he loses honorably, and the way to heaven is open. In *The Five Indras* we have the God's Little Finger, or Garuḍa's Single Feather: a mere glance of Rudra paralyzes the quondam king of the Gods,[127] and he finds himself buried with four previous Indras.

This is new mythology. The epic encompasses both old and new, to be sure, but its main business is the legend of men who were heroes.

On Myth and Epic—4. Legends Old and New: Sequels

An Old Legend and Its Sequel: Gālava

Nahuṣa, successively a human king, sovereign of the Gods, boa-constrictor, and dweller in heaven, is not the only king in the Lunar Dynasty to be toppled for his pride. *Hubris* runs in the family: his grandfather was Purūravas, who stole fire from heaven and aspired

123. E.g., 3.31 ff.
124. 5.158.9.
125. 3.13 ff.
126. 1.189.
127. 1.189.16.

to loving a Goddess;[128] his son was Yayāti, who was thrown out of heaven.

Yayāti was a fabulous figure who was not allowed to depart from the epic. In the *Beginning* there are two stories: one deals with his life on earth with all its intriguing detail, and ends with his retirement to the forest after he has cursed his five senior sons and installed the youngest, Pūru, as king;[129] the other, *The Latter Days of Yayāti*,[130] is a sequel only in the sense that it describes Yayāti's vicissitudes after death, not because it was inspired by the first story. He was clearly at one time a culture hero about whom several stories could be told.

Yayāti's fall from heaven is legendary. When Kṛṣṇa sees his father Vasudeva fall from the sky-ship Saubha in an illusionist trick that is played on him, confusion seizes him: "It was the very likeness of my father tumbling down, like Yayāti tumbling down from heaven to earth when his merit was exhausted" (II.264). Yayāti's fall became so much a part of legend that its location was venerated: there is a *tīrtha* called "Yayāti's Fall" (II.375), by the river Pārā, "on whose bank Nahuṣa's son Yayāti fell in the midst of the honest" (II.402). We know the names of these honest men: Pratardana, Vasumanas, Aṣṭaka, and Śibi or Śaibya (I.84 ff.). The *Mahābhārata* has not forgotten them: "In their tasks [people] have protectors, as Yayāti had in Śaibya and others" (II.452). Yayāti's fall is probably also commemorated by the *tīrtha* of Plakṣāvataraṇa, "the descent upon the *plakṣa* [wavy-leaved fig] tree," which "the wise say is the gate to the ridge of heaven" (II.463), for thanks to Śaibya and others Yayāti went, after his fall there, straight back to heaven again. "King Yayāti fell," the hunter tells the brahmin, "and he was rescued by his daughter's good sons" (II.635). Clearly Yayāti's fall was proverbial, and so was his resurgence, thanks to his daughter's sons.

So far we have only heard of Yayāti's sons, four of whom were banished to the corners of the earth while Pūru held sway in the center in Kurukṣetra.[131] In the present story they are reduced to two, Pūru and Yadu, "who fostered two dynasties," namely that of the Pauravas = Kauravas, and of the Yādavas.[132] Now a daughter by the name of Mādhavī is introduced.

Before she and her father appear on the scene, there is an involved narrative that begins with another installment in the ongoing saga of Vasiṣṭha and Viśvāmitra, where Vasiṣṭha is really the God Dharma. Viśvāmitra, at present still a royal sage, is practicing *tapas*, when Vasiṣṭha appears looking for a meal. Viśvāmitra takes so long

128. 1.70.17 ff.; Purūravas too fell afoul of the brahmins because of pride and greed.
129. 1.79.1.
130. 1.81 ff.
131. 1.81 ff.
132. 5.118.12.

preparing it that Vasiṣṭha eats with other ascetics. When Viśvāmitra comes with the hot rice, Vasiṣṭha laconically says, "I ate. You wait a while." He stays away a hundred years, while Viśvāmitra waits, stockstill, with the steaming platter on his head. His student Gālava attends to him meanwhile. Vasiṣṭha returns, and calls Viśvāmitra a "brahmin seer": henceforth the latter is a brahmin.[133] Viśvāmitra thereupon dismisses Gālava, who, however, keeps trying to press a guru's gift on his teacher. Exasperated, Viśvāmitra snaps, "Give me eight hundred moon-white horses with a black ear each!"[134]

While this may seem a uniquely imaginative demand, such demands are hereditary in Viśvāmitra's family. When King Gādhi of Kānyakubja, Viśvāmitra's father, obtains a daughter, the Bhṛgu brahmin Ṛcīka solicits her. The king replies: "There is a custom in our lineage, which began with our forefathers: we demand as bride price a thousand white horses, each with a black ear." Ṛcīka obtains the horses promptly from Varuṇa at the Ford of the Horses (3.115.9 ff., II.444).

Viśvāmitra's eight hundred horses are a slightly more modest demand, but enough to baffle the penniless Gālava. The discomfited ascetic gets the help of his friend, Garuḍa, who describes the four directions,[135] and upon Gālava's request takes him to the East. After more adventures Gālava and Garuḍa encounter Viśvāmitra, who pointedly repeats his demand.[136] Garuḍa now steers his friend to Yayāti, the richest king on earth, to ask for alms sufficient to buy the horses. While appreciating the honor, Yayāti confesses that his resources have dwindled; instead, he will give in alms his daughter Mādhavī, who "shall establish four lineages."[137]

Gālava and Garuḍa go with Mādhavī to Haryaśva of Ayodhyā, who is not wealthy enough to provide the whole eight hundred horses, but is ready to rent Mādhavī from Gālava for two hundred horses, in order to beget one heir. He begets Vasumanas. Gālava fetches Mādhavī back, takes her to Divodāsa of Kāśi, where the scene repeats itself; Divodāsa begets Pratardana,[138] Then on to Uśīnara, who begets Śibi.[139] When Gālava has thus acquired six hundred horses, Garuḍa discloses that the search is over. He tells the history of the horses: how King Gādhi demanded them from Ṛcīka as bride price for his daughter Satyavatī. Gādhi later gave the horses away to brahmins who sold two hundred of them to each of the above kings. The

133. 5.104.12 ff.
134. 5.104.26.
135. 5.106 ff.
136. 5.111.20 f.
137. 5.113 f.
138. 5.115.
139. 5.116.

remaining four hundred drowned in the river Vitastā.[140] So Gālava should rent Mādhavī to Viśvāmitra in lieu of the balance of two hundred horses for an heir of his own. Viśvāmitra agrees and begets Aṣṭaka.[141]

Gālava, indentured to Viśvāmitra for the guru's gift, is now free and departs for the forest. Mādhavī, indentured to Gālava by her father in lieu of a brahmin's alms, is now free and returns to her father. Yayāti holds a *svayaṃvara* for her, but she chooses the forest, where she lives like a doe.[142] After a long life Yayāti dwells in heaven, commits the sin of pride and falls back to earth. "Let me fall among good men," he wishes, sees four kings in Naimiṣa Forest, and descends in their midst down the column of fire rising from their sacrifice.[143] The four press their merit upon him; Yayāti, a baron, declines. Mādhavī wanders by, like a grazing doe, and identifies the four kings as her sons, Yayāti's daughter's-sons. Gālava too happens by and makes it unanimous: Yayāti accepts the merit they press upon him and reascends to heaven.[144]

What are we to make of all this, and how does this story of *Gālava* relate to *Yayāti* and *The Latter Days of Yayāti*? Dumézil has with great enthusiasm tackled the story and has much to say about it.[145] As so often there is much incandescence in his writing, which I can express only in a metaphor. It is as though I am guided with a candle by a courteous, even solicitous host through ancient caverns whose features he describes to me with eloquent erudition, more features than I can readily make out, but I am inclined to believe him. Then, led out among my own trees, I blink my eyes and wonder what I saw.

In the matter of Yayāti his incandescence illumines more than elsewhere. I too consider Yayāti's story an ancient myth of an original king founding the kingdoms of earth directly through his sons, as in *Yayāti*, or indirectly through his daughter's sons, as in *Gālava*. All the many references to his regal magnificence, his sacrificial munificence, his fall and resurgence outside the epic-specific stories of the *Mahābhārata* about him show that the events of his life were still proverbial. Already an ancient king in *Ṛgveda* 1.31.17, he has relations with Devas and Asuras alike. He remains a figure productive of legends and their verbifications: the story of *Yayāti* is an extremely well-told story. The "Fall of Yayāti" not only produced places of pilgrimage worthy of the munificent sacrificer, but also became a vehicle for the description of the circumstances of transmigration first

140. 5.117.1 ff.
141. 5.117.14 ff.
142. 5.118.1 ff.
143. 5.119.9 ff.
144. 5.119.28.
145. *Mythe et épopée* 2: 272 ff.

adumbrated in the oldest Upaniṣads.[146] His resurrection to heaven was attributed in the most direct fashion to the surviving merits of his life on earth: his grandsons. Yes, I hope that Dumézil is right and that he had no less glorious a past than he had a life and a future.

More than elsewhere, too, Dumézil's application of the three functions to the four grandsons of Yayāti makes good sense.[147] Vasumanas, "he whose mind is on wealth," represents the *vaiśya* and his "wont to give," the great virtue of that class. Pratardana the warrior king, with his merit of glory in war, is surely the *kṣatriya*. Aṣṭaka, the son of a warrior become brahmin, a performer of the grand sacrifices, pays fine homage to the class of the brahmins. Śibi is a bit less precise: while in tradition he is the generous giver of alms par excellence, here his merit is that of *satya*; perhaps this *satya-ṛta* is the value that overarches the three classes—which would make good orthodox sense: the same notion is found in *Bṛhadāraṇyaka Upaniṣad* 1.4.11–14.[148]

Nevertheless, the student of the *Mahābhārata* must do more than look for myth, whether ancient or future. While recognizing it as material, sometimes raw material, of the narrative, the narrative itself is his object. And within the narrative I regard *Gālava*, however ancient and "authentic" some of its elements may be, as a sequel. The stories of *Yayāti* and his *Latter Days* are told outside the context of the epic: they simply are adduced to establish one of the beginnings of the dynasty. On the other hand, *Gālava* may still be somewhat out of direct context (it is not part of the epic events, for how could it be?), yet it is adduced as a warning: Duryodhana should cease being obdurate, for his obstinacy might well lead to trouble—witness Gālava.

The severity of an Indian teacher toward his student was (and is) proverbial. The candidate's studies were sufficiently traumatic to have inspired a whole festive homecoming ritual to mark their end, the *samāvartana*; and his gratitude, relief, or both, demanded a dramatic gift of the guru's choice.[149] The rite of initiation simply was not complete without this *dakṣiṇā*. It could be an easy present, or a difficult one. Gālava's insistence in pressing a present on a character like Viśvāmitra is, to say the least, imprudent, and he suffers for it. So will Duryodhana suffer for his imprudent obstinacy toward the Pāṇḍavas.

This is the principal burden of the story as far as the *Mahābhārata*

146. 1.85; see J. A. B. van Buitenen, "Some Notes on the Uttarayāyāta," *Adyar Library Bulletin*, 1968.

147. *Mythe et épopée* 2: 243 ff., esp. pp. 278 ff.

148. There *dharma*, sc. *kṣatradharma*, is equated with *satya*.

149. J. C. Heesterman, "The Return of the Vedic Scholar," *Pratidānam* (Festschrift Kuiper) (The Hague, 1968), pp. 436 ff.

is concerned. The impossible task is exemplified by drawing on older mythology and legend: Viśvāmitra's brahminhood is once more explained. The black-eared white horses which the Bhṛgu Ṛcīka paid up to Viśvāmitra's father as bride price are recast as the price her temporary husbands pay for Mādhavī. The generosity of an impoverished Yayāti, so proverbial, justifies his gift of his daughter in lieu of alms. The daughter now in this narrative context gives birth to four heroic kings, who will catch Yayāti when he falls, and send him back to heaven.

Once more, then, old narrative has been used for new purposes. The brahmin Viśvāmitra's desire to teach Gālava his last lesson, with all the far-reaching, unpremeditated consequences of it, is the point of the story of *Gālava*. Kings labor to help Gālava get the horses to satisfy one brahmin's whim, and in the process obtain heirs; in the end the brahmin is satisfied, and everybody is free to return to the forest: Viśvāmitra and Gālava to perform *tapas*, the four sons to sacrifice, Yayāti to fall down and reascend, and Mādhavī herself to roam like a doe.

Dumézil attaches great importance to her name Mādhavī, which he connects with derivatives from *madhu* "honey, mead," in the meanings of "honey-rich flower" and "intoxicating drink," both attested. He goes on to connect her, progenitrix of kings, with Medb, the famous queen of Irish lore, who has been considered the personification of the royalty of Ireland. Her name too is cognate with words for inebriation.[150] There are indeed striking resemblances, but that of the name may be purely coincidental. She is not the only woman in the *Mahābhārata* to bear the name; she shares it with five others. It is more likely to be a name like Kausalyā, Kaikeyī, Mālavī, Vaidehī, Kālingī, Aikṣvākī, Gāndhārī, etc., indicating country or tribe of origin. Mādhavī then would simply signify "the Mādhava woman."

New Legend—A Sequel: Ambā

After Bhīṣma has renounced throne and marriage and consequently installed his younger brother Citrāngada and, upon his death, the youngest, Vicitravīrya, as king in Hāstinapura, he is concerned about the continuity of the Kuru lineage. Hearing that the king of the Kāśis is holding a *svayaṃvara* for his three daughters, he goes to the affair, abducts all three on his chariot, fights a fierce battle with the king of Śālva, and returns triumphant to the City of the Elephant.[151]

These three sisters are called Ambā, Ambikā, and Ambālikā, variations on the vocative *ambe, amba*, a hypocorism for "mother, mommy." Like so many persons referred to in the *Mahābhārata*, these

150. Dumézil, pp. 340 ff.
151. 1.96.

three Ambās may have a considerable antiquity. They may well have given rise to an old epithet of Rudra, *tryambaka*:[152] "he of the three mothers," which was later reinterpreted as "three-eyed." There is nothing in the *Mahābhārata* to shed light on this question. On the contrary, the epic splits up the collective three Ambās almost immediately.

As soon as Bhīṣma arrives with them in his city, Ambā, the eldest, discloses that she had chosen Śālva for her husband at the *svayaṃvara*. After consulting the brahmins, Bhīṣma lets her go.[153] We hear no more about her till the end of this Book 5, when Bhīṣma recounts her later life. The occasion is Duryodhana's question why Bhīṣma will not fight the Pāñcāla warrior Śikhaṇḍin. He replies with a fantastic tale.[154]

When Ambā is let go by Bhīṣma, she makes at once for Śālva to present herself to the king as his bride. Śālva refuses her: she has been won by Bhīṣma and he will not have a second-hand wife. Her pleas go unheard, and she seeks shelter with hermits. The hermits see Śālva's point, though they commiserate with Ambā's plight. The rejected bride refuses to return to Bhīṣma, or her father. She weighs the evidence and singles out Bhīṣma as the cause of her misery. She will seek his death. How she will do that remains in question, until Akṛtavraṇa visits the hermits, hears Ambā's story and advises her to seek help from Rāma, "who will come tomorrow."[155]

Rāma promises Ambā his help in forcing either Śālva or Bhīṣma to take her in. She insists that he address Bhīṣma. He goes to Kurukṣetra, but Bhīṣma refuses to give in. A lengthy battle between Rāma and Bhīṣma ensues, in which both are evenly matched. Both fall repeatedly. At one time Bhīṣma's charioteer is killed; Bhīṣma falls, but is caught by eight brahmins, while his mother the Ganges guards his chariot.[156] The same eight brahmins appear in his dream with a weapon that would put Rāma to sleep, but not kill him.[157] Rāma's ancestors appear to warn him off: "Bhīṣma is a Vasu."[158] He is prevented from using it by Nārada with the consent of the eight seers.[159] Rāma and Bhīṣma make their peace.

Rāma confesses his failure to Ambā, who vows to kill Bhīṣma herself. She immerses herself in *tapas*. The Ganges appears and curses her to become a miserable stream, the river Ambā. Thanks to her

152. This epithet appears as early as *ṚV*. 7.59.12; cf. Macdonell, p. 74.
153. 1.96.
154. *Ambā*, 5.170 ff.
155. 5.175.13.
156. 5.183.11 ff.
157. 5.184.
158. 5.186.10 ff.
159. 5.186.1 ff.

tapas she retains one half of her body. At last Rudra appears and promises that she shall kill Bhīṣma when she is reborn in Drupada of Pāñcāla's house. She burns herself on a funeral pyre, her last words being: "For Bhīṣma's death!"[160]

So far the story is fairly straightforward. True, what might have been a tragic story soon gets bogged down in talk. The introduction of Rāma is unexpected: he has long since retired[161] and is the venerated inhabitant of a *tīrtha* on Mount Mahendra in the Eastern Ghāṭs.[162] Why he should suddenly interest himself in a rejected maiden of the *kṣatriya* class which he had destroyed "thrice seven times" remains a mystery. This "last battle,"[163] which as far as the *Mahābhārata* is concerned is a posthumous one, can only cloud his memory. With curiosity we note that someone has remembered that Bhīṣma is a reborn Vasu;[164] the "eight brahmins" are, of course, his brother-Vasus. It all sounds epigonic.

After this the story becomes positively droll. King Drupada, once more, is sonless, and he does *tapas* for Bhīṣma's death, as he once did for Droṇa's.[165] Śiva appears to him, and prophesies a child which will first be a girl, then a man. Drupada's wife becomes pregnant, and gives birth to a girl, who is treated like a boy, with male sacraments and a masculine name; only Drupada and his wife know the truth. She is given a boy's training. When she comes of age, they look for a bride and find one in the daughter of King Hiraṇyavarman of Daśārṇa.[166] The secret now necessarily gets out. Hiraṇyavarman sends an envoy declaring war and consults his allies, who agree to march with him, if Śikhaṇḍin is a girl. Drupada stages a public scene, pretending that he himself was also deceived. He becomes very religious, but his wife prods him to act first, pray later.[167]

Meanwhile Śikhaṇḍin, knowing herself to be the cause of all the trouble, goes into the forest to kill herself. In the forest she encounters the Yakṣa Sthūṇākarṇa, who agrees to lend her his manhood and to assume her womanhood, but only for a brief span. Hiraṇyavarman, already before the walls of the fortress-city Kāmpilya, sends a last envoy announcing battle. Drupada dispatches his own envoy asserting Śikhaṇḍin's manhood; it is enthusiastically certified by courtesans delegated by Hiraṇyavarman.

Shortly thereafter Kubera comes visiting Sthūṇa, who fails to show

160. 5.188.17 f.
161. Cf. 1.121.
162. 3.115.1 f.
163. 5.186.13 ff.
164. 1.91.
165. 1.155.
166. It speaks to the novelty of *Ambā* that this king is otherwise unknown to the *MBh.*
167. 5.192.10 ff.

up. Told why—shame over his womanhood—Kubera lays a curse on him: he shall be a woman in perpetuity. But he mitigates so horrendous a curse: Sthūṇa will be a woman until Śikhaṇḍin dies. When Śikhaṇḍin comes back to the Yakṣa to return his manhood, the Yakṣa reports it all to him. Henceforth Sikhaṇḍin is a man. Therefore, since Śikhaṇḍin had once been a woman, Bhīṣma will not kill him.

In spite of the rather remarkable report of a sex change in one of the great warriors of the *Mahābhārata*, it is astonishingly underplayed elsewhere in the text. Outside this story there are five references to it. In the late list of peculiar births (all culled from the *Mahābhārata*) in *The Descent of the First Generations* (1.37.83–106), one final *śloka* is devoted to him (ibid. 104): "Śikhaṇḍin was born a girl child, from Drupada, but later became a man: the Yakṣa Sthūṇa changed her into a man, to do her a favor." This reference is clearly derived from *Ambā*. Another reference in 6.16.15: "The pure-spirited [Bhīṣma] has said: 'I will not kill Śikhaṇḍin, for he is reported to have been a woman before, therefore I must avoid him in battle.'" A third in 6.82.26: Śikhaṇḍin attacked Bhīṣma, and "ignoring Śikhaṇḍin on the battlefield in consideration of his womanhood, Bhīṣma attacked the Sṛñjayas." A fourth in pretty much the same context: "Smilingly Bhīṣma again and again refused to engage the Pāñcālya, recalling Śikhaṇḍin's womanhood."

The fifth reference is in 6.104.40 ff.: "When Śikhaṇḍin hit him very hard, Bhīṣma looked at him and, though enraged, remained unwilling; he said jeeringly, 'Hit me if you wish, or don't. I will not fight with you in any fashion. You are still the same woman Śikhaṇḍinī that the Creator made you!'"

All the references center around Bhīṣma's imminent death; only in that connection is Śikhaṇḍin's erstwhile womanhood memorable. Arjuna uses Śikhaṇḍin as a human shield and then shoots Bhīṣma dead, for Śikhaṇḍin's female past makes him invulnerable to Bhīṣma. There is no reference here at all to indicate that Śikhaṇḍin is a born-again Ambā, not even in 1.37.104. The story of *Ambā* is occasioned by Bhīṣma's statement that he will not fight Śikhaṇḍin; only then it transpires that Śikhaṇḍin is Ambā reborn.

Since there is no evidence that the story of *Ambā* was independent epic lore, I assume that it developed within the *Mahābhārata*. Its starting point was Śikhaṇḍin's curious invulnerability to Bhīṣma, either because he was in fact born a woman, or because he just was invulnerable and therefore might once have been a woman. But which woman?

A fond preoccupation with the heroes of the epic produced one answer: he must have been Ambā, who had been forgotten too early. For what could have become of her when she left Hāstinapura for

Śālva? She could only have been rejected, since she was legally taken in *āsura* marriage by the fact of Bhīṣma's abduction.

–Then what became of her? She could hardly go back to Bhīṣma, whom she herself had asked to let her go, and who had formally, with the brahmins' consent, abandoned her. Nor could she go back to her father: she would be the laughing stock of the clan,[168] a woman condemned for life to spinsterhood. She must have remained on her own, a woman who had two chances at a prestigious marriage and was cheated out of both–a miserable relict seeking vengeance. And vengeance on whom but Bhīṣma?

–But what could a mere woman do to a Bhīṣma?

–She must have sought male help.

–But who was powerful enough to stand up to a Bhīṣma?

–Remember Rāma, the scourge of the *kṣatriyas*?

–But Rāma has retired!

–So it will be his last battle; it will end in a standoff, for after all Bhīṣma survived it.

–But then what? Whom could Ambā turn to?

–A God, by *tapas* of course, so she gets a boon that she shall be reborn and kill Bhīṣma.

–But it says that Śikhaṇḍin was born a woman!

–So, a sex change as the fulfillment of the boon; a boon is like a curse, the swearer can stipulate anything he wants.

–How could this possibly work? A baby's sex is the first thing anybody looks at!

–The parents keep it a dead secret.

–But her father is Drupada–remember Śikhaṇḍin is supposed to be a Pāñcālya–and a king will want to marry off a son as soon as possible to profit by the alliance.

–So he marries her off.

–This is incredible!

–Yes, of course the secret will be out then and cause a lot of strife, but the God's word comes true. At the last possible moment there will be a little miracle.

–Just like that?

–Hardly: a Yakṣa helps out.

–This is unheard of! What happens to the Yakṣa?

–Well, Kubera curses him in eternity.

–This is hardly fair!

–Oh, the Yakṣa gets his manhood back.

–Well, yes, it just could have happened.

The point I wish to make with this *monologue intérieur* of a

168. 5.174.11 ff.

storyteller trying to tie up one loose end of the *Mahābhārata* is that within the half millennium of the composition of the text, a minor element – minor only in terms of the five references, not in its consequence, which is Bhīṣma's death – could create a new legend, an instant tradition, which is acceptable not only because it is entirely epigonic in character, drawing on materials already there, but also because it is so utterly appropriate: the great Bhīṣma, fearfully famed for his abjuration of all women, in the end finds his undoing at the hand of one of them, whom he had cheated out of her rightful marriage. It has no precursors, and to my knowledge no successor. This last battle of Rāma is not part of his later biography as an *avatāra* of Viṣṇu.[169]

The story of *Ambā* uses elements exclusively from the *Mahābhārata*: the person of Ambā herself; Bhīṣma's abduction; her choice of Śālva, not even dignified by a proper name;[170] Bhīṣma's disdain for Śikhaṇḍin, and his consequent death; Bhīṣma's relationship with the Vasus; Rāma's friend Akṛtavraṇa as announcer of Rāma's arrival on the following day; Rāma's contention with *kṣatriyas*; Rāma's warning by his Fathers;[171] Rāma's retirement to Mt. Mahendra; Śiva's giving of dubious boons;[172] Drupada's attempt to get a son to kill an enemy. To it are added novel elements, which makes the conclusion of *Ambā* read like a secular *kathā*: how a friendly though foolish Yakṣa lent his manhood to a girl for a few days, and came deservedly to grief because of that – though, thankfully, not forever.

If we were to take this story seriously as simultaneous to the epic portions of the *Mahābhārata*, we would ultimately have to lay the death of Bhīṣma at the fragrant door of the Yakṣa Sthūṇākarṇa's mansion in a wood off Kāmpilya. I, among my trees of different ages, find this view of the enchanted forest absurd.

Myth and Epic – 5. Instructions

Vidurā and Her Son: Instruction as a Call to Arms

After listening to the echoing sounds of the story of *Ambā* in this series of essays about epic and myth, history and change, let us hark back to the sound of the epic as at one time it was heard, and also address ourselves to the issues of the didactic intentions of the *Mahābhārata*. For despite all the stress I have placed on the epic intentions of our text, I do not for a moment deny that in the course

169. Even the fullest account of this *avatāra* that I know of in the *Purāṇas*, *Bhāgavata Parāṇa* 9.15 f., does not pick up this episode.

170. Śālva is the name of his people; his proper name seems to be Saubha (so once in 5, 178, 10), if the Saubha king of 3.15 ff. is the same one.

171. This is clearly a part of the Rāma-Kārtavīrya *kṣatriya* massacre story; cf. 1.2.1 ff.; 3.117.1 ff.; cf. also the parallel *Aurva* story, 1.170.13 ff.

172. 1.189.41 ff.

of time it also acquired a didactic purpose. But while accepting the didacticism of what Hopkins called the "pseudo-epic,"[173] we should at least attempt to delineate to what specific purposes this teaching was applied.

One instance of such teaching is the text portion called *The Instruction of Vidurā's Son*. It is interesting because, like many such instances, it is presented not as part and parcel of the *Mahābhārata*, but as a quotation from elsewhere, an *itihāsaṃ purātanam* which "they quote" (*udāharanti*) on a topic that emerges from the text.[174]

After Kṛṣṇa's unsuccessful embassy to the Kauravas, he pauses to bid Kuntī, his father's sister, the mother of the Pāṇḍavas, farewell, and to ask for a message for her sons. Kuntī's most important message is for her eldest son Yudhiṣṭhira, and her language is powerful:

> Unearth your ancestral share that lies buried, strong-armed son! Do it with persuasion, bribery, subversion, punishment, or policy. Is there anything harder for me than, with my own relatives destitute, having to hope for the dole of *others*, after giving birth to you, delight of your enemies? Fight by the Law of kings, don't drown your grandfathers![175]

With relish she quotes a mother from another epic, Vidurā, "a famous, radiant, and irascible lady of high birth," who "once berated the son of her womb when he lay about dejectedly after his defeat at the hands of the king of Sindhu."[176]

Said Vidurā:

> Where did you come from? Neither I nor your father begot you! Too cowardly for anger, barely hanging on to a low branch, you are a man with the tools of a eunuch! You can feel sorry for yourself for the rest of your life, but if you want better, shoulder the yoke. Don't despise yourself, don't be satisfied with little. Plan great things, don't be afraid, have some backbone! Get up, coward, don't lie there defeated![177]

In this vein she continues for 130 glorious *ślokas*, in a martial, even bellicose Sanskrit that is highly idiomatic. This is the sound of ancient epic, hardly intended to "express certain abstract ideas through stories," but to stir the hearts and raise the courage of warriors. The fact that this language is placed in the mouth of a mother, Vidurā, and is quoted with approbation by another mother, Kuntī, to put spine into her son tells us that the old epic was not for men only. In

173. *The Great Epic*, passim.
174. It is the standard opening of many didactic inserts.
175. 5.130.30.
176. 5.131.4.
177. 5.131.5 ff.

the *Mahābhārata* too Draupadī regularly sounds more vindictive and belligerent than her husbands, with the possible exception of Bhīma.[178]

The compilers, or perhaps just the caption writers, of the *Mahābhārata* call Vidurā's harangue an "instruction," but it is clearly not didactic in the sense that other text portions are. The text must have survived because it was a stirring piece of *kṣatriya* oratory. At its provenance one can only guess. It is presented as a segment from another lay, of Saṃjaya and the king of Sindhu, which, like the *Bhārata* itself, went by the name of *Jaya*.[179] At one time there likely was a warlike literature of "Triumphs," and it is good to find, in a happily surviving segment like this, the encouragement to believe that before the *Mahābhārata* was "myth" there were epics. Nevertheless, in the *Mahābhārata* this inspiring fragment functions only as an "instruction."

Dhṛtarāṣṭra's Vigil: Instruction as Caution

For a categorically different kind of instruction, we may compare the well-nigh interminable sermon to which Vidura subjects his brother Dhṛtarāṣṭra, when the king cannot get to sleep on the eve of Saṃjaya's ambassador's report. Instead of mother Vidurā's thundering broadsides we have brother Vidura's relentlessly incessant rainy-season pitter-patter of peanuts of wisdom that should have lulled to sleep the most insomniac of worriers. The theme is all too familiar to readers of didactic Sanskrit: the blessings of virtue, the perils of vice. For this literature not only does not shy away from repetitiousness and redundancy, it is blissfully unaware of it. The chapters of Vidura's instruction provide one of the longest *longueurs* of the *Mahābhārata* so far. But we are here not to complain, but to try to explain why at some time a need for this lecture was felt, and by whom.

The immediate connections are obvious enough: "sagacious Vidura" is the wisest of the Kurus. He has always known, and frequently predicted,[180] where Duryodhana's enmity toward the Pāṇḍavas would end: in utter disaster for the Kurus. Vidura is the closest to an Indian "maternal uncle" that the Pāṇḍavas have at the Kaurava court; Duryodhana has his real maternal uncle in Śakuni. Vidura was there to warn the Pāṇḍavas about Duryodhana's likely trickery during their semi-exile in Vāraṇāvata.[181] He was the only one to raise his voice against the dicing match.[182] When the Pāṇḍavas have left for the forest, he accuses Dhṛtarāṣṭra of duplicity;

178. Even Bhīma seems to lapse temporarily in 5.72 ff.
179. Cf. 1.34.15; 20.
180. E.g., 1.197.1; 2.52.11.
181. 1.133.5 ff.
182. 2.55 ff.

when Dhṛtarāṣṭra berates him for his partiality and disowns him, Vidura joins the Pāṇḍavas in the forest until his brother repents and sends Saṃjaya to fetch him back.[183] He has other opportunities in *The Book of the Effort* to speak up; but his influence, always weak, has waned to nil. Nevertheless, he is now given a last chance to try to sway Dhṛtarāṣṭra, and he tries his best: every lecture ends with a peroration on the justice of the Pāṇḍavas' cause.[184]

This is the immediate setting, but there is more background, or, rather, more foreground now. The *Mahābhārata* in its present form has grown uneasily reluctant to start this war: the entire *Book of the Effort* is as much about the effort to prevent, or at least stall, the war as to raise arms. The political persuasiveness that Kṛṣṇa tries to exert is preceded by Vidura's moral persuasiveness. It is the exact opposite of mother Vidurā's instruction as a call to arms. Kṛṣṇa's own embassy is punctuated by narratives that keep stressing the unwisdom of rashness. In the end all these efforts, successively frustrated, become a more and more impressive testimony to the undesirability as well as the inevitability of this war.

I rather doubt that this effort at stalling is a narrative device to increase suspense on the part of the listener or reader. Nor does it tactically serve any purpose: no more armies are raised or new coalitions formed during this interval. No, this entire Book speaks to this inevitable, for already recorded, war as an acute moral embarrassment. Another, perhaps a new, sensibility finds expression here, one that a Vidurā would have scorned, and that Kuntī, in her envoy to Yudhiṣṭhira, will ignore. There is a *horror* of this war. This sensibility continues to express itself: at the moment of engagement there is the *Bhagavadgītā*,[185] followed by Yudhiṣṭhira's last call on the Kauravas.[186] And all this laying of the *onus* of this war on the Kauravas is not, as Holtzmann would argue, a transparent late attempt to whitewash the Pāṇḍavas, aggressors but victors—in the end the Pāṇḍavas themselves do not come off as simon-pure. What is present in the reflections of *The Book of the Effort* is the knowledge of the futility of this war, and an endeavor—it is there now in prospect; later, when the war is over, in retrospect—to deal with it as a moral lesson.

This war has been coming forever. There is a time for all things, a time for warning, a time for comfort. Vidura's instruction is one to caution; Sanatsujāta's, which follows it immediately, is one to console.

183. 3.5; 7.
184. 5.33.14 f.; 34.80 ff.; 35.66 ff. etc.
185. 6.23 ff.
186. 6.41.

Sanatsujāta: Instruction as Consolation

Vidura's sermon to Dhṛtarāṣṭra ends on an unexpected note. The king asks, "Is there anything, Vidura, that you have left unsaid?"[187] Vidura replies, "The ancient and eternal youth Santsujāta has proclaimed that there is no death."[188] Dhṛtarāṣṭra presses his brother to reveal this wisdom. Vidura demurs: he is the son of a *śūdra* woman and thus not entitled to speak. But he calls Sanatsujāta with his mind and asks him, "Pray do speak to [Dhṛtarāṣṭra], so that upon hearing it this Indra among kings may be translated beyond happiness and misery, and . . . so that old age and death do not overwhelm him . . . ."[189]

Sanatsujāta belongs with Sanatkumāra, Sanātana, and Sanaka to a Purāṇic group of four divine youths (*kumāra*), not born of woman but directly from Brahmā's mind. They are quite shadowy, but now and then they emerge as teachers, like Sanatkumāra in *Chāndogya Upaniṣad* 7, and Sanatsujāta here.

The *Sānatsujātīya* had a minor reputation as a philosophical classic. A Śankara has written a commentary on it,[190] and Deussen and Strauss, too, include it in their *Vier Philosophischen Texte des Mahābhāratam*.[191] The text certainly deserves more study than it has received and my few remarks below must be regarded as quite preliminary.

The *Sānatsujātīya* should probably be best approached as a brief, late-upaniṣadic text that very early attracted to itself, by way of appendix, commentary, and continuation, other texts that were considered to be of the same inspiration, not unlike the *Maitrāyaṇīya Upaniṣad*.[192] The text is in poor shape, also in the critical edition, which diverges here greatly from the Vulgate; this is a sign of early popularity, which subjected it to reinterpretations.

Its core seems to be the *triṣṭubh* verses of the beginning, in which the problem of death is addressed. This is followed, in *ślokas*, by reflections on *brahman* and wisdom, on the twelve vices and twelve virtues, and on *brahmacarya*. It ends with a mystical hymn on the manifestations of the Supreme, partly in *triṣṭubhs*, with the refrain: "The yogins behold the sempiternal blessed Lord."[193]

Whatever its provenance, the intention of *Sanatsujāta* in the *Mahābhārata* is upaniṣadic. It is probably for this reason that the

187. 5.41.1.
188. 5.41.2.
189. 5.41.8.
190. Published in Sri Sankaracharya, *Memorial Edition*, Volume XIII (Srirangam, no date), pp. 171 ff.
191. Paul Deussen and Otto Strauss, *Vier Philosophischen Texte des Mahābhāratam* (Leipzig, 1906).
192. J. A. B. van Buitenen, *The Maitrāyaṇīya Upaniṣad* (The Hague, 1961).
193. 5.45.1 ff.

teaching is attributed to Sanatsujāta, as Sanatkumāra is the teacher in *Chāndogya Upaniṣad* 7.[194] Thus it is Vedic in character, and it does not behoove a Vidura, the son of a *śūdra* woman, to promulgate it.

The instruction embodies a *jñāna*, an insight, which transcends the *vijñāna*, discursive knowledge, which Vidura has just set forth. It also offers consolation in its central tenet, which is that there is really no death, a thought of some comfort before a holocaust. Thus it functions in a manner comparable to the *Bhagavadgītā*, which begins with expounding that there really is no killing.[195]

Sanatsujāta maintains that "non-death" (*amṛtyu*), i.e., the conquest of what earlier texts called *punarmṛtyu* "re-death," comes about by conquering folly, which is distraction, through *ātmāvasannaṃ brahmacaryam*, the study-practice of the *brahman*, which is "sunk," absorbed, into the *ātman*.[196] This *yoga*—the word is not used yet—is here as elsewhere contrasted with the normal practice of ritual by those who "covet the fruits of their acts" (*karmodaye karmaphalānurāgās*), and who in consequence "follow after the *karman* resulting" (*tatrānu yānti*) and so "do not cross Death" (*na taranti mṛtyum*), i.e., do not cross over the realm of rebirth and death to the farther shore of non-death, of release from rebirth.[197] On the other hand, there is "he who thinks and destroys those fruits as they try to arise" (*yo'bhidhyayann utpatiṣṇuni* [sc. *phalāni*] *hanyād*), i.e., the one who, by having the proper mental attitude, the *buddhi*, destroys the fruits of his acts, that is to say, his *karman*, before this has a chance to come into being, but who is nevertheless not *pratibudhyamānah*, not "of contrary *buddhi*,"[198] not antagonistic to acting as such, out of disrespect (*anādareṇa*) for ritual acts.[199] Such a one is indeed himself "Death," inasmuch as "like Death, he eats them [the fruits of acts] aborning" (*mṛtyur ivātti bhūtvā*), i.e., destroys the fruits of his acts as they take on being.[200] This teaching concludes with the confident upaniṣadic *śravaṇaphala*, the "reward of listening to the instruction": "So, wise is the one who forsakes his desires."[201]

We have here in a nutshell the message of the *Gītā*: acts bind to the extent that you perform them because of the fruits they will yield; abjure the fruits by *buddhiyoga* and *asanga*, and you will incur no

194. Sanatkumāra promulgates to Nārada similarly a wisdom higher than ordinary erudition, ending: "The seer does not see death, etc.," an intriguing parallel (7.26.2).

195. *BhG*. 2.

196. 5.42.6.

197. 5.42.8.

198. Though *pratibudhyamāna* normally has the meaning of "awakening, becoming alert and enlightened," I take *apratibudhyamāna* here as "not having a contrary opinion," which suits the context better.

199. 5.42.9ab.

200. 5.42.9c.

201. 5.42.9d.

karman while performing acts. This teaching is mystically, but not incomprehensibly, cast in a context of thought associations about death: death as *this* death, and as continual death by *karman*; non-death by conquest of death through conquest of *karman* before it can arise; so that the *abhidhyāyan*, the *buddhiyukta*, becomes the death of *karman*. Be it conceded that all this is concisely, even densely put, but it is all there.

What interests me here is not the inevitable question whether these lines were condensed from the teaching of the *Gītā*, or the *Gītā* expanded from such verses, or whether, as is most likely, both texts are parallel statements of the solution of a serious ideological dilemma: if acts equal *karman* which equals *saṃsāra*, why act? What is interesting in the context of the purposes of such instructions in the didactic portions of the *Mahābhārata* is that both the *Sānatsujātīya* and the *Bhagavadgītā* have discovered a new ethical justification for the act, which is this war; it is a very subtle argument: Yes, this act is a task that cannot be shirked. And if this act be done as task, not for the rewards it yields, it shall have no unfavorable consequences for the soul.

This instruction must have been a comfort to Dhṛtarāṣṭra, as it will be to Arjuna.

Contents

5(49) *The Book of the Effort*

5.1–21 (B. 1–21; C. 1–644)
1 (1; 1). After Abhimanyu's wedding the Pāṇḍavas and their allies hold a council (1–5). Kṛṣṇa recalls Duryodhana's villainy and Yudhiṣṭhira's rectitude; an envoy should be sent to persuade Duryodhana to return half the kingdom (5–25).
2 (2; 27). Rāma agrees, but counsels a humble approach; after all, it was Yudhiṣṭhira's fault that he lost at the dicing (1–10).
3 (3; 41). Sātyaki protests: Yudhiṣṭhira had no choice, and the others are still playing tricks (1–10). If need be, the kingdom should be recovered by force (10–20).
4 (4; 64). Drupada agrees with Sātyaki; they should send out messengers and raise armies (1–25). He offers his house priest as envoy (25).
5 (5; 90). Kṛṣṇa, while stressing his own neutrality, declares his support of this plan and departs (1–10). The Pāṇḍavas and Kauravas start war preparations; the kings mobilize (10–15). Drupada sends his priest as envoy (15).
6 (6; 109). The envoy is instructed: he should try to estrange Bhīṣma, Droṇa, and Kṛpa from Duryodhana (1–15).
7 (7; 129). Arjuna and Duryodhana travel the same day to Dvārakā to seek Kṛṣṇa's alliance. The latter is asleep

when they arrive. Duryodhana, the first to arrive, sits by his head, Arjuna by his feet. On awaking he sees Arjuna first (1–5). Kṛṣṇa offers them either his army, or himself as a noncombatant. (5–15). Arjuna chooses Kṛṣṇa, Duryodhana the army (15–20). Duryodhana then approaches Rāma, who wishes to remain neutral, but Kṛtavarman joins him (20–30). Arjuna returns with Kṛṣṇa (30–35).

8 (8; 172). Śalya of Madra sets out to join the Pāṇḍavas. Learning this, Duryodhana builds elegant rest houses on his itinerary (1–10). On hearing that not Yudhiṣṭhira but Duryodhana built them, Śalya gives him a boon: Duryodhana chooses an alliance with Śalya (10). Traveling on to Yudhiṣṭhira, Śalya tells him what has occurred; Yudhiṣṭhira asks him to demoralize Karṇa when he acts as his charioteer (10–25). Śalya consents. Attempting to console Yudhiṣṭhira (25–35), he tells him the story of Indra's victory.

9–18 (B, 9–18; C, 227–569). The Victory of Indra.

19 (19; 570). Yuyudhāna Sālyaki joins Yudhiṣṭhira (1–5). So do Dhṛṣṭaketu of Cedi, Jayatsena of Magadha, and the king of Pāndya. With the armies of Virāṭa and Drupada, Yudhiṣṭhira has seven armies (1–10). Bhagadatta, Bhūriśravas, Śalya, Kṛtavarman, Jayadratha, Sudakṣiṇa, Nīla, Vinda, Anuvinda, the Kekayas join Duryodhana for a total of eleven armies (10–30).

20 (20; 603). The envoy arrives in Hāstinapura. He conveys his message that the Pāṇḍavas do not want war but demand their kingdom (1–15).

21 (21; 624). Bhīṣma supports him, pointing to Arjuna's might (1–5). Karṇa protests: the Pāṇḍavas have not carried out the covenant and should return to the forest (1–15). Dhṛtarāṣṭra decides to send his bard Saṃjaya as envoy to Yudhiṣṭhira (15–20).

Vaiśaṃpāyana said;

5.1.1 When the Kaurava heroes had celebrated
Abhimanyu's wedding with their joyous party,
They rested four dawns with confidence;
Thereupon they repaired to Virāṭa's hall.

The opulent hall of the king of the Matsyas

Was wondrous with choicest of jewels and gems,
With thrones set out, and fragrant with flowers—
It was there that repaired those eminent kings.

The two kings of men, Drupada and Virāṭa,
Then seated themselves on the thrones in front,
With the ancient, by all kings respected
Grandfather* of Rāma and Janārdana.**

Close by the king of Pāñcāla sat
The champion Sātyaki with Rauhiṇeya,***
And near to the Matsya king were seated
Janārdana and Yudhiṣṭhira.

5 And all King Drupada's sons sat there
and Arjuna, Bhīma, and Mādrī's twins,
Pradyumna and Sāmba, heroes in war,
And Virāṭa's son with Abhimanyu.

All Draupadī's sons had seated themselves—
All heroes who were the likes of their fathers
In gallantry, beauty, and strength of arms—
On handsome thrones that sparkled with gold.

When those great warriors were sitting thus
In their colorful robes and dazzling jewels,
That king-filled opulent hall was shining
Like the sky that is covered with spotless planets.

They held converse such as suited their concourse
With manifold tales, these heroes of men,
And the kings for a while were sunk in reflection
While they looked expectant at Kṛṣṇa's face.

They ceased conversing, those lions of kings,
Assembled by Mādhava**** there in the cause
Of the Pāṇḍava's task, and they lent their ears
To his meaningful speech of great consequence.

Kṛṣṇa said:

10 It is known to you all, my lords, how this
Yudhiṣṭhira was defeated with tricks
By Subala's son, and his kingdom taken,
And a covenant made to live exiled.

* = Śini.
** = Kṛṣṇa.
*** = Bala-Rāma.
**** = Kṛṣṇa.

They were capable fiercely to conquer the earth,
But they stood by their truth and carried it out,
These sons of Pāṇḍu and Bharata chiefs—
That abominable vow of thirteen years.

How they spent the difficult thirteenth year
In your vicinity undiscovered,
While bearing with intolerable hardships,
You know full well how they spent it all.

This being the case, think of what will profit
The Dharma's son and Duryodhana,
And profit the Kurus and Pāṇḍavas,
Consistent with Law, correct, earning fame.

King Dharma is not one to covet the realm
Of even the Gods, if it were under Unlaw;
He would strive for lordship in even some village
If it were consistent with Law and Profit.

15 We know that the kings' ancestral domain
Was plundered by Dhṛtarāṣṭra's sons
In a manner deceitful, but nevertheless
Submitted to great, unendurable hardship.

Dhṛtarāṣṭra's sons did not vanquish the Pārtha
In battle by virtue of their own splendor;
But still the king as well as his brothers
Desires to see them hale and hearty.

The sons of Kuntī, the sons of Mādrī,
These heroes of men have only the wish
To regain what the Pāṇḍavas won for themselves
By defeating and forcing the kings of the earth.

You know how they* tried by various means
To kill these foe-endurers when children,
Unholy and fearful, they sought to seize
Their domain—it's a matter of common knowledge.

Observing the full-grown greed of them
And the spirit of Law of Yudhiṣṭhira,
And seeing their family piety,
You must now decide, together and singly.

20 They have always been avowed to the truth,
And accomplished correctly the covenant:

* = the Kauravas.

Therefore, if now they are treated falsely,
They might kill Dhṛtarāṣṭra's sons altogether.

On learning of the king's* mistreatment by them,
Their friends will all rally to their side,
Engage them in battle and bring them down,
And while being killed, kill off the embattled.

If it is your view nonetheless that they
Are too few to be able to vanquish them,
Still, banding together and joined by their friends,
They will yet strive to destroy them all.

At present the mind of Duryodhana
Is still unknown, what he plans on doing.
As long as the enemy's mind is not known,
How could you decide what best had be done?

Therefore let depart from here a pure,
Law-minded, well-born, and undistracted
Ambassador able to persuade them
To return to Yudhiṣṭhira half the kingdom.

Vaiśaṃpāyana said;
25 Having heard Janārdana speak his word
Full of Profit and Law, mild, equable,
His senior brother raised his voice
And applauded his speech most strongly, O king.

Baladeva said:
2.1 Your lordships have heard from Gada's elder**
A speech consistent with Profit and Law,
Of benefit to Ajātaśatru,***
Of profit to King Duryodhana.

Relinquishing half the kingdom, the sons
Of Kuntī heroically strive for his good;
Dhṛtarāṣṭra's son, by giving up half,
Shall rejoice with all of us joyfully.

By obtaining half the heroes of men—
If the others indeed act honorably—
Will be surely placated and find new joy,
There'll be peace among them and the subjects will profit.

* = Yudhiṣṭhira.
** = Kṛṣṇa.
*** = Yudhiṣṭhira.

It would please me if somebody were to go
And bring peace to the Kurus and Pāṇḍavas,
In order to learn Duryodhana's mind
And explain the words of Yudhiṣṭhira.

5 He must greet the Kaurava hero Bhīṣma,
The majestic son of Vicitravīrya,*
And Droṇa and son, and Vidura, Kṛpa,
The prince of Gāndhāra,** and the son of the *sūta*,

And all Dhṛtarāṣṭra's other sons
With their prominent strength and eminent learning,
Who all abide by their personal Laws,
World heroes who've aged in wisdom and years.

When they have all foregathered there
And the elders and citizens are assembled,
He must speak his word in most humble fashion
To suit the cause of the son of Kuntī.

Under no condition should they be hectored:
They have grasped their profit while resting on strength
Yudhiṣṭhira was approached like a friend,
And lost his domain while distracted by dicing.

Yudhiṣṭhira had been warned by his friends,
The Kaurava heroes, for he *could* not dice;
Yet he challenged the son of the king of Gāndhāra
Who himself was a master at playing the dice.

10 There were thousands of other gamesters whom
Yudhiṣṭhira could have defeated at dice,
Yet he left them aside and made his challenge
To Saubala, who then defeated him.

He was being played by his counter-player
And the dice were always hostile to him;
He lost his head and was soundly defeated,
And for that is Śakuni not to blame.

Therefore let him speak in the humblest fashion
To Vaicitravīrya*** and flatter him much:
In this way that man might be able to sway
Dhṛtarāṣṭra's son for the good of his cause.

* = Dhṛtarāṣṭra.
** = Śakuni.
*** = Duryodhana.

Vaiśaṃpāyana said:

While the Mādhava hero was thus holding forth
The champion Sātyaki flew in a rage
And berating those words of his thoroughly,
Himself raised his voice in wrathful speech.

Sātyaki said:

3.1 A man speaks in the manner of his soul, and you speak after the
shape of your inner soul! Brave men there are and also cowards:
both steady factions can be found among men. In the very same
lineage a eunuch and a hero may be born, as in the same tree one
branch yields fruit and the other none. It is not for me to protest your
words, plough-bannered one! But I protest to those who listen to you
5 speak, Mādhava. For how does one dare to speak even the slightest
ill of the King Dharma in the midst of a gathering without expecting
danger? Expert gamblers challenged that great-spirited man, and
beat him. He did not know the dice, he trusted them; was that a
lawful win? If they had come to his house and defeated Kuntī's son
while he was gaming with his brothers, then they would have
conformed to the Law. But by challenging a king who was bent on
the baronial Law and then defeating him with trickery—could they
indeed have acted more handsomely!

How then, after having staked all and now finally freed from his
forest sojourn, should he prostrate himself for coming into his
10 patrimony? Yudhiṣṭhira would not even have to plead too much at
all with others were he to covet their riches! Are they beholden to
the Law, are they not greedy for kingship who claim that the
Kaunteyas were discovered, while in fact they had completed their
sojourn? Bhīṣma pleaded with them, so did the great-spirited Droṇa,
but they refused to hand over to the Pāṇḍus their ancestral property.
I'd plead with them violently in battle with sharp arrows and drop
them at the feet of the great-spirited Kaunteya; and if they refuse to
prostrate themselves before the sage king, they'll go with their
15 councilors to Yama's seat, for they can no more bear the brunt of a
furious Yuyudhāna who is eager to fight than mountains can bear
the impact of the thunderbolt. Who indeed can withstand the Gāṇḍīva
bowman in battle, who the discus-wielder, or me, and who the
unassailable Bhīma? And what man who hopes to live can attack
the Yama-like twins of the hard bows, that illustrious pair, or
Dhṛṣṭadyumna Pārṣata? Or the five Pāṇḍaveyas* who foster
Draupadī's fame, those berserkers who equal the Pāṇḍus in stature
and valor? And the great archer Saubhadra,** unassailable even to

* = the Pāṇḍavas' sons by Draupadī.
** = Abhimanyu.

the Gods, and Gada, Pradyumna, and Sāmba, equal to Time,
20 thunderbolt, and fire? We here shall cut down Dhṛtarāṣṭra's son on
the battlefield with Śākuni and Karṇa, and anoint the Pāṇḍava!

There is no Unlaw at all in killing off enemies who are lying in ambush, but begging from foremen brings on Unlaw and infamy! Do not be slow to fulfill the desire of Yudhiṣṭhira's heart: the Pāṇḍavas must regain the kingdom Dhṛtarāṣṭra relinquished to them. So either let Pāṇḍu's son Yudhiṣṭhira have his kingdom, or let them all be killed in battle and sleep the long sleep on the flat of the earth!

Drupada said:

4.1 So no doubt will it be, strong-armed Sātyaki. Duryodhana will not
hand over the kingdom meekly, and Dhṛtarāṣṭra will comply with
him, for he loves his son; and so will Bhīṣma and Droṇa from poverty,
and Rādheya and Saubala* from folly. But in my judgment it was
not proper for Baladeva to speak as he did, for that applies to a man
who from the first wanted to act wisely. The Dhārtarāṣṭra should not
at all be addressed gently, for I know that he has evil intentions and
5 will not be swayed by gentleness. Talking gently to the ill-minded
Duryodhana is like being kind to an ass and rough to a cow. The
scoundrel thinks that one who speaks kindly is impotent: if we are
peaceable, the fool will think that he has won his cause.

What we should do is this, and spare no effort. We should send
word to our allies to raise troops for us. Let swift-moving messengers
go to Śalya, Dhṛṣṭaketu, mighty Jayatsena, and all the Kekayas.
Duryodhana is certain to send word to all of them too, but men who
10 are strict and have been loyal will accept the first bid. Therefore
hasten and be the first to exhort those Indras among men, for I think
that the task that is to be borne will be a heavy one. Let word at
once be sent to Śalya and the kings loyal to him, and to King
Bhagadatta who dwells by the eastern ocean, to Amitaujas, Hārdikya,
Ugra, and Āhuka, the farsighted Malla, and Rocamāna, my lord.
Bṛhanta should be fetched, and King Senābindu, Pāpajit, Prativindhya,
Citravarman, Suvāstuka, Bāhlīka, Muñjakeśa, and the overlord of
15 Cedi, Supārśva, Subāhu, and the great warrior Paurava, the rulers of
the Śakas, Pahlavas, and Daradas, the Kāmbojas, Ṛṣikas, and the
Western Anūpakas, Jayatsena, the king of the Kāśis, the kings of the
Five Rivers, the unassailable son of Kratha, the mountain kings,
Jānaki, Suśarman, Maṇimat, Pautimatsyaka, the king of the Pāṃsu,
the valiant Dhṛṣṭaketu, Auḍra, Daṇḍadhāra, and gallant Bṛhatsena,
Aparājita, Niṣāda, Śreṇimat, Vasumat, Bṛhadbala of august might,
Bāhu, victor over enemy cities, the mighty King Samudrasena with
20 his son, Adāri, Nadīja, King Karṇaveṣṭa, Samartha, Suvīra, Mārjāra

* = Karṇa and Śakuni.

and Kanyaka, Mahāvīra, Kadru, Nikara and the frightful Kratha,
Nīla, Vīradharman and the gallant Bhūmipāla, Durjaya, Dantavakra,
Rukmin, Janamejaya, Āṣāḍha, Vāyuvega, and King Pūrvapālin,
Bhūritejas, Devaka, and the son of Ekalavya, the Kārūṣaka princes
and valiant Kṣemadhūrti, Uddhava, Kṣemaka, King Vāṭadhāna,
25 Śrutāyus, Dṛḍhāyus, and the mighty son of Śālva, and Kumāra the
chief of the Kalingas, berserk in war—let word at once be sent to them,
for that I think is best.

And this brahmin, O king, my house priest, must at once be dispatched to Dhṛtarāṣṭra. Imprint on him the words with which Duryodhana should be addressed, and Lord Śaṃtanava and Dhṛtarāṣṭra should be addressed, and the most sagacious Droṇa.

Vāsudeva said:

5.1 These words indeed are appropriate for the yoke-bearer of the
Somakas, and will bring success to the cause of the august Pāṇḍava.
This is indeed the first thing to do if we wish to follow the right
course. A man would be foolish if he were to act otherwise. However,
we ourselves owe the Kurus and Pāṇḍus the same loyalty, no matter
how the Pāṇḍavas and the others see fit to behave. We all, like you,
have been fetched here for the wedding, and now that the wedding
5 is over we shall return happily to our houses. You yourself are the
oldest of the kings in age and learning, and we are like pupils to you,
no doubt of that. Dhṛtarāṣṭra has always thought highly of you, and
you are friendly with both the teachers, Droṇa and Kṛpa. You are the
one to send them word in the Pāṇḍava's interest, and whatever word
you send will surely be all right with all of us. If then the bull of the
Kurus makes peace as he rightly should, there will be no great loss of
brotherly feeling on the part of the Pāṇḍus. But if Dhṛtarāṣṭra's son
out of arrogance and folly does not make peace, then, after you have
10 sent for the others, summon us too. . . . Then the slow-witted fool,
Duryodhana, will with councilors and relations meet his fate for
having angered the Gāṇḍīva bowman!

Vaiśampāyana said:

Thereupon King Virāṭa, having treated the Vārṣṇeya hospitably,
allowed him to depart home with his escort and relatives. When
Kṛṣṇa had gone to Dvārakā, the Pāṇḍavas, headed by Yudhiṣṭhira,
and King Virāṭa made preparations for war. Virāṭa, his relatives, and
and King Drupada sent messengers to all the lords of the earth. On
receiving word from the bulls of the Kurus, the Matsya, and the
Pāñcāla, the powerful lords of the earth foregathered joyfully.
15 Upon hearing that a large army was gathering for the sons of
Pāṇḍu, Dhṛtarāṣṭra's son too assembled the kings. The entire earth
was astir with kings that marched in the Kurus' or the Pāṇḍavas'

cause, O king. Troops of champions arrived from hither and yon and shook Goddess Earth with her mountains and forests. The king of Pāñcāla with Yudhiṣṭhira's approval thereupon sent his own priest, who was old in years and wisdom, to the Kurus.

Drupada said:

6.1 Of all creation the creatures that breathe are best, of the breathing
creatures the intelligent are best, among the intelligent, men are best,
and of men the brahmins. Among the brahmins those who are
learned in the Veda are best, and among those learned in the Veda
those are best who have achieved understanding. You yourself, sir, I
consider the finest of those who have achieved understanding. You
are of distinguished lineage, age, and learning, and in wisdom you
are not the lesser of Śukra and Āngirasa. You know fully how the
Kaurava acts, and how acts Yudhiṣṭhira Pāṇḍava, the son of Kuntī.
5 The Pāṇḍavas were, with Dhṛtarāṣṭra's foreknowledge, deceived by
their enemies, and though cautioned by Vidura, the king catered to
his son alone. For Śakuni, a seasoned gambler, deliberately challenged
Kuntī's son, who did not know the dice, yet uprightly abode by the
way of the baronage. After having thus tricked Dharma's son
Yudhiṣṭhira, they will under no circumstances return his kingdom to
him of their own accord. But when you address Dhṛtarāṣṭra with
words consistent with the Law, you will surely sway the hearts of his
warriors. Vidura too will carry out your words and estrange Bhīṣma,
10 Droṇa, and Kṛpa. Then with his councilors estranged and his
warriors reluctant, Dhṛtarāṣṭra will have the task of guiding them
back to their common cause.
Meanwhile the Pārthas will happily devote their full attention to
military matters and to the building up of supplies; but the others,
while they are disunited and you hang about, will doubtlessly not
attend to army business in the same fashion. This I see as the
principal purpose of your embassy. Also, after meeting with you,
Dhṛtarāṣṭra just might follow your lawlike words. You yourself are
a man of Law, and acting toward them in a lawly spirit, you should
dwell, with those who are disposed to compassion, on the hardships
15 of the Pāṇḍavas; and speaking to the elders of the family Law that
their ancestors observed, you will—I have no doubt about that—
alienate their hearts from Dhṛtarāṣṭra. You have nothing to fear
from them, for you are a Veda-wise brahmin, sent on an embassy,
and old to boot. At the conjunction of Puṣya and the hour of Jaya,
depart quickly to the Kauraveyas to ensure the success of the
Kaunteya's cause.

Vaiśaṃpāyana said:

With those instructions of the great-spirited Drupada, his house priest, who was perfect in deportment, started for the City of the Elephant.

Vaiśaṃpāyana said:
7.1 After Kṛṣṇa and Baladeva Mādhava had left for Dvāravatī with all
the hundreds of Vṛṣṇis, Andhakas, and Bhojas, the king the son of
Dhṛtarāṣṭra* learned through envoys and commissioned spies about
all the doings of the Pāṇḍavas. Hearing that the Mādhava** had
returned, he himself* departed for Dvārakā city, with fine, wind-fast
horses and not too large an escort. That very same day Dhanaṃjaya,
son of Pāṇḍu and Kuntī, also traveled quickly to the lovely city of
the Ānartas.
5 When the tigerlike men, both scions of Kuru, arrived in Dvārakā,
they approached and found Kṛṣṇa sleeping. While Govinda was asleep
Suyodhana entered and sat down on a throne at Kṛṣṇa's head. After
him the spirited Diademed One*** entered too and stood, bowing and
folding his hands, at Kṛṣṇa's feet. On waking the Vārṣṇeya saw the
Diademed One first. He bade both of them welcome, and after
honoring them duly Madhusūdana asked for the reason of their
coming. Then Duryodhana said to Kṛṣṇa with a laugh, "In this
10 approaching war you should come to my aid, for you bear me equal
friendship with Arjuna, and you are equally allied with us, Mādhava.
I was the first to come to you today, Madhusūdana, and the strict
who observe precedence join forces with the one who was the first to
come. You are on earth the very first of the strict, Janārdana, and
always esteemed: maintain the conduct of the strict!"

Kṛṣṇa said:
I have no doubt that you have come first, but it was Dhanaṃjaya
Pārtha whom I saw first, king. Since you came first and I saw him
15 first, I shall lend my help to both of you, Suyodhana. But it is said
that the first choice goes to the youngest, therefore Dhanaṃjaya
Pārtha should choose first. I have a large multitude of cowherds who
match my strength, famed as the Nārāyaṇas, all veteran warriors.
Those troops, who are unassailable in war, will go to the one, and
I myself, as noncombatant and with weapons downed, will go to the
other in this conflict. Pārtha, you choose first from among the two,
whatever pleases you better, for by Law you have the first choice.

Vaiśaṃpāyana said:
At these words of Kṛṣṇa, Kuntī's son Dhanaṃjaya chose Keśava
20 who would not fight in the war. Duryodhana was extremely pleased
to win the thousand thousands of warriors, Bhārata, knowing that
Kṛṣṇa was excluded from the war. Having gained the entire army,
the king of terrible might went to the mighty son of Rohiṇī.**** He told
him the reason for his coming, and Śauri replied to the Dhārtarāṣṭra,
"Everything I said before at Virāṭa's wedding party should be known

* = Duryodhana.
** = Kṛṣṇa.
*** = Arjuna.
**** = Balarāma.

to you, tigerlike man. For your sake I spoke to restrain Hṛṣīkeśa,*
O scion of Kuru, saying again and again that I was friendly with both
25 parties. Kṛṣṇa did not agree with my assertion, and I myself cannot
for a moment do without Kṛṣṇa. Looking to Vāsudeva I have decided
to ally myself with neither the Pārthas nor Duryodhana.

"You have been born in the dynasty of the Bhāratas, which is
honored by all the kings: go and wage war according to the baronial
Law, bull of the Bhāratas!"

At these words Duryodhana embraced the plough-armed Rāma and
knowing that Kṛṣṇa had excluded himself from the war, he thought
that victory was assured. Dhṛtarāṣṭra's son the king went to
30 Kṛtavarman, and Kṛtavarman gave him a grand-army. In the midst
of the entire awesome army the scion of Kuru returned home
joyously and brought happiness to his friends.

When Duryodhana had gone, Kṛṣṇa said to the Diademed One,
"What was in your mind that you chose me when I will not fight?"

Arjuna said:

There is no doubt that you are able to kill them all, and I too can
kill them alone, best of men. You are famous throughout the world,
and the glory of this war will go to you. I too aspire to glory,
therefore I have chosen you. It has been my desire to have you as
my charioteer, a desire of lengthy nights—pray bring my wish about!

Vāsudeva said:

35 It is fitting that you compete with me, Pārtha! I shall be your
charioteer, let your wish come true!

Vaiśaṃpāyana said:

So, accompanied by Kṛṣṇa and in the midst of the flower of the
Dāśārhas, the Pārtha returned joyfully to Yudhiṣṭhira.

Vaiśaṃpāyana said:

8.1 Śalya, on hearing from the messengers, marched with a large army
to the Pāṇḍavas, king, accompanied by his warrior sons. His army
camp stretched for about a league and a half, for so large was the
force that this bull among men supported. His champions wore
colorful armor, bore colorful banners and bows, wore colorful
ornaments, and rode colorful chariots and mounts. Bull-like barons
by the hundreds and thousands, in native dress and adornment, were
5 the captains of his army. Terrifying the creatures and shaking the
earth, he marched his army slowly with frequent rests to where the
Pāṇḍava was.

When Duryodhana learned that the great warrior was coming with
a large host, he hastened to him in person and paid homage to him.
Duryodhana had lodges built in his honor in pleasant environs,

* = Kṛṣṇa.

sparkling with gems and well-decorated. When Śalya stopped at those lodges, Duryodhana's ministers honored him like an Immortal at every place with all due homage. Then he reached another lodge effulgent like the mansion of a God. Provided with choice and superhuman thrills, Śalya's head swelled, and he despised the Sacker of Cities.* The bull among barons questioned the servants most happily, "Which of Yudhiṣṭhira's servants have built these lodges? Let the builders be brought in, for I think they deserve a reward." Thereupon Duryodhana, who had been hidden, showed himself to his maternal uncle. Upon seeing him and knowing the effort he had made, the king of the Madras embraced him and, pleased, said to him, "Take whatever you desire!"

Duryodhana said:

Be true to your word, honest man! Let a veritable boon be granted to me: pray be the commander of my entire army!

Vaiśaṃpāyana said:

"Done!" said Śalya, "What else can I do?" "Done!" answered Duryodhana and repeated it. He took leave from Śalya and returned to his own city. Śalya went to the Kaunteyas to tell them what he had done.

When Śalya reached Upaplavya, he entered the headquarters and saw all the Pāṇḍavas there. The strong-armed Śalya on meeting with the sons of Pāṇḍu accepted, as was proper, the water to wash his feet, guest water, and a cow. The king of the Madras, slayer of enemies, first asked about their health, then embraced Yudhiṣṭhira with great joy, and also the happy Bhīma and Arjuna and both twins, who were his sister's sons. Sitting down on a stool Śalya said to the Pārtha, "Are you still in good health, scion of Kuru, tiger among men? How fortunate that you are freed from your exile in the forest, greatest of victors. You have done a very difficult thing, living in the empty forest, king, with your brothers and Kṛṣṇa here, Indra of kings. You have also accomplished the difficult, dreadful life in concealment. For one who has been thrown from his kingdom it is all misery, for where would he find happiness? But after this great misery that was brought about by the Dhārtarāṣṭra you will attain to happiness, king, when you have killed your enemies, enemy-burner. Great king, overlord of men, you know the facts of life, that is why it is not in you to act from greed, son!" Thereupon the king told him of his encounter with Duryodhana, O Bhārata, and of the entire promise he had made and the boon he had bestowed.

Yudhiṣṭhira said:

You did well, heroic king, to carry out cheerfully what you had promised Duryodhana in so many words. But, bless you, there is one

* = Indra.

thing I wish you to do, lord of the earth. Surely you are the equal of Vāsudeva in battle, great king, and when the chariot duel of Karṇa and Arjuna befalls, you will no doubt have to act as Karṇa's charioteer, best of princes. If you wish to do me the favor, king, protect Arjuna. Obscure the splendor of the *sūta*'s son, which will bring us victory. It is not a proper thing to do; still agree to do it, uncle!

Śalya said:

Listen, Pāṇḍava, bless you. You ask me that I obscure the splendor
of that evil son of a *sūta* on the battlefield. I am certain to be his
charioteer in the fight, for he has always thought me Vāsudeva's
30 equal. When he is eager to fight, tiger of the Kurus, I shall talk to
him discouragingly and belittle him, so that he will lose pride and
splendor, Pāṇḍava, and be easy to kill—this I promise as truth! I shall
do what you ask me, son, and whatever else I can do in your cause.
The misery you suffered with Kṛṣṇa at the dicing, the insults that the
son of the *sūta* uttered, the trouble with Jaṭāsura and Kīcaka,
resplendent prince, all the unholy hardships that Draupadī suffered
35 like Damayantī—all this misery will end in happiness, hero. Do not
fret over it, for fate is stronger. Indeed, great-spirited men find
troubles, Yudhiṣṭhira; even Gods have had their troubles, lord of the
earth. Indra, the great-spirited king of the Gods, and his wife also
experienced great unhappiness, so we hear, King Bhārata.

5(49a) The Victory of Indra

5.9–18 (B, 9–18; C, 227–550)

9 (9; 227). To spite Indra, Tvaṣṭar creates a three-faced son Viśvarūpa, who threatens to swallow the universe. Indra sends Apsarās to seduce him, but they fail (1–15). Indra kills him with the thunderbolt, but his remains stay effulgent (15–20). Indra urges a woodcutter to cut off the three heads (20–30). Birds issue from the severed heads (30–35). Enraged, Tvaṣṭar engenders and empowers Vṛtra, who swallows Indra but loses him while yawning (35–45). Embattled, Indra retreats; the Gods invoke Viṣṇu (45–50).

10 (10; 290). Indra and the Gods beseech Viṣṇu (1–5). Viṣṇu tells them to make a truce with Vṛtra, then he will help Indra kill him (5–10). Vṛtra demands conditions which seemingly make betrayal impossible (10–30). When Indra sees Vṛtra at twilight by the sea, he kills him with foam that has been entered by Viṣṇu (30–35). Under the burden of brahmin murder (Viśvarūpa) and treason (Vṛtra), Indra retreats to the waters. Drought now reigns (35–45).

11 (11; 342). The Gods decide to anoint the human Nahuṣa as their king; he receives the boon that he will assume the power of anyone he looks at (1–5). Nahuṣa, turned libertine, covets Indra's wife Śacī (5–15). She turns to Bṛhaspati who promises help (15–20).

12 (12; 368). Pressed by Nahuṣa, the Gods come to fetch Śacī (1–15). Bṛhaspati advises her to stall Nahuṣa (15–30).

13 (13; 401). Śacī asks Nahuṣa for time to find out about Indra; he grants it (1–5). The Gods beseech Viṣṇu, who says Indra should sacrifice to him; he does so and is cleansed (5–15). Nahuṣa still rules, and Indra disappears (15–20). Śacī invokes the Whisper (20–25).

14 (14; 428). Śacī follows the Whisper to a pond where she finds Indra inside a lotus fiber. She exhorts him to kill Nahuṣa (1–15).

15 (15; 446). Indra tells Śacī to demand that Nahuṣa ride a palanquin carried by seers (1–5). She does and Nahuṣa is delighted to comply (5–20). Śacī calls on Bṛhaspati to fetch Indra; he calls on Fire and orders a search. Fire fails, but has not explored the waters. Bṛhaspati orders him to do so (20–30). Fire demurs (30).

16 (16; 483). Bṛhaspati praises Fire (1–5). Fire enters the waters and finds Indra in a lotus fiber. Bṛhaspati praises Indra, who becomes strong (5–15). Bṛhaspati asks his help against Nahuṣa. Kubera, Yama, Soma, and Varuṇa join Indra; they demand a share in the sacrifice; so does Fire (15–30).

17 (17; 520). Agastya appears and reveals that Nahuṣa has been toppled because he erred on Vedic mantras *and kicked Agastya's head. He is cursed to be a boa constrictor on earth (1–15). The universe congratulates Indra (15–20).*

18 (18; 544). Indra bestows a boon on Angiras, and reigns happily (1–5). Śalya exhorts Yudhiṣṭhira (10–15). The story is praised (15–20). Śalya promises to demoralize Karṇa and joins Duryodhana (20–25).

Yudhiṣṭhira said:
9.1 How was it, Indra of kings, that the great-spirited Indra found dire
trouble with his wife? That I wish to know.
Śalya said:
Listen, king, to the ancient story of yore, how Indra and his wife
found trouble, O Bhārata.

There was Tvaṣṭar Prajāpati, the best of the Gods and a great
ascetic, and they say he created a three-headed son to spite Indra;
and with his three dreadful faces, which resembled sun, moon, and
5 fire, this resplendent Universal Being* coveted Indra's rank. With one
mouth he studied the Vedas, with one he drank wine, and with one
face he looked as though swallowing all of space. A meek and
controlled ascetic, intent on Law and austerity, he practiced great
and severe self-mortification that was difficult to accomplish, enemy-
tamer. Seeing the power of austerity and the substance of this
boundlessly splendid Triśiras, Indra became desperate, fearing that he
might become Indra: "How to addict him to pleasure and stop him
from austerities? If that three-faced creature grows, he will swallow
the three worlds." The wise God reflected much, bull of the Bharatas,
10 then he ordered the Apsarās to seduce the son of Tvaṣṭar, "Go and
hasten to addict Triśiras to the pleasures of the flesh and seduce him
forthwith. In the raiment of love and with your full hips, seduce him
with your ravishing allurements, bless you, and appease my fear.
I feel sick, beautiful women, quickly take this terrible fear away
from me!"
The Apsarās said:
We shall do our best to seduce him, Śakra, so that you will have
nothing to fear, slayer of Vala! That ascetic who sits there as though
burning things with his eyes, we shall all go and seduce him, God.
We shall try to put him in our power and take away your fear!
Śalya said:
15 Dismissed by Indra they went to Triśiras. There the beautiful
nymphs attempted to stir his lust with all manner of allurements,
exhibited their dances, displayed their charms, pranced about; but
the ascetic did not become excited and controlled his senses,
imperturbable as the full ocean. They put forth their best efforts and
returned to Śakra. Folding their hands they all said to the king of the
Gods, "It is impossible to sway this unapproachable man from his
self-control, my lord. Do whatever is next to be done, sir."
Wise Śakra paid respects to the Apsarās, dismissed them and
20 thought about a means to kill the great-spirited Triśiras. Pondering in
silence the heroic king of the Gods, both determined and sagacious,

* = Viśvarūpa.

decided, "I shall smite him this very day with my thunderbolt, and he will soon cease to exist. A growing, though still weak enemy should not be ignored by a stronger man." Having made up his mind, informed by the scriptures, and having firmly resolved on slaying him, Śakra hurled his firelike, awesome, and terrifying bolt angrily at Triśiras. Hit hard by the thunderbolt, Triśiras fell dead as a mountain peak, shaken loose, falls on earth.

Indra, seeing him lying like a boulder where he had been struck
by the bolt, found no shelter but was set afiire by the other's
splendor: though killed, he so blazed forth with splendor that he
25 looked alive. Then Śacī's Consort saw a woodcutter thereabouts at
work, and Pāka's Chastiser said quickly to him, "Cut off his heads
at once; do as I tell you!"

The woodcutter said:

He is very big-shouldered; my axe will not cut through. Moreover, I cannot do a deed which the strict condemn.

Indra said:

Have no fear. Do quickly as I tell you, for by my grace your axe shall become like a thunderbolt.

The woodcutter said:

For whom am I to know you who have done this grisly deed today? Tell me truly, I wish to hear it.

Indra said:

I am Indra, the king of the Gods, woodcutter. You must know me. Do as I have told you, axeman, do not tarry.

The woodcutter said:

30 How is it you are not shamed by this cruel deed, Śakra? Having
killed the seer's son, are you not afraid of brahmin murder?

Indra said:

Later I shall perform a difficult Law to cleanse myself. This was a mighty enemy whom I have killed with my thunderbolt. Even now I am distraught, woodcutter; I still fear him. Quickly cut off his heads, and I will do you a favor. People will give you at the sacrifice the head of the victim as your share. This is your favor, woodcutter; quickly do what I want.

Śalya said:

Having heard these words of great Indra, the woodcutter cut off
35 the heads of Triśiras with his axe. When they had been cut off there
issued from Triśiras heathcocks and partridges and sparrows on all
sides. From the mouth with which he had studied the Veda and drunk
the Soma, heathcocks swiftly flew away. Partridges flew out of the
mouth which had made him look as though drinking up all of space,
Pāṇḍava. From the mouth of Triśiras which he used to drink liquor
sparrows flew away, bull of the Bharatas.

With the heads cut off Maghavat was rid of his fever and happily
40 went to heaven, while the woodcutter too went home. But when
Tvaṣṭar Prajāpati learned that Śakra had killed his son, his eyes
reddened with rage, and he said: "Inasmuch as he has done harm
to my austerity-practicing son, who was always forgiving and
controlled, was master of his senses and had no guilt, therefore I shall
engender Vṛtra so that he may slay Śakra. Let the worlds witness my
puissance and the great power of my austerities, and so let the Indra
of the Gods witness, that evil-spirited wicked heart!" That most
glorious ascetic touched water, poured an oblation into the fire,
created the grisly Vṛtra and said to him, "Enemy of Indra, grow by
the power of my austerity!" He grew up, propping up the sky,
resembling sun and fire. "What do I do?" he said, risen like the sun
of doomsday. "Slay Indra!" he was told, and he went to heaven.

45 Thereupon there ensued a most gruesome and protracted battle
between the raging Vṛtra and Vāsava, O best of the Kurus. The heroic
Vṛtra lay hold of God Indra of the Hundred Sacrifices and, filled with
fury, opened his maw and swallowed him. But when Śakra had been
swallowed by Vṛtra, the mettlesome Gods, disturbed, created the Yawn
to be Vṛtra's perdition; and when Vṛtra yawned, the Slayer of Vala
gathered up his limbs and came out of the gaping maw. Ever since
in these worlds the yawn has dwelled in breathing creatures. Seeing
Śakra come out, all the Gods rejoiced. Once more the battle of Vṛtra
and Vāsava began, the terrible and very lengthy battle of the enraged
pair, bull of the Bharatas.

50 When Vṛtra, burgeoning with strength, swelled in that battle by
the power of Tvaṣṭar's austerities, Śakra wisely retreated; and at his
retreat the Gods fell to the deepest despair. Driven witless by the
splendor of Tvaṣṭar they all joined Śakra and sought counsel from the
hermits, Bhārata. Bemused by fear, they pondered upon their task,
king, and all went in their thoughts to the great-spirited and
imperishable Viṣṇu. All sat on the peak of Mount Mandara, desirous
of slaying Vṛtra.

Indra said:

10.1 The entire indestructible universe is permeated by Vṛtra, for
nothing can stand up to him. In olden times I was capable of doing
it, but now I am impotent. What can I do now, bless you? He seems
to me very hard to overcome. This great-spirited, splendiferous
creature is of boundless valor in battle: he may well devour the
entire three worlds with Gods, Asuras, and men. Therefore, celestials,
listen to what I have resolved upon. Let us approach the seat of
Viṣṇu and consult together with the great-spirited God—then we
shall find the means of slaying that miscreant!

Śalya said:

5 At these words of Maghavat the Gods and the hosts of seers sought mercy with the merciful God, the mighty Viṣṇu. Panic-stricken by Vṛtra they all said to Viṣṇu, sovereign of the Gods, "Thou hast bestridden the three worlds with three strides. Thou hast fetched the Elixir, Viṣṇu, and killed the Daityas in battle. Having smitten the great Daitya Bali, thou hast made Śakra the overlord of the Gods. Thou art the master of all the worlds, this universe is strung upon thee, for thou, God, art the Great God, honored by all the worlds. Be thou the recourse of Indra and the Gods, O highest of the Immortals. The entire world has become permeated with Vṛtra, O slayer of Asuras!"

Viṣṇu said:

10 Of necessity I must do what is most beneficial to you. Therefore I shall explain a plan, whereby Vṛtra shall cease to exist. Go ye with seers and Gandharvas to the lair of him who wears all forms. Act toward him with conciliation, then you shall vanquish him. By virtue of my splendor, O Gods, Śakra will proceed and I shall invisibly enter his supreme weapon, the thunderbolt. Go, good Gods, with the seers and Gandharvas, and quickly contract a truce between Vṛtra and Śakra.

Śalya said:

Thus addressed by the God the seers and celestials departed
15 together, placing Śakra at their head. All those august beings then approached Vṛtra who, ablaze with splendor, set fire to the ten regions. Then the Gods and Śakra set eyes on Vṛtra, who seemed to devour the three worlds, the sun, and the moon. The seers drew nearer and spoke to Vṛtra these friendly words, "The entire universe is permeated by your splendor, invincible one! You are unable to vanquish Vāsava of abundant valor. It has been a very long time that the two of you have been fighting, and all the creatures, with Gods, Asuras, and men, are suffering from it. Let there be friendship between you and Śakra forever, Vṛtra, and you will attain to happiness and the everlasting worlds of Śakra."

20 Hearing the seers' words the very powerful Asura Vṛtra replied to them all, bowing his head, "What all of you, my lords, and all the Gandharvas have said I have heard. Now listen to me too, blameless ones. How can there be peace between Śakra and me? How can there be friendship between our two splendors, Gods?"

The seers said:

For the strict to meet be desired at least once.
What later must be shall later be.
One does not transgress a pact with a strict man.
Therefore of the strict be a meeting desired.

Of the strict the encounter is firm and eternal;
The wise must speak to profit in hardships;
To meet with a strict man is to great profit:
Therefore the wise one will not kill the strict one.

25 Indra is respected by the strict and is the abode of those who are
great-spirited; for he is a speaker of the truth, undejected, wise in the
Law, and well-assured. Therefore let there be eternal peace between
Śakra and you, and thus you must have faith and not resolve
otherwise.

Śalya said:

When the refulgent Vṛtra heard the words of the great seers, he
replied, "Surely I owe you reverend ascetics respect. Let everything
I say here be carried out, Gods; then I shall do all that these bulls
30 among the twiceborn are asking. I am not to be slain by Śakra and
the Gods with matter dry or wet, rock or wood, thunderbolt or
weapon, by day or by night, Indras among priests. Such a pact with
Śakra will please me forever." "Certainly!" replied the seers, O bull
of the Bharatas.

When this compact had been made, Vṛtra was happy. Śakra, filled
with resentment, remained constantly on the alert, pondering on the
means that were appropriate for the killing of Vṛtra. The Slayer of
Vala and Vṛtra,* perturbed, kept watching for an opening. Then
upon a time he saw the great Asura on the ocean shore, at twilight,
when the hour had come that is lovely and parlous. The blessed lord
thought of the boon that the great-spirited one had been granted:
"It is grisly twilight now, and neither day nor night. I surely can
35 kill him now, my all-grasping enemy! If I do not kill Vṛtra with
deceit today, that powerful and gigantic great Asura, I shall find no
rest."

As he thought this way while keeping Viṣṇu in mind, he saw
foam there in the ocean, piled up like a mountain: "This is neither
dry nor wet, nor is it a weapon. I shall throw it at Vṛtra, then he
shall instantly perish." Quickly he threw the foam at him with the
thunderbolt, and Viṣṇu entered the foam and destroyed Vṛtra.

When Vṛtra had been killed, the skies cleared up, a salubrious
40 wind began to blow, and the creatures rejoiced. The Gods,
Gandharvas, Yakṣas, Rākṣasas, Snakes, and the great Seers praised
great Indra with various lauds. Paid honor by all beings and
conferring peace on all beings, Law-wise Vāsava, in joyous spirits
now that his enemy was killed, paid homage with the deities to
Viṣṇu, who is the greatest in the three worlds. After the puissant
Vṛtra, terrifier of the Gods, had been slain, Śakra was overcome by

* = Indra.

his falsehood and became greatly depressed; he had already taken on the burden of brahmin murder in the case of Triśiras. The Indra of the Gods went to the end of the worlds and, bereft of consciousness and wits, was no longer aware of anything, being pressed down by his guilt. He dwelled concealed in the Waters, writhing like a snake.

Thus, when Indra had become lost, afflicted by the dread of brahmin murder, the earth looked ravaged, her trees gone, her wilderness dried up. The streams of the rivers dwindled and the ponds
45 stood empty. Panic seized all creatures because of the drought, and the Gods and all great seers trembled sorely. Kingless, the entire world was beset by disasters, and the Gods became afraid: "Who shall be our king?" In heaven Gods and seers were now without a King of Gods, and none of the Gods set their minds on kingship.

Śalya said:

11.1 Thereupon all the seers and the thirty lordly Gods said, "Let us anoint the majestic Nahuṣa to be the king of the Gods." They all went and said, "Be thou our king, sire!" Nahuṣa replied to the Gods and hosts of seers accompanied by the Ancestors, O king, while seeking his own advantage, "I am weak and unable to protect you. It is the powerful man who becomes king, and power indeed has always been Śakra's." Once more the Gods, headed by the seers, said, "Guard your kingdom of heaven reinforced with our austerities. No doubt we stand
5 in awesome fear of one another. Be anointed, O Indra of kings, be the king of heaven. If Gods, Dānavas, Yakṣas, Seers, Rākṣasas, Ancestors, Gandharvas, and Ghosts come within your range of vision, you shall with your eyes seize their splendor for your own and become strong. Always putting Law first, be the overlord of all the worlds and the herdsman of the brahmin seers in heaven!"

When Nahuṣa obtained this rare boon and attained to kingship in heaven, he became lust-driven, though he had always been law-spirited. In all the gardens of the Gods and in the parklands of Nanda, on Mount Kailāsa, the ridge of the Himālaya, Mounts Mandara, Śveta, Sahya, Mahendra, and Malaya, and by oceans and rivers
10 Nahuṣa, being the king of the Gods, played many games in the midst of the Apsarās and the maidens of the Gods, and listened to many kinds of divine stories that captivated heart and ear, and to all manner of music and songs of sweet melodies. Viśvāvasu, Nārada, the hosts of Gandharvas and Apsarās, and the six seasons in bodily form attended upon the Indra of the Gods, while a fragrant breeze blew, lovely and pleasantly cool.

While the great-spirited Nahuṣa was thus at play, divine Śacī, the beloved queen of Śakra, came before his eyes. And when he had seen her, he wickedly said to all the courtiers, "Why doesn't this Goddess,

15 the queen of Indra, wait on me? I am the Indra of the Gods and the
sovereign of the world! Śacī must come to my house at once."
Hearing this the Goddess spoke desperately to Bṛhaspati: "Protect me
from Nahuṣa, brahmin, I seek shelter with you! You always say that
I am endowed with all marks that betoken luck, Brahmā; you say
that as the beloved of the king of the Gods I partake of perfect bliss,
and that, being a devoted wife avowed to her husband, I shall never
be a widow. So have you spoken before—now make your words
come true! Never before, my lord, have you spoken idly; may it
therefore be true what you have said, best of the twiceborn."
20 Thereupon Bṛhaspati replied to Indrāṇī, who was numb with fear,
"Goddess, what I have said of you shall certainly be true. Soon you
shall see the king of the Gods Indra return here. I tell you the truth,
you have nothing to fear from Nahuṣa. I shall shortly reunite you
with Śakra."

Then Nahuṣa heard that Indrāṇī had sought refuge with Bṛhaspati
Angiras, and the king was furious.

Śalya said:

12.1 Knowing that Nahuṣa was enraged, the Gods, led by the seers,
spoke to the king of the Gods, whose aspect was dreadful, "King of
the Gods, shed your wrath! When you are angry, O lord, the world
with Asuras and Gandharvas, Kiṃnaras and great Snakes, trembles.
Shed your wrath, good sir, the likes of you do not anger! The Goddess
is the wife of another, be gracious, lord of the gods! Turn your mind
away from evilly molesting another's wife. You are the king of the
5 Gods, bless you, protect the subjects with Law!" Thus addressed
by the Gods and seers, Nahuṣa did not heed their words, being
befuddled with lust.

Then the overlord of the Gods spoke to the deities concerning Indra, "Indra once violated Ahalyā, the glorious consort of a seer, while her husband was alive: why did you not stop him? Indra has of old perpetrated many cruelties, lawless deeds, and deceptions: why did you not stop him? The Goddess shall wait on me, and that will be best for herself, and so things will always be well with you too!"

The Gods said:

We shall bring Indrāṇī as you wish, lord of heaven. Shed your wrath, hero, be pleased, king of the Gods!"

Śalya said:

10 The Gods and the seers, having thus spoken, O Bhārata, then went
to Bṛhaspati to tell Indrāṇī the unholy message: "We know that
Indrāṇī has come for shelter to your house, and that you have
granted her safety, O Indra of priests, best of divine seers. The Gods,
Gandharvas, and seers placate you, splendid one: Indrāṇī must be

handed over to Nahuṣa. Nahuṣa, the resplendent king of the Gods, is superior to Indra: let the fair-hipped and fair-complexioned woman choose him for her husband!"

At these words the Goddess shed loud tears, and sobbing miserably she said to Bṛhaspati, "I do not want to have Nahuṣa for my husband and abandon my master. I have come to you for refuge, brahmin, save me from great danger!"

Bṛhaspati said:

I shall not give up a woman who has come for shelter, Indrāṇī. That is my resolve. I do not give you up, blameless woman, who are law-wise and law-wonted. Especially being a brahmin, I do not want to do the forbidden, for I have heard the Law, practice truth, and know the ordinance of the Law. I shall not do it. Go, best of Gods! Hear what Brahmā long ago sang in this matter:

"His seed will not grow at seeding time,
His rain will not rain at the time of the rains,
If he hands an afraid refugee to his foe;
And when he needs rescue he shall not find it.

"That witless man finds his harvest barren,
That mindless man will be cast from heaven,
Who delivers a refugee who is afraid,
And the Gods shall refuse whatever he offers.

"Before their time his offspring will perish,
His Fathers will banish him forever,
If he hands an afraid refugee to his foe,
The Gods and Indra will hurl him their bolt."

Knowing this well I shall not hand over Śacī Indrāṇī, who is famed in the world as the beloved queen of Indra. Let be carried out, best of Gods, what is of profit to her and of benefit to me, for I shall not hand over Śacī.

Śalya said:

Thereupon the Gods said to Bṛhaspati, chief of the Angirases, "Counsel us, Bṛhaspati, what better course we should take."

Bṛhaspati said:

Let the fair Goddess ask Nahuṣa for some delay, which will be of advantage to Indrāṇī as well as us. Time authors many obstacles; Time will lead on Time. Nahuṣa is prideful and powerful on account of his boon.

Śalya said:

When he had thus spoken, the Gods said pleased, "Brahmin, you have spoken well; this will be good for all celestials, best of the twiceborn, and let the Goddess be placated." Then the Gods, led by

the Fire, all said to Indrāṇī, attentively wishing for the good of the
world, "You carry the entire universe of standing and moving
30 creatures. You are a devoted wife and true. Go to Nahuṣa: King
Nahuṣa, who lusts after you, will soon perish, Goddess, and Śakra
will resume the overlordship of the Gods."

Having made her decision for the furtherance of the cause, Indrāṇī bashfully went to Nahuṣa of dreadful aspect. And Nahuṣa, seeing her endowed with youth and beauty, was excited, that villain whose mind had been transported by lust.

Śalya said:

13.1 When the king of the Gods Nahuṣa saw her, he said, "I am the
Indra of all three worlds, sweet-smiling Śacī! Love me as your
husband, fair-hipped and fair-complexioned woman." At these words
of Nahuṣa the Goddess, who was devoted to her husband, shuddered
from terror like a plantain in a wind gust. Bowing to Brahmā and
folding her hands at her forehead, she spoke to the king of the Gods,
whose aspect was dreadful, "I want to gain some time from you, lord
of the Gods, for it is not known what has happened to Śakra or
5 where he has gone. After the truth of the matter has become known,
or if it cannot be found out, I shall wait on you, my lord, this I
declare to you as truth."

Nahuṣa rejoiced at Indrāṇī's words.

Nahuṣa said:

So shall it be, full-hipped woman, just as you have told me. You must come when you know—you will remember your oath.

Śalya said:

With Nahuṣa's leave the fair Goddess strode out and wretchedly
she went to Bṛhaspati's dwelling. Upon hearing her words the Gods,
headed by Fire, consulted together diligently in Śakra's cause, best of
kings. Meeting with the God of Gods, the puissant Viṣṇu, the
10 eloquent Gods said to him dejectedly, "Śakra, the king of the hosts
of Gods, is in the power of brahmin murder. You are our last resort,
sovereign of the Gods! The first-born Lord of the Universe, you have
become Viṣṇu for the protection of all creatures. After Vāsava killed
Vṛtra by the grace of your prowess, he was covered with brahmin
murder, O best of the hosts of Gods. Instruct how he may be
released."

Viṣṇu, hearing these words of the Gods, replied, "Śakra must
sacrifice to me. I shall purify the Thunderbolt-Wielder. When the
Chastiser of Pāka has offered a holy Horse Sacrifice, he shall return
to being Indra with nothing to fear. By his own deeds the wicked
Nahuṣa will come to perish. You must endure him unweariedly for
15 some time yet." After hearing this propitious and truthful speech of
Viṣṇu, which was like Elixir, all the hosts of Gods with teachers and
seers strode to the region where Śakra lay swallowed up by fear.

There unfolded the glorious Horse Sacrifice of the great-spirited Indra
that would cast out the brahmin murder for his purification, O king.
He distributed the brahmin murder over the trees, rivers, mountains,
earth, and women, Yudhiṣṭhira. And having cast it out and distributed
it, Vāsava, the lord of the Gods, lost his fever, was purified of evil,
and was his own master again. The Slayer of Vala, seeing that Nahuṣa
was not to be shaken from his rank, that he fed on the vigor of all
20 creatures and was unassailable because of the gift of the boon, he,
the heroic Consort of Śacī, once more disappeared and, invisible to all
creatures, wandered about biding his time.

When Śakra had disappeared, Goddess Śacī was filled with sorrow
and wailed piteously, "Woe Indra! If I have given gifts, offered
sacrifices, and satisfied my gurus, or if there be truth in me, then
I shall have but one husband! I shall pay worship to this auspicious
and divine Night that has fallen in the Northern Course, and my
desire must come true." The Goddess thereupon attentively worshiped
the Goddess Night, and by virtue of her devotedness to her husband
25 and her truthfulness she brought forth the oracular Whisper. The
Goddess said to the Whisper, "Show me the place where the king of
the Gods is. Be truth seen by truth!"

Śalya said:

14.1 The Whisper attended to the good and beautiful Goddess when she
saw that she, endowed with youth and beauty, waited on her.
Indrāṇī happily paid honor to her and asked, "I wish to know you;
who are you, fair-faced one?"

The Whisper said:

I am the Whisper, Goddess. I have come and appeared to you, since
I am satisfied with your truth. You are a devoted wife and possessed
of restraint and self-control. I shall show you God Śakra, the Slayer of
Vṛtra. Follow me quickly, bless you, and you shall see the chief of
the Gods.

Śalya said:

5 Indrāṇī then followed the Goddess, who had started. Passing
beyond the forests of the Gods and many mountains, she crossed the
Himālaya and went to its northern flank. She came to a sea many
leagues wide and went to a large island wooded with various trees
and creepers. There she saw a divine pond that was covered with all
kinds of birds, lovely, a hundred leagues wide and as many long.
Five-colored celestial lotuses, about which bees were buzzing, were
blowing there by the thousands, Bhārata. She broke the stalk of a
lotus and entered it with the Whisper; and there she saw the God
of the Hundred Sacrifices, who had entered into a fiber.

10 When she saw her lord in a very tiny body, the Goddess and the
Whisper themselves became tiny in form. And Indrāṇī praised Indra
for his famous feats of yore. Upon her praise the God Sacker of Cities

said to Śacī, "Why have you come and how did you discover me?"
Thereupon she related the acts of Nahuṣa: "When he attained to
Indrahood, he became drunk with power; and filled with pride, the
villain cruelly said to me, O God of the Hundred Sacrifices, 'Wait on
me!' and he set a time for me. If you do not save me, lord he will put
me in his power. He outraged me, Śakra, and so I have come to you.
Kill that gruesome Nahuṣa, strong-armed Indra, for his intentions are
15 evil. Reveal yourself, slayer of Daityas and Dānavas! Recover your
splendor, my lord, and govern the kingdom of the Gods!"

Śalya said:

15.1 At these words of Śacī the blessed lord replied, "This is not the
time for valor. Nahuṣa is most powerful; he has been strengthened by
the seers with oblations to Gods and Ancestors, glowing woman! But
I shall set to work a plan, Goddess, and you pray carry it out, a secret
task, my lovely, which you must not talk about anywhere. Go to
Nahuṣa, woman of the slender waist, and say to him when you are
alone, 'Lord of the world, come to me on a wagon drawn by the
seers!" Say to him, 'That way I shall be pleased and submit to you.' "
5 Told thus by the king of the Gods, his lotus-eyed wife said, "So
shall it be!" and betook herself to Nahuṣa. When Nahuṣa saw her,
he said surprised, "Be welcome, full-hipped woman! What can I do,
sweet-smiling one? Love me, who love you, my pretty! What do you
desire, spirited woman? My lovely of the slender waist, I shall do
what you want done. Don't be bashful, fair-hipped Goddess, have trust
in me, I swear by the truth that I shall do what you say."

Indrāṇī said:

I am waiting out the time you have allowed me, lord of the world.
Thereafter you shall be my husband, overlord of the Gods! Ponder
10 upon what I want done in my heart, king of the Gods. I will tell you
what, sire, if you will do me this favor. Carry out what I say with
affection; then I shall be yours to command! Indra had horses for
mounts, and elephants and chariots—now I want from you, overlord
of the Gods, an unprecedented carriage, such as neither Viṣṇu nor
Rudra have, or the Asuras and Rākṣasas. My lord, great king, let all
the seers together carry you on a palanquin, for that will pleasure
me, my king! Don't just be the equal of Asuras and Gods, capture
the splendor of all with your prowess, by a mere glance at them. No
one shall dare stand before you boldly!

Śalya said:

At these words, they say, Nahuṣa rejoiced, and the king of the
15 Gods replied to the blameless woman, "That is indeed an
unprecedented carriage that you describe, fair-skinned Goddess; it
pleases me mightily! I am your slave, my lovely. Surely one who
employs seers as beasts is not one of little prowess! I am a powerful

ascetic, the lord of future, past, and present. When I am wroth the
world ceases, everything rests on me—Gods, Dānavas, Gandharvas,
Kiṃnaras, Snakes, and Rākṣasas. All the worlds, sweet-smiling one,
are no match for my anger! I take for myself the splendor of anyone
whom I perceive with my eye. Therefore I shall carry out your words,
Goddess, no doubt of that. The Seven Seers shall carry me, and all the
brahmin seers. Behold our greatness and affluence, fair-skinned one!"
20 Having thus spoken he dismissed the fair-faced Goddess. That
unbrahminic, powerful, lust-ridden villain, who was besotted by the
gift of the boon, yoked the seers, who were self-controlled to his
celestial chariot, and had them carry him about.
When Nahuṣa had dismissed Śacī, she said to Bṛhaspati, "Little of
the time that Nahuṣa allowed me is left. Quickly search for Śakra;
show compassion to me who love him." "Certainly," replied the
blessed lord Bṛhaspati to her; "you have nothing to fear from the
evil-minded Nahuṣa, for he shall not last long. The vile man is lost—
ignorant of the Law, he is slain by the sages' carrying of him, my
25 lovely. I shall offer an oblation to destroy the evil spirit, and uncover
Śakra. Have no fear, be blessed!" Thereupon the splendid Bṛhaspati
made the fire blaze and according to the rite offered a superb oblation
in order to discover where the king of the Gods might be. Out of it
arose the blessed God Fire in person and assumed a wondrous
womanly form. Suddenly he disappeared. With speed beyond
imagining he searched the regions and the by-regions, mountains,
forests, earth, and sky, and returning after a mere instant went on
to Bṛhaspati.

The Fire said:

Bṛhaspati, I can find the king of the Gods nowhere. The waters
alone remain, and I cannot enter the waters: they are out of my
reach, Brahmā. What else can I do for you?

Śalya said:

30 The Guru said to him, "Enter them, splendid One!"

The Fire said:

I cannot enter the waters, it will be my perdition! I seek refuge
with you, hail to you, splendid One! Fire has sprung from water, the
baronage from brahminhood, iron from rock: their ubiquitous power
vanishes before their sources.

Bṛhaspati said:

16.1 Thou, Fire, art the mouth of all the Gods, thou art the Carrier of
the Oblation. Thou art within all creatures and thou runnest
concealed as their witness. The sages call thee one, and again they
call thee triple. Were the world deserted by thee it would perish that
instant, O oblation-carrying Fire. The bramins after paying homage to
thee go the sempiternal course they have won with their deeds,

together with their wives and sons. Thou alone carriest the oblation, thou alone art the ultimate oblation. To thee they offer the Sessions and the sacrifices at the supreme ritual.

5 Having made the three worlds, thou offering-carrier,
Thou cookest them blazing when the time has come.
The begetter of this entire vast world,
Thou, God of the Fire, art its final foundation.

Thou, Fire, they call the clouds, and thou art the lightning flashes. The flames that issue from you burn all the creatures. On thee rest all the waters, on thee this whole world. Nothing in the three worlds is hidden from thee, O purifier. Everyone loves his mother, so enter the waters fearlessly. I shall make thee grow with eternal brahmic spells.

Śalya said:

At this praise of Bṛhaspati, the supreme sage the blessed Fire spoke pleased this excellent word, "I shall show you Śakra—this I declare to you as the truth!"

10 Having entered the waters, including oceans and ponds, the Fire went to the lake where the God of the Hundred Sacrifices was lying. There he searched the lotuses, bull of the Bharatas, and found Indra in the middle of a fiber. Quickly he returned and said to Bṛhaspati, "The lord is hidden inside a lotus fiber in a very tiny body." Accompanied by Gods, seers, and Gandharvas, Bṛhaspati went and praised the Slayer of Vala for his ancient feats.

"Thou wert the killer of the grisly Asura Namuci, and of Śambara
15 and Vala, both of dreadful prowess. Grow, thou of the Hundred Sacrifices, destroy all foes! Rise up, Thunderbolt-Wielder, behold the Gods and seers assembled! Great Indra, by killing the Dānavas thou hast rescued the worlds, O lord. Resorting to the foam of the waters that was strengthened by the splendor of Viṣṇu, thou hast slain Vṛtra of yore, king of the Gods, lord of the world!

By all creatures, desirable one, thou art
To be worshipped, none in the world is your equal.
Thou, Śakra, supportest the creatures all,
Great feats hast thou wrought in the cause of the Gods.

Protect the Gods and the worlds, great Indra, gain strength!"

When he had thus been praised, Indra grew very slowly, and resuming his own body, he became filled with strength. The God said
20 to the Guru Bṛhaspati, who was waiting for him, "What is there left that need be done for you? The great Asura Tvāṣṭra* is dead, and so is the giant Vṛtra, who wanted to swallow the world."

* = Triśiras.

Bṛhaspati said:

The human king Nahuṣa has attained to the kingship of the Gods by the splendor of the Gods and the hosts of seers, and oppresses us grievously.

Indra said:

How did Nahuṣa attain to the rare kingship of the Gods, Bṛhaspati, of what austerities possessed, and of what puissance?

Bṛhaspati said:

The frightened Gods desired a Śakra
When thou hadst relinquished Indra's high station.
And the Gods, the Fathers, the hosts of the seers
And the throngs of Gandharvas foregathered all.

They went and spoke to Nahuṣa, Śakra:
"Be thou our king and herd our world!"
Then Nahuṣa said, "I have not the power—
With splendor and *tapas* ye must make me swell."

25 And the Gods at his words did as he had asked:
He became a king of dreadful prowess.
Now king of the world, he has made the ascetics
His beasts and thus evilly travels the worlds.

His horrible poisonous eye robs splendor—
You must never set eyes on Nahuṣa!
All the frightened Gods are running in hiding
Lest they should glance upon Nahuṣa.

Śalya said:

As the best of the Angirases, Bṛhaspati,
Was speaking, Kubera, the guard of the world,
And ancient Yama, Vivasvat's son,
King Soma and Varuṇa came there too.

When they there had gathered, they said to great Indra,
"How lucky that Tvāṣṭra and Vṛtra are dead,
How lucky we see thee hale and unscathed,
With thine enemies finally slain, O Śakra!"

Then Śakra replied in the proper fashion,
Exhorting them so they'd leave Nahuṣa:
"The God-king Nahuṣa is dread-looking,
Please give me your aid in subduing him!"

30 They answered, "Nahuṣa is dread-looking,
His eyes are poison, we fear him, O God.
If thou wert to vanquish this Nahuṣa, king,
Then we should deserve our share, O Śakra!"

Quoth Indra, "So be it. The lord of the waters,
Kubera and Yama attain the great Unction
Today together with this person himself:
We shall vanquish the dread-eyed Nahuṣa!"

Thereupon the Fire said to Śakra, "Bestow
On me also a share, and I shall give you aid!"
And Śakra replied, "You shall have it too:
One share for Indra-and-Fire at the rite!"

Upon reflection the blessed lord Great Indra, the Chastiser of Pāka, gave Kubera the overlordship of all the Yakṣas and their riches, Vaivasvata* that of the Ancestors, and Varuṇa that of the waters; this boon-granting Śakra did with due honor.

Śalya said:

17.1 Now, while the sagacious king of the Gods was thinking with those World Guardians about a means of killing Nahuṣa, the blessed ascetic Agastya appeared. He saluted the Indra of the Gods and said, "With good fortune dost thou thrive, because Viśvarūpa has been killed and the Asura Vṛtra slain! And by good fortune, too, Nahuṣa has been toppled from his divine kingship, O Sacker of Cities, and by good fortune do I look upon you with all your enemies slain, Slayer of Vala!"

Indra said:

Be welcome, great seer, I am pleased at the sight of you. Pray accept from me the foot water, the rinsing water, the *arghya*, and the cow!

Śalya said:

5 When that good hermit, a bull among brahmins, had been honored and seated, the lord of the Gods joyfully interrogated him: "I wish to hear you tell, best of the twiceborn, sir, how Nahuṣa of the evil resolve was ousted from heaven.

Agastya said:

Śakra, listen to the happy news of how the ill-spirited King Nahuṣa, villainous and prideful of his strength, was toppled from heaven. The lordly divine seers and untainted brahmin seers, wearied of carrying that evil-doer Nahuṣa around, raised a question to him, God, greatest of victors: "The *mantras* that have been promulgated by Brahmā for the Sprinkling-of-the-Cows, are they authentic or not?" they asked, O Vāsava. And Nahuṣa, his wits befuddled by darkness, replied, "No."

The seers said:

10 You are engaged in Unlaw, you do not know the Law: to us they are authentic, as it has been formerly declared by the great seers!

* = Yama.

Agastya said:

While he was arguing with the hermits, Vāsava, this man, pressed
down by his Unlaw, touched me on the head with his foot. Because
of that he forfeited splendor and fortune, Consort of Śacī! And I said
to this perplexed and fear-ridden man, "For as much as you have
despoiled the pure *brahman* that was uttered by the ancients and has
been observed by the brahmin seers; as you have touched me on the
head with your foot; and as you have made the unassailable seers,
the likes of Brahmā, your beasts of burden to carry you about,
therefore vanish from heaven, deprived of light, evil one, and fall
15 down to the flat of the earth with your merit exhausted! For ten
thousand years you shall wander in the shape of a large snake; and
when the years are full, you shall regain heaven." Thus the scoundrel
was cast from divine kingship, enemy-tamer, and now we thrive with
good fortune, Śakra—that thorn of brahmindom is gone! Consort of
Śacī, return to heaven and protect the worlds, with your senses
mastered and your enemies slain, amidst the praises of the great
seers!

Śalya said:

Thereupon, in the midst of the hosts of great seers, the Gods, who
were greatly contented, and the Ancestors, Yakṣas, Snakes, Rākṣasas,
Gandharvas, the maidens of the Gods, all the throngs of the Apsarās,
the lakes, rivers, mountains, and oceans, O lord of the people, all
approached and said, "With good fortune dost thou flourish, slayer
of your enemies! The evil Nahuṣa has luckily been dispatched by the
20 sage Agastya. By good luck that doer of evil has been made into a
snake on the face of the earth."

Śalya said:

18.1 Śakra then, lauded by the hosts of Gandharvas and Apsarās,
mounted that Indra of elephants, Airāvata, who bore all the marks.
The effulgent Fire was there, and the great seer Bṛhaspati, and Yama,
Varuṇa, and the God of Riches Kubera. Surrounded by all the Gods
and by Gandharvas and Apsarās, Lord Śakra, the Slayer of Vṛtra,
went to the Three-World.

Reunited with Indrāṇī, the King of the Gods, He of the Hundred
Sacrifices, was possessed of perfect bliss and reigned again as king.
5 The blessed Lord Angiras appeared there and honored the Indra of
the Gods with spells from the *Atharvaveda.* Happily the Good Lord
Indra then bestowed a boon on Atharvāngiras: "In this Veda the
citation will be Atharvāngirasa by name, and you shall obtain a
share in the sacrifice." Having thus honored Atharvāngiras, the good
Lord of the Hundred Sacrifices, the King of the Gods, dismissed him,
O great king. Indra paid homage to all Thirty Gods and the austerity-
rich seers, O king, and happily ruled his subjects by the Law.

10 Thus it was that Indra and his consort found troubles and out of a
desire to slay his enemies lived a life of concealment. It must not
excite your wrath that you have found hardship in the wilderness,
Indra of kings, with Draupadī and your great-spirited brothers. So
shall you too regain your kingdom, Bhārata, Indra of kings, just as
Śakra did after slaying Vṛtra, O joy of the Kauravas. The evil-doer
Nahuṣa of wicked mind, that hater of brahmindom, was smitten by
Agastya's curse and has been removed for years without end: so too
your evil-spirited enemies, Karṇa, Duryodhana, and the others, will
15 quickly go to their perdition. Then you shall enjoy the sea-girt earth,
hero, with Draupadī and your brothers, O lord.

This story of *The Victory of Indra*, which measures up to the *Veda*,
should be heard by a king who wishes to triumph, while his armies
stand arrayed. For that reason I have told you about the Victory,
greatest of victors: great-spirited men grow when they are praised,
Yudhiṣṭhira. It spells the doom of the great-spirited barons,
Yudhiṣṭhira, through the fault of Duryodhana and the strength of
Bhīma and Arjuna. He who recites *The Victory of Indra* diligently, is
washed of his evil, wins heaven, and rejoices here and hereafter.
20 That man will be in no danger of enemies, not remain without sons,
meet with no calamity, and find a long life, in which he shall meet
victory, and no defeat at all!

Vaiśaṃpāyana said:

When Śalya had thus reassured the king, O bull of the Bharatas, that best of the bearers of the Law paid proper homage to him. Kuntī's son, strong-armed Yudhiṣṭhira, upon honoring Śalya's words, replied to the king of the Madras, "You will no doubt become Karṇa's charioteer and obscure his splendor by your praises of me!"

Śalya said:

I shall do as you tell me, and whatever else is in my power.

5(49) The Book of the Effort (continued)

Vaiśaṃpayana said:

19.1 Thereupon the hero Yuyudhāna, the great champion of the Sātvatas, came with a large, four-membered army to Yudhiṣṭhira. His brave and powerful warriors, who hailed from many countries, ornamented the army as they brandished their manifold weapons. The army glistened with flashing battle-axes, slingshots, spears, javelins, maces, lances, hatchets, missiles, spotless sabres and swords, bows, helmets, all sorts of arrows wiped with oil. Adorned with all that weaponry the cloudlike army had the aspect of a monsoon cloud with lightning flashing. That grand-army entered Yudhiṣṭhira's troops, king, and vanished in them like a little stream in the ocean.

Likewise the powerful bull of the Cedis, Dhṛṣṭaketu, took a grand-army and joined the boundlessly august Pāṇḍavas. Mighty Jayatsena of Magadha, Jarāsaṃdha's son, joined the King Dharma with one grand-army. Also the Pāṇḍya, O Indra of kings, went to Yudhiṣṭhira's side surrounded by many warriors that dwelled on the ocean shore. His army looked surpassing handsome in that gathering of troops, O king, with fine gear, and mighty. Drupada too had an army adorned with champions from many countries and his own warrior sons. Likewise army commander Virāṭa, king of the Matsyas, went over to the Pāṇḍavas with the chiefs of the mountain tribes. From everywhere a total of seven grand-armies, astir with manifold flags, joined the great-spirited Pāṇḍus, ready to fight the Kurus, and they brought joy to the Pāṇḍavas.

No less joy did King Bhagadatta bring to the Dhārtarāṣṭra, whom he gave a whole grand-army. His unassailable force, made up of Chinese and Mountain Men, shone as a forest of *karṇikāras* shines with golden *kancana* trees. The champion Bhuriśravas, too, and Śalya joined Duryodhana, O joy of the Kurus, with a grand-army each. Kṛtavarman Hārdikya and the forces of the Bhojas and Andhakas went to Duryodhana with one grand-army. His troops shone with those tigerlike men, who wore garlands of wild flowers, as a wood with *must* elephants at play. The kings that dwelled by the Sindhu and in Suvīra came led by Jayadratha, shaking the mountains. Their multitudinous grand-army appeared like many-colored rainclouds swept by the wind. Sudakṣiṇa the Kāmboja joined the Kauravya with a grand-army, along with the Greeks and Scythians, O lord of the people. The mass of his army appeared like a swarm of locusts, and when it reached the Kaurava forces it disappeared among them. King Nīla of Māhiṣmatī arrived with the heroes of the South, who brandished dark weapons. Both kings of Avanti, surrounded by a mighty force, came to Suyodhana with a grand-army each. The tigerlike Kekayas, the five brother-kings, also hurried thither with a grand-army, gladdening the Kauravya. From everywhere three other armies converged, the forces of great-spirited princes, O bull of the Bharatas. Thus eleven grand-armies turned to Duryodhana, eager to find the Kaunteyas, stirring with manifold flags.

There was not enough room in Hāstinapura, Bhārata, sire, even for the principal kings and their chief warriors. The entire vast land, rich in treasure and grains, of the Five Rivers—all of the Jungle of the Kurus, the Rohitaka Forest, the whole Desert Country, Ahicchattra,

Mount Kālakūṭa, the bank of the Ganges, O Bhārata, Vāraṇa, Vāṭadhāna, and the Yāmuna hills—was completely overrun by the army of the Kauraveyas.

Such was the army beheld by the priest whom the king of Pāñcāla had sent to the Kauravas.

Vaiśaṃpāyana said:

20.1 Drupada's priest approached the Kauravya and was hospitably
received by Dhṛtarāṣṭra, Bhīṣma, and Vidura. He asked about the
good health of all of them, then spoke as follows in the midst of all
the army leaders.
"All of you know the eternal Law of the kings; but, known though
it be, I shall repeat it to lead up to my statement. Dhṛtarāṣṭra and
Pāṇḍu are known to be the sons of the same father, and to have
5 equal rights to the patrimony, there is no doubt of that. It is the sons
of Dhṛtarāṣṭra who now possess the ancestral heritage, but why
indeed have the sons of Pāṇḍu not obtained their paternal share?
This is the case: you know that the Pāṇḍaveyas never received their
patrimony, which was appropriated by the Dhārtarāṣṭra. Many a
time have the others made attempts on the lives of the Pāṇḍaveyas
with murderous means, but as they had life left to live, they could
not be dispatched to Yama's domain.
"The great-spirited brothers fostered a new kingdom with their
own resources, but it was robbed from them deceitfully by the lowly
Dhārtarāṣṭras and Saubala. This one here* approved even of an act
like that, and the Pāṇḍavas were forced to live in the forest for
10 thirteen years. The heroes and their wife, outrageously mistreated in
the assembly hall, suffered many more terrible hardships in the forest.
Then, in the city of Virāṭa, like men who had undergone another
birth, these great-spirited men endured extreme hardship, as though
they were the evildoers.
"All of them have now put behind them all the previous injuries,
and the bulls of the Kurus now wish only for reconciliation with the
Kurus. Their friends, fully aware of how they acted and how
Duryodhana did, should please win over Dhṛtarāṣṭra. For the heroes
do not want war with the Kurus—the Pāṇḍavas want what is theirs,
15 without devastating the world. Whatever the reason the Dhārtarāṣṭra
gives for waging war, it is not to be credited. Indeed, they are so much
stronger, for as many as seven grand-armies have gathered ready to
fight with the Kurus and are waiting for his orders. There are other
tigerlike men equal to a thousand grand-armies—Sātyaki and
Bhīmasena and the puissant twins. On one side are gathered eleven
armies, but on the other side stands strong-armed Dhanaṃjaya of
the many forms.

* = Dhṛtarāṣṭra.

"Just as the Diademed One outclasses all armies, so does the strong-armed Vāsudeva the illustrious. The multitude of their armies, the prowess of Dhanaṃjaya, and the sagacity of Kṛṣṇa—what man, knowing them, would want to fight? You, sirs, must according to Law and covenant render to them what is to be rendered. Let Time not pass you by!"

Vaiśaṃpāyana said:
21.1 Upon hearing his words illustrious Bhīṣma, aged in wisdom,
applauded him and spoke these timely words: "How fortunate that
all the Pāṇḍavas and their relations are in good health, how
fortunate that they have allies and are intent upon the Law! How
fortunate that these brothers, the joys of the Kurus, desire peace, and
how fortunate that they, along with Dāmodara, do not want war!
All you have said is the truth, no doubt of that. But you have spoken
5 too bluntly, I think, because you are a brahmin. No doubt the
Pāṇḍavas have suffered hardships here and in the forest, and no
doubt too they have by Law a claim on their father's property.
"The Diademed Pārtha* is powerful, an expert armsman of great
strength—who could withstand Pāṇḍu's son in battle, were he the
Thunderbolt-Wielder himself, let alone other archers? I think that
he is capable of all three worlds!"
While Bhīṣma was still speaking, Karṇa irately and boldly cut him
off, and with a glance at Duryodhana said, "No creature in the
world can fail to know all that, brahmin! What is the point of saying
10 it again and again? On Duryodhana's behalf, Śakuni defeated Pāṇḍu's
son Yudhiṣṭhira at the time at dicing, and according to the covenant
Yudhiṣṭhira went to live in the forest. Without heeding the covenant
the prince now wants the ancestral kingdom, relying on the might of
the Matsyas and Pāñcālas. O wise one, Duryodhana will not give up
out of fear as much as a foot of land, but if Law were to command it,
he would make over the entire earth even to an enemy! If they want
their ancestral kingdom back, they will have to live in the forest as
covenanted. Thereafter let them dwell in Duryodhana's lap with
nothing to fear! Their present notion is against the Law; it is plain
15 foolishness! Or if the Pāṇḍavas want to cast aside the Law and make
war, they will remember my words when they encounter these chiefs
of the Kurus."
Bhīṣma said:
Who are you to talk, Rādheya? Pray remember that feat when the Pārtha by himself defeated six chariot warriors in battle! If we do not act as this brahmin has advised, we shall surely be killed on the battlefield and eat the dust!

* = Arjuna.

Vaiśaṃpāyana said:

Dhṛtarāṣṭra prayed and placated Bhīṣma, scolded Rādheya, and
spoke as follows: "Bhīṣma Śāṃtanava has spoken for our good, for
20 the good of the Pāṇḍavas and of the entire earth. After due reflection
I shall send Saṃjaya to the Pārthas. You, sir, must return at once
to the Pāṇḍavas." After treating him hospitably, the Kauravya sent
him back to the Pāṇḍavas; and summoning Saṃjaya to the assembly
hall, he spoke these words.

5(50) The Embassy of Saṃjaya

5.22–32 (B. 22–32; C. 645–970)
22 (22; 645). Dhṛtarāṣṭra, addressing Saṃjaya, comments on the Pāṇḍavas' lot, their mutual loyalty, Arjuna's power, and their allies, especially Kṛṣṇa (1–30). He fears Yudhiṣṭhira most (30). He tells Saṃjaya to go to the Pāṇḍavas and speak discreetly (35).
23 (23; 685). Arriving in Upaplavya, Saṃjaya greets Yudhiṣṭhira, who welcomes him and asks about all the Kauravas' health (1–15). He hopes they remember the Pāṇḍavas' prowess (15–25).
24 (24; 713). Saṃjaya praises Yudhiṣṭhira's manners, cites Dhṛtarāṣṭra's discomfiture and his hopes for peace (1–10).
25 (25; 723). Yudhiṣṭhira mentions his allies who are waiting to hear Saṃjaya's message (1). Saṃjaya greets all. He extols the Pāṇḍavas, who are just and who should join Dhṛtarāṣṭra in his desire for peace (1–15).
26 (26; 738). Yudhiṣṭhira, not unaccommodating, points out that Dhṛtarāṣṭra, living luxuriously, has always favored Duryodhana and his band and wants to keep the kingdom (1–15). But all know they cannot hold on to the kingdom (15–25).
27 (27; 767). Saṃjaya pleads for moderation on Yudhiṣṭhira's part (1–15). With his allies he can win, but it would be family slaughter (15–25).
28 (28; 794). Yudhiṣṭhira stresses that the Law is on his side, and seeks the advice of Kṛṣṇa (1–10).
29 (29; 809). Kṛṣṇa points out that action is better than inaction on Yudhiṣṭhira's part (1–15). The Pāṇḍavas are acting rightly against Duryodhana's rapacity: they were looted of their property in full view

of the Kauravas and were abused, especially Draupadī (15–35). He announces his intention to plead with the Kauravas himself (35–40). If he fails, war is certain (40–50).
30 (30; 867). Saṃjaya makes his farewells (1). Yudhiṣṭhira sends greetings to everyone (1–45), with a warning to Duryodhana (45).
31 (31; 916). Yudhiṣṭhira ends on a conciliatory note: he will be satisfied with five villages (1–20).
32 (32; 939). Saṃjaya returns to Hāstinapura and meets and greets Dhṛtarāṣṭra: he reports that the Pāṇḍavas are well but unyielding (1–10). Dhṛtarāṣṭra must accept responsibility (10–20); he is to blame for his son's folly (20–30).

Dhṛtarāṣṭra said:

22.1 They say that the Pāṇḍavas, Saṃjaya,
Have reached Upaplavya. Go there and find out.
You must kindly salute Ajātaśatru:
"How fortunate that you have come to this town!"

You must call them all blessed for having completed
That difficult sojourn they did not deserve;
And soon they shall be at peace with us:
Though deceived they are friendly disposed to us.

I have never, O Saṃjaya, seen on the part
Of the Pāṇḍavas any deceptiveness.
Having won all their wealth with strength of their own,
The Pāṇḍavas offered it all to me.

For, however closely examining them,
I can find no fault to blame on the Pārthas;
They always act with Law and Profit;
Loving comforts, they yet indulge no desires.

5 They endure heat and cold, and hunger and thirst,
They subdue sleep, laziness, anger, and joy
And distraction with wisdom and fortitude;
The Pāṇḍavas strive toward Law and Profit.

They part with their wealth for their friends when it suits,
Long usage does not wear thin their friendship.
The Pārthas give honor and wealth where it fits,
No one hates them in Ajamīḍha's line,

Except that wicked, uneven, and foolish
Duryodhana and despicable Karṇa:
They engender the heat of those great-souled men,
Whom they first had deprived of their comforts and pleasures.

Accustomed to comforts and energetic,
Duryodhana thinks that his acts were right;
But only a fool would think that their share
Can be taken from them as long as they live.

Ajātaśatru's footsteps are followed
By Arjuna, Keśava, Sātyaki,
The Wolf-Belly, twins, and all the Sṛñjayas:
It were better to give it to him than to war.

10 The left-handed archer, the Gāṇḍīva bowman,*
Alone on his chariot lashes the earth;
And unassailable Keśava Viṣṇu**
Is the great-souled sovereign of the three worlds.

What mortal man would stand before him
Among all Gods most worthy of praise,
Who sows out his monsoon-resonant arrows
That swiftly course like a flock of birds?

The Gāṇḍīva bowman alone on his chariot
Subdued the North and the Northernmost Kurus.
The Left-handed Archer plundered their wealth,
And made them his soldiers and payers of tribute.

In the Khāṇḍava Forest the Left-handed Archer
With Gāṇḍīva defeated the Indra-led Gods;
And Phalguna* offered the wood to the Fire God,
Increasing the Pāṇḍavas' honor and fame.

No wielder of clubs is the equal of Bhīma,
No elephant-rider matches him.
On the chariot, they say, he is Arjuna's peer,
In his arms is the strength of a myriad tuskers.

15 Well-trained, full of vigor, implacable foe,
He'd angrily burn Dhṛtarāṣṭra's son;
This powerful, intransigent man
Even Indra himself is unable to vanquish.

The sagacious, powerful, deft-handed twins,
Those brothers well-trained by Phalguna,
Like vultures that shatter a flock of birds
Will surely leave none of the Kurus alive.

* = Arjuna.
** = Kṛṣṇa.

In the midst of the Pāṇḍavas, Dhṛṣṭadyumna
Is vigorously striding like one of them;
He, the joy of the Somakas, with his council
Has devoted his life to the Pāṇḍavas' triumph.

Virāṭa, the overlord of the Śālvas,
Their long-time host whom they served, now old,
With his sons has chosen the Pāṇḍavas' side,
And is, I have heard, Yudhiṣṭhira's friend.

Expelled from the rule of the Kekaya country,
The five brothers are powerful men with the bow,
And wanting the realm of the Kekayas,
They follow the Pārthas, eager for war.

20 All the heroes among the rulers of earth
Have been gathered intent on the Pāṇḍava's cause.
I hear that the champions are loyal to him
And with love have chosen for Dharma the king.

The mountain men, they who live by the passes,
And the well-born, pure-lined warriors on earth,
And the gallant Mlecchas of various weapons
Have gathered intent on the Pāṇḍava's cause.

King Pāṇḍya the boundless, the equal of Indra,
Accompanied in battle by plenty of barons,
That great-souled man has chosen his cause,
That champion on earth whose heat is resistless.

I hear Sātyaki, who learned weaponry
From Arjuna, Droṇa, and Vāsudeva,
And Kṛpa and Bhīṣma, the match of Pradyumna—
I hear that he too is intent on his cause.

The Cedis and Kārūṣakas have joined him too,
With their bands of most tempestuous kings.
That one among them who blazed like the sun,
The glorious, lustrous king of the Cedis,*

25 Who they thought could not be halted in war,
The greatest on earth of the drawers of bowstrings,
That most vigorous man among barons was smitten
By Kṛṣṇa and forcibly, forcefully crushed.

Increasing the Yādavas' honor and fame,
He broke of yore Śiśupāla in battle,
Of whom the Karūṣaka chieftains, those lords
Among men, together extolled the fame.

* = Śiśupāla.

But deeming Kṛṣṇa invincible
While he rode his chariot yoked with Sugrīva,
They deserted the Cedi king, running away
Like puny game at the sight of a lion.

He rose with vehemence counter to Kṛṣṇa
While he hoped to win a chariot duel—
And lay lifeless, slain by Vāsudeva,
Like a *karṇikāra* tree felled by a gale.

What they told me of Keśava's gallantry
In the cause of the Pāṇḍavas, Saṃjaya,
And remembering other exploits of this Viṣṇu,
I find no peace, Gavalgana's son.

30 No enemy would withstand those ever
Whose leader were that Vṛṣṇi lion;
And with fright does my heart shudder when I hear
The two Kṛṣṇas have joined on a single chariot.

Pray my dull-witted son with his contrary mind
Does not in a fight fall afoul of them;
Pray that pair will not, Saṃjaya, burn down the Kurus,
As Indra and Viṣṇu the host of the Daityas.
For I deem Dhanaṃjaya Śakra's peer
And the Vṛṣṇi hero the eternal Viṣṇu.

Kuntī's son Pāṇḍava Ajātaśatru*
Who delights in the Law, is modest and bold,
This spirited man Duryodhana wronged—
Pray he does not in anger set fire to the Kurus.

I am not as afraid of Arjuna, Kṛṣṇa,
Not even of Bhīma and the twins,
As I forever am fearful, O bard,
Of the wrath of that fury-kindled king.

He possesses austerity, continence—
The plans of his mind are sure to succeed,
Of his wrath on the battlefield, knowing it just,
I am utterly fearful now, Saṃjaya.

35 So go fast with your chariot on your mission
And on reaching the host of the king of Pāñcāla,**
You should ask the health of Ajātaśatru
Again and again, and speak with affection.

* = Yudhiṣṭhira.
** = Drupada.

When you meet with Janārdana too, my friend,
That lordly and generous man of the brave,
You must ask him his health at my behest:
"Dhṛtarāṣṭra wishes the Pāṇḍavas peace."

For there is not a word of Vāsudeva
That Kuntī's son would not carry out.
He is dear to them, Kṛṣṇa, they count him their own;
And ever attentive he knows of their tasks.

On meeting the Pāṇḍavas, Saṃjaya,
Janārdana, Yuyudhāna, Virāṭa,
You should ask their health at my behest
And likewise all five of Draupadī's sons.

Whatever you think is opportune with them,
And what profitable for the Bhāratas,
That, Saṃjaya, say in the midst of the kings,
If it does not arouse them and lead to war.

Vaiśaṃpāyana said:

23.1 Upon hearing these words of King Dhṛtarāṣṭra, Saṃjaya went to Upaplavya to visit the boundlessly august Pāṇḍavas. He approached the law-spirited King Yudhiṣṭhira and prostrated himself first. Then the son of the *sūta* spoke.

Gāvalgani Saṃjaya, son of a *sūta*
Said faithfully to Ajātaśatru,*
"How fortunate, king, that I see you healthy
With all your companions, the equal of Indra.

"Of your health inquires from you Ambikā's son,
The wise and ancient King Dhṛtarāṣṭra.
Is the first of the Pāṇḍavas, Bhīma, healthy,
And Dhanaṃjaya and both sons of Mādrī?

5 And the Princess Kṛṣṇā, Drupada's daughter,
Faithful spouse of heroes and mother of sons,
The spirited lady of whom you seek
The desires of your heart and hope for good luck?

Yudhiṣṭhira said:

Gāvalgani Saṃjaya, welcome to you!
With a happy heart I salute you, bard.
Indeed I declare my good health to you,
I am well, good sage, and so are my brothers.

* = Yudhiṣṭhira.

It's been long since I heard of the health, O bard,
Of the Kuru elder, King Bhārata.*
It's as though I am seeing the king in person
By seeing you, Saṃjaya, with affection.

Our ancient Grandfather, full of spirit,
Great sage endowed with all good virtues,
Is he healthy, my friend, is Kauravya Bhīṣma,
And does he persist in his previous tenor?

Is King Dhṛtarāṣṭra, the father of sons,
Great-souled Vaicitravīrya still well?
And Pratīpa's scion King Bāhlika,
Is he in good health, O son of a *sūta*?

10 Is Somadatta keeping good health,
And Bhūriśravas, Satyasaṃdha, and Śala,
And Droṇa and son, and the brahmin Kṛpa,
Great archers all, are they too well?

Those sagacious men steeped in all knowledge,
The very best of the bowmen on earth,
Do they, good friend, receive their due honor?
Are the bowmen perchance all free of sickness,

They vie with the Kurus, O Saṃjaya,
Those youths who carry their bows in the land
And in whose realm dwells Droṇa's son,
That handsome archer of steady habits?

Is Yuyutsu, the son of a commoner wench,
That sagacious son of the king, in good health?
And is councilor Karṇa healthy, my friend,
Whose guidance that fool Suyodhana follows?

The aged ladies, the Bhārata mothers,
The kitchen women, the wives of the slaves,
The daughters-in-law, boys, sisters, and nephews
And the daughters' sons, are they keeping truth?

15 Does the king continue in his old ways
With the keep and support of the brahmins, my friend?
I hope Dhṛtarāṣṭra's son has not
Cut off my gifts to the twiceborn, bard?

Does King Dhṛtarāṣṭra with his son
Overlook the transgressions of brahmin folk,
But not for some reason, he being their road,
Overlook any shortages in their lives?

* = Dhṛtarāṣṭra.

It's the high, bright light in the world of the living
That by the creator was set for the creatures.
If fools do not restrain their greed
There will be a total collapse of the Kurus.

Does King Dhṛtarāṣṭra and his son
Take care of his ministers' livelihood?
No foes in the guise of friends wish to live
In discord, having but one for their friend?

Pray, none of the Kauravas, friend, relate
Of any offence of the Pāṇḍavas?
When people see bands of *dasyus* assembled,
Do they think of the Pārtha,* the warrior leader?

20 Friend, do they recall the straight-flying shafts
With their roaring whirr, that were fixed to the bow-string
By that tensely vibrating archer and then
Shot off from his tall Gāṇḍīva bow?

For I have not seen anyone on earth
Or heard of one Arjuna's equal or better,
The thrust of whose hand equals sixty-one
Well-robed, keen-bladed, stone-whetted arrows.

The ferocious club-wielding Bhīmasena
Who causes the hosts of his foes to quake,
Do they recall of him how he would ravage
Like a rutting elephant down in a reed bed?

Sahadeva, the son of Mādrī, defeated
In Dantakūra the assembled Kalingas,
Shooting with both the right and the left,
Do they chance to remember the powerful man?

He rode out on my mission, Nakula did,
Gāvalgaṇi Saṃjaya, while you watched,
And he brought the West into my sway:
Do they chance to remember that son of Mādrī?

25 That defeat that befell in the Dvaita Forest,
When they came on their ill-guided cattle tour
And Bhīmasena and Jaya* set free
The fools who had walked into enemy power,

While I stood guard over Arjuna's back
And the twins and Bhīma defended his wheels—
The Gāṇḍīva bowman defeated the foes
And came out unscathed—do they chance to recall him?

* = Arjuna.

But one good deed does not, surely, suffice
To render, O Saṃjaya, everything right,
If we are unable with all our soul
To sway that son of Dhṛtarāṣṭra.

Saṃjaya said:
24.1 This is, Pāṇḍava, what you are capable of:
You ask, Kuru chief, about Kurus and people!
The spirited men are well, my friend,
Those chiefs of the Kurus you ask about.

There are good old men with the Dhārtarāṣṭra,
And then there are villains, O Pāṇḍava.
But the Dhārtarāṣṭra'd enrich even foes,
Why then should he plunder the shares of the brahmins?

If he acts toward you in a lawless way
As one harming the harmless, it would not be right.
Dhṛtarāṣṭra and sons would be threats to their friends,
If he wickedly hated you who are honest.

He does not condone it and is deeply pained,
The old man is grieving, Ajātaśatru.
For he hears indeed from the brahmins he gathers
That betraying a friend is the worst of sins.

5 They remember you, God among men, at their meetings,
And Jiṣṇu* at battles, that warrior leader.
When the sound of conches and drums is raised,
They remember the club-wielding Bhīmasena.

They remember the twin sons of Mādrī as well,
Who fly all around in the midst of the battle,
Incessantly showering armies with arrows,
Those warriors who cannot be shaken in war.

I think, O king, that no one can know
What the future will bring to a man as his lot,
If you who are with all virtues endowed
Found hardship and misery, Pāṇḍava.

You yourself will make up for it all and still more
With the aid of your wisdom, Ajātaśatru.
No Indra-like son of Pāṇḍu will ever
Abandon the Law for pleasure's sake.

You yourself with your wisdom, Ajātaśatru,
Will make the peace that shall bring shelter

* = Arjuna.

To Pāṇḍavas, Kurus and Sṛñjayas
And the other kings who have rallied to them.

10 Now hear from me, O king, the words
That Dhṛtarāṣṭra told me at night,
The words of your father, Ajātaśatru,
When he had gathered his sons and his council.

Yudhiṣṭhira said:

25.1 The Pāṇḍus and Sṛñjayas have assembled
With Janārdana, Yuyudhāna, Virāṭa.
Gavalgaṇi, son of the bard, speak up
And relate Dhṛtarāṣṭra's message to us.

Saṃjaya said:

Ajātaśatru and Wolf Belly too,
Dhanaṃjaya and the twin sons of Mādrī,
I salute you and Vāsudeva Śauri,
Cekitāna, Virāṭa and Sātyaki,

And you, the ancient king of Pāñcāla,*
Dhṛṣṭadyumna Pārṣata Yājñaseni,
Pray all lend your ear to this word of mine—
I shall speak to the benefit of the Kurus,

The King Dhṛtarāṣṭra, welcoming peace,
Has had me hurriedly yoke my chariot.
May it please the king, his brothers and sons,
And his kinsmen: peace to the Pāṇḍavas!

5 You are gifted with every virtue, ye Pārthas,
With steadiness, mildness and honesty.
You are high-born, gentle and generous,
Restrained by shame, decisive in acts.

Mean acts are not befitting to you,
For such is your mettle, ye Bhīmasenas!
Any evil on your part would glare like a drop
Of collyrium fallen upon a white cloth.

Who knowingly would commit a deed
Entailing total devastation,
Productive of evil, infernal, destructive,
Where victory only amounts to defeat?

They are blessed who act for the sake of their kin;
Your sons, your friends, your kinsmen they are,

* = Drupada.

Who would shed their lamented lives in your cause—
For thus is the Kurus' welfare assured.

If you, Pārthas, continue to chastise the Kurus,
Bring down all your foes and subjugate them,
Your life would be the same as death,
For to live with your kinfolk dead is not right.

10 For who would be able to vanquish you
Supported by Keśava,* Cekitāna,
And Sātyaki, guarded by Pārṣata's** arms,
Had he Indra to help him with all the Gods?

Or who would be able to vanquish the Kurus,
Protected by Bhīṣma and Aśvatthāman
By Droṇa, by Śalya and Kṛpa and others,
Protected by Karṇa with all the kings?

The army of King Dhārtarāṣṭra*** is mighty:
Who could attack it and fail to die?
I myself do not see how any good
Would come from defeat, or victory.

But why would the Pārthas like low-born churls
Commit any act of lawlessness?
I bow placating to Vāsudeva
And the Lord of Pāñcāla, ancient king.

I fold my hands and pray and beseech you:
How to prosper the Kurus and Sṛñjayas?
For there is not a word of you, Vāsudeva
That Dhanaṃjaya ever would fail to do.

15 His life he would give if asked, so what not?
Then this do I say, sage, to finish my task:
The king who is guided by Bhīṣma desires
That he be completely at peace with you all!

Yudhiṣṭhira said:
26.1 What words have you heard from me, Saṃjaya,
What warlike words, that you fear for war?
No war, my friend, is better than war:
Who would go to war, bard, if he had found peace?

If every wish of his heart would come true
For a man who did nothing, O Saṃjaya,

* = Kṛṣṇa.
** = Dhṛṣṭadyumna.
*** = Duryodhana.

I know that he would do nothing at all;
And what is more frivolous than going to war?

Why would a man knowingly go to war?
Who cursed by his fate would choose for war?
The Pārthas who hanker for happiness act
For the fullness of Law and the common weal.

He who hopes for happiness rising from acts
(And to act with troublous means is to suffer)
Wishes pleasure to gain and grief to avoid,
Is enslaved to the pleasuring of his senses:
The longing for pleasure consumes one's body,
And spurred by it, misery is its reward.

5 As a fire whose glow has been kindled will grow
Even greater in power if fuel is added,
So desire grows more if its object is gained,
Like a butter-fed fire it will not be sated—
See the pile of the pleasures of King Dhṛtarāṣṭra,
And compare it with our diminished lot!

No lord of inferior bodies he,
He hears not the sound of lesser men's songs,
He smells not the smell of inferior garlands,
He has never known inferior salves.

He has never worn inferior clothing:
So why did he drive us away from the Kurus?
And here and now having shaken us off
Desire still consumes the heart in his body.

It is wrong that the king who is partial himself
In others expects nonpartisanship;
He receives from others exactly the same
Behavior he finds in himself toward *them*.

He who at the end of the dewy season
Sets fire closeby at the height of summer
Among dense dead trees so it grows with the wind
Will come to sure grief if he tries to escape.

10 Having gained full power now King Dhṛtarāṣṭra
Wails piteously, Saṃjaya—for what reason
But for taking his son's misguided advice,
That villainous fool who is bent on deceit!

Untrustworthy himself, Suyodhana flouted
Most trustworthy Vidura's good advice;

And King Dhṛtarāṣṭra to favor his son
Embarked upon lawlessness, knowing it well.

Bard, King Dhṛtarāṣṭra has paid no heed,
Out of love for his son, to that wisest of Kurus
The learned and eloquent Vidura,
That virtuous man who yet wished him well.

His son is an envious humbler of pride,
Self-seeking and rash, overreaching Profit
And Law, foul-spoken, a prey to his wrath,
A lecher who prospers the evil of heart.

He is contrary, heeding no betters, vindictive,
An evil betrayer of friends, O bard—
And King Dhṛtarāṣṭra to favor that son
Shed Profit and Law, though he *saw* full well.

15 It occurred to me, Saṃjaya, while I was gambling,
"Pray let not the Kurus meet with disaster,"
When Vidura voicing his sage advice,
Got no approval from Dhṛtarāṣṭra.

As long as they followed the mind of the Steward
No dangerous times overtook the Kurus;
As long as they followed Vidura's wisdom,
Their kingdom enjoyed great opulence.

Now learn from me, bard, who are the advisers
Of that avaricious Dhārtarāṣṭra:
Duḥśāsana, Śakuni, the son of the *sūta*,*
Behold his folly, Gāvalgaṇa's son!

I fail to see, in spite of my searching,
How the Kurus can thrive and the Sṛñjayas;
Dhṛtarāṣṭra has taken power from the others
And sent farsighted Vidura wandering.

Dhṛtarāṣṭra and son have now set their hopes
On a great, unrivaled kingdom on earth.
When this is the case, no peace can be had;
He thinks that my wealth is all too close.

20 If Karṇa regards it a feasible thing
To take up his arms against Arjuna—
There have been great battles of war in the past,
Why was Karṇa then not a haven to them?

* = Karṇa.

Suyodhana knows it, and Karṇa does,
Our grandfather knows it and so does Droṇa,
And so do the other Kauravas too,
That there is no archer like Arjuna.

The Kauravas all know fully well,
And so do the other kings that have gathered,
That Duryodhana only can do his wrongs
If foe-tamer Arjuna is not there.

So the Dhārtarāṣṭra thinks that he can
Wrest my tied-up wealth from the Pāṇḍavas?
With his nine-ell bow the Diademed One,*
Aware of his plans, goes to battle with him!

The Dhārtarāṣṭras survive for as long
They don't hear the crackling snap of Gāṇḍīva.
Ignoring the force of a furious Bhīma
Suyodhana thinks that his goal is attained.

25 Not Indra himself could, friend, take away
My power while Bhīmasena's alive,
And Dhanaṃjaya, Bard, and Nakula,
And that hero of mine, Sahadeva, as well.

If the ancient king and his son, O Bard,
Accept the case and adopt the spirit,
Then, Saṃjaya, all those Dhārtarāṣṭras
Will not perish consumed by the Pāṇḍavas' wrath.

You know the hardships that we have suffered:
In honor of you I forgive them all.
You know what we got from the Kauravas,
And how we behaved to Duryodhana.

Today we still behave the same:
As you have declared I will be appeased:
But I *must* have my reign in Indraprastha,
Let Bhārata chief Suyodhana grant it!

Saṃjaya said:

27.1 Your actions forever are based on the Law,
And they are in the world deemed famous, O Pārtha.
But the torrent of life is a transient thing,
Seek not to destroy it, Pāṇḍava!

If the Kurus refuse short of war to return
Your kingdom to you, Ajātaśatru,

* = Arjuna.

It is better, I deem, to beg in the land
Of the Andhaka-Vṛṣṇis than reign by war!

The life of a man is a torrent, but brief,
Of perpetual suffering, and volatile,
Insufficient to sate man's zest for life;
Thence, Pāṇḍava, perpetrate no sin.

Upon a man there prey the desires
Which form an obstruction to Law, lord of men.
If a man perseveringly strikes them down,
Then he finds in this world high praise without blame.

5 The thirst for possessions shackles one, Pārtha,
The Law of the man who yearns for them dwindles.
He who chooses the Law is enlightened by it,
He who hankers for objects, diminished by them.

If he places the Law ahead of his acts,
He shines like the sun with great effulgence.
By lacking in Law a man may obtain
All of earth and yet sink with his evil resolve.

You have learned the Veda and practiced the *brahman*,
You have offered oblations and given to brahmins;
Though knowing that that is the highest estate,
You have given yourself many years to pleasure.

He who lives for his pleasure beyond sound measure
And does not act in the practice of Yoga,
Is too direly deprived when his wealth is exhausted,
And spurred by desire he wallows in grief.

So he who, involved in the search for possessions,
Abandons the Law and resolves on Unlaw
And dumbly declines to believe in hereafter,
That fool, shedding body, burns after death.

10 There is in the afterworld no disappearance
Of the acts that were done, whether good or evil;
In front of the doer proceed his deeds—
And after them follows the one who did them.

Your acts are known to be pure as the food
That with proper rite is given to brahmins—
Food tasty and fragrant and hallowed by faith—
At *śrāddha* performances liberally paid for.

All acts are done in this field, O Pārtha,
After death there is nothing left to be done;

The acts you have done go with you hereafter,
Those great good acts that are praised by the strict.

One is rid of death there, and old age and fear,
No hunger and thirst, no things that displease,
No longer anything set as your task
Except for the purpose of pleasing the senses.

Such, Indra of men, is the fruit of our deeds,
And it rises from anger and rises from joy.
For a short-lived pleasuring of the heart
Do not abandon the world for too long.

15 At the end of the acts there is good name,
Truth, self-control, honesty, gentleness,
Aśvamedha, *Rājasūya*, and Oblation—
But do not go to the limit of evil.

Therefore, ye Pārthas, if following custom
You must do evil deeds after all this time—
Is that why you dwelled many years in the forests,
For a troublous sojourn dictated by Law?

You could without exile have yoked the army
You formerly had under your command;
The Pāñcālas who always have been your allies,
And Janārdana and Yuyudhāna the hero.

The king of the Matsyas on a chariot of gold,
Virāṭa along with his warrior sons,
And the kings that you formerly had defeated,
Would all together have rallied to you.

With mighty companions, ablaze with your army,
With Arjuna's homage and Vāsudeva's,
Striking down the choicest of foes in the field,
You'd have humbled the pride of the Dhārtarāṣṭra.

20 Why have you increased the might of your foes,
Why have you reduced your allies to few,
Why have you sojourned many years in the forests,
If you now out of time wish to fight, O Pārtha?

A foolish man, Pāṇḍava, fights, or a man
Unknowing of Law leaves the pathway to welfare,
Or a man of wisdom who knows the Law,
Might stray from well-being, driven by wrath.

But, Pārtha, *your* mind is not set on Unlaw,
You do not from anger commit what is wrong:

Then surely, what is the reason that you
Wish to do this deed which runs counter to wisdom?

A bitter headache, not born from disease,
That steals one's fame and gives rise to misdeeds,
Is the wrath the strict swallow but not the lax:
Great king, appease and swallow it!

Now who would desire what leads but to evil
(Forgiving is better than hugging your comforts)
Where Bhīṣma Śāṃtanava is to succumb
And Droṇa is slain along with his son?

25 Kṛpa, Śalya, Vikarṇa, the son of Somadatta,
Viviṃśati, Karṇa, Duryodhana:
Having killed all those, what will be the pleasure
You will find in it, Pāṇḍava, tell me that!

Having gained all of earth to her borders of oceans
You shall yet not escape old age and death,
Nor happiness, king, or unhappiness:
As you know all this, do *not* wage war!

If it is for the sake of your councilors' wishes
That you wish to commit a mistake like this,
Give them all that you have and run away!
Don't stray from your path, the Road of the Gods!

Yudhiṣṭhira said:

28.1 Undoubtedly, Saṃjaya, is it true
That the Law is the highest of acts as you say.
However, you should not blame me before
You are sure it is Law I practice or Unlaw.

The sages discern with their minds the case
Whether Unlaw is wearing the guises of Law,
Or if what is Law appears to be Unlaw,
Or again whether Law has the right guise of Law.

Thus in emergencies Law and Unlaw,
Applied to one's livelihood, share the same aspect:
The proof of the first alternative is
The Law of emergencies—learn it from me.

When one's natural pattern is lost, one should seek
What will help him to do the acts that he lacks;
So the man in distress, though still in his pattern;
They both are, Saṃjaya, open to blame.

5 The Ordainer's ordained a rite of repair
For brahmins who wish to make right what was wrong.
Those who fell to inaction in their distress
Or misaction are, Saṃjaya, open to blame.

The proper vocation is set forever
For the strict non-brahmin and non-Vedic folk,
So the wise can determine the facts of the matter:
From them one can know the proper solution.

Our fathers and those who preceded them
Our grandsires and ancestors meant it thus,
And those seekers of wisdom who did their task
It is not in the end an Unlaw, I think.

I do not, Saṃjaya, covet by Unlaw
Whatever there is of wealth on the earth,
Or whatever wealth with the Thirty Gods,
Or Prajāpati's heaven, the World of Brahmā.

A master of Law, skilled, worldly-wise,
Sagacious Kṛṣṇa, attendant of brahmins,
Advises all manner of powerful
Rājanyas and *bhojas* upon this earth.

10 The glorious Keśava must advise me
Whether I'm not to blame when I give up war,
Or desert my own Law when I *do* wage war:
Vāsudeva has both parties' profit at heart.

The Caitrakas, Śinis, and Andhakas,
The Kaukuras, Sṛñjayas, Vṛṣṇis, and Bhojas
All wait on the counsel of Vāsudeva,
And subduing their foes they gladden their friends.

Ugrasena and all other Andhaka-Vṛṣṇis,
All Indra-like men, are guided by Kṛṣṇa.
The spirited men have the valor of truth,
The powerful Yādavas take their pleasure.

Obtaining Kṛṣṇa as brother and guide,
The Kāśi king Babhru, on whom Vāsudeva
Has showered his wishes, as after the summer
The cloud on the creatures, has found great fortune.

Friend, such an adviser has Keśava been,
We know that he knows to decide upon action.
Most virtuous Kṛṣṇa is dear to us,
I shall not trespass on Keśava's word.

Vāsudeva said:

29.1 It is my desire that the Pāṇḍavas,
O Saṃjaya, prosper, I wish them well!
Likewise I always hope for the growth
Of Dhṛtarāṣṭra and his many sons.

It has always, Saṃjaya, been my desire—
And I told them not different—that there be peace.
For that, I hear, is dear to a king,
And I think it is best for the Pāṇḍavas.

The Pāṇḍava* has, to be sure, displayed
A most difficult peacefulness, Saṃjaya.
Dhṛtarāṣṭra and sons having been so greedy,
Why should not a quarrel arise over that?

Ascertaining here, Saṃjaya, the fact of the Law
You learn it from me and Yudhiṣṭhira.
Then why do you speak to belittle the Pārtha,
Who is vigorous in fulfilling his tasks,
Who, as is well-known, guides wisely his household,
And from the beginning has acted correctly?

5 On the matter at hand and its proper ruling
The brahmins have had diverse opinions:
Some say that one's acts bring success hereafter,
Some reject them and hold that success follows knowledge.
It is known to the brahmins that he who knows food
And then fails to eat it will still go hungry.

It is only such knowledge as brings about acts
That is found to bear fruit and not other knowledge.
And the act itself bears visibly fruit:
One's thirst is appeased by the drinking of water.

The rite is enjoined by virtue of action,
The act is contained in it, Saṃjaya.
I do not hold anything higher than acting;
To prate otherwise is feeble and vain.

By their acts do the Gods in the other world shine,
By his act does the Wind blow here on earth;
Ordaining the days and the nights by his acts,
The Sun rises daily unwearyingly.

Unwearied the Moon goes through fortnights and months,
Through constellations and asterisms;
Indefatigably does the kindled Fire
By his act blaze forth for the good of the creatures.

* = Yudhiṣṭhira.

10 Untiringly does the Goddess Earth
With her own strength carry her heavy load;
Unweariedly do the rivers carry
Their water and sustain all the creatures that be.

Untiringly does the Slayer of Vala
Of opulent splendor shower his rains,
Making noisy the skies, and he practices *brahman*,
Desiring the chieftainship of the Gods.

Abandoning pleasure and heart's desires
Has Śakra by acting become the chief,
Protecting the truth and the Law undistracted;
By cultivating the virtues all
Of self-control, patience, equity, pleasure,
Has Maghavat* reached the high rule of the Gods.

Bṛhaspati practices diligently,
With his spirit honed, the life of the *brahman*,
Abandoning happiness, mastering senses,
And so he became the guru of Gods.

By their act do the contellations shine,
The Rudras, Ādityas, the Vasus, and All-Gods,
King Yama, Kubera Vaiśravaṇa,
Gandharvas and Yakṣas and Apsarās bright;
Observing the *brahman*, the Vedas and rites
The Hermits shine forth in yonder world.

15 Knowing this is the Law for all in the world,
For brahmins, barons and commoners,
Why do you, knowing the lore of the knowing,
Toil, Saṃjaya, in the Kaurava's cause?

Understand his constant devotion to Scripture,
To the Horse Sacrifice and the Rājasūya;
He is occupied too with armor and bow,
With handguards, chariots, and weaponry!

If the Pārthas knew of a means to their end
Without having to slaughter the Kauravas,
They would virtuously protect the Law
And force Bhīmasena to act like an Āryan.

But when they perform their ancestral task
And meet their death by the power of fate,
While fulfilling their task as far as they could,
Then their very end would be worthy of praise.

* = Drjuna.

And since you seem to know everything,
I should like to hear you give us the answer
Whether Law commands a king to wage war
Or Law commands him not to wage war.

20 You should take account first, Saṃjaya,
Of the four-class division and the duties of each,
And then when you hear the Pāṇḍavas' duty
You may praise or blame according to fancy.

A brahmin should study and sacrifice
And give and visit the sacred fords,
And teach and officiate for those deserving,
And accept such gifts as are known to him.

The baron should offer the subjects protection,
Act under the Law, make gifts, be alert,
Perform oblations, and learn all the Vedas,
Take a wife and virtuously govern his household.

The *vaiśya* should study and undistracted
Earn wealth with farming, cow-herding, and trade
And save it, do favors for brahmins and barons
And by Law and with virtue govern his household.

As the ancient Law of the *śūdra* is known
That he serve and pay honor to brahmin folk;
Both study and sacrifice are forbidden;
Untiring he always should strive for his welfare.

25 A king should protect all classes without
Distractions and yoke them each to his task,
Be not given to lusts and be fair to the subjects
And not comply with lawless desires.

If there be someone who is better than he,
A person endowed with all the virtues,
He should chastise the lesser man, acting with knowledge,
But not covet his land, for that is not right.

When one cruelly covets the land of another
And, angering destiny, seizes power
Then this shall be a cause of war for the kings;
For that were sword, bow, and armor created:
By Indra were warfare, weapons, and bows
And armor created to slaughter the *dasyus*.

Where a thief steals property without witness,
Where another steals it by force and in public,

They both are equally guilty of crime:
What sets Dhṛtarāṣṭra's son apart?
He out of mere greed considers *that* Law
Whatever he pleases, a prey to his rage!

The Pāṇḍavas had their inherited share—
Why should suddenly others now rob us of it?
If we fight in this matter our death will be praised:
To inherit a kingdom precedes over conquest.
Relate, O Saṃjaya, those old Laws
To the Kauravas seated in their own realm.

30 They are fools and caught in the power of death
Who have rallied inanely to Dhṛtarāṣṭra;
Once more behold that vilest of acts
That the Kurus committed amidst their assembly.

The Kauravas headed by Bhīṣma ignored it
When the Pāṇḍavas' dear wife Draupadī
That glorious woman of virtue and conduct,
Was seized upon by a lecher, and wept.

If the Kurus assembled there, young and old,
At that time had tried to prevent this deed,
Dhṛtarāṣṭra would surely have done me a favor,
And it would have been a good deed for his sons!

Duḥśāsana, trampling all rules, brought Kṛṣṇa
In the midst of the hall of her fathers-in-law!
Once brought there she spoke so pitifully
And found no protector but Vidura.

The kings were too pusillanimous
To be able to voice their protest in the hall;
It was only the Steward who, knowing the Law
And speaking accordingly, scolded the nitwit.

35 You did not yourself talk Law in the Hall—
Are you now to lecture the Pāṇḍava?
But Kṛṣṇā herself did this beautiful thing,
This difficult thing, when she met the assembly,
With which she extracted the Pāṇḍavas
And herself from their straits as a boat from the ocean.

When the *sūta*'s son in the hall spoke to Kṛṣṇā,
Who stood there before her fathers-in-law,
"You have no more recourse left, Yājñasenī,
Repair to the house of the Dhārtarāṣṭra!

Your men are defeated, they no more exist,
Choose another man, beautiful wench, for your husband!"

Then this insolent, shaftlike, stingingly burning,
Outrageous word that Karṇa spoke
Cut to the bone through the weak in the heart
And lodged with Bībhatsu Phalguna.*

When they readied to don their black antelope skins,
Duḥśāsana spoke these scathing words,
"You are no more than barren sesamum seeds,
You are lost to hell for a very long time!"

Said Śakuni, king of Gāndhāra, the trickster,
To the Pāṇḍavas when they were playing at dice,
"You lost Nakula, what have you left to stake?
Now gamble for Kṛṣṇā Yājñasenī!"

40 You know yourself the unspeakable words
That were said at the dicing game, Saṃjaya,
I propose to go to the Kurus myself,
And settle the matter before it is lost.

If without hurting the Pāṇḍavas' cause
I succeed in bringing peace to the Kurus,
It will be a deed of high merit and import
And they will be saved from the noose of death.

When I speak my sagacious words, which delight
In the Law, full of meaning, and causing no harm,
Dhṛtarāṣṭra's men will heed it before me,
And the Kurus will honor me for having come.

If not, then Phalguna* riding his chariot
And Bhīmasena, armored for war,
Will set fire to the worthless Dhārtarāṣṭras,
Who will burn, be sure, for their witless act.

45 Dhṛtarāṣṭra's son spoke cutting words
To the Pāṇḍaveyas who were defeated;
But purposeful, wielding his club, Bhīmasena
Will in time remind Duryodhana.

The wrathful Duryodhana is the great tree,
With Karṇa the trunk, and Śakuni the branches,
Duḥśāsana is its blossom and fruit,
And the root Dhṛtarāṣṭra, the dumbfounded king.

* = Arjuna.

The lawful Yudhiṣṭhira is the great tree,
The trunk is Arjuna, Bhīma the branches,
The twin sons of Mādrī the blossom and fruit,
And the root is the *brahman* and brahmindom.

The King Dhṛtarāṣṭra and sons are the forest,
And the Pārthas the tigers, Saṃjaya,

do not cut down the forest with its tigers, and don't banish the tigers from the forest. The tiger perishes without the forest, and the forest without its tigers is cut down. Therefore the tiger should stand guard over the forest and the forest protect its tiger. The Dhārtarāṣṭras are of the nature of creepers, Saṃjaya, and the Pāṇḍavas are *śāla* trees; a creeper never grows without clinging to a big tree.

50 The Pārthas stand ready to obey, and the enemy-tamers stand ready to fight. Let King Dhṛtarāṣṭra do what he has to do. The great-spirited, law-abiding Pāṇḍavas are still at peace, but they are robust warriors. Relate it all truthfully, wise one.

30.1 *Saṃjaya said:*

Farewell I bid you, king of kings,
Good fortune! I go now, Pāṇḍava.
I hope my partisan heart has not
Made me say anything to give you offense.

With farewells to Janārdana, Bhīmasena,
To Arjuna, Mādrī's sons, Cekitāna,
And Śatyaki, bless you, I now must go.
Look upon me, kings, with kindly eyes!

Yudhiṣṭhira said:

With our leave go safely, Saṃjaya,
You have never given me any offense.
They know and we know that you are a man
Of probity when you speak in assembly.

A competent envoy, Saṃjaya, are you,
Kind-spoken, and friendly, insightful and good.
Your mind is never beclouded, O bard,
And though told the truth you do not anger.

5 You will never hurt with scathing remarks,
Never give a bitter or acid address;
We know that your speech is informed by the Law
And meaningful, bard, not intended to hurt.

To us you are the friendliest envoy;
Besides you, Vidura's welcome here:

In previous days we constantly saw you,
You are as a friend Dhanaṃjaya's equal!

After journeying swiftly from here, attend
On deserving brahmins, O Saṃjaya,
Of pure vigor, erudite schoolmen all,
Who are born from good lines and endowed with all virtues,

And on studious brahmins and mendicants,
And ascetics who steadfastly live in the woods:
Salute all elders on my behalf,
And likewise ask the health of the others.

You must meet with King Dhṛtarāṣṭra's chaplain,
His preceptors and sacrificial priests,
You must meet with them, friend, and as they deserve
Inquire of the health of each of them, bard.

10 Salute in our name our beloved preceptor,
Who never goes wrong for all his compliance,
Who desiring the Vedas, practiced the *brahman*
And restored the weapon lore—gracious Droṇa.

Inquire of the health of Aśvatthāman,
Who made his studies and follows the Law,
Who restored in its fullness the lore of the weapons,
An impetuous man like the son of Gandharvas.

Go also to Śāradvata's* lodgings,
Great warrior, chief of those learned in weapons,
And mentioning me repeatedly, you
Must, Saṃjaya, touch his feet with your hand.

And touching the feet of the greatest of Kurus,
In whom harmless valor resides and *askesis*,
Just wisdom, steadfastness, learning, and mettle,
You should make mention of me to Bhīṣma.

And the Kuru guide with the eyesight of wisdom,**
Sage, learned, who sees to the needs of the old,
To that ancient king you must with my greetings
Convey my good health, O Saṃjaya.

15 Dhṛtarāṣṭra's eldest and slow-witted son,
A fool and a scoundrel of villainous habits,
Who now is the ruler of all of earth,
Suyodhana—ask, friend, about his health.

* = Kṛpa.
** = Dhṛtarāṣṭra.

His younger brother of equal folly,
And always, Saṃjaya, matching his habits,
Great archer and bravest of Kaurava champions,
Duḥśāsana—ask, friend, about his health.

The eminent sage, in all matters wise
Of deep understanding, endowed with all virtues,
Who always has hated the thought of war
Ask, friend, of the health of that son of a *vaiśya*.

That one unmatched at cutting and dicing,
Smart trickster, expert at the dice and the game,
Who cannot be beaten at dicing matches,
Citrasena—ask, friend, about his health.

The one whose only desire it has been
That there might be peace for the Bhāratas,
That wise old bull of the Bāhlikas
As before may graciously greet me again.

20 He whom many of choicest of talents adorn,
Of wide erudition but never harsh,
Who from love endures indignities,
Somadatta—I think him worthy of honor.

Somadatta's son, most worthy of Kurus,
Is a brother and friend to us, Saṃjaya,
Great archer and first of chariot warriors,
Do ask him his health and his family's.

And those other ranking Kaurava youths,
Who are sons and grandsons and brothers to us,
If you happen to meet them, whatever the way,
Do ask them their health on my behalf.

Whoever the kings that the Dhārtarāṣṭra
Has gathered to battle the Pāṇḍavas,
Vasātis, Śālvakas, Kekayas,
Ambaṣṭhas as well as the chief Trigartas,

The Eastern champions, the Northern, the Southern,
The Western along with the kings from the mountains,
Who mean no harm, of right habits and conduct,
Do ask them all, friend, how well they are keeping.

25 Mahouts and horsemen and chariot warriors,
And the footmen too, great masses of Āryans—
To them all convey that my health is good,
And of all inquire if they're keeping well.

Likewise all the king's appointed officials,
His chamberlains, those who marshal his army,
The ones who are charged with income and outgo,
And the grandees who ponder upon his affairs,

The mountain king of Gāndhāra, Śakuni,
Unmatched at cutting and playing at dice,
Who raises the pride of the Dhārtarāṣṭra,
Do ask, good friend, that hypocrite's health.

And the hero who hopes with a single chariot
To vanquish invincible Pāṇḍavas,
Unequaled deluder of the deluded,
Vaikartana*—friend, do ask his health.

Our loyal ally, our guru, our servant,
Who has been a father and mother and friend,
The farsighted Vidura, plumbless of spirit,
Inquire of the health of him, our adviser.

30 The elderly women, the ones of virtue,
Who are, Saṃjaya, known as mothers to us,
Pray meet with all those elderly women,
And pray salute them on our behalf.

"Ye whose sons are alive, are your sons perchance
Correctly and gently treating you?"
Speak thus to them, Saṃjaya; afterward tell them
That Ajātāśatru and sons are well.

The women you, Saṃjaya, know for our wives there,
Them all you should ask, friend, how they are faring.
"Are you well protected, perfumed and reproachless,
And undistracted in household chores?

"Are you nicely behaved to your parents-in-law,
Do you live good lives and live them in comfort?
Do you seek to arrange the ways of your lives
So your husbands remain compliant with you?"

Those you, Saṃjaya, know for our daughters-in-law,
Those virtuous women of wellborn stock,
Tell them when you meet them, "Yudhiṣṭhira
Salutes you with grace, ye mothers of children!"

35 And, Saṃjaya, do in their houses embrace
The young girls, saluting them on my behalf:
"May you have handsome husbands compliant with you,
And may you yourselves comply with your husbands!"

* = Karṇa.

And ask the courtesans how they are doing:
"Adorned, well-wardrobed and well-perfumed,
Always pleasant and pleasured and comforted—
Are your visits but brief and your words but brief?"

The slave girls' sons and the slaves of the Kurus
And the many dependent hunchbacks and cripples,
Do tell that I am still in good health,
And ask them about their sorry good health:

"Have you still been able to keep your old jobs?
Does the Dhārtarāṣṭra give you some comforts?
You who lost a limb, you simples, you dwarfs,
Does the Dhārtarāṣṭra treat you gently?"

And the blind and the oldsters and the others as well,
The many who just have their hands to live by,
Do tell them that I still am in good health,
And ask them about their sorry good health:

40 "Don't be frightened by life's misery,
Which is no doubt due to evil of yore!
After taming my foes and helping my friends,
I shall give you support with housing and food.

"I still have good fruits from the brahmins to come,
And surely I shall have more in the future:
I see that you all will be able-bodied—
Pray tell the king when you have succeeded."

The orphaned, the weak and the ill of mind
Who all the time are absorbed in themselves,
And those who are wretched in every way,
You must ask in my name for their health, my friend.

And the others who rallied to the Dhārtarāṣṭras,
Who, son of the bard, came from many lands,
When you see them, or anyone worthy to see,
Inquire if they're keeping invariably well.

All those who have come or are just arriving,
Kings, envoys that rally from every region,
Ask all, good bard, about their good health,
And later convey that *I*'m keeping well.

45 There are no warriors found on the earth
Like the ones that the Dhārtarāṣṭra has got;
But the Law is eternal and my mighty Law
Is to extirpate all my enemies.

Once more tell, Saṃjaya, Dhārtarāṣṭra
Suyodhana this last word of mine:
The desire that is burning the heart in your body
To rule the Kurus without a rival,

There is neither rhyme nor reason to it!
We are not the kind that pleases you:
You either return Indraprastha to us,
Or you fight, brave chief of the Bhāratas!

Yudhiṣṭhira said:

31.1 The Placer governs the good and the evil, the young and the old,
the weak and the strong, Saṃjaya. The lord grants learning to a child
and childishness to a learned man, he grants it all when in the
beginning he pours out the seed. Enough of further instruction—you
will tell it the way it is, now that we have taken counsel with each
other quite happily. Son of Gavalgaṇa, go to the Kurus, salute the
5 mighty Dhṛtarāṣṭra, touch his feet, and inquire about his health. Tell
him, when he is seated in the circle of the Kurus, "Sire, by the might
of you alone do the Pāṇḍavas live happily. By your grace, enemy-
tamer, they acquired a kingdom while they were still young. Having
established them first in a kingdom, you must not now ignore them
so that they perish." (For nobody deserves to have all there is for his
alone, Saṃjaya.) "Father, we shall live together. Don't fall into the
power of the enemies!"

Likewise salute with your head Bhīṣma Śāṃtanava, the grandfather
of the Bhāratas, praising my name. After greeting him tell our
grandfather, "Sire, you once rescued Śaṃtanu's lineage when it was
10 drowning. Now, dear grandfather, act by your own judgment once
more in such a fashion that your grandchildren live in mutual
harmony." Speak likewise to Vidura, the councilor of the Kurus:
"Speak to peace, friend; Yudhiṣṭhira means well." Then you should
tell the intransigent Prince Suyodhana, flattering him again and
again as he sits in the midst of the Kurus, that we shall endure the
misery of the occasion on which he saw us ignore Kṛṣṇā when she
came alone into the hall—"lest we slaughter the Kurus!" The
Pāṇḍavas have also borne with previous and later hardships though
15 they were stronger; the Kurus know all this. "That you cast us out
into exile, wrapped in deer hides, that misery we forgive, lest we
slaughter the Kurus. We have overlooked the fact that Duḥśāsana,
with your approval, strode in and seized Kṛṣṇā by her hair in the hall.
But, enemy-burner, we must receive our proper share in return: bull
among men, turn away your greedy mind from another's possessions!

"Thus, there shall be peace, king, and mutual harmony. Return to
us who want peace even a corner of your kingdom: Kuśasthala,

Vṛkasthala, Āsandī, Vāraṇāvata, and whatever you choose as the
20 fifth and last portion. Give five villages to the five brothers,
Suyodhana!" So, sagacious Saṃjaya, shall there be peace between us and our kinsmen. "Let brother follow brother, let father be united with son, and let the Pāñcālas smilingly foregather with the Kurus. I wish we may see the Kurus and Pāñcālas unharmed. Friend, bull of the Bharatas, we shall all be happily at peace! I am as capable of peace as I am of war, Saṃjaya, as capable of Law as of Profit, of gentleness and as of toughness!"

Vaiśaṃpāyana said:

32.1 Upon being dismissed by the Pāṇḍava, Saṃjaya, having carried
out the entire command of the great-spirited Dhṛtarāṣṭra, departed; and reaching Hāstinapura he swiftly entered. Coming to the inner chambers he said to the doorkeeper,

"Announce me to Dhṛtarāṣṭra, porter,
I have come from the side of the Pāṇḍavas;
You will tell him, steward, if he's awake—
I wish to arrive with the king's foreknowledge."

The doorkeeper said:

Here is Saṃjaya, sire, I bow to you;
He stands at the gate and wishes to see you.
Your envoy has come from the Pāṇḍavas;
Give orders, king, what he is to do.

Dhṛtarāṣṭra said:

5 Tell him I am happy and ready for him,
Let Saṃjaya enter and be bid welcome.
I have never before been unready for him,
So why, steward, should he remain at the gate?

Vaiśaṃpāyana said:

With the king's permission the bard's son entered
The large chamber protected by wise, brave Āryans
And drew near to King Vaicitravīrya
On his lion throne with folded hands.

Saṃjaya said:

I Saṃjaya bow to you, king of the earth!
I have come from seeing the Pāṇḍavas:
Yudhiṣṭhira, Pāṇḍu's spirited son,
Salutes you and asks you about your health.

He fondly inquires about your sons
And asks, Are you pleased with your sons and grandsons,

With your kinsmen too and your councilors, sire?
And with all others who live off you?

Dhṛtarāṣṭra said:
I greet you, Saṃjaya, on your arrival
And Pārtha Ajātaśatru with pleasure.
Is the king keeping well, and are his sons,
His household and his Kaurava brothers?

Saṃjaya said:
Pāṇḍu's sons and his household are keeping well;
And even more than you knew him before
He pursues pure Profit and Law and is learned,
High-minded, insightful, and steady of habits.

With the Pāṇḍava mildness surpasses the Law
And the Law he deems higher than piling up wealth;
The Pārtha will not yield to pleasures and comforts
That are lacking in Law, sire, know that of him.

Like a wooden puppet strung on a string
So a man gestures, handled by others:
When I see the Pāṇḍava's bitter reverses
I think *karman* is fate that exceeds the man.

Having seen the error that you have committed,
With its evil outcome and unspeakable horror,
I think that as long as a man desires
What is seemly, so long does he win renown.

Ajātaśatru abandoned evil
As a snake its worn-out, useless slough;
Heroic Yudhiṣṭhira's splendor is his
Forever, to you has he passed the guilt.

Come learn, my king, what deed you have wrought,
Ignoble and lacking in Law and Profit;
You have earned only notoriety, king;
You cannot remove it, it will travel with you.

Not heeding them you hope to retain
A dubious prize while you look to your son;
The report of your Unlaw is abroad in the land:
This deed was not, Bhārata, worthy of you.

One wanting in wisdom, lowborn, cruel,
Vindictive and weak in baronial lore,
Such a man will not overcome disaster,
One who lacks in vigor and is unschooled.

One who is born high, law-minded, and famous,
Learned, leading a good life, master of self,
Bears up with Profit and Law intertwined:
Nowhere else can he flee from the power of fate.

For how could one with the best of counsels,
Sure guide to Profit and Law in disaster,
Well-disciplined, lacking not one of the spells,
Not foolish, commit a cruel deed?

20 Your councilors have assembled and sit
Together, as always intent on your tasks;
They have conceived a firm conviction–
All hell has burst loose for the Kurus' destruction.

The Kurus would instantly cease to exist,
If Ajātaśatru countered the evil
With evil, while passing the evil to you;
And the blame in the world would go to yourself.

And was it beyond the domain of the Gods
That the Pārtha set eyes on yonder world?
He ascended to it and was highly honored–
No doubt, no human enterprise counts.

King Bali examined the fruits of acts,
Non-being and being, the present and transient,
And failing to find the farther shore,
Concluded that nothing but Time was the cause.

Eyes, ears, the nose, and skin and tongue,
These are the seats of human perception;
When the Thirst is quenched the senses are happy;
One should, carefree and happy, goad them on.

25 Not so, say others: a person's act,
If well employed, takes on form as it should:
By the act of the father and mother begotten
The child grows normally by eating food.

What is pleasant, unpleasant, happy, or wretched
And praise and blame are a person's lot;
The one scolds the other when he has done wrong;
And gives him praise if he acted right.

I blame you for the Bhāratas' discord;
This surely will be the end of your offspring;
Would that, because of your error, it not
Burn up the Kurus as fire burns deadwood.

You alone in the world are falling into
The power of sons that were born to you;
At the time of the dicing you praised the lecher—
Behold: without peace extinction is his.

By preferring untrustworthy men, O king,
And rejecting the trustworthy ones, lord of men,
You are now too feeble, O Kauraveya,
To protect your endless, opulent land.

30 The speed of the chariot has shaken me up,
I am tired: with your leave I shall lie on my bed.
Tomorrow the Kurus shall hear in assembly
The message Ajātaśatru has sent.

5(51) *Dhṛtarāṣṭra's Vigil*

5.33–41 (B. 33–41; C. 971–1576)
33 (33; 971). Dhṛtarāṣṭra summons Vidura, to whom he explains that Saṃjaya has denounced him and that he cannot sleep until he has heard the message which he is to receive the next day (1–10). Vidura should remain with him in the interval, sharing his wisdom with Dhṛtarāṣṭra (10–15). Vidura discourses on the wise man (15–25), on the fool (25–35), on things that come in ones, twos, etc., through tens (40–80), and on the virtues of a good ruler (80–100), ending with an admonition to give in to the Pāṇḍavas (100).
34 (34; 1094). On Law and Profit (1–50), the mastery of the senses (50–65), the vice of verbal abuse (70–75), the virtues of Yudhiṣṭhira (80).
35 (35; 1181). On honesty: the colloquy of Virocana and Sudhanvan. Virocana's wife Keśinī asks her husband whether brahmins or Dānavas are superior; being a Dānava, he answers: the Dānavas (1–5). The matter will be resolved on the morrow when the brahmin Sudhanvan will come. Sudhanvan, however, refuses to sit with Virocana (5–10). They wager their lives on their respective rank (10–15). They go to Virocana's father Prahrāda for arbitration; he receives them (15–20). Sudhanvan presses Prahrāda, who decides for Sudhanvan; the latter presents his son's life to him (20–30). Vidura continues with more saws, ending with praise for the Pāṇḍavas (30–75).

36 (36; 1260). The Colloquy of Atri and the Sādhyas on wisdom; more saws (1–20). Dhṛtarāṣṭra asks Vidura what makes a family great: the virtues of good family and general morality (20–45). On virtue and vice (45–65), the need to protect the Pāṇḍavas (65–70).
37 (37; 1334). The seventeen futilities (1–5); on straight advice (5–15), masters and servants, good character (15–35). The evil of quarreling with the Pāṇḍavas (35–40). The five strengths (45–50), and the perils of contempt (50–55).
38 (38; 1398). On hospitality (1), proper purchases and diet (5), treasures to be guarded (10), a king's counsel (15). A king's forbearance (20), good conduct (30–40).
39 (39; 1446). Dhṛtarāṣṭra states that he cannot abandon his son (1–5). Vidura replies that the wicked must be abandoned, but kinsmen supported: he should give the Pāṇḍavas some villages and treat them well (5–25), or he will regret it (25–30). The virtues of deportment (30–35); on morality (35–45), luck (45–50), austerity (50–55), moderation (60–65).
40 (40; 1532). On law-abiding action (1), good luck tokens (5), contentment (10). Karman *follows the man after death (10–15); on self-control (15–20), the duties of the classes (25). Dhṛtarāṣṭra, despite himself, cannot abandon his son (25–30).*
41 (41; 1565). He asks for more knowledge; Vidura replies that being the son of a śūdra *woman he may not speak of higher matters, but Sanatsujāta will come (1–5).*

Vaiśaṃpāyana said:

33.1 The wise King Dhṛtarāṣṭra said to his doorkeeper, "I want to see Vidura, bring him here at once." The messenger dispatched by Dhṛtarāṣṭra said to the Steward, "Our lord the great king wishes to see you, sage." At these words Vidura went to the king's palace and said, "Announce me to Dhṛtarāṣṭra, doorkeeper!"

The doorkeeper said:

Vidura has come at your command, Indra of kings. He wishes to see your feet. What is he to do? Command me.

Dhṛtarāṣṭra said:

5 Let the sagacious and farsighted Vidura enter! I am never unready to see him.

The doorkeeper said:

Enter the inner chambers of the wise king, Steward, for the king tells me he is never unready to see you.

Vaiśaṃpāyana said:

Vidura, entering Dhṛtarāṣṭra's chamber, said with folded hands to the king, who was brooding, "I, Vidura, have come at your behest, wise king. If there is anything to be done, here I am. Command me!"

Dhṛtarāṣṭra said:

Saṃjaya has returned, Vidura. And after berating me he left.
Tomorrow he will deliver Ajātaśatru's message in the assembly hall.
10 I do not know what the message of the Kuru hero is, and it burns
my limbs and makes me sleepless. Tell me what you think is good for
a sleepless and hot man to hear, for you, friend of us, are experienced
in Law and Profit.

> Since Saṃjaya returned from the Pāṇḍavas,
> My mind has not known the peace that it should;
> All my faculties are in disorder now,
> While I brood on what he is going to say.

Vidura said:

Sleeplessness happens to him who is attacked by a stronger foe, to one who is weak and lacks the means, to him who has lost his all, to a lover, and to a thief. Surely you are not touched by any of these disasters, O king? Or are you burning because you covet the possessions of another?

Dhṛtarāṣṭra said:

15 I wish to hear from you words that bespeak the Law and lead to
the ultimate good, for you are the only one deemed wise in this
lineage of royal seers.

Vidura said:

The mark of a wise man is that he cultivates praiseworthy acts
and avoids the blameworthy, that he is not heterodox but has faith.
He is called wise whom neither anger, joy, pride, false modesty, nor
vainglory draw away from his purpose. He is called wise whose plan
and counsel are unknown to his enemies, and whose actual deeds
only are known to them. He is called wise whose plans are not
obstructed by heat and cold, fear and love, wealth and poverty.
20 He is called wise whose transmigrating spirit obeys Law and Profit
and who chooses Profit over Pleasure. The wise, O bull of the
Bharatas, wish to act as they can, then act as they can, and do not
despise anything.

> Understanding quickly he listens with patience;
> He pursues his profit with knowledge, not lust;
> Unless asked to he mixes in no one's affairs;
> This is the premier sign of a wise man.

People of wise minds do not want what they cannot have, do not bemoan what has been lost, and are not confused in adversity. He is called wise who proceeds upon his decision, does not stop in the
25 midst of his task, does not waste time, and controls himself. The wise, O bull of the Bharatas, are attracted to noble deeds, perform acts conducive to prosperity, and do not mutter against their well-wishers. He is called wise who does not exult when he is honored, nor burns when he is despised, but remains as imperturbable as a Ganges lake. That man is called wise who knows the nature of all creatures, the practice of all acts, and the expedients of men. He is called wise whose speech is eloquent, whose conversation is varied, who is quick to understand, imaginative, and fast in expounding a text. He whose learning serves his intelligence, whose intelligence serves his learning, and who does not violate the standards of an Āryan earns the renown of being wise.

30 He is called a fool who is not learned yet vain, poor yet proud, and hopeful of gain without action. He is called a fool who abandons his own purpose, promotes another man's purpose, and acts falsely in the cause of a friend. Him they call a nitwit who hankers after the undesirable, despises the desirable, and hates a stronger man. Him they call a nitwit who treats an enemy as a friend, hates and harms a friend, and perpetrates evil. A fool, bull of the Bharatas, postpones his tasks, hesitates over everything, and takes long over a quick
35 matter. A nitwit, the lowest of men, enters unbidden, talks much unasked, and puts his trust in the vigilant. He who blames others when he himself is at fault and who gets angry without having power is a most stupid man. He is called confused who, without knowing his own strength, wishes to obtain without work that which is unattainable and devoid of Law and Profit. Him they call a nitwit, king, who teaches one who is not his pupil, subserves a destitute man, and seeks out the ignoble. But he is called wise who goes around without pride after obtaining great wealth, knowledge, or power.

40 Who is more cruel than he who eats well alone, dresses handsomely alone, without sharing with his dependents? One man commits evil deeds but many experience the fruit thereof; the latter are free of guilt, while the doer is tainted by it. A single arrow shot by an archer may or may not kill, but the intelligence displayed by an intelligent man can kill a kingdom and its king. Having with the one decided upon the two, subdue the three with the four, master the five, know the six, avoid the seven, and you will be happy. A poisoned meal kills one, a sword kills one, but the leaking of counsel kills king, kingdom,
45 and people. One should not eat tasty food alone, reflect upon one's affairs alone, go on a journey alone, wake alone amidst the sleeping. The One without a second, which you do not comprehend, king, is

the truth, the staircase to heaven, a lifeboat in the sea. The forgiving have one flaw, none other is found: people think that the forgiving man is incompetent. The one Law is the highest good, the one forgiveness the ultimate peace, the one wisdom the highest insight, the one *ahiṃsā* the path to happiness.

Earth eats up these two, as a snake eats up animals dwelling in
holes: an unaggressive king and a brahmin who does not make
50 pilgrimages. By two actions does a man shine in this world: by never
speaking cuttingly and by not making requests of bad people. There
are two kinds of people, tiger among men, who put their trust in
others: women who love a man loved by another, and people who
honor a person honored by others. There are two sharp thorns that
sap the body: for a poor man to covet and for a powerless man to
rage. Two kinds of men rank above heaven: a master who is forgiving
and a poor man who is generous. Property that has been rightfully
acquired is misused in two ways: by giving it to an unworthy man
and by not giving it to a worthy one.

50 There are three measures, bull of the Bharatas, that they say apply
to men: low, middling, and good, thus know the Veda-wise. There
are three kinds of people, king: good, bad, and middling; one should
properly charge to them three kinds of tasks. Three hold no property,
king: the wife, the slave, and the son, whatever they obtain belongs
to him who owns them.

> They say, and a *paṇḍit* should know, that a king
> Who is powerful should avoid these four;
> He should not consult with dimwitted men,
> Woolgatherers, sloths, and flattering bards.
>
> Let, friend, these four live with you at home
> At the householder's stage, if fortune has blessed you:
> A kinsman who's old, one of rank but distressed,
> A friend who is poor, and childless sister.

60 Bṛhaspati mentioned four instant events when Indra of the Thirty
Gods questioned him; learn them from me, great king: the intention
of the Gods, the understanding of the intelligent, the humility of the
learned, and the ruin of the wicked.

A man should tend five fires religiously, bull of the Bharatas:
father, mother, fire, self, and guru. By honoring these five does one
obtain fame in this world: Gods, ancestors, men, mendicants, and
guests. Five will follow you wherever you may go: friends, enemies,
65 neutrals, those you live on, and those who live off you. If one of the
five senses of mortal man springs a leak, then his knowledge seeps
away through it, like water from the bottom of a water bag.

A man who wants to prosper should avoid these six vices: sleepiness, sloth, fear, anger, laziness, and procrastination. A man should avoid these six like a leaking boat in the ocean: a teacher who does not teach, a priest who has not studied, a king who fails to protect, a wife who is abusive, a cowherd who wants a village, and a barber who wants the forest. But six virtues a man should never give up: truthfulness, liberality, alertness, compliance, patience,
70 and steadiness. He who achieves mastery of these permanent six qualities in himself and subdues his senses is not affected by evil, let alone disasters. These six live off six others: thieves off the careless, physicians off the sick, wanton women off lechers, priests off sacrificers, a king off the querulous, and the learned always off fools.

A king should at all times avoid the seven vices which spring from addiction and because of which otherwise firmly established princes mostly perish: women, dice, the hunt, liquor, abusive language in the fifth place, cruel punishment, and abuse of wealth.

75 There are eight portents of a person's ruin: first that he hates brahmins, quarrels with brahmins, takes brahmin property, wants to kill brahmins, delights in berating them, does not welcome praise of them, does not remember them in his tasks, and protests when solicited by them: these eight faults a wise man who uses his intelligence should avoid. These eight are the fresh butter of joy, Bhārata, found to give great pleasure when they obtain: encounter with friends, a large inflow of wealth, the embrace of a son, sexual
80 intercourse, pleasant conversations at the appointed time, high rank within one's own herd, the attainment of desired goals, honor in society.

The wise man who knows the dwelling of the nine gates, three pillars, and five witnesses, which is governed by the soul, is the greatest sage.

There are ten who do not know the Law; learn who they are, Dhṛtarāṣṭra: the drunk, careless, insane, tired, angry, hungry, hasty, timid, greedy, and lustful. Therefore the wise man should not incline to these states. On this they cite the ancient story which was chanted by the Asura king Sudhanvan for the sake of his son.

> The king who abandons anger and lust
> And bestows his largess on worthy men;
> Discriminates, studies, and is quick to act,
> To him all people turn as their standard.
>
> If he knows how to comfort the people and does
> Employ his staff on known criminals,
> If he knows his measure and is benign,
> All fortune will visit such a king.

He does not despise a very weak foe,
But treats him strictly with intelligence,
He seeks no quarrel with persons in power,
But marches in season to war and is wise.

If reduced to distress, he never wavers,
But undistracted exerts his efforts;
In control of himself, he endures times of grief:
Such an eminent man sees his rivals defeated.

Forever is happy the man who avoids
A profitless sojourn away from his home,
Consorting with scoundrels, caressing strange wives,
Pride, thievishness, treachery, drinking of liquor.

90 He pursues his goals not too zealously;
When questioned he only relates what is true;
He quarrels not about trifling things,
And wisely he angers not when not honored.

If one does not protest but takes pity instead,
And if he, when weak, does not act hostile,
If he talks not too much and pardons a quarrel,
He will everywhere win people's praise.

Him who never puts on a prideful appearance
Or to others boasts of his manliness,
Or excitedly speaks in abusive language,
The people make him a friend of theirs.

They deem him the greatest of nobly behaved men
Who does not fire up a forgotten feud,
Does not climb up his pride nor fades away,
Or thinks in a rage, "I am badly off!"

A person of noble behavior will not
Display great pleasure when he is lucky
Or relax at another's unhappiness,
Or after his gift be sorry for it.

95 If he, knowing the high and the low, tries to foster
Local customs and covenants and caste Laws,
Then wherever he goes he always achieves
A superior rank with the public at large.

That man of intelligence ranks as the best
Who shuns arrogance, folly, jealousy, misdeeds,
Insults to the king, wide feuding, betrayal,
And converse with the drunk, the insane, and the evil.

The deities seek to elevate him
Who practices self-control, purity, piety,
Auspicious acts, rites of reparation,
Good repute with the people, and daily tasks.

If he weds in his rank and not beneath him
Is friendly and deals and converses with equals,
And gives first place to the quality,
He is wise and his ways are well-conducted.

No ill fortune will strike that man of soul
Who eats measuredly, sharing with his dependents,
Sleeps little but does not limit his work,
And if he be asked gives even to foes.

100 If a person's intentions are apt to do harm
The people will never know what he did
As long as his counsel is kept and observed:
He will not in the slightest be hurt in his purpose.

If intent on the peace of all creatures he stays
Mild, truthful, liberal, pure in his being,
He is recognized among his kinsmen
As a gracious amulet to his kind.

A man very diffident with himself
Is soon a guru to all the world;
Immense in prestige, attentive, and kindly,
He shines with his splendor alike to the sun.

To five Indra-like sons who were born in the woods
To Pāṇḍu the king, who was burned by a curse,

You have reared as children and given instruction—
They now wait for your orders, Ambikā's son!

If you render to them their accustomed kingdom,
And rejoice with your sons, friend, finally happy,
You shall no more be to Gods and to men
Of questionable honesty, Indra on earth!

Dhṛtarāṣṭra said:
34.1 What should a sleepless and hot man do in your view, tell me that, for among us you, my friend, are experienced in Law and Profit, and honest.

Instruct me properly, Vidura,
What you in your wisdom consider wholesome
For Ajātaśatru, you noble of heart,
And what will be best for the Kauravas.

Apprehensive of evil and forecasting evil
I ask you the question with anxious heart:
Declare to me wholly and truthfully, sage,
The entire desire of Ajātaśatru.

Vidura said:

Even without being asked one should speak up to him whom one does not wish to see defeated, whether it be good or bad, hateful or pleasant. Therefore I shall tell you, sire, as I wish the Kurus well—listen as I speak words that are beneficial and consistent with the Law.

Never set your mind on actions which succeed through deceit and the use of bad expedients. The wise man does not tire out his mind, if an action that was taken correctly and with the right means does not succeed, king. As actions have consequences, one should look at the consequence and act after due deliberation; don't act in haste. Looking at the aftereffect and consequences of actions and one's own competence, one may decide either to act or not. A king who does not know what criteria to apply to place, gain, loss, funds, people, and reprisals does not remain long in his kingship. He attains kingship who diligently looks for the criteria I mentioned with a knowledge of Law and Profit. One should never take inappropriate action, thinking, "Mine is the kingdom," for lack of discipline kills a king's fortune as surely as old age kills physical beauty.

A fish, leaping to the mere appearance, swallows the iron hook that is clothed in a fine morsel, and does not look at the consequence. He who seeks prosperity looks for what can be eaten, and considers how the eatable will digest if eaten, and whether this eatable will be beneficial when it has been digested. If one plucks unripe fruits from a tree, he does not get the juice from the fruit, and he also loses the seed; but if one takes a ripe fruit at the time it has ripened, he gets the juice from the fruit and the fruit from the seed. Just as the bee takes the honey but spares the flower, so one should take property from people without hurting them. Pluck flower after flower, but don't cut the root, like a garland-merchant in a pleasance and not like the charcoal-burner.

Think about prospective actions, testing them with questions like "How do I profit if I do it, and how if I don't?" and then do it or don't. Some matters should not be acted upon, and are always like that, for any personal effort expended on them will be pointless. Other matters may yield great results though they may lack much root: those the wise man tackles at once and he puts no obstacle in their way. If a man sees everything straight, as it were drinks it in with his eyes, his subjects love him even if he sits still and silent. When one favors the world in all four ways, with eye, thought, speech, and act, the world favors him correspondingly. But if the creatures fear

him as game animals fear the hunter, he may have gained all earth
to her borders of seas, but he is deserted.
25 A man may come into an ancestral kingdom by his own splendor,
but if he sticks to bad policies he causes it to collapse as the wind
shreds a cloud. Treasure-filled earth promotes and increases the
fortunes of a king who practices the Law that the strict have
practiced from the beginning. But for one who abandons the Law
and adopts the lawlessness, the world shrinks like a hide that is put
on a fire. The same effort should be made to protect one's own realm
as is made to crush another's. Find a kingdom by Law, protect it by
Law, and you will not lose, or be lost by, your Law-rooted fortune.
30 Does one obtain any substance at all from the babblings of a
madman and the crawling of a child; does one get gold from a rock?
The wise man will sit and collect the good sayings and deeds of the
prudent, as a gleaner his gleanings. Cows see with their noses, the
brahmins with their Vedas, kings with their spies, all the rest with
their eyes. A cow that is hard to milk suffers much discomfort, but
no one, king, disciplines an easy milker. People do not heat what
bends unheated; they do not force wood to bend that bends of itself.
35 By this parable the wise man bows to the stronger, and to Indra bows
the one who bends to the stronger. Cattle have the rain god for their
patron, kings their kin for their friends, husbands are the women's
friends, the Veda is the brahmins' friends. Law is preserved by truth,
knowledge by practice, beauty by washing, family rank by conduct.
Rice is saved by measure, horses by exercises, cows by constant
watching, a woman by poor clothes. Family rank is no criterion, if
one has no manners, for even among the lowest-born manners stand
40 out. Without end is the disease of one who envies others their wealth,
beauty, courage, descent, happiness, and loving reception.

If you are afraid because you do wrong things, forget what should be done, or are confused at the wrong time, don't drink what makes you drunk. Those prone to get drunk get drunk on knowledge, wealth, and good birth; but the same are the triumphs of the strict. Let the strict ask the lax for a bit of a favor just once, and the notoriously lax consider themselves strict. The strict are the guide of those who have soul, the strict guide the strict, the strict guide the lax, but never do the lax guide the strict. A well-dressed man wins over the assembly, the owner of cattle is above having to share his meal, the man with the cart overcomes the road, the man of good habits vanquishes all. Good habits are the core of a person; if he loses them, he profits from neither life, wealth, nor relatives. Of the rich the main dish is meat, of the middling it's cow's milk, bull of Bharatas, of the poor it's salt. Yet the poor always eat better: hunger sweetens their dishes, and that is rare among the rich. It is generally

found in the world that the rich have no appetite, but the poor,
50 O Indra of kings, digest even wood. The fear of the lowest classes is
to have no job, of the middle ones it is death, of the highest mortals
the greatest fear is dishonor. The intoxication with power is worse
than drunkenness with liquor and such, for he who is drunk with
power does not come to his senses before he falls.

People are plagued by their senses, if they act without restraint to
attain their desires, as stars are plagued by the planets. If one is
dragged along as the victim of his natural five senses, his adversities
wax like the moon in the bright fortnight. He who wishes to control
his councilors without controlling himself, and to control his enemies
55 without controlling his councilors, perishes willy-nilly. If he first
conquers himself as though he were a country, he will not vainly
conquer both councilors and enemies. Fortune favors that wise king
very greatly who has mastered himself, controls his councilors, raises
his staff against criminals, and acts after due deliberation.

> A chariot, king, is a person's body:
> The soul is the driver, the senses his horses;
> Undistracted by his fine horses a driver
> Who is skilled rides happily, if they are trained.

Senses out of control suffice to bring one to grief, as untrained and
disobedient horses bring a driver to grief on the road. A fool who,
guided by his senses, sees profit arising from the unprofitable and the
60 unprofitable from profit mistakes misery for happiness. If one gives up
Law and Profit and falls under the sway of his senses, he is soon
deserted by fortune, life, wealth, and wife. He who owns riches but is
owned by his senses is toppled from his estate by his triumphant
senses. One oneself should search for the self, with mind, spirit, and
senses subdued, for the self is one's friend and the self is one's foe.
Like two large fish held in fine-gauze net, desire and anger, O king,
tear apart one's wisdom. If one collects the necessities while looking
to Law and Profit, then, having made his collection, he prospers
65 happily. He who without subjugating the five inner enemies that
destroy his judgment seeks to subdue his other foes is set upon by his
foes. We see that ill-spirited kings are murdered by their own actions,
because they have no control over their senses and because of their
wanton lust for kingship. Just as the wet gets burned with the dry
because it is mixed with the dry, so a guiltless man receives the same
punishment as the guilty if he does not cease consorting with them.
Therefore one should not keep company with the wicked. If out of
folly a man fails to subdue his five rearing senses with their five
purposes, disaster devours him.

Compliance, uprightness, purity, contentment, kindly speech, self-
70 control, truthfulness, and ease are not of the wicked. The lowliest do

not have self-knowledge, ease, endurance, steadfastness in the Law,
guarded speech, and liberality, Bhārata. Fools seek to harm the wise
with abuse and slander: the speaker takes the guilt, while the
forgiving man is free. Of the evil, harm is the strength; of kings
authority; of women obedience; of the virtuous forgiveness. Controlling
one's speech is considered the most difficult thing, for there is not
much meaningful and varied that can be said. Varied speech that is
well-turned brings on good results, while a bad tongue leads to
75 adversity. A wood pierced with arrows and struck with an axe grows
again, but the loathsome wound that abusive speech strikes never
heals. Arrows of various kinds may be pulled from a body, but the
thorn of speech cannot be extracted, for it sticks in the heart.

> From the mouth fly forth the arrows of speech,
> Hit by which one suffers by day and by night;
> They hit another in his weak spots—
> The wise do not shoot them at enemies.

When the Gods want to defeat a man they take away his wit and he
sees matters upside down. When his wit has been despoiled and
destruction looms, his wrong policy, which appears right to him,
does not leave his heart.

80 The wit of your sons is perverted, Bhārata, by their enmity for the
Pāṇḍavas, and you do not realize it. Endowed with the marks, fit to
be the king of even the three worlds, Yudhiṣṭhira, your pupil, must
reign, Dhṛtarāṣṭra! Over and above all your sons he is honored by
destiny; he is possessed of splendor and insight, and he knows the
nature of Law and Profit. The first of those that uphold the Law, he
has endured many hardships, O Indra of kings, out of gentleness,
compassion, and respect for you.

Dhṛtarāṣṭra said:

35.1 Speak, O sage, more words that conform to Law and Profit. I am
not sated of listening to you, for you are speaking here in various
ways.

Vidura said:

There is the practice of taking baths at all the sacred fords, and then there is honesty toward all creatures: maybe both are equal, and maybe honesty wins out. Act honestly toward your sons at all times, my lord; thus you will gain the highest rewards on earth, and after death heaven. A man, tiger among men, exults in heaven for as long as his virtuous name is celebrated among the people.

5 On this point people cite the ancient legend, the colloquy of
Virocana with Sudhanvan in the case of Keśinī.

Keśinī said:

Are the brahmins superior, Virocana, or the sons of Diti? Or rather, with whom would Sudhanvan decline to sit on a couch?

Virocana said:

Being the scions of Prajāpati, we are superior, Keśinī, we are the best! Ours, in fact, are these worlds—who are the Gods, who are the twiceborn?

Keśinī said:

Sit here; we shall wait in this audience hall, Virocana. Sudhanvan will be coming in the morning, so I will see the two of you together.

Virocana said:

I shall do so, my dear, do as you say, timid girl. Tomorrow morning you shall see Sudhanvan and me together.

Sudhanvan said:

10 Son of Prahrāda, I accept the golden seat from you, now that I have met you; but I will not sit with you!

Virocana said:

Let them fetch you a wooden board, or a bundle or cushion of grass! You are unworthy of sitting with me, Sudhanvan.

Sudhanvan said:

Even your father sits below me when I sit with him! You are a child spoiled at home, you know nothing!

Virocana said:

Let us bet gold, cows, and horses, and whatever wealth there is with the Asuras, Sudhanvan. With that stake we shall ask the question of those who know!

Sudhanvan said:

Keep your gold, cattle, and horseflesh, Virocana! Let us bet our lives and ask the question of those who know.

Virocana said:

15 Having wagered our lives, where shall we go? For I shall not stand ever before Gods or humans!

Sudhanvan said:

Having wagered our lives we shall go to your father. Prahrāda will not lie even in the cause of his son.

Prahrāda said:

There these two appear together who have never joined before. Like two angry cobras they come here by the same road! Why are you walking together? You have never walked together before! Virocana, I ask you, why are you friends with Sudhanvan?

Virocana said:

I am not friends with Sudhanvan. We have bet our lives. Prahrāda, I ask you a question, and speak no lie!

Prahrāda said:

20 Let them fetch water and the honey dish for Sudhanvan. Brahmin, you deserve my welcome; a white cow has been fattened!

Sudhanvan said:

Water and the honey dish were offered me for the road. Prahrāda, you resolve the question that we are asking of you.

Prahrāda said:

Another son, you stand here as witness, brahmin? When the two
of you debate a question, who am I to argue? I ask you, Sudhanvan,
what night does the false arbiter spend who would neither speak the
truth nor lie?

Sudhanvan said:

A false arbiter will spend the night that a superseded wife spends,
or one who lost at the dicing, or one whose body is exhausted with
25 his burden. The false arbiter spends the night of one forbidden the
city and staying hungry outside the gate and seeing many enemies.
With a lie about a goat he kills five, with a lie about a cow ten,
with a lie about a horse a hundred, with a lie about a man a
thousand. . . . If he lies about gold, he kills those born and unborn,
with a lie about land he kills everything. Don't lie about land!

Prahrāda said:

Angiras is better than I and Sudhanvan than you, Virocana. His
mother is better than yours, therefore you have been won by him,
Virocana, this Sudhanvan now owns your life. Sudhanvan, I want
you to give Virocana back.

Sudhanvan said:

30 As you have chosen the Law and not spoken a lie out of love, for
that I give you the rare present of a son, Prahrāda. Here is your son
Virocana, Prahrāda, my gift to you. He shall wash my feet before the
princess.

Vidura said:

Therefore, O Indra of kings, you must not tell a lie about land. Do
not leap to perdition along with your sons and councilors by straying
after your son. The Gods do not protect like a herdsman by taking a
stick: to him whom they wish to protect they deal wisdom. A person's
affairs prosper to the extent that he sets his mind on good things, no
doubt about that.

35 No hymns will save from calamity
An illusionist who works with deceit;
As birds that are fledged abandon the nest
So the hymns abandon him in his last hour.

They say that one should shun spiritous liquor,
Broad feuds and quarrels, discord with one's spouse,
A breach with one's kinsmen, harm to a king,
A dispute between sexes, a road that goes wrong.

These seven are not to be called in witness:
A palmist, a merchant who has been a thief,
A trapper of birds, a physician,
An enemy, friend, and lastly an actor.

A proud *agnihotra*, a prideful silence,
A prideful learning, a rite done with pride,
Are four that may not inspire any fear
Yet are dangerous if they are wrongly enacted.

An arsonist, poisoner, pimp, seller of Soma, arrow-wright, soothsayer,
40 harmer of friends, paramour, abortionist, defiler of his guru's bed, a
brahmin who drinks liquor, a scathing speaker, impure man, heretic,
reviler of the Veda, self-server, apostate, a wealthy niggard, and he
who harms when asked for help are equal to brahmin-murderers.
Gold is proved by a straw fire, a good man by the yoke, a strict man
by his conduct, a brave man in danger, a steady man in hardships,
and friends and foes in grievous disaster. Old age robs beauty, hope
robs steadiness, death robs life, envy robs lawfulness, anger robs good
luck, subservience to the ignoble robs character, lust robs modesty,
pride robs everything. Good fortune rises from auspicious beginnings,
grows from bold action, takes root with dexterity, and stands firm
with self-control.

45 Eight virtues illumine a man: intelligence, good birth, self-control,
learning, prowess, reticence, liberality where possible, and gratitude.
These are powerful virtues, friend, but one virtue forges them
together: when the king treats a man with honor, this virtue
outshines them all. These eight, O king, are in the world of men the
portents of the world of heaven; four of them are innate with the
good, the other four are pursued by the good: sacrifice, liberality,
study, and austerity are innate in the good; self-control, truthfulness,
uprightness, and gentleness are pursued by the good.

There is no assembly where there are no elders, there are no
elders if they do not expound the Law, there is no Law where there
50 is no truth, there is no truth if it is shot through with falsehood. Truth,
beauty, learning, knowledge, good birth, character, vigor, wealth,
bravery, and eloquence are the ten sources of social grace. The man
of ill repute reaps ill, doing ill; the man of good repute reaps good,
doing good. Evil that is perpetrated time and again destroys one's
wits, and once his wits are lost a man does nothing but evil. Good
done time and again cause one's wits to prosper, and when his wits
prosper a man does nothing but good. The envious man, the malicious
man, the cruel man, and the querulous man soon meet with great
55 hardships while pursuing their evil ways; a man without envy and
who keeps his wits while pursuing his good ways meets no hardship,
only happiness, and he shines everywhere.

He who learns wisdom from the wise is a sage, and, gaining Law and Profit in his wisdom, he can strive for happiness. By day one must do what makes one sleep happy at night; in the eight months he should do what makes him weather the rains happily. In the prime of his youth he should do what will give him a happy life in old age, and all his life he should do what will make him happy hereafter. People praise food that has been digested, a wife past her youth, a hero with no more battles, and an ascetic who has gone the whole way.

60 A flaw that is covered up with ill-gotten wealth remains open and
another bursts forth. The guru is the controller of the self-possessed,
the king of the criminal, and Yama Vaivasvata of those who sin in
secret. The origins of seers, rivers, and great-spirited lineages cannot
be recovered, nor can that of women and ill conduct. A generous
man devoted to the brahmins, a man honest toward his male kin,
and a baron partaking of heaven long rule the earth, O king. Three
kinds of men pluck the golden bloom of the earth: a hero, a man of
65 learning, and a man who knows how to serve. Acts of intelligence
are the best, acts of the arms are middling, acts of the skin the worst,
and those of carrying burdens even worse.

How can you hope to prosper when you have given power to the mindless Duryodhana, Śakuni, Duḥśāsana, and Karṇa? The Pāṇḍavas are endowed with all virtues, bull of the Bharatas! They treat you like a father, so treat them like sons!

Vidura said:

36.1 On this issue people quote this ancient story we have heard, the
Colloquy of Ātreya and the Sādhyas.

Of yore the Sādhya Gods interrogated a great seer of strict vows, when he was wandering about in the guise of a swan. "Great seer," they said, "we are the Sādhya Gods. We see you, but cannot guess who you are. We know you are steadfast and wise in learning—pray speak a noble word of wisdom."

The swan said:

I have learned, Immortals, that this is one's task: to be steady and
serene and to pursue truth and Law; having undone all the knots of
the heart, one should bring both the pleasant and the unpleasant
5 under control. When abused, do not abuse: if you endure it, the
wrath will burn up the abuser, and you yourself reap the other's
merit. Do not insult, do not despise a foe, do not betray a friend, nor
serve the lowly; be not too proud or lacking in conduct, avoid harsh
and scathing words. Rough words burn a man's vitals, bones, heart,
and life away; therefore one should at all times avoid harsh and
scathing speech, if he delights in the Law. Know that he is the most
ill-favored of men who hurts people with thorn-like words, wounding,
rough, and harsh—such a one carries death on his lips.

When an enemy hits one sorely with very sharp arrows that burn like sun and fire, and one though bloodied survives it, then, if he is wise, he knows that the other has thereby surrendered his merit to him. If one serves a strict man or a wicked one, an ascetic or a thief, then just as cloth is tinged by the dye, he is tinged by them. The Gods longingly await the coming of him who does not reply to slander or make others reply, who when struck does not strike back or have others strike, and who does not wish ill to him who wants to kill him. They say that, in the first place, not to speak is better than speaking; that if one speaks, he should speak the truth, in the second place; if he speaks the truth, it should be pleasant, in the third; if he speaks the truth that pleases, it should be informed by Law, in the fourth place. A man becomes like the ones he converses with, like the ones whom he serves, or like what he desires to be.

One is free of whatever one turns away from; by turning away from everything one experiences not the slightest unhappiness. He is not vanquished and does not wish to vanquish others, he carries on no feuds and does not strike back; even-natured at either praise or blame, he does not grieve and he does not rejoice. He is a great man who wishes everyone to fare well, has no ill will, speaks the truth, and is gentle and controlled; middling is he who does not placate an unworthy man, gives what he has promised, and knows what has been done well and ill; the mark of the lowest man is that he cannot be swayed, strikes instead of teaching, does not turn away from the influence of anger, is ungrateful, friendless, and ill-spirited. The worst is he who gives no credence to whatever good others do to him, distrusts himself, and discards his friends. If one wishes the best for himself, he should cultivate the best and, at the right time, the middling, but never the lowest. One may gain futile wealth through strength, constant effort, shrewdness, and enterprise, and still not fully earn praise or attain to the conduct of great families.

Dhṛtarāṣṭra said:

Gods, men who have grown old and wise in Law and Profit, and those of great learning aspire to great families. I ask you this question, Vidura, what makes a family great?

Vidura said:

Those are the great families of correct conduct in which are found the seven virtues of austerity, self-control, *brahman* study, sacrifices, pure marriages, and the daily donations of food. Great are those families in which neither conduct nor womb is deficient, which practice the Law by the grace of good habits, which aspire to distinguished renown in their lineages, and which give up all falsehood. Families lose rank by failing to sacrifice, by bad marriages, by neglect of the Veda, and by transgression of the Law. Families lose rank by despoiling what is owed to the Gods, plundering the property

of brahmins, and offending the brahmins. Families lose rank by
oppressing and maligning brahmins, O Bhārata, and by stealing what
has been entrusted to them. Families that own cattle, men, and
horses do not attain to the name of *family* when they are lacking in
good conduct, but families that do not fall short in conduct though
they be of small means bear the name of *family* and reap great
renown.

30 May no one in our family carry on a feud, may no king's councilor
steal another's property, betray a friend, cheat, or lie, or eat ahead of
the ancestors, Gods, and guests. He of us who would strike a
brahmin, he of us who would hate a brahmin, he of us who would
practice husbandry shall have no concourse with us. Grass, room on
the floor, water, and in the fourth place a friendly word are never
lacking in the houses of the strict: they are offered with total faith,
wise king, in the houses of law-observing men of merit to provide
hospitality. Even a small *syandana* tree can support a weight that
other trees cannot; likewise men in great families when thus
burdened are capable of assuming weights that other people cannot.
35 He is not a friend whose anger one fears or who is to be treated with
circumspection; but he is a friend whom one can trust like a father—
others are mere relations. If someone, though unrelated, behaves as
a friend, then he is a relative, a friend, a refuge, and an ultimate
resort. If one is fickle of mind, fails to attend to the aged, and has a
changeable nature, he will always have difficulty making friends.
Possessions desert the fickle-minded man who is not master of himself
and is swayed by his senses, as wild geese desert a dry pond. To
anger at nothing and calm down for no reason is not in the character
of the good; it is behavior like that of a wind-tossed cloud.
40 Beasts of prey will not touch the corpses of ingrates who have not
treated their friends well and have not made them content. Ask
favors from friends, whether you are rich or poor: one does not
discover without asking whether they are strong or weak. Grief
destroys beauty, grief destroys strength, grief destroys wisdom, grief
brings on disease. Nothing is gained by sorrowing, the body just
suffers, and one's enemies exult: do not give in to grief.

Again and again man dies and is born,
Again and again man rises and falls;
Again and again man asks and is asked,
Again and again man mourns and is mourned.

45 Happiness and misery, good fortune and bad, profit and loss, death
and life touch everyone in turn—therefore a wise man neither rejoices
nor grieves. These six senses are volatile: wherever one of them turns
a man's spirit leaks away like water from a leaky pot.

Dhṛtarāṣṭra said:

I have treated the king who shines like a high thin flame with falsehood. He will put an end in battle to my stupid sons. Everything is always upset and my heart is always upset.
Speak, sage, whatever words will not upset me.

Vidura said:

I see no peace, prince sans blame, outside knowledge and austerity,
50 the mastery of the senses, and the loss of greed. One fends off fear
with knowledge; one discovers great things through austerity; and
one finds knowledge through obedience to his guru and peace
through relinquishment. Aspirants to release roam about here on
earth, not depending on the merit of gifts and the merit of Vedic
practice, free from love and hatred. At the end of studies well-learned,
battles well-fought, acts well-done, austerities well-observed, happiness
increases.

Those who have separated from their kinsmen never find sleep,
well-made though their beds may be; they get no pleasure from
women, king, or from the praises of minstrels and bards. Those who
have broken with kin never observe the Law; those who have broken
find no happiness; those who have broken place no value on respect;
55 those who have broken do not welcome peace. To those who have
broken with kin apt advice is not palatable; acquisition and
preservation do not apply to them; they have no refuge whatever,
king of men, but in death.

As milk is to be expected from cows, asceticism from the brahmin,
and fickleness from women, so danger is to be expected from
kinsmen. Good men use the metaphor of the many long thin threads
which together can hold many burdens because of their multitude.
Dhṛtarāṣṭra, bull of the Bharatas, kinsmen are like firebrands which
separately only smoke but which together burn brightly. Those who
hector brahmins, women, kinsmen, and cows fall as ripe fruits from
60 their stalks, Dhṛtarāṣṭra. A lone tree, however big, strong and deep-
rooted, can be shattered in branch and trunk by a violent wind; but
well-rooted trees crowded together can outlast the strongest winds
because they support one another. So enemies regard a lone man,
however endowed with virtues, as vulnerable, even as the wind
regards the lone tree. Kinsmen prosper by supporting one another
and relying on one another likc lotuscs in a pond. Not to be killed
are brahmins, cows, women, children, kinsmen, those whose food
65 one has eaten, and those who seek refuge. There is no greater virtue
in a man even if rich than good health: good luck to you, for the
sick are like the dead. Anger is like a sharp headache arising from
no disease, harsh, biting, ugly, and resulting in evil: the good swallow
it and the evil do not—swallow it, great king, and calm down. Those
plagued by sickness do not care about rewards; they have no use for

the sense objects; the sick are always miserable and do not know the
comforts of wealth or happiness.
I told you before, but you did not take my advice, king, when you
saw Draupadī won at the dicing: "Stop Duryodhana." I said, "stop
him from gambling! The wise shun crookedness. It is not strength if
it runs counter to gentleness: a mixed Law should be pursued
diligently. Fortune based on cruelty dwindles, but if both gentle and
70 bold it descends to sons and grandson. Let the Dhārtarāṣṭras protect
the Pāṇḍavas, and Pāṇḍu's sons must protect yours. Let the Kurus
live in happiness and wealth with the same enemies and friends, the
same counsel. You are now the pillar of the Kauravas, Ājamīḍha;
on you rests the house of Kuru. Protect your own repute, friend, by
guarding the young Pāṇḍavas, who have suffered from their forest
sojourn. Ally the Kauravas with Pāṇḍu's sons lest your enemies seek
out an opening. They all stand by the truth, God among men; stop
Duryodhana, king of men!"

Vidura said:
37.1 Manu Svāyaṃbhuva, O son of Vicitravīrya, Indra among kings,
named these seventeen kinds of men who beat the air with their fists
or try to bend Indra's unbendable rainbow or the sun's unbendable
rays. There is the one who teaches one unteachable; who gets angry;
who is overloyal to him who is hostile; who fails to guard his women
(good luck to you!); who asks what may not be asked; who brags;
who, though wellborn, does what he should not do; who, though
weak, feuds with somebody stronger; who speaks to someone who
does not believe him; who covets what may not be coveted, Indra
5 among men; a father-in-law who jokes with his daughter-in-law;
one who expects esteem when living with his wife; who sows seed
in another man's acre; who slanders a woman; who having received
says he does not remember; who, having given, boasts upon being
asked; and who seeks benevolence from an evil man: these persons
pursue the wind with noose in hand. One must treat a man according
to who he is and how he acts in what, that is the Law. The magician
should be treated with magic, the good should be welcome with good.
Dhṛtarāṣṭra said:
While it is said in all the Vedas that a man's life span is a hundred
years, what is the reason one does not attain the entire span?
Vidura said:
Too much talk, too much pride, no renunciation, anger, rapacity,
10 and the betrayal of friends are the six swords that cut short the life
of the embodied; it is they that kill a man, not death—good luck to
you. He who goes to the wife of a man who trusts him, who violates
his teacher's bed, a brahman who marries a *śūdra* woman or drinks
liquor, he who kills a refugee are all equal to a brahmin-murderer.

Revelation says that a rite of reparation must be performed for consorting with such. That sage goes to heaven who is a liberal householder, whose words are not shot through with falsehood, who eats only after sacrificing, does nothing harmful or disadvantageous, avoids discord, is grateful, true, and gentle.

Easy to find, king, are people who always say nice things, but
15 hard to find is a speaker of unpleasant but apt advice. A king has a friend in a person who looks to the Law and, ignoring what his master likes or dislikes, gives unpleasant advice when that is appropriate. For the sake of the family abandon a man, for the village abandon a family, for the country abandon a village, for the soul abandon the earth. One should protect one's wealth in case of disaster, one's wife with one's wealth, and oneself with both wife and wealth.

At the time of the dicing I told you, king,
That it was not right, O Pratīpa's scion;
But that displeased you, Vaicitravīrya,
As a wholesome herb displeases a sick man.

You have vanquished the peacock-like Pāṇḍavas
With the Dhārtarāṣṭras who are like crows;
Abandoning lions and herding jackals
You will come to rue it, king of men.

20 The servants have confidence in a master
Who does not get angry all the time
At servants who loyally see to his welfare,
And they do not desert him even in straits.

One should not attempt to woo the stranger
By stopping his servant's living wages,
For thwarted in what they are used to, his housemates,
Once friendly, desert him if lacking in comforts.

Considering first all the chores to be done
And setting a wage that he can afford,
He should win to himself appropriate allies,
For allies accomplish what's hard to achieve.

The one who tirelessly does his tasks
While knowing full well his master's intentions
And speaks for his good, is loyal and noble
And knows his own strength should be treated as self.

If a servant is told but pays no attention,
Or if he talks back when given his orders
And argues with you and thinks he is smart,
He should be dismissed without further delay.

25 They say that an envoy should have eight virtues:
He should be without pride, quick-acting, and manly,
Compassionate, polished, unbribable,
Not sickly, and noble in using the language.

A sensible man will never feel free
To enter a stranger's house the wrong hour,
Nor stand at night concealed at a crossroads,
Nor solicit a woman of baronial rank.

Do not contradict a man in disguise,
Whose counsel is mixed, whose company bad,
Don't say that you put no trust in him,
But give him a pretext and quote some reasons.

Do not transact with a man of compassion,
A king, or whore, or a king's dependent,
Son, brother, or widow with little sons,
A soldier or one who has loyal supporters.

Ten virtues adorn the man who bathes:
Strength, beauty, pure accent and vowels,
Fine touch, fine smell, and cleanliness,
Luck, delicacy, and beautiful women.

30 Six virtues adorn him who limits his meals:
Good health, longevity, well-being, vigor,
No sickness to plague his offspring either,
And no one berates him for gluttony.

One should not lodge in one's house a man
Who is gluttonous, idle, or widely disliked,
Full of tricks or cruel or dressing unseemly,
Or one who knows not the right place and time.

However in need do never solicit
A miser, a slanderer, one unstudied,
A man fallen low, one respecting the worthless,
A cruel, a rancorous man and an ingrate.

There are six kinds of people one should not serve:
Those of vile occupation, the garrulous,
Habitual liars and disloyal men,
The alienated and arrogant.

Profit depends on a helper and the helper depends on profit; they
35 are interdependent and do not succeed without each other. After one
has begotten sons and acquitted them of debts, after arranging some
sort of livelihood for them and marrying all his daughters well, one

should live in the forest and seek the hermit's life. A prince should do what benefits all beings and brings himself happiness, for that is the root on which Law and Profit prosper. If one has intelligence, power, splendor, mettle, resilience and resolve, why should he fear that he might find no living?

Behold the evil consequences in quarreling with the Pāṇḍavas, for whom even Śakra and the Gods tremble: enmity with sons, an ever-anxious life, the loss of repute, and the joy of your foes. Indra-like king, the wrath of Bhīṣma, Droṇa, and King Yudhiṣṭhira when fully
aroused would cause the world to collapse like a white comet
40 streaking across the sky. Your one hundred sons, Karṇa, and the five
Pāṇḍavas can rule the ocean-girt earth. The Dhārtarāṣṭras are a forest, king, and Pāṇḍu's sons I regard as tigers: do not cut down the forest with its tigers, and do not drive the tigers from the forest. There would be no forest but for its tigers, and no tigers but for their forest; for the forest is protected by its tigers, and the forest protects its tigers.

The wicked and evil-minded do not wish as urgently to know the virtues of others as their vices. If one wishes his Profit to work out
fully, he should from the beginning stick to the Law, for Profit does
45 not stray from the Law, as the Elixir does not stray from heaven. To
him whose soul is averse to evil and set upon the good, everything becomes known, whether it be cause or effect. When one practices Law, Profit, and Pleasure at the right time he finds the aggregate of Law, Profit, and Pleasure here and hereafter. By controlling the rising force of wrath and joy, a baron becomes the vessel of good fortune, king, and will not be perplexed in emergencies.

Learn from me that men always have five kinds of strength, and the strength of their arms has been said to be the least of them. The winning of good advisors—and good luck to thee!—is called the
second strength. Those who seek victory call the winning of wealth
50 the third. The inborn strength of father and grandfather, the strength
of good birth, is known as the fourth. But the highest kind of strength by which all the others are encompassed is said to be the strength of wisdom. If a man tries to offend and seeks to overpower another man, then, with the enmity thus contracted, he cannot feel secure, though he be far away. What wise man can be confident about women, kings, snakes, Vedic knowledge, the well-wishers of his enemy, comforts, and life span? There are no healers or herbs for him who
has been hit by the arrow of intelligence: neither oblation, spells,
55 blessings, sorcerers, nor medicines can help him. A man should not
despise a snake, fire, a lion, or the son of a noble lineage, Bhārata, for they are all very powerful. Fire is a great power in the world; it is hidden in wood but does not consume it, as long as it is not

kindled by others. But when it is drilled and kindled from the tree, then it quickly burns with its power that tree and the forest and the rest. Likewise men who have been born in good families have the power of fire: they lie patiently and inoffensively as fire in wood.

You and your sons are like creepers, and Pāṇḍu's sons are *śāla* trees: no creeper ever grows without clinging to a tall tree.

60 King, you and your sons are together the forest,
And the forest lions the Pāṇḍavas:
A forest is doomed when empty of lions,
And without the forest the lions die.

Vidura said:

38.1 When an old man arrives, the spirit of a youth departs upward,
but he regains it by rising to meet him and greeting him. To a good
man who arrives he should gravely present a stool, bring water,
wash his feet, ask about his health, convey his own situation, and
offer food with full attention. The noble say that one's life is in vain,
if someone who knows the spells does not accept the water,
madhuparka, and cow at his house because of his greed, fears, and
grudge. A physician, arrow-wright, unchaste man, thief, cruel man,
drunkard, abortionist, soldier, and seller of the Veda do not deserve
the water as guests, even if they are dear to the host.
5 Not to be sold are salt, cooked food, curds, milk, honey, oil, *ghee*,
sesamum seeds, meat, roots and fruits, vegetables, dyed cloth, any
perfumes, and molasses. He who is not given to anger, holds clay
and gold as alike, discards grief, is beyond friendship and enmity,
praise and blame, pleasure and displeasure, and roams about
uninvolved is a true mendicant. He is a prominent and meritorious
ascetic who lives on wild rice, roots, nuts, and greens, is completely
master of himself, needs not to be urged to the fire rituals, and while
dwelling in the forest looks diligently to his guests.
If you offend an intelligent man, don't take comfort in living far
away: long are the arms of the intelligent man with which, he, when
hurt, will hurt you back. Mistrust the distrusted, and do not trust the
trusted too far: from trust there arises a danger that cuts down the
10 very roots. One should not be envious; he should guard his wife,
share his property, speak kindly, be smooth and pleasant-spoken
toward women, but not come under their spell. Worthy of honor,
noble, holy, and ornamental, women are the treasures of a house;
therefore they should be especially guarded. One should entrust the
women's quarters to the father, the kitchen to the mother, the cattle
to one valued like himself, but do the ploughing himself; he should
look after traders through his servants, after the brahmin through
his sons.

Fire springs from water, baronage from brahmindom, iron from
rock: their ubiquitous power vanishes before their sources. Men of
good family who are always virtuous live patiently and inoffensively
15 as fire in wood. A king whose counsel neither outsiders nor insiders
know but who himself has eyes everywhere, will long enjoy dominion.
He should not speak of what he will do but show his works of Law
and Profit only when they are done: then his counsel will not be
breached. His plans should be made while he climbs a mountain top,
or steals out on the roof, or secludes himself in a desert. One who is
not a friend should not know his ultimate plan, Bhārata, nor an
unlearned friend or a learned man without self-control; for the
attainment of profit and the keeping of the counsel rest upon the
minister. A king whose counsels are a secret and all whose works his
associates know only when they have been done succeeds without
question.

20 He who in his folly commits acts that are forbidden forfeits even
his life as his acts miscarry. The performance of approved acts brings
happiness, while their nonperformance brings much regret.
Independent is the country of him, king, who knows about increase,
decrease, and stability, knows the state of the six properties, and who
possesses habits that are not despised.

The country of a king whose pleasure and displeasure bear fruit,
who himself looks after his tasks and who himself has full information
about his treasury, holds treasure. A king should be content with his
title and umbrella: he should bestow his spoils on his dependents and
25 not keep everything for himself. Brahmin knows brahmin, husband
knows wife, a prince his minister, a king a king. An enemy who
deserves death is not to be released when he has come to your side,
for if he is not killed, he will soon be dangerous. One should at all
times make an effort to control his anger with deities, kings, brahmins,
the old, the young, and the sick. A sensible man should avoid the
pointless quarrels that fools seek: thus he earns fame in the world and
no disaster besets him. No more than women want a eunuch for a
husband do people want a master whose grace has no consequence
and whose wrath does not matter.

30 Cleverness does not always lead to gain nor stupidity to poverty;
the sage and no one else knows the turns that affairs take in the
world. Disasters soon beset him whose conduct is ignoble, who is
foolish, malcontented, without Law, foul-spoken, and irascible.
Honesty, liberality, strict observance of covenants, and correctly
addressed speech draw the creatures near. An honest, competent,
grateful, clever, and upright man, even though his treasury has
35 dwindled, wins a retinue. Steadfastness, serenity, self-control, purity,
compassion, kind speech, and loyalty are the seven kindling sticks of
fortune.

The one who does not share his property and who is wicked,
ungrateful, and shameless, that vilest of men should be shunned in
the world, king of men. As in a snake-infested house, the man does
not sleep peacefully who, while himself at fault, angers the guiltless
folk of his dwelling. Those who pose a threat to one's prosperity when
they are offended should be appeased like Gods. All possessions
attached to women, reckless people, or ignoble men are in danger.
40 The country where a woman, a child, or a gambler rules sinks
helplessly as a stone raft in a river. Them I call wise who are attached
to the general principles rather than the specifics, Bhārata, for specifics
are contingent. That man lives no more whom gamblers praise,
songsters praise, and harlots praise.

Abandoning these mighty archers, the boundlessly august Pāṇḍavas,
you have devolved the grand dominion of the Bhāratas upon
Duryodhana. You shall soon see him toppled from it as Bali, deluded
by the drunkenness of power, was toppled from the three worlds.

Dhṛtarāṣṭra said:

39.1 Man is not the master of destiny,
But a wooden doll that is strung on a string,
The creator has made him subject to fate;
So speak on, for indeed I pay heed to your words.

Vidura said:

By speaking out of turn even Bṛhaspati incurred disesteem for his
intelligence, and contempt, Bhārata. The one becomes beloved for his
gifts, the other for his pleasant words, the third for his power of spells
and herbs, but he who is loved is loved. A hateful man is not good,
not intelligent, not learned: with the loved one are the good works,
5 with the hateful one the evil. Great king, it is no loss if the loss brings
on gain; but that should be considered a loss upon which still more
is lost. There are some who are rich in virtue, others in wealth;
avoid the rich in wealth, Dhṛtarāṣṭra, who are devoid of virtue.

Dhṛtarāṣṭra said:

All that you say is beneficial for posterity and approved by the
wise. But I cannot abandon my son—where there is Law there is
triumph.

Vidura said:

One who is naturally endowed with virtues and possessed of good
manners will never do the slightest harm to creatures. Those who
delight in speaking ill always jump to the chance when others
decline or prosper by fomenting quarrels between one and the other.
10 With those the very sight of whom is harmful and association with
whom dangerous, accepting gifts is harmful and proffering them
dangerous. Avoid people known to be wicked, whose company is

disapproved, and who have other grave faults. When a friendship
comes to an end, the affection of the lowly man dies, and so do its
fruits and the pleasure that lay in the friendship. He turns to
slandering and strives to destroy, and even if the offense was slight,
he finds no peace in his folly. A wise man will observe matters
intelligently with his mind and keep a wide distance from consorting
with such lowly and cruel people who have not mastered themselves.

15 He who favors a kinsman who is poor, wretched, and sick waxes
in sons and cattle and earns unending fame. Kinsmen should be
helped to prosper by those who wish for their own well-being and
the prosperity of their lineage; therefore, Indra among kings, comport
yourself well. By treating your kinsmen well, king, you shall be yoked
with affluence, bull of the Bharatas, for even flawed kinsmen deserve
protection, how much more then virtuous kin who yearn for your
grace: lord of the people, behave with grace toward the poor
Pāṇḍavas. Give them some little villages for them to live on, my lord,
and thus, ruler of men, you will earn fame in the world. You are an
20 old man, friend—protect your sons; I must speak for your own good,
for know that I wish you well. No one who aims at prosperity should
quarrel with kin, bull of the Bharatas, but he should enjoy his
comforts with kin. Kinsmen should eat, talk, and have pleasure with
one another, and not in any way quarrel. In this world kinsmen save
and kinsmen ruin: it is the good ones who save, the evil that ruin.
Be good to the Pāṇḍavas, Indra of kings, giver of pride, and
surrounded by them you will become invincible to your foes.
25 If a kinsman suffers from adversity while he has a prosperous
kinsman, the latter, like a hunter with blood-smeared hands before
a deer, takes on the other's evil.

Later you will rue it, best of men, when you hear that they or
your sons have been killed; think about that. Don't do at the outset
what in the end will make you climb in bed and suffer, for life is
unstable. No one but Bhārgava does not stray, but in all intelligent
persons there is a perception of consequences. If in the past
Duryodhana did a bad thing, then you, as the family elder, should
30 repair it. By putting them in their rightful place in the world you
will be free of guilt and praiseworthy to the wise.

If one gives deep thought to the good utterances of deliberate
people about consequences and decides on his tasks accordingly,
he will long stand in good repute. Graceful deportment kills bad
manners, valor conquers calamity, patience always conquers anger,
right conduct overcomes ill omens. One should judge a family by its
retinue, acreage, dwelling, staff, food, and dress, king. The affection
of the pair whose thoughts, secrets, and insights match endures
35 forever. The wise man should avoid the evil-minded man who has

formed no insight, like a well covered by straw; friendship for such a one dies. Nor should a wise man contract a friendship with the arrogant, foolish, violent, rash, and lawless; rather hope for a friend who is grateful, law-abiding, true-spoken, noble, loyal, self-controlled, dignified, and humble. The withdrawal of the senses is no different from death; their total withdrawal would fell even Gods.

Gentleness to all creatures, contentment, patience, poise, and respect for one's friends add to one's life span. It is the life rule of the noble to wish to replace a badly run affair with one better run by relying on his intelligence. A man who knows how to deal with the future, is firmly resolved in the present, and knows the consequences of his deeds of the past will not be parted from his wealth. One is carried off by what he constantly pursues in action, thought, and speech; therefore he should pursue the good. Undertaking what is propitious, perseverance, learning, resilience, uprightness, and the continual serving of good men bring prosperity. Refusal to despair that misery will ever cease is the root of good fortune and happiness; the undespairing man becomes great and attains to complete bliss. There is nothing whatever more elevating and edifying, friend, than a powerful man's forgiveness in all matters at all times. A powerless man must forgive everything, and so should also a man of power, but for reasons of Law. If gain and loss are the same for him his patience is always firm. Pursue the Pleasure by which neither Law nor Profit are diminished; don't follow the life rule of fools.

No luck dwells in those who are afflicted with misery, easily distracted, heretical, lazy, uncontrolled, and unenterprising. The evil-minded oppress the honest man who from honesty is modest, thinking he has no power. Luck is afraid to approach too liberal a donor, too gallant a champion, the man of too many vows, and the fool who prides himself on his cleverness. The Vedas have their fruit in the *agnihotra*; learning in good habits and behavior; wives in pleasure and sons; wealth in gifts and consumption. If one performs the rites that secure the world hereafter with ill-gotten wealth, he does not acquire their fruit after death because his wealth was badly come by. Those who still have life to live have nothing to fear in wilderness, forest, and difficult passes, in dire emergencies or confusion, or from upraised weapons.

Resilience, self-control, competence, alertness, bearing, memory, and enterprise after due deliberation—know that these are the roots of prosperity. Austerity is the strength of ascetics, the *brahman* the strength of the knowers of the *brahman*, hurt the strength of the wicked, forgiveness the strength of the virtuous. These eight do not interfere with a vow: water, roots, fruit, milk, oblation, the pleasure of a brahmin, the behest of a guru, and medicine. Do not do to

another what is disagreeable to yourself: this is the summary Law;
the other proceeds from desire. Conquer anger with mildness, evil
with good, the miser with liberality, the lie with truth. Do not place
trust in women, crooks, sloths, cowards, berserkers, braggarts,
60 thieves, ingrates, and heretics. These four increase for one who
practices the proper mode of greeting and always attends on his
elders: reputation, life span, fame, and vigor.

Do not set your mind on riches that require too much toil, the
transgression of the Law, or submission to the enemy. Pitiful is the
man without knowledge, pitiful the childless couple, pitiful the hungry
subjects, pitiful the kingless kingdom. Travel ages the embodied, rain
ages the mountains, lack of intercourse ages women, the scathing
word ages the mind. The Vedas are stained by the lack of transmission,
the brahmin by lack of vows, the good woman by curiosity, women
65 by being away from home, gold by silver, silver by tin, tin by lead,
lead by dirt. Do not conquer sleep with more sleep, women by
lechery, fire by feeding it, liquor by drinking. Fruitful is the life of
him who has won friends by giving, enemies in battle, wives with
food and drink.

Those who have thousands live and so do those who have
hundreds; give up your desire, Dhṛtarāṣṭra, there is no way one
cannot live. All the rice, barley, gold, cattle, and women on earth
70 are not enough for one man; observing this be not fooled. King, once
more I tell you, you will do well by your sons, by holding yours and
Pāṇḍu's as equal.

Vidura said:

40.1 Quickly does fame visit the good man who, at the bidding of good
men, does his task without self-interest and without straining his
power; for the good, when serene, are able to bring happiness. He
who even without warning abolishes a grand affair that is tainted by
lawlessness sleeps peacefully, casting off miseries as a snake casts off
its worn-out slough. A lie in a high place, treason against a king, and
consistent dishonesty before a guru are equal to brahmin murder.
One word of malcontentment, death, and quarrelsomeness kill
fortunes; disobedience, haste, and boastfulness are all three the
5 enemies of wisdom. How can the pleasure-seeker find wisdom? The
wisdom-seeker has no pleasure; the pleasure-seeker should give up
wisdom, the wisdom-seeker pleasure. Fire is never sated of wood, the
ocean is never sated of rivers, or death of creatures and a pretty-eyed
woman of men. Hope kills steadfastness, death kills prosperity, anger
kills fortune, niggardliness kills reputation, heedlessness kills cattle,
king, and one irate brahmin kills a kingdom.

One should always keep in the house a goat, brass, a chariot,
honey, antidotes, a bird, a priest, an old relation, and a friend fallen

on hard times. Manu has said that for good luck one should keep at home a goat, a bullock, sandalwood, a lute, a mirror, honey and butter, iron, copper, a conch shell, gold, musk, and *rocana* pigment
10 for the purpose of honoring Gods, brahmins, and guests. And this holy and superior word do I speak to you, elevated above all: never give up the Law out of desire, fear, or greed, or for the sake of life itself. The Law is eternal, happiness and misery are not; life is eternal, but its carriers are not: relinquishing the noneternal, stand firm on the eternal; be content, for contentment is the greatest good.

Behold the powerful and puissant kings: after ruling the earth filled with wealth and riches, they forsook their kingdoms and vast comforts and fell into the power of death. King, parents lift up and carry out of their house their dead son, so painfully reared, and, weeping piteously with hair disheveled, they cast him in the middle
15 of the pyre like a piece of wood. Someone else enjoys the wealth of the dead man as the birds and the fire consume his remains. One goes to the world hereafter with two companions: one's merits and one's evil. Kinsmen, friends, and sons cast away and go back, but the deeds he himself has done follow the man who has been thrown into the fire. Above this world and below the next there is a large blinding darkness which bewilders the senses; know this and do not attain to it, king.

If you carry out correctly all these words you have heard you shall gain superb fame in the world of the living and have nothing to fear hereafter and here. The soul is a river, O Bhārata: merit forms its sacred fords, the truth its water, steadfastness its banks, self-control its waves: bathing in it, the man of merit is purified, for the soul is
20 holy and the eternal water is the water. Build a boat of steadfastness and cross safely the river with its crocodiles of lust and anger, the water of the five senses, and the rapids of rebirth. He who asks the advice of a relative grown old in wisdom, Law, knowledge, and age concerning what one should do or not, after paying him due homage, will never be confused. Protect your penis and belly with gravity, head and foot with the eye, eye and ear with the mind, mind and speech with deeds. A brahmin who always has water, always wears his sacred thread, always studies, always avoids food that has fallen on the ground, who speaks the truth to his guru and does his deeds does not fall out of the world of Brahmā. A baron who, after studying the Vedas, kindling the fires, offering up sacrifices, and protecting the creatures, cleanses his inner soul with weapons in the cause of cows
25 and brahmins and falls in battle, goes to heaven. The *vaiśya* who has studied, distributed his wealth at the right time over brahmins, barons, and dependents, and smelled the sacred smoke purified by the three fires, enjoys after death the bliss of the Gods in heaven. The *śūdra* who pays homage correctly to brahmindom, baronage, and the *vaiśya*

class and satisfies them, will, when he abandons the body, enjoy the pleasures of heaven without worries, for his evil will have been burned off.

I have set forth to you the Law of the four classes; listen to me tell the reason why: Pāṇḍu's son has fallen short of baronial Law; enjoin you upon him, king, the Law of kings.

Dhṛtarāṣṭra said:

It is indeed as you always are saying, and my mind too, friend,
responds to your words. My spirit favors the Pāṇḍavas, but when I
30 meet Duryodhana, it turns away. No mortal can go beyond what is
fated for him. It is fate that acts, I think, and personal effort is futile.

Dhṛtarāṣṭra said:

41.1 Is there anything, Vidura, that you have left unsaid? Tell me, since
I am eager to hear, for you speak wonderfully.

Vidura said:

Dhṛtarāṣṭra, the ancient and eternal youth Sanatsujāta has proclaimed that there is no death, Bhārata. That foremost of all who have spirit shall declare to you, great king, all that clings to the heart, overt or hidden.

Dhṛtarāṣṭra said:

Do you then not know what the eternal youth will tell me? You must tell me, Vidura, if you have that wisdom left.

Vidura said:

5 I have been born from a *śūdra* womb, therefore I cannot say any
more than this. But I know the eternal wisdom of the youth. For he
who speaks even of mysteries is not reproved by the Gods, if he has
been born a brahmin. That is why I speak to you like this.

Dhṛtarāṣṭra said:

Tell me, Vidura, how can I with this body and on this spot meet with the ancient and eternal youth?

Vaiśaṃpāyana said:

Vidura sent his thoughts to the seer of strict vows and knowing that he was being thought of he appeared, O Bhārata. Vidura received him with the rite that is found in the Rules, and when the other had rested and was sitting at ease, he said to him, "Blessed lord, there is a doubt in Dhṛtarāṣṭra's mind which I am unable to explain. Pray do you speak to him, so that upon hearing it this Indra among kings may be translated beyond happiness and misery, and gain and loss, the pleasant and the hateful, so that old age and death do not overwhelm him, nor fear and indignation, hunger and thirst, intoxication and power, and hatred, sloth, desire, anger, and rise and decline.

5(52) *Sanatsujāta*

5.42–45 (B. 42–46; C. 1576–1790)
42 (42; 1577). Dhṛtarāṣṭra asks Sanatsujāta why he teaches that there is no death. Sanatsujāta replies that distraction equals death (1–5). One should neutralize karman *by not desiring the fruits of action (5–10). Death rises from passion (10). The worlds hereafter are determined by* karman *(15). The knowledge of* brahman *is brought about by high morality; there is a need for austerity (15–30).*
43 (43; 1627). The Veda cannot save a man from evil, but it leads the knower to better rebirth (1–5). The twelve, and again six, vices; the twelve vows; the eighteen vices; the six forms of relinquishment (5–20); the eight defects that distract (20). There are many Vedas, but one truth (20–25). This truth gives knowledge of the brahman, *on which one should meditate (30–35).*
44 (44–45; 1684). This is achieved by brahmacarya *with a guru; rules of* brahmacarya *behavior (1–15).* Brahman *is without color, beyond elements and Veda; it is the foundation of the universe (15–20).*
45 (46; 1737). The yogins behold the Lord mystically as the seed of the universe, the sun, the unmanifest (1–5), the full, the supreme, the swan, the Person (5–15), the truth, the Elixir (15–20). It is the I, the ātman *(25).*

Vaiśaṃpāyana said:

42.1 The wise and great-spirited King Dhṛtarāṣṭra
Acknowledged the words that Vidura'd spoken,
And wishing to gain the highest insight
He questioned in secret Sanatsujāta.

Dhṛtarāṣṭra said:

Sanatsujāta, I hear that you teach
That indeed there is no death at all,
Yet Gods and Asuras studied the *brahman*
To achieve non-death—so which is the truth?

Sanatsujāta said:

Some hold non-death comes about by the rite,
While some maintain that there is no death.

Now listen to me, king, while I explain,
So that you may cherish no doubts about it.

Baron, both these truths are primordial!
The death that the seers believe in is *folly*.
I say to you distraction is death:
To be never distraught is to live forever.

5 The Asuras lost by being distracted;
Undistracted, they were the *brahman* itself.
Yet death is no tiger that eats the creatures—
No shape is ever perceived of death.

Some hold Yama is Death, but others another;
But non-death is study sunk in the soul.
The God holds sway in the world of the Fathers,
Being safe to the safe, unsafe to the unsafe.

It is from his mouth that there issue for men
Wrath, Distraction, and Death as Folly;
The ones that are fooled and under his sway
Depart from here and fall back again.

It is after him that the Gods collapse
And hence that Death has acquired his name;
They who covet the fruits of their acts follow after
The *karman* resulting, and do not cross Death.

He who thinks and destroys those fruits as they try
To arise, not hostile by disrespect,
He is Death, for like Death, he eats them aborning.
So he who knows thus forsakes his desires.

10 The man who runs after his desires perishes with his desires; if he can lay aside his desires, he can shake off any passion. This lusterless darkness is for all creatures hell; as though possessed they eagerly rush to it and fall into the pit.

The notion of *I* first kills him off,
Love and hatred possess him and kill him again;
They steer the befuddled ones to their death,
But the firm cross death with their fortitude.

If a man, baron, thinks of nothing at all,
It's a tiger of straw that cannot attack him;
Your soul if bemused by anger and greed
That is death itself within your own body.

Aware that it's thus that death is born
One standing in knowledge fears no death;

Death dies for him if the object dies,
As the mortal dies when gaining death's object.

Dhṛtarāṣṭra said:

15 There are those who here do not follow the Laws,
There are those as well who follow the Laws:
Now does the evil destroy the Law,
Or is it the Law that destroys the evil?

Sanatsujāta said:

There are two fruits experienced here,
The fruits of the Law and its opposite;
The sage discards Unlaw with Law,
So know from him that Law wins out.

Dhṛtarāṣṭra said:

The eternal worlds that they say accrue
From the Law of the twiceborn who act well
They say these have different boundaries—
That, sage, must result from deeds once done.

Sanatsujāta said:

The brahmins who do not compete in strength as strongmen do, hereafter shine in the world of heaven.

That place where a brahmin thinks that food and drink are most
plentiful, like grass in the rainy season, that place he will not regret.
20 Where people present unholy danger to one and he keeps silent,
without acting as though it were nothing to him, he and no one else
is superior. If one does not become aggravated before someone who
keeps silent and does not consume the property of brahmindom, then
his food is regarded as food for the strict. Just as a dog, always to its
own peril, eats its own vomit, so they eat their vomit by living off
their own power. The brahmin thinks: "Let my way of life remain
unknown," then nothing will be found out even if he live among
his kin.

What brahmin can thus kill the inner soul? It is because of such
25 conduct, baron, that he sees some *brahman* that dwells in him. A
brahmin should be unwearied, esteemed for not accepting gifts,
unobstructed, educated in reality rather than appearance as a
brahman-knowing sage. The twiceborn who are not wealthy in
worldly goods, but wealthy in Vedas, are unassailable and unshakable;
know that they form the *brahman*'s body. Whosoever knows that all
the Gods have been properly sacrificed to is not the equal of a
brahmin, for he has to exert himself in this matter. Truly esteemed is
he whom they esteem while he does not exert himself. When
esteemed he does not regard it, and does not fret at not being
esteemed. One who is esteemed should think, "The wise bestow

esteem in the world." When not esteemed, one should think, "The
foolish, proficient only in the ways of the world, who do not know
30 the Law, will not esteem an estimable man." Esteem and austerity
never run together, for this world is that of esteem and the yonder
one that of austerity. In this world good fortune is the abode of
happiness, but it is an obstacle on the road. The good fortune in
brahman, O baron, is very hard to obtain by one devoid of insight.
They say that there are doors of many kinds, which are hard to
protect, to this fortune. These six: truth, uprightness, modesty, self-
control, purity, and knowledge, are destructive of pride and delusion.

Dhṛtarāṣṭra said:
43.1 If a brahmin who has learned the Hymns, the Formulas, and the
Veda of the Chants commits evil, is he tainted or not?

Sanatsujāta said:
The Chants, Hymns, and Formulas do not save him from evil *karman*, O sage—I am not speaking idly to you. The Hymns do not save from evil the deceiver who works with illusion. As birds whose wings have been fledged desert the nest, so the Hymns desert him in the end.

Dhṛtarāṣṭra said:
If the Vedas cannot save the Veda-wise, O sage, then why the eternal prattling of brahmins?

Sanatsujāta said:
5 The austerity practiced in this world is seen to yield fruit in
another. For brahmins these worlds are achieved when austerities
are thriving.

Dhṛtarāṣṭra said:
How is it that austerities are either thriving or not? Explain this, Sanatsujāta, so that we may know.

Sanatsujāta said:
The one is that which has the twelve vices, anger, etc., and the
six, cruelty, etc., O king; the other is that which possesses the twelve
virtues of Law, etc., which are known to the twiceborn from their
texts. Anger, desire, greed, delusion, possessiveness, compassion,
discontent, pride, grief, lust, jealousy, and abhorrence are the twelve
human vices a man should avoid. Every single one of them, O Indra
among kings, waits about a man looking for an opening, as a hunter
10 with a deer. The boastful, envious, cunning, vindictive, fickle, and
heedless—these six, when present, make people wicked in their Law;
they do no good in difficult situations. Libertinage, scheming, hatred,
pride of cunning, regrets after gifts, feeble pusillanimity, praising one's
own, dislike for women are the seven cruel vices. Law, truthfulness,

self-control, austerity, lack of envy, modesty, forebearance,
contentment, sacrifice, gift, steadfastness, and learning are the twelve
great vows of the brahmin. He who travels with all these twelve is
able to sway all of earth; if he is distinguished by three, two, or one
he should be known to possess nothing.

Self-control, relinquishment, heedfulness – on them rests
immortality; sagacious brahmins say that these are headed by truth.
15 There are eighteen vices that endanger self-control: contrariness in
what is done or not done, mendacity, malcontentment, lust,
acquisitiveness, covetousness, anger, grief, thirst, greed, treachery,
jealousy, possessiveness, regrets, gloating, forgetfulness, slander, and
vanity; the strict call that self-control which is free from these vices.
The six forms of relinquishment are the best: if one does not rejoice
when gaining something pleasant; if one does not fall to misery when
something unpleasant happens; if he gives a worthy supplicant who
asks for no one but his beloved wife and sons that which he asks for,
though the other says the unsayable, that is known as the third
20 virtue; if he relinquishes his possessions; if he does not enjoy them
wantonly; and if he is not without property for rituals. As a man
with the mind of a pupil is such a renouncer who, though
propertied, is possessed of all virtues.

Eight defects hurt heedfulness and should be avoided: those that
derive from the five senses, from the mind, from the past, and from
the future. Freed from them one becomes happy. Only austerity
devoid of these defects and possessed of these virtues thrives, as you
asked me. What else do you want to hear?

Dhṛtarāṣṭra said:

Some persons are said to have up to four Vedas with Story as the
fifth, others have four Vedas, still others three or two, then there are
those who have one and others who have no Hymns at all. Which
of these should I regard as a brahmin?

Sanatsujāta said:

25 Because of ignorance of the One Veda there are many Vedas of the
one truth. Any one of them is based on the truth, Indra of kings.
Thus without abolishing the Veda they aim their insight at the Great
One. If gifts, Vedic learning, and sacrifice are practiced out of greed,
then the ritual intention of the practitioners who have fallen away
from the truth becomes false. Therefore a sacrifice should be
undertaken only out of consideration for the truth. When a man
performs it with mind, speech, or act, he is successful in his intention
and is in charge of his intentions. One should practice the vow of the
consecrated sacrificer without being secretive about his intention.
The name *Satyam* is achieved by derivation from its root: *satyam*, or

truth, is the highest goal of those who are *sat*, or strict.
Knowledge is evident, austerity obscure. One should know a
brahmin who recites a lot as simply a great reciter: do not therefore,
baron, regard a brahmin as high just for his prattling; only one who
does not stray from the truth should be known as a brahmin.
30 Atharvan chanted what are called the Hymns of old at the creation
of the seers; they who learned them were the hymnists; but they do
not know the One who is known from the Veda of the One to be
known. No one *truly* knows the Veda, merely the letter, king. A Veda
knower does not know its spirit. *He* knows the One to be known who
stands on the truth.

I hold that brahmin for a clever narrator who, with his doubt
resolved, narrates all doubts. The search for the One does not go
forth to the east, nor to the south, nor this way, nor horizontally, nor
no way at all. One should reflect upon it while keeping *mauna*, or
silence, and not move even in thought; then the *brahman* that rests
35 in the inner soul will come to him. One becomes a *muni*, or hermit,
by keeping *mauna*, or silence, not by dwelling in the forest. He who
knows the Immutable One is said to be the greatest hermit. One is
called a grammarian because of the grammatical analysis of all
meanings. He to whom the worlds are evident sees everything. The
brahmin who stands on the truth sees *brahman*, baron, by following
the Vedas in succession; this I declare to you.

Dhṛtarāṣṭra said:

44.1 Sanatsujāta, this discourse on *brahman*, which bears upon the
supreme, includes everything. This superb discourse is very rare
among desirable things. Therefore, speak your word to me, youth.

Sanatsujāta said:

This *brahman*, about which you query me so very joyously, cannot be attained by one who hurries. I shall proclaim to you the ancient knowledge of the unmanifest, which is achieved by the spirit with *brahmacarya*.

Dhṛtarāṣṭra said:

You say that the eternal knowledge of the unmanifest is achieved with *brahmacarya*. This knowledge is not some act that is to be undertaken here at a given time; it dwells here already, noble sir. How may one attain to the immortality that is *brahman*'s?

Sanatsujāta said:

They who conquer their desires in this world, while patiently
observing this stance on *brahman*, pull the self out of the body, as a
5 stalk out of *muñja* grass, for they are firm in *sattva*. Father and
mother make one's body, Bhārata, but the birth that is instructed by
the teacher is the true birth that knows of no aging and dying. They
who, having entered the teacher's womb and become an embryo,

observe *brahmacarya*, become here on earth the practitioners of the śāstras, and when they shed the body they attain the highest Yoga.

One should regard as father and mother the teacher who fills the
ears with truth, while practicing the truth and bestowing immortality;
knowing his deeds, one should not harm him. Always paying heed to
his guru, a student should pursue his study, pure and undistracted.
He should not cherish pride or anger—that is the first quarter of
brahmacarya. The second quarter is stated to be that he do what
pleases his teacher, even at the cost of life and wealth, with thought,
10 speech, and deed. As the third quarter it is declared that his conduct
toward the guru's wife be the same as to the guru, acting as
instructed and pleasingly so. The fourth quarter of *brahmacarya* is
that in reporting to his teacher he should sagely not say, "I did not
do it"; he may think like that but not say it.

He should present to his teacher whatever property comes to him while he lives like that; for the strict it then grows many times over. And this is the conduct also toward the teacher's son. While living thus, he prospers in the world, he obtains many sons and a firm footing; the skies rain forth for him, and many people will dwell with him in turn in *brahmacarya*.

With such *brahmacarya* the Gods attained godhead, the wise and
15 exalted seers the world of Brahmā, the Gandharvas and Apsarās their
beauty; with this *brahmacarya* the sun was born of yore. He who lies
down and makes his whole body burst while practicing austerities,
king, will thereby transcend folly and become wise and in the end
put a stop to death. Finite are the worlds that people conquer by the
acts they have performed, baron, but the sage attains to the whole
brahman—there is no other way to go.

Dhṛtarāṣṭra said:

Appears it like white, like red, or like dark, jet black, or brown? What color is the immortal, immutable spot that the wise brahmin beholds?

Sanatsujāta said:

It appears not as white, or red, or black or ironlike, or sun-hued.
Neither in the earth nor in the sky is it found, and the water in the
20 ocean does not carry it. It is not in the stars or clinging to lightning,
and its color is not seen in the clouds; it is not in the wind or the
deities, not found in the moon or the sun. It is not in the Hymns, not
in the Formulas, not in the Atharvans, nor can it be found in the
impeccable Chants, whether the *rathantara* or *bārhata*, king, and it is
not seen in the *mahāvrata*, that stable thing. Beyond darkness it has
no farther shore to cross to; death dies in it at the time of death; it is
thinner than a razor's edge but larger even than the mountains. It is
the foundation, the immortal, the worlds, the *brahman*, the glory:
from it are the creatures born, in it they are dissolved. It is whole,

and large, and soaring fame—sages hold that they are the products of speech. On it is this whole universe established, and they who know it have conquered death.

Sanatsujāta said:

45.1 That seed, that great burning light, that grand glory from which
the sun shines forth, that the Gods adore—the yogins behold the
sempiternal blessed Lord.

From the seed springs the *brahman*, and the *brahman* waxes by the seed—the yogins behold the sempiternal blessed Lord.

> Water from water amidst the ocean,
> The two Gods lie upon the sky;
> The centripetal and centrifugal,
> They both bear up the earth and the sky—

the yogins behold the sempiternal blessed Lord.

> And both the Gods carry heaven and earth,
> The seed carries space and the universe,
> From it do regions and rivers flow,
> In it the vast oceans have their source—

the yogins behold the sempiternal blessed Lord.

5 Standing in the wheel of the chariot that is stable and working
unfailingly, with a blazing crest—that divine ageless being the horses
carry in the sky—the yogins behold the sempiternal blessed Lord.

> Compareless is that form of his,
> No one beholds him with his eye,
> But they who with wisdom, mind and heart
> Gain knowledge of him have become immortal—

the yogins behold the sempiternal blessed Lord.

> The lordly ones course the terrifying
> Sweet twelvefold river guarded by Gods—

the yogins behold the sempiternal blessed Lord.

The bee collects and drinks the half-month honey; among all creatures the Lord has made it the oblation—the yogins behold the sempiternal blessed Lord.

Becoming wingless birds they alight on the gold-leafed *aśvattha* tree and fly out each in his own direction—the yogins behold the sempiternal blessed Lord.

10 From the full they pull the full, from the full they make the full,
from the full they take the full, yet the full is always left full—the
yogins behold the sempiternal blessed Lord.

From it rises the wind and in it it subsides; from it spring Fire and Soma, on it is stretched the breath. By it one knows all, and we cannot say what it is—the yogins behold the sempiternal blessed Lord.

Prāṇa swallows *apāna*, moon swallows *prāṇa*, sun swallows moon, the highest swallows the sun—the yogins behold the sempiternal blessed Lord.

The swan as it ascends does not lift one foot; if it did, there would be neither death nor immortality—the yogins behold the sempiternal blessed Lord.

15 Thus the great-spirited God: this Person swallows the fire; if one knows that Person, his soul will come to no harm—the yogins behold the sempiternal blessed Lord.

If he spread his thousand thousands of wings and flew up and went into the middle most center, he'd be swift as thought—the yogins behold the sempiternal blessed Lord.

His form is beyond the range of the eye,
And only the very pure-mettled behold him;
The well-wishing sage sees him with the mind;
Who resort to him have become immortal—

the yogins behold the sempiternal blessed Lord.

Like snakes in the thicket the mortals hide him
By virtue of learning or good behavior;
Only foolish people are fooled by them,
So that they mistake the road to danger—

the yogins behold the sempiternal blessed Lord.

It would always be rendered existent and nonexistent, so whence would there be death and immortality?

But truth and lie are based on the truth;
Of what is and is not the root is the same—

the yogins behold the sempiternal blessed Lord.

20 Among men it is never seen as the same
By honest folk and dishonest men;
Let him know that it's equal to the Elixir,
And being thus yoked let him search for the honey—

the yogins behold the sempiternal blessed Lord.

Abuse does not torment his heart,
Nor unlearned lessons, the unoffered rite:
The mind should take on the lightness of *brahman*,
The wise acquire an insight of him—

the yogins behold the sempiternal blessed Lord.

If one sees oneself in all creatures yoked to their various tasks, why should he worry anymore? As much use as there is in a large well where there is a flood of water, so much use is there in all the Vedas for the brahmin who knows.

> The great-spirited soul with the size of a thumb
> Cannot be seen where it lies in the heart;
> Unborn it tirelessly roams day and night,
> The sage sits serenely knowing it.

25 I am I, I am mother, father, son, I am the soul of all whether existent or not. I am the ancient grandfather, father, and son, Bhārata. You live in my soul, you are not mine, I am not yours.

> My soul is the place, my soul is the birth,
> I'm the ageless foundations the Vedas declare.

Subtler than the subtle, of friendly mind, I wake in the creatures. They know the father who is placed in the lotus of all creatures.

5(53) The Suing for Peace

5.46–69 (B. 47–71; C. 1791–2580)
46 (47; 1791). In the morning the Kauravas assemble in the hall and seat themselves (1–10). Saṃjaya arrives (10–15).
47 (48; 1809). At Dhṛtarāṣṭra's request Saṃjaya reports Arjuna as saying that refusal to return the kingdom to Yudhiṣṭhira will mean war (1–10). Duryodhana shall rue the consequences of the might of Bhīma (10–15), Nakula, the Draupadeyas, Sahadeva (20–25), Abhimanyu, Virāṭa and sons (25–30), Śikhaṇḍin, Dhṛṣṭadyumna, Sātyaki (30–45), and Arjuna himself (45–60). Arjuna has chosen Kṛṣṇa, whose glorious battles are detailed (60–80). The Pāṇḍavas have been cheated and Law is now on their side: the Dhārtarāṣṭras are doomed: all signs point to that (80–100). The Kauravas should desist (100).
48 (49; 1917). Bhīṣma relates the might of Nara and Nārāyaṇa, who defeated the Daityas; they have returned as Arjuna and Keśava, who are as one (1–20): Duryodhana is all but lost and Karṇa is no help (20–25). Karṇa protests (25–30). Bhīṣma points to Karṇa's past failures (30–40). Droṇa argues in the same vein (40–45).

49 (50; 1967). Dhṛtarāṣṭra asks about Yudhiṣṭhira's authority; Saṃjaya replies that it is total (1–5). At Dhṛtarāṣṭra's question about Yudhiṣṭhira's allies Saṃjaya collapses (5–10). Reviving, Saṃjaya reports on Yudhiṣṭhira's forces (10–45).
50 (51; 2018). Dhṛtarāṣṭra fears Bhīma, whose prowess he describes (1–45). The Kauravas are indeed doomed by fate; he himself is powerless (45–60).
51 (52; 2085). Dhṛtarāṣṭra describes Arjuna's greatness (1–15).
52 (53; 2106). He praises Yudhiṣṭhira's rectitude: they should strive for peace (1–15).
53 (54; 2121). Saṃjaya agrees but fears it is too late now: too many wrongs have been done to the Pāṇḍavas; Duryodhana should be kept down (1–30).
54 (55; 2143). Duryodhana replies. When the Pāṇḍavas went to the forest, allies joined them and plotted attack. At that time Duryodhana consulted his elders, who reassured him: the Kauravas could stand up to anybody (1–20). Now the Kauravas are even stronger, the Pāṇḍavas weaker: Yudhiṣṭhira now wants only five villages (20–25). Bhīma is not all that strong: Duryodhana can beat him (30–40). The Kauravas are great men (40–50), and outnumber the others by a third (50–65).
55 (56; 2214). Duryodhana asks about Yudhiṣṭhira's war preparations. Saṃjaya replies that he expects to triumph (1–5) and describes the horses of Arjuna, Bhīma, Sahadeva, and Nakula (5–15).
56 (57; 2232). At Dhṛtarāṣṭra's question Saṃjaya enumerates Yudhiṣṭhira's allies (1–10), and relates who is going to be pitted against whom (10–25). Dhṛtarāṣṭra predicts the Kauravas' defeat (25–35). Duryodhana protests: he will triumph (35–40). Dhṛtarāṣṭra asks who is the Pāṇḍavas' chief inspirer. It is Dhṛṣṭadyumna, who gave Saṃjaya the message that the Kauravas should come to terms with Yudhiṣṭhira (40–60).
57 (58; 2295). Dhṛtarāṣṭra urges Duryodhana to return the Pāṇḍavas' land (1–5). Duryodhana vows war, which he describes as a grand ritual. He will not give them a pinprick of land (10–15). Dhṛtarāṣṭra gives warning (15–25).
58 (59; 2323). Saṃjaya describes Kṛṣṇa and Arjuna together (1–15). Kṛṣṇa gave Saṃjaya a message: Arjuna is invincible (15–25).

59 (60; 2359). Dhṛtarāṣṭra tries to sway Duryodhana (1–20).
60 (61; 2382). In a rage Duryodhana boasts of his own divine powers (1–20). He will defeat them (20–25).
61 (62; 2411). Karṇa speaks equally boastfully (1–5). Bhīṣma ridicules him (5–10). Karṇa swears that he will not fight until Bhīṣma lies dead (10). Bhīṣma laughs it off (10–15).
62 (63–64; 2429). Duryodhana supports Karṇa (1–5). Vidura tells the fable of two birds which took off with a fowler's net; but they quarreled and were caught (5–10). Kinsmen must not quarrel. Another parable is told, of the mountain men who, on seeing priceless honey across a ravine, were so eager to get at it that they perished in the ravine. Duryodhana will likewise perish (10–30).
63 (65; 2482). Dhṛtarāṣṭra warns Duryodhana (1–15).
64 (66; 2498). Saṃjaya reports Arjuna's message: make peace or perish (1–15).
65 (67; 2513). Duryodhana rejects the message. Dhṛtarāṣṭra questions Saṃjaya in private about their relative strength. Saṃjaya wants Gāndhārī and Vyāsa present; they come (1–5).
66 (68; 2523). Saṃjaya describes Kṛṣṇa's divinity (1–15).
67 (69; 2538). Saṃjaya points to his own bhakti *for Kṛṣṇa which gives him superior insight (1–5). Dhṛtarāṣṭra implores Duryodhana to seek Kṛṣṇa's mercy; he refuses (5). Gāndhārī, Vyāsa, and Saṃjaya join in; there is praise of Kṛṣṇa (5–15).*
68 (70; 2560). The names of Kṛṣṇa (1–10).
69 (71; 2574). Dhṛtarāṣṭra hymns Kṛṣṇa (1–5).

Vaiśaṃpāyana said:

46.1 While the king was thus discoursing with Sanatsujāta and the sagacious Vidura, that night went by. At dawn, all the kings happily came into the assembly hall to gaze upon the bard. All of them, led by Dhṛtarāṣṭra, went into the king's beautiful hall, for they wished to hear the Pārthas' message, which was informed by Law and Profit. The deep hall was plastered white and adorned with a court of gold, bright like the moon and very splendid, sprinkled with sandalwood
5 water, spread with stools of gold and wood, precious stones, and ivory that were well-covered with cushions.

Bhīṣma, Droṇa, Kṛpa, Śalya, Kṛtavarman, Jayadratha, Aśvatthāman,

Vikarṇa, Somadatta, Bāhlika, sagacious Vidura, and warlike Yuyutsu
—all these princely champions assembled, bull of the Bharatas, and,
placing Dhṛtarāṣṭra at their head, filed into the hall. Duḥśāsana,
Citrasena, Śakuni Saubala, Durmukha, Duḥsaha, Karṇa, Ulūka, and
Viviṃśati placed the intransigent Kuru king Duryodhana at their
head and entered the hall, king, as the Gods enter the dwelling of
10 Indra. Sire, with those champions of bludgeon-like arms entering,
that hall appeared like a mountain cavern with lions.

Having made their entrance into the hall, the great archers, who shone in assemblies, radiant like the sun, took their precious seats; and when all the kings were seated, Bhārata, the gate-keeper announced that the son of the bard had arrived: "Our envoy has swiftly returned on the chariot on which he went to the Pāṇḍavas with the five horses from Sindh." Wearing his earrings, he jumped off the chariot and quickly entered the hall, which was filled with great-spirited princes.

Saṃjaya said:

15 Kauravas! Know that I have come back from the Pāṇḍavas. The sons of Pāṇḍu salute all the Kurus according to age. The Pārthas greet their elders and contemporaries like friends, and according to age they hail with honor their juniors. Learn, princes, what I have to say after going to the Pāṇḍavas on the instructions of Dhṛtarāṣṭra.

Dhṛtarāṣṭra said:

47.1 I ask thee, Saṃjaya, 'midst these kings
For the words that Dhanaṃjaya spoke, that chief
Of warriors always undaunted of mettle,
Great-spirited robber of evil men's lives.

Saṃjaya said:

Let Duryodhana listen then to the words
That Arjuna spoke, quite ready for battle,
Great-spirited hero Dhanaṃjaya,
With Yudhiṣṭhira's leave and in Keśava's hearing.

Fully confident, knowing the strength of his arms,
And poised in the presence of Vāsudeva,
The bellicose Diademed One said to me:
"Tell the Dhārtarāṣṭra amidst the Kurus,

"In the hearing of all those kings as well
Who have gathered to kill the Pāṇḍavas—
Give voice to the message entire that I send
So the king and his councilors hear it all."

5 As eagerly surely as all the Gods
Lend ear to their thunderbolt-wielding king,

So listened the Pāṇḍus and Sṛñjayas
To the capable speech of the Diademed One.

Quite ready for battle Gāṇḍīva bowman
Arjuna said with red lotus eyes:
"If the Dhārtarāṣṭra fails to surrender
The realm to Yudhiṣṭhira Ājamīḍha,
Then surely there has been evil committed
That is yet unatoned by the Dhārtarāṣṭras.

"To battle with Bhīma and Arjuna,
With the Aśvins' sons and Vāsudeva,
With the son of Śini who has taken up arms,
With Dhṛṣṭadyumna and with Śikhaṇḍin,
With the Indra-like Yudhiṣṭhira
Who with one cross thought can burn heaven and earth—

"If Duryodhana fancies to battle with them,
Then the Pāṇḍavas' purpose is amply fulfilled!
Do nothing to help the Pāṇḍavas' cause,
Rather come and make war, if you fancy that!

"If the Pāṇḍava, heeding the Law, bedded down,
Exiled to the woods, on a bed of sorrow,
Dhṛtarāṣṭra's son shall lie down and die
On a sorrier bed that shall be his last.

10 "Dhṛtarāṣṭra's son has governed the Kurus
And Pāṇḍavas wickedly outside the Law,
While he with modesty, wisdom, and penance,
Gifts, self-control, wrath, concern for the Law,

"And, though tricked, with respectful and upright stance,
With austerity, self-control, strength, and Law,
And speaking the truth and friendly, though lied to,
Endured the hardships that knew no bounds!

"When the Pāṇḍavas' eldest, whose soul is honed
And whose mind excited, unleashes the wrath
That has seethed for many dread years on the Kurus,
Dhṛtarāṣṭra's son shall rue that he warred.

"As the black-trailed fire that is lit in the summer
Blazing forth burns down a deadwood's trees,
Yudhiṣṭhira shall with a glance burn down
Duryodhana's host when his fury is kindled.

"When the Dhārtarāṣṭra beholds Bhīmasena
In battle spewing the venom of rage,

The intransigent, club-wielding Pāṇḍava
Of terrible speed, he shall rue this war.

15 "When Bhīma, wielding his club, sets upon
Duryodhana's army, of fearful aspect
A mighty lion invading a cowpen,
And smites them, Duryodhana'll rue this war.

"When he, weapon-wise, fearless in gravest peril,
And crushing the enemy host in the clash,
On one chariot counters a flood of them,
Cutting down with his bludgeon the masses of footmen,

"And, grinding the many hosts with his furor,
He shatters the force of the Dhārtarāṣṭra,
That champion, like felling a wood with an axe,
Then the Dhārtarāṣṭra shall rue this war.

"Beholding his massive forces scattered,
Like a village of mostly straw-built huts
Consumed by a fire, or a ripe patch of grain
By lightning fire ravaged, their champions slain,

"Their faces averted and panic-stricken,
For the most part in flight and with hardly a fighter
Still daring, laid waste by the club fire of Bhīma,
Then the Dhārtarāṣṭra shall rue this war.

"When that greatest of champions, Nakula,
That trick fighter, pulls with his right from the quiver
And mows down many hundreds of chariot warriors,
Then the Dhārtarāṣṭra shall rue this war.

"For that wretched woods bed that Nakula slept on—
Though used to his comforts—a very long time,
While hissing hard like a furious cobra,
The Dhārtarāṣṭra shall rue this war.

"Beholding the heroes on chariots bright
Attack his own host on King Dharma's* behest,
Abandoning self in the killing of kings,
The Dhārtarāṣṭra shall later repent.

"When the Kaurava sees the five child heroes,
Not like children at all in the use of their weapons,
Abandoning life to fight the Kekayas,
Then the Dhārtarāṣṭra shall rue this war.

* = Yudhiṣṭhira.

"When mounted upon his resistless chariot
With the noiseless axles and golden stars,
With trained steeds yoked, killer Sahadeva
With arrow floods scatters the heads of the kings,

"And the Dhārtarāṣṭra beholds him mounted
Rolling into the perilous fight and attacking
All quarters with weapons he knows so well,
Duryodhana then shall rue this war.

"Restrained by modesty, clever and truthful,
Endowed with great strength and firm in all Laws,
Swift-acting impetuous Sahadeva
On his way to Śakuni shall slaughter the folk.

"When he sees all of Draupadī's sons, great archers,
Sharp warriors and heroes in chariot battles,
Who advance like cobras of virulent poison,
Then the Dhārtarāṣṭra shall rue this war.

"Abhimanyu, the killer of enemy heroes—
When he like a cloud pelts the foes with his shafts,
And, an armsman like Kṛṣṇa, plunges in,
Then the Dhārtarāṣṭra shall rue this war.

"When he sees Abhimanyu, a child but no child
In gallantry, storm on the enemy host
Like death, that matchless and weapon-wise youth,
Then the Dhārtarāṣṭra shall rue this war.

30 "When the agile Prabhadraka youths, whose might
Is like that of lions, experienced fighters,
Smite the Dhārtarāṣṭras with all their hosts,
Then the Dhārtarāṣṭra shall rue this war.

"When the aged Virāṭa and Drupada, storming,
Great warriors, each with his force to the foe,
Each espy Dhṛtarāṣṭra's men and their ranks,
Then the Dhārtarāṣṭra shall rue this war.

"When the weapon-wise Drupada flails away
And riding his chariot angrily cuts
With his arrows in battle the heads of the youths,
Then the Dhārtarāṣṭra shall rue this war.

"When Virāṭa, the killer of enemy heroes,
Penetrates your army where it is weakest,
Spearheading his tough-looking Matsya host,
Then the Dhārtarāṣṭra shall rue this war.

"When he sees the fierce-looking eldest of the Matsyas,
The chariot warrior son of Virāṭa,
Who has donned his mail in the Pāṇḍava's cause,
Then the Dhārtarāṣṭra shall rue this war.

35 "When Śaṃtanu's eminent son* has fallen,
The Kaurava champion, felled by Śikhaṇḍin,
Then without a doubt I declare to you,
Our enemies shall live no more.

"When the armored Śikhaṇḍin, mowing down warriors,
On his chariot makes his attack on Bhīṣma,
With celestial horses trampling the fighters,
Then the Dhārtarāṣṭra will rue this war.

"When he sees in the midst of the Sṛñjaya ranks
At their head the gloating Dhṛṣṭadyumna,
To whom the sagacious Droṇa revealed
The secret weapon, Duryodhana'll rue it.

"When that measureless army commander, who matches
His enemies, felling the Dhārtarāṣṭras,
With his arrows attacks on the battle field Droṇa,
Then the Dhārtarāṣṭra shall rue this war.

"He's the strong, wise, modest, and spirited hero,
The chief of the Somakas, darling of fortune.
The foe shall never hold out against us
Whose leader and guide is the Vṛṣṇi lion.

40 "Let him say to the people, 'Choose no more!'
For we have chosen the grandson of Śini
For our helper, this Sātyaki, chariot warrior,
Unrivaled, fearless, weapon-wise, strong.

"When ordered by me the chief of the Śinis
Like a rain cloud showers the enemies,
With a blanket of arrows smothers the fighters,
Then the Dhārtarāṣṭra shall rue this war.

"When eager to battle he musters his firmness,
That strong-bowed, long-armed, great-spirited man,
Then like cows which smell the smell of a lion
The enemies shrivel as fronting a fire.

"That strong-bowed, long-armed, great-spirited man
Could sever the mountains and shatter all worlds;
An experienced fighter whose hands are quick,
He shines like the sun that stands in the sky.

* = Bhīṣma.

"That lionlike Vṛṣṇi, that Yādava,
Possesses a subtle and versatile yoga
In weapons, as high as they praise any yoga,
With all great virtues is Sātyaki gifted.

45 "When Suyodhana sees the chariot of gold,
Yoked with four white steeds, on the battlefield,
The chariot of Sātyaki Mādhava,
Then that foolish and uncontrolled churl shall rue it.

"When he sees the chariot, gem-studded, golden,
With white steeds yoked, with the monkey banner,
On the battlefield driven by Keśava,
Then that foolish and uncontrolled churl shall rue it.

"When that shallow brain hears the great, ugly sound
Of the bow Gāṇḍīva, striking my wrist guard,
That equals the crack of a thunderbolt strike,
As in the grand battle I brandish it,

"Then that asinine son of Dhṛtarāṣṭra,
Of the wicked heart and evil companions,
Shall rue it, seeing his darkening army
Under arrow rains breaking apart like a cow herd.

"When, like lightning leaping out of the cloud,
Killing thousands of enemies in the encounters,
My bow spews shafts striking vitals and bones,
Then the Dhārtarāṣṭra shall rue this war.

50 "When he sees clouds of arrows fly from the string,
Let loose by Gāṇḍīva, with sharp-pointed piles,
Taking elephants, horses, and armored men,
Then the Dhārtarāṣṭra shall rue this war.

"When the fools see our enemies' arrows deflected
By arrows of mine, or turned around,
Or slantwise pierced and cut by my razors,
Then the Dhārtarāṣṭra shall rue this war.

"When the arrows propelled by my arms strike home
And, as birds pluck fruits from the tops of the trees,
Pluck off the heads of his youthful warriors,
Then the Dhārtarāṣṭra shall rue this war.

"When he sees his fighters topple from chariots,
From horses and mountainous elephants,
Hit and felled by my arrows in the arena,
Then the Dhārtarāṣṭra shall rue this war.

"When I, like gaping death to the killers,
Dispatch with the flaming rain of my arrows
The masses of enemy footmen and chariots
On every side, then the fool shall rue it.

55 "When he sees his troops completely bewildered,
Cut up by Gāṇḍīva, obscured by the dust
From my chariot, flying in all directions,
Then that addle-brain shall later repent it.

"Duryodhana'll see all his soldiers maimed,
Knowing not where to turn, bereft of their wits,
With their horses and heroes and elephants slain,
Athirst, in terror, their mounts exhausted,

"Wailing piteously, killed or about to be killed,
Their hair, bones, skulls all scattered about,
Like the half-finished work of God the Creator,
And the foolish churl shall rue the sight.

"When the Dhārtarāṣṭra beholds on my chariot
The bow Gāṇḍīva, and Vāsudeva,
My steeds, my celestial conch Pāñcajanya,
The inexhaustible quivers, me, Devadatta,

"When disbanding the gathered ranks of the *dasyus*,
And ushering in another new Eon,
I burn like a fire the Kauraveyas,
Dhṛtarāṣṭra shall rue it with his sons.

60 "With his brothers and sons and army that fool,
To his sovereignty lost and a prey to his wrath,
And shivering now that his pride has been humbled,
The slow Dhārtarāṣṭra shall later repent it.

"One morning when I had done with my prayers
And done with the water, a brahmin said kindly,
'There awaits you a difficult task, son of Pṛthā.
You must fight with your enemies, left-handed archer.

" 'Let either the bay-horsed, bolt-hurling Indra,
Destroying the enemies, go in your front,
Or let Vāsudeva protect your rear
On his chariot yoked with his steed Sugrīva.'

"I chose, over Indra the Thunderbolt-Wielder,
In this battle for Vāsudeva as helper,
And *I* found Kṛṣṇa to kill the *dasyus*,
But I think that the Gods arranged it for me!

"For whoever Kṛṣṇa wishes to triumph
With nary a thought, without fighting himself,
He surely surpasses all enemies,
Be they Indra and Gods, not to think now of humans.

65 "He is ready to swim with his arms 'cross the ocean,
Across the salt water's measureless girth,
Who hopes to defeat in a war Vāsudeva,
The splendid, surpassing champion Kṛṣṇa.

"He who wishes to split with his palm the mountain,
The great White Mountain piled up with rock,
Will surely shatter his hand and nails
But not do a thing to the mountain itself.

"He who hopes to defeat Vāsudeva in battle,
Might well try to extinguish a fire with his hands,
Or put a stop to the sun and the moon,
Or forcibly rob the Gods of the Elixir.

"He devastated the realm of the kings,
And on one chariot abducted alone
The glorious Rukmiṇī of the Bhojas,
Who bore the great-spirited Raukmiṇeya.*

"Impetuously he churned up Gāndhāra,
And having defeated all Nagnajit's sons,
He freed from his fetters by force that friend
Of the Gods whose name is Sudarśanīya.

70 "At Kavāṭa he smote the king of the Pāṇḍyas,
And smashed the Kalingas at Dantakūra;
The city Vārāṇasī, burned by him,
Stayed many a year without a protector.

"The king of Niṣāda named Ekalavya,
Whom others had deemed invincible in war,
Lay slain by Kṛṣṇa and robbed of his life
Like Jambha who, furious, stormed at the mountain.

"He felled Ugrasena's wicked son,
Who blazed in the midst of the Andhaka-Vṛṣṇis,
With Baladeva as second and gave
The kingdom back to Ugrasena.

"With magic he battled the sky-going Saubha,
The terror-inspiring Śālva king;
At the gate of the Saubha he caught with his arms
The hundred-killer—what mortal can face him?

* = Pradyumna.

"Then there was that fortress of Prāgjyotiṣa,
The Asuras' dread, impregnable city:
There the powerful earth-born Naraka
Stole Aditi's beautiful jeweled earrings.

75 "The Gods with Śakra combined to retrieve them
But failed to match him and fled in terror;
And witnessing Keśava's gallantry,
His might and irresistible weapons,

"Aware of this Keśava's real nature,
They charged this Kṛṣṇa with killing the *dasyus*;
Vāsudeva agreed to that difficult task,
For among his perfections he owned dominion.

"At Nirmocana city he slew six thousand
And cleft with a will the sharp-edged fetters;
Then smiting Mūru and Rākṣasa hosts,
The champion entered Nirmocana.

"It was there that then the battle ensued
Of mighty demon and mightier Viṣṇu;
He lay slain by Kṛṣṇa and robbed of his life,
Like a *karṇikāra* felled by the wind.

"Thus having retrieved the jeweled earrings,
And slain Mūru and earthborn Naraka,
Sagacious, covered with fortune and glory
And of unequaled prowess, Kṛṣṇa returned.

80 "Upon seeing the terrible feat he had wrought
In the battle the Gods lavished boons on him,
'No fatigue shall afflict you whenever you battle,
Upon water and sky shall be your footprint,

" 'No weapon shall ever enter your body!'
And with these boons was Kṛṣṇa contented:
Such is the immeasurable Vāsudeva,
In whom are all virtues, so powerful.

"That invincible, endlessly puissant Viṣṇu
Dhṛtarāṣṭra's son seeks to overpower!
When his evil soul makes attempts on him,
He endures even that for he looks to us.

"If he thinks he can start and foment a quarrel
That would run its course between Kṛṣṇa and me,
And plunder the Pāṇḍavas' property,
He'll find out the truth when he goes to war.

"Obeisance to Śaṃtanu's son the king,
To Droṇa obeisance and Droṇa's son,*
To the son of Śaradvat** who has no rivals—
I covet the kingdom and fight for it!

85 "Methinks that the Law shall point the weapon
At who lawfully fights with the Pāṇḍavas;
The sons of Pāṇḍu were cheated at gambling
By savage men and have waited twelve years.

"Having found long hardship ordained in the forest
And lived one year a life of concealment,
On a sudden the Pāṇḍavas' life is begrudged
By the Dhārtarāṣṭras, usurping their place.

"If they were to defeat us in fighting this war,
With the help of the Gods even, headed by Indra,
Then Unlaw is better practiced than Law
And certainly no more good will be done.

"If he thinks that a man is not bound by his acts,
If he thinks we are not superior to him,
Then I hope with the aid of Vāsudeva
To slay Duryodhana and his gang.

"Even if no *karman* be bound on a man,
If a person have no *karman* that's his,
Then keeping the one and the other in view
The Dhārtarāṣṭra's defeat will be just.

90 "Ye Kurus, I tell you this obvious truth:
The Dhārtarāṣṭras shall die in this war;
If they seek their goal without waging a war,
Then let them desist, and they will survive.

"Having smitten the Dhārtarāṣṭras and Karṇa,
I shall conquer the Kauravas' kingdom entire;
So do what you have to do and as you can,
And enjoy while you may your dear wives and your sons.

"We too have elderly brahmins with us,
Men of learning, deportment, and family,
Who are spellers of years and steeped in the stars
And know to decide on the stellar conjunctions,

"The higher and lower secrets of fate,
Celestial riddles, zodiac, hours—

* = Aśvatthāman.
** = Kṛpa.

Of the Kurus and Śṛñjayas do they predict
The colossal collapse, and the Pāṇḍavas' triumph!

"Our Ajātaśatru* already considers
Success achieved in taming our foes;
Janārdana too, who envisions the hidden,
The lionlike Vṛṣṇi, foresees no risk.

95 "I myself know well the shape of the future,
And undistracted I look with my mind—
My ancient vision is unimpaired:
The Dhārtarāṣṭras will die in this war.

"My Gāṇḍiva gapes without being held,
My bowstring shudders without being touched,
My arrows jump from the mouths of my quivers
And again and again they want to fly off.

"My dagger serenely pops out of its sheath
Like a serpent that sheds its worn-out slough;
In my banner are gruesome voices that ask:
'When, Diademed One, will your chariot be yoked?'

"In the night are howling the jackal packs
And down from the skies fly Rākṣasas,
The animals, jackals, whitenecks, and crows,
The vultures and kites and hyenas come out,

"And flights of Garuḍas fly behind
When they see my chariot yoked with white steeds,
And alone I shall shower my arrows and take
All the warrior kings to the world of the dead.

100 "As I set my various arms on their courses,
Like fire in the summer that ravages forests,
My pillar-ear missile, Paśupati's weapon,
The Brahmā projectile, the one Śakra found,

"Set on slaughter and sending my swift shafts forth,
I shall leave of these creatures no remnant at all,
I shall find my peace, and I shall be exulted
For good—you tell them, Gavalgana's son!"

That Dhārtarāṣṭra aspires to feud
With those with whose help he has always challenged
His enemies, even if Gods led by Indra
Took their side—behold Duryodhana's madness!

* = Yudhiṣṭhira.

Old Bhīṣma, Śaṃtanu's son, and Kṛpa,
Sagacious Vidura, Droṇa and son,
They all have said it and so shall it be,
Let the Kauravas all enjoy a long life.

Vaiśaṃpāyana said:
48.1 When all those kings had foregathered, O Bhārata, Bhīṣma
Śāṃtanava spoke these words to Duryodhana, "Bṛhaspati and
Uśanas once attended on Brahmā. Indra and his Maruts, the Vasus,
Aśvins, Ādityas, Sādhyas, the Seven Seers in the sky, the Gandharva
Viśvāvasu, and the bright throngs of the Apsarās bowed and
approached the Grandfather, who is the elder of the worlds. The
celestials surrounded and waited upon the lord of the universe.
5 Thereupon the two ancient Gods, the seers Nara and Nārāyaṇa, went
out, drawing out the minds and vigor of the celestials. Bṛhaspati
questioned Brahmā: 'Who are these two? They do not wait on your
pleasure! Tell us, Grandfather.'
Brahmā said:
" 'These two ascetics, who illuminate heaven and earth, blazing
and shining, powerfully pervading and surpassing, are Nara and
Nārāyaṇa, who roam from world to world. Strengthened by their
austerities, they possess great mettle and prowess. This pair indeed
eternally brings joy to the worlds, honored by Gods and Gandharvas,
for the destruction of the Asuras.' "
Vaiśaṃpāyana said:
10 Having heard this Śakra went to the spot where the two were
performing austerities, in the company of all the hosts of Gods led by
Bṛhaspati. Since at that time the celestials lived in grisly fear because
of war between Gods and Asuras, he asked Nara and Nārāyaṇa for a
boon. They said to him, "Choose." Śakra said, "Help us!" O best
of the Bharatas, and they replied to him, "We shall do what you
want."
With their help Śakra vanquished the Daityas and Dānavas. In
Indra's battle, enemy-burner Nara slew the enemies, Paulomas and
15 Kālakhañjas, by the hundreds and thousands. Standing on his
spinning chariot on the battlefield Arjuna cut off with a bear arrow
the head of Jambha, who was swallowing the sacrifice. He scourged
Hiraṇyapura on the ocean shore after killing in battle sixty thousand
Nivātakavacas. That conqueror of enemy cities bested Indra and the
Gods, then the strong-armed Arjuna sated Jātavedas. Nārāyaṇa too
killed many others in that battle.

Behold! The two champions have returned and joined together as
the great heroes and warriors Vāsudeva and Arjuna. It is said that
they are the ancient Gods Nara and Nārāyaṇa, invincible in the

20 world of men even to Indra, Gods, and Asuras. Kṛṣṇa is said to be
Nārāyaṇa and Phalguna Nara. Nara and Nārāyaṇa are one being
made into two. With their feats they have earned imperishable and
enduring worlds, but they take on new births time and again in this
world or that, when it is time to give battle. That is why Nārada
has said, "The deed shall be done," for he, who knows the Veda,
told it all to the circle of the Vṛṣṇis.

Duryodhana, when you see Keśava with conch shell, discus, and
club in his hands and the terrible archer Arjuna holding his weapons,
the two everlasting, great-spirited Kṛṣṇas standing on one chariot,
25 then, my son, you will remember my words. Would that the
destruction of the Kurus did not loom, but your spirit, son, has
veered away from Law and Profit! If you will not heed my words,
you shall hear that very many have fallen, for all the Kurus wait
on your opinion alone. Of only three do *you* accept the views, bull
of the Bharatas: of Karṇa, who has been cursed by Rāma, that low-caste son of a *sūta*; of Śakuni Saubala; and of that base and evil
brother of yours, Duḥśāsana.

Karṇa said:

Long-lived grandfather, do not talk of me like that! For I abide by
the Law of the baronage without forsaking my own. Where have I
30 conducted myself ill that you berate me? The Dhārtarāṣṭras know of
no misdeeds of mine anywhere, rather all that I do is to please King
Dhṛtarāṣṭra as well as Duryodhana, for he controls the kingdom.

Vaiśaṃpāyana said:

Upon hearing Karṇa's reply Bhīṣma Śāṃtanava spoke once more,
addressing great King Dhṛtarāṣṭra, "This fellow boasts all the time
that he will kill the Pāṇḍavas, and he is not worth a fraction of the
great-spirited sons of Pāṇḍu. The disaster that is coming to your
ill-spirited sons is the work of Karṇa, realize that—of this wicked son
35 of a *sūta*. Your nitwit son Suyodhana relies on him and has only
contempt for those enemy-taming and valiant sons of Gods. Now
what rare feat has he achieved in the past that matches any one
accomplished by any of the Pāṇḍavas? When he saw his own dear
brother killed with much gallantry by Dhanaṃjaya by the city of the
Matsya king, what did *he* do? Dhanaṃjaya in fact attacked all the
Kurus together, routed them and cut away the cattle—was this one
away on a trip? When your son was captured by the Gandharvas on
their cattle expedition, where was the *sūta*'s son then who now struts
40 like a bull? Wasn't it the Pārtha, the great-spirited Bhīma, and the
twins who came and vanquished the Gandharvas? There are a good
many lies, bull of the Bharatas, that this braggart who has always
lacked in Law and Profit likes to voice! Good luck to thee!"

When Bhāradvāja heard Bhīṣma's words, he saluted Dhṛtarāṣṭra in

the midst of the kings and said to him, "Sire, best of the Bharatas, do
as Bhīṣma says, and do not follow instead the advice of those who
seek their own profit. I think we should negotiate with the Pāṇḍavas
45 before we wage war. I know that Arjuna Pāṇḍava will do everything
that he has said and that Saṃjaya has reported, for that archer has
no equal in all three worlds!"

But without heeding Bhīṣma's and Droṇa's wise advice the king questioned Saṃjaya about the Pāṇḍava. It was then, when the king failed properly to answer Bhīṣma and Droṇa, that all the Kurus lost hope of their lives.

Dhṛtarāṣṭra said:

49.1 What did King Pāṇḍava, son of Dharma, say when he heard that these many armies were massing against his cause? What does Yudhiṣṭhira, although ready for war, hope from this enterprise? From among all his brothers and sons, at whose face does he look in his worries? Who among his law-abiding kin are the ones who restrain him, counseling war or peace, while the law-wise king remains enraged at the deceit these fools perpetrate against him?

Saṃjaya said:

It is at the king's face that the Pāñcālas and Pāṇḍavas look, at
5 Yudhiṣṭhira's, good luck to thee—he rules them all. The chariot
columns of the Pāṇḍavas and Pāñcālas in separate detachments salute Yudhiṣṭhira when he comes. The Pāñcālas salute the Kaunteya of blazing splendor, like the rising sun, like a ready mass of splendor. The Pāñcālas, Kekayas, and Matsyas, down to the cowherds and shepherds, salute Yudhiṣṭhira Pāṇḍava, who brings them joy. Brahmin ladies, princesses, and the commoners' daughters crowd together in play to gaze upon the Pāṇḍava, who is girt for war.

Dhṛtarāṣṭra said:

Saṃjaya, tell what forces the Pāṇḍavas have mustered against us, what of Dhṛṣṭadyumna and his army, how strong are the Somakas?

Vaiśaṃpāyana said:

10 Thus questioned in the hall where the Kurus were assembled, Gavalgana's son heaved deep long sighs and seemed to be lost in thought. Then as fate would have it, faintness overcame the bard, and a man in the assembly of the kings spoke up, "Mahārāja, Saṃjaya has fallen on the ground in a faint! He is unconscious and senseless and does not utter a word."

Dhṛtarāṣṭra said:

Surely Saṃjaya saw the warrior sons of Kuntī and his mind is upset over those tigerlike men.

Vaiśaṃpāyana said:

Saṃjaya regained consciousness, and breathing freely again he said to great King Dhṛtarāṣṭra in the hall where the Kurus were assembled,

"Indra among kings, I have seen the warrior sons of Kuntī, emaciated by the constraints of living in the house of the Matsya king. Hear, great lord, whom the Pāṇḍavas have mustered against you. The Pāṇḍavas have mustered Ajātaśatru, who for neither anger, fear, lust, profit, nor specious argument ever forsakes the truth, the law-spirited king, first of the upholders of the Law and the standard for what is the Law. The Pāṇḍavas have mustered against you Bhīmasena, who has no equal on earth in the strength of his arms, the archer who brought all the kings of the earth into his power; the Wolf-Belly, son of Kuntī, who was a haven for the others and saved them from the man-eater Hiḍimba when they had escaped from the lacquer house; the Wolf-Belly, son of Kuntī, who was a haven for the others when the king of Sindhu abducted Yājñasenī;* who, when all the Pāṇḍavas were being burned alive in Vāraṇāvata, set them free—him they have mustered against you. The one who killed the Krodhavaśas when, to do a favor for Kṛṣṇā, he penetrated dread and craggy Mount Gandhamādana and in whose arms reside the mettle and vigor of ten thousand elephants—him they have mustered against you!

"The Pāṇḍavas have mustered against you in the war Vijaya, who of yore, seconded by Kṛṣṇa, with great valor defeated the warring Sacker of Cities in order to sate Jātavedas,** and who gratified in a battle the Great God himself, the trident-wielding Sleeper of the Mountain, the God of Gods, Consort of Umā. The Pāṇḍavas have mustered Vijaya*** against you, the archer who subjugated all kings of earth. The warrior Nakula, that marvelous fighter, who conquered the West which is peopled by Barbarians, that handsome hero and superb archer, the son of Mādrī—him the Pāṇḍavas have mustered, Kauravya. The Pāṇḍavas have mustered against you Sahadeva, who in battle conquered the Kāśis, Anga, Magadha, and Kalinga. The one whose prowess is matched by but four men on earth—Aśvatthāman, Dhṛṣṭaketu, Pradyumna, and Rukmi—him the Pāṇḍavas have mustered against you, Sahadeva, the younger son who brought joy to Mādrī, a hero among men.

"Ye Kurus, they have mustered against you the armsman Śikhaṇḍin, who in a previous life was the daughter of the king of the Kāśis; who, wishing to assassinate Bhīṣma, performed dread austerities, died, and was reborn the daughter of the Pāñcāla, and by fate became a man, knowing, O tigerlike king, the virtues and vices of man and woman—the Pāñcāla who, berserker in war, assailed the Kalingas. The woman whom a Yakṣa, so we hear, changed into a man to kill Bhīṣma: that terrible archer the Pāṇḍavas have mustered.

"They have mustered against you the five princely Kekaya brothers,

* = Draupadī.
** = the Fire God.
*** = Arjuna.

the champions with the well-polished armor. The Vṛṣṇi hero
Yuyudhāna, long-armed, swift, and steadfast fighter whose valor is
his truth, has declared war on you. The Pāṇḍavas have mustered for
this war the same Virāṭa who at the time gave the great-spirited men
shelter. The warrior lord of the Kāśis, who is king in Vārāṇasī, has
become their champion; they have mustered him against you. The
youthful, great-spirited Draupadeyas, invincible in battle, whose touch
40 is like a cobra's, the Pāṇḍavas have mustered, and Ahbimanyu,
Kṛṣṇa's match in gallantry and Yudhiṣṭhira's in self-control. The
Pāṇḍavas have mustered the glorious warrior Dhṛṣṭaketu, son of
Śiśupāla, who, furious and irresistible in war, has no match in
gallantry. The Pāṇḍavas have mustered against you Vāsudeva, who
is the refuge of the Pāṇḍavas as Vāsava is of the Gods, as well as
Śarabha, the brother of the king of Cedi, Karakarṣa, Sahadeva, son of
Jarāsaṃdha, and Jayatsena. Splendid Drupada, who leads a large
army, stands ready to fight at the risk of his life in the cause of the
45 Pāṇḍavas. Building on these and many other kings of the East and
the North, hundreds of them, King Dharma stands prepared.

Dhṛtarāṣṭra said:

50.1 All the ones you have mentioned are men of great enterprise, yet
all of them together are one to one with Bhīma. I have as great a
fear of Bhīmasena angry and intolerant as a sturdy antelope has of a
tiger. I wake through all the nights heaving deep, hot sighs from fear
of the Wolf-Belly, as a weak animal fears a lion, for I see no one in
this army who could endure in battle that strong-armed man, whose
splendor matches Śakra's. This son of Pāṇḍu and Kuntī is truculent,
determinedly hostile; he does not laugh at jokes; he is mad; he looks
5 straight ahead, bellowing his roar. His speed, enterprise, arms, and
strength are all great, and he will put an end to my stupid sons in
battle. When he brandishes his club, his enemies are struck with
paralysis in their thighs; the bull of the Kurus is like staff-wielding
Death in battle.

In my mind I see his steel club adorned with gold, like the upraised
staff of Brahmā. Bhīma will stride among my troops like a powerful
10 lion among herds of antelope. From his boyhood on, this voracious,
recalcitrant man of cruel valor has, all by himself, displayed violence
toward my sons. It upset my heart when Duryodhana and the others
as boys were crushed by him in fights as by an elephant. My sons
have always been oppressed by his gallantry; it is he, Bhīma, who
has been the cause of the breach, Bhīma of terrible prowess. I see
Bhīma before me on the battlefield, raging with fury and devouring
the ranks of men, elephants, horses. With weapons he is the equal of
Droṇa and Arjuna, in speed the equal of the wind—tell me, Saṃjaya,
about the irate champion Bhīmasena!

15 It was more than they deserved, I think, that this enemy-slaying,
spirited man did not kill all my sons at the time. How shall a human
withstand his impact in battle, if he slaughtered Yakṣas and Rākṣasas
of terrific strength? Even as a child the Pāṇḍava was never in my
control, Saṃjaya, so how much less now that he has been made to
suffer by my evil sons? He is tough and because of his toughness he
might break but not bend. Level-eyed, with knitted brow, wide-
shouldered, irresistible, light-skinned, tall as a palm—why should the
Wolf-Belly be appeased? Bhīmasena stands a span taller than Arjuna,
20 in speed he overtakes racing horses, in strength he outmatches
elephants! This middlemost son of Pāṇḍu rumbles when he speaks,
his eyes are honey-colored, his strength is great. I have heard from
the lips of Vyāsa himself that in truth the Pāṇḍava was like that in
shape and strength even as a child. With his iron mace an angry
Bhīma, greatest of fighters, will shatter chariots, elephants, horses,
and men. Wrathful, always impetuous, ferocious, and cruel in his
valor, he has been slighted in the past for acting counter to my
wishes. How will my sons stand up to his heavy, well-ringed, gold-
studded iron club, when it swings out, killing hundreds, thudding a
25 hundredfold? Friend, only fools would attempt to cross that shoreless,
plumbless, impassable ocean called Bhīmasena, an ocean stormy with
arrows. Thinking they are clever, these children do not listen to my
pleas, and, having eyes only for the honey, they do not see the
pitfalls. If they want to wage war on the Wind in human form, they
must have been prodded by the Placer, as game by a lion. How can
my sons stand up to the swing of that boundlessly powerful shattering
steel bludgeon that measures four cubits and has six edges? Spinning
his club, breaking the heads of elephants, licking the corners of his
30 mouth, shedding tears of rage, aiming and striking his hits, yelling his
terrifying roars, falling upon the furious elephants that counter him
and echoing their bellows, plunging into the chariot courses and
smiting my best troops—will any of my offspring escape him, blazing
like fire? Cutting a path and putting my army to flight as though he
were dancing, he will, strong-armed, club in hand, show the end of
the Eon. Like a rutting elephant breaking flowering trees, the Wolf-
Belly will rout my sons' army on the battlefield. Robbing the chariots
of their men and pennants, breaking the drumskins, crushing
35 charioteers and riders, that tigerlike man will, just as the heavy
pressure of the Ganges overruns the manifold trees near the water
on her banks, overrun the great army of my sons, Saṃjaya! Pressed
by Bhīmasena's might my sons, retainers, and kings will surely fall
into his power, Saṃjaya. It was he who, entering King Jarāsaṃdha's
inner apartments, felled the mighty king with Vāsudeva's help. This
entire Goddess Earth had been overpowered by the powerful king of
Magadha, who thereupon oppressed her. The Kurus, thanks to

Bhīṣma's majesty, and the Andhaka-Vṛṣṇis, thanks to their policy, did not fall under his sway—or was it just fate? Pāṇḍu's son with his strong arms went there swiftly and the unarmed champion killed the king—what could top that? Just as a cobra spits out the venom that has been collecting for a long time, so he will let loose his splendor upon my sons in war, Saṃjaya. Bhīmasena with club in hand will slaughter my sons as great Indra, the chief of the Gods, once slaughtered the Dānavas with his thunderbolt. I see the Wolf-Belly, irresistible and inescapable, whose speed and prowess are fierce, attack with eyes redder than copper. What man could hold his ground before Bhīma even if the latter were without club, bow, chariot, and armor, fighting with his bare arms? Bhīṣma, the brahmin Droṇa, and Kṛpa Śāradvata know as I do the might of that cunning man. Knowing the vow of the Āryan and unwilling to break their pledges, those bull-like men will stand firm in the vanguard of my troops. Fate always prevails, especially over man's efforts: for even though I see the others' triumph, I do not bridle my sons. The great archers, starting on the ancient road that leads to Indra, will abandon their lives in the tumult and preserve their fame on earth. The Pāṇḍavas are to my sons as these are to them—grandsons of Bhīṣma and pupils of Droṇa and Kṛpa. Whatever gifts and offerings we have made to these three old men, they will surely repay, for they are noblemen. For a brahmin who has taken up arms and wants to fulfill the Law of the baronage, so they say, death is the ultimate boon. Indeed, I pity them all, who want to do battle with the Pāṇḍavas: the great danger foretold by Vidura at the outset is now upon us. I do not think, Saṃjaya, that knowledge thwarts grief: when grief is overwhelming, it thwarts knowledge instead. Even the detached seers, watching the weal of the world, rejoice at its happiness and grieve at its grief. How much more then I, who in a thousand ways am attached to my sons, kingdom, wife, grandsons, and kinsmen? Of what in the end am I capable in this great danger, for I see in my thoughts the perdition of the Kurus. This great disaster for the Kurus seems to have begun with the dicing. That slow-witted hankerer after power perpetrated his evil out of greed. This, I think, is the Law of the rushing of Time which lasts beyond the end: all are fixed to the wheel like its rim, there is no escape for anyone. What am I to do, how am I to do it, where am I going, Saṃjaya? The foolish Kurus are perishing in the clutches of Time. Powerless before the death of my one hundred sons, friend, I hear the wailing of the women—why, let death seize me too!

> As a blazing fire in the season of summer,
> Propelled by the wind, burns down the deadwood,
> So the Pāṇḍava, wielding his club, will likewise,
> Supported by Arjuna, kill my sons.

Dhṛtarāṣṭra said:

51.1   He, from whose lips we have never heard an untruthful word and whose warrior is Dhanaṃjaya, his can be the rule even of the three worlds! Ceaselessly I ponder but I do not see anyone who on his chariot could counter the Gāṇḍīva bowman on the battlefield. There is not a single person who is the match of the Gāṇḍīva archer when he shoots his reeds, shafts, and arrows. Let the heroic bulls among men Droṇa and Karṇa stand up to him and they might have a slight chance because of their greatness of spirit, but there will be no

5   victory for me in this world. Karṇa is compassionate and rash, the Teacher is old and venerable, and the indefatigable Pārtha of the hard bow is capable of opposing both. There would be a terrible battle, but no victory on anyone's part. For all are weapon-wise champions and have earned great fame. They might refuse the overlordship over all the Immortals, but not victory. Surely peace will reign only if they are killed, or Phalguna is killed; yet neither Arjuna's defeat is at hand, nor his slayer. How will his fury calm down when he has risen against my dim-witted sons? There are others who know arms and are vanquished or vanquish, but for Phalguna we hear of nothing but total victory. He challenged the Thirty-three Gods and sated Fire in the Khāṇḍava Forest. He triumphed over all the Gods! I know of

10   no time he was defeated. To him whose charioteer is Hṛṣīkeśa, his equal in character and conduct, victory is assured as it is to Indra. We have heard that the two eager Kṛṣṇas and the mighty bow Gāṇḍīva, all three of fiery power, have now joined on one chariot. We have no bow like that at all, no warrior, no charioteer, but the dimwits who follow Duryodhana's lead don't see it. The burning thunderbolt, when striking the head, may leave some remnant, Saṃjaya, but the arrows shot by the Diademed One leave nothing. There Phalguna already appears, shooting, killing, ripping the heads

15   from the trunks with his raining arrows. Will the fire of his shafts, blazing everywhere, kindled by Gāṇḍīva, not burn down the army of my sons? I have a vision of the Bhārata army panicked by the rattle of the left-handed archer's chariot and shivering in its multitude. Just as fire burns deadwood and grows and spreads everywhere with tall flames fanned by the wind, so he shall burn down my troops.

> When, spewing his volleys of sharpened arrows,
> The Diademed One stands poised for battle,
> He shall be irresistible Death created
> By our Ordainer to massacre all.

> When I hear incessantly of all the many
> Signs which occur in the seats of the Kurus
> Or around them or after the start of the war,
> Then surely perdition has come to the Kurus!

Dhṛtarāṣṭra said:

52.1 As valorous and hopeful of victory as all the Pāṇḍavas, so are
their allies who risk their lives and hold out for victory. You yourself
have spoken to me of those valiant foes, the Pāñcālas, Kekayas,
Matsyas, Magadhans, and the Vatsa kings. Kṛṣṇa, most high in all
the worlds, the mighty man who could bring into his power all these
worlds with their Indra, is bent upon the Pāṇḍavas' triumph. Sātyaki,
who rapidly acquired the art in its entirety from Arjuna himself, that
descendant of Śini will stand on the battlefield sowing his arrows like
5 seeds. Dhṛṣṭadyumna Pāñcālya, that great warrior of cruel feats, will
wage war on my forces with his supreme knowledge of weapons.
Friend, I am frightened of Yudhiṣṭhira's ire, of Arjuna's prowess, of the
twins, and of Bhīmasena: those Indras among men have cast out
their superhuman net in the middle of my army and will kill it off—I
rue it already, Saṃjaya!

Pāṇḍu's son is a handsome and spirited man; he has the luster of
luck, the effulgence of the *brahman*; he is wise; his insights are well-
formed; and he is inspirited with the Law. He is well-supplied with
friends and councilors, with horses to yoke and with men to yoke
10 them, with brothers, fathers-in-law, and sons who are great warriors.
Perseverance he possesses, and secrets he keeps, that tigerlike
Pāṇḍava; he is gentle and generous and modest, and his word is his
strength. He is greatly learned, has made his soul, attends to his
elders, has mastered his senses—what fool will like a moth want to
throw himself into that blazing fire of a man, endowed with all
virtues, as into a well-kindled fire? A fool is bound to die if he does
not avoid the Pāṇḍava fire! That king is a tall thin flame with the
glow of refined gold, and he shall put an end to my nitwit sons in
the battle.

Not to war were best, I think—listen to me, Kurus! If there be war,
15 the destruction of our entire lineage is assured. This is my last
attempt at peace, to appease my mind. If you do not want war, let
us then strive for peace. Yudhiṣṭhira will not ignore you, if you sue
for peace, for he loathes lawlessness, pointing at me as the cause of it.

Saṃjaya said:

53.1 Mahārāja Bhārata, it is exactly as you say: it is foreseeable that
Gāṇḍīva will destroy the baronage in a war. But this I fail to
understand in you who are always reasonable: that, in spite of
knowing the mettle of the Left-handed Archer, you yet submit to
your son. It is too late now, Mahārāja! It is you who have always
been to blame, for from the very beginning you have disparaged the
Pārthas, bull of the Bharatas. If one is a father and a good friend
whose heart is always guided well, he should practice what benefits

his sons—he who betrays is not called a guru. At the time of the
dicing you gloated like a little boy, Mahārāja, when you heard that
5 they had been beaten: "We have won! We have gotten it!" You
ignored that the Pārthas were scathingly talked to; you did not
perceive your own downfall while knowing full well that they
themselves had won the entire kingdom. Only the Field and the Jungle
of the Kurus are your ancestral domain, Mahārāja, and it was only
later that you obtained all of earth when those heroes had conquered
it. The Pārthas handed over to you the earth they had conquered
with the might of their arms, and now you think you conquered it
yourself, greatest of kings. The Pārtha brought back your sons when
they had been devoured by the king of the Gandharvas and were
10 drowning in a sea without boats. Like a little boy you gloated, sire,
when the Pāṇḍavas had been tricked at the game of dice and went
in retreat to the forest. Even oceans dry up before Arjuna when he
rains his many volleys of sharp arrows, let alone men born of flesh.
Of archers Phalguna stands first, of bows Gāṇḍīva is best, of all
creatures Keśava is chief, of all discuses Sudarśana, of standards his
standard, the shining monkey, is the greatest. Carrying all these on
his chariot in battle, the man of the white horses shall annihilate us,
king, like the upraised wheel of Time. His is now the entire earth,
sire, bull of the Bharatas, he is the king, O best of kings, who has
15 Bhīma and Arjuna for his warriors. The Kauravas led by Duryodhana
will go to their perdition when they see your army mostly slain by
Bhīma, and drowning; for your sons, mighty Mahārāja, and the
kings who follow them will panic before Bhīma and not be
victorious.

Now the Matsyas no longer respect you, nor do all the Pāñcālas
and Kekayas; and all the Śālveyas despise you, for all have gone over
to the Pārtha, knowing the valor of that sagacious prince. For
wronging these men who do not deserve to die and are possessed of
the Law, that evil man your son should be restrained by any means,
Mahārāja. He is not worth grieving over! At the time of the dicing
I told you and Vidura told you! All this lamenting of yours about
the Pāṇḍavas, Bhārata, as though you were powerless, Indra of kings,
is pointless!

Duryodhana said:

54.1 Have no fear, great king, do not feel sorry for us, for we are
capable of defeating our enemies in war, mighty prince! When the
Pārthas had retreated to the forest, Madhusūdana came to them with
a vast circle of troops that had crushed enemy kingdoms—the
Kekayas came; Dhṛṣṭaketu, Dhṛṣṭadyumna Pārṣata, and many other
kings followed the Pārthas. The great warriors gathered not far from

Indraprastha and together they reviled you and the Kurus. They banded together and, led by Kṛṣṇa, paid homage to their neighbor Yudhiṣṭhira where he was seated on an antelope skin, Bhārata. The kings told him to take back the kingdom and they were ready to uproot you and your following. When I heard this, I told Bhīṣma, Droṇa, and Kṛpa, being fearful of the destruction of my kinsmen, king, bull of the Bharatas: "It is my opinion that the Pāṇḍavas will not stand by the covenant, for Vāsudeva wants to extirpate us completely. With the exception of Vidura, all of you great-spirited men are to be killed. The law-wise Dhṛtarāṣṭra, the chief of the Kurus, is not to be killed. Janārdana, after having destroyed us completely, wishes to make the Field of the Kurus a single kingdom under Yudhiṣṭhira.

"The time has come now, but for what? Submission? Flight? Or shall we fight back at the enemies at the risk of our lives? If we fight back, we are certain to be defeated, for all the kings of earth are under Yudhiṣṭhira's sway. Our kingdom is disaffected, our allies are angry, we are reviled by all kings and all our kinfolk. There is no shame in submission to relatives for years everlasting. Nevertheless, I am sorry for my father, the lord of the people, who has the eyesight of insight: because of me he has found grief and come upon trouble without end. Indeed, your sons have blocked the others in order to please me—you have always known that, best of men. The warlike Pāṇḍavas will seek revenge by eradicating the house of Dhṛtarāṣṭra and his councilors!"

Thereupon Droṇa, Bhīṣma, Kṛpa, and Droṇa's son said in reply, O Bhārata, knowing that I was much worried and my senses were upset: "When others threaten us, we have nothing to fear, enemy-burner. The others are not able to defeat us in battle, prince. Each of us singly can defeat any of the kings. Let them come! We shall wipe out their pride with sharp arrows. In the olden days Bhīṣma alone irately defeated all the kings when his father had died, on a single chariot, Bhārata. The chief of the Kurus slew very many of them in anger and out of fear they then sought refuge with Devavrata himself! This Bhīṣma is more than capable, when seconded by us in battle, to vanquish the enemy, so rid yourself of your fear, bull of the Bharatas!"

That was the decision of those boundlessly august men, at a time when the entire earth was in the power of their enemies. Now those men are unable to defeat us in battle: the party of the enemy is split; the Pāṇḍavas have lost their prowess. Earth now rests on us, bull of the Bharatas. The kings, who have been brought in by me, are of one purpose in happiness and grief. They would enter the fire in my cause, they would enter the ocean, enemy-burner, all kings would—realize that, chief of the Kurus! They are laughing at you for your apprehensions, as though you were a madman, for your many fearful lamentations while you extol the foe. Every one of these kings is capable of meeting the Pāṇḍavas, and everyone knows that of himself. Let the fear that besets you depart! Not even Vāsava would be able to slay our entire army, even by Brahmā the Self-existent it is not to be shattered.

Yudhiṣṭhira has abandoned his city and only wants five villages, for he fears my army and might, my lord. The capacity you assume in Kuntī's son Wolf-Belly simply is not there, Bhārata, you don't know my strength, Bhārata! No one on earth equals me in club fighting, no one has outmatched me and no one will! Intently and at great pain I have crossed to the other shore of the art, therefore I have nothing to fear from Bhīma and the others. When I studied with him, Saṃkarṣaṇa concluded, "Duryodhana has no peer in club fighting." In battle I am Saṃkarṣaṇa's equal, and in might his better on earth. Bhīma will never withstand the blows of my club in battle. The one blow I will angrily deal to Bhīma, king, will speed him to Vaivasvata's dreadful domain. I wish I could see the Wolf-Belly brandishing his club, king! That is what I have hoped for for a very long time. Felled by my club on the battlefield, Pṛthā's son Wolf-Belly will lifelessly tumble to the ground with his limbs shattered. Mount Himālaya itself, hit once by my club, would crumble into a hundred thousand pieces! He knows it as well as Vāsudeva and Arjuna, that the final conclusion is that nobody matches Duryodhana with the club. So shed your fear about Bhīma in battle, for I shall dispatch him, do not worry, sire! When he has been slain by me, bull of the Bharatas, many warriors of equal measure and more will overpower Arjuna. Bhīṣma, Droṇa, Kṛpa, Droṇa's son, Karṇa, Bhūriśravas, the king of Prāgjyotisa, Śalya, the king of Sindhu Jayadratha are each of them capable of killing the Pāṇḍavas, Bhārata. All of them will send the others to Yama's seat instantly. Why should the entire army of the kings be unable to defeat Dhanaṃjaya alone? There is no reason. The masses of arrows, by hundreds and thousands, shot by Bhīṣma, Droṇa, Droṇa's son, and Kṛpa will speed the Pārtha to Yama's realm. Grandfather Bhīṣma Gāngeya was born from Śaṃtanu the equal of a brahmin seer, Bhārata, and is hard to assail even for Gods; for his father told him graciously: "You will not die before you wish." Droṇa was born in a trough from the brahmin seer Bharadvāja, and from Droṇa has Drauṇi been born, O great king, a master of arms. Kṛpa, this greatest of teachers, who was begotten by the great seer Gautama from a reed stalk—this illustrious man is, I think, unslayable. These three men, not born from a human womb, one a father, one a mother, one a maternal uncle, and Aśvatthāman who, great king, stands as my champion—all of them, Mahārāja, godlike

great warriors—would harass even Śakra in an encounter, bull of
the Bharatas! And in my view Karṇa equals Bhīṣma, Droṇa, and
Kṛpa: Rāma has acknowledged him as his peer, Bhārata. Karṇa had
bright, sparkling earrings, with which he was born, and great Indra
begged them from the enemy-burner for Śacī in exchange for the
infallible spear, great king, which is most terrifying. When
Dhanaṃjaya is embraced by the spear, how will he live? My triumph
is assured, king; it is as plain as a fruit lying in my hand, and the
total defeat of our enemies on earth is a matter of course!
In a single day Bhīṣma here kills ten thousand, Bhārata, and
55 Droṇa, Drauni, and Kṛpa are great archers who match him. The
Sworn Bands of barons have pledged, enemy-burner, "We shall take
Arjuna, or Dhanaṃjaya shall take us." The kings, my lord, think that
they are well-matched to kill the Left-handed Archer—so how is it,
sire, that you needlessly shrink away? When Bhīmasena has been
slain, who else of the others will fight on, Bhārata? Tell me this, if
you know the answer, enemy-burner! They have all the five brothers,
and Dhṛṣṭadyumna and Sātyaki: these seven warriors are the main
strength of the enemy. But our superior champions are Bhīṣma,
60 Droṇa, Kṛpa, and so forth: Droṇa's son Karṇa Vaikartana,
Somadatta, Bāhlīka, the king of Prāgjyotisa, Śalya, the king of Avanti,
Jayadratha, Duḥśāsana, Durmukha, Duḥsaha, O lord of the people,
Śrutāyus, Citrasena, Purumitra, Visiṃśati, Śala and Bhūriśravas both,
and your son Vikarṇa. I have mustered eleven grand-armies, sire,
while the enemy has fewer—seven in all. How can I lose? "A force
less by a third can be fought," quoth Bṛhaspati, and my armies
outnumber the enemy's by a third, king. I see that the enemy is
outnumbered by many ratios, while my own has the advantage of
65 many ratios, lord of the people. Knowing all this, the superiority of
my force and the inferiority of the Pāṇḍavas, you should not be
confused!

Vaiśaṃpāyana said:

Having spoken, that victor of enemy cities once more questioned
Saṃjaya, for he wished to find out what matters suited the day,
Bhārata.

Duryodhana said:

55.1 Now that Yudhiṣṭhira has mustered seven grand-armies, Saṃjaya,
what is he planning to do in concert with the kings to prepare for war?

Saṃjaya said:

Sire, Yudhiṣṭhira is most happily preparing for war, and Bhīmasena,
Arjuna, and the twins exhibit no fears. The Terrifier, son of Kuntī,
wishing to try out his spells, has yoked his divine chariot, illumining
all quarters. We have seen him girt, like a monsoon cloud bright with
5 lightning, and, reflecting on his spells, he told me joyfully, "Behold

this portent—we shall triumph, Saṃjaya!" I know it is exactly as the Terrifier spoke to me.

Duryodhana said:

You blithely praise the Pārthas, who were beaten at dice! Tell me, what kind of horses does Arjuna's chariot have, and what kind of flag?

Saṃjaya said:

Bhauvana, together with Śakra, and Tvaṣṭar, along with the Placer, created beautiful and colorful things, my prince, lord of your people. With their divine wizardry they made beautiful shapes for the flag, costly, celestial, large, and light.

In all directions, sideways and upward,
That flag of his covers the span of a league;
If surrounded by trees, it does not get caught,
For such is the wizardry Bhauvana wrought.

10 Just as in the sky the rainbow sparkles
Many-colored, and what it is we know not,
In such fashion has Bhauvana wrought that flag—
Its form displays a plenty of shapes.

As smoke through obstructions rises up to the sky
Wearing many a form and a body of fire,
In such fashion has Bhauvana wrought that flag—
No weight is too much for it, no obstruction.

He has fine white horses as fast as the wind
That are docile, divine, Citrasena's gift;
There will always be a full hundred of them,
Even when some are killed: that is an old boon.

The king likewise has yoked to his chariot
Big, ivory-colored ones, matching his might;
Bhīmasena has mounts that are antelope-hued
Whose speed on the battlefield matches the wind.

Sahadeva drives horses whose bodies are spotted
And whose colorful backs are partridge-colored:
His kind brother Phalguna gave them to him—
They better the steeds of his champion brother.

15 Bay coursers, the gift of great Indra, carry
Mādrī's son, strong Nakula Ājamīḍha;
They equal the wind in their speed and they carry
The hero like Indra, the Slayer of Vṛtra.

Large steeds that match them in age and valor
And have no peers in velocity, drive

Draupadī's sons and Subhadrā's son,
Fine horses bestowed on them by the Gods.

Dhṛtarāṣṭra said:
56.1 Saṃjaya, whom did you see assembled there, for their various
purposes, to give battle to my son's army in the cause of the
Pāṇḍava?
Saṃjaya said:
I saw Kṛṣṇa arrive, the first of the Andhaka-Vṛṣṇis, and Cekitāna
and Yuyudhāna Sātyaki. The latter two warriors, who pride
themselves on their manliness, have joined the Pāṇḍavas with a force
of one grand-army each. Drupada, the king of Pāñcāla, came with a
grand-army amidst his ten heroic sons, Satyajit and the rest, who are
5 headed by Dhṛṣṭadyumna, to increase the Pāṇḍavas' fame; he came
under the protection of Śikhaṇḍin after he had clothed the persons of
all his soldiers. Virāṭa arrived with his sons Śankha and Uttara, and
with Sūryadatta and his other champions, who are led by Madirāśva;
the king came accompanied by brothers and sons and joined the
Pārtha surrounded by a grand-army. Jārāsaṃdhi of Magadha and
King Dhṛṣṭaketu of Cedi came, each with a grand-army. All the five
Kekaya brothers, parading their blood-red standard, joined the
10 Pāṇḍavas with a grand-army. These in their numbers are the men
whom I have seen assembled to fight the army of Dhṛtarāṣṭra in the
Pāṇḍava's cause. The sagacious Dhṛṣṭadyumna, who knows the
formations of men, Gods, Gandharvas, and Asuras, is in command
of Yudhiṣṭhira's forces.
Sire, Bhīṣma Śāṃtanava has been allotted to Śikhaṇḍin for killing,
and Virāṭa with the Matsya spearmen are to support him. The mighty
king of the Madras has fallen to the eldest son of Pāṇḍu, though some
said they thought the two were mismatched. Duryodhana, with his
sons and one hundred brothers, have fallen to Bhīmasena as his share,
15 and so have the eastern and southern kings. Arjuna's lot is Karṇa
Vaikartana, as are Aśvatthāman, Vikarṇa, and Jayadratha of Sindh;
the Pārtha took also as his share all those who are unassailable and
pride themselves on their prowess. The five princely Kekaya brothers,
great archers all, took the Kekayas for their portion to fight in the
war. The Mālavas, Śālvas, Kekayas, and Trigartas are theirs, too,
and so are the two sworn champions. All the sons of Duryodhana
and Duḥśāsana are taken by Subhadrā's son, and also King Bṛhadbala.
20 Those great bowmen the Draupadeyas, with their standard wrought
of gold, will, led by Dhṛṣṭadyumna, assail Droṇa. Cekitāna wants to
fight Somadatta in a chariot duel; Yuyudhāna is to do battle with the
Bhoja Kṛtavarman. Mādrī's son Sahadeva, the champion who roars
in battle, has made it his share to kill brother-in-law Saubala.

Ulūka Kaitavya and the Sārasvata bands are assigned to Madravatī's
son Nakula. Other kings who counter them in battle, the sons of
Pāṇḍu will assign according to who challenges whom, sire.
25 This is the way the troops have been distributed lot by lot. Now
you and your son should not waste time before taking
countermeasures.

Dhṛtarāṣṭra said:

Lost are my sons, all of them, those fools, those crooked gamblers
who will have to fight mighty Bhīma in a pitched battle! All the kings
of the earth have been consecrated by the Law of Time and will fly
into the fire of Gāṇḍīva as moths into a flame. I already can see the
army routed by those great-spirited avengers! Who is going to follow
an army that has been shattered by the Pāṇḍavas on the battlefield?
For they are all champion warriors of fame and fieriness, equal in
30 their fierce splendor to sun and fire, triumphant in war, who have
Yudhiṣṭhira as their guide, Madhusūdana as their guardian, the two
heroic Pāṇḍavas, the Left-handed Archer and the Wolf-Belly, as their
warriors, and Nakula, Sahadeva, Dhṛṣṭadyumna Pārṣata, Sātyaki,
Drupada, Dhṛṣṭadyumna's son, Uttamaujas of Pāñcāla, and the
undefeatable Yudhāmanyu, Śikhaṇḍin, Kṣatradeva, Virāṭa's son
Uttara, the Matsyas, the Cedis, the Kāśyas and all the Sṛñjayas,
Virāṭa's son Babhru, the Pāñcālas, the Prabhadrakas—from whom
not even Indra would be able to wrest the earth if they were
35 unwilling, heroes seasoned in war, able to cleave mountains—all
these men of virtue and superhuman heat my evil sons want to
fight, Saṃjaya, while I stand by weeping!

Duryodhana said:

We of both parties are of the same stock, we both walk the earth,
so why do you think that victory can only go to the Pāṇḍavas?
Grandfather, Droṇa, Kṛpa, undefeatable Karṇa, Jayadratha,
Somadatta, and Aśvatthāman are cunning archers, whom even
Indra with the Immortals is unable to defeat in battle, father, let alone
the Pāṇḍavas! All of earth has been created for me to put the
Pāṇḍavas to flight, those noble steadfast champions, who are like fires
40 themselves. The Pāṇḍavas cannot even face my troops, for I am fully
capable of fighting the Pāṇḍavas and their sons. All these kings who
wish to please me, Bhārata, will stop them like antelopes with a net.
The Pāñcālas and Pāṇḍavas will be overrun by my large column of
chariots and my showers of arrows.

Dhṛtarāṣṭra said:

My son is raving like a madman, Saṃjaya, for he will not be able
to defeat in battle Yudhiṣṭhira the King Dharma! Bhīṣma indeed has
always known how strong the famous, great-spirited and law-wise
45 Pāṇḍavas and their sons really are. That is why I do not favor war

with those men of great spirit. But tell me once more about their
moves, Saṃjaya. Who is causing the impetuous Pāṇḍavas to blaze
up, those fiery archers, as fire is made to blaze with a butter
oblation?

Saṃjaya said:

It is Dhṛṣṭadyumna who is always inciting them, Bhārata, crying:
"Fight, best of the Bharatas, do not shy away from war! Whatever
kings Dhṛtarāṣṭra's son has secured and will mass together in a
horrendous battle like a sea of armor—I alone shall devour them,
when they are angrily arrayed for battle with their followers, as a
50 whale devours the fish of the sea. I shall put a stop to Bhīṣma, Droṇa,
Kṛpa, Karṇa, Droṇa's son, Śalya, and Suyodhana, just as the
floodline halts the ocean!"

When he spoke thus, the law-spirited King Yudhiṣṭhira said,
"Pāñcālas and Pāṇḍavas alike all depend on your fortitude and
bravery—be our savior in this war! I know, strong-armed warrior,
that you stand firm by the Law of the baronage and alone are a
sufficient match for the bellicose Kauravas. What you desire, enemy-burner, shall redound to our profit! With a thousand men one should
buy the one who holds his ground and shows his heroism to the foe
who, broken, runs away from the battlefield, looking for shelter—and
that is the point, you man of wise policy. You are a champion, a hero,
a paladin, bull among men, the savior of those who panic in battle,
no doubt of that!"

55 When the law-spirited Yudhiṣṭhira Kaunteya had thus spoken,
fearless Dhṛṣṭadyumna pronounced these words to me: "Bard, tell all
the men who are Duryodhana's warriors—the Kurus of Pratīpa's
lineage, the Bāhlīkas and Śāradvats, the *sūta*'s son, Droṇa and his
son, Jayadratha, Duḥśāsana, Vikarṇa as well as King Duryodhana—

"Go quickly and give to Bhīṣma this word:
'You must come to terms with Yudhiṣṭhira,
Lest Arjuna slay you, the ward of the Gods,
Go plead with the Pāṇḍavas, lord of the earth!'

60 "There is no warrior on earth like the Left-handed Archer, the son
of Pāṇḍu, supreme master of arms. For the celestial chariot of the
Gāṇḍīva bowman is protected by the Gods. No man can defeat him;
don't set your heart on war!"

Dhṛtarāṣṭra said:

57.1 The Pāṇḍava glows with baronial prowess and might, he has been
chaste since his boyhood; and with him these fools want to wage war
in spite of my lamentations! Duryodhana, best of the Bharatas,
turn away from war, for there are no circumstances in which war is

condoned, enemy-tamer. Half the earth should suffice you, for you and your councilors to live on. Return to Pāṇḍu's sons what is rightfully theirs, enemy-tamer, for all the Kauravas regard it as just that you make your peace with Pāṇḍu's great-spirited sons. Come look at this army of yours, son: it is a disease that saps you, but in your folly you don't realize it! For I do not want war, Bāhlīka does not want war, nor Bhīma, Droṇa, Aśvatthāman, Saṃjaya or Somadatta, Śalya, Kṛpa, Satyavrata, Purumitra, Jaya, Bhūriśravas—no one wants war! They on whose firmness the Kauravas fall back when harassed by enemies, they do not welcome this war, and that should please you, my son. You yourself do not seek it willingly; Karṇa makes you do it, and the evil Duḥśāsana, and Śakuni Saubala.

Duryodhana said:

I am not putting the burden of war on you, or on Droṇa, or on Aśvatthāman, or on Saṃjaya, or on Vikarṇa, or on Kāmboja, or on Bāhlīka, Satyavrata, Purumitra, Bhūriśravas, or any others of your party, when *I* make this challenge! I and Karṇa, father, have laid out the sacrifice of war and here we stand consecrated with Yudhiṣṭhira as the victim, bull of the Bharatas. This chariot is the altar, this sword the spoon, this club the ladle, this armor the *sadas*. My steeds are the four sacrificial priests, my arrows the *darbha* grass, my fame the oblation! Having offered up ourselves in war to Vaivasvata, O king, we shall triumphantly return, covered with glory, our enemies slain. I, Karṇa, and my brother Duḥśāsana, we three, father, will kill Pāṇḍavas in battle. I shall kill the Pāṇḍavas and rule the earth. I should rather surrender my life, wealth, and realm, steadfast king, than ever dwell together with the Pāṇḍavas! We shall not cede to the Pāṇḍavas as much land as you can prick with the point of a sharp needle, father!

Dhṛtarāṣṭra said:

I am sorry for all of you, good men, if you are ready to follow this fool on the road to the kingdom of Yama! I reject Duryodhana! Like tigers among herds of antelopes, these champion warriors, these sons of Pāṇḍu, will close ranks and kill all your leaders. It seems to me all running upstream—the Bhārata army dismembered and crushed by Yuyudhāna of the long arms, like a woman molested. Overflowing the already brimful force of the Pārtha, Mādhava Śaineya will stand on the battlefield, sowing his arrows like seed. Bhīmasena will be in the vanguard of the warriors, who will cling to him as to a reassuring bulwark. When you see the mountainous war elephants brought down by Bhīma, their tusks in pieces, their temples cut and dripping with blood, when you see them on the battlefield like pulverized mountains, and you yourself are in terror of Bhīma's touch, you shall remember my words. When you see your army burned down by

Bhīmasena and your chariots and elephants broken and killed, when you see the devastation like a trail of fire, you shall remember my words. If you do not make peace with the Pāṇḍavas, great peril will be upon you, and instead you will find your peace when you have been killed by Bhīmasena's club. When you see the army of the Kurus felled on the battlefield like a large forest that has been cut, then you shall remember my words.

Vaiśaṃpāyana said:

After the king had spoken thus much to all the kings, he again turned to Saṃjaya, great king, and asked—

Dhṛtarāṣṭra said:

58.1 What did the great-spirited Vāsudeva and Dhanaṃjaya have to
say? Tell me, sage, I want to listen to you.

Saṃjaya said:

Sire, listen as I tell you how I found Kṛṣṇa and Dhanaṃjaya, and what the heroes said, Bhārata.

I entered the sacred chambers of these God-like men humbly,
looking at my toes and folding my hands, in order to talk with them,
king. Abhimanyu himself and the twins are not allowed near the
5 place where the two Kṛṣṇas, Kṛṣṇā, and Saytabhāmā are staying. Both
men were drunk with mead, both were anointed with sandalwood
paste and wore garlands, fine robes, and the adornment of celestial
ornaments. There was a large golden bench on which the enemy-
tamers were seated, sparkling with all kinds of precious stones, which
was covered with colorful carpets.

I noticed that Keśava's feet rested in Arjuna's lap, and great-
spirited Arjuna's feet lay on Kṛṣṇā and Satyabhāmā. The Pārtha
pointed me then to a golden footstool, which I touched with my
hand before sitting down on the ground. When the Pārtha removed
his blessed feet from the stool I saw on their soles straight lines that
10 ran upward. Upon seeing these two dark and large young men, tall
like the trunk of a *śāla* tree, sitting on one bench, I was struck by
great fear. They are like Indra and Viṣṇu—the fool does not realize
it because he clings to Droṇa and Bhīṣma and listens to Karṇa's
bragging. I then became convinced that the will of the King Dharma
would prevail, if these two waited on his orders.

Welcomed with food and drink, presented with a cloth, and well
treated, I folded my hands at my head and gave Arjuna the message.
The Pārtha nudged Keśava's well-marked foot with one hand that was
accustomed to arrow and bow, in order to prompt him to speak.
15 Kṛṣṇa, who matches Indra's bravery, sitting straight like Indra's
banner, adorned with all his jewels, thereupon addressed me. This
eloquent speaker's words were gladdening and fitting, but though
gentle, frightening and perilous for Dhṛtarāṣṭra's men. And I listened

to this speech of him, who deserved to speak; it was delivered in
clearly articulated words that made their point, but, in the end,
dried up my heart.

Vāsudeva said:

Saṃjaya, you should carry this message to the wise Dhṛtarāṣṭra
within the hearing of the elder of the Kurus and of Droṇa. "Offer up
plentiful sacrifices, give fees to the brahmins, take pleasure in wives
20 and sons, for great danger is upon you! Surrender your properties
to worthy recipients, beget sons who are born from love, do favors
for your friends, for the king is hastening to his triumph!" When I
was far away, Kṛṣṇā cried out: "Ah, Govinda," and that left me with
a debt, a debt now old, which will not depart from my heart. Because
of that I now second him who wields the effulgent, unassailable
Gāṇḍiva, the Left-handed Archer, who has a feud with you. And
who is there who wishes to argue with the Pārtha, with me as his
helpmate, were he the Sacker of Cities himself, unless he is
encompassed by Time? With his arms he could lift the earth, with his
fury burn down these creatures, and from their heaven topple the
25 Gods—who could defeat Arjuna? Neither among the Gods, Rākṣasas,
or men, nor among Yakṣas, Gandharvas, and Snakes do I see anyone
who could counter Arjuna in battle. That great marvel which is
recounted, the encounter of the one and the many at the city of
Virāṭa, is sufficient proof! It is sufficient proof that the son of Pāṇḍu,
all by himself, broke them all at the city of Virāṭa and put them to
flight in all directions. In no one but the Pārtha is found such force,
power, might, speed, deftness, perseverance, and fortitude!

Saṃjaya said:

Thus spoke Hṛṣīkeśa and brought joy to the Pārtha with his words,
thundering like the Chastiser of Pāka in the sky when the monsoon
30 breaks. And having listened to Keśava's words the Diademed Arjuna
of the White Horses himself gave voice to great words, and they were
terrifying.

Vaiśaṃpāyana said:

59.1 The king who had the eyesight of wisdom, having heard Saṃjaya's
words, began to consider them as to advantage and disadvantage.
And after considering them in detail, weighing advantage and
disadvantage precisely and sagaciously, wishing victory for his sons,
and judging strengths and weaknesses according to the facts, the wise
king began to assess the parties' relative power. Considering that the
Pāṇḍavas had the upper hand and greater might on the human and
divine sides, and the Kurus less power, he addressed Duryodhana.
5 "Duryodhana, this worry of mine is never laid to rest, for I know
it is a matter of palpable truth, not of inference. All creatures have an
overriding love for their sons and do all they can to please and profit

them. Likewise we observe in general that those who have been
benefited want to return greater pleasure to their benefactors. Thus
the Fire God, remembering Arjuna's doings in the Khāṇḍava, will
assist him in this utterly terrible war of the Kurus and Pāṇḍus.
Dharma and many other celestials will rally to the Pāṇḍavas out of
10 love for their sons. Seeking to protect them from the danger of
Bhīṣma, Droṇa, Kṛpa, and the others, they will, I am convinced, wax
wroth with the fury of lightning. The Pārthas cannot be opposed when
they are joined by the Gods, and they are tigerlike men to boot,
powerful enough in their mere human characters, and past masters
of arms.

"That man who wields the superb divine bow, irresistible Gāṇḍīva,
and carries Varuṇa's great inexhaustible quivers filled with arrows;
whose divine banner, never entangled and always blazing trails like
fire, bears the monkey; whose chariot has no equal in splendor on
four-bordered earth and with its monsoonlike sound strikes terror in
15 his enemies when people hear its thunder; whose prowess the entire
world has decided is superhuman and whom the kings know to be
the conqueror even of Gods on a battlefield; who has been seen to
sow out in a blink of the eye five hundred arrows, shooting and
landing them far away, the Pārtha whom Bhīṣma, Droṇa, Kṛpa,
Droṇa's son, King Śalya of the Madras, and the neutral kings call an
enemy-taming tiger of a warrior when he stands ready to fight,
invincible even to superhuman kings; who in one burst shoots five
hundred reeds, the Pāṇḍava who is the peer of Kārtavīrya in the
20 power of his two arms—this Arjuna, an archer protected by Indra
and Upendra, I see in my mind slaughtering us in a shattering battle.

"All this I ponder days and nights, Bhārata, and I go sleepless and
without comfort out of worry over the peace of the Kurus. Total
destruction looms for the Kurus, when it is clear that nothing remains
but peace to end this feud. I am always for peace with the Pārthas,
my son, not for war, for I know that the Pāṇḍavas will always be
more powerful than the Kurus.

Vaiśaṃpāyana said:

60.1 The intransigent Dhārtarāṣṭra, upon hearing his father's words,
flew into great rage, and he said, "Cast aside your fears, greatest of
kings, if you think that the Parthas are impossible to deal with when
joined by the Gods! The Gods have become Gods because they are
impervious to love and hatred, malice and greed, and ignore all
sentiments: so have Vyāsa Dvaipāyana and the great ascetic Nārada
5 told us, as well as Rāma Jāmadagnya. The Gods never act, like
humans, out of love or greed, compassion or hatred, bull of the
Bharatas. So if the Fire, the Wind, Dharma, Indra, and the Aśvins

were to act out of love, they would come to grief. Therefore you should not harbor such worries at all, Bhārata, for Gods never concern themselves with other than divine affairs. It would never do for the Godhead of the Gods to be judged by the criterion of their love, hatred, and greed. When the Fire surrounds all the worlds on all sides, wishing to burn them down, I put a spell on it and it praises me!

"Supreme indeed is the fiery might the celestials possess, but my own the Gods cannot match, know it, Bhārata. While the world looks on, I shall with my incantations steady the earth's mountains and peaks if they are shattered. The terrifying, thundering gale and avalanche of rocks that spell the destruction of the sentient and insentient, the standing and moving—I shall stay them any time, before the eyes of the world, out of sheer compassion for the creatures. Chariots and foot soldiers will march over water that I have frozen, any time at all: I am the sole mover of the affairs of Gods and Asuras! Whatever may be the country in which I have business with my grand-armies, the waters will speed me there, wherever I want. In my domain no danger lurks from snakes and such, king; because of me, no fearful things beset the sleeping creatures. Parjanya rains when they wish for those who dwell in my domain. All my subjects are most law-abiding and there is nothing that plagues them. The Aśvins, Wind, Fire, the Slayer of Vṛtra and his Maruts, and the God Dharma are unable to protect those whom I hate. For if they were capable of saving my foes with their august might, the Pārthas would not have suffered for thirteen years. I swear to you, neither Gods nor Gandharvas, neither Asuras nor Rākṣasas are able to save the ones I hate. Whatever good or evil I have ever wished upon friends and enemies alike has never failed to befall. Whatever I have said should befall, O enemy-burner, has never failed to befall. Therefore people know that I am a speaker of truth. My greatness, renowned everywhere, witnessed by the world—I proclaim it to you to comfort you, king, not to praise myself. Never before have I bragged, king, for to praise oneself is the act of the mean.

"You shall hear that I have defeated Pāṇḍavas, Matsyas, Pāñcālas, Kekayas, Sātyaki, and Vāsudeva. Just as rivers on reaching the ocean perish entirely, so upon reaching me they shall perish with their followers. In me are superior wisdom, superior might, superior prowess, superior knowledge, and superior Yoga, which lift me above them. Grandfather, Droṇa, Kṛpa, Śalya, and Śala, whatever they know about weapons is lodged with me."

Having spoken thus, O Bhārata, he once more questioned Saṃjaya belligerently, enemy-tamer, in order to find out when the time would be ripe for his tasks.

Vaiśaṃpāyana said:

61.1 Not heeding the son of Vicitravīrya
Who thus kept asking about the Pārthas,
Now Karṇa addressed Dhṛtarāṣṭra's son
To cheer him in this Kaurava meeting.

"When Rāma of old found out that I lied
To obtain from him the Brahmā-Head missile,
He said to me, "When at the end of your days
You call it you will not remember it!"

Albeit I had wronged him, it was with a bow
That the guru of seers put his curse on me,
Though the seer of fiery splendor was able
To set all of earth with her oceans on fire!

"And later his mind was placated by me
With a student's obedience and masculine valor.
That weapon is still completely with me—
I am capable therefore; the burden is mine.

5 "In a blink of the eye, by the grace of the seer,
I shall get to Pāñcālas, Karūsas, and Matsyas,
And slay the Pārthas with sons and grandsons,
And attain to the worlds that my weapons have won.

"Let grandfather tarry and stay with you,
And Droṇa, and all chief leaders of men.
I shall march with a force of my finest of troops
And slaughter the Pārthas—the burden is mine!"

But while he was saying this, Bhīṣma rejoined:
"Your wits are beclouded by Time, you braggart!
Don't you realize, Karṇa, that once the chief
Has been slain, Dhṛtarāṣṭra's sons will be dead?

"The mere account of Dhanaṃjaya's feat
When, with Kṛṣṇa as second, he set on fire
The Khāṇḍava, surely suffices to check
Your ambitious selves and your partisans!

"That selfsame spear which the lord of the Thirty,
Great-spirited Indra, bestowed on you,
You will see it in ashes, fallen and shattered,
Struck down with his discus by Keśava.

10 "That snake-mouth arrow which shines about you,
Which you zealously honor with beautiful garlands,

Will be hit by the arrows of Pāṇḍu's son
And along with yourself come to nought, O Karṇa.

"Vāsudeva himself guards the Diademed Hero,
The slayer of Bāṇa and Bhauma, O Karṇa,
A killer he, in ferocious battles,
Of enemies, equal or better than you!"

Karṇa said:
No doubt that the lord of the Vṛṣṇis is as
You describe him, great-souled, and greater yet . . .
But let me reply to this bit of an insult,
Let grandfather hear the result of that:

I shall down my weapons, and grandfather shall
But see me in court and not in battle.
Not before you have gone to your peace yourself
Shall all these kings see my prowess on earth!

Vaiśaṃpāyana said:
'Twas thus he spoke, magnificent bowman,
And he left the assembly and went to his place.
But Bhīṣma laughed and amidst the Kurus
Said this to Duryodhana, O king:

15 "This *sūta*'s son, how he keeps his promise!
How will he discharge that burden he mentioned?
Rather watch now, as rank arrayed against rank,
Reeds flying, the ruin of the world springs from Bhīma.

" 'I shall,' so he said, 'by the thousands and myriads
Keep on killing the enemy warriors all,
While Avanti, Kalinga, and Jayadratha
Stand by with Bāhlīka and Vedidhvaja!' "

"At the time when before the blameless Lord Rāma
Saying he was a brahmin, he got that missile,
That time his *dharma* and *tapas* were lost
To Vaikartana, vilest now of all men!"

When Bhīṣma the king had had his say,
And Karṇa had gone after downing his weapons,
Vaicitravīrya's dimwitted son
Duryodhana spoke to Śāṃtanava.

Duryodhana said:
62.1 The Pārthas are the same as other men, born just as they are, so why do you think that victory is theirs solely? We are all born the

same from human wombs, grandfather, so how do you know that victory will go to the Pārthas? I am not relying on you for my triumph, nor on Droṇa, Kṛpa, Bāhlīka, and the other kings. I, Karṇa Vaikartana, and my brother Duḥśāsana will kill the five Pāṇḍavas in battle with sharp arrows. Then, O king, I shall satisfy the brahmins with grand rituals of plentiful stipends, and with cattle and horses and wealth!

Vidura said:

Son, we have heard the ancient ones tell of a bird catcher who put out his net on the ground to snare birds. Now two equally strong birds got caught in that net, but they held on to the net and took to the sky. When the fowler saw them flying in the sky, he was not put out but ran after them. A certain seer, who had finished his
10 morning duties in his hermitage, saw that hunter running after the birds he wanted, they up in the sky, he pursuing them earthbound. The hermit then questioned him with this verse, Kauravya:

> "It seems like a wonderful marvel, O hunter, to me
> That you, a pedestrian, run after birds in the sky!"

The fowler said:

These two birds can take my net as long as they stay together, but as soon as they start quarreling, I'll get them!

Vidura said:

And, being destined to die, those two birds began to quarrel, and when they fought the silly things fell on the ground. Ensnared by the nose of death they fought on furiously, and the fowler approached unnoticed and seized them both.

15 So when kinsmen get to quarreling over possessions, they fall victim to their enemies, like these birds, because of their quarreling. Kinsmen should eat together, talk together, riddle together, come together, but never contend with one another. When kinsmen, happy of heart, wait on their elders, they are as unapproachable as a forest protected by lions. But they who have obtained wealth that stretches and stretches, and yet act meanly, hand their fortune over to their haters, bull of the Bharatas! Kinsmen, Dhṛtarāṣṭra, bull of the Bharatas, are like firebrands which only smoke when separated but blaze forth together.

20 I shall tell you about something else that I once saw happen on a mountain, and when you have heard it, do what is best. We were traveling to the Northern Mountain with mountain men and Godlike brahmins who were sorcerers, herbalists and conjurers. We headed for Mount Gandhamādana, which, being one vast stretch of groves, is lit up with phosphorescent herbs and visited by Siddhas and Gandharvas. There we all saw yellow honey, but not bees' honey,

lying on a craggy, barren precipice, measuring a jarful, guarded by
poisonous snakes. The honey, a great favorite of Kubera, was such
25 that if a mortal tasted it he became immortal; if a blind man tasted
it, he regained his sight, and an old man became young again. That
is what those brahmins who knew herbs said.

When the mountain men saw it, they wanted it, king, and they
perished in that craggy, snake-infested mountain ravine.

In the same way this son of yours wants the earth for himself. He
sees the honey, but in his folly does not see the ravine. Duryodhana
wants to fight with the Left-handed Archer, but I do not see that he
has the might and the prowess for it. Singlehandedly he conquered
earth on his chariot—now the hero is waiting patiently, watching
30 your face. Drupada, the king of the Matsyas, and an enraged
Dhanaṃjaya will leave no survivors, like fires raging in the wind.
Dhṛtarāṣṭra, take King Yudhiṣṭhira on your lap, for when the two
parties battle, victory is not assured to either.

Dhṛtarāṣṭra said:

63.1 Duryodhana, my son, give thought to what I shall say to you. Like
a traveler who does not know the way, you think that the wrong
turn is the right way. The force of the five great-spirited sons of
Pāṇḍu, which you are seeking to frustrate, is as massive as that of
the five elements. You cannot know the first son of Kuntī, Yudhiṣṭhira,
who lives by the Law, without facing your last journey. You plot
against Bhīmasena Kaunteya, who has no equal in the world as a
5 killer in battle, as a tree might plot against a gale! What man who
has his wits about him would fight in a war with the Gāṇḍīva
bowman, foremost of all bearers of arms as the Meru is of all
mountains? Whom could Dhṛṣṭadyumna Pāñcālya not hack down,
shooting arrows in the midst of the enemy, as the king of the Gods
shoots his thunderbolt? Sātyaki, too, unassailable, highly esteemed
among the Andhaka-Vṛṣṇis, and devoted to the Pāṇḍaveya's cause,
will devastate your army. What man by his wits would fight the
lotus-eyed Kṛṣṇa, who by comparison transcends the three worlds?
For he has on one side his wives, kinsmen, relations, self, and this
10 earth, and Dhanaṃjaya on the other. Vāsudeva, unconquerable
master of himself, is where the Pāṇḍava is; and the Pāṇḍava's army,
which earth herself cannot withstand, is where Keśava is. Stand by
the words of your honest friends, son, who speak to your profit; pay
heed to old Bhīṣma Śāṃtanava, your grandfather. Obey what I say;
I speak for the good of the Kurus. Droṇa, Kṛpa, Vikarṇa, and
Mahārāja Bāhlīka think as I do—pay attention to them, for they are
all versed in the Law and bear you equal love, Bhārata. The fact that
your force was shattered along with that of your brothers at the city

of Virāṭa, before your very eyes, after they had let go of the cattle in panic—the great marvel that is recounted of the battle of the one and the many at that city, is sufficient proof. Arjuna wrought that alone—how much more will they achieve all together! Recognize your fellow-brethren, and provide them with a living!

Vaiśaṃpāyana said:

64.1 After the wise Dhṛtarāṣṭra had said this to Suyodhana, the lordly king again questioned Saṃjaya, "Tell me the rest, Saṃjaya, what Arjuna said after Vāsudeva had spoken, for I am most curious."

Saṃjaya said:

After listening to Vāsudeva's speech, Kuntī's invincible son Dhanaṃjaya now spoke while Vāsudeva was listening, "Go to grandfather Śāṃtanava and Dhṛtarāṣṭra, O Saṃjaya, to Droṇa, Kṛpa, Karṇa, and Mahārāja Bāhlīka, to Drauṇi, Somadatta, and Śakuni Saubala, to Duḥśāsana, Śala, Purumitra, Viviṃśati, Vikarṇa, Citrasena, Jayatsena the king, to Vinda and Anuvinda, the two Avanti princes, and Durmukha Kaurava, the untamable Saindhava and Bhūriśravas, to King Bhagadatta and King Jalasaṃdha

"And all other kings who have banded together
To fight in the cause of the Kauravas,
Who are doomed to die in the Pāṇḍavas' fire
Having rallied to Dhārtarāṣṭra, O bard—

"Salute them and ask their health as is proper,
And give them my message when they are assembled.
In the midst of the kings, you, Saṃjaya, tell
That most evil of scoundrels Suyodhana,

"Intransigent, ill-witted son of the king,
Dhṛtarāṣṭra's greedy and evil-souled son,
And proclaim to him this my word entire
Where he stands with his councilors, Saṃjaya—"

Having thus commenced, Dhanaṃjaya then
Declared to me, while glancing at Kṛṣṇa,
Declared this word full of Profit and Law—
The sagacious Pārtha with long, red eyes—

"You have heard with attention the words that has spoken
The great-spirited valiant chief of the Madhus,
And in like vein convey you my words
Where the kings in their multitudes stand together:

" 'Strive together with all your determination
That no sacrifice be made in holocaust

Which fumes with our arrows, chants with our chariots,
Pouring forth your troops with the spoon of our bows:

" 'When you fail to return to enemy-killer
Yudhiṣṭhira what he claims as his share,
I shall send you with horse, foot, and elephant
With my sharpened shafts to the land of the dead!' "

I bade hasty farewell to four-armed Hari
And bowed my homage to Arjuna,
And returned, O king with the glow of Immortals,
To bring to your presence that powerful word.

Vaiśaṃpāyana said:
65.1 When Duryodhana Dhārtarāṣṭra refused to accept that message and all remained silent, the kings rose up. And after all kings on earth had risen, great king, the king began to question Saṃjaya in private, hoping for victory for his sons in whose power he was, to reach a conclusion about himself, the others, and the Pāṇḍavas.

Dhṛtarāṣṭra said:

Gāvalgani, tell us the substance and weakness
Of our own army so far as we have it.
You know full well how the Pāṇḍavas stand:
Where are they ahead and where behind us?

The strengths of both parties, you know it all;
Of Profit and Law you know the decisions.
I am asking you, Saṃjaya, tell me all,
Which ones of the two will perish in battle?

Saṃjaya said:

I will not tell you as long as we're private,
For you'll bear me a grudge for it, Mahārāja!
Bring in your father, whose vows are sharp,
And Queen Gāndhārī, O Ājamīḍha.

They are Law-wise, sagacious judges both,
And they will discard any grudge of yours, king.
In their presence alone I shall tell you then
Vāsudeva's and Arjuna's thought entire.

Vaiśaṃpāyana said:
Divining the thought of Saṃjaya and his son, the wise Kṛṣṇa Dvaipāyana repaired there and said:

Now, Saṃjaya, tell Dhṛtarāṣṭra the answer
And fully reply to the question he asks—

Tell all that you know in this matter precisely
About Vāsudeva and Arjuna.

Saṃjaya said:

66.1 Arjuna and Vāsudeva, highly esteemed archers both, have of their
free will taken on another existence and are equal to the annihilation
of all. The discus of the spirited Vāsudeva, which for the nonce is
hidden in the sky, works by magic, my lord. While it is concealed
from the Pāṇḍavas, they respect it highly. Listen to me as I tell you
in brief their strengths and weaknesses.
Janārdana Mādhava has, as though in play, defeated Naraka,
5 Śambara, Kaṃsa, and the king of Cedi, all of gruesome aspect. This
Supreme Person, whose soul is superior, has, by a mere act of will,
brought earth, atmosphere, and heaven into his power. King, time
and again you have asked me about the Pāṇḍavas to learn their
strengths and weaknesses—now listen as I tell you. Put the entire
world on one side and Janārdana on the other, and Janārdana exceeds
the entire world in substance. Janārdana could reduce this world to
ashes with a thought, but not the entire universe could render
Janārdana ashes. Wherever there is truth, wherever Law, wherever
modesty and honesty, there is Govinda. Where Kṛṣṇa stands there is
10 victory. As though in play, Janārdana, Supreme Person, soul of the
creatures, keeps earth, atmosphere, and heaven running. Setting up
the Pāṇḍavas as his disguise and beguiling as it were the world, he
wishes to burn down your sons, who are befuddled and prone to
lawlessness. The blessed Keśava by his own Yoga makes go around
and around, ceaselessly, the Wheel of the World, the Wheel of the
Eons. In truth, I tell you, the blessed Lord alone governs time and
death, and the standing and moving creatures. Hari, the great Yogin,
though he rules the world, yet undertakes acts like any powerless
15 peasant. Thus Keśava beguiles the worlds with his own Yoga, but
men who seek mercy with him are not deceived.

Dhṛtarāṣṭra said:

67.1 How is it that you know the Mādhava as the great Lord of all the
worlds, and how is it that I do not? Explain this to me, Saṃjaya.

Saṃjaya said:

Sire, you do not have the knowledge, but my knowledge is not wanting. Devoid of the knowledge and obfuscated by darkness, you do not recognize Keśava. By this knowledge, my friend, I know Madhusūdana of the three Eons as the God who is the unmade Maker, beginning and end of the creatures.

Dhṛtarāṣṭra said:

Gāvalgani, what is this *bhakti* which you always bring to

Janārdana and by virtue of which you recognize Madhusūdana of the three Eons?

Saṃjaya said:

5 I do not cherish *māyā*—hail to thee!—and I do not feign the practice of Law. Having become pure by *bhakti* I know Janārdana from scripture.

Dhṛtarāṣṭra said:

Duryodhana! Seek the mercy of Hṛṣīkeśa Janārdana! We trust in Saṃjaya, son, seek refuge with Keśava!

Duryodhana said:

If the blessed Lord Keśava who is Devakī's son, were to destroy the world while testifying to his friendship for Arjuna, I could even now not seek him out!

Dhṛtarāṣṭra said:

Down goes this son of yours, Gāndhārī, with his evil-ridden mind, his envy, his wicked soul, his contempt for the words of his betters!

Gāndhārī said:

10 Power-crazy, evil-minded transgressor of your elders' commands, abandoning power and life, your father and me, fool, increasing your enemy's pleasure and adding to my sorrow, you shall remember your father's words when Bhīmasena strikes you down!

Vyāsa said:

King, you are beloved of Kṛṣṇa—listen to me, Dhṛtarāṣṭra. Saṃjaya is your envoy and he shall yoke you to your weal. He knows Hṛṣīkeśa, the old one and the new, and he shall set you free from great danger, if you care to listen to him attentively, Vaicitravīrya, men are beclouded with the darkness of wrath and joy, and, being bound by manifold nooses, are not content with their own possessions. Again and again they fall into Yama's power bewildered by their lusts. And like the blind led by the blind, they are carried off by their
15 own acts. There is this path of one direction by which the wise go forth; when one sees it, one overcomes death; a great man does not attach himself.

Dhṛtarāṣṭra said:

Come, Saṃjaya, tell me the path where all danger ceases, by which I may reach Hṛṣīkeśa and attain to ultimate peace.

Saṃjaya said:

One of unmade soul can never know Janārdana, whose soul is made. But the performance of one's rites is not the way unless the senses are mastered. The single-minded relinquishment of one's love for the objects of the excitable senses, undistracted attention, and avoidance of injury are the womb of knowledge, there is no doubt. Be consistently and unwearyingly in control of your senses, king, let your
20 spirit not stray, but check it hither and yon. This mastering of the

senses the brahmins know as constant wisdom. This is the wisdom and the path by which the wise go forth. Men cannot reach Keśava with unbridled senses, king. The self-controlled man who is learned in the scriptures finds, by virtue of Yoga, serenity in the truth.

Dhṛtarāṣṭra said:

68.1 Again tell me, Saṃjaya, at my bidding about the Lotus-eyed One. When I know the meaning of his names and deeds I may reach the Supreme Person, my friend.

Saṃjaya said:

Indeed I have heard the propitious explanation of the God's names—as far as I can know; for Keśava is beyond the measure of knowledge.

He is *Vāsudeva*, because he clothes the creatures, because he is
wealth, because he is the womb of the Gods. Inasmuch as he is
known for his masculinity, he is called *Viṣṇu*. Know, Bhārata, that
he is *Mādhava* because of his hermithood, meditation, and Yoga, and
inasmuch as he dissolves all beings he is *Madhuhan* and *Madhusūdana*.
5 *Kṛṣi* betokens the earth, and *ṇa* expresses bliss; and since Kṛṣṇa
combines them both he is the eternal *Kṛṣṇa*. The lotus is the highest
abode, everlasting, undecaying, never-ending—so he is the *Lotus-eyed*
One, because he is of such nature. He is *Janārdana* because he
terrifies the *dasyus*. Since his vigor never gives out and he never lacks
in vigor, he is, for this vigor, *Sātvata*. He is *Bull-eyed*, because he is
bull-like. Inasmuch as he has not been born from a mother, he is the
Unborn, the vanquisher of armies. They know him as *Dāmodara*,
because he tames the Gods with his self-luminousness. He has become
Hṛṣīkeśa because of his joy, his happiness, his lordship of pleasures.
As he carries heaven and earth in his arms, he is known as the
Great-armed One. He is *Adhokṣaja*, because he never shrinks downward,
10 and is known as *Nārāyaṇa*, because he is the course of men. He is
Puruṣottama, because he fills up and brings down. They call him *All*,
because he is the source and dissolution of all that is existent and
nonexistent, and because he always knows all. Kṛṣṇa stands firm on
truth and truth stands firm on him, and Govinda is truth beyond
truth—therefore he has the name of *True*. Because of his striding he is
Viṣṇu, because of his triumphing he is *Jiṣṇu*, because of his eternality
Ananta, and because of his finding cows *Govinda*. He makes the unreal
real, and thereby confuses the creatures.

Such is he, constant in Law, the blessed Lord, and he shall come with the hermits, he, Great-armed Acyuta, to avoid bloodshed.

Dhṛtarāṣṭra said:

69.1 How I, Saṃjaya, envy those who have eyes,
For they shall see Vāsudeva before them,

Illumining all with his wondrous form,
Setting light to all the corners of space!

Giving voice to words to be heeded with care
By the Bhāratas, blissful to Sṛñjayas,
To be seized without blame by those wishing to live
And not to be seized by those who are doomed—

Sole champion of Sātvatas, coming to us,
He the bull who is the Yādavas' guide,
The killer and shaker of enemies,
Who of all that hate him robs the fame—

The Kurus assembled now shall set eye
On the great-souled, lovable killer of foes,
Who will speak in words that spell no bloodshed,
That best of the Vṛṣṇis, beguiling my sons—

The most sempiternal and all-wise seer,
An ocean of words, the jar of ascetics,
The fair-winged Garuḍa Ariṣṭanemi,
The lord of the creatures, abode of the world—

The ancient Person of thousand heads,
Beginningless, middleless, endless, all-glorious,
The Placer of seed, the Unborn Begetter—
With Him, higher than high, do I seek refuge.

The begetter who built and made the Three Worlds,
The Gods and Asuras, Rakṣas, and Snakes,
The chief of all wise kings of men—
With Indra's junior seek I refuge.

5(54) The Coming of the Lord

5.70–137 (B. 72–139; C. 2581–4725)
70 (72; 2581). Yudhiṣṭhira seeks Kṛṣṇa's help against Dhṛtarāṣṭra's apparent perfidy (1–15). He discourses upon the discomforts of being poor (20–30), and the virtues of modesty (30–35). Action is mandatory, even though it means war, which is evil (35–65), but surrender is pointless (65–75). He asks Kṛṣṇa's advice (75). Kṛṣṇa replies that he himself will try to make peace (75–80). Yudhiṣṭhira demurs (80), Kṛṣṇa insists, and Yudhiṣṭhira agrees (85–90).
71 (73; 2675). Kṛṣṇa doubts the Kauravas' good faith;

they deserve death (1–10). Duryodhana has dishonored himself and should be killed (10–20). Kṛṣṇa will seek to make peace, but expects war: all signs point to it (20–30).
72 (74; 2717). Bhīma urges diplomacy (1–10): eighteen famous kings have defiled their lineages, and so has Duryodhana; but he should be appeased (10–20).
73 (75; 2740). Kṛṣṇa chides Bhīma for his leniency in spite of his well-known rancor (1–10). Is Bhīma panicking? (10–20).
74 (76; 2763). Angrily Bhīma recounts his might; he is fearless (1–15).
75 (77; 2782). Kṛṣṇa calms him down: action is necessary, though the outcome is doubtful (1–10). Kṛṣṇa will try his best (10–20).
76 (78; 2802). Arjuna speaks up with greater hopes of success (1–5). He gives Kṛṣṇa full freedom to deal with Duryodhana as he sees fit (5–20).
77 (79; 2822). Kṛṣṇa discourses on fate and human enterprise (1–5). He expects no peace (5–20).
78 (80; 2844). Nakula gives Kṛṣṇa complete freedom of action, but he should speak strongly (1–15).
79 (81; 2862). Sahadeva speaks of his rage (1), and Sātyaki supports him, to everyone's applause (1–5).
80 (82; 2871). Draupadī speaks up for war (1–15) and recounts her grievances (15–40). Kṛṣṇa promises the death of her enemies (40–45).
81 (83; 2920). Kṛṣṇa prepares to leave (1–10). His chariot is described (10–20). There are favorable portents; the seers honor Kṛṣṇa (20–25). He departs with a final message from Yudhiṣṭhira: to comfort Kuntī (25–45); from Arjuna: he will kill all their enemies (45–50). Bhīma roars out (55). Kṛṣṇa on his way meets and salutes the seers, who have come to watch the negotiations (55–70).
82 (84; 2993). Many marvels occur when Kṛṣṇa progresses (1–10) to Śālibhavana (15) and Vṛkasthala, where he camps (20–25).
83 (85; 3022). Dhṛtarāṣṭra orders a grand reception for Kṛṣṇa and has many traveling lodges built, but Kṛṣṇa ignores them (1–15).
84 (86; 3040). Dhṛtarāṣṭra speaks of many gifts to Kṛṣṇa (1–20).
85 (87; 3061). Vidura accuses Dhṛtarāṣṭra of

hypocrisy: he should offer Kṛṣṇa peace (1–15).
86 (88; 3078). Duryodhana is against any gifts (1–5). Bhīṣma counsels peace through Kṛṣṇa (5–10). Duryodhana threatens to capture Kṛṣṇa (10–15); Bhīṣma is aghast (15–20).
87 (89; 3101). Kṛṣṇa arrives in Hāstinapura, where all come out to observe him (1–10). He enters the palace and is received honorably; after courtesies he leaves (10–20) and visits Vidura (20–25).
88 (90; 3128). In the afternoon he visits Kuntī, who asks after her sons whose erstwhile greatness she recounts (1–40), and after Draupadī, whom she praises (40–50). She speaks of her grief, which she blames on her father (50–70). She gives her sons strong messages (70–85); Kṛṣṇa comforts her (85–95). She wishes him success (100).
89 (91; 3236). Kṛṣṇa repairs to Duryodhana's palace, where he accepts a seat but declines sharing a meal (1–10). Duryodhana asks why: Kṛṣṇa will eat only when he has succeeded (10–15). Duryodhana protests (20). Kṛṣṇa berates Duryodhana; he will eat with Vidura (15–30). At Vidura's the Kauravas arrive to plead with Kṛṣṇa, but he does not relent (35–40).
90 (92; 3278). Vidura warns Kṛṣṇa against Duryodhana, who will be adamant (1–25).
91 (93; 3308). Kṛṣṇa replies that he is aware of it, but he has to make the attempt: he has to help his friends (1–20).
92 (94; 3330). In the morning Duryodhana fetches Kṛṣṇa, who rides up to the hall in state (1–25). He is received solemnly (25–35). The seers arrive and are seated (40–45); the others are seated and silence falls (45).
93 (95; 3384). Kṛṣṇa's address to Dhṛtarāṣṭra: he seeks peace; he recalls the greatness of the dynasty. Falsity is unseemly as well as disastrous, while peace is possible and advantageous: with the Pāṇḍavas the Bhāratas will be the greatest power on earth (1–25). War will be a holocaust (25–35). The Pāṇḍavas have kept their promises and now plead for Law (35–45). Kṛṣṇa urges that Law be served (40–60).
94 (B. 96; C. 3448–3500) Dambhodbhava.
95–103 (B. 97–105; C. 3501–713) Mātali.
104–21 (B. 106–23; C. 3714–4120) Gālava.

122 (124; 4121). At Dhṛtarāṣṭra's request Kṛṣṇa speaks directly to Duryodhana: he should heed his father's desire for peace (1–15), and shun bad advisers (15–25). It is profitable for him to make up with the Pāṇḍavas, who are more than a match for him (25–35), lest the Kauravas perish (55–60).
123 (125; 4186). Bhīṣma supports Kṛṣṇa (1–5), as do Droṇa (10–15) and Vidura (15–20). Dhṛtarāṣṭra too pleads that Duryodhana meet with Yudhiṣṭhira (20–25).
124 (126; 4214). Bhīṣma and Droṇa together pray for peace to avoid bloodshed (1–15).
125 (127; 4232). Duryodhana denies to Kṛṣṇa any guilt on his part (1–5). The Kauravas are invincible; it is a baron's honor to be felled in battle (10–20). He will return no land to the Pāṇḍavas (20–25).
126 (128; 4259). Kṛṣṇa threatens war to avenge the Pāṇḍavas and Draupadī for all the wrongs done them by Duryodhana (1–20). Duḥśāsana warns that the Kauravas may betray Duryodhana (20). Duryodhana leaves the hall (20–25), while Bhīṣma protests (30). Kṛṣṇa counsels the Kauravas to restrain Duryodhana, just as Kṛṣṇa himself once eliminated Kaṃsa and the Gods fettered the Asuras (30–45).
127 (129; 4309). Dhṛtarāṣṭra has Gāndhārī fetched and complains about her son (1–5). She has Duryodhana brought in and berates Dhṛtarāṣṭra for his weakness, then Duryodhana for his greed (5–30). He should make peace with the Pāṇḍavas: they have suffered enough (30–45). The Kauravas will fight only halfheartedly (45–50).
128 (130; 4364). Duryodhana and his henchmen plot to capture Kṛṣṇa (1–5). Sātyaki surmises the plan and tells Kṛtavarman and Kṛṣṇa (5–15); Vidura tells Dhṛtarāṣṭra (15–20). Kṛṣṇa says he can match them (20–30). Dhṛtarāṣṭra sends for Duryodhana and scolds him (30–35), followed by Vidura who praises Kṛṣṇa (35–50).
129 (131; 4418). Kṛṣṇa reveals his power to Duryodhana: the hosts of Gods and Pāṇḍavas appear from his body (1–10). There are portents (10–15). Kṛṣṇa leaves on his chariot; Dhṛtarāṣṭra confesses his impotence (12–15). Farewells are said (25–30).
130 (132; 4459). Kṛṣṇa visits Kuntī and tells her what has happened, and asks for messages for her sons (1). Kuntī commands Yudhiṣṭhira to heed the Law (1–10).

Kings influence their times (10–15). Yudhiṣṭhira should restore his past greatness (15–30).
131–34 (B. 133–36; C. 4434–643) The Instruction of Vidura's Son.
135 (137; 4644). Kuntī's messages for Arjuna (1–5), Bhīma (5–10), Draupadī (10), the twins (10–15), last admonitions and farewell (15–20). Kṛṣṇa departs after talking to Karṇa privately (20–30).
136 (138; 4676). Bhīṣma inveighs against Duryodhana and pleads for peace (1–15). All portents are adverse (20–25).
137 (139; 4704). Bhīṣma and Droṇa voice their misgivings about the coming war (1–20).

Vaiśaṃpāyana said:
70.1 When Saṃjaya had gone back, Yudhiṣṭhira the King Dharma said
to the Dāśārha, bull of all Sātvatas. "It is time now for friends,
Janārdana. I see no one but you to help us through our perils. For
only by relying on you can we fearlessly demand our share from the
Dhārtarāṣṭra, emboldened as he is by his confusions, and from his
councilors. Just as you, enemy-tamer, protect the Vṛṣṇis in all
emergencies, so you should protect the Pāṇḍavas. Save us from this
great danger!"
The blessed Lord said:
5 I am here, strong-armed prince, say to me what you want to say,
and I shall do all you ask, Bhārata.
Yudhiṣṭhira said:
You have heard what Dhṛtarāṣṭra and his sons have in mind, for
all that Saṃjaya told me is what Dhṛtarāṣṭra himself is thinking; in
Saṃjaya his soul stands revealed. An envoy speaks as he is told; he
deserves death if he speaks differently. Covetous, going about with a
wicked mind, dealing others less than himself, Dhṛtarāṣṭra looks for
peace with us without giving back our kingdom. At Dhṛtarāṣṭra's
command we have lived in the forest for twelve years, and one more
10 autumn, in concealment, on the assumption, my lord, that
Dhṛtarāṣṭra would stand by his covenant with us. We have not
broken the agreement—the brahmins know it full well. Old King
Dhṛtarāṣṭra does not see his Law, or if he does, he still follows out of
love the orders of his foolish son. The king submits to Suyodhana,
and greedily looking out for his own advantage, Janārdana, he treats
us falsely.What can be more painful than that I am not able to look
after my mother and friends? With the Kāśis, Cedis, Pāñcālas,
Matsyas, and you, Madhusūdana, on my side, I asked for five villages—

15 Kuśasthala, Vṛkasthala, Māsandī, Vāraṇāvata, and any other village
as the fifth and last, Govinda. "Father," I said, "give me five villages
or towns where we will live together and where the Bhāratas must
leave us alone." And the evil Dhārtarāṣṭra did not even allow me that
much, thinking he owns it all. What is more grievous than that? If
a man who is born and bred in a high lineage covets the possessions
of others, his greed kills his good sense, and once his good sense is
gone, shame goes. Shame destroyed kills Law, Law killed kills
fortune, fortune killed destroys the man: poverty is the death of a
man.
20 Kinsmen, friends, and priests turn away from a poor man, friend,
as birds from a tree without bloom and fruit. It is like death, my
friend, if kinsmen turn away from a man as though he had fallen
from rank, just as life and breath leave a dead man. Śambara has
said that there is no state worse than seeing no food for today and
tomorrow. Wealth, they say, is the highest Law; everything is based
on wealth. In this world the wealthy are alive and the poor are dead.
If you, relying on your strength, rob a man of his wealth you destroy
his Law, and his Profit and Pleasure as well, along with the man
25 himself. There are men who choose death when they reach that
state; some go forth to a village, some to the forest, some to their
ruin. Some grow insane, others surrender to their enemies, others
become the slaves of others, all because of wealth. The loss of fortune
is a calamity worse than death for a man, for fortune is the cause of
Law and Pleasure, while natural death is the eternal way of the
world, applying to all creatures, and no one is excepted.
A man who has always been poor does not suffer as one who had
30 a lovely fortune and, while used to his comforts, lost it, Kṛṣṇa. When
he has fallen on hard times by his own fault, he blames Indra and
all the Gods, but never himself. Not even all the scriptures wipe out
that shame in him. He gets angry at his dependents, he reviles his
friends. Rage possesses and stupefies him. Having lost his senses he is
driven to cruel deeds. To lapse further into evil he cultivates
miscegenation and that leads to hell. It is the final stage of evildoers.
Unless he wakes up in time, Kṛṣṇa, he is heading for hell; only
wisdom is his awakening: with the eye of wisdom only he does not
35 fail. For when he has regained his good sense, he looks to the
scriptures and, when firm in the scriptures, to Law. Then modesty
becomes his finest limb. For a modest man abhors evil, and his
fortune thrives. One is a man to the extent he has modesty. Constant
in the Law, serene of soul, always carrying the yoke of his tasks, he
does not set his mind on lawlessness and does not wallow in evil.
A shameless and insensate person is neither woman nor man; he
has no title to Law and becomes like a *śūdra*. A man who has

modesty sustains the Gods, the Fathers, and himself: for this he
becomes immortal, which is the final stage of those who do good.
40 All this you see quite clearly in me, Madhusūdana: you have seen
how I passed those nights fallen from kingship. There is no way at all
that we can relinquish our fortune. If we die in our efforts, that is all
right. Our first course of action, Mādhava, is to assure that we and
they may enjoy our common fortune at peace with one another and
on an equal footing. The stage beyond that will cause gruesome
disaster and ruin, when we regain our realms by killing the Kauravas.
However unrelated and ignoble an enemy is, Kṛṣṇa, he does not
deserve to be killed, let alone men such as they, for they are kinsmen
45 mostly, friends and gurus, and to kill them is a most evil thing.

But what is pretty in war? It is the evil Law of the barons, and we
have been born in the baronage. It is our Law, be it Lawless; any
other way of life is forbidden to us. The *śūdra* obeys, the *vaiśya* lives
by trade, we live off killing, the brahmin prefers his begging bowl.
Baron kills baron, fish lives on fish, dog kills dog—behold, Dāśārha,
the Law as it has come down. In war there is always discord; on the
battlefield the spirits take leave. Force merely extends policy; victory
and defeat rest on chance. Life and death are not a creature's choice;
50 unless his time has come, he finds neither happiness nor suffering,
best of the Yadus. One man may kill many, or many kill one; a
coward may kill a hero, an infamous scoundrel a famous champion.
Victory goes to either and to either goes defeat. The same is true of
decline. If you run away from it, there is death and ruin.

War is evil in any form. What killer is not killed in return? To the
killed victory and defeat are the same, Hṛṣīkeśa. I don't think that
defeat is different from death; the victor too is surely diminished: in
55 the end some others will kill a loved one of his; and behold, when
he has lost his strength and no longer sees his sons or brothers a
loathing for life will engulf him completely, Kṛṣṇa. It is the modest
warriors, noble and with a sense of compassion, who are killed in
war, and the lesser men escape. There is always remorse after the
killing of others, Janārdana. The aftermath is evil, for survivors do
survive. The survivors regain their strength and themselves leave no
survivors but aim at total annihilation to put an end to the feud.
Victory breeds feuds, for the defeated rest uneasy. But easy sleeps the
60 man who serenely has given up both victory and defeat. He who has
started a feud never sleeps well, for his heart is ill at ease, as in a
snake-infested dwelling. If he exterminates everyone, he is deprived
of glory and reaps eternal infamy among all creatures. For feuds,
however long ago they may have been contracted, do not die down:
there will be people to pass the word until a new man is born in the
family. Nor is one feud laid to rest with another one, Keśava; it

rather grows stronger, just as fire blazes up with the oblation, Kṛṣṇa. There is no way to appease a feud, in the end one always remains vulnerable: that is the inescapable flaw of those who seek their advantage. For heroism is a powerful disease that eats up the heart, and peace is found only by giving it up or by serenity of mind. On the other hand, if final tranquillity were ignited by the total eradication of the enemy, that would be even crueler, Madhusūdana.

But peace through renunciation is but death without the fact, because the risk of death remains for enemy and self. We want neither to renounce our kingdom nor ruin the family. Peace by surrender is preferable. Those who strive at all do not want war; only if their peaceful overtures are rebuffed is war inevitable. When negotiations fail, the consequences are dreadful. The wise have noticed that it is the same as in a mess of dogs. It starts with a wagging of tails, then a bark, a bark in reply, backing off, baring the teeth, loud barking, and then the fight; and the stronger one wins and eats the meat, Kṛṣṇa. It is the same with people, there is no difference at all. It is always the same thing that the stronger does to the weaker: disregard and aggressiveness—and the weak man surrenders. Father, king, and elder always deserve respect, and therefore Dhṛtarāṣṭra deserves our respect and homage, Janārdana. But Dhṛtarāṣṭra's love for his son is great, Mādhava, and as long as he is in his son's power, he will violate our surrender.

What do *you* think; Kṛṣṇa, now that the time has come? How, Mādhava, can we avoid falling short in Profit *and* Law? For in this miserable affair whom else can we quietly consult but you, Madhusūdana, best of men? Who is our friend, our well-wisher, knowing the course of all affairs, but you, Kṛṣṇa, a friend who knows all the answers?

Vaiśampāyana said:

At these words Janārdana replied to King Dharma, "I myself shall go to the assembly of the Kurus in the cause of both of you. If I make peace without hurting your cause, I shall gain very great merit, king, and the action will have great consequences. I shall free the Kurus and Sṛñjayas from the noose of death, free the Pāṇḍavas and Dhārtarāṣṭras, and all of earth."

Yudhiṣṭhira said:

I do not agree, Kṛṣṇa, that you should go to the Kurus. Suyodhana will not accept your advice, however well-spoken. The entire baronage of earth obeys Suyodhana and is assembled there. I don't want you to descend in their midst, Kṛṣṇa. Not a thing in the world would comfort us, not divinity—let alone happiness—not the overlordship of all Immortals, if you were frustrated, Mādhava.

The blessed Lord said:
85 Great king, I know the wickedness of Dhṛtarāṣṭra's son, but this
way we shall stand unblamed before all the kings on earth. All the
kings combined do not suffice to stand up to me in battle, if I am
angry, any more than other animals before a lion. Or if they act
untoward to me in any way, I shall burn down all the Kurus! My
mind is made up. My going there will not be profitless in any case,
Pārtha: we shall gain something sometime, if it only turns out that
you escape the blame.

Yudhiṣṭhira said:
If it please you, Kṛṣṇa, godspeed! Go to the Kurus, and I shall
90 watch you return successfully and safely. Viṣvaksena, go to the Kurus
and appease the Bhāratas, my lord, so that we all may live together
in happiness and friendship. You are a brother, you are a friend, dear
to the Terrifier and to me. Your friendship is never suspect—
godspeed, go for our good! You know us, you know the others, you
know Profit, you know the words. Tell Suyodhana whatever redounds
to our profit, Kṛṣṇa. Whatever sound advice is consistent with the
Law, you can give them that, Keśava, whether it be for peace, or
war.

The blessed Lord said:
71.1 I have listened to Saṃjaya, and I have heard your good words.
I know their entire intention as well as yours. Your spirit is bent on
Law, theirs on hostility. You will honor whatever can be gained
without war. Mendicancy is not a baron's business, lord of the people.
All those who observe the life stages have said what a baron should
beg: victory, or death on the battlefield, as the Placer has ordained
5 for eternity. That is the baron's Law, and cowardice is not extolled. For
livelihood is impossible by giving in to cowardice, Yudhiṣṭhira. Stride
wide, strong-armed king! Kill the foe, enemy-tamer! Over-covetous,
contracting friendships with others by living side by side with them
over a long time, the Dhārtarāṣṭras have found allies and built up
their strength, enemy-burner.

There is not a chance that they will treat you on an equal footing,
lord of the people, for they think that with Bhiṣma, Droṇa, Kṛpa, and
so forth they are stronger. As long as you treat them with kindness,
king, they will keep your kingdom away from you, enemy-tamer. No
sympathy, no pusillanimity, no reasons of Law and Profit will move
10 the Dhārtarāṣṭras to do your desire, enemy-tamer. Let this be proof to
you, Pāṇḍava, that when they left you in your loincloth, they did not
regret their misdeed. Before the eyes of grandfather, Droṇa, and the
sagacious Vidura, indeed all the Kuru chiefs, that blackguard did not

shrink in shame from his act of cruelty, when he had cheated you with sleight of hand at the dicing, you, a king generous with gifts, gentle, self-controlled, Law-loving, and true to your vow. Have no scruples with a man of such character and behavior. They deserve death at anybody's hands—how much more then at yours, Bhārata! He hurt you and your brothers with vile words, when he boastfully
15 and gloatingly said to his brothers, "Now the Pāṇḍavas have absolutely nothing to call their own! Not even their own names and family name will survive. After a long time they will meet their undoing and having lost their natures return to nature!"

Voicing such scathing words and more, he boasted amidst his kinsmen while you went forth to the forest. They who had been assembled there, on seeing you who were guiltless, sat in the hall with tears in their throats or crying openly. The kings and brahmins did not congratulate him; no, all there in the hall blamed
20 Duryodhana. For a man of family, enemy-plougher, there are shame and death, and death is preferred to the shame of a wicked life, king. That very moment, king, when he stood condemned for his shamelessness before all the kings on earth, he was dead, Mahārāja! It takes little to kill one who behaves like that—a tree with its roots cut and precariously balanced on the base of its trunk! He should be killed like a snake, that evil-minded man ignoble to all the world. Kill him, enemy-tamer! Don't hesitate, king! But, in any case it is worthy of you, and pleasing to me, prince sans blame, that you are ready to prostrate yourself before your father and Bhīṣma.

25 I myself shall go and resolve the doubts of all those who are still of two minds about Duryodhana, king. In the midst of the kings I myself shall extol your manly virtues, and his transgressions. When they hear me speak words that are beneficial and consistent with Law and Profit, all the kings of the various countries of earth shall know of you that "he is a great-spirited speaker of truth!" and know of him that he acts out of greed. Among town and country folk, including the old and the young, I shall put all blame on him at the
30 meetings of the four classes. When you are suing for peace, you will incur no Unlaw—the kings will revile the Kurus and Dhṛtarāṣṭra. What is left to be done when he is deserted by the world? What else is left to be done with Duryodhana gone, king?

With this in mind I shall go to all the Kurus and, without hurting your cause, strive to make peace and note their reaction. And when I have observed the war effort of the Kauravas, I shall leave and return to bring you victory, Bhārata! In any case I expect only war with the others, for all the portents pointing that way are clear to me.

35 The cries of beasts and fowl are fearsome;
At the onset of night elephants and horses

Assume fearful shapes, and also the fire
Shows manifold colors betokening evil,
And this would not be so unless dread death
Had arrived to destroy the world of men.
Let all your warriors ready their arms,
Their arrows and armor and elephants,
Their banners and chariots, finish their training
And sit ready on horse, car, and elephant.
All the gear that is needed for warfare, king,
Make sure that all is at hand and complete.

Duryodhana now is unable to give
You in any fashion as long as he lives
The prosperous realm that once was yours
And he stole with the dice, O chief of the Pāṇḍus!

Bhīmasena said:

72.1 Speak with them in whatever way the Kurus will be prompted to accept peace, Madhusūdana; do not frighten them with war! Duryodhana is truculent, always in a rage, resentful of other people's prosperity, and spirited: don't talk to him harshly, treat him gently! Evil by nature, in mind no better than a *dasyu*, drunk with the intoxication of power, engaged in a feud with the Pāṇḍavas, shortsighted, cruel-spoken, quick to deceive, with merciless power, he'd die before sharing his wealth, and he will not give up what he thinks is his. To make peace with such a man is, I think, most difficult, Kṛṣṇa. He turns down even his friends, he has given up Law, he loves the lie, he strikes down the words and the plans of his well-wishers. A prey to his rage, obeying a wicked nature, he follows by instinct evil ways like a snake goaded with straw stalks. You know what armies Duryodhana has, what character, what nature, what strength, and what valor. There was a time when the Kurus and their sons were tranquil, and we too were like Indra's elders, rejoicing with our relations. Now because of Duryodhana's fury, Madhusūdana, the Bhāratas will burn as the forests burn with fire at the end of winter.

There are eighteen kings known, Madhusūdana, who extirpated their kinsmen, friends, and relations. At the turn of the Eon of the Law, Bali became the king of the Asuras, who prospered and blazed with splendor. Udāvarta became king of the Haihayas, Janamejaya of the Nīpas, Bahula of the Tālajanghas, the prideful Vasu of the Kṛmis, Ajabindu of the Suvīras, Kuśarddhika of the Surāṣṭras, Arkaja of the Balīhas, Dhautamūlaka of the Chinese, Hayagrīva of the Videhas, Varapra of the Mahaujasas, Bāhu of the Sundaravegas, Purūravas of the Dīptākṣas, Sahaja of the Cedi-Matsyas, Bṛhadbala of the Pracetas, Dhāraṇa of the Indra-Vatsas, Vigāhana of the Mukuṭas, Śama of the

Nandivegas – and they all defiled their dynasties. Vile men they were
to their lineages when they rose at the end of the Eon, Kṛṣṇa.
Now this Duryodhana has been gathered up by Time, a vile, evil
man, to be the coal that burns up our lineage and that of the Kurus
at the end of the Eon. Therefore speak mildly and softly, as consistent
with Law and Profit, mostly compliant with his wishes, not
20 disdainfully with overbearing haughtiness. All of us would bow before
Duryodhana, Kṛṣṇa, and follow him humbly rather than destroy the
Bhāratas. Act so that he along with the other Kurus becomes
indifferent to us, Vāsudeva, lest disaster strike the Kurus. Speak to
old grandfather and the men in the hall, Kṛṣṇa, so that there be
brotherliness among the brethren and the Dhārtarāṣṭra be appeased.

That is what I say, and the king approves. Arjuna does not want war, for there is great compassion in Arjuna.

Vaiśaṃpāyana said:

73.1 When strong-armed Keśava heard these words of Bhīma, which
were without precedent in their leniency, he laughed aloud. Thinking
that now mountains had become light and fire cold, Śauri, Rāma's
younger brother, who holds the Śārnga bow, now, in order to incite
the Wolf-Belly with his words, as the wind fans a fire, spoke to
Bhīmasena, who was sitting there flooded with compassion: "At all
other times you advocate only war, Bhīmasena, wishing to grind
5 down the cruel Dhārtarāṣṭras, who delight in murders. You never
sleep, but stay awake and lie face down, enemy-killer, and always
speak in words that are fearsome, unappeased, and hurtful, while
you sigh, burning with a firelike fury, with your mind perturbed like
a fuming fire, Bhīma. You lie down apart, groaning like a feeble man
under too heavy a load. People who do not know better even think
you are a madman! You run around breaking uprooted trees like a
grazing elephant, stomping the earth with your feet and groaning,
Bhīma! You take no pleasure in these people, you rather lie away
from them, Pāṇḍava, and welcome no one else, ever, day or night.
10 Suddenly you smile or sit by yourself as though weeping, or you sit
with your eyes closed for a long time, resting your head on your
knees. Or you may be seen knitting your brow and licking your lips
all the time, Bhīma, and it is all because you are enraged.

" 'Just as the sun is seen in the east, spreading light,' you said,
'and just as it sets in the west, circling the polar star with its rays, so
I swear – and I shall not break my word – I shall attack rancorous
Duryodhana and kill him with my club!' So you spoke amidst your
brothers and swore it by the club you held. Is that the same spirit
15 which is now bent on appeasement, enemy-burner? Aho! Has panic
at last found you, Bhīma, because now that war is at hand you seem

to see signs that point this way or that way? Aho! Do you see
unfavorable portents, Pārtha, in dreams or while awake, and that is
why you want peace? Aho! Are you a eunuch that you dare not
hope for manhood in yourself? You are attacked by cowardice, that
is why your mind is awry! Your heart is palpitating, your mind
despairs, your thighs are paralyzed, that is why you want peace!
Indeed, inconstant is a mortal's volatile mind like a tumor on a
20 *śālmali* tree that sways in the wind. This attitude is as unnatural to
you as human speech is to cows, it drowns the hearts of Pāṇḍu's
sons like shipwrecked sailors! It is as marvelous to me as the walking
of mountains that you should speak words so unlike you, Bhīmasena!
"Look at your own feats, Bhārata, and your birth in high family.
Rise up. Do not despair, hero, be firm! This is not like you, this
weariness, enemy-tamer! A baron does not obtain what he does not
grab by force!

Vaiśaṃpāyana said:

74.1 When Vāsudeva talked to him like this, the other, always angry
and impatient, ran like a fine horse and replied at once, "You mistake
completely what I want to do, Acyuta! You have lived with me long
enough to know how I am. I am utterly at ease in battles, and my
bravery lives up to my words, Dāśārha! Or perhaps you do not know
me after all, like a shipwrecked man floating in a lake, and that is
why you are attacking me with words that are wide of the mark.
How could anybody who knows me, Bhīmasena, speak as wildly as
5 you, Mādhava, are pleased to do? So I shall tell you something, scion
of the Vṛṣṇis, about my own manhood and my strength which
nobody matches.
"To be sure, it is not an Āryan's way to praise himself, but I will
tell you of my strength, for I am stung by your insults. Look, here is
earth, there is heaven, Kṛṣṇa, in which the creatures live, immovable,
infinite foundations and mothers of all—if these two should ever
angrily collide, like two rocks I would hold them apart, with their
standing and moving creatures, with these two arms! Look at the
space between these two arms like heavy bludgeons: I do not see a
10 man who, once caught in it, could escape. Himālaya and Ocean and
the thunderbolt-wielding Slayer of Vala himself could not, the three
of them together, rescue the man I have got when I use my strength.
I can kill all the barons who lie in ambush for the Pāṇḍavas; I
trample them all down into the earth with the flat of my feet! No,
you cannot fail to know my might, Acyuta, how I vanquished the
kings and subdued them. Or if you really do not know me like the
light of the rising sun, you shall find out when I plunge into the
turmoil of battle. Why do you insult me with harsh words as though

lancing a wound, prince sans blame? I tell you what I know, but be
15 sure I am more than that. You shall, when the crowded battle goes
on, on the day of bloodshed, see the elephant and chariot drivers and
riders annihilated! You and all the world shall see me furiously
finishing off brave bulls of the barons, pulling away the best of the
best. No, my marrow is not sinking and my heart does not tremble—
I have no fear of the fury of all the world! It is only good-heartedness
that makes me compassionately endure all hardships, Madhusūdana,
lest the Bhāratas find their perdition from us!"

The blessed Lord said:

75.1 I talked as I did out of affection, to find out your intention, not to
reproach you, display my wit, vent my anger, or voice my doubt.
I know your greatness of spirit, I know your strength, I know your
feats. I am not trying to be overbearing with you. I imagine in you a
virtue, Pāṇḍava, a thousand times greater than you imagine in
yourself. Bhīma, you are the kind of man to be born in a lineage
honored by all kings, to be surrounded with relatives and friends.
5 People who want to know how a doubtful Law distinguishes
between what is fate and what human effort do not reach a firm
conclusion, Wolf-Belly. The same factor which causes a man to
succeed in his affairs also causes his fall, for human action is always
doubtful. Matters that are judged one way by wise men, who would
be able to see the flaws, turn out the other way, like the changing
direction of a veering wind. A human action, however well counseled
and conducted and however correctly carried out, may be opposed by
fate. Also, human action countervails against what fate does or leaves
10 undone—like cold and heat, rain, hunger, and thirst, Bhārata. And
again, an action personally taken by a man who has the right insight
may not be hindered by fate. These are the three characteristics of
fate and human effort. The world cannot live by any other means
than action, Pāṇḍava, and the man who knows this will carry on,
whatever the result be of both his effort and fate. He who has come
to realize this carries on with his actions, and does not waver at
failure, nor rejoice at success.
This is all I meant to say, Bhīmasena: we must not count on
complete success in a war with the Kurus. One should not be too
quick letting go of the reins if luck changes contrarily, and succumb
to despair and exhaustion—that is what I mean to say.
15 Tomorrow morning I shall go to Dhṛtarāṣṭra, Pāṇḍava, and attempt
to make peace without hurting your cause. When they do make peace,
fame without end will be mine, your desire will be done, and their
ultimate well-being assured. If the Kurus stick to their position and
do not agree with what I say, there shall be war and work of terror.

In that war the burden will be on you, Bhīmasena, and the yoke on
Arjuna, while the others are pulled along. I shall be the chariot-
driver of the Terrifier in that war. That is Arjuna's desire, for I myself
20 do not want to fight. It was because I was not sure of your mind,
Wolf-Belly, that I prodded you, saying, "Don't act like a eunuch!"
and lighted up the fire of your splendor.

Arjuna said:
76.1 Yudhiṣṭhira himself has said what there is to say, Janārdana.
Listening to what you say, enemy-burner, it appears to me that you
do not think it will be easy to make peace, my lord, whether because
of Dhṛtarāṣṭra's greed, or because of our lack of resources. You think
at once that a man's might is of no consequence and that without
manly action no fruit ripens. What you say may be so or not so; but
5 nothing should be looked on as impossible. Besides, you think that
our miserable state of affairs has from the beginning been our
weakness. Well, *they* have been acting all along, and still have no
results to show for it. When correctly carried out an action does have
consequence, my lord. Move in such a way, Kṛṣṇa, that we find
shelter with the others. You are the very best friend of Pāṇḍavas and
Kurus, hero, as Prajāpati is of Gods and Asuras. Bring about what is
healthy for Kurus and Pāṇḍavas—I do not think it is difficult for you
to do what is good for us. If so, your task will be carried out,
Janārdana: you will accomplish it by the mere act of your going, no
10 doubt of that. If you wish to deal with that scoundrel one way or the
other, hero, let it be as you wish. Whether it will be shelter with
them for us, or whatever you want to effect, the desire in your mind
will weigh heavy with us, Kṛṣṇa. Does that evil-minded man not
deserve death with his sons and relations? He did not tolerate the
fortune he saw at the hall of the son of Dharma, and unable to find
a means according to Law, stole it cruelly with the aid of a cheater
at dice. How can a man who has been born a holder of the bow
among the barons decline when challenged, even though he lose his
15 life? When I saw us lawlessly defeated and sent forth into the forest,
this Suyodhana became mine to kill, Vārṣṇeya.
It is no wonder what you wish to do in the cause of your friends—
but how will the main task be carried out, by gentleness or feud? Or
if you think that it is better they are slaughtered immediately, let it be
done at once, and don't hesitate about it. For you know how that
fiend molested Draupadī in the middle of the hall, you know that the
others allowed it, Mādhava. I cannot believe that such a man would
20 treat the Pāṇḍavas fairly—it is like seed cast on salty soil. Therefore,
whatever you think fitting and good for the Pāṇḍavas, do it quickly,
Vārṣṇeya, and leave the rest to us.

The blessed Lord said:

77.1 It is as you say, strong-armed Pāṇḍava; still all of it depends on the
two kinds of actions, Terrifier. A fertile, cleared acre may be all
prepared by the farmer, but without rain it will fail to yield a crop,
Kaunteya. On this some might say that human effort does help, like
irrigation made possible by hard work, yet in that case too one might
surely find that the water dries up due to fate. Our great-spirited
forefathers have decided this in their wisdom: that the affairs of the
5 world are contingent on both fate and human effort. I myself shall
do the utmost that human agency allows, but I am unable in any
way to take care of fate.

This miscreant carries on after throwing out both Law and truth,
and he is not at all bothered by that kind of behavior. And his
councilors encourage his most wicked design—Śakuni, the *sūta*'s son,
and his brother Duḥśāsana. He is not going to agree to peace if it
means giving up the kingdom, before he is killed with his followers,
Pārtha. King Dharma refuses to give up the kingdom by surrender,
10 but that ruffian will not hand it over at his asking. I do not think it
is even worthwhile telling him Yudhiṣṭhira's demands—King Dharma
has himself given the reason not to, Bhārata. That evil Kaurava is
not going to do anything of the sort, and if it is not done, he deserves
to be killed by anyone, even by me and all the world, Bhārata, for
he mistreated you all when children. The evil-spirited brute has looted
your kingdom, for he could not find peace, the vile man, once he had
seen that fortune at Yudhiṣṭhira's. Time and again he has sought to
15 estrange me from you, but I never accepted his foul design. You know
quite well, strong-armed prince, what is uppermost in his mind, and
also that I want to do King Dharma a favor. Yet you are suddenly
suspicious, as though you did not know for sure, Arjuna! You also
know the divine secret which was ordained by Ordinance, Pārtha—so
how could there be shelter with the others? Whatever I can do with
word or deed, Pāṇḍava, I shall do it, Pārtha, but I expect no peace
with the others. And that expedition last year, that cattle robbery,
did he talk of wanting such shelter then, even when asked by Bhīṣma?
20 That very day they were defeated when you put your mind to
vanquishing them! Suyodhana is not content to part with the smallest
bit for the shortest time!

At any rate, I have to carry out King Dharma's mandate—the
evil doings of that scoundrel are once more to be considered. . . .

Nakula said:

78.1 King Dharma, who knows the Law and is a generous man, has
said it in many ways, and it is in fact consistent with Law, Mādhava.
Bhīmasena, too, knowing the king's mind, has spoken of peace,

Mādhava, but also the power of his arms. You have also heard what
Phalguna had to say, and you yourself have repeatedly stated what is
my own view, hero.

Now that you have heard what others think, ignore it all and do
5 what you think the time requires, best of men. There is an opinion
for every occasion, but a man has to do himself what the time
demands, enemy-tamer. A matter may be thought of one way, yet
actually happen in another. People in this world do not stick to their
opinions forever, best of men. We had one set of opinions while we
were living in the forest, another set when we were incognito, Kṛṣṇa,
and yet another now that we are out in the open. When we were
roaming about in the forest at the time, Varṣṇeya, we were not so
set upon the kingdom as we are now. When you heard that we had
returned from our forest exile, Janārdana, these seven grand-armies
10 were brought together by your grace, hero. What man would not
tremble at the sight of these tigerlike men, whose strength and
prowess are beyond imagining, and who have taken up their arms for
battle?

So, should you speak amidst the Kurus tactfully and timidly, so that
that fool Suyodhana does not get upset? Here are Yudhiṣṭhira,
Bhīmasena, the unvanquished Terrifier, Sahadeva, I, you Keśava, and
Rāma, and puissant Sātyaki, Virāṭa and his sons, Drupada and his
household, and Dhṛṣṭadyumna Pārṣata, the gallant king of the Kāśis,
and King Dhṛṣṭaketu of Cedi: what mortal of flesh and blood would
15 fight back at them on the battlefield? Simply by going there you will
no doubt accomplish, strong-armed lord, the desired purpose of King
Dharma. Vidura, Bhīṣma, Droṇa, and Bāhlīka are able to understand
what is good for them when you tell them, lord sans blame. And they
will bring King Dhṛtarāṣṭra around, and that miscreant Suyodhana
with his councilors. With Vidura listening and you speaking,
Janārdana, what matter can the two of you not bring to a halt
when it is rolling down the road?

Sahadeva said:

79.1 What the king has said is the sempiternal Law, but see to it that
there be war, enemy-tamer! Even if the Kurus should want peace
with the Pāṇḍavas, you should still provoke war with them, Dāśārha!
How could my rage at Suyodhana subside without bloodshed after
seeing the Princess of Pāñcāla manhandled in the hall? If Bhīma,
Arjuna, and King Dharma stick with the Law, I want to fight him in
battle, and begone with the Law!

Sātyaki said:

5 The sagacious Sahadeva speaks the truth, strong-armed lord! Only
when Duryodhana is killed will my anger with him be appeased.

You know that when you saw the wretched Pāṇḍavas wear bark and deerskin, your anger too flared up. Therefore what this champion bull among men, this son of Mādrī says, best of men, is the opinion of all of us warriors.

Vaiśaṃpāyana said:

While the shrewd Yuyudhāna was still speaking, a terrifying lion's roar rose from all the warriors there. On all sides the heroes applauded his words shouting "Right! Right!" and gladdened the scion of Śini with their truculence.

Vaiśaṃpāyana said:

80.1 After hearing the words of the king, consistent with Law and
Profit, and beneficial, Kṛṣṇā now spoke to the Dāśārha, who was
seated, looking wan with grief. The daughter of King Drupada, with
her long jet-black hair, applauded Sahadeva and the warrior Sātyaki.
Seeing even Bhīmasena in favor of peace, she was utterly dejected,
and with tears filling her eyes the spirited woman said, "You know
well, strong-armed, Law-wise Madhusūdana, how the Pāṇḍavas were
5 toppled from their happiness by the trickery of Dhṛtarāṣṭra's son and
his councilors, Janārdana, and what counsel the king gave Saṃjaya
in secret. You also know, Dāśārha, what Yudhiṣṭhira told Saṃjaya,
for you have heard it all, radiant lord: "Father," he said, "let five
villages be given us, Kuśasthala, Vṛkasthala, Māsandī, Vāraṇāvata,
and whatever other village you like as the fifth and last, strong-armed
lord." Duryodhana and his friends were to be told this, Keśava, and
Suyodhana heard the demand but did not comply with it, though
10 Yudhiṣṭhira was modest and wanted peace, Dāśārha. If Suyodhana
wants peace only if he does not have to give back the kingdom, it is
not worth going there and making peace, Kṛṣṇa. For, strong-armed
lord, the Pāṇḍavas along with the Sṛñjayas are quite able to cope
with Dhārtarāṣṭra's terrible and furious troops. When neither
conciliation nor generosity amounts to anything with those people,
I should show them no mercy, Madhusūdana! Enemies that are not
appeased by conciliation or generosity should be made to feel the
rod, Kṛṣṇa, if we want to save our lives. Therefore hurl a big rod at
them at once, Acyuta, you, the Pāṇḍavas and the Sṛñjayas, strong-
15 armed lord! It will bring profit to the Pārthas, glory to yourself, and
great happiness to the baronage, Kṛṣṇa. For a baron, if he follows
his own Law, should kill a baron who has become greedy, and a
non-baron too, with the exception of a brahmin even if he is a
criminal, friend; for the brahmin is the guru of all classes and
partakes of the best offerings. Those who know the Law know that
just as it is a sin to kill one who does not deserve it, so a sin is found
in not killing one who does deserve it. So see to it, Kṛṣṇa, that this

sin does not touch you, the Pāṇḍavas, and the Sṛñjayas with their
troops, Dāśārha!
20 "It has been said often enough, but I repeat it confidently,
Janārdana: has there been a woman like me on earth, Keśava?
Daughter of King Drupada, risen from the middle of the altar, sister
of Dhṛṣṭadyumna, and a woman dear to you, Kṛṣṇa, who, as
daughter-in-law of the great-spirited Pāṇḍu, entered into the lineage
of the Ājamīḍhas, chief queen of the sons of Pāṇḍu, who in holy
radiance equal five Indras! Five warrior sons have I borne by the
five heroes, who by Law are to you as Abhimanyu himself, Kṛṣṇa.
Yet I, a woman of such standing, was grabbed by the hair and
molested in a men's hall, while the sons of Pāṇḍu looked on and you
25 were alive, Keśava! And while the Kauraveyas, the Pāñcālas, the
Vṛṣṇis were alive, I was put in the middle of the hall and made a
slave of vile men! The Pāṇḍavas watched it without showing anger
or doing anything, so it was you I desired in my heart, Govinda,
crying, Save me! When my venerable father-in-law the king said to
me, 'Choose a boon, Princess of Pāñcāla, for I think you are deserving
of boons!' I said, 'Let the Pāṇḍavas with chariots and weapons go
free from slavery!' and they were set free, but to live in the forest,
Keśava.
"Janārdana, you are well aware of those grievances—save me
30 again, lotus-eyed one, with brothers, kinsmen, and relations! Am I
not by Law the daughter-in-law of both Bhīṣma and Dhṛtarāṣṭra?
Yet I became a slave! A curse on Bhīmasena's strength, a curse on
the Pārtha's bowmanship, if Duryoduana stays alive for another hour,
Kṛṣṇa! If you find favor in me, if you have pity on me, direct your
entire fury at the Dhārtarāṣṭras, Kṛṣṇa!"
Saying this, the black-eyed, heavy-hipped woman gathered up with
her left hand the side of her hair, which was soft and curled at the
ends, beautiful to look at and jet-black, perfumed with fine scents,
35 showing all the good marks, and glossy like a cobra; and the lily-
eyed one approached the lotus-eyed one with an elephant's steps.
Eyes filled with tears, Kṛṣṇā spoke to Kṛṣṇa. "This hair was pulled by
Duḥśāsana's hands, lotus-eyed lord; remember it at all times when
you seek peace with the enemies! If Bhīma and Arjuna pitifully
hanker after peace, my ancient father will fight, and his warrior sons,
Kṛṣṇa! My five valiant sons will, led by Abhimanyu, fight with the
Kurus, Madhusūdana! What peace will my heart know unless I see
40 Duḥśāsana's swarthy arm cut off and covered with dust! Thirteen
years have gone by while I waited, hiding my rage in my heart like
a blazing fire. Pierced by the thorn of Bhīma's words, my heart is
rent asunder, for now that strong-armed man has eyes for the Law
only!"

Long-eyed Kṛṣṇā spoke with her throat choked by tears, and she
shivered and wept aloud, sobbing, with tears sprinkling her breasts.
And the woman of the broad hips shed tears from her eyes like
45 liquefied fire. Strong-armed Keśava said to her soothingly, "Soon,
Kṛṣṇā, you shall see the women of the Bhāratas weep! They shall,
timid woman, weep for their kinsmen and relatives who are killed.
They at whom you are enraged, radiant woman, have already lost
their friends and troops. I along with Bhīma, Arjuna, and the twins
will act as Yudhiṣṭhira orders and as ordained fate allows. If the
Dhārtarāṣṭras, cooked in the fire of Time, do not listen to my words,
they shall lie killed on the earth as fodder for dogs and jackals. Mount
Himālaya may walk, Earth split into a hundred pieces, Heaven fall
with its stars, before my words are false! I promise you this truth,
Kṛṣṇā: stop your tears, for soon you shall see your husbands
rejoined with their fortune and their enemies slain."

Arjuna said:
81.1 You are now the best friend of all the Kurus. You have always
been the dear ally of the two parties. Health must be restored between
Pāṇḍavas and Dhārtarāṣṭras, and you, Keśava, are capable of making
peace between them. Hence, lotus-eyed one, go to the intransigent
Suyodhana in the cause of peace, and say to the Bhārata what need
be said, enemy-killer. If you speak to him of wholesome health
according to Law and Profit, and he does not accept your advice, he
will succumb to the power of fate.
The blessed Lord said:
5 Indeed I shall go to King Dhṛtarāṣṭra with a desire to obtain what
is due by Law, beneficial to us, and healthy for the Kurus.
Vaiśaṃpāyana said:
Then, when darkness had lifted, and an unclouded sun had risen,
at the hour of Maitra with the sun shining mild, in the month of
Kaumuda under the star of Revatī, when autumn ended and winter
began, in the season when crops abound and happiness rules, this
best of men of mettle was ready. Janārdana listened to the benedictions
of holy sound and blissful truth by the confident brahmins, as Vāsava
listens to the seers bless him. Janārdana performed the morning rites,
10 bathed, purified and adorned himself, and worshiped sun and fire. He
touched a bull on the back, saluted the brahmins, circumambulated
the fire, looked at auspicious things before him. Then Janārdana,
having acknowledged the Pāṇḍava's words, addressed Śini's grandson
Sātyaki, who was seated: "Have the conch, discus, and mace put in
the chariot, as well as the quivers, javelins, and striking weapons,
for Duryodhana, Karṇa, and Saubala have evil souls, and a stronger

man should ignore no enemy however common."

On hearing Keśava's wish, his servants ran about to yoke up the chariot of him who bears discus and club. The chariot shone like the blazing Doomsday fire and traveled like a bird, with two wheels resembling sun and moon to adorn it. It bore a fine flag with pennants. The flag was large, sporting half-moons and full moons, fish, deer, and fowl, all kinds of flowers, and was colorful with all its gems and stones—large, shining like the morning sun, and beautiful to the eyes. The chariot had a fine staff variegated with gold and jewels, and was well provided with gear, unassailable, covered with tiger skins—destroying the fame of enemies and increasing the joy of the Yadus. They yoked to it his steeds Sainya, Sugrīva, Meghapuṣpa, and Balāhaka, all freshly washed and accoutred with a full complement of harnessings. The chariot, which had a good sound, was emblazoned with the Garuḍa standard, even further adding to the glory of Kṛṣṇa.

Śauri ascended that chariot, which resembled a peak of the Meru and thundered like clouds and drums, as after death a man of merit ascends a celestial chariot. He had Sātyaki ascend after him, and then the best of men started out, filling earth and sky with the sound of his chariot. In an instant the weather cleared and the sky was unclouded. A favorable wind blew and all the dust settled. Beasts and fowl, auspiciously circling on the right, followed upon the departure of Vāsudeva. Cranes, woodpeckers, and wild geese winged all around, following Madhusūdana, with cries that spelled good luck. Great offerings, with oblations and *mantras*, were poured into the fire, and it became smokeless with flames perambulating it. Vasiṣṭha, Vāmadeva, Bhūridyumna, Gaya, Kratha, Śukra, Nārada, Vālmīka, Maruta, Kuśika, Bhṛgu—brahmin seers and divine seers—all circumambulated Kṛṣṇa, the younger brother of Indra, the bringer of joy to the Yadus.

Thus honored by these lordly throngs of great seers and holy men, Kṛṣṇa set out toward the seat of the Kurus. And as he went forth, Kuntī's son Yudhiṣṭhira followed him, and so did Bhīmasena, Arjuna, the twin sons of Mādrī and Pāṇḍu, the valiant Cekitāna, and King Dhṛṣṭaketu of Cedi, Drupada, the king of the Kāśis, the warrior Śikhaṇḍin, Dhṛṣṭadyumna, Virāṭa and his sons, and the Kekayas. All these barons sped the bull of the barons to help him succeed. After following Govinda for a while, illustrious Yudhiṣṭhira the King Dharma then spoke to him in the presence of the kings. Him who never followed wrong counsel because of love, or fear, or greed, or self-interest, always steady of spirit, never covetous, Law-wise, steadfast, full of insight into all creatures, him, Keśava, lord of all beings, majestic God of Gods, endowed with all virtues and marked with the Śrīvatsa curl, him the Kaunteya embraced and gave a message.

"The woman," he said, "who from our childhood on fostered us, wonted to fasts and austerities, always prone to auspicious rites, devout in her homage to deities and guests and in her obedience to her gurus, a loving mother to her sons and beloved of us, Janārdana, who, enemy-plougher, saved us from Suyodhana's danger, and from great threat of death rescued us as a ship rescues the shipwrecked from the ocean, who for our sake, Mādhava, suffered hardships constantly, though she deserved none—ask her her health! Comfort and comfort her drowning in grief for her sons, and when you have greeted her, embrace her while praising the Pāṇḍavas. Little though she deserved it, from the day she was wed she has seen nothing but hardships and deceptions from her family-in-law, and she has suffered.

"Will there ever be a time, Kṛṣṇa, a reversal of this sorrow, when I may bring happiness to my much-injured mother, enemy-tamer? When we went forth, she ran after us, miserably yearning for her sons, but we left the weeping woman behind and went into the forest. A person cannot ever die from grief, if mother is still alive, Keśava, looked after by the Ānartas but deeply hurting with the sorrow of her sons. Pray salute her, Lord Kṛṣṇa, at my bidding, and also Dhṛtarāṣṭra Kauravya and the kings who are older than we. Embrace Bhīṣma, Droṇa, Kṛpa, and Mahārāja Bahlīka, Drauṇi, Somadatta, and all the other Bhāratas one by one, and the sagacious Vidura, chief councilor of the Kurus, who is of unfathomable mind and wise in the Law, Madhusūdana."

After Yudhiṣṭhira had thus spoken to Keśava in the presence of the kings, he took his leave and returned after circumambulating Kṛṣṇa. But the Terrifier strode on and he said to his friend, bull among men, killer of enemy heroes, invincible Dāśārha, "Govinda, all the kings know about the matter of half the kingdom, which we settled at our final consultations. If he gives it ungrudgingly, with courtesy and without disdain, it would be a welcome gesture to me, strong-armed lord, and they would be saved from great danger. But if the Dhārtarāṣṭra, ignorant of the right means, acts differently, I shall of a certainty put an end to the barons, Janārdana!"

When the Wolf-Belly heard what the Pāṇḍava said, he was thrilled with joy, and that son of Pāṇḍu shivered again and again from rage. Trembling, the Kaunteya bellowed forth mighty roars, for Dhanaṃjaya's words had much excited his spirits. And hearing his roars the archers shivered and all the mounts dropped dung and urine. Having thus spoken to Keśava and thus voiced his

determination, Arjuna embraced Janārdana, took his leave and
turned back. And while all the kings returned to their camp,
Janārdana happily took wing, driving Sainya and Sugrīva; and
Vāsudeva's horses under Dāruka's whip seemed to sip the road and
devour the sky.

60 On the way Keśava of the strong arms saw seers blazing with
brahminic luster, who stood on both sides of the road. Janārdana
quickly alighted from his chariot and saluted them, and with due
honor he said to all those seers, "Is good health abroad in the
worlds, is the Law observed, do the other three classes abide by the
brahmins' behest?" Paying homage to them, Madhusūdana resumed,
"Reverend sirs, where have you reached perfection? What path has
brought you here? Is there something you want done? What can I
do for you? For what purpose have your worships come down to
earth?"

65 Jāmadagnya approached Madhusūdana, and, as an old comrade in
good deeds, embraced Govinda and said to him, "The divine seers of
meritorious acts, the learned brahmins, the royal seers, and the
honorable ascetics, O Dāśārha, once were witnesses of the ancient
battle of Gods and Asuras, radiant lord. Now they all wish to see the
barons of earth foregathered, and the kings sitting in the hall, and
yourself speaking the truth, Janārdana. We are coming to watch this
grand spectacle, Keśava, and to listen to the words of Law and Profit
which you, Mādhava, will speak to the Kurus in the midst of the
70 kings, enemy-burner. Bhīṣma, Droṇa, and the others, the sagacious
Vidura and you yourself, tiger of the Yādavas, will meet in
assembly. Of you and them, Mādhava, we wish to hear the divine,
truthful and beautiful speeches, Govinda! Farewell, strong-armed
lord, we shall see you again. Travel a safe road, hero, we shall see
you in the hall."

Vaiśaṃpāyana said:

82.1 Ten enemy-harassing chariot champions carrying arms
accompanied the son of Devakī on his progress, with a thousand foot
soldiers and riders, enemy-killer, and hundreds more of servants with
ample provisions, king.

Janamejaya said:

How did the great-spirited Madhusūdana Dāśārha progress? And
what portents were there when the august lord went forward?

Vaiśaṃpāyana said:

Then hear from me the marvels, the celestial, fateful, and prodigious
5 portents, that befell at the great-spirited Kṛṣṇa's departure. In a clear
sky there was thunder and lightning; without clouds Parjanya rained
fierce showers behind him. The great and noble rivers that flow east

reversed their course. Space was upside down and no directions could
be made out. Fires flared up, king, earth shook, wells and jars by the
hundreds brimmed over and poured forth water. The entire world was
covered with darkness, and dust obscured all points of space. A
mighty noise exploded in the sky, but not a body was to be seen
10 anywhere, king; it was a great marvel. A fierce southwesterly gale
strafed Hāstinapura, uprooting numbers of trees, with horrifying
howls. Everywhere the Vārṣṇeya went there blew a pleasant breeze,
Bhārata, everything was favorable, a shower of blossoms rained
down, there were lotuses aplenty, the road stretched smoothly without
discomfort and clear of sharp grasses and thistles. Wherever the
strong-armed man went, he was hailed by brahmins with honey
dishes and flowers, while he showered largess. Along the road women
came up to the great-spirited savior of all and scattered fragrant
forest flowers over him.

15 He passed by lovely Śālibhavana, where all crops stood plentiful, a
happy and most law-abiding settlement, bull of the Bharatas, and as
he went on he saw villages with ample livestock, lovely and satisfying
to the heart, and cities and various kingdoms. Always happy and
friendly city people, who were protected by the Bhāratas and therefore
safe and healthy and ignorant of any evil design of enemy circles,
came in crowds to see Viṣvaksena arrive from Upaplavya, and they
all honored the famous lord, who, blazing like fire, had come to their
land as a guest, with the honors he deserved.

20 Keśava, slayer of enemy heroes, came at last to Vṛkasthala, when
an unclouded sun grew red with scattered rays. He alighted from his
chariot, quickly did the proper ablutions, had the chariots unyoked,
and sat down for the evening rites. Dāruka unharnessed the horses,
attended to them according to custom, and after loosening all their
gear, took off their armor and let them go. When he had gone
through all that, Madhusūdana said, "We shall spend the night here,
while we are on Yudhiṣṭhira's business." Learning his wish, the men
25 set up camp and soon procured finc food and drink. The notable
brahmins in the village, noble, well-descended, modest, and observing
brahminic occupations, O king, approached the great-spirited
Hṛṣīkeśa, tamer of enemies, and paid homage to him respectfully
with blessings and benedictions. After their homage they offered the
great-spirited Dāśārha, renowned in all worlds, their treasure-filled
houses. The lord said, "No more!"; he treated them as they deserved,
entered their dwellings, and returned with them. Keśava then feasted
the brahmins on delicious food, and, after eating with them all, spent
the night comfortably.

Vaiśaṃpāyana said:

83.1 Dhṛtarāṣṭra had learned from his messengers that Madhusūdana
was coming and he spoke to the strong-armed Bhīṣma with proper
respect, and to Droṇa, Saṃjaya, and the sagacious Vidura, and to
Duryodhana and his councilors he spoke, thrilled with joy, "Joy of
the Kurus! We hear of a great and marvelous wonder! Women and
children and oldsters talk about it from house to house; others
recount it devoutly; still others do so in crowds, as various accounts
5 run through squares and halls—that the victorious Dāśārha* is
coming in the Pāṇḍava's cause! Madhusūdana* deserves our respect
and homage in every way; for in him walks the world, for he is the
lord of the creatures. In him, the Mādhava,* reside fortitude, prowess,
wisdom, and august might. He is to be honored as the best of men,
for that is the sempiternal Law. When honored he brings happiness,
unhappiness when not. When Dāśārha the enemy-tamer is satisfied
with our attentions, we, among all kings, shall attain all our wishes
entire!

"Enemy-burner, see to it that he receives honors this very day.
10 Let lodges be built on his way filled with all he desires. Son of
Gāndhārī, make sure that he takes pleasure in you, strong-armed
prince. Or what do you think, Bhīṣma?"

Bhīṣma and all the others applauded the words of Lord Dhṛtarāṣṭra
and cried, "Excellent!" Knowing they approved, King Duryodhana
thereupon undertook to assign sites for lodges. In spot after lovely
spot they built numerous lodges, well-arranged, that were filled with
all kinds of treasure: colorful seats of various attractions, women,
15 perfumes, ornaments, and fine garments, superior food and drink, a
variety of food and very fragrant garlands—the king donated it all.
Especially in the village of Vṛkasthala King Kaurava** set up a lovely
lodge with much treasure for Dāśārha to spend the night.

Having arranged all this, worthy of Gods and superhuman beings,
King Duryodhana reported to Dhṛtarāṣṭra. But Keśava Dāśārha
ignored all those lodges and their comforts, and went on to the seat
of the Kurus.

Dhṛtarāṣṭra said:

84.1 Steward, Janārdana is on his way here from Upaplavya. He is
spending the night in Vṛkasthala and will be here in the morning.
Overlord of the Āhukas, leader of all Sātvatas, the great-minded,
puissant, and lordly Janārdana Mādhava is the ruler and herdsman

* = Kṛṣṇa.
** = Duryodhana.

of the wealthy house of the Vṛṣṇis, indeed the blessed grandfather
of all three worlds. The Vṛṣṇi-Andhakas heed his wisdom happily, as
5 the Ādityas, Vasus, and Rudras heed Bṛhaspati's. I shall extend my
homage to the great-spirited Dāśārha for you to see. Listen, law-wise
Vidura, I shall tell you.

I shall give him sixteen golden chariots, each yoked with four fine
steeds from Bactria of solidly jet-black coloring. I shall give Keśava
eight pole-tusked war elephants with running temples, each with
eight handlers. I shall present him with a hundred beautiful golden-
skinned slave girls who have never given birth, and as many male
slaves. I shall give him eighteen thousand soft cashmere sheepskins
10 that have been brought to me by the hill people, and thousands of
yak hides from the Chinese country, as many as Keśava deserves. Day
and night shines this translucent gem: I shall present it to Keśava,
for he deserves it. I shall give him a mule cart that flies eighteen
leagues a day. Every day I shall give him eight times the food that
his men and mounts can eat. All my sons and grandsons, except
Duryodhana, shall go out to meet the Dāśārha adorned with
15 handsome chariots. Finely ornamented and beautiful courtesans of
the first rank will go out on foot by the thousands to meet the lordly
Keśava. Pretty nubile girls will go from the city to Janārdana, and
they shall go unveiled. The whole citizenry, women, men, and
children, shall gaze upon the great-spirited Madhusūdana as on the
sun itself!

Let his road everywhere be emblazoned with large flags and
pennants, and sprinkled with water and swept of its dust! (he
ordered). Let Duḥśāsana's mansion, which is better than
20 Duryodhana's, be at once decorated beautifully for him, for it is
adorned with handsome pavilions, and lovely and sound, and it
abounds in treasures in all seasons. All my wealth and Duryodhana's,
too, is in that house—all the Vārṣṇeya deserves should be given him,
no doubt of that!

Vidura said:

85.1 King, you are highly esteemed by all three worlds as the best of
men, you are honest and greatly respected by the people, Bhārata.
In whatever you say, now that you are in the last stretch of your life,
based either on scripture or reasoning, you are secure, for you are
old. The subjects know, Mahārāja, that Law is in you as lines are in
rock, light in the sun, waves in the ocean. Everyone is always honored
because of the multitude of your virtues, prince, so strive continuously
5 with your relatives to protect those virtues! Take the course of
honesty, lest you destroy in many ways your kingdom, your sons,
and grandsons, and the friends who are very dear to you.

However much you want to present to Kṛṣṇa as your guest, the
Dāśārha deserves it all and more, even the entire world! But I touch
myself and swear that you do not want to give it to Kṛṣṇa for reasons
of Law or to show your friendship. It is a deception, a lie, a cover,
king of plentiful stipends! I know your design, king, which is
concealed under your outward acts. The Pāṇḍavas want five little
villages, king, only five, and you do not want to give them to them.
10 Who will make peace then? But with this wealth you want to draw
the Vārṣṇeya, and split him from the Pāṇḍavas with this subterfuge. I
tell you the truth: by neither treasure, nor effort, nor abuse can he be
estranged from Dhanaṃjaya. I know Kṛṣṇa's greatness, I know his
firm loyalty, and I know that he will not abandon Dhanaṃjaya, who
is as dear to him as his life. Janārdana will want from you no more
than a full jar of water, no more than water to wash his feet, no more
than an inquiry after his health. So offer the great-spirited man, who
deserves it, true hospitality, king, for Janārdana is worthy of honor.
15 Keśava is coming to the Kurus hoping for one benefit: so give him
that for which he is coming, king. The Dāśārha wants peace between
you and Duryodhana and the Pāṇḍavas, Indra of kings. Do as he
says. You are their father, they are your sons, king. You are old, the
others are young. Act like a father to them, for they act toward you
like sons!

Duryodhana said:
86.1 It is all very true what Vidura says about Kṛṣṇa: Janārdana is
inseparably attached to the Pāṇḍavas. But all these various gifts you
want to make to Janārdana in the name of hospitality, they should
not be given at all, Indra of kings! It is neither the time nor the place
for them. Surely Keśava deserves it all, but Adhokṣaja will think that
you honor him out of fear, king. I am firmly convinced, lord of the
people, that a sagacious baron should avoid doing anything that
5 might bring him disdain. Divine Kṛṣṇa of the lotus eyes is indeed
most worthy of the homage of all three worlds, that I know full well.
But no gifts should be made to him. That is the proper course to take,
for once war has been undertaken no peace is made by pretending
there is no war.

Vaiśaṃpāyana said:
Upon hearing his words Bhīṣma, grandfather of the Kurus, replied
to King Vaicitravīrya, "Whether he is treated well or not, Kṛṣṇa will
not get angry. Though he himself be slighted, Keśava is unable to
slight the other. No one can undo, with any means, whatever he has
10 made his task. We should do without hesitation what the strong-
armed lord tells us to do, and make peace with the Pāṇḍavas, with
Vāsudeva as our savior. Being law-spirited, Janārdana is sure to say

what is good for Law and Profit. You and your relations must speak to him as friends."

Duryodhana said:

King, there is no circumstance in which I could share this fortune, which is solely mine, with the Pāṇḍavas and go on living with the living, grandfather! Listen to what I have determined is my important task: I shall take captive Janārdana, who is the last resort of the Pāṇḍavas. With him in fetters, the Vṛṣṇis, the earth, and the
15 Pāṇḍavas will submit to me. Tomorrow morning he will be here. Tell me sir, by what means Janārdana can be prevented from finding out, so that no harm comes to us.

Vaiśaṃpāyana said:

When Dhṛtarāṣṭra and his councilors heard these dreadful words of threat to Kṛṣṇa, they were hurt and perturbed. Dhṛtarāṣṭra told Duryodhana, "If you are the protector of your subjects, don't talk like that! This is not the sempiternal Law! Hṛṣīkeśa is an envoy and our dear friend. He means no harm to the Kauraveyas, so how does he deserve being held?"

Bhīṣma said:

Dhṛtarāṣṭra, this demented son of yours is possessed! His friends
20 plead with him, and still he chooses disaster over profit! This evil man with his evil followers has gone off the road, and you obey him, brushing off the advice of your friends! If this vile son of yours and his councilors touch Kṛṣṇa of unsullied deeds, they'll meet their end instantly. I refuse to listen to any more nonsense from this evil, cruel brute who has thrown over the Law!

Vaiśaṃpāyana said:

The ancient chief of the Bhāratas rose with extreme rage. And Bhīṣma, whose prowess was his truth, strode away.

Vaiśaṃpāyana said:

87.1 The next morning Kṛṣṇa rose, performed the morning rites, took leave from the brahmins and started for the city. All the villagers of Vṛkasthala bade farewell to the strong-armed lord at his departure, O king, and returned home. The sons of Dhṛtarāṣṭra in their finery—all except Duryodhana—and Bhīṣma, Droṇa, Kṛpa, and so forth met him when he arrived, and so did numerous townspeople, sire, eager
5 to see Hṛṣīkeśa, some coming in various vehicles, others on foot. He met them on the road, and, surrounded by Bhīṣma of unsullied deeds and by Droṇa and the Dhārtarāṣṭras, went into the city. In Kṛṣṇa's honor the town was spruced up and the royal roads were lavishly decorated. No one stayed home, king, bull of the Bharatas, woman, or oldster, or babe in arms, for they all wanted to see Vāsudeva. There were no men on the road; they were all lying on the ground,

king, for so great was their awe at the entrance of Hṛṣīkeśa. Even the
very big houses crowded with beautiful women seemed to sway on
their foundations under the burden. And Vāsudeva's fast coursers
had to slow down, for the royal road was thronged with people.
The lotus-eyed enemy-plougher entered Dhṛtarāṣṭra's white house,
which was adorned with pavilions. Kṛṣṇa strode through three palace
enclosures, then the enemy-tamer went up to King Vaicitravīrya. At
the Dāśārha's approach the glorious king with the eyesight of
wisdom rose up together with Droṇa and Bhīṣma. Kṛpa, Somadatta,
and Mahārāja Bāhlika all rose from their seats and honored
15 Janārdana. The scion of the Vṛṣṇis drew near to famous King
Dhṛtarāṣṭra and Bhīṣma and saluted them at once. Madhusūdana
Mādhava extended his own greetings according to age in the order of
Law and met with the kings. Then Janārdana met with Droṇa and
his son, famous Bāhlika, Kṛpa, and Somadatta. There was a large
and mighty throne there, finely wrought and gilded, and there Acyuta
sat at Dhṛtarāṣṭra's behest. The priests of Dhṛtarāṣṭra offered the cow,
the honey dish, and the water to Janārdana according to the rules.
20 Govinda, having been received hospitably, jested with the Kurus and
sat there in friendly conversation, while the Kurus surrounded him.
Then the glorious enemy-tamer, having been honored by
Dhṛtarāṣṭra, excused himself to the king and left. After meeting in
proper fashion the Kurus in their assembly, the Mādhava made his
way to the dwelling of Vidura. Vidura received Janārdana with all the
blessings, and he saluted the Dāśārha and waited on him with all he
desired. After receiving Govinda as a proper host, Vidura, who knew
all the Laws, asked Madhusūdana about the health of Pāṇḍu's sons.
25 To his dear and sagacious friend the Steward, constant in the Law
and without flaws, the most wise Dāśārha, who saw it all before him,
then told in full the vicissitudes of the Pāṇḍavas.

Vaiśaṃpāyana said:
88.1 After meeting with Vidura, Janārdana Govinda, tamer of enemies,
went in the afternoon to his father's sister. When she saw Kṛṣṇa
come with the luster of a serene sun, Pṛthā embraced him and,
remembering the Pārthas, began to weep. Seeing now after a long
time Govinda Vārṣṇeya, who was a companion of her mettlesome
sons, Pṛthā shed tears; and when Kṛṣṇa was seated after his
hospitable reception, she spoke to that lord of warriors choking with
tears and with a dried-out mouth—
"Keśava, how have the great-spirited sons of Pāṇḍu lived in the
5 forest, a life they did not deserve? From boyhood they were eager to
obey their elders, to one another they were respected friends and of
the same mind; but driven from their rule by deceit, they went into

the desolate forest, although they deserved the company of people. They had subdued their angers and their joys, they were brahminic, they spoke the truth—then the Pārthas relinquished pleasures and comforts and, leaving me behind in tears, took my heart with its roots with them as they went into the forest.

"How, my friend, have they lived in the forest that teems with lions, tigers, and elephants? I always cherished them, as children deprived of their father—how have they lived in the vast forest seeing *neither* of their parents? From childhood on the sons of Pāṇḍu used to wake up to the sound of conches, kettle drums, flutes, and hand drums, Keśava! At home they were always awakened by the trumpeting of elephants, the whinnying of horses, and the clatter of chariot wheels, honored with the music of conch and drum accompanied by flute and lute, and the sound of the Blessing of the Day by the brahmins. They would honor the twiceborn with clothes, largess and jewelry, while the great-spirited brahmins in turn would bless them with chants and benedictions. They used to wake up, greeted by the praise of the honored and honorable, from beds of *ranku* hides in the finest palaces. Surely, Janārdana, they could not get to sleep in the great forest, listening to the sounds of predators, in a life they did not deserve. They had woken up to the sound of drums, conches, and flutes and the sweet songs of women and the praise of bards and minstrels—how could they wake up to the cries of wild beasts in the forest?

"A modest man, firm in his truth, restrained, compassionate to the creatures, in control of love and hatred, he walks the path of the strict. He bore the hard yoke of Ambarīṣa, Māndhātar, Yayāti, Nahuṣa, Bharata, Dilīpa, and Śibi Auśīnara, the royal seers of antiquity; his character and behavior adorned him, he knew the Law and kept his word, he could have been the king of all three worlds with all the qualities he possesses. Law-spirited Ajātaśatru with the complexion of pure gold, best among all the Kurus in Law, learning and conduct—how is Yudhiṣṭhira, Kṛṣṇa, of the pleasing mien and the long arms?

"And Wolf-Belly, with the vigor of a myriad elephants and the vehemence of a gale, the truculent son of Pāṇḍu, always dear to his brother and pleasing him, the heroic slayer of Kīcaka and his kinsmen, Madhusūdana, and of the Krodhavaśas, Hiḍimba, and Baka, in valor the equal of Śakra, in speed the equal of a wind gust, in anger the match of the great God, Bhīma, first among fighters, the enemy-burner who controlled his anger, strength, and impatience, the Pāṇḍava, master of himself in spite of his fury, who obeys his brother's behest—that mass of splendor, storm flood of power, boundlessly august, great-spirited Bhīmasena who strikes terror with his appearance, Janārdana—tell me, Vārṣṇeya, how is Wolf-Belly now?

"And the middlemost Pāṇḍava, Arjuna, who with his two bludgeon-like arms, Kṛṣṇa Acyuta, rivals the thousand-armed Arjuna and always bests him, Keśava, who in a single volley shoots off five hundred arrows, who is the equal in bowmanship of King Kārtavīrya, in splendor of the sun, in self-control of the great seers, in patience of the earth, in prowess of Indra, who, Madhusūdana, with his might brought the Kurus their vast, lustrous, glorious overlordship of all the kings, the dreadful strength of whose arms the Kauravas respect, the Pāṇḍava, greatest of all warriors, whose valor is his truth, the refuge of the Pāṇḍavas as Vāsava is of the Gods—your brother and friend, how is Dhanaṃjaya now?

"Compassionate to all creatures, restrained by modesty, a great master of arms, gentle and delicate, law-abiding and dear to me, all this is the great archer Sahadeva, a champion who shines in battle, obedient to his brothers, Kṛṣṇa, a youth well-versed in Law and Profit. His brothers always laud the conduct of the great-spirited Sahadeva, whose deportment is always proper, Madhusūdana. Tell me, Vārṣṇeya, of heroic Sahadeva, son of Mādrī, chief of warriors, who defers to his elder brothers and obeys me.

"That delicate youth and champion, that handsome Pāṇḍava, dear to all his brothers, Kṛṣṇa, like their own life, a model warrior and great archer, strong Nakula, is he in good health, Kṛṣṇa, my calf, who has prospered on comforts? Will I ever see Nakula again, O strong-armed one, used to his pleasures, undeserving of sorrows, a delicate warrior? I found no peace when I was without Nakula for as long as a blink of an eye, hero, now look at me—I live!

"And Draupadī, beloved of all my sons, Janārdana, high-born, of fine character and endowed with all virtues, a true woman who chose the life of her husbands over that of her sons, and left her dear sons behind to follow the Pāṇḍavas, born of high family, honored with all she could desire, a lady beautiful in all respects—how is Draupadī, Acyuta? Draupadī has five husbands, champions all, fighters the likes of Fire, and great archers, and she knows only misfortune! This is the fourteenth year that I have not seen true-spoken Draupadī, who herself must be worn out with worries about her own sons.

"Surely, no man enjoys happiness because of the good deeds he has done, if Draupadī, of such high conduct, does not enjoy happiness without end! The Terrifier is not dearer to me than Kṛṣṇā, nor is Yudhiṣṭhira, or Bhīmasena and the twins. When I saw her in the assembly hall, it was a sorrier thing than anything I had experienced before—when all the Kurus watched, Draupadī stood there, outside the wind, in the presence of her fathers-in-law, in her single garment, in that assembly hall where a vile man had had her

brought, indulging his anger and greed. In that very place Dhṛtarāṣṭra
and Mahārāja Bāhlīka, Kṛpa and Somadatta and the dispirited Kurus
were present, but in that whole assemblage I respect only the
Steward, for one is an Āryan by what he does, not by his knowledge
or wealth. And the Steward, that great-spirited, strong-armed,
profound man, is adorned by a character that supports the worlds!"

Full of both sorrow and joy at seeing Govinda come, she recited
all her many griefs.

55 "Could the vices of ancient kings, gambling and deer-hunting,
possibly give *them* pleasure, enemy-tamer? It burns me that the sons
of Dhṛtarāṣṭra molested Kṛṣṇā, in the hall, in the presence of the
Kurus, in a way that was sick unto death! And then their banishment
from the city and their forest life, enemy-tamer—yes, I have harbored
a great many sorrows, Janārdana!—their life in concealment and
their separation from their youngsters! Nothing hurts me *and* my
sons more, enemy-tamer, than the fact that we are now tricked for
the fourteenth year! If there is no happiness growing from suffering,
blossom and fruit are dead. Never have I made any distinction between
60 Dhārtarāṣṭras and Pāṇḍavas: and by this truth I swear to, Kṛṣṇa,
may I see you and the Pāṇḍavas survive this war with your enemies
slain and fortune around you! Not that they can be defeated, their
mettle being what it is.

"I am not blaming myself, or Suyodhana, but my father, who paid
me out to Kuntibhoja as crooks pay out. I was a little girl, playing
with my ball, and your grandfather gave me to Kuntibhoja, friend to
magnanimous friend! I have been cheated by my father and my
fathers-in-law, enemy-tamer, unhappy beyond the limit! Kṛṣṇa, what
has life profited me? When I gave birth to the Left-handed Archer,
there was a voice in the night that said: 'Thy son shall conquer earth,
65 and his fame shall reach to heaven. After killing the Kurus in a war
between peoples and obtaining the kingdom, Dhanaṃjaya, son of
Kuntī, shall with his brothers offer up the three sacrifices.'

"I have never doubted it, praise be the Law that ordains, to great
Kṛṣṇa praise; the Law upholds the creatures forever! If there *is* any
Law, Vārṣṇeya, then the truth shall prevail, and you shall make it
all happen entirely, Kṛṣṇa. I am a widow, Mādhava, I have lost my
possessions, I have enemies, but nothing hurts me like being without
my sons. What peace does my heart know as long as I do not see
Dhanaṃjaya the Gāṇḍiva bowman, greatest of all that bear arms?

70 "This is the fourteenth year, Govinda, that I have not seen
Yudhiṣṭhira and Dhanaṃjaya, the twins and Wolf-Belly! People hold
a *śrāddha* for those who have disappeared, as though they are dead.
In effect they are dead to me, and I to them, Janārdana.

"Tell the king, Mādhava, tell the law-spirited King Yudhiṣṭhira:

'Your Law is dwindling fast, don't be a hypocrite, little son!' Vāsudeva, I live here as a burden of *others*, a curse on me! Life without secure foundation is better still than living by begging!

"Then tell Dhanaṃjaya and Wolf-Belly, who is always ready: 'I, a
75 baroness, bore you for a purpose, and the time is now. If, when the
time has come, time passes you by, you'll end up with cruelty,
however high the world holds you now. If you stoop to cruelty, I
shall leave you forever, for, when the time has come, one should be
ready to relinquish life itself.'

"Say to the twin sons of Mādrī, who have always embraced the
Law of the baronage: 'Choose yourselves the joys that only bravery
earns, be it at the cost of your lives!' For, best of men, it is the
possessions obtained with bravery that best please the man who lives
by the Law of the baronage.

"So go, strong-armed man, and say to Arjuna Pāṇḍava the hero,
80 greatest of bearers of arms: 'Walk the path of Draupadī!' For you
know that when Bhīma and Arjuna are enraged beyond measure,
they are like death and can send even Gods on the last journey. It
was an insult to them that Kṛṣṇā stood in the hall and Duḥśāsana
and Karṇa abused her. Duryodhana assailed the headstrong
Bhīmasena while the chief Kurus looked on, and he shall witness the
result of that. For Wolf-Belly, once he is embroiled in a feud, finds no
peace; with Bhīma no feud is appeased, however old, before the
enemy-plougher has put an end to his enemies.

"Not the hurt of the theft of the kingdom, not that defeat at the
dice, not the exile of my sons have caused me as great pain as the
85 knowledge that that large, dark woman stood in the hall in her single
garment and had to listen to those abusive words! What could hurt
me more? That beautiful woman who was ever devoted to the Law
of the baronage, was in her period, and Kṛṣṇā found no one to
protect her, though her protectors were there.

"But I and my sons have you as protector, Madhusūdana, and
Rāma, strong of the strong, and Pradyumna the warrior; and so I
can endure all this sorrow now, best of men, as long as the
unassailable Bhīma and never-retreating Arjuna live!"

Śauri, the Pārtha's friend, consoled the grieving Pṛthā, his father's
sister, who was overwhelmed with the afflictions of her sons: "Is there
90 a woman in the world like you, father's sister? The daughter of King
Śūra, who entered the House of the Ājamīḍhas, a highborn woman
who like a lotus was transplanted from pond to pond, a mistress of
all high qualities and honored highly by your husband, the mother
of heroes, the wife of a hero, crowned by all the virtues—sagacious
woman, one like you can endure both happiness and misery! Sleep
and sloth, anger and joy, hunger and thirst, cold and heat, the

Pārthas have conquered them all, and still, like heroes, they aim for happiness. The Pārthas have given up the pleasures of villagers. The pleasures they want are those of heroes and, full of vigor and power,
95 they are not content with just a little. The steadfast seek the extreme, while those that want the pleasures of villagers seek the mediocre. The steadfast rejoice in the greatest human hardships and joys beyond the average; they delight in the extremes, not in the middle. They say that attaining the extreme is happiness, and that which lies between the extremes is suffering.

"The Pāṇḍavas and Kṛṣṇā salute the lady. They convey that they are in good health and ask about yours. You shall soon see the Pāṇḍavas healthy and successful in all their affairs, masters of the entire world, with their enemies slain and fortune around them!"

Comforted, Kuntī replied to Janārdana, controlling the darkness of incomprehension, though still overcome with grief over her sons,
100 "Madhusūdana, do whatever is good for them in whatever way you see fit, strong-armed Kṛṣṇa, without hurting the Law and without deception, enemy-tamer. I know the power of your truth and your high birth, Kṛṣṇa, and of the wisdom and valor you show in establishing your friends. In our family you are the Law, you are the truth, you are great ascetic power, you are the savior, you the great Brahman—on you rests everything. It will be as you say: in you will be the truth."

Govinda took leave of her, and circumambulated her; then the strong-armed lord departed for Duryodhana's houses.

Vaiśaṃpāyana said:

89.1 After taking leave of Pṛthā and circumambulating her, Govinda Śauri, enemy-tamer, went to Duryodhana's house, which looked like the palace of the Sacker of Cities, decked with great splendor. He strode through three enclosures unchecked by the doorkeepers, then the famous man ascended to the palace which like a cloud in the sky rose high as a mountain peak and blazed with wealth. There, surrounded by the Kurus and thousands of kings, he saw the strong-
5 armed son of Dhṛtarāṣṭra seated on a throne. And he saw Duḥśāsana, Karṇa, and Śakuni Saubala seated close to Duryodhana.

The Dāśārha drew near, and the famous Dhārtarāṣṭra rose up with his councilors, welcoming Madhusūdana. Keśava Vārṣṇeya met with the Dhārtarāṣṭra and his councilors, and with the kings who were present there, according to their seniority. Then Acyuta seated himself on a finely ornamented golden couch that was spread with all kinds of coverlets. The Kaurava, after presenting him with the cow and
10 the honey dish, thereupon offered him his house and realm. All the Kurus and the kings offered their services to Govinda, who sat with

the luster of a tranquil sun. King Duryodhana now invited the Vārṣṇeya, greatest of victors, to share a meal, but Keśava declined.

Duryodhana Kaurava said to Kṛṣṇa in the assembly of kings in soft tones that promised villainy, while looking at Karṇa, "Janārdana, why do you not accept this food, drink, clothing, and bedding, which have been fetched for you? You have given both parties your help, you wish both well, you are the beloved ally of Dhṛtarāṣṭra, Mādhava! For you know Law and Profit truly and wholly. I wish to hear your reasons, bearer of discus and mace!"

At these words the wise Govinda of the lotus eyes grasped his own sturdy arm and replied in a voice that sounded like flood and cloud, with words that were fully articulated, not swallowed or dropped or slurred, "Envoys eat and accept homage when they have succeeded. When I have succeeded, you and your councilors shall honor me, Bhārata."

The Dhārtarāṣṭra replied to Janārdana, "It is not right for you to act improperly toward us. Whether you be successful or not, Madhusūdana, we still try to honor you, and cannot, Govinda. Nor do we know the reason, Madhusūdana, why you have disdained the homage which we offer you in a spirit of friendship, best of men. We have no feud with you, Govinda, nor a quarrel. Considering this you ought not to speak as you do!"

Janārdana replied to the Dhārtarāṣṭra, looking him and his councilors in the face and laughing, "I would not transgress the Law out of love, fury, hatred, self-interest, argument, or greed. Food is to be accepted either out of affection, or because of need. But neither do I have affection for you, king, nor am I in need! King, you have hated the Pāṇḍavas from birth without cause, your brethren who have treated you kindly and who glory in all virtues. This senseless hatred of the Pāṇḍavas is out of place. The Pāṇḍavas abide by the Law; who can say anything against them? He who hates them hates me; he who follows them follows me; for know that I have become of one soul with the Law-observing Pāṇḍavas. They call him the vilest of men who, a prey to lust and anger, in his folly hates and seeks to thwart a man of virtue. He who, a slave to self and anger, wants to look upon kinsmen of high virtue with folly and greed will soon lose his fortune. And he who with kindness subjugates men of quality, even though in his heart he dislikes them, will for a long time rest on his fame. All this food I consider spoiled for me and inedible. I have decided I shall eat only the Steward's food." And with these words to the indignant Dhārtarāṣṭra, the strong-armed lord walked out of Duryodhana's resplendent palace. Out strode the strong-armed, wise Vāsudeva, and he went to stay at the house of great-spirited Vidura.

35 Droṇa, Kṛpa, Bhīṣma, Bālika, and other Kurus came to the strong-
armed lord where he stayed at Vidura's. The Kurus came and said to
Madhusūdana, "Vārṣṇeya, we are offering you our houses and
treasures!" And splendid Madhusūdana said to them, "Your worships
must all go, I am being done all the honor I want." The Kurus left
and the Steward did his best to honor the unvanquished Dāśārha
with all he desired. The Steward fetched pure and fine foods and
40 drinks aplenty for the great-spirited Keśava. Madhusūdana first sated
the brahmins with it and also gave superb gifts to the scholars of the
Veda. Then, like Indra with his retinue of Maruts, he enjoyed Vidura's
pure and fine food.

Vaiśampāyana said:
90.1 At night when Kṛṣṇa had eaten and relaxed, Vidura said, "Keśava,
it was not a wise decision of yours to come. Dhṛtarāṣṭra's son has
thrown Law and Profit to the winds; he is an impetuous fool,
Janārdana, belittling others and exalting himself, ignoring the
commandments of his elders, trampling the dictates of Law—an evil
madman possessed, Janārdana, wicked and out of the control of his
betters! He is driven by desire, he thinks he is clever, he betrays his
friends, he suspects everybody, he does not do what he should do.
5 He is ungrateful to others, scoffs at the Law, loves to lie—a man with
these many flaws and more will not be advised by you but out of
sheer contrariness refuse to accept what is best for himself. He looks
at earth's levy of armies, the fool, and thinks he has it made,
Madhusūdana, without looking at himself. The dimwitted Dhārtarāṣṭra
has decided that Karṇa alone is able to defeat all others, and he will
not come to peace. He sets the greatest store by Bhīṣma, Droṇa, Kṛpa,
Karṇa, Droṇa's son, and Jayadratha, and does not set his mind on
peace. Janārdana, the Dhārtarāṣṭras, and Karṇa have made up their
minds that the Pārthas cannot look Bhīṣma, Droṇa, and Kṛpa in
the eye.
10 "While you are striving for peace and hope for brotherliness, all
the sons of Dhṛtarāṣṭra are agreed that they will not return to the
Pāṇḍavas what is theirs, Keśava. They are determined and it is
pointless to talk to them. When good and bad advice are all the
same, Madhusūdana, a wise man holds his tongue, like a singer
before a deaf audience. You should not talk to them; they are
ignorant fools who overstep the bounds, Mādhava; you should no
more talk to them that a brahmin talks to *cāṇḍālas*. Relying on his
strength, he is fool enough not to follow your advice, so your words
15 will be useless. It does not seem right to me, Kṛṣṇa, for you to
descend among all those villains where they are huddling together;

it does not seem right for you to warn them off, when they are ill-intentioned, untaught, numerous, and villainous. He will not accept what is best for himself, for he has never heeded his elders and he is emboldened by delusions of wealth, proud of his youth, and intransigent. He also has a strong army. If you speak, Madhusūdana, he will mistrust you completely and not follow your advice. Janārdana, all the Dhārtarāṣṭras are convinced that even Indra and the
20 Immortals cannot defeat their army now. When they are so disposed, and moved solely by desire and anger, your words, however effective, will have no effect.

Duryodhana stands in the midst of his army
Of elephants, chariots and horses, the fool,
And without a sense of foreboding he thinks
That all of earth has been conquered by him.

Dhṛtarāṣṭra's son has set his sights
On an empire on earth without any rivals.
No peace can be gained from one so decided
Who thinks he can hold all the wealth that he found.

All warriors of earth have gathered together
And the kings have joined with the rulers of countries
In Duryodhana's cause to war on the Pārthas:
Earth is overturned and cooked by Time!

They have old feuds with you, all of them,
You have robbed these kings of their properties, Kṛṣṇa;
Out of terror for you these heroes rely
On the Dhārtarāṣṭras and stick with Karṇa.

25 All warriors, eager to war on the Pārthas,
Will risk their lives with Duryodhana,
And for you then to enter and sit in their midst
Is, heroic Dāśārha, far from my mind!

Enemy-plougher, why should you go in amidst these vile men, where they are huddled together? But in any case, strong-armed lord, not even the Gods can best you. I know your power, manhood, and spirit, enemy-killer. I have the same affection for you as for the Pāṇḍavas, Mādhava, and I speak out of love, great respect, and friendship.

The blessed Lord said:

91.1 You have spoken as a man of wisdom should speak, as a man of vision should speak; you have spoken to me as a friend like you should speak to a friend like me, truly and consistent with Law and

Profit, as it befits you; you have spoken to me like a father or mother.
What you tell me is true, to the point, and right. Now listen to the
reason why I came, Vidura, and pay attention.
5 Steward, I came to the Kauravas with full knowledge of the
wickedness of Dhṛtarāṣṭra's son and the enmity of the barons. But
magnificent would be the Law of him who were to set free the whole
upside-down earth with horses, chariots, and elephants! Even if a
man, while trying to the best of his ability, cannot accomplish a task
of Law, he still—and I have no doubt of that—gains the merit of that
Law; for the Law-wise know that a man may plot some evil deed,
yet not agree to do it, and thus not incur the fruit of that misdeed.

So I too shall attempt to make peace without dissembling, Steward,
to stop a war between the Kurus and Sṛñjayas, who are doomed to
perish. This very disaster of the greatest horror is now upon the
Kurus, and it is the doing of Karṇa and Duryodhana, but they are
10 all involved. The wise know that he who does not run to the rescue
of a friend who is plagued by troubles and does not try to help him
as far as he can is guilty of cruelty. Go as far as grabbing him by the
hair to keep a friend from committing a crime, and no one can blame
you, for you tried your best.

The Dhārtarāṣṭra and his councilors should accept my advice,
Vidura, which is appropriate, healthy, beneficial, and in keeping with
Law and Profit. For I shall strive for the good of Dhārtarāṣṭras and
Pāṇḍavas alike, without any dissembling, and of all the barons on
earth. If Duryodhana distrusts me when in fact I am attempting to
15 do what is right, the affection of my heart shall be free from debt. If a
friend does not intervene in a breach between kinsmen as best he
can, but stays aloof, the wise know that he is not a friend. Those
ignorant of the Law, or foolish, or hostile will not say of Kṛṣṇa that
he failed to try and stop the enraged Kurus and Pāṇḍavas when he
could.

No, I have come to help the cause of both parties, and having
made the attempt I shall be without blame before all men. If that
child hears my healthy advice that speaks to both Law and Profit
and does not need it, he shall be the victim of his fate.

If I can make peace between Kurus and Pāṇḍus
Without hurting the cause of the Pāṇḍavas,
I shall have earned outstanding merit
And set free the Kurus from certain death.

20 And if Dhṛtarāṣṭra's sons will heed
The sage and apposite words I speak
For their Law and Profit, which save their health,
The Kurus shall praise me for having come.

Also, all the kings of earth together do not suffice to stand up to me in battle when I am angry, no more than deer stand up to a lion!

Vaiśaṃpāyana said:

Having thus spoken, the bull of the Vṛṣṇis, fountain of joy for the Yadus, lay down on a bed that was gentle to the touch.

Vaiśaṃpāyana said:

92.1 While these two sagacious men were thus conversing, the starry
night went by propitiously. It was as though with reluctance that the
great-spirited Vidura, listening to the varied talk of Law, Profit, and
Pleasure of boundlessly splendid Keśava in apt conversations, and
Kṛṣṇa himself saw the night pass. Then many bards and minstrels
with clear voices awakened Janārdana Keśava with the sound of
5 conches and drums. The Dāśārha, bull of all the Sātvatas, rose and
performed all the necessities of the morning. After bathing and
murmuring the formulas and offering into the fire, the Mādhava,
well-adorned, worshiped the rising sun.
Thereupon Duryodhana and Śakuni Saubala came to the
unvanquished Kṛṣṇa Dāśārha, while he was worshiping the dawn,
and told him that Dhṛtarāṣṭra was in the assembly hall with Bhīṣma
and the Kurus, and all the kings of earth: "They are waiting for you,
Govinda, as in heaven the Immortals wait for Śakra!" Govinda
10 greeted them both with the kindliest courtesy. Then, when the sun
had fully risen, Janārdana, enemy-tamer, presented the brahmins
with gold, clothes, cows, and horses. After the unvanquished Dāśārha
had given away largess and stood waiting, his charioteer arrived and
greeted him. Knowing that the divine chariot was ready, which was
capable of making the sound of a monsoon cloud and was ornamented
with all manner of gems, the spirited Janārdana circumambulated the
fire and the brahmins, put on his Kaustubha jewel, and, blazing with
superb fortune, Kṛṣṇa Śauri, joy of all Yadus, ascended the chariot,
15 surrounded by Kurus and guarded by his Vṛṣṇis. Vidura, who knew
all the Laws, ascended after the Dāśārha, the chief of all breathing
creatures and first of all upholders of the Law. Duryodhana and
Śakuni Saubala followed Kṛṣṇa the enemy-burner on a second chariot.
Sātyaki and Kṛtavarman and the Vṛṣṇis rode behind Kṛṣṇa on
chariots, horses, and elephants. As they proceeded, their rattling
chariots, provided with golden accoutrements and yoked with the
finest steeds, sparkled brightly. In a while the sagacious Kṛṣṇa, ablaze
with good fortune, came upon the main road, which was swept and
20 sprinkled, and walked by royal seers. While the Dāśārha progressed,
drums were struck and conches blown and other instruments
sounded. Youthful champions of all the world, striding like lions,
enemy-burners, went along around Śauri's chariot. Preceding Kṛṣṇa

were many thousands of men in colorful and wondrous dress,
carrying swords, javelins, and other weapons. Over a hundred
elephants and horses by the thousands followed the unvanquished
Dāśārha hero on his progress. The whole town of the Kurus had
come to the road, eager to see Janārdana, tamer of enemies, with
25 oldsters and young people and womenfolk. The mansions were so
crowded with women who had come out on the balconies in large
numbers that they seemed to sway under the burden.

Slowly he went on amidst the praises of the Kurus, lending his ear
to various addresses and returning honor where fitting, while looking
about him, until he reached the hall; and all the skies resounded with
the sounds of the conches and flutes of Keśava's escort. The entire
assembly of boundlessly splendid kings quivered with joy in
anticipation of Kṛṣṇa's arrival. As Kṛṣṇa drew nearer, the kings
shuddered on hearing the clangor of the chariot, which boomed like
30 a raincloud. The bull of all Sātvatas then reached the gate of the hall;
and Śauri descended from his chariot as from a peak of Mount Kailāsa.
Then he entered the hall, which loomed like a mountain or a cloud,
blazing with splendor, the image of the seat of great Indra. The
glorious man took Vidura and Sātyaki each by the hand, outshining
with his luster the Kurus, O king, as the sun outshines the stars.
Duryodhana and Karṇa were in front of Vāsudeva, and behind Kṛṣṇa
were Kṛtavarman and the Vṛṣṇis. Following Dhṛtarāṣṭra's lead
Bhīṣma, Droṇa, and the others all rose from their seats and honored
35 Janārdana. At the Dāśārha's entrance the wise and glorious king with
the vision of insight stood up with Bhīṣma and Droṇa; and when
great King Dhṛtarāṣṭra, lord of the people, stood up, the thousands
of kings rose all around. At Dhṛtarāṣṭra's command a seat had been
arranged for Kṛṣṇa, wrought with gold and handsome all over.

Smiling, the Law-spirited Mādhava greeted the king, Bhīṣma, and
Droṇa and the other kings according to seniority; and all kings on
earth and the Kurus paid Keśava Janārdana proper homage when he
40 had come into the hall. Standing amidst the kings, the enemy-burner
Dāśārha, conqueror of enemy cities, saw the seers hovering in the
sky. While watching the seers, headed by Nārada, the Dāśārha said
softly to Bhīṣma Śāṃtanava, "Sire, the seers have come to watch this
earthly assembly. They should be invited and honored with seats and
full hospitality. No man can sit before they are seated. Let homage be
paid at once to these sages, whose souls have been perfected."
Śāṃtanava, seeing the seers at the gate, hurriedly ordered the
45 servants: "Seats!" and they brought large and wide smooth seats
that sparkled with gold and gems. When the seers had seated
themselves and accepted the guest gift, Kṛṣṇa himself sat down, and
so did the kings then. Duḥśāsana showed Sātyaki his ranking seat,

and Vivimśati brought a golden stool for Kṛtavarman. Not far from
Kṛṣṇa, Karṇa and Duryodhana, great-spirited and truculent, shared
the same seat. Śakuni, prince of Gāndhāra, guarded by his Gāndhāras
50 took his seat with his son, O lord of the people. The sagacious Vidura
sat down on a gem-encrusted stool covered with a white deerskin, so
close that he touched Śauri's seat.

All the kings on earth gazed long at the Dāśārha and were not sated watching Janārdana as though drinking Elixir. Janārdana, dark as flax blooms and robed in yellow, glistened in the middle of the hall like a sapphire set in gold. All fell silent, intent upon Govinda, and not a man there said anything anywhere.

Vaiśampāyana said:

93.1 While all those kings were sitting in silence, Kṛṣṇa, teeth sparkling,
began to speak in a voice that sounded like a drum. Like a cloud at
the end of the hot season the Mādhava, while facing Dhṛtarāṣṭra,
spoke so that the whole hall heard him.

"Bhārata! May there be peace between Kurus and Pāṇḍavas
without any war effort on the part of the heroes—this is what I have
come to accomplish. Sire, I have no other statement to make to you
that could more redound to your benefit, for you yourself, enemy-
5 tamer, know all there is to know. This lineage of yours is today the
highest among all kings, gifted with learning and conduct, enhanced
by all good qualities, O king. The Kurus are distinguished by their
sense of compassion, their sympathy for others, their lack of cruelty,
Bhārata, their uprightness, forebearance, and truthfulness. In a lineage
so noble and great, king, anything unseemly, especially on your part,
is out of character. For you, chief of the Kurus, are the chief
restrainer of the Kurus when they stray into falsity, with either
outsiders or kin, friend.

"Kauravya! Your sons led by Duryodhana have turned their backs
10 on Law and Profit and have strayed into cruelty. They are misguided,
they have overstepped the bounds, their minds have been carried
away by greed with regard to their own closest relatives, and you
know it, bull of the Bharatas. A terrifying disaster is looming for the
Kurus, which, if ignored, shall cause the destruction of the earth,
Kauravya. But it can be appeased, Bhārata, if you want that, for to
my mind, bull of the Bharatas, peace is not difficult. Peace depends
on you, king, and on me, lord of the people: steady your sons,
Kauravya, and I shall steady the others. Your sons and their followers
have to obey your command, Indra of kings, and it is mightily
15 profitable for them to submit to your authority. What benefits you,
king, benefits the Pāṇḍavas, who wait on your word while I am
trying for peace. Ponder it all yourself and act accordingly, lord of

the people: you can unite the Bhāratas, king of the country! Sire, protected by the Pāṇḍavas, abide by Law and Profit, for they cannot be defeated as they are, however much you may try, my king.

"Not Indra himself and the Gods—let alone human kings—would be able to vanquish you if protected by the great-spirited Pāṇḍavas! If you had on your side Bhīṣma, Droṇa, Kṛpa, Karṇa, Viviṃśati,
20 Aśvatthāman, Vikarṇa, Somadatta, Bāhlīka, the Saindhava, the Kālinga, and the Kāmboja Sudakṣiṇa, *and* Yudhiṣṭhira, Bhīmasena, the Left-handed Archer, the twins, the mighty Sātyaki, and the warlike Yuyutsu, who in his right mind would start a war with them, bull of the Bharatas? With the Kurus and the Pāṇḍavas, enemy-killer, you can become the paramount lord of the earth, unassailable to your enemies! The kings of the earth, now your equals or betters, king of the earth, will ally themselves with you, enemy-tamer! Then, guarded by sons, grandsons, brothers, fathers, and friends on all sides, you
25 will be able to live a happy life. Put them first, treat them well as before, and you shall enjoy all of earth entire, king of the earth. For together with all the Pāṇḍavas and your own sons, Bhārata, you shall defeat all other enemies; it is all your gain. Enemy-burner, you shall enjoy the land that they have won for you, if you are united with sons and councilors, king of men.

"But, if there be war, Mahārāja, it will be a holocaust, king, a holocaust for both sides, and what Law do you perceive in that? Tell me, king, bull of the Bharatas, what happiness will you find, with
30 the Pāṇḍavas or your mighty sons slain in battle? They are all heroes, expert armsmen, eager to fight, the Pāṇḍavas and your people—protect them from great peril. We shall no more see any of the Kurus and Pāṇḍavas, when on both sides the champions lie wasted on the battlefield, struck from their chariots by chariot fighters. For the kings of earth have closed rank, best of kings, and, overpowered by rage, will slaughter your people! Save the world, king, do not let your people die! When you come back to normalcy, there can be a respite, joy of the Kurus. Save all these nobles, pure, generous, modest, and of high lineages, who are allied with one another; save them, king,
35 from great peril. Let these kings join one another in a spirit of peace, let them eat and drink together, and return home in their handsome robes and beautiful garlands, bull of the Bharatas, and, while honoring one another, bury their grudges and feuds, enemy-burner. Now that so much of your life span is past, let there once more be the good feeling for the Pāṇḍavas which you had before, bull of the Bharatas. As children deprived of their father they were reared by yourself: protect them as well as your sons, for that is fitting, bull of the Bharatas, now and forever. When they had lost their father, you yourself reared them, bull of the Bharatas; now protect them as well

as your sons, as is fitting. For they deserve your protection, particularly in a calamity, lest both your Law and your Profit be mortally wounded, bull of the Bharatas.

40 "Sire, the Pāṇḍavas salute and placate you. And they say to you: 'At your honor's behest we and our followers have suffered misery while we lived in the forest for these twelve years, and also for a thirteenth year living unknown among people. We were determined, king, thinking that our father would stand by the covenant. We have not broken the compact: the brahmins know it full well, father. Therefore stand by your covenant with us, bull of the Bharatas! We have suffered enough, king; now we should regain our share of the kingdom. Pray save us, joining Law and Profit correctly. For looking
45 upon you as our guru we have endured many hardships. Act toward us like a father or mother. The mode of a student's conduct toward his guru is of grave import, Bhārata. For if we stray, it is our father who puts us straight: set us on the right path, king, and you too, remain on yours!

"And to this assembly, bull of the Bharatas, your sons say: 'Among assemblymen who know the Law the unseemly is out of place. Where Law is killed by Unlaw, where truth is killed by lie, there the assemblymen who witness this are themselves killed. When a Law pierced by Unlaw comes to an assembly and they do not cut out the thorn, the assemblymen themselves are pierced. Law uproots them as a river uproots the trees on its banks.'

50 "Bull of the Bharatas, they are speaking the truth, looking to the Law and sitting in silent reflection, and the Law is what is proper. What else can you reply to them, lord of the people, but that you will return their share to them? Let the kings who are sitting here in assembly speak out, if I have considered Law and Profit and spoken the truth. Bull of the barons, set these barons free from the noose of death! Make peace, best of the Bharatas, do not fall victim to anger. Give the Pāṇḍavas their paternal portion as is just, and enjoy henceforth your pleasures with your sons, your task fulfilled. You know that Ajātaśatru always stands by the Law of the strict and that
55 he acts toward you and your sons accordingly, king of men. He whom they had plotted to burn, he who was cast out, he whom you and your sons banished to Indraprastha, now once more relies on you. While living in his city he subjugated all the kings and placed you at their head, king, and he never overreached you. While he was acting thus, Saubala played the final trick on him, for he wanted to seize his kingdoms, treasure, and grain. Reduced to such a state and seeing Kṛṣṇā brought into the hall, Yudhiṣṭhira of immeasurable soul yet did not swerve from the Law of the baronage.

"I wish the best for you and them, Bhārata, of Law, Profit, and

60 Pleasure. Do not destroy your subjects, king. Restrain your sons who
have gone too far in their greed, thinking the profitless profitable and the profitable profitless to themselves. The enemy-taming Pārthas stand ready to obey, and they stand ready to fight. Take your stand, enemy-killer, on what is healthiest for you."

All the kings applauded his words in their hearts, but no one came to the fore to speak.

5(54a) Dambhodbhava

5.94 (B. 96; C. 3448–500)
94 (96; 3500). Rāma speaks. King Dambhodbhava, conceited, searches earth for his match, in spite of the remonstrations of the brahmins (1–10). They tell him of the invincible heroes Nara and Nārāyaṇa, who are now retired as ascetics on Mt. Gandhamādana (10–15). Dambhodbhava marches out and finds the pair, whom he asks for a match. They first decline (15–20), then agree: Nara picks up some reed stalks with which he hits Dambhodbhava's troops in the eyes, ears, and noses (20–30). Dambhodbhava prostrates himself (30–35). Rāma reveals that Arjuna and Kṛṣṇa are Nara and Nārāyaṇa (35–40).

Vaiśaṃpāyana said:

94.1 When the great-spirited Keśava had spoken, all the assemblymen
sat frozen with goose flesh, and all the kings thought in their hearts, "What man could reply to that?" And while all those kings remained silent, Rāma Jāmadagnya spoke up in the assembly of the Kurus: "King, listen to this one parable and trust it is true. When you have heard it, take to heart what is best for you, if indeed you think so."
5 Of yore there was a universal king by the name of Dambhodbhava,
who, so we have heard, enjoyed the entire earth. This mighty warrior used to rise every morning when the night had passed, and sit there questioning the brahmins and barons. "Is there a man," he would say, "be he a serf, or a commoner, or a baron, or even an arms-bearing brahmin, who is my equal or better in battle?" The king went about the earth with this question, thinking of nobody else, so drunk was he with great pride.

Now learned brahmins who feared nothing and were not cowed
10 tried to stop the king who kept boasting all the time, but though

restrained he kept questioning the twiceborn, prideful and drunk with his fortune. The brahmins, ascetic, great-spirited, and observing the vows of the Veda, spoke blazing with anger to that braggart king, "King, you will never emulate two lionlike men who have fought battles in many incarnations!" At these words the king again interrogated those brahmins: "Where are those heroes? Where were they born? What did they do? Who are they?

The brahmins said:

Nara and Nārāyaṇa, two ascetics, so we have heard, who have
15 come to the world of men. Fight with them, king. It is said that both great-spirited men, Nara and Nārāyaṇa, are performing indescribably severe self-mortifications on Mount Gandhamādana.

Rāma said:

The king mustered a large army with six divisions and impatiently marched out to the region where the two undefeated heroes dwelled. He found the best of men wasted with hunger and thirst, held together by their veins, and emaciated by cold winds and the heat of the sun. He approached them, clasped their feet and asked their health. They welcomed the king with roots and fruit, a seat, and water, then addressed him, "What needs to be done?"

Dambhodbhava said:

20 I have conquered earth with my two arms, slain all my enemies, and now I have come to this mountain to fight with you. Let that be the guest gift. I have wanted this for a long time.

Nara and Nārāyaṇa said:

Best of kings, anger and greed are banished from this hermitage. There is no fighting in this retreat, whence weapons, whence malice? Seek your fight elsewhere: there are many barons on earth.

Rāma said:

Despite their words he insisted. Though they excused themselves and placated him many times, Dambhodbhava, eager to fight, challenged the two ascetics. Thereupon Nara took a fistful of reeds, Kaurava, and said: "Come and fight then, bellicose baron! Take up all your arms and array your army. I shall relieve you of your faith in war for evermore!"

Dambhodbhava said:

25 If you think that a sufficient weapon to deal with us, ascetic, I shall fight you nevertheless, for I have come wanting to fight.

Rāma said:

Upon saying this, Dambhodbhava pelted the ascetic on all sides with a shower of arrows, wishing to kill him with his army. The hermit rendered useless the gruesome arrows the king shot, though they were capable of cutting up the bodies of enemies, and warded them off with his reeds. Then he cast forth at him his terrible reed

weapon, which was impossible to counter, and a miracle happened:
that hermit marksman by his magic power hit the eyes, ears, and
noses of the troops with his reeds.
30 When the king saw the sky white with massed reeds, he fell at
Nara's feet and said, "Blessings be upon me!" Nara, safe refuge for
those who sought it, O king, said to him, "Be brahminic and Law-
spirited, and do not act thus again. Do not, possessed with pride,
abuse anyone ever, be he lesser or better than you. That, king, will
be your highest good. Achieve wisdom, discard greed and selfishness,
possess yourself, and, self-controlled, forgiving, gentle, and safe,
protect your subjects, king. Go with my blessing, you have my leave,
do not act this way again. At our behest ask the brahmins their
35 health!" Thereupon the king saluted the feet of the two great-
spirited hermits and returned to his city and piled up much Law.
"Very great was the feat that Nara wrought of yore, and Nārāyaṇa
was still greater than he, because of his very many holy qualities.
Therefore shed your pride, king, and go to Dhanaṃjaya before he puts
an arrow on his great bow Gāṇḍīva. He has the Kākudīka, Śuka,
Nāka, Akṣisaṃtarjana, Saṃtāna, Nartana, Ghora, and the
Ājyamodaka weapon in the eighth place. All men hit by these
weapons go to their death, or gesticulate insanely, go out of their
40 minds, fall asleep, jump about, or vomit, urinate, cry, or laugh without
stopping. Countless are the Pārtha's virtues and Janārdana surpasses
him.
"You yourself have known him as Kuntī's son Dhanaṃjaya, but
know, great king, that Arjuna and Keśava, champions and bulls
among men, are Nara and Nārāyaṇa. If you know this and do not
distrust me, make a noble resolve and make peace with the Pāṇḍavas,
Bhārata. If you think it is best that there be no breach with you, then
make peace, best of the Bharatas, and do not set your mind on war.
45 Your lineage, best of the Kurus, is highly esteemed on earth, and
must remain so. Be blessed, and ponder your own interest."

5(54b) Mātali

5.95–103 (B. 97–105; C. 3501–713)
95 (97; 3501). Kaṇva speaks, glorifying Kṛṣṇa and urging Duryodhana to make peace (1–10). Indra's charioteer Mātali has a nubile daughter, for whom he cannot find a suitable husband; he descends to the earth (10–20).

96 (98; 3522). He meets Nārada, who will be his guide; they visit Varuṇa (1–5). Nārada describes Varuṇa's world, inhabited by defeated demons and divine weapons (5–25).
97 (99; 3547). The World of the Elephants, with the city of Pātāla, Asura fire, the elephants Airāvata, etc., Daityas, ascetics, and a mysterious egg (1–20).
98 (100; 3567). Hiraṇyapura of the Daityas with beautiful mansions (1–20).
99 (101; 3586). The World of the Garuḍas, many of whom are enumerated (1–15).
100 (102; 3602). Rasatala with the cow Surabhi and her offspring; she was born from the ocean when it was churned (1–15).
101 (103; 3617). Bhogavatī of the Snakes, many of whom are enumerated (1–15). Mātali spies a handsome Snake, Sumukha, after whom he inquires as a prospective son-in-law (15–25).
102 (104; 3643). Nārada introduces Mātali to Sumukha's grandfather Āryaka (1–10). Āryaka relates that Sumukha's father was eaten by Garuḍa, who soon will return for Sumukha himself. Mātali remains firm in his desire (10–20). He takes Sumukha to Indra, who is being visited by Viṣṇu. Viṣṇu tells Indra to give Sumukha the Elixir; Indra gives him longevity (20–25).
103 (105; 3674). Garuḍa is enraged and berates Indra, boasting of his might (1–15). Viṣṇu intervenes and asks Garuḍa to support his right arm. Garuḍa collapses and asks for mercy (15–20). Likewise Duryodhana should not challenge the Pāṇḍavas (20–25). Duryodhana pays no heed (25).

Vaiśaṃpāyana said:

.1 After hearing Jāmadagnya speak, the venerable seer Kaṇva, too, spoke to Duryodhana in the assembly of the Kurus: "Brahmā, grandsire of the world, is indestructible and eternal, and so are the blessed seers Nara and Nārāyaṇa. Of all the Ādityas, Viṣṇu alone is everlasting, invincible, unending, eternal lord and master. The others, sun, moon, earth, water, wind, fire, space, planets, and constellations, are subject to death; when the end of the world comes, they abandon the universe and die, and all are created over and over again. Others, like men, game, fowl, animals, and other creatures inhabiting the

world of the living, are quick to die. Kings, having for the most part
enjoyed their fortunes, at the end of their life span return to death
to reap the reward of good and bad deeds.
"You should make peace with the sons of Dharma; let the Pāṇḍavas
and Kurus rule the world. Suyodhana, do not think you are strong,
10 for the strong are judged by the strong, Kaurava: among the strong
just strength is not strength, Kaurava; all the Pāṇḍavas are strong,
for they have the prowess of Gods.
"On this they quote this ancient story of Mātali, who searched for
a suitor to whom to give his daughter."
Mātali is the name of the esteemed charioteer of the king of the
three worlds. In his household there was one girl, world-famous for
her beauty, known by the name of Guṇakeśī, and lovely as a Goddess.
In beauty and luster she surpassed all other women. Knowing that it
was time to marry her off, Mātali and his wife gave much worried
15 thought to the matter, king. "Fie upon the growing up of a daughter
in the families of men of grave habits, elevated, renowned, and rich in
character. A daughter puts in jeopardy three good families at once:
her mother's, her father's, and that into which she marries. With my
mind's eye I have fathomed and searched the worlds of both Gods
and men, but no one of Gods, Daityas, Gandharvas, or men pleases
me as a suitor, nor one of the many seers."
At night Mātali consulted with his wife Sudharmā and decided to
20 journey to the world of the Snakes: "Neither among Gods nor men
do I see a suitor equal in beauty to Guṇakeśī, but surely there will be
someone among the Snakes." Having consulted Sudharmā, he
circumambulated her, kissed his daughter on the head and entered
earth.

Kaṇva said:

96.1 On his way Mātali happened to encounter the great seer Nārada,
who was journeying to visit Varuṇa. Nārada said to him, "Where are
you going, sir? On an errand of your own, charioteer, or on orders of
the God of the Hundred Sacrifices?" At this question of Nārada, who
was traveling, Mātali told him of his business with Varuṇa, and
Nārada said, "Let us travel together. I have left heaven to visit the
5 Lord of the Waters. I shall explain everything to you while I show
you the surfaces of the earth. When we find some suitable suitor
there, we shall both approve him, Mātali."
Mātali and Nārada plunged together into earth, and the great-spirited pair visited the World Guardian, who is the Lord of the
Waters. Nārada received the honors due a divine seer and Mātali
those due to great Indra. In cheerful spirits they mentioned their
business and with Varuṇa's leave explored the World of the Snakes.

Nārada gave the charioteer a complete explanation of all the creatures that dwell inside the earth.

Nārada said:

10 You have now seen Varuṇa, my friend, amidst his sons and
grandsons. Observe the seat of the Lord of the Waters, which is
beautiful everywhere and opulent. This is the wise son of Varuṇa, lord
of the Cows, who surpasses him in character, conduct, and purity.
He loves this son Puṣkara of the lotus eyes, this handsome and
good-looking man, whom the daughter of Soma chose as her husband,
she whom they call Jyotsnākālī, a second Śrī in beauty. It is said that
he, the son of a Cow, was made the eldest son of Āditya himself.

Behold the solid golden palace of Vāruṇī, by obtaining which the
15 *sura* Gods became Suras, O friend of the king of the Suras. And all
these radiant weapons you see, Mātali, are those of the Daityas who
were ousted from kingship. Being indestructible, as they say, the
weapons still survive, Mātali, and, now won by the Gods, require great
power to be used. Here live the tribes of the Rākṣasas and Bhūtas,
who wielded celestial weapons but were defeated by the previous
Gods. Here a brilliant fire lies awake in the sea of Varuṇa, and also
Viṣṇu's discus, which is permeated by smokeless fire. Here is the bow
made of rhinoceros horn, which has been fashioned for the
destruction of the world; because it is always guarded by the Gods,
20 it is known as the bow Gāṇḍīva. Whenever the occasion arises, it
wields the power of a hundred thousand vital breaths, always and
assuredly.

This is the first-born Staff, created by Brahmā who speaks the
brahman, which punishes those kings allied with the Rākṣasas who
otherwise escape punishment. This is the mighty weapon of the kings
of men invigorated by Śakra, a glorious tool in the hands of the sons
of the King of the Waters. Here in the umbrella room stands the
umbrella of the King of the Waters, which rains cool water all around
like a cloud. The water that falls from this umbrella is pure as the
25 moon, but being obfuscated by darkness it cannot be seen. Many are
the wonders that may be seen here, Mātali, but to examine them
further would interfere with our business; therefore let us go on at
once.

Nārada said:

97.1 Here, at the navel of the World of the Elephants, rises the city
renowned as Pātāla, which is inhabited by Daityas and Dānavas.
Standing and moving creatures which are washed down by the waters
and enter it scream loud screams in their terror. Here is the Asura
fire which always burns, feeding on water, but it knows its limits,
bound as it is by its range of action. It is here that the Gods, after

defeating their enemies, drank the Elixir and deposited it, hence it is
5 from here that the waning and waxing of the moon appear. Here is
the divine Horse Head, which at every joint of time emerges in a
golden hue and fills the world with water.

Since all forms in which water appears rain down here, this
superb city is known as Pātāla. It is from here that Airāvata, well
disposed to the world, drinks water with its trunk and then splashes
it on the clouds, which great Indra then causes to rain forth cold
water. Here dwell sea monsters in many shapes and forms, which lie
in the water, drinking the light of the moon. Here many denizens of
Pātāla are dead by day, being pierced by the rays of the sun, but live
10 at night, charioteer: every day the moon when it rises, surrounded
by rays, touches the liquid of the Elixir, and by this touch revives the
creatures. Here, too, dwell the Daityas prone to lawlessness, who,
bereft of their fortune by Vāsava, are now fettered and suppressed by
Time. Here the great lord of all beings named Bhūtapati performed the
severest austerities for the well-being of all creatures.

Here also dwell those brahmins who, emaciated by the study and
transmission of the Veda, observed the vow of the cows, great seers
who abandoned life and won heaven. He is said to observe the vow
of the cow who lies down anywhere, feeds on anything, and covers
15 himself with anything whatsoever. Airāvata, the king of elephants,
and Vāmana, Kumuda, and Añjana, chiefs of elephants, were born
in the lineage of Supratīka.

See if someone here pleases you as a suitor because of his virtues. Then we shall make an effort, Mātali, and go to him and choose him. Here there is this egg, blazing as it were with its luster, which has been lying here in the water since the creation of the creatures without breaking or moving. I have never heard the tale of its birth or creation, and nobody knows its father or mother. They say that at the end of time a vast fire will explode from it that burns down the entire universe, Mātali, with its standing and moving creatures.

Kaṇva said:

20 Hearing Nārada's question Mātali said, "No one pleases me; let us
quickly go elsewhere.

Nārada said:

98.1 This grand city is renowned Hiraṇyapura of the Daityas and
Dānavas, who roam around with a range of a hundred illusions.
Created by Maya in his mind and built by Viśvakarman with no little
effort, it hugs the surface of Pātāla. One time the august Dānavas
lived here when they had been granted a boon, employing their
thousands of illusions. Śakra could not overpower them, nor any
other one among the World Guardians, Varuṇa, Yama, and the Lord

5 of Riches. The Asuras and Kālakhañjas, who sprang from the footstep
of Viṣṇu, and the Nairṛtas and Wizards, who sprang from the Veda
of Brahmā, tusked and gruesome-looking, with the speed and power
of the wind, and possessing the prowess of magic, live here, protecting
themselves. Here dwell the Nivātakavaca Dānavas, berserkers in war,
and you know that Indra cannot put them down. Many a time you,
Mātali, and your son Gomukha broke down before them with Śacī's
consort Śakra and his son.

Mātali, look at those golden and silver mansions, fashioned and
10 adorned with consummate skill, green with beryl, red with coral,
white with sun quartz, and sparkling with diamonds. They shine as
though made of earth or mountain or rock or the stars themselves.
They appear sunlike, and resemble a blazing fire, colorful with gem-
encrusted lattice work, rising tall and compact. It is impossible to
describe the form, material, and quality of these palaces, which are
perfect in proportion and style.

Look at the pleasances of the Daityas, the beds and jeweled, costly
10 vessels and seats, the cloud-shaped hills with creeks, and the freely
moving trees that blossom and yield fruit at will. Is there anyone
here, Mātali, who attracts you as a suitor? Or if you wish, let us go
to another part of earth.

Kaṇva said:

Mātali replied to his questions, "Divine seer, I ought not to do
anything displeasing to the celestials. The Gods and Dānavas are
brothers embroiled in an everlasting feud. How could I desire an
alliance with the enemy side? Let us rather go some other place—I
should not look at Dānavas: I know of myself that I am inclined
enough to give her away!

Nārada said:

99.1 This is the World of the Garuḍas, the birds that feed on the Snakes,
which know no fatigue in valor, traveling, or carrying burdens. This
race has multiplied from the six sons of Vinatā's son Garuḍa,
charioteer, from Sumukha, Sunāman, Sunetra, Suvarcas, the king of
birds Surūpa, and Subala, O Mātali. Hundreds and thousands of
families, descended from the King of Birds, have been born and reared
by the dynasts of the House of Vinatā, who themselves were born in
5 the lineage of Kaśyapa and increased its prosperity. They are all
endowed with fortune, all marked with the Śrīvatsa whorl, all strive
toward good fortune, while maintaining their strength. By their deeds
they are barons, ruthlessly feeding on Snakes, and because of their
destruction of their kinsmen do not attain to brahminhood.

I shall mention the principal ones by name, Mātali, listen. This
race is highly praised because they honor Viṣṇu. Viṣṇu is their deity;

Viṣṇu is their recourse; Viṣṇu is always in their hearts; Viṣṇu is
always their goal. There are Suvarṇacūḍa, Nāgāśin, Dāruṇa,
10 Caṇḍatuṇḍaka, Anala, Anila, Viśālākṣa, Kuṇḍalin, Kāśyapi,
Dhvajaviṣkambha, Vainateya, Vāmana, Vātavega, Diśācakṣus, Nimeṣa,
Nimiṣa, Trivāra, Saptavāra, Vālmīki, Dvīpaka, Daityadvīpa, Sariddvīpa,
Sārasa, Padmakesara, Sumukha, Sukhaketu, Citrabarha, Anagha,
Meghakṛt, Kumuda, Dakṣa, Sarpānta, Somabhojana, Gurubhāra,
Kapota, Sūryanetra, Cirāntaka, Viṣṇudhanvan, Kumāra, Pāribarha,
Harita, Susvara, Madhuparka, Haimavarṇa, Malaya, Mātariśvan,
15 Niśākara, and Divākara. These sons of Garuḍa I mention only by
way of example; they are the principal ones in renown and vigor.
If you have no liking for them, let us go on, Mātali. I shall take you
to a region where you may find what you want.

Nārada said:

100.1 This is the seventh level of earth, named Rasātala, where Surabhi
dwells, the mother of the cows who was born from the Elixir and is
always flowing with milk, which is the source of all good things on
earth—the single matchless taste drawn from the essence of all six
tastes. This flawless cow arose from the mouth of Grandfather of yore,
when he, sated with Elixir, regurgitated its quintessence. From a
stream of her milk falling on the surface of the earth the Sea of Milk
5 was created, a supreme, superb means of purification, which on its
shores is surrounded by patches of foam like blossoms: there dwell the
good seers called Foam-Drinkers. They are called Foam-Drinkers
because they live on that foam, Mātali, and observe severe austerities;
and the Gods are afraid of them.

From Surabhi four other milch cows were born, in each of the
regions, Mātali, who dwell there as the protectresses of the regions
and are known to support them. Surabhi's daughter Surūpā supports
the East, Haṃsakā the South; the western region of Varuṇa is
sustained by Subhadrā, always very powerful and assuming all forms,
10 Mātali; the cow called Sarvakāmadughā maintains the northern
region, famed for its Law, Mātali, which is named after Ilavila's son.

The Gods conjoint with the Asuras churned the water of the ocean,
which was mixed with their milk, after making Mount Mandara the
churning pole; and they extracted the Vāruṇī liquor, Lakṣmī, and
the Elixir, Mātali, and the king of horses Uccaiḥśravas, and that jewel
of gems Kaustubha.

Surabhi yields as her milk the Nectar for the Nectar-Drinkers, the
Libation for the Libation-Drinkers, the Elixir for the Elixir-Drinkers.
On this there was of old a verse sung by the denizens of Rasātala,
an ancient verse still heard and sung by the learned:

15 Neither in the world of the Snakes
Nor heaven or paradise
Is the living as easy as in
The World of Rasātala!

Nārada said:

101.1 This is the city of Bhogāvatī ruled by Vāsuki, which is as lovely as
the beautiful city of the king of Gods, Amarāvatī. Here dwells Śeṣa,
the Snake who carries Earth forever by virtue of his supreme and
most potent austerities. That powerful Snake, who resembles in bulk
the White Mountain and is decked with all manner of ornaments,
carries a thousand on his head and has a tongue of flames. Here live
Surasā's sons, the Snakes, happily in their multitudinous shapes and
5 adornment, marked with gems, *svastikas*, circles, and gourds.
Numbering in the thousands, they are all strong and terrifying by
nature; some have a thousand heads, some five hundred faces, some
a hundred heads, some three, or ten, and others again seven, with
mighty coils and mighty bodies, coiling like curving mountains. There
are here many thousands, millions, and tens of millions of Snakes,
just in one lineage. Hear who are their chiefs.

There are Vāsuki, Takṣaka, Karkoṭaka, Dhanaṃjaya, Kāliya,
10 Nahuṣa, Kambala, Aśvatara, Bāhyakuṇḍa, the Snake Maṇi, Apūraṇa,
Khaga, Vāmana, Elāpatra, Kukura, Kukuṇa, Āryaka, Nandaka,
Kalaśa, Potaka, Kailāsaka, Piñjaraka, and the Snake Airāvata,
Sumanomukha, Dadhimukha, Śankha, Nanda, and Upanandaka,
Āpta, Koṭanaka, Śikhin, Niṣṭhurika, Tittiri, Hastibhadra, Kumuda,
Mālyapiṇḍaka, the two Padmas, Puṇḍarīka, Puṣpa, Mudgaraparṇaka,
Karavīra, Pīṭharaka, Saṃvṛtta and Vṛtta, Piṇḍāra, Bilvapatra,
15 Mūṣikāda, Śirīṣaka, Dilīpa, Śankhaśīrṣa, Jyotiṣka, Aparājita, Kauravya,
Dhṛtarāṣṭra, Kumāra, Kuśaka, Virajas, Dhāraṇa, Subāhu, Mukhara,
Jaya, Badhira, Andha, Vikuṇḍa, Virasa, and Surasa.

These and many others are known as Kaśyapa's sons. Look,
Mātali, to see if anyone pleases you as a suitor.

Kaṇva said:

Mātali, now, who had been staring attentively at one Snake and
appeared delighted with him, asked Nārada, "This one who is
standing in front of Āryaka and Kauravya, radiant and handsome,
20 of what lineage is he the scion? Who is his father, his mother? From
what Snake does he derive? Of what family is he the grand standard?
With his application, fortitude, beauty, and age he attracts my heart,
divine seer, as a worthy husband for Guṇakeśī!"

Noticing Mātali's pleasure at seeing Sumukha, Nārada then
conveyed his standing, birth and feats: "He is a princely Snake, born

in Airāvata's line, by the name of Sumukha, the well-esteemed grandson of Āryaka on his father's side, and of Vāmana on his mother's. His father is the Snake Cikura, who was recently reduced
25 to the five elements by Vinatā's son Garuḍa." Hereupon Mātali said happily to Nārada, "This fine Snake pleases me as a son-in-law, friend. Let us make an effort, for this prince of the Snakes delights me enough for me to give him my daughter, hermit!"

Nārada said:

102.1 This is Mātali, the charioteer and good friend of Śakra. He is pure, full of character and virtue, vigorous, valiant and strong. Besides being his charioteer, he is Śakra's friend and adviser, hardly the lesser of Vāsava in battle after battle. He drives the superb chariot Jaitra, which is yoked with a thousand bay horses, in the battles of Gods and Asuras, using only his wits. Vāsava triumphs over his foes with his arms after *he* has defeated him with the horses. After *he* has struck first, the Slayer of Vala makes his strike.

5 He has a fine-hipped daughter, peerless on earth in beauty, endowed with character, conduct, and virtues, who is known as Guṇakeśī. While he was determinedly roaming the three worlds, my lord of an Immortal's luster, your grandson Sumukha took his fancy as the husband of his daughter. If it so pleases you, dear Āryaka, best of Snakes, you should not delay but at once decide to accept the maiden. May the fine-waisted Guṇakeśī be to your family as Lakṣmī is to Viṣṇu's and Svāhā to the Fire's. Therefore welcome Guṇakeśī for your grandson: she equals him in stature as Śacī matches Vāsava.
10 Although bereaved of his father, we choose Sumukha out of respect for you and Airāvata and for his qualities of character, purity, self-control, and so on. Now that Mātali has come in person, determined to marry off his daughter, it is but meet that you do him honor too.

Kaṇva said:

With his grandson being chosen and his son dead, Āryaka was both happy and sad when he replied to Nārada, "Divine seer, do not think that I do not prize your words, for who would not wish to be allied with this friend of Śakra? However, great hermit, I am troubled by the weakness of the foundation of such an alliance, for he who begot his body, my son, has, O illustrious lord, been devoured by
15 Garuḍa, and we all mourn his fate. Moreover, when Garuḍa went, my lord, he said: "In another month I shall devour Sumukha." We know his determination—it will surely come to pass. And thus my joy has been killed by the words of Suparṇa."

But Mātali said to him, "I have made up my mind: I have chosen your son's son Sumukha to be my son-in-law. This Snake must come with me and Nārada and see Vāsava, the lord of the three worlds and

king of the Gods. I shall find out how much of his life span remains
20 and do my best to obstruct Suparṇa, good Snake. Let Sumukha come
with me to the king of the Gods—and blessing be on you, Snake—for
the success of our task."

Thereupon he took Sumukha, and all these august persons visited Śakra, the illustrious king of the Gods, where he was sitting; and by chance the blessed lord, four-armed Viṣṇu, was also there. Nārada then related everything regarding Mātali. Viṣṇu said to the lord of the worlds, the Sacker of Cities, "Give him the Elixir and make him equal to the Immortals. Thus, by your desire, Mātali, Nārada and Sumukha will all obtain their cherished desire, Vāsava." The Sacker of Cities reflected upon Garuḍa's prowess and said to Viṣṇu, "*You* give it!"

Viṣṇu said:

You are the master of the worlds, whatever moves or stands. Who, my lord, would dare undo what you have given?

Kaṇva said:

Śakra did give the Snake a very long life, but the Slayer of Vṛtra and Vala did not bestow on him a taste of the Elixir. And receiving the boon Sumukha's face became radiant. And he married and went home at his pleasure. Nārada and Āryaka too, having succeeded in their task, returned home joyfully after saluting the illustrious king of the Gods.

Kaṇva said:

103.1 Then mighty Garuḍa heard what had happened, Bhārata—Śakra's
gift of a long life to the Snake. Furious, the bird Suparṇa flew to
Vāsava, stopping the three worlds with the heavy wind of its wings.

Garuḍa said:

My lord, why, after giving me of your own free will a boon when
I was in danger of starvation, have you now contemptuously reneged
on it? The Placer, who is the lord of all creatures, has, ever since the
creation of all creatures, ordained what I should feed on—why have
5 you now rescinded his edict? I have chosen the great Snake and set
the date: I have to support my vast offspring with him. Now that this
intention has been frustrated, I cannot kill another. You play
wantonly, king of the Gods, by your own whims. I shall die now,
and so shall my people and the servants in my house—you can be
pleased, Vāsava! But I deserve no less, Slayer of Vala and Vṛtra, I
who became another's servant while I was king of the three worlds!
As long as you are there, lord of the Gods, Viṣṇu is not the cause of
my servitude, for in you, Vāsava, king of the three worlds, is kingship
10 vested forever. I too have a daughter of Dakṣa as my mother, Kaśyapa
as father, I too can carry all the worlds with ease. My strength too is
vast and unassailable by any creatures. I too have wrought great
exploits in the war with the Daityas. I too have killed Daityas—

Śrutaśri, Śrutasena, Vivasvat, Rocanamukha, Prasabha, and
Kālakākṣa. Do you despise me because I go about zealously on your
younger brother's flagpole and carry him also? Who else is capable of
the burden; who else is stronger than I; who, though superior, carry
15 him and his relations? I have lost your respect, Vāsava, and his as
well, now that I have been contemptuously turned away from my
meal.

Of all the sons of Aditi, who possess strength and prowess, you
surely are by far the strongest: still I carry you untiringly with a
single feather. Think about that quietly, friend—who is the strongest?

Kaṇva said:

When he who carries the chariot wheel heard these menacing
words of the bird, he said to Tārkṣya in order to shake up the
unshakable, "Garutman, you are quite feeble and you think yourself
20 strong! Stop praising yourself in our presence, bird! Not the entire
universe is capable of carrying my body: I myself carry myself, and
you as well. So then support this one right arm of mine. If you can
carry it, your boasting bears fruit."

Thereupon the blessed lord laid his arm on the bird's shoulder, and
the bird collapsed under the weight, confounded out of its wits. It
seemed to the bird that this one arm weighed as much as the entire
earth with its mountains. Yet Acyuta, who was far stronger than that,
did not push it down with his full strength and did not rob the bird
25 of its life. The bird, unwinged, spread-eagled, upset, and confused,
shed feathers under the pressure of the heavy weight. With its head
the bird, the son of Vinatā, bowed to Viṣṇu and, confounded out of its
wits, said wretchedly, "Blessed lord, with the well-shaped arm which
you freely extend and which equals the substance of the world, you
have pushed me to the surface of the earth. Pray forgive, O God, this
befuddled and dimwitted bird, burnt by the fire of strength, which
dwells on your flagpole. I did not know, my Lord God, your extreme
strength, and therefore I thought that no one equaled my own
power."

30 Then the blessed Lord took mercy on Garutman and in a kindly
voice said, "Do not do it again."

"Likewise you too, son of Gāndhārī, live only as long as you do
not assail the heroic sons of Pāṇḍu in battle, little son. Bhīma, greatest
of fighters, the mighty son of the Wind, and Dhanaṃjaya, the son of
Indra—whom will they not kill on the battlefield? Viṣṇu, Wind, Śakra,
Dharma, and the Aśvins, these Gods you can in no way face. Therefore
stop the hostilities and make peace, prince. Protect your lineage
35 through Vāsudeva as your savior. The great ascetic Nārada has been
a witness to all the greatness of Viṣṇu, who is no other than he who
bears the discus and the club."

Vaiśaṃpāyana said:
Duryodhana, who had listened with sighs and frowns, looked at Rādheya and laughed out loud. Flouting Kaṇva's words, the evil man slapped his elephant trunk of a thigh and said, "I shall do as the creator has made me, as the future and my course dictate. What does all this prattling help?

5(54c) Gālava

5.104–21 (B. 106–23; C. 3714–4120)
104 (106; 3714). Janamejaya asks why nobody stopped Duryodhana on his evil course. Vaiśaṃpāyana replies that Nārada did try (1). Nārada warns Duryodhana not to be obdurate like Gālava (5). The God Dharma as Vasiṣṭha asks food from Viśvāmitra, who is practicing tapas *(5–10). Viśvāmitra takes a long time and Vasiṣṭha eats elsewhere; he orders Viśvāmitra to wait with the food for his return; meanwhile Viśvāmitra's student Gālava looks after him (10). After a hundred years Vasiṣṭha returns and eats the food. Pleased, he calls Viśvāmitra a brahmin: thus Viśvāmitra becomes a brahmin (15). Viśvamitra dismisses Gālava, who keeps pressing his guru to demand a gift. Viśvāmitra asks for eight hundred white horses with a black ear each (15–25).*
105 (107; 3741). Gālava is at his wits' end, when Garuḍa appears to help him (1–15).
106 (108; 3761). Garuḍa describes the eastern quarter (1–15).
107 (109; 3779). He describes the southern quarter (1–20).
108 (110; 3801). He describes the western quarter (1–15).
109 (111; 3821). He describes the northern quarter (1–20).
110 (112; 3850). Gālava asks Garuḍa to take him to the East, but is overcome by Garuḍa's speed (1–15). He complains about his debt to Viśvāmitra. They alight on Mt. Ṛṣabha (15–20).
111 (113; 3873). There a brahmin woman, Śāṇḍilī, is doing tapas*; she feeds them (1). Garuḍa wakes up with his wings shorn: Śāṇḍilī's punishment for his unspoken desire to take her to heaven. Upon Garuḍa's prayers she restores the wings (1–15). The two return and meet*

Viśvāmitra, who reminds Gālava of his debt (15–20).
112 (114; 3896). Garuḍa advises Gālava to beg from King Yayāti, to whom he introduces Gālava (1–10) and explains his friend's debt (10–15).
113 (115; 3917). Yayāti confesses he has fallen on hard times (1–5), but will give Gālava his daughter Mādhavī, who will bear four founders of dynasties (5). Gālava accepts her and tries to trade her to King Haryaśva for eight hundred horses (5–20).
114 (116; 3938). Haryaśva has only two hundred such horses, which he will trade for one son by Mādhavī. Vasumanas is born (1–15), and Gālava takes Mādhavī back.
115 (117; 3960). They go to Divodāsa where the story is repeated; Pratardana is born (1–15).
116 (118; 3981). They go to Auśīnara; Śibi is born (1–20).
117 (119; 4002). Garuḍa congratulates Gālava, who rejoins that he is still two hundred horses short. Garuḍa tells him that of the original one thousand horses only six hundred remain (1–5). He should lend Mādhavī to Viśvāmitra in lieu of two hundred horses; he agrees (5–10). Viśvāmitra accepts and begets Aṣṭaka. Gālava dismisses Mādhavī and Garuḍa (10–20).
118 (120; 4026). Yayāti holds a svayaṃvara *for Mādhavī at Prayāga; she chooses the forest where she lives like a doe (1–10). Yayāti dies and goes to heaven (10). Because of his pride Yayāti loses recognition in heaven (15–20).*
119 (121; 4048). Deprived of all recognition, Yayāti is dropped from heaven; he asks that he may fall among good men (1–5). At that time his four daughter's-sons are performing a Vājapeya sacrifice in the Naimiṣa Forest. Yayāti floats down the column of fire from the sacrifice. He identifies himself (5–15). His grandsons press their merit on Yayāti, who declines (15). Mādhavī arrives and identifies his grandsons. Gālava also arrives. Yayāti now accepts the merits of his grandsons, Madhavī, and Gālava (20–25).
120 (122; 4078). Vasumanas bestows the merits of his generosity, forbearance, and maintenance of the sacred fires (1–5), Pratardana those of his warfare (5), Śibi those of his veracity (5–10), Aṣṭaka his merits as sacrificer (10). Yayāti rises from the earth (15).

121 (123; 4097). Yayāti reascends to heaven and is joyously received; Brahmā welcomes him back (1–5). Upon Yayāti's question Brahmā reveals that he lost heaven because of his pride (10–15). Nārada pleads with Duryodhana not to be stubborn and prideful (15–20).

Janamejaya said:

104.1 This man so stubbornly prone to catastrophe, crazed by his greed for the property of others, a friend to ignoble men, resolved upon his own death, the cause of the grief of his kinsmen: adding to his relatives' sorrows, inflicting pain on his friends, and increasing the joy of his enemies—why did his relations not restrain this man from his evil course out of affection? Or why did not the venerable grandfather stop him, as he loved his family?

Vaiśaṃpāyana said:

Indeed, the venerable Bhīṣma did speak words that were fitting, and Nārada too had much to say. Listen.

Nārada said:

5 Rare indeed is a friend who listens, rare a friend with good advice, for wherever the needy friend is, the needed friend is not. Your friends should be heard, I think, joy of the Kurus, and stubbornness abandoned, for obstinacy is a most dangerous course.

On this point they cite this ancient story of how stubbornness was the undoing of Gālava.

In the olden days the God Dharma himself, having become the blessed seer Vasiṣṭha, came to Viśvāmitra, who was practicing austerities, in order to try him. In the guise of one of the Seven Seers, he came, King Bhārata, to Kauśika's hermitage, hungry and in search
10 of a meal. Anxious, Viśvāmitra cooked a *caru* dish of rice, and because of the trouble he took over it, the other did not wait till it was ready but ate the food that other ascetics proffered him.

Finally Viśvāmitra came out carrying the hot rice. "I ate," Dharma said; "you wait a while," and the blessed Lord left. And so the illustrious Viśvāmitra stood there, O king, and carried the cooked food on his head, holding it with both hands. He stood there like a pillar, close to the hermitage, motionlessly feeding on the wind. A hermit, Gālava by name, painstakingly attended on him out of respect and esteem, affectionately wishing to please Viśvāmitra.

15 A hundred years went by before Dharma returned to Kauśika in Vasiṣṭha's guise, wishing for a meal. He saw the food that the great wise seer Viśvāmitra had continued to carry on his head while he lived on the wind. Dharma accepted the food, which was still hot and

fresh, ate, and said, "I am pleased, brahmin seer!" and then the hermit departed. Thus, because of these words of Dharma, Viśvāmitra relinquished his baronial estate and attained brahminhood. And he was pleased.

Thereupon, being satisfied with the obedience and devotion of his
ascetic student Gālava, Viśvāmitra said to him, "Calf, you have my
20 leave. Go wherever you wish, Gālava." Happily Gālava replied to the
good hermit, the illustrious Viśvāmitra, in a winning voice, "What gift should I fetch you to recompense you for acting as my guru? For only that human rite succeeds which is recompensed with stipends; for when the stipends have been paid, the strict man enjoys the acquittal of his debt. The stipend is the rite's reward in heaven, and it is said to be one's peace. What shall I bring as guru's gift? Speak, master!" The blessed Lord Viśvāmitra, aware that he had already been rewarded by Gālava's obedience, repeatedly urged him, "Go now. Go!"

Nevertheless, in spite of Viśvāmitra's repeated urgings that he go,
25 Gālava replied as often, "What shall I give?" Viśvāmitra became
somewhat vexed with the ascetic Gālava's stubborn insistence and said, "Give me eight hundred moon-white horses with a black ear each! Go now, Gālava, and don't be long!"

Nārada said:

105.1 When Gālava had been told this by the wise Viśvāmitra, he could
not sit or lie or eat. Skeletal, greenish, lost in worry and anxiety, grieving beyond measure and burning with exasperation, he complained, "Where are there any wealthy friends, where riches, where a treasure-trove? Where do I get eight hundred moon-white horses? How can I hope to eat, where hope for happiness? Though
5 I am alive, my hopes are shattered—what does it profit me to live? I
shall go to the ocean shore, or far beyond earth, and give up life. What profit is there in living? Where shall a man who is destitute, unfulfilled, deprived of all rewards, carrying the burden of debt, find the happiness he cannot hope for? For one who has consumed the wealth of his friends, which they offered him with affection, and is unable to repay them, death is better than living. If one does not do what he has to do after promising that he would, he is burned by his falseness and his offerings come to nought. There is no beauty to the liar, to the liar no sons are born, no power has the liar—where will
10 he find the good life? Where does an ungrateful man win renown,
where position, where happiness? Let there be no faith placed in the ingrate; for the ungrateful there is no expiation.

"A penniless crook has no life, for where does the crook find

support? The crook who reduces to nought a good deed done to him
surely meets his perdition. I am a crook, an ingrate, a wretch, and a
liar, if, after completing my student tasks, I do not obey my guru's
command. I shall make an incomparable effort and then give up my
life. Never before have I sought anything from the celestials, and all
the Thirty Gods respect me for this at the sacrificial spread. But now
I will go to that highest of deities, the God who is the lord of the
three worlds, Viṣṇu-Kṛṣṇa, the best course of those who must go,
15 him by whose grace all comforts have their place, since he pervades
all Gods and Asuras. I want to see him with all my heart, that eternal
great Yogin."

When he said this, his friend Garuḍa, the son of Vinatā, appeared
to him and joyfully said to him, in order to do him a kindness, "I
regard you as my friend, and friends should help their esteemed friend
to attain the desire he craves, if they have the means. I do have the
means, brahmin. I have talked earlier with Vāsava's younger brother
on your behalf, and he has done my desire. Come, sir, let us go. I
shall take you, if you please, to the end of the world. Hurry, Gālava!"

Suparṇa said:

106.1 Gālava, I have received instructions from the God whose origin is
unknown. Tell me, to which region shall I go first for a visit, to the
East, or South, or the western quarter, or the North, best of the
twiceborn? Where shall I go, Gālava? It is from the East that the sun
rises, which gives being to all worlds. There the austerities of the
Sādhyas take place at dawn. There the first thought was born and the
entire universe was permeated by it, there are the two eyes of the
5 Law and there is the Law itself established, through whose mouths
the oblation is offered and spreads over all regions. It is the gate of
the journey of the day, where of yore, O best of brahmins, the
daughters of Dakṣa gave birth to the creatures; the region where the
sons of Kaśyapa prospered, and the fortune of the Gods is rooted, and
Śakra was consecrated king of the Gods, brahmin seer, and the Gods
piled up ascetic power. It is for this reason that the East is called the
First Quarter, since in the first days it was the first to be covered by
the Gods. Hence the man who wishes happiness should perform the
first divine rites, while the ancient gaze upon the eastern quarter.

10 Here the blessed Lord, who gives being to the worlds, first sang the
Vedas, here the *sāvitrī* was first pronounced by Savitar to the students
of the *brahman*. Here the Sun bestowed the *yajus* formulae, best of the
twiceborn; here at sacrifices the Soma is drunk by those Gods who
have obtained that boon; here the oblation-carrying fires, when
satiated, partake of their own source; here Varuṇa descended to
Pātāla and obtained his fortune; here of yore took place the birth,

firm establishment, and death of ancient Vasiṣṭha, bull of the twiceborn; here occurred ten times ten times the birth of the syllable OM.

It is in the East that the hermits drink the Soma in the *havirdhāna* barn, and that the boar and other beasts of the forest are consecrated by Śakra as the portion of the lesser Gods. And here the rising sun irately kills all malevolent and ungrateful men and Asuras. This is the Gate of the Three Worlds, of heaven and of happiness—the eastern quarter. Let us go there, if you wish, for this favor I must do for him whom I obey. Speak, Gālava, and I will go. Hear now about another quarter.

Suparṇa said:

107.1 In ancient times Vivasvat presented in the course of a *śrauta* rite, so we hear, this region to his guru as his *dakṣiṇā*, and hence it is called the *dakṣiṇā*, the southern quarter. It is here that the party of the Deceased Ancestors of the three worlds is established and that, as they say, the *uṣmapa* Gods have their dwelling. Here dwell, with the Ancestors, the Viśve Devas who, when being honored with sacrifices in the worlds, obtain the same portions thereof. They call this the second Gate of the Law, brahmin. Time here is reckoned by instants and moments. The divine seers always live here, as well as the ancestral and all the royal seers, without a care. It is here that one hears of Law, truth, and *karman*, for here goes he who sinks in himself through *karman*, best of brahmins. This is the region, eminent brahmin, where everyone goes, but being obfuscated by ignorance, they do not attain to happiness. Here many thousands of Nairṛta demons, created hostile, must be faced by those who failed to perfect their souls, bull of the twiceborn. Here, in the arbors of Mt. Mandara and in the dwellings of the brahmin seers, the Gandharvas sing songs that entice mind and thought, brahmin. Here Raivata went to the forest, without wife, councilor, and kingdom, when he heard the sāmans intoned in chant. Here Sāvarṇin and the son of Yavakrīta set the brahminic boundary which the sun does not transgress. Here Pulastya's son Rāvaṇa, king of the Rākṣasas, practiced austerities and chose invulnerability from the Gods as his boon. Here Vṛtra's behavior made him Śakra's foe. Here comes all breathing creatures to return to the five elements, here men of evil acts are cooked, Gālava. Here the river Vaitaraṇī is covered by those who sought to cross it, here one goes to the limit of misery after having gone the limit of pleasure. Upon its return here the sun streams down tasty water, while at reaching the solstice under the stars of Dhaniṣṭhā, it gives forth snow. It was here, Gālava, that long ago, when I was starving and searching for food, I obtained two large embattled creatures, an elephant and a

tortoise. Here the great seer Śakradhānu was born from the sun, the
one whom they know as the divine Kapila, who consumed the sons
of Sagara. Here the perfected brahmins called Śivas, who mastered
the Veda to its end, learned all the Vedas with their Appendices and
attained to Yama's realm. Here is the city of Bhogavatī, ruled by
20 Vāsuki, the Snake Takṣaka, and also Airāvata. Here one encounters,
at the time of death, a vast darkness which is not pierced even by the
sun or black-trailed fire itself. You yourself will travel this road of
misery, Gālava. Tell me if you want to go. Or else, hear from me about
the West.

Suparṇa said:

108.1 This region is the favorite of King Varuṇa, the Lord of Cows, and is
forever the abode of the King of the Waters, indeed his source. It is
here that later in the day the sun dispels its own light, and thus this
quarter is known as the Late Quarter, best of brahmins. Here the
blessed God Kaśyapa consecrated Varuṇa to the kingship of water
creatures and the rule of the sea. After drinking here all six juices of
Varuṇa, the moon is rejuvenated at the beginning of the bright
5 fortnight and dispels the darkness. Here the Wind drove the Daityas
to flight and fettered them, and now they sleep, still panting, under
the oppression of the great Snakes, brahmin. Here the mountain called
Asta receives the loving sun, and from it the western dusk then
spreads. From here issue forth, at the close of the day, night and sleep
as if to steal away half the life span of the world of the living. It was
here that Śakra aborted the Goddess Diti while she was asleep, bearing
her offspring; whereof sprang the band of the Maruts. Here the roots
of the Himālaya reach as far as eternal Mt. Mandara, and not in a
10 thousand years does one reach their end. Here Surabhi, having come
to the shore of the ocean by Mt. Kāñcana and the river Kāñcana,
poured forth her milk. Here in the middle of the ocean can be seen
the trunk of Svarbhānu, resembling the sun, who tries to kill sun
and moon. Here too is heard the wide-ranging sound of Suvarṇaśiras
of the yellow body hair, when he sings forth, invisible and beyond
measure. Here stands Harimedhas' daughter Dhvajavatī in the sky at
the command of the sun, who said, "Stay where you are!" Here wind,
fire, water, and air, O Gālava, lose their unpleasant touch by day and
15 at night. From here on the course of the sun is askew. Here all
celestial bodies enter the orb of the sun, and after making their orbit
for twenty-eight nights with the sun, emerge once more from the sun
to be in conjunction with the moon. Here is the eternal source of the
rivers, from which the ocean springs, here abide the waters of the
three worlds, which are the dwelling place of Varuṇa. Here, too, is
the abode of the King of the Snakes Ananta, here the incomparable

seat of beginningless and endless Viṣṇu. Here is the dwelling of the
Wind, the friend of Fire, and that of the great seer Kaśyapa Mārīca.
20 Thus I have described to you the western road in my account of
the Quarters. Shall we go, Gālava? Tell me, what is your mind, best
of brahmins?

Suparṇa said:
109.1 Inasmuch as one is saved from evil and partakes of the supreme
good, therefore this quarter is called the Northern, the Saving Quarter
by the wise. The road to the field of the northern gold, Gālava, is
known to run between the West and the East. In this most excellent
Northern Quarter, bull of the Bharatas, no people live who are not
gracious, have no control over themselves, or do not abide by the
Law.

Here Kṛṣṇa-Nārāyaṇa and Jiṣṇu, the best of men, dwell in a
5 hermitage at Badarī, as does the eternal Brahmā. Here, on the crest
of the Himālaya, dwells the Great God in all eternity, here the Moon
was consecrated king of the brahmins. Here the Great God received
the Ganges, when she fell from the sky, and bestowed her on the
world of men, great scholar of the Brahman. Here the Goddess
practiced austerities in order to win the Great God. Here desire, anger,
mountain, and Umā took being; here the God of Wealth was
consecrated on Mt. Kailāsa as overlord of the Rākṣasas, Yakṣas, and
Gandharvas, O Gālava. Here is the lovely Caitraratha forest, here the
hermitage of the Vaikhānasas, here the river Mandākinī, here
10 Mt. Mandara, O bull of the brahmins. Here is the Saugandhika forest
guarded by the Nairṛtas, with meadows and banana groves, and here
is the Saṃtānaka range. Here are the celestial chariots of the
perpetually self-controlled Siddhas, who move where they please;
chariots befitting them, which they enjoy as they wish, Gālava.

Here are the Seven Seers and the divine Arundhatī. Here is the
star of Svāti and here does it rise. Here is fixed grandsire Dhruva,
embarked on his sacrifice; the celestial bodies, moon and sun, revolve
around him daily. Here good brahmins guard the Gate of Gāyantikā,
15 the great-spirited and true-spoken hermits named Dhāmas; their
origin is not known, nor their shape, nor the ascetic power they have
accumulated. Here are their thousand of orbits that may be enjoyed
at will, Gālava.

Whenever a man penetrates beyond here he is dissolved, Gālava,
first of the twiceborn. Nobody else has gone there before, bull among
brahmins, except God Nārāyaṇa and the imperishable Jiṣṇu Nara.
Here is the abode called Kailāsa of Ilavila's son and here were born
the ten Apsarās called Vidyutprabhās. Here the Step of Viṣṇu was
placed by the striding Viṣṇu as he bestrode the three worlds—it is in

20 the North, brahmin. Here, at Uśirabīja, King Marutta offered up
sacrifice, best of the twiceborn, where the Golden Pond lies. Here the
spotless, holy, and divine lotus pond of the Himālaya waits in person
upon the great-spirited brahmin seer Jīmūta. Having presented that
entire vast wealth of his to the brahmins, the great seer chose the
forest Jīmūtavana and departed for it. Here the World Guardians
gather every morning and evening, bull of the brahmins Gālava, and
cry out "Who has any need of what?"
Thus this Northern Quarter for its various virtues is famed as the
25 Best, and it is the best in all rites. So have I described in detail the
quarters to you, good friend, all four in succession—to which of them
do you want to go? I am ready, best of brahmins, to show you the
regions and all of earth, brahmin. Mount me, twiceborn one!

Gālava said:
110.1 Garutman, foe of the kings of the Snakes, fair-winged Suparṇa, son
of Vinatā, take me to the East, Tārkṣya, where the two eyes of the
Law are. First go to that quarter which you described first, for you
have declared that the deities are present there. You have truly set
forth that both truth and the Law are there. I wish to meet with all
the deities and again I wish to visit the Gods, younger brother of
Aruṇa.

Nārada said:
Vinatā's son said to the brahmin, "Then mount me!"—and the
hermit Gālava mounted Garuḍa.

Gālava said:
5 As you travel, O eater of Snakes, your beauty shines like that of
Vivasvat himself in the morning, the thousand-rayed Bringer of Light.
I see how the trees, toppled by the wind of your wings, break away
and pursue you in your wake, Bird. With the storm of the wind you
raise you seem to pull with you all of earth with her oceans and
forests, mountains and wildernesses, O roamer of the skies! The
unrelenting hurricane of your tempestuous wingbeat lifts skyward the
water of the sea with its fish, serpents, and crocodiles. Shoals of fish
I see churned up with like bodies and faces, and whales and
10 swallowers of whales, and serpents with the faces of men. The roar of
the ocean deafens my ears, I hear nothing, I see nothing, I do not
know what I am doing here! Please go slowly, remember you may
kill a brahmin! I don't see the sun, good friend, nor the horizons or
the sky, I see only darkness, bird. I cannot make out your body, I only
see your eyes, bird, like two noble gems. I cannot see your body or my
own, but I do see fire rising ever higher from the sea. Suddenly my
eyes are blown out and their light extinguished! Stop now! You have
15 been going a long time, son of Vinatā! I really have no reason at all

to go, eater of Snakes. Stop, tempestuous bird, I cannot stand your speed. I have promised my guru eight hundred shining moon-white stallions with a black ear each, but now I see no way to acquit myself of them, and so I do see my way clear to the abandonment of my life. I have no property at all, or a wealthy friend—not that even great wealth could wipe out my debt.

Nārada said:

While Gālava babbled much and miserably in this fashion, the son
20 of Vinatā replied laughing, while speeding on, "You aren't too clever,
brahmin-seer, if you want to kill yourself. One's time is not of one's
own choosing, for Time is paramount. Why have you not told me
this before? There is a good way to accomplish this. . . .

"Here on the breast of the sea is the mountain called Ṛṣabha. After we have rested and eaten here, we shall return, Gālava."

Nārada said:

111.1 The brahmin and the bird lit on a peak of Mt. Ṛṣabha, and they saw the brahmin woman Śāṇḍilī practicing austerities there. Suparṇa and Gālava saluted her, and she welcomed them; and they sat down on spread grass. They quickly ate cooked food, which had been consecrated with a thrown-offering and a spell; and both fell asleep on the ground, overcome by the food.

After a while Suparṇa woke up and wanted to go; then the bird
5 saw that his wings had fallen off. The bird was a mere ball of flesh
with a face and feet. When Gālava saw him he asked sadly, "What
has happened to you? How long shall we now have to stay here?
Did you think some thought that hurt the Law? Surely I could not
have been a trifling aberration on your part!"

Suparṇa replied to the brahmin, "I did have the notion of taking this sorceress to the seat of Prajāpati, and the Great God, and sempiternal Viṣṇu, where Law and Sacrifice reside, so that she could live there too.

10 "I prostrate myself before you, my lady, and pray you that indeed I had this thought, to my grief to be sure, but it was just to do you a kindness! It was out of respect for you that I did something that displeased you. But be it well done or ill done, pray forgive with magnanimity!"

Placated, she said to the king of birds and bull of brahmins, "Fear
not, you are Suparṇa, Suparṇa. You slighted me, calf, and I do not
suffer slights. From his worlds shall tumble the miscreant who slights
me! Innocent of any blemishes and blameless in my ways, I have
15 embraced strict conduct and thus achieved the highest perfection. With
conduct one gains Law, with conduct one gains wealth, with conduct
one gains fortune; conduct defeats bad augury.

"Now, long-lived bird, go hence as you please. Never despise a

woman even if she is despicable. You shall be strong and powerful as
before." Thereupon his two wings grew even larger than before, and
with Śāṇḍilī's leave he went as he had come. Gālava, however, had
not come across horses of that description.

Then Viśvāmitra happened to see Gālava on the road, and that
20 greatest of speakers said to him in Garuḍa's presence, "The time has
come for you to acquit yourself of the guru's gift you have promised,
or do you think otherwise? I shall wait this much longer. Find a way
to succeed, brahmin!"

Suparṇa said to Gālava, who was most distressed, "Now I myself
have indeed heard what Viśvāmitra said. Come, best of the twiceborn.
Let us take counsel together, Gālava. You cannot sit until you have
given him his entire gift."

Nārada said:

112.1 Suparṇa, greatest of birds, then said to the dejected Gālava, "Since
gold, fashioned in earth by fire and purified by wind, entirely consists
in *hira*, therefore it is called *hiraṇya*. Wealth is *dhana*, because it puts
and keeps man in place—wealth abides forever in the three worlds.
Under the constellations of the Foot of the Stool, with Śukra as lord
of riches, Śukra bestows on men the wealth that they have earned
with their thoughts. Guarded by Aja Ekapād, Ahi Budhnya, and the
Lord of Riches, treasure cannot be obtained if it is unobtainable, bull
5 among brahmins. Without wealth you have no chance to obtain
those horses. Beg a king for wealth, a king born in a dynasty of royal
seers, who without depriving his citizens can make our hearts
content.

"Now there is a king, a friend of mine born in the dynasty of the
Moon. Let us approach him, for he has the greatest fortune on earth.
It is the royal seer Yayāti, son of Nahusa, whose valor is his truth.
At my word and your request, he will give. He once had a fortune as
vast as that of the Lord of Riches; but by giving some of it up, he
sagely cleansed his wealth."

While they were so conversing and pondering the possible, they
10 reached King Yayāti in Pratiṣṭhāna. After receiving the guest gift and
other hospitality, as well as excellent food, Vinatā's son was asked
the purpose of his coming. "Nāhuṣa," he said, "this is my good friend
Gālava, an ocean of austerities. For myriads of years he has been the
student of Viśvāmitra. When his teacher dismissed him, this venerable
brahmin, out of a desire to make some return gift, asked him, 'What
should I give you as a guru's gift?' He asked many times, and his
teacher became a little exasperated and said: 'So give!' while fully
knowing that his means were limited. 'Give me eight hundred shining
15 thoroughbred moon-white horses with a black ear each. Make this
your guru's gift, Gālava, if you please!

"That is what the ascetic Viśvāmitra told him irately. Now this bull

among brahmins is consumed with great anxiety, for he is unable to
make the return gift, and so he seeks help from you. When he has
accepted an alms from you, tiger among men, and is rid of his
trouble, he shall acquit himself of his debt to his guru and practice
great austerity; and he shall apportion a share of his austerities to
you. To the brim he shall fill you who are already full of a royal
seer's austerities. For, ruler of men and lord of the earth, as many
hairs as there are on the body of a horse, so many worlds receive
20 those who give away a horse. He is a fit vessel to receive, you a fit
vessel to give: it will be like milk poured into a conch shell!"

Nārada said:

113.1 Upon these fine and fitting words of Suparṇa, the king pondered
deeply and at last made his decision. A performer of thousands of
sacrifices, a most bountiful lordly giver, Yayāti, king of Matsyas and
Kāśis made his reply. Seeing his dear friend Tārkṣya and the great
brahmin Gālava, and reflecting that he was a model of austerity
and that the begging itself would be renowned as high praise indeed
for himself—"These two have come straight to me, bypassing the
5 other kings of the dynasty of the Sun!"—he said, "Today my birth
has borne fruit, today my lineage has been saved, today this country
of mine has been rescued by you, Tārkṣya, bird sans blame! But I
want to tell you, friend, I am not as wealthy now as you have known
me before, for my wealth has dwindled, friend. Yet I cannot render
your coming fruitless, bird, nor dare I frustrate the expectations of this
brahmin seer. I shall give something that will accomplish his task,
for one who comes and leaves with his hopes dashed burns down
a family.

"They say, Vainateya, that nothing in the world is a greater evil
than saying 'I have nothing' and killing the hope of him who asked
10 'Pray give!' A man of honor who has been cut off with his hopes
dashed and his purpose undone harms the sons and grandsons of
him who fails to do what he is asked. Therefore, Gālava, take this
young daughter of mine, as beautiful as a child of the Gods,
observant of all the Laws, always coveted for her beauty by Gods,
men, and Asuras. For she shall establish four lineages. Kings will
surely give even their kingdoms as her bride price, let alone eight
hundred black-eared horses! Accept from me this my daughter
Mādhavī. It is my desire, my lord, that I shall have daughter's sons."

15 Gālava accepted the maiden, and saying, "Let us look further," he
departed with the bird, taking the maiden along. Said the bird, "You
have found the gate to the horses!" and he took leave of Gālava and
went to his own dwelling place.

When the king of birds had departed, Gālava went on with the
maiden, wondering about kings capable of paying the bride price. He

decided to go to good King Haryaśva Ikṣvāku of Ayodhyā, heroic
leader of a four-membered army, possessor of treasuries, granaries,
and troops, beloved of his citizens, a friend to the brahmins, peaceably
20 looking after his subjects and practicing a high austerity. Gālava the
brahmin approached Haryaśva and said, "This maiden of mine shall
increase families with offspring. Accept her as your wife for a bride
price, Haryaśva. I shall quote you her price. Listen and give thought
to it."

Nārada said:

114.1 King Haryaśva thought many thoughts, and, heaving a deep hot
sigh for the offspring he craved, the good king said, "She is high in
the six high points, slim in the seven slim points, deep in the three
deep points and red in the five red spots. A vision to many Gods and
Asuras, a spectacle to many Gandharvas, she is endowed with many
signs of good augury and capable of bearing many children. She is
capable of giving birth to a Turner of the Wheel! Tell me her bride
price, best of twiceborn, but bear in mind the limits of my wealth."

Gālava said:

5 Give me eight hundred native-born, well-built, moon-white horses
with a black ear each, then this beautiful long-eyed maid shall be
the mother of your children, as the kindling block is the womb of the
offering fires!

Nārada said:

Hearing his words King Haryaśva, who was smitten with desire,
spoke—royal seer to brahmin seer—regretfully to Gālava, "I have
two hundred such horses at hand for you, though I have hundreds
of other desirable steeds in my pastures. I shall beget a single son on
her, Gālava—accord me this desire as a boon!"
10 When the maiden heard this, she said to Gālava, "A certain
speaker of spells once gave me a boon that after each childbirth I
would be a virgin again. Give me to the king and take the fine horses.
You shall have the full eight hundred from four kings, and I shall have
four sons in all. You should collect the prize for your guru with my
help—at least that is what I think, best of brahmins. What do you
think?" At the girl's words the hermit Gālava made his reply to King
15 Haryaśva, "Take the maiden, Haryaśva, first among kings, and beget
one son for a quarter of the bride price."

The king accepted the girl and paid homage to Gālava. And in due
place and time he obtained the son he wanted, by the name of
Vasumanas, who became a king richer than the Vasus, resembling
one of the Vasus, a giver of wealth.

In time the sagacious Gālava returned, and he approached and
addressed Haryaśva, who was in high spirits, "Sire," he said, "a son
has been born to you in the likeness of the morning sun. It is now

time for me, best of kings, to go begging from another king."
20 Haryaśva, who was as true to his promises as to his prowess, handed
back Mādhavī, since those horses were hard to find. Mādhavī
relinquished that blazing regal fortune and at will became a virgin
again, and she followed after Gālava. The brahmin said, "Keep the
horses for the time being," and departed with the girl to King
Divodāsa.

Gālava said:

115.1 There is a mighty king named Divodāsa, the princely overlord of the Kāśis, the son of Bhīmasena. Let us both go there, my dear. Come quickly and do not worry. The king is law-abiding, self-controlled, and true-spoken.

Nārada said:

The hermit approached the king, who received him properly. Thereupon Gālava exhorted the king to beget offspring.

Divodāsa said:

I have already heard about this, brahmin, why say more? As soon
5 as I heard about the matter, good brahmin, I was set on it. It does me
great honor that you passed by other kings and came to me. It shall
doubtless come to pass. I have the same wealth of horses, Gālava,
so I too shall beget one prince on her.

Nārada said:

The good brahmin assented and gave the maiden to the king, who
accepted her with the proper rite. The royal seer made love to her as
the Sun to Prabhāvatī, as Fire to Svāhā, Vāsava to Śacī, Moon to
Rohiṇī, Yama to Dhūmorṇā, Varuṇa to Gaurī, the Lord of Riches to
10 Ṛddhi, Nārāyaṇa to Lakṣmī, the Ocean to the Ganges, Rudra to
Rudrāṇī, and the Grandfather to the Altar. Or as Vasiṣṭha's son to
Adṛśyantī, Vasiṣṭha himself to Akṣamālā, Cyavana to Sukanyā,
Pulastya to Saṃdhyā, Agastya to the Princess of Vidarbha, Satyavān
to Sāvitrī, Bhṛgu to Pulomā, Kaśyapa to Aditi, Rcīka's son to Reṇukā,
Kauśika to the daughter of the Himālaya, Bṛhaspati to Tārā, Śukra
to Śataparvā, Bhūmipati to Bhūmi, Purūravas to Urvaśī, Ṛcīka to
15 Satyavatī, Manu to Sarasvatī. And while King Divodāsa made such
love to her, Mādhavī gave birth to one son, Pratardana.

Then, when the time had come, the venerable Gālava came to Divodāsa and said to him, "Sire, return the maiden to me, but let the horses stay here while I go elsewhere for a bride price, O king." And at the agreed time the law-spirited King Divodāsa, who lived by the truth, returned the maiden.

Gālava said:

116.1 So the famous Mādhavī abandoned her riches, became a virgin and, being true to her word, followed the brahmin Gālava. Upon reflection

Gālava, still preoccupied with his task, went to the city of the Bhojas
to visit King Auśīnara. He went and said to the king, whose valor
was his truth, "This maiden shall bear you two princely sons. You
shall attain your goal, here and hereafter, by begetting in her two
5 sons the likes of sun and moon, king. But you must pay me as her
price four hundred moon-white horses, each with a black ear, O sage
who know all the Laws. I do this for a guru's gift—I myself do not
need those horses. Do it if you can, great king, do not hesitate. You
are childless, royal seer—beget two sons, O king! Save yourself and
all your ancestors with the lifeboat that is a son. He who enjoys the
reward of a son is not cast from heaven, royal seer, and does not
go to the gruesome hell where the sonless go."

King Uśīnara, having listened to those and other varied words of
10 Gālava, made this reply to him, "I have heard the words you have
spoken, Gālava. Where my heart is eager, fate is powerful: I have only
two hundred such horses, good brahmin, though I have grazing a
good many thousands of others. I too shall beget one son on her,
Gālava. I shall go the way that others have gone, brahmin, and pay
you the same price, best of brahmins. My wealth exists for my
townspeople and countryfolk, not for my enjoyment. For he who
squanders other people's property on his own lust, O man of Law,
15 earns neither Law nor Fame. I shall accept her, give her to me, sir,
this princess like the child of Gods, so one son will be born to me."

The good brahmin Gālava paid homage to this King Uśīnara, who
had said much that was beautiful. Having given her to Uśīnara,
Gālava went forth to the forest. And the king enjoyed her as a virtuous
man enjoys his prosperity, in mountain caves and by river falls, in
colorful gardens and woods and groves, on lovely terraces and palace
rooftops, in windowed mansions and secluded chambers.

20 In time a son was born like the morning sun, that good king who
is famed as Śibi. And the brahmin Gālava returned, took back the
maiden, and went on to visit the son of Vinatā, O king.

Nārada said:

117.1 With a laugh Vinatā's son said to Gālava, "How fortunate that I
see you have succeeded, brahmin!" Upon hearing the bird's words,
Gālava told him that a quarter of his task remained undone.
Whereupon Suparṇa, first of all that flies, rejoined to Gālava, "Do
not try any further. It will not work for you; for formerly Ṛcīka
sought Gādhi's daughter Satyavatī in Kānyakubja for his wife, Gālava,
5 and was told: 'Sir, give me a thousand moon-white horses with a
black ear each.' Ṛcīka promised so and went to Varuṇa's dwelling,
obtained the horses at the Ford of the Horses and gave them to the
king. At the performance of a *puṇḍarīka* sacrifice the king gave them

to the brahmins, and several kings bought them from them, two
hundred each. The remaining four hundred, good brahmin, were
taken by the river Vitastā while they were being led across. So the
rest being unobtainable, no more can ever be had, Gālava. Present
this woman to Viśvāmitra in lieu of two hundred horses, along with
the six hundred you have, law-spirited man, then, bull among
brahmins, you will have done your task and be rid of your confusion."
10 Gālava agreed, and taking the horses and the maiden went with
Suparṇa to Viśvāmitra.

Gālava said:

Sir, accept these six hundred horses and this maiden for the remaining two hundred. She has borne three law-obeying sons to royal seers, and you, best of men, will beget a fourth. Thus the full eight hundred horses shall be yours, so that I am acquitted of my debt and can pursue austerities as I please.

Nārada said:

Viśvāmitra looked upon Gālava, the Bird, and the full-hipped
13 maiden and said, "Gālava, why did you not give this woman to me
to begin with? I would have had four sons to prosper my line! Indeed,
I accept this maiden of yours for the reward of a single son. All the
horses remain in my hermitage."

Lustrous Viśvāmitra, making love with her, begot a son, Aṣṭaka,
son of Mādhavī. Viśvāmitra imbued his son, as soon as he was born,
with Profit and Law and gave him the horses. Thereupon Aṣṭaka
departed for a city resembling the city of the moon, while Kauśika
himself returned the maiden to his student and left for the forest.
20 Gālava, in high spirits now that he had paid off the stipend, said
to the maiden while Suparṇa stood by, "You have borne one son who
is royal in generosity, another who is a hero, a third who is dedicated
to truth and Law, and one more who is a sacrificer. Therefore go,
full-hipped woman: you have saved your father with sons, you have
saved four kings and myself as well, slim-waisted Mādhavī!"

Gālava gave Suparṇa, eater of Snakes, leave to go, turned the maiden over to her father, and departed for the forest.

Nārada said:

118.1 King Yayāti, intending to hold a bridegroom choice for her,
traveled to a hermitage at the confluence of the Ganges and Yamunā,
with Mādhavī mounted on a chariot and decked with garlands and
chaplets, and Pūru and Yadu accompanied their sister to that
hermitage. There was a gathering there of Snakes, Yakṣas, men,
birds, and deer, and of the denizens of the mountains, trees, and
woods. The forest teemed with the princes of diverse peoples and
5 countries, and it was filled everywhere with Brahmā-like seers. But,

when all the suitors were announced, the fair-complexioned woman
passed by all of them and chose the forest as her bridegroom. Yayāti's
daughter descended from the chariot, bowed to her relatives, went to
the holy forest and practiced austerity. By means of various fasts,
observances, and restraints, she made light of herself and lived like
a doe. She grazed soft green sprouts of the color of beryl, fine grasses
pungent and sweet, she drank the choice waters, tasty and pure,
10 cool and unmuddied, of holy streams, she roamed in forests deserted
by lions, where deer were king, empty and dense and left alone by
fires, alongside fawns, like a hind of the woods, and so practiced
much Law, decked with chastity.

Yayāti, in the manner of the ancient kings, lived for many
thousands of years before succumbing to the Law of Time. Pūru and
Yadu, best of men, fostered two dynasties, and by them Nahuṣa's son
was established in this world and the next. Arriving in heaven King
Yayāti gloried, and like a great seer the mighty prince rejoiced in the
choicest rewards of heaven.

15 After the passage of many times many thousands of years amongst
grand royal seers and great seers who were seated there, Yayāti, his
mind befuddled and his wit seized by wonderment, fell to despise all
men, Gods, and hosts of seers. God Śakra the Slayer of Vala found
him out, and all the royal seers intoned, "Fie! Fie!" When they now
saw Nahuṣa's son, there was hesitation, "Who is he? Of what king?
How did he get to heaven? What feat perfected him? Where did he
acquire ascetic power? In what manner is he known in heaven, and
20 who knows him?" Thus the kings who dwelled in heaven asked
uncertainly of one another about King Yayāti when they saw him.
The hundreds of keepers of the celestial chariots, the keepers of the
gates, and the keeper of the seats replied to their questions, "We do
not know him." All had their knowledge clouded and none recognized
the king. Instantly the king had lost his prestige.

Nārada said:

119.1 Then, divested of his rank, toppled from his seat, with heart
atremble, savaged by the fires of grief, his garlands withered, his
knowledge slipped, his diadem and upper armlets dropped, dizzied,
slack in all his limbs, with ornaments and robe awry, no longer
visible, and seeing and not seeing the others, void with an empty
mind, he was about to tumble to the flat of the earth. "What unclean
thoughts have I thought, soiling the Law," he wondered, "which
5 caused me to fall from rank?" But the kings, Siddhas, and Apsarās
there no longer saw Yayāti, who had lost his footing and tottered.

Then a person came, the expeller of those whose merit has expired,
and at the behest of the king of the Gods, O king, he said to Yayāti,

"Besotted with pride, you despise everyone else. Your pride has lost you heaven; you are unworthy of it, son of a king. You are unknown now. Go," he said, "and fall!" "Let me fall among good men!" said the son of Nahuṣa about to fall, and he considered his course, that first of travelers.

At that very hour the king saw four bull-like kings in the Naimiṣa
10 Forest and he fell in their midst. Pratardana, Vasumanas, Śibi
Auśīnari, and Aṣṭaka were sating the lord of the Gods with a
Vājapeya sacrifice. Yayāti smelled the smoke that rose from the
sacrifice—a ready gate to heaven—and fell to the earth. The king
floated down the flowing river of smoke that joined heaven and earth
like the Ganges, and fell in the midst of those four eminent sacrificers,
who were his own relatives and resembled the World Guardians. King
Yayāti fell amid those lionlike kings, who were like grand offering
fires, in that holy sanctuary.
15 All the kings questioned him, who was the image of beauty: "Who
are you, and whose kinsman, and from what country and city? Are
you a Yakṣa, or God, or Gandharva, or Rākṣasa, as you are not of
human form? What purpose are you pursuing?"

Yayāti said:

I am Yayāti the royal seer, now fallen from heaven with my merit exhausted. Thinking, "May I fall among good men," I have fallen among you, sirs.

The kings said:

Then let this desire of yours come true, bull among men. Accept the fruits of sacrifice and the Law of all of us!

Yayāti said:

I am not a brahmin rich from accepting gifts; I am a baron! Nor does my spirit incline to the pillaging of the merit of others.

Nārada said:

20 It was at this very time that the kings espied Mādhavī, who had
come as a wandering doe, and they greeted her and said, "What is
the purpose of your coming? What command of yours must we carry
out? For we all are at our orders, we are your sons, ascetic woman."
Mādhavī on hearing their words approached her father Yayāti with
the greatest joy and saluted him. Seeing her sons with heads bent, the
ascetic said: "These my sons are your daughter-sons, not strangers.
They shall rescue you, that is the ancient decree. I am your daughter
Mādhavī, king, now living like a doe. I too have accumulated Law—
25 accept half of it. Since all men partake of the reward of having
offspring, king, therefore they desire to have daughter-sons, like you,
king of the earth."

Thereupon all the kings saluted their mother with their heads, bowed before their maternal grandfather and spoke in like manner. Filling the earth with their incomparable, loud, and affectionate sounds the kings rescued their grandfather, who had fallen from heaven. Gālava, too, arrived there, and he said to the king, "Ascend to heaven with an eighth portion of my ascetic power, sire!"

Nārada said:

120.1 As soon as Yayāti, bull among men, was recognized by those good
men, he regained his celestial stature, and his fever abated. Wearing
divine garlands and robes, adorned with celestial ornaments, endowed
with divine fragrance and virtue, he did not touch earth with his feet.
Then Vasumanas, famed in the world for his generous gifts, first
raised his voice and spoke to the king, "Whatever I have obtained in
the world by my irreproachable standing with all classes, that I shall
5 give away and bestow on you; the fruit of wonted generosity, the
fruit of wonted forgiveness, and the fruit of maintaining the fires I
bestow on you."
Pratardana, bull among barons, also spoke, "Whatever fame arising
from baronial Law I have attained in the world by my constant delight
in the Law and constant devotion to warfare, and the fruit of my
title of hero I bestow upon you."
Sagacious Śibi Auśīnara spoke his honeyed word, "As I have never
uttered a lie to even children or women, or in bantering talk, or in
the midst of battles, calamities, and emergencies, so go to heaven by
10 virtue of that truth! As I would sooner give up my life, kingdom,
works, and comforts than my truth, king by that truth go to heaven.
As I have pleased Law with my Truth, Fire with my truth, Śakra with
my truth, king, by that truth go to heaven."
Now the royal seer Aṣṭaka, the law-wise son of Kauśika and
Mādhavī, spoke to Yayāti, who had offered up many hundreds of
sacrifices, "Sire, I have piled up *puṇḍarīkas* and *gosavas* by the
hundreds, as well as Vājapeya sacrifices—now obtain the fruit of
them. I have no jewels, no riches, no other possessions that have not
been used up in sacrificing—by that truth go to heaven!"
15 While his grandsons were speaking to the king of men, he rose
ever higher from the earth toward heaven. And in this manner all the
kings by virtue of their good deeds swiftly rescued resplendent Yayāti,
who had fallen from heaven. By means of their own Law, sacrifices,
gifts, and feats those grandsons, born in four royal dynasties and
prospering their lineages, caused their wise maternal grandfather to
ascend to heaven.

The kings said:

Sire, we are your daughter's sons possessed of the Law and virtue of kings, and of all Laws and virtues—rise to heaven, O king!

Nārada said:
121.1 Thus lifted up to heaven by those good kings of generous stipends,
Yayāti dismissed his grandsons and reentered heaven. Showered with
a rain redolent of all kinds of flowers, embraced by a pleasant breeze
of holy fragrance, he ascended to the eternal domain he had earned
with his grandsons' fruits; and increased by his own works, he blazed
forth with superb luster. Sung and danced to by throngs of
Gandharvas and Apsarās, he was joyously received back in heaven to
5 the beat of drums. Lauded by diverse Gods, royal seers, and celestial
bards, welcomed with fine hospitality, saluted by deities, he reaped the
fruits of heaven.

And Grandfather spoke to the joyous and serene king as though
sating him with his words, "By your acts in the world you have
collected the full fourfold measure of the Law, and this world is
immutably yours. Your fame is once more eternal in heaven because
of your good works, royal seer. The minds of all who dwell in heaven
were covered with darkness, so that they did not recognize you; and
unrecognized, you were cast out. Rescued by your grandsons with
love, you have now returned here and resumed the station you had
earned with your own works—immovable, eternal, holy, supreme,
permanent, and untransitory."

Yayāti said:
10 Reverend sir, I have a doubt. Pray remove it, for I cannot ask
anyone else, Grandfather of the world. I had earned great fruits,
lasting many thousands of years, fostered by my protection of my
subjects, won with the floods of countless sacrifices and gifts. How
then could all that be exhausted in a short time, so that I was cast
out? My lord, you know the eternal worlds I had won!

Grandfather said:
The fruits, lasting many thousands of years, which were fostered by
the protection of your subjects and which you had earned with the
floods of countless sacrifices and gifts, were exhausted by just this one
flaw, for which you were cast out, Indra among kings: the celestials
15 pronounced their "Fie!" on you for your self-pride. This world cannot
become eternal, royal seer, if there be pride, brute strength, injury,
crookedness, or deceit. You, king, are not to despise either the
elevated or the lowly or the middling. To those who are consumed
by self-pride no one is ever an equal.

The man who shall narrate your fall and reascension shall
overcome all adversity, let there be no doubt of that.

Nārada said:
Such was the flawed state to which of yore Yayāti was reduced

because of his self-pride, and Gālava likewise because of his obduracy,
O king. People who desire their own well-being should listen to friends
who wish them well, and not be stubborn, for stubbornness brings
20 on perdition. Therefore you too, son of Gāndhārī, must avoid pride
and anger. Make peace with the Pāṇḍavas, hero! Get rid of your
rancor, king!

Whatever is given, O prince, what is done,
What *tapas* observed, what offerings made,
Is never forfeited and never it dwindles,
No other enjoys it but the doer alone.

When this great incomparable tale, esteemed
By dispassionate men of wide erudition,
Is studied detailedly, their spreading insight
Into the Three Pursuits will conquer the earth.

5(54) The Coming of the Lord (continued)

Dhṛtarāṣṭra said:

122.1 It is indeed precisely as you say, Nārada, and so I too wish it to be,
but I am powerless, my lord.

Vaiśaṃpāyana said:

Having said this, O Bhārata, he addressed Kṛṣṇa, "Keśava, you have told me what is good for heaven and this world, conducive to the Law, and conforming to reason. But I cannot act on my own, good friend, and my desire is never done. Well, try your best, strong-armed Kṛṣṇa, best of men, to win over this fool Duryodhana who flouts my commandments, and you shall have done your friends a very great service, Janārdana."

5 The Vārṣṇeya turned to the truculent Duryodhana, and knowing
all the principles that govern Law and Profit, he spoke these kindly
words, "Duryodhana, best of the Kurus, listen to what I have to say
in your own interest and that of your followers, Bhārata. You have
been born in a high lineage, man of wisdom, therefore I pray thee
act well, since you have learning and deportment and are exalted in
all virtues. It is the low-born, mean-souled, cruel, and shameless men
who act as you propose, my son. In this world the proceedings of the
strict are looked upon as consistent with Law and Profit, while those
10 of the lax are regarded as perverse, bull of the Bharatas. Now your

conduct in this matter often appears perverse—your lawless obduracy is heinous and murderous. Bhārata, there has been repeated infamy on your account; now, if you gave up this profitless course, you would do what is best for yourself, as well as release your brothers, retainers, and friends from a lawless and inglorious course of action, enemy-tamer.

"Make your peace, tigerlike man, bull of the Bharatas, make your
peace with the sagacious and heroic Pāṇḍavas, who are enterprising,
self-controlled, and well-informed. That would be beneficial and
agreeable to the wise Dhṛtarāṣṭra, to Grandfather, Droṇa, sagacious
15 Vidura, Kṛpa, Somadatta, the sage Bāhlīka, Aśvatthāman, Vikarṇa,
and Saṃjaya, O lord of your people, and to your kinsmen and most
of your friends. In peace, son, the whole world will find shelter. You
have modesty, high birth, learning, and no cruelty, my son, so abide
by the commandment of your father and mother, bull of the
Bharatas!

"They consider that most profitable which a father commands,
Bhārata. Everyone remembers his father's command in a dire
emergency. Your father prefers that you treat with the Pāṇḍavas, my
friend, and you and your councilors should prefer the same course,
best of Kurus. If a man after hearing the advice of his friends does not
20 follow it, it will burn him later as though he had eaten *kiṃpāka*. A
mortal who out of plain foolishness does not follow the best advice,
but procrastinates, loses his purposes and lives to regret it. But he who
listens to what is best for him and, abandoning his own opinion, acts
accordingly, prospers in this world. He who does not accept the words
of his well-wishers because it is repugnant to him, but listens to
advice that really runs counter to his true interest, falls victim to his
enemies. If a man shoves aside the judgment of the strict to follow
25 that of the lax, his friends will soon mourn his undoing. He who
abandons superior advisers and caters to inferior ones falls into bad
trouble with no hope of rescue. Earth curses him, Bhārata, who
listens to the wicked and not to his friends, behaves wrongly, and
chooses strangers over kin.

"You have broken with those heroes and now seek succor from
others who are uninformed, incompetent, and fools to boot, bull of the
Bharatas. What man on earth but you would reject his kinsmen, great
warriors the likes of Śakra, and hope for rescue from others? From
birth you have always put down the Kaunteyas, but they never got
30 angry at you, for the Pāṇḍavas are law-spirited. From birth the
Pāṇḍavas have been treated wrongfully, friend, yet these glorious
men have treated you correctly, strong-armed prince. You should
treat them likewise, bull of the Bharatas! Do not succumb to anger
at close relatives. The undertakings of the wise are consistent with the

Three Pursuits, Bhārata bull, but when all three are impossible to carry out at the same time, men follow Law and Profit. If those two cannot be reconciled, a sagacious person follows the Law, a middling man prefers Profit, a fool the Pleasure of discord. If a man, driven by his senses, abandons Law out of greed, and strives after Profit and Pleasure by foul means, he perishes. Even if he strives for Profit and Pleasure he should still practice the Law from the start, for neither Profit nor Pleasure ever part company with Law. They say that Law alone is the means to all three, lord of your people, and if one strives by that means, he grows rapidly like a fire in a hollow tree. You, bull of the Bharatas, are striving for grand lustrous sovereignty accepted by all kings, but your way is wrong, friend. One who treats wrongfully those who treat him correctly cuts down himself as a tree with an axe. One should not cut off the opinion of a person whose defeat one does not seek: the mind of a wise person who is not cut off is set upon well-being. One should never rule out anyone in the three worlds who is willing to risk his life, not even an ordinary one, let alone the bull-like Pāṇḍavas. Once fallen victim to intolerance, a man loses his bearings: what is too long will be cut to size; you see the proof, Bhārata.

"It is more profitable for you to unite with the Pāṇḍavas than with the wicked, son, for if you are friends with them you will obtain all that you desire. Best of kings, while enjoying the land conquered by the Pāṇḍavas, you yet discard the Pāṇḍavas and seek help from strangers. Bhārata, you hope for prosperity while vesting authority in such as Duḥśāsana, Durviṣaha, Karṇa, and Saubala, but they are no match for you in the knowledge of Law and Profit, and no match for the Pāṇḍavas in bravery. Not all the kings and yourself combined are sufficient to face a furious Bhīmasena in battle. This entire troop of kings around you, friend, this Bhīṣma, Droṇa, Karṇa, Kṛpa, Bhūriśravas, Somadatta's son, Aśvatthāman, Jayadratha—they are all incapable of withstanding Dhanaṃjaya. For an angry Arjuna is unconquerable by all Gods and Asuras, men and Gandharvas. Do not put your mind to battle—or is there a single man to be found in this whole army of kings who could meet Arjuna on the battlefield and go home in one piece?

"What is the point of wholesale slaughter, bull of the Bharatas? Find one man at whose victory, victory is yours. What man can fight him who defeated Gods, Gandharvas, Yakṣas, Asuras, and Snakes in the Khāṇḍava Tract? Likewise there is the report of that great miracle near Virāṭa's city with the one and the many—it is sufficient proof. Yet you hope to vanquish the indefatigable, unassailable, unfallen Jiṣṇu, the mighty hero Arjuna in battle. Again, who is able to challenge the Pārtha, seconded by me, when he faces him, were he

the Sacker of Cities himself? With his arms he could pull out the
earth, in anger burn these creatures, hurl the Gods from their heaven,
the man who can defeat Arjuna in battle!

"Look at your sons, your brothers, your kinsmen, your relations,
best of the Bharatas: don't let them die for you. Let the Kauravas
survive, lest the entire dynasty perish. Don't let yourself be called a
family murderer, and lose all honor, lord of men! Those warriors will
install you alone as Young King and your father King Dhṛtarāṣṭra
60 as Senior King. My friend, do not reject the Fortune that is ready to
join you: by giving the Pāṇḍavas half you will amass a vast fortune.
Follow the advice of your friends and make peace with the Pāṇḍavas—
as a friend to friends you will obtain all that is good for a long time.

Vaiśaṃpāyana said:

123.1 After listening to Keśava's words, O bull of the Bharatas, Bhīṣma
Śāṃtanava addressed the truculent Duryodhana, "Kṛṣṇa has spoken
to you out of a desire to make peace between his friends. See it his
way, my son, and do not give in to anger. You will never attain to
well-being, or happiness, or prosperity, unless you do what the great-
spirited Keśava says. Strong-armed Keśava has told you how to profit
under Law, my son; pursue that profit, king, lest you lead your
subjects to ruin.

5 "This splendid fortune of the Bhāratas that blazes among all kings
you are about to destroy out of mean-mindedness, while Dhṛtarāṣṭra
is still alive. You yourself, your councilors, sons, cattle, relatives, and
friends, you are about to put them all perversely to death by ignoring
the truthful and meaningful words of Keśava, your father, and the
sagacious Vidura, O best of the Bharatas. Do not travel the low road
as a foul, evil-minded family murderer. Do not give pain to your
father and mother!"

Then Droṇa spoke to Duryodhana who, indulging his truculence,
10 sat there panting heavily, "The words that Keśava has spoken, my
son, are informed with Law and Profit, and so are Bhīṣma
Śāṃtanava's, heed them, king of men! Two calm wise men of great
learning who wish you well have spoken to your benefit: accept their
words, enemy-tamer. Do, man of wisdom, what Kṛṣṇa and Bhīṣma
say, do not embrace the words of the frivolous-minded, enemy-burner.
The ones who are inciting you have never acted in your interest.
When there is war, they will tie the feuds of others around your neck.
Do not murder all the Kurus, your sons and brothers. Realize that
15 when Vāsudeva and Arjuna are there, that force is invincible. The
opinion of your friends Kṛṣṇa and Bhīṣma is right: if you do not
accept it you shall regret it, Bhārata. Arjuna is even greater than
Jāmadagnya predicted, and Devakī's son Kṛṣṇa is unconquerable

even by the Gods. But what good does it do to speak of your
happiness and comfort, bull of the Bharatas! You have been told
everything – go ahead and do as you please, for I cannot tell you
any more, best of the Bharatas."

In this exchange of words the Steward Vidura now looked at the
intransigent Duryodhana Dhārtarāṣṭra and said, "Duryodhana, bull
of the Bharatas, I feel no grief over you, but I am sorry for these two
20 oldsters, Gāndhārī and your father, who will live unprotected with
you as their hard-hearted protector; they have lost their friends and
and advisers, and, as helpless as unwinged birds, they will roam this
earth sorrowfully as beggars after begetting such a miscreant, the
assassin of his family!"

Then King Dhṛtarāṣṭra spoke to Duryodhana, who was sitting with
his brothers, surrounded by kings, "Listen, Duryodhana, accept what
the great-spirited Śauri has said, for it is entirely beneficial, protective
of your profit and safety, and permanent. For with this Kṛṣṇa of
unsullied deeds as our helper we shall, among all kings, accomplish
25 all our cherished plans. My son, go to Yudhiṣṭhira with the full
support of Keśava. Perform the act that will bring all good luck and
health to the Bharatas. Go to your meeting, with Vāsudeva as your
sacred crossing, my son. I think the time has now come; do not miss
your chance. If you rebuff Keśava, who is suing for peace and argues
in your cause, you will not fail to lose."

Vaiśaṃpāyana said:

124.1 After hearing Dhṛtarāṣṭra speak, Bhīṣma and Droṇa again spoke in
support of him to Duryodhana, who disobeyed his father's orders, "As
long as the two Kṛṣṇas have not donned armor, as long as Gāṇḍīva
still rests, as long as Dhaumya has not offered the host of the enemy
into the fire of the army, as long as modest Yudhiṣṭhira, the great
archer, does not cast a baleful glance at your troops, so long may we
be spared bloodshed. As long as we do not see the mighty bowman
Bhīmasena Pārtha take his place among his ranks, so long may we
5 be spared bloodshed. As long as he does not go on his patrols to the
army's delight, as long as he does not knock off on the battlefield the
heads of elephant warriors with his hero-killing club like the fruits of
a tree that have been ripened by Time, so long may we be spared
bloodshed. As long as Nakula, Sahadeva, Dhṛṣṭadyumna Pārṣata,
Virāṭa, Śikhaṇḍin, and Śiśupāla's son, fully armed masters of arms
and fast archers, do not invade us as crocodiles invade the ocean, so
10 long may we be spared bloodshed. As long as no dread vulture-
fletched arrows strike into the delicate bodies of the kings, so long
may we be spared bloodshed. As long as no mighty iron shafts, sent
by far-aiming and fast-shooting archers, do not hit the sandalwood

and aloe-anointed, gold-plate and necklace-decked chests of our
warriors, so long may we be spared bloodshed.

"May Yudhiṣṭhira the King Dharma, elephant among kings, receive
you by the hands when you salute him with your head. May that
king of princely stipends place his right hand, which is marked with
pennant, elephant, goad, and banner, on your shoulder in the cause
of peace, bull of the Bharatas. May he, when you are seated, slap
15 your back with his red-lacquered, jewel-fingered hand. May the tree-
shouldered, strong-armed Wolf-Belly embrace and greet you
conciliatorily in the cause of peace, bull of the Bharatas. Saluted by
all three, Arjuna and the twins, you must greet them back with
affection, king, kissing them on their heads. Upon the spectacle of you
united with your heroic Pāṇḍava brethren, let the kings of men weep
tears of joy, let the good fortune of all be proclaimed in the capital
cities of the kings, let earth be enjoyed in a spirit of brotherhood, and
let your fever abate."

Vaiśaṃpāyana said:

125.1 Upon hearing these unpalatable words in the assembly of the
Kurus, Duryodhana replied to famous strong-armed Vāsudeva,
"Keśava, before you speak, first give matters some thought! You
abuse and revile only me, without grounds, because you have
declared yourself loyal to the Pārthas. But, Madhusūdana, did you
examine the strength and weakness of our cases before blaming me?
You, the Steward, the king, the teacher and Grandfather put the
5 blame only on me and on no other prince. I do not perceive any
wrongdoing on my part, yet all of you and all the kings hate me.
On reflection I fail to see any terrible wrong I have done, enemy-
tamer, any wrong at all. The Pāṇḍavas agreed happily to the dicing,
Madhusūdana, and then lost the kingdom to Śakuni—was that my
fault? Whatever riches the Pāṇḍavas forfeited in the game I allowed
them to take back then and there, Madhusūdana. It was not my
fault that the invincible Pārthas lost the game and retreated to the
forest, greatest of victors.

10 "Besides, by reason of what insult do they now quarrel, impotently
but blithely, as though with enemies, Kṛṣṇa? What have we done to
them? To avenge what wrong do the Pāṇḍavas and Sṛñjayas seek to
kill the Dhārtarāṣṭras? No threat in word or deed can make us tremble
and cower, even when in danger from Indra! I do not see a man who,
following the Law of the baronage, could hope to vanquish us in a
battle, enemy-killer. For Bhīṣma, Kṛpa, Droṇa, and their troops
cannot be bested in battle even by the Gods, let alone the Pāṇḍavas.
15 And if we, following our own Law, meet our death by the sword in
a war, Mādhava, when our time has come, it will mean heaven. This,

Janārdana, is the highest Law for us who are barons, that we lie on
the battlefield on a bed of arrows. If we obtain a hero's bed on the
battlefield, Mādhava, without bowing to the enemy, we shall not rue
it. Who was ever born in a noble house who, abiding by the Law of
the baronage, would bow to anyone out of fear, with regard only for
his life? 'One should raise oneself, not cower,' said Mātanga, 'for to
raise oneself is a man's way. One should break in one's joints rather
20 than bend to anyone,' and that saying is cherished by those who hope
for well-being. A man like me bows only to the Law and the brahmins,
and that rule he should obey all his life without heeding anybody.
That is the Law of the barons, and that has always been my view.
"Keśava, as long as I am alive they will not get the portion of the
kingdom that my father once allowed them. As long as Dhṛtarāṣṭra
lives, Janārdana, we and they should hold down our swords and live
25 off him, Mādhava. Even if this inalienable kingdom was once given
away, whether from ignorance or fear, when I was a child and
dependent, Janārdana, it can no longer be had by the Pāṇḍavas, scion
of Vṛṣṇi. As long as I am alive, strong-armed Keśava, I shall not
surrender as much as a pin-prick of land to the Pāṇḍavas, Mādhava!"

Vaiśaṃpāyana said:
126.1 Rolling his eyes in anger, the Dāśārha replied mockingly to
Duryodhana in the assembly of the Kurus, "You shall have your wish,
you shall find a hero's bed! Stand firm with your counselors; there
shall be a holocaust! You think you have not wronged the Pāṇḍavas,
fool? Hear it all, ye kings! When you burned with envy for the wealth
of the great-spirited Pāṇḍavas, you and Saubala plotted a dicing game,
5 Bhārata. How could your kinsmen, exalted and admired by good men
and not crooked in their ways, attend such a lawless dicing match
with that crook, O man of wisdom, a game joyless and destructive to
the strict, source of the quarrels and vices of the wicked? It was you
who heedlessly started that evil, heinous dice game, along with good
men who now were siding with crooks. What man but you could
find it in himself to molest the wife of a kinsman, fetch Draupadī to
the hall, and speak to her as you did? You manhandled the queen
10 of Pāṇḍu's sons, high-born, high-bred, dearer to them than life! All
the Kurus know how the Kaunteyas were abused by Duḥśāsana in the
assembly of the Kurus, when those enemy-burners were departing for
the forest. What righteous man would act in so contemptible a way
toward his own relatives, whose conduct was impeccable, who are
innocent of all greed, and always abide by the Law? Karṇa,
Duḥśāsana, and you repeatedly resorted to the language of cruel and
ignoble churls!
"When they were boys, you did your best to burn them with their

mother in Vāraṇāvata, but you did not succeed. Afterward the
Pāṇḍavas and their mother lived a very long time in hiding in
15 Ekacakrā, in a brahmin's house. Using any means at all, poison,
snakes, fetters, you made attempts to destroy them, and you failed.
Now, with such a mentality toward the Pāṇḍavas, but always
dissembling, are you *not* at fault in regard to the great-spirited
Pāṇḍavas? After cruelly perpetrating many misdeeds against the
Pāṇḍavas, you, an ignoble hypocrite, are now at odds with everyone.
Your father and mother, Bhīṣma, Droṇa, and Vidura all have told
you and told you to make peace, prince, but you do not.

"There is very great profit for both you and the Pārtha in peace,
20 but you do not want it—out of sheer frivolity, what else? You will
find no shelter, king, if you overstep the advice of friends. What you
are doing is lawless and dishonorable!"

While the Dāśārha was thus speaking to the intransigent
Duryodhana, Duḥśāsana spoke up in the assembly of the Kurus, "It
seems that if you do not treat with the Pāṇḍavas voluntarily, the
Kauravas are going to tie you up and hand you over to Yudhiṣṭhira!
Bhīṣma, Droṇa, and your own father are ready to proffer the three
of us to the Pāṇḍavas, Vaikartana, you, and me!" When he heard his
brother's words, Suyodhana Dhārtarāṣṭra rose irately and, hissing
25 like a great snake, strode out, heeding no one, whether Vidura,
Dhṛtarāṣṭra, great King Bāhlīka, Kṛpa, Somadatta, Bhīṣma, Droṇa,
or Janārdana; out strode the shameless scoundrel, unbridled like an
untaught lout, vainglorious despiser of honorable men.

When they saw the bull-like man depart, all his brothers, their
councilors, and other princes followed him. Bhīṣma Śāṃtanava, seeing
Duryodhana rise angrily in the hall and leave, said to him, "He who
abandons Law and Profit and indulges his wild impulses will soon be
30 mocked in his distress by his ill-wishers. This vile son of King
Dhṛtarāṣṭra is ignorant of what is right and aberrant in his pride of
kingship, a prey to anger and greed. Janārdana, I think the entire
baronage is now cooked by Time, for all the princes and their
councilors follow him in their folly."

Hearing Bhīṣma's words the valiant lotus-eyed Dāśārha spoke to
all who remained, Bhīṣma, Droṇa, and others, "It is the grave fault
of all the elders of the Kurus that they do not forcibly restrain this
addlebrained king in his abuse of power. Tamers of your enemies,
I think the time has come to do just that, and if it is done, everything
35 may still turn out for the better. Listen, men sans blame, what I shall
say before you is for your own good—if indeed you agree that it is in
your own interest, Bhāratas.

"The wicked and uncontrolled son of King Bhoja in a fit of anger
seized power while his father was still alive. This Kaṃsa, this son of
Ugrasena, deserted by his relatives, I punished in a great battle for

the good of his kinsmen. Thereupon I and the other kinsmen with
proper ceremony once more installed Ugrasena Āhuka as a king who
increased the baronage of the Bhojas. By abandoning the single
Kaṃsa for the sake of the family, all Yādavas, Andhakas, and Vṛṣṇis
prospered and lived in happiness, O Bhārata.
40 "Also, when Gods and Asuras were arrayed for battle and weapons
were raised, Parameṣṭhin Prajāpati lifted his voice; while the worlds
were split in discord and perishing, Bhārata, the blessed God Creator,
who gives being to the worlds, spoke, 'The Asuras, Daityas, and
Dānavas will be defeated; the Ādityas, Vasus, and Rudras will dwell
in heaven. Gods, Asuras, men, Gandharvas, Snakes, and Rākṣasas
will furiously slay one another in this war.' Judging thus, Parameṣṭhin
Prajāpati spoke to Dharma, 'Fetter the Daiteyas and Dānavas and
45 give them to Varuṇa.' Dharma then at Parameṣṭhin's behest fettered
all the Daiteyas and Dānavas and gave them to Varuṇa. In his turn
Varuṇa, the Lord of the Waters, bound the Dānavas with the fetters
of Law and his own nooses; and ever since he has guarded them
carefully in the ocean.

"Likewise fetter ye Duryodhana, Karṇa, Śakuni Saubala, and
Duḥśāsana, and give them to the Pāṇḍavas. 'For the family abandon
a man, for the village abandon a family, for the country abandon a
village, for the soul abandon the earth.' King, if you fetter Duryodhana
and make peace with the Pāṇḍavas, the barons will not perish in your
cause, bull of the barons!"

Vaiśampāyana said:

127.1 When King Dhṛtarāṣṭra had heard Kṛṣṇa's words, he spoke quickly
to Vidura, wise in all the Laws, "Go, my friend, and bring the
sagacious and far-sighted Gāndhārī. Together with her I will bring
around our wayward son. If she can appease that evil spirit and evil
mind, we shall be able to abide by the words of our friend Kṛṣṇa.
She might be able to show that greed-ridden man, with his evil
5 intentions and friends, the right path, if she uses the right words. She
may avert, for our safety and comfort, our looming dire predicament
that Duryodhana is bringing on for a long time to come."

Upon hearing the king's words, Vidura fetched far-sighted Gāndhārī at Dhṛtarāṣṭra's behest.

Dhṛtarāṣṭra said:

This evil-spirited son of yours flouts my commandment, Gāndhārī. Out of greed for power he mocks both power and life. An intemperate churl, he has left the hall with his wicked friends, the fool, ignoring the words of his friends.

Vaiśampāyana said:

When she heard her husband's words the glorious Gāndhārī, the daughter of a king, replied with a view to the greatest profit for all,

10 "Fetch my sick son, who craves the kingdom, immediately, for the
kingdom cannot be ruled by a man who scoffs at Law and Profit.
You yourself are very much to blame in this matter, Dhṛtarāṣṭra, for
out of love for your son you followed his mind, while knowing that he
is evil. Now, obsessed with greed and anger and deluded, he can no
longer forcibly be turned around by you. Dhṛtarāṣṭra has reaped the
fruit of handing over the kingdom to an evil-minded greedy nitwit
with wicked friends. How could a sensible man loverlook a breach in
his own family? Enemies will worst you when you have broken with
15 your kin. Great king, when misfortune can be averted with persuasion
or gifts, who would bring down his staff on his own kinsmen?"

At the mother's words and on Dhṛtarāṣṭra's orders, the Steward
again ushered the truculent Duryodhana into the hall. He reentered
the hall with copper-red eyes and hissing angrily like a snake,
expecting fully what his mother would say. Upon seeing her wayward
son enter, Gāndhārī reproachfully made this appropriate speech,
"Duryodhana, listen to what I have to say, little son, in your own
and your followers' interest in order to bring happiness in the future.
20 By making peace you honor Bhīṣma, your father, and me, as well as
your well-wishers from Droṇa onward. A kingdom, man of wisdom,
cannot be obtained, protected, and enjoyed by one's own whim, bull
of the Bharatas; for one who is not in control of his senses does not
keep his kingdom for long. It is the wise man, in control of his senses,
who guards his kingdom. Greed and anger drag a man away from
his profits; by defeating these two enemies a king conquers earth.
To be lord and master is a great task; the wicked may court kingship
25 but cannot keep it for long. He who desires greatness should subject
his senses to Law and Profit. A man's spirit grows when he subdues
his senses, as a fire grows by burning kindling wood. If they are not
firmly ruled they lead easily to ruin, as unruly, unchecked horses
lead an inept charioteer astray. If one hopes to control one's councilors
without controlling oneself, then, with self and councilors out of
control, one helplessly comes to ruin. But if one conquers oneself first
as if the self were a country, then he does not seek to conquer his
councilors and enemies in vain. Fortune smiles on him who rules
himself, conquers his councilors, lowers his staff on wrongdoers, acts
30 with circumspection, and remains steadfast. Lust and anger in the
body rip reason to pieces, like two big fish caught in a fine-meshed
net. Lust and anger in full growth make the Gods, in fear of discord,
close the gate of heaven on him who travels there. The king who
knows how to conquer completely lust, anger, greed, bombast, and
pride conquers the earth. A king should always be intent on
controlling his senses, if he wants Law, Profit, and the defeat of his

enemies. He who overcome by lust or out of anger acts wrongly
toward his own or others has no one to stand by him.
35 "You will happily enjoy the earth, my son, along with the wise and
heroic Pāṇḍavas, who are as one, uprooters of their enemies. It is
true what Bhīṣma Śāṃtanava and Droṇa the warrior have said:
Kṛṣṇa and the Pāṇḍava are invincible. Seek the help of strong-armed
Kṛṣṇa of unsullied deeds, for Keśava is graciously disposed to the
happiness of both parties. A man who does not follow the advice of
well-wishing friends who are wise and learned is the delight of his
enemies. There is no good in a war, no Law and Profit, let alone
happiness; nor is there victory in the end—don't set your mind on
war.
40 "Bhīṣma, your father, and Bāhlīka, my sagacious son, gave the
sons of Pāṇḍu part of the kingdom out of fear of a breach, enemy-
tamer. You now see the result of that gift, since you enjoy the entire
earth which those heroes have emptied of rivals. Give the sons of
Pāṇḍu what is coming to them, enemy-tamer, if you and your
advisers are content to lord it over half of the kings. Half the earth
suffices you and your men to live on; and when you abide by the
advice of your friends, you will gain fame, Bhārata. A war with the
illustrious, self-possessed, intelligent Pāṇḍavas, who have mastered
45 their senses, will cast you out of great happiness, son. Dispel the anger
of your friends and rule the kingdom fittingly after giving the sons
of Pāṇḍu their share, bull of the Bharatas. Be it enough now that
they have been repressed for thirteen years—lay to rest the grudge
that has been fed by lust and anger, sagacious man. The rancorous
son of the *sūta*, who hopes for the success of your cause, is not able
to stand up to the Pārthas, nor is your brother Duḥśāsana. When
Bhīṣma, Droṇa, Kṛpa, Karṇa, Bhīmasena, Dhanaṃjaya, and
Dhṛṣṭadyumna are enraged, the subjects are done for, that is certain.
Do not in the thrall of truculence attempt to slaughter the Kurus, son,
for all of earth is involved in the holocaust, either on your side or on
50 that of the Pāṇḍavas. If you foolishly think that Bhīṣma, Droṇa, Kṛpa,
and the others will fight with all their might—it will never happen.
To these self-possessed men kingship, affection, and rank count the
same with the Pāṇḍavas as with you; but the Law transcends all
three. Even if they will lay down their lives out of fear of forfeiting
the king's dole, they will not be able to look King Yudhiṣṭhira in the
face. We do not find in the world that greed creates a fortune, so
calm down, bull of the Bharatas, and be done with greed, son."

Vaiśaṃpāyana said:
128.1 But Duryodhana paid no heed to his mother's sensible words and

once more angrily left for the company of the unrestrained. Leaving the assembly hall the Kaurava took counsel with King Śakuni Saubala, the cunning gambler; and this course of action occurred to Duryodhana, Karṇa, Śakuni Saubala and, in the fourth place, Duḥśāsana: "Before fast-acting Janārdana captures us with the aid of King Dhṛtarāṣṭra and Śāṃtanava, it is time for us to overpower Hṛṣīkeśa forcibly and lay hold of that tigerlike man as Indra laid hold of Vairocani. When the Pāṇḍavas hear that the Vārṣṇeya has been taken captive, they will be dispirited and immobilized like cobras whose fangs have been broken, for that strong-armed warrior is the shelter and armor of them all. When the boon-granting bull of all the Sātvatas has been seized, the Pāṇḍavas and Somakas will lose their impetus. Therefore, over the protests of Dhṛtarāṣṭra, we shall keep fast-acting Keśava prisoner and attack the enemies!"

Sagacious Sātyaki, who knew how to read signs, soon divined the evil plan of the foul-minded crooks, and for that reason he came out accompanied by Hārdikya. He told Kṛtavarman, "Yoke up the army at once. Close ranks and wait at the gate of the hall in full armor, until I have talked to Kṛṣṇa of unsullied deeds." The warrior reentered the hall, as a lion a mountain cave, and told the great-spirited Keśava of the plot. Then he spoke to Dhṛtarāṣṭra and Vidura and with a smile told them the plan: "Those fools want to perpetrate a deed that runs counter to Law and Profit and is abhorrent to honest men! There is no way they can succeed. These deluded rogues have got together in the past to commit crimes, a prey to lust and anger and slaves to grudge and greed. And now the nitwits seek to capture lotus-eyed Kṛṣṇa, as children and idiots try to capture a blazing fire in a piece of cloth!"

Far-sighted Vidura, when he heard Sātyaki's words, said to strong-armed Dhṛtarāṣṭra in the assembly of the Kurus, "Time is wrapping up all your sons, enemy-burning king, ready as they are to commit a heinous, impossible crime. For indeed! they plan to ambush and capture the Lotus-eyed One himself, the younger brother of Vāsava! If they attack that indomitable and invincible tiger among men, they will no more survive than moths attacking a fire. If Janārdana wants to, he will dispatch all these strivers to hell as an angry lion dispatches small game! But Kṛṣṇa will never do anything that is frowned upon; that best of men Acyuta will not stray from the Law."

When Vidura had spoken, Keśava lifted his voice, looking at Dhṛtarāṣṭra, while his friends listened together, "Sire, if those angry men try to subdue me by force, allow them to try me, and me to try them. I can subdue all those raging churls without doing anything I might be blamed for. Greedy for the Pāṇḍavas' wealth, your sons will forfeit their own. If that is what they want, Yudhiṣṭhira's task is done, for this very day I'll capture them and their followers, King

Bhārata, and hand them over to the Pārthas. What would be wrong
about that? Yet, Bhārata, I will not in your presence do anything
blameworthy that grows from anger and evil intentions, great king.
If this is what Duryodhana wants, so be it—I for one allow any and
all covenants, Bhārata."

30 When Dhṛtarāṣṭra heard this, he said to Vidura, "Fetch at once
that wretch Suyodhana obsessed with the kingdom along with his
friends, councilors, brothers, and followers, to see if once more I can
take him down the path." The Steward again brought in the
reluctant Duryodhana with his entourage of brothers and kings.
Thereupon King Dhṛtarāṣṭra addressed Duryodhana, who was
surrounded by Karṇa, Duḥśāsana, and kings, Malicious brute, with
your vile band of friends, you are conspiring with evil henchmen to
35 perpetrate a crime! A heinous, infamous crime, abhorrent to all
decent people, such as only deluded defilers of their families like you
could conceive! So you, in league with your evil helpers, want to
ambush the indomitable and invincible Lotus-eyed One? Indeed! Like
a child asking for the moon, you, fool, want to get him whom even
the Gods with Vāsava could not overpower! You do not know Keśava:
Gods, men, Gandharvas, Asuras, or Snakes cannot face him in battle.
No hand can stay the wind, no hand can touch the moon, no head
can carry earth, no force can capture Keśava!"

40 After Dhṛtarāṣṭra had spoken, Vidura the Steward too addressed
Duryodhana Dhārtarāṣṭra, looking balefully at that intransigent man,
"At the Gate of Saubha the chief of apes named Dvivida buried
Keśava under a mighty avalanche of rocks. However valiantly he did
his best to capture Mādhava, he could not hold him there—and now
you want to overpower him! At Nirmocana great Asuras bound him
with six thousand fetters and could not hold him—and now you
want to overpower him! At Prāgjyotiṣa, Naraka and the Dānavas
45 could not hold Śauri, and now you want to overpower him! When
he was a mere babe, he killed Pūtanā and held up Mount Govardhana
to save the cows, bull of the Bharatas. He has slain Ariṣṭa, Dhenuka,
the powerful Caṇūra, Aśvarāja, and the evil-doer Kaṃsa. He has slain
Jarāsaṃdha, Vakra, the heroic Śiśupāla, and Bāṇa, and slaughtered
kings in battle. He has vanquished King Varuṇa and boundlessly
august Pāvaka, and when he stole the *pārijāta* flowers, defeated Śacī's
Consort himself. When sleeping in the one vast ocean he slew Madhu
and Kaiṭabha, and in another birth slew Hayagrīva.

50 "He is the Unmade Maker, cause of all manly prowess. Whatever
Śauri wishes he does effortlessly. No, you do not know Govinda
Acyuta of the awesome strides, a mass of splendor, undefeated like
a furious venomous serpent. Assailing, as a moth assails fire, this
strong-armed Kṛṣṇa of unsullied deeds, you and your councilors
shall not live!"

Vaiśaṃpāyana said:
129.1 When Vidura had spoken, Keśava, mighty killer of enemy hordes,
said to Duryodhana Dhārtarāṣṭra, "Since you in your folly think of
me as just one man, Suyodhana, you seek to overpower and capture
me, miscreant. But in this very spot stand all the Pāṇḍavas, the
Andhakas, and Vṛṣṇis, here the Ādityas, Rudras, Vasus, and great
seers." Saying this Keśava, killer of enemy heroes, laughed out loud.
While the great-spirited Śauri was laughing, the Thirty Gods sprang
thumb-sized from his body, lightning-like and with the glow of fire.
5 Brahmā appeared on his brow, Rudra on his chest, the World
Guardians on his four arms; Agni issued from his mouth. The
Ādityas appeared, the Sādhyas, Vasus, Aśvins, Indra and his Maruts,
the All-the-Gods, and the shapes of Yakṣas, Gandharvas, and
Rākṣasas. On two of his arms Saṃkarṣaṇa and Dhanaṃjaya appeared,
the archer Arjuna on the right and plough-bearer Rāma on the left.
Bhīma, Yudhiṣṭhira, and the two sons of Mādrī issued from his back,
and the Andhakas and Vṛṣṇis headed by Pradyumna were in front of
Kṛṣṇa with their mighty weapons raised. The conch, discus, mace,
10 spear, horn bow, plough, and the sword Nandaka were visible, and all
manner of weapons upraised, blazing all around in Kṛṣṇa's many
hands. From his eyes, nose and ears flickered most dreadful flames
that smoked, and rays as though from the sun burst forth from his
pores.

When they saw the awesome person of great-spirited Keśava, the
kings shut their eyes with trembling hearts, except Droṇa, Bhīṣma,
sagacious Vidura, the lordly Saṃjaya, and the seers and ascetics—the
blessed Lord Janārdana had given them divine eyesight. At the sight
of that great miracle of Mādhava on the floor of the hall the drums
15 of the Gods sounded forth and a shower of flowers fell. The entire
earth shook and the ocean quaked. The kings fell into the greatest
astonishment, bull of the Bharatas.

Then the tigerlike enemy-tamer withdrew his real form, his divine, wondrous, brilliant richness. He took Sātyaki and Hārdikya by the hand and, with the leave of the seers, Madhusūdana departed. Nārada and the other seers disappeared and went—another miracle in that continuing spectacle.

Seeing him leave, the Kauravas and the kings followed that tiger
among men, as the Gods follow the God of the Hundred Sacrifices.
20 Ignoring the whole circle of kings, Śauri of measureless spirit strode
out like fire trailed by smoke. Then on his large bright chariot, hung
with little bells, colorful with gold lattice work, swift and thunderous
like a monsoon cloud, covered with bright tigerskins and circled by a
bumper bar, to which Sainya and Sugrīva were yoked, Dāruka arrived.
The great warrior Kṛtavarman Hārdikya likewise appeared riding his

chariot, that honored hero of the Vṛṣṇis. While enemy-tamer Śauri
was standing in the chariot pit ready to start, great King Dhṛtarāṣṭra
25 once more spoke to him, "Janārdana, you have seen how much power
I hold over my sons; it is before your very eyes, and nothing is
hidden, enemy-plougher. Knowing that I wish and strive for peace
among the Kurus, and aware of my condition, you must not suspect
me. I have no evil designs on the Pāṇḍavas, Keśava, for you know the
words I spoke to Suyodhana. All the Kurus and kings of the earth
know that I strive for peace with all my heart, Mādhava."

Thereupon the strong-armed hero said to King Dhṛtarāṣṭra, Droṇa,
30 Grandfather Bhīṣma, the Steward, Bāhlīka, and Kṛpa, "You have
witnessed what happened in the assembly of the Kurus, how that
foolish lout repeatedly rose in anger. Rightly does King Dhṛtarāṣṭra
call himself powerless! I bid all of you farewell; I shall return to
Yudhiṣṭhira." With this salute Śauri, bull among men, departed on
his chariot, and those great archers, the heroic bulls of the Bharatas,
followed him—Bhīṣma, Droṇa, Kṛpa, the Steward, Dhṛtarāṣṭra,
Bāhlīka, Aśvatthāman, Vikarṇa, and the warrior Yuyutsu. And on
his large, bright, tinkling chariot he went before the eyes of the Kurus
to his father's sister Pṛthā.

Vaiśaṃpāyana said:

130.1 He entered her house, greeted her feet, and recounted briefly what
had happened in the assembly of the Kurus.

Vāsudeva said:

Much worthy of acceptance and reasonable was said by the seers
and myself, but that man refused to accept it. This whole family,
being in Duryodhana's power, is cooked by Time. I bid you farewell,
my lady; I shall speed back to the Pāṇḍavas. What am I to tell the
Pāṇḍavas on your behalf? Tell me, wise woman; I shall do what you
say.

Kuntī said:

5 Keśava, tell the law-spirited King Yudhiṣṭhira, "Your Law has
greatly declined; do not go wrong, my son. Since you have mere rote
learning of the Veda without understanding or insight, your mind is
possessed by mere recitation and looks but to a single Law. Come,
heed the Law that was created by the Self-existent: the baron was
created from his chest, to live by the strength of his arms, to act
always mercilessly for the protection of his subjects.

Hear this parable I have heard from the elders. In olden times
Vaiśravaṇa once offered the earth to the royal seer Mucukunda, for
he was pleased with him, but the other declined to accept: "I wish to
enjoy such kingship as is earned by the strength of my arms."
10 Vaiśravaṇa was happily surprised. Later King Mucukunda did rule

the earth, having obtained it by the prowess of his arms, while he
stuck fully to the vow of the baronage.

Bhārata, a king acquires a quarter of the merit of the Law that his
subjects practice when well protected by their king. When a king
practices his Law, he is worthy of divinity; when he practices
lawlessness, he only goes to hell. Strict government applied by a ruler
according to his own Law constrains the four-class order and
restrains the people from breaking the Law. When a king pursues
strict government perfectly and completely, then the best of eras
15 begins, the Kṛta Age. Have no doubt whether the time causes the
king, or the king causes the time: it is the king who is the cause of
the times. The king is the creator of the Kṛta Age, of the Tretā and
the Dvāpara, and the king is the cause of the fourth Age. By causing
the Kṛta, a king enjoys heaven beyond measure, by causing the
Tretā a king enjoys heaven, though not beyond measure. By setting
in motion the Dvāpara he enjoys it but moderately. A wicked king
dwells in hell for years without end; for the world is touched by a
king's flaws, and the king by the world's.

Look to the kingly Laws that befit your heritage, for the conduct
20 by which you wish to stand was not that of the royal seers. A king
infected by cowardice, who does not act ruthlessly, does not win the
reward that results from the protection of his subjects. Neither Pāṇḍu
nor I nor Grandfather have ever prayed that you be blessed with the
wisdom you live by; the blessings I asked were sacrifice, generosity,
austerity, heroism, offspring, greatness of spirit, and the enjoyment of
strength forever. There was constant *svāhā*, constant *svadhā*; and
Ancestors and Gods thus duly pacified have graciously given long
life, wealth, and sons. Parents as well as the deities always hope in
their sons for liberality, learning, sacrificing, and protection of the
subjects.

25 Whether it be Law or not, you are born to it by the very fact of
birth. You are knowledgeable and high-born, but a victim of your
failure in living, son. When earthlings who go hungry find a liberal
and courageous king, they flock to him contentedly—what higher
Law is there? On reaching kingship a lawlike king should draw on
all kinds of people, on the one by gifts, the other by force, the third
by kindliness. A brahmin should live on alms, a baron should protect,
the commoner should acquire wealth, the serf should serve them all.
Begging is forbidden you, farming is unseemly—you are a baron, the
savior from wounds, living by the strength of your arms!

30 Unearth your ancestral share that lies buried, strong-armed son!
Do it with persuasion, bribery, subversion, punishment, or policy. Is
there anything harder for me than, with my own relatives destitute,
having to hope for the dole of *others* after giving birth to *you*, delight

of your enemies? Fight by the Law of kings, don't drown your grandfathers! Do not, with your merit exhausted, take an evil turn with your brothers!

5(54d) *The Instruction of Vidurā's Son*

5.131–34 (B. 133–36; C. 4494–643)
131 (133; 4494). Kuntī speaks. Queen Vidurā berates her son Saṃjaya, who is dejected after having been defeated by the king of Sindhu. He should regain his pride, blaze brightly if briefly (1–25), cultivate his ambitions, and save his country (25–40).
132 (134; 4359). He must not give up (1–10): his mother is now destitute (10–20). He should rather risk his life than do nothing (20–40).
133 (135; 4580). Saṃjaya protests her harshness; she replies she must speak up (1–10). It is the baron's duty to fight or die (10–15). Saṃjaya protests that he has no more means (20). She replies that he can rise again (20–35).
134 (136; 4622). A king should never appear frightened (1–5). He still has a hidden treasury (5–10). Saṃjaya resolves to fight, and wins (10–15). The merits of the story (15–20).

Kuntī said:

131.1 On this they quote this ancient story, the Colloquy of Vidurā and her Son, O enemy-tamer, how she was able to speak to his benefit and well-being.

Vidurā was a famous, radiant, and irascible lady of high birth, avowed to the Law of the baronage, fortunate and far-sighted, and well-known in the councils of the kings as erudite and learned. This Vidurā, who was true-spoken, once berated the son of her womb when he lay about dejectedly after his defeat at the hands of the king of Sindhu, depressed, ignorant of Law, increasing his enemies' joy.

5 "Where did you come from? Neither I nor your father begot you! Too cowardly for anger, barely hanging on to a low branch, you are a man with the tools of a eunuch! You can feel sorry for yourself for the rest of your life, but if you want better, shoulder the yoke! Don't

despise yourself, don't be satisfied with little. Plan great things, don't
be afraid, have some backbone! Get up, coward, don't lie there
defeated! With no pride at all, you are the delight of all your enemies
and the sorrow of your relatives. A rivulet is soon filled, the paws of a
mouse are soon filled, a coward is soon satisfied and content with
very little. Are you going to die like a dog, without breaking the
snake's fang, or are you going to fight back even if it means risking
10 your life? Will you circle unafraid in the sky like a hawk and wait for
a hole in the enemy, screeching or silent? Why do you lie about like
a corpse as though lightning has struck you? Get up, coward, don't lie
there defeated! Don't fade away as a wretch, be famed for your deeds.
Don't stay in the middle or lower or all the way down, stand mighty!
Blaze up, if only for an instant, like a firebrand of *tinduka* wood, don't
just smolder like a chaff fire—do you want to live the fugitive life of a
crow? Better to flame briefly than to smoke long. Let in no king's
house be the birth of a man-child as meek as a she-mule. As long
as a man does manly deeds and runs the final race, he wins acquittal
15 of the Law and has nothing to be ashamed of. Whether he wins or
loses, it is no matter to the wise: he goes on to the next task and
does not think that his life is all he has. Either show courage, or go
a certain route. When you have put Law first, what price life?
Castrate, your rites and gifts and all your fame are lost! When the
root of joy is cut, what price life? One who is sinking and about to
fall should grab his enemy by the shin, and even if he has lost his
footing, not despair at all. One should lift the yoke and excel, mindful
of the achievement of thoroughbreds. Win mettle and honor, know
your manliness! Raise up your family that has sunk because of you.
20 If people do not talk about a man's acts as miracles, he is merely
another addition to the pile of humanity, he is neither man nor
woman. A man whose gifts, austerity, bravery, learning, or gains
are not reported with awe is his mother's excrement. One is a man by
deeds that best others in their learning, austerity, fortune, or
gallantry. Do not pursue the vile living of the begging bowl,
contemptible, dishonorable, wretched, which only cowards practice.
No relative lives happily who has for his relative a thin man whom
enemies welcome and the world despises, foul of food and dress,
25 the 'look-what-I-got' kind, destitute, living on next to nothing, next
to nothing himself.

"Exiled from the realm, deprived of all pleasures of life, fallen from rank, counting for nothing, we shall perish by doing nothing. Saṃjaya, I have given birth to you as a Kali under the fraudulent disguise of a son who acts contrary to his class among the strict. May no woman ever bear a son like you, without anger, without enterprise, without manhood, the joy of your enemies! Don't smolder—

blaze up! Attack with a vengeance and slay the enemies. Blaze on the
30 head of the enemy, an hour or an instant. One is a man to the extent
of his truculence and unforgivingness. The forgiving man, the meek
man is neither woman nor man. Contentment kills off good fortune,
and so do compassion, sloth, and fear. Without ambition no man
achieves great things. Liberate yourself from these vices of deception.
Steel your heart and hunt for what is yours. A man is called a *puruṣa*
because he is a match for a city; he who lives like a woman is
misnamed a man. A hero of vigorous mettle, who valiantly strides
like a lion, may meet his appointed fate, yet his subjects rejoice at
35 his obsequies. He who seeks his fortune while foregoing comfort and
happiness soon brings joy to his councilors."

The son said:

If you have no regard for me, what use is all of earth to you, what
use ornaments, or pleasures, or life itself?

The mother said:

Let your enemies obtain the worlds of those who wail, "What
now?" but let your friends travel to the worlds of the self-respecting!
Do not follow the way of life of the spineless wretches who are
deserted by their servants and live on the rice ball of others. May
brahmins and friends live off you, son, as the creatures live off the
40 monsoon and Gods off Indra. He lives a meaningful life on whom all
creatures live as on a tree with ripe fruit, Samjaya. Blessed is the life
of him by whose exploits his relatives live happily, as the Thirty by
Śakra's. The man who lives grandly, relying on the strength of his
own arms, obtains fame in this world, and the good goal in the next.

Vidurā said:

132.1 If in your present condition you want to forsake your manhood,
you will soon go the way of the dispossessed. A baron who clings to
life without displaying to the highest degree possible his talent by his
feats, him they know for a thief. Though meaningful, appropriate,
and to the point, my words do not reach you, as medicine does not
reach a dying man. Surely the king of Sindhu has many contented
followers, but from weakness they sit about numb, waiting for
5 disaster to strike. Others will lose heart when they watch your
prowess, after you have put resolve in the growing ranks of your
friends everywhere. Unite with them and prowl the haunts of
mountain fastnesses waiting for the time of his downfall, for he is not
beyond aging and death. You are a Saṃjaya in name only, I see no
victory in you. Live up to your name, my son, be not misnamed. A
clairvoyant and wise brahmin said of you while you were still a child:
"After meeting great misfortune he shall rise again." Recalling his
prediction I am hoping for you to win, and therefore I am talking to

10 you now as I will again and again. He by whose perseverance in his
goals others thrive, he is assured success when he pursues his goals
circumspectly. Be minded to give battle and do not retreat, in the
knowledge that your forebears too saw fortune and misfortune.
Śambara has said that there is no sorrier state than not knowing
where today's and tomorrow's meal will come from. Worse than the
death of a husband or son, he said, is poverty, which is continual
death.

I was born in a great family and went from one pond to another,
a mistress highly honored by my husband with all good things.
15 Formerly my friends used to see me in costly garlands and ornaments
and robed in the finest raiment—now they find me penniless. Saṃjaya,
when you see me and your wife enfeebled, life will hold no more
meaning for you. Will you want to live when you see menials,
servants, teachers, priests, and chaplain leave us for want of wages?
If I do not see today, as I did before, your laudable and famous
enterprise, what peace will my heart know? When I am to say no to
the brahmins, my heart will be rent asunder, for neither I nor my
20 husband have ever denied the brahmins. Others depend on us, but
we depend on no one; if I have to live dependent on others, I'll take
my life.

In the shoreless ocean, be our shore; on a boatless sea, be our
boat. Make a place to stand where there is none, revive us who are
dead. You can be a match for all your enemies, if you do not cling
to life; but if you persist in this eunuch's course, despondent and
demoralized, then take your wretched life. A hero attains fame by
killing just one enemy. Indra became Great Indra by merely killing
Vṛtra: he obtained Great Indra's soma cup and became master of the
25 worlds. When, roaring his name in battle, challenging enemies in
armor, putting a fine army to flight, or killing a great warrior, a hero
wins great fame in a good fight, then his enemies tremble and bow
low. Cowards helplessly shower upon an able warrior, who is ready
to risk his life in battle, all the wealth he desires. Whether it means
the fearful ruin of a kingdom or gambling away their lives, good
warriors do not spare an enemy at hand. Kingship is the door to
heaven—indeed the Elixir itself—and it has closed on you, on the
path that has room for only one: knowing this, fly at your enemies
30 like a firebrand. Kill the foes in battle, king, protect your own Law,
let no illustrious enemy ever see you cower amidst our sorrowing
people and jubilant foes. Let me not wretchedly look upon you as a
wretch. Boast of your riches as before, while lying with the maidens
of Suvīra; do not dejectedly fall into the hands of the maidens of
Sindhu! If a young man like you, endowed with beauty, learning,
and birth, noted and famed in the world, acts contrary, like a bullock

when it has to bear the yoke, it is no less than death, I think. If I see
you flatter the enemy and crawl behind him, what peace does my
heart know? No one in this family has ever walked behind another:
you should not live carrying another's yoke!
I indeed know the eternal heart of the baronage as proclaimed by
35 our forebears and theirs, and our descendants and theirs. No one
born a baron here, and knowing the Law of the baronage, will either
out of fear or hope for a living bow to anyone else. Hold up your
head and do not bow: standing tall means manhood—rather break
in the middle than bend! Proud of heart, you should go about like a
rutting elephant, bowing before brahmins and always to the Law,
40 Saṃjaya. Subduing the other classes and striking down all evildoers,
a baron should be the same as long as he lives, with allies or without.

The son said:

133.1 Your heart is made into an iron ball, merciless, war-mongering,
intransigent mother. Accurst the code of the baron, for which you
berate me, your only son, as though I were a stranger! If you do
not have regard for me, what use is all of earth to you, what use
your ornaments, what of pleasures or life itself?

The mother said:

All the undertakings of the wise, my son, are for Law and Profit;
5 it is in view of them alone that I have exhorted you, Saṃjaya. The
great moment has come when you have to decide on your course: if
you do not go to your task now that the time has come, then,
dishonored, you will commit an act of extreme cruelty. Saṃjaya,
if I were not to speak up when you are touched by dishonor, my
love would be a she-ass's love, powerless and pointless. Abandon the
course that fools follow and the strict despise: it is the great ignorance
to which creatures cling. But if you choose the way of the strict, you
will be dear to me, going no other course than that which has the
virtue of both Law and Profit, recognizes both fate and human
action, and is taken by the strict. A man rejoicing in a son or
grandson who is ill-mannered and unenterprising forfeits the fruit of
10 offspring. Lowly people who do not do what they ought to do, and
do what is forbidden, do not find happiness here or hereafter.
The baron has been created to fight and win, Saṃjaya, to act
sternly at all times in the protection of his subjects; whether in
victory or death he obtains the world of Indra. But in Śakra's blessed
abode there is not that happiness which a baron tastes in subjugating
his enemies. Let the spirited man who is brought down many times
bide his time, burning with anger while fostering his desire to
vanquish his foes. In what other way will he find peace than by either
15 abandoning his life or felling his enemies? In this world a sagacious

man holds a trifle unacceptable: he for whom a trifle is acceptable will surely become trifling and unacceptable to the world. In the absence of desirable possessions a man acquires no luster and soon turns into nothing himself, like the Ganges flowing into the ocean.

The son said:

You should not voice such thoughts, mother, especially not to your son. Look only for compassion, like a deaf mute.

The mother said:

It is a great pleasure to me that you think so! You who need scolding scold me, and I scold you the more. I shall honor you when you have killed all the Saindhavas—for I see your total victory at hand!

The son said:

20 How can I win without treasury and allies? That is my sorry state
and I know it well. My heart has turned away from kingship as a
criminal's heart from heaven. But if you do see any means in your
mature judgment, then I beg you to tell me precisely. I shall follow
your advice exactly.

The mother said:

Son, do not despise yourself for past misfortunes. Riches suddenly
appear from nowhere, and present riches disappear the same way.
Nor can the foolish acquire riches just by being indignant over their
absence. The fruit of any action is always impermanent. They who
know it is impermanent may prosper or may not; but they who do
25 not act never prosper. Lack of trying has one consequence: nothing;
trying has two: there either is a result or not. He who knows
beforehand that all matters are impermanent pushes away growth
and success to his own disadvantage.

Making up his mind without trepidation that "this is going to
happen," a man should wake, rise, and yoke himself to actions that
bring prosperity, after auspicious rites with brahmins and Gods. A
sagacious king soon rises again, son: fortune returns to him as the
sun to the east. I see you are edified by my illustrations, examples,
and many encouraging words: now show your mettle, for you are
30 able to grasp the manly purpose you cherish. Keep your eye attentively
on those who are angered, greedy, weakened, insulted, humiliated,
and competitive: in this manner you can split up large forces as a
gathering storm scatters clouds. Bc thc first to give gifts, rise at
daybreak, speak gently: people will do you favors and surely place
you first. As soon as an enemy knows that his rival is ready to lay
down his life, he shrinks away from him as from a snake that has
got into his house. If one knows that the enemy is too courageous
to subdue, he should warn him off, and the same effect is
35 accomplished: by obtaining a breathing space by means of warnings,

one can increase his wealth; and allies will flock and cling to a man of wealth. On the other hand, son, relations desert him whose wealth has slipped away: they do not stick with him but abhor him. If one makes a friend of the enemy and comes to trust him it is inconceivable that he will regain his kingship.

The mother said:

134.1 The king should never be afraid in an emergency; and even if he
is frightened, he should not act like a frightened man. For if people
see their king frightened, they all become frightened themselves: the
kingdom, the ministers, and the army each make up their minds
separately. Some may then join the enemies, others merely desert
their king, while still others who had been humbled before will try
to strike back. Only his best friends stick with him, powerless and
hoping for better times, like a cow whose calf is fettered. They sorrow
5 after his sorrow, as for relations who have departed. Even those who
had been honored, even those considered friends before, covet the
kingdom of a king who has met with disaster. Do not be frightened,
lest your friends desert you in your fears.

I have spoken to embolden you, as a strong man to one weaker, to
test your mettle, prowess, and resolve. If you understand what I have
said, and if what I have said is right, then harden yourself and rise
to victory, Saṃjaya! We still have a large treasury unknown to you.
No one but I knows about it, and I'll make it available to you. You
still have many hundreds of friends, Saṃjaya, steadfast in happiness
10 and sorrow, hero, each worth a hundred, who will not retreat. Such
are the true companions and enemy-ploughing councilors of an
ambitious man who steadily moves upward.

The son said:

Hearing even from a nitwit a speech of such wonderful words and meanings, would a man not cast off darkness? With you as my guide, who see future and past, I must carry this yoke in the water and hurry up the slope. As I wished to hear from you every single word, I have sat mostly silent, contradicting you here and there, not satiated as though with Elixir received from a relative at the time of a disaster. Now I shall exert myself to subdue the enemies and to win victory!

Kuntī said:

15 Like a fine horse hurling along prodded by the arrows of her
words, he carried out her instructions exactly so.

This awe-inspiring and incomparable exhortation, which makes one's mettle swell, a minister should repeat to a king who despairs under the pressure of his enemies. This history called *Victory* should

be heard by him who wishes to triumph; and having heard it he will
soon conquer the earth and shatter his enemies. It causes the birth
of a son, it causes the birth of a hero: a pregnant woman who hears
it again and again is sure to bear a hero, a champion in learning,
austerity, self-control, an ascetic, blazing with the luster of brahman,
20 honored with applause, fiery, strong, lordly, a great warrior, daring,
unassailable, an invincible conqueror. A chastiser of the wicked and
protector of the law-abiding that baroness shall bear, a hero whose
valor is the truth.

5(54) The Coming of the Lord (continued)

Kuntī said:

135.1 Keśava, tell Arjuna: "When you were born, my little son, I was
sitting in the hermitage surrounded by women. Then there was a
Voice in the sky, divine and enchanting: 'Kuntī, your son will be the
like of the God of the Thousand Eyes. He shall vanquish in battle all
the gathered Kurus and, seconded by Bhīmasena, overturn the world.
Your man-child shall conquer earth and win heaven-touching fame
after killing the Kurus on the battlefield, with Vāsudeva as his
5 companion. He shall recover the paternal portion that was lost and
with his brothers illustriously offer up the three sacrifices.' "

Acyuta, if I know indeed the true-spoken Terrifier, the powerful,
indomitable Left-handed Archer, then it must be as the Voice has
predicted, Dāśārha! If indeed there is Law, then this shall become
true, Vārṣṇeya! And you, too, Kṛṣṇa, shall so bring about everything.
I myself do not call into question what the Voice has predicted. I
bow to the great Law—the Law maintains the creatures. Say this
to Dhanaṃjaya.

And to the ever ready Wolf-Belly this: "The time has come for
which a baroness gives birth, for bull-like men do not falter when they
10 encounter a fight." You have always known Bhīma's spirit: that
enemy-plougher has no peace until he has put an end to his enemies.

Kṛṣṇa Mādhava, say to the glorious and beautiful Kṛṣṇā, the
daughter-in-law of the great-spirited Pāṇḍu, who knows all the
niceties of Law: "Famous and distinguished daughter of a dynasty, it
is meet and proper that you have behaved toward all my sons
according to the truth."

Address as follows the twin sons of Mādrī, both devoted to the Law
of the baronage, "Choose over life itself such happiness as is earned

by gallantry! The riches achieved by gallantry always please the
heart of a man who lives by the Law of the baronage, best of men.
15 Who could forgive that before your very eyes the Princess of Pāñcāla,
who had accumulated the merit of all the Laws, was harshly insulted?
Not the rape of the kingdom, not the defeat at dice, not the
banishment of my sons to the forest grieves me, as it grieves me that
that great dark woman, weeping in the hall, had to listen to insults!
While in her period the fair-hipped Kṛṣṇā, always devoted to baronial
Law, found no protector there, though she had protectors."

Strong-armed Kṛṣṇa, say to the tigerlike Arjuna, greatest of all
20 bearers of arms: "Walk the path of Draupadī!" For you know that
Bhīma and Arjuna like two enraged Yamas could speed even the Gods
on the last journey. It was humiliating to both that Kṛṣṇa was taken
to the hall and Duḥśāsana abused Bhīma, while the Kuru heroes were
watching. Remind him of that. Ask the Pāṇḍavas, Kṛṣṇā, and their
sons how they are faring, and tell them in turn that I am in good
health, Janārdana. Travel a safe path, and protect my sons.

Vaiśaṃpāyana said:

Strong-armed Kṛṣṇa saluted and circumambulated her, then he
went out striding like a lion. He dismissed the Kuru bulls, Bhīṣma and
the others, had Karṇa mount his chariot, and rode off with Sātyaki.
25 When the Dāśārha had departed, the Kurus gathered together and
talked about that wondrous miracle that had happened with Kṛṣṇa.
"All of stupefied earth is enmeshed in the snares of death," they said,
and "It comes to an end because of Duryodhana's madness."

Leaving the city the best of men rode off, and for a long time talked
with Karṇa. Then the joy of all the Yādavas dismissed Rādheya and
urged his horse to great speed. Driven by Dāruka, the horses seemed
to drink up space and ran with the speed of thought and wind.
30 Covering the road swiftly like fast kites, they carried the Śārnga
bowman to Upaplavya while the sun stood high.

Vaiśaṃpāyana said:

136.1 After listening to Kuntī's words, the great warriors Bhīṣma and
Droṇa said to the insubordinate Duryodhana, "Tiger among men, you
have heard Kuntī's matchless and meaningful speech, which she made
in dead earnest in Kṛṣṇa's presence. The Kaunteyas will obey it with
Vāsudeva's consent. They will no longer make peace without the
kingdom, Kaurava. Youabused the Pārthas and Draupadī, when they
5 were caught in the noose of the Law and had to bear it. But with the
armsman Arjuna, the toiling Bhīma, Gāṇḍīva, the two quivers, the
chariot, the banner, and Vāsudeva as companion, Yudhiṣṭhira will
forgive no more. You have seen yourself, strong-armed man, how
the crafty Pārtha vanquished everyone in battle by the city of Virāṭa.

He used his *raudra* missile and burned with the missile's fire the
gruesome Nivātakavaca Dānavas. Karṇa and the others and you
yourself in your armor and chariot were set free at the Cattle
Expedition—the example suffices.
"Best of the Bharatas, make peace with your brethren the
Pāṇḍavas, and save all of earth which is caught in the maw of death.
10 Your elder brother is a man of Law, affectionate, gentle-spoken,
honest—wipe out your guilt and go to that tiger among men. When
the Pāṇḍava sees you lay down your bow, the illustrious man will
smooth his brow and bring peace to our dynasty. Go with your
councilors to that son of a king and embrace him. Salute the king as
before, enemy-tamer, and then let Kuntī's son Yudhiṣṭhira, elder
brother of Bhīma, clasp you in friendship with his hands as you greet
him. Let Bhīma, first among fighters, with the shoulders, arms, and
thighs of a lion, of the long round arms, embrace you with those
15 arms. Lotus-eyed, lion-necked Guḍākeśa Dhanaṃjaya Pārtha, son of
Kuntī, let him greet you then. Let the tigerlike sons of the Aśvins,
peerless in beauty on earth, rise up for you in homage and affection
as for an elder. And let the kings, headed by the Dāśārha, shed tears
of happiness. Abandon your pride, king, and join with your brethren
and then rule the entire earth with your brethren. Let the kings all go
home after joyously embracing one another. Stop warring! Indra
among kings, listen to the reasoning of friends, for surely war
betokens the destruction of the barons.
20 "The stars are hostile, the signs of animals and birds are ominous,
diverse portents are seen, hero, that spell the doom of the baronage—
there are omens with us that bode the destruction of us above all.
Your army is being pelted by blazing meteors, the mounts are joyless
and seem to weep, lord of the people. There are vultures about,
circling your troops. Neither the city nor the king's palace look as
before, and jackals with unholy howls prowl the flaming horizon.
Follow the words of your father and mother and us who wish you
25 well, for on you, strong-armed man, depend war and peace. If you
do not follow the advice of your friends, enemy-plougher, you shall
rue it when you see your army tormented by the shafts of the Pārtha.
When you hear the great roar of the hissing and bellowing Bhīma
and the sound of Gāṇḍīva, you shall remember my words—when you
do, my advice will finally sound right to you."

Vaiśaṃpāyana said:
137.1 At these words Duryodhana was dispirited; he shifted his eyes,
hung his head, creased his brow, but said not a word. Seeing him
dispirited, the two bull-like men glanced at each other and spoke in
reply to his silence—

Bhīṣma said:
What greater cause for grief than that we shall have to fight
against the obedient, compliant, brahminic Pārtha, who keeps his
promises!
Droṇa said:
I hold Dhanaṃjaya higher than my son Aśvatthāman, king, and
5 there is greater humility in that ape-crested man. If I shall have
to fight with Dhanaṃjaya, who is dearer to me than my son, in order
to maintain the Law of the baronage—a curse on a baron's life! The
Terrifier, for whom no archer in the world is a match, is better than
any other bowman by my own grace. A betrayer of friends, one
evil-natured, heretical, dishonest, or crooked finds no more honor
among the strict than an addlebrain at a sacrifice. An evil man,
though warned from evil, wants evil; a good man, though tempted
by evil, wants good. Though treated treacherously, *they* still act
friendly, while *your* flaws, chief of the Bharatas, only lead to your
10 downfall. The elder of the Kurus has spoken to you, I have, Vidura
has, and so has Vāsudeva, yet you do not see your salvation.
"I have got the strength," you think and hope forcibly to make
your crossing, as though crossing in the rainy season the flooding
Ganges with its sharks, dolphins, and crocodiles! You think you are
now dressed in Yudhiṣṭhira's robe, while you merely have greedily
snatched his fortune like a cast-off garland. Who, ruling a kingdom,
outlives the son of Pāṇḍu and Pṛthā, him* who though banished to
the forest, was yet followed by Draupadī and surrounded by his
armed brothers? King Dharma shone even upon meeting Ailavila, on
15 whose command all kings wait like servants. After reaching Kubera's
seat and obtaining treasures, the Pāṇḍavas are now marching on your
opulent kingdom and demand kingship.
We have made our gifts, we have done our oblations, we have gone
through our studies, we have satisfied the brahmins with largess, we
have lived our lives—both of us have: know that we have carried
out our tasks. But you, abandoning happiness, kingdom, friends, and
riches, will wage war on the Pāṇḍavas, and you will reap disaster.
You cannot defeat the Pāṇḍava for whose triumph a Draupadī hopes,
she true-spoken and of awesome vows and austerities, a Goddess!
How can you defeat the Pāṇḍava, best of all bearers of arms, who
has Janārdana as his councilor, and Dhanaṃjaya for his brother?
20 How will you defeat the heroic Pāṇḍava of severe austerities, who
has for his companions brahmins of great fortitude, who have
mastered their senses?
I shall repeat, as a friend must who wishes to do anything to save
the life of a friend who is drowning in an ocean of disaster. Stop this

* = Yudhiṣṭhira.

warring, make your peace with these heroes, so that the Kurus may rise! Do not, with your sons, councilors, and troops, march out to defeat!

5(55) *The Temptation of Karṇa*

5.138–48 (B. 140–50; C. 4726–5096)
138 (140; 4726). Dhṛtarāṣṭra asks Saṃjaya what Kṛṣṇa had to say to Karṇa (1). Saṃjaya speaks: Kṛṣṇa tells Karṇa that by rights Karṇa is Pāṇḍu's son, for he was Kuntī's premarital son (1–10). The Pāṇḍavas will recognize him as rightful king, and Kṛṣṇa himself will consecrate him with the Pāṇḍavas' happy assistance. His will be the power and the glory (10–25).
139 (141; 4755). Karṇa replies that yes, he has the rights, but Kuntī cast him out (1–5). Adhiratha and Rādhā have showered him with love (5–10). Duryodhana has been his generous patron: to change sides now would be dishonorable (10–15). Kṛṣṇa should keep this matter quiet (15–20). Yudhiṣṭhira will triumph (20–25). Karṇa describes the war in terms of a grand sacrifice (25–50). May all barons fall and ascend to heaven (50–55).
140 (142; 4813). Kṛṣṇa smiles at Karṇa's rejection of the kingdom, nay earth itself (1). The war will spell the end of the eon (1–15). Karṇa should prompt the start of the war in seven days, on the Day of Indra (15). The fallen kings will go to heaven (20).
141 (143; 4833). Karṇa recounts all the adverse omens in Duryodhana's camp and the favorable portents in Yudhiṣṭhira's (1–25). He has had a dream presaging Yudhiṣṭhira's triumph (25–40). Kṛṣṇa agrees that the end is near. Karṇa bids Kṛṣṇa adieu (40–45). Kṛṣṇa rides off (45).
142 (144; 4885). Vidura speaks to Kuntī of his despair (1–5). She too finds only evil in this family war (10–15). She will try to soften Karṇa, the circumstances of whose birth she recounts (15–25). Kuntī goes to the Ganges, where Karṇa is worshiping the sun (25–30).

143 (145; 4917). Karṇa greets her. She recalls that he is her son and should join his real brothers as a Pārtha (1–10).
144 (146; 4929). The sun god supports her (1). Karṇa replies: Kuntī has deprived him of his dues as a kṣatriya *(1–5). It would be shameful now to change sides (5–15). He will spare the Pāṇḍavas but fight Arjuna: if either falls, Kuntī will still have five sons (15–20). Kuntī pleads with him to keep this promise (20–25).*
145 (147; 4956). Back in Upaplavya, Kṛṣṇa and the Pāṇḍavas hold counsel. Yudhiṣṭhira asks how the Kauravas reacted to Duryodhana's truculence (1–10). Kṛṣṇa replies: Bhīṣma recounted the history of the dynasty since Śaṃtanu: that king's desire to have more sons, Bhīṣma's oath, Vicitravīrya's installation and death, the subjects' pressure on Bhīṣma to become king, Bhīṣma's firm refusal (10–30), Vyāsa's service, Dhṛtarāṣṭra's blindness and consequent disqualification, Pāṇḍu's legitimate succession, the Pāṇḍavas' legitimate heritage; Duryodhana should give them half the kingdom (30–40).
146 (148; 5001). Kṛṣṇa reports Droṇa's words: Pāṇḍu bequeathed the realm to Dhṛtarāṣṭra and Vidura before departing for the forest. The kingdom was united, and Duryodhana should not break up family rule (1–15). Vidura then told Bhīṣma either to avert the impending war or return to the forest (15–25). Gāndhārī then spoke: The kingdom is rightfully the Pāṇḍavas' and Yudhiṣṭhira must rule (25–35).
147 (149; 5040). Dhṛtarāṣṭra finally addressed Duryodhana, recounting the dynastic history from Prajāpati and Yayāti. Yayāti's son Yadu was disinherited although the eldest; so was Devāpi, because of a skin disease (1–25). So was Dhṛtarāṣṭra himself, because of his blindness. Pāṇḍu succeeded and now Yudhiṣṭhira is heir (25–35).
148 (150; 5077). Duryodhana paid no heed. Kṛṣṇa has tried everything possible, but to no avail, and now sees no course but war (1–15).

Dhṛtarāṣṭra said:
138.1 Saṃjaya, before Madhusūdana rode out amidst princes and
councilors, he had Karṇa mount his chariot. What did that slayer of
enemy heroes say to Rādheya inside the chariot, what blandishments
did Govinda offer the *sūta*'s son? Relate to me what Kṛṣṇa, with his
voice roaring like a flood or a cloud, said to Karṇa, whether gently
or sharply?

Saṃjaya said:
Hear from me, Bhārata, what Madhusūdana of the boundless spirit
5 had to say to Rādheya in the course of their conversing, in words that
were smooth and gentle, friendly, informed with Law, truthful, and
helpful, to be cherished in the heart.

Vāsudeva said:
Rādheya, you have attended to brahmins learned in the Veda, and
you have questioned them about truths without demurring. You,
Karṇa, know the sempiternal sayings of the Veda, and you are well-
grounded in the subtleties of the scriptures regarding the Law.

Now, those who know the scriptures teach that the son born to a
woman before her marriage is as much counted the son of her wedded
husband as the son she bears in marriage. You, Karṇa, were born
that way: under Law you are the son of Pāṇḍu. Under the constraint
10 of the books of the Law, come with me and you shall be a king. The
Pārthas are your kin on your father's side, the Vṛṣṇis on your
mother's side: recognize, bull among men, both these lineages of
your kinsmen!

Come with me today, my son; the Pāṇḍavas shall have to recognize
you as the Kaunteya senior to Yudhiṣṭhira. The five Pāṇḍavas shall
clasp your feet as your brothers, and so shall the five sons of
Draupadī, and the unvanquished son of Subhadrā. The kings and the
sons of kings who have trooped together in the Pāṇḍava's cause, and
15 all the Andhaka-Vṛṣṇis shall clasp your feet. Baronesses and daughters
of kings shall bring golden, silver, and earthen vessels, herbs, all
seeds, all gems and shrubs for your inauguration. And at the sixth
turn you shall lie with Draupadī!

Today brahmins representing all four Vedas shall consecrate you,
assisted by the very priest of the Pāṇḍavas, while you are seated on
the tiger skin: so shall the five Pāṇḍava brothers, bulls among men,
the Draupadeyas, the Pāñcālas, and Cedis. I myself shall consecrate
you King and Lord of the Land, and Kuntī's son Yudhiṣṭhira shall be
your Young King. Kuntī's law-spirited son Yudhiṣṭhira shall mount
the chariot of state behind you, holding the white fan.
20 Kaunteya! Mighty Bhīmasena Kaunteya himself shall hold the
grand white umbrella over you, the King consecrated! Arjuna shall

drive the chariot drawn by his white horses, tinkling with hundreds of bells and covered with tiger hides. Abhimanyu, Nakula, Sahadeva, and the five Draupadeyas shall always be at your beck and call.

The Pāñcālas will follow your banner, and the great warrior
Śikhaṇḍin, and I myself will follow you; and all the Andhaka-Vṛṣṇis,
the Dāśārhas, and Daśārṇas shall be your retinue, lord of the people!
Enjoy your kingship, with your Pāṇḍava brothers, amidst prayers and
25 oblations and manifold benisons. The Draviḍas and Kuntalas shall be
your vanguard with the Āndhras, Tālacaras, Cūcupas, and Veṇupas.
Bards and minstrels shall today sing your praises in many a song.
And the Pāṇḍavas shall proclaim the Triumph of Vasuṣeṇa.

You, Kaunteya, surrounded by the Pārthas as the moon by the stars, reign you over the realm and bestow blessing on Kuntī! Your friends shall shudder with joy, your enemies with fear. Today, let there be brotherhood between you and your Pāṇḍava brothers!

Karṇa said:

139.1 I have no doubt at all, Keśava, that you are speaking to me out of
friendship and affection, and so as a friend have my best interests at
heart, Vārṣṇeya. I understand it all: under the Law, under the
constraints of the scriptures concerning the Law I am, as you hold,
the son of Pāṇḍu, Kṛṣṇa. An unmarried maiden conceived me by the
Sun, Janārdana, and at the behest of the Sun she abandoned me at
5 birth. Yes, Kṛṣṇa, under Law I was born the son of Pāṇḍu. But Kuntī
cast me out as though I had been stillborn! And Adhiratha, a *sūta*, no
sooner did he see me than he carried me to his home, Madhusūdana,
and proffered me to Rādhā, with *love*! Out of *love* for me the milk of
Rādhā's breasts poured forth at once, and she accepted my piss and
shit, Mādhava! How could a man like me deny her the ancestral
offering? A man who knows the Law and always took care to listen
to the scriptures on the Law? Adhiratha, the *sūta*, thinks of me as his
son, and my *love* demands that I think of him as my father.

He had my birth rites performed, Mādhava, by the Rules found in
10 Scripture, out of *love* for his son, Janārdana. He had the brahmins
name me Vasuṣeṇa, and when I was old enough, he married me to
wives, Keśava. I have sons and grandsons by them, Janārdana, and
my heart has bonds of *love* with them, Kṛṣṇa!

Govinda, neither joy nor fear, nor all of earth nor piles of gold can
make me a traitor to my word. For thirteen years I have enjoyed
unrivaled royal power in Dhṛtarāṣṭra's lineage by relying on
Duryodhana. I have offered up much and often, but always with
sūtas. I have performed domestic and marital rites, but always with
15 *sūtas*. Duryodhana has raised arms and prepared for war with the
Pāṇḍavas, because he relies on me, Kṛṣṇa of the Vṛṣṇis. Therefore he

has confidently chosen me to be the main opponent of the Left-handed Archer in a chariot duel in the war, Acyuta. Neither death nor capture, neither fear nor greed can make me break my promise to the sagacious Dhārtarāṣṭra, Janārdana. If I now refuse to enter the chariot duel with the Left-handed Archer, Hṛṣīkeśa, it will bring both me and the Pārtha disgrace in the world.

No doubt you mean well, Madhusūdana, and no doubt, either, that
20 the Pāṇḍavas will accomplish everything, with your guidance. So you should suppress word of our taking counsel here, best of men; that would be best, I think, joy of all the Yādavas. If the law-spirited king of strict vows knows that I am Kuntī's first-born son, he will not accept the kingdom; and if I were then to obtain this large, prosperous kingdom, I would hand it over to Duryodhana, Madhusūdana, enemy-tamer! Let the law-spirited Yudhiṣṭhira be king forever, he who has Hṛṣīkeśa as his guide, Dhanaṃjaya as his warrior. His is the earth who has the great warrior Bhīmasena, Nakula, Sahadeva, the
25 Draupadeyas, O Mādhava, and Uttamaujas, Yudhāmanyu, Satyadharman, Somaki, Caidya and Cekitāna, the unvanquished Śikhaṇḍin, the firefly-colored Kekaya brothers, the rainbow-hued Kuntibhoja, that great warrior, and Bhīmasena's uncle, and the warrior Senājit, Śankha son of Virāṭa, and you as his treasury, Janārdana. Great is this gathering of the baronage that has been achieved, Keśava. And this kingdom, blazing and renowned among all kings, has now been won.

Vārṣṇeya, the Dhārtarāṣṭra will hold a grand sacrifice of war. Of this sacrifice you shall be the Witness, Janārdana, and you shall be
30 the Adhvaryu priest at the ritual. The Terrifier with the monkey standard stands girt as the Hotar; Gāṇḍīva will be the ladle; the bravery of men the sacrificial butter. The *aindra, pāśupata, brāhma,* and *sthūṇākarṇa* missiles will be the spells employed by the Left-handed Archer. Saubhadra, taking after his father, if not overtaking him, in prowess, will act perfectly as the Grāvastut priest. Mighty Bhīma will be the Udgātar and Prastotar, that tigerlike man who with his roars on the battlefield finishes off an army of elephants. The eternal king, law-spirited Yudhiṣṭhira, well-versed in recitations and oblations, will
35 act as the Brahmán. The sounds of the conches, the drums, the kettledrums, and the piercing lion roars will be the Subrahmaṇyā invocation. Mādrī's two glorious sons Nakula and Sahadeva of great valor will fill the office of the Śamitar priest. The clean chariot spears with their spotted staffs will serve as the sacrificial poles at this sacrifice, Janārdana. The eared arrows, hollow reeds, iron shafts and calf-tooth piles, and the javelins will be the Soma jars, and the bows the strainers. Swords will be the potsherds, skulls the Puroḍāśa cakes,

40 and blood will be the oblation at this sacrifice, Kṛṣṇa. The spears and
bright clubs will be the kindling and enclosing sticks; the pupils of
Droṇa and Kṛpa Śāradvata the Sadasyas. The arrows shot by the
Gāṇḍīva bowman, the great warriors, and Droṇa and his son will be
the pillows. Sātyaki shall act as Pratiprasthātar, the Dhārtarāṣṭra as
the Sacrificer, his great army as the Wife. Mighty Ghaṭotkaca will be
the Śamitar when this Overnight Sacrifice is spun out, strong-armed
hero. Majestic Dhṛṣṭadyumna shall be the sacrificial fee when the
fire rite takes place, he who was born from the fire.
45 The insults I heaped on the Pāṇḍavas, to please Duryodhana, those
I regret. When you see me cut down by the Left-handed Archer, it
will be the Re-piling of the Fire of their sacrifice. When the Pāṇḍava
drinks the blood of Duḥśāsana, bellowing his roar, it will be the Soma
draught. When the two Pāñcālyas fell Droṇa and Bhīṣma, that will be
the Conclusion of the sacrifice, Janārdana. When the mighty
Bhīmasena kills Duryodhana, then the great sacrifice of the
50 Dhārtarāṣṭra will end. The weeping of the gathered daughters-in-law
and granddaughters-in-law, whose masters, sons, and protectors have
been slain, with the mourning of Gāndhārī at the sacrificial site now
teeming with dogs, vultures, and ospreys, will be the Final Bath of
this sacrifice, Janārdana.
May these barons, old in learning and days, O bull among barons,
not die a useless death for your sake, Madhusūdana. Let the full
circle of the baronage find their death by the sword on the Field of
the Kurus, holiest in all three worlds, Keśava. Ordain here, lotus-eyed
Vārṣṇeya, what you desire, so that the baronage in its totality may
ascend to heaven.
55 As long as the mountains will stand and the rivers flow, Janārdana,
so long and forevermore shall last the sound of the fame of this war.
Brahmins shall in their gatherings narrate the Great War of the
Bhāratas, proclaiming the glory of the barons.
Keśava, lead the Kaunteya to the battle, and keep this council of
ours secret, enemy-burner.

Saṃjaya said:

140.1 Having heard Karṇa's reply, Keśava, slayer of enemy heroes, smiled;
then he laughed and said, "Does the offer of a kingdom not tempt
you, Karṇa? Do you not wish to rule the earth I am giving you?"

There is not a shadow of doubt remaining
That victory's sure of the Pāṇḍavas:
The Pāṇḍava's banner of Triumph is out,
The terrible king of the apes has been raised!

Celestial art did Bhauvana fashion:
It is raised like the banner of Indra himself;
It shows many creatures that terrify,
Celestial creatures that horrify.

5 It is never entangled in rocks or trees,
Upward and across it stretches a league;
The illustrious flag of Dhanaṃjaya, Karṇa,
Is raised with a glow that resembles the fire's.

When you see the man of the white horses on the battlefield with
Kṛṣṇa driving his chariot, employing the missiles of Indra, Fire, and
Wind, and hear the whip-crack of Gāṇḍīva as of a thunderbolt, then
there will be no more Kṛta Age, no more Tretā, no more Dvāpara.
When you see Kuntī's son Yudhiṣṭhira on the battlefield, protecting
his grand-army with spells and oblations, unassailable like the sun
burning the host of the enemy, then there will be no more Kṛta, no
10 more Tretā, no more Dvāpara. When you see the mighty Bhīmasena
on the battlefield, dancing his war dance after drinking Duḥśāsana's
blood, like a rutting elephant that has killed a challenging tusker,
then there will be no more Kṛta, no more Tretā, no more Dvāpara.
When you see Mādrī's warrior sons on the battlefield, routing the
army of the Dhārtarāṣṭras like elephants, shattering the chariots of
enemy heroes as they plunge into the clash of arms, then there will
be no more Kṛta, no more Tretā, no more Dvāpara. When you see
on the battlefield Droṇa, Śāṃtanava, Kṛpa, King Suyodhana, and
15 Jayadratha Saindhava storming to the attack and halted by the
Left-handed Archer, then there will be no more Kṛta, no more Tretā,
no more Dvāpara.

Go hence, Karṇa, and say to Droṇa, Śaṃtanava, and Kṛpa: this is a propitious month, with fodder and fuel plentifully at hand, abounding with ripe grains and plants, with plenty of fruit and hardly any mosquitoes. There is no mud, the water is tasty, the weather is pleasant, neither too hot nor too cold. Seven days from now it will be New Moon: let then the battle be joined, for they say that that is the Day of Indra.

Likewise say to all the kings who have come to battle, "I shall
20 accomplish for you all that you desire." The kings and princes who
follow Duryodhana's orders will, in finding their death by the sword,
attain to the highest goal.

Saṃjaya said:

141.1 Upon hearing Keśava's words, benevolent and propitious, Karṇa paid homage to Kṛṣṇa Madhusūdana, and said, "Why, strong-armed man, did you seek to delude me when you knew already? The total destruction that looms for the earth is caused by Śakuni, me, Duḥśāsana, and Dhṛtarāṣṭra's son King Duryodhana. There is no doubt, Kṛṣṇa, that a great battle impends between the Pāṇḍavas and Kurus, grisly and mired in blood. The kings and princes who follow Duryodhana's orders will journey to Yama's realm, burned by the fire of the weapons in the war. Many nightmarish dreams are being seen, Madhusūdana, and dreadful portents and calamitous omens, hair-raising and manifold, which presage that victory will be Yudhiṣṭhira's and defeat Duryodhana's, Vārṣṇeya. The luminous planet Saturn is sharply threatening the constellation Rohiṇī, menacing the creatures even more. Mars, in retrograde position to Jyeṣṭha, is aiming for Anurādhā, Madhusūdana, as though pleading for the peace of friendship.

Surely great danger is at hand for the Kurus, Kṛṣṇa, for the planet threatens Citrā in particular, Vārṣṇeya. The spot on the moon is distorted, while Rāhu is about to attack the sun. Meteors are falling from the sky with hurricanes and earthquakes. The elephants are trumpeting, the horses are shedding tears and take no pleasure in water and fodder, Mādhava. When such portents appear, they say a horrendous danger is near that will destroy the creatures, strong-armed one. Horses, elephants, and men are eating little in all the armies of the Dhārtarāṣṭra, Keśava, yet their feces are massive. The wise say that that is a sign of defeat, Madhusūdana. They say, Kṛṣṇa, that the mounts of the Pāṇḍavas are in good spirits and that the wild beasts are circumambulating their camp, a sign of victory, but all animals go the reverse way around the Dhārtarāṣṭra, Keśava, and there are also disembodied voices, a sign of his defeat. Peacocks, flower birds, wild geese, cranes, *cātakas*, and *jīvaṃjīvaka* flocks follow the Pāṇḍavas, while vultures, crows, *baḍas*, kites, ghouls, jackals, and swarms of mosquitoes follow the Kauravas.

In the Dhārtarāṣṭra's armies there is no sound of drums, but the drums of the Pāṇḍavas sound forth unstruck. The wells in the Dhārtarāṣṭra's camp gurgle like bullocks, presaging his defeat. The God rains a rain of flesh and blood. A brilliant Gandharva city hovers nearby with walls, moats, ramparts, and handsome gate towers. A black mace obfuscates the sun at dawn and dusk, predicting great danger, and a single jackal howls horrifyingly, a sign of Duryodhana's defeat. Black-necked birds hover terrifyingly, then fly into the dusk, a sign of his defeat. He hates first of all the brahmins, Madhusūdana, and then his elders and loyal retainers, a sign of his defeat. The eastern horizon is blood-red, the southern darkling like swords, and the western mud-colored like an unbaked pot, Madhusūdana. All the horizons of the Dhārtarāṣṭra are on fire, Mādhava, and with these portentous signs they foredoom great danger.

I had a dream in which I saw Yudhiṣṭhira and his brothers ascend
to a thousand-pillared palace, Acyuta. All wore white turbans and
white robes, and I saw that they all had beautiful stools. In my vision
I saw you drape the blood-fouled earth with entrails, Kṛṣṇa Janārdana.
30 A boundlessly august Yudhiṣṭhira mounted a pile of bones and
joyously ate rice mixed with *ghee* from a gold platter. I saw
Yudhiṣṭhira swallow the earth which you had served him—clearly
he shall enjoy the rule of the earth. Wolf-Belly of the terrible feats
had climbed a steep mountain and with his club in hand the
tigerlike man seemed to survey this earth—clearly he shall destroy
us all in a great battle. I know, Hṛṣīkeśa, that where there is Law
there is triumph. Dhanaṃjaya carrying Gāṇḍīva had mounted a white
35 elephant, together with you, Hṛṣīkeśa, blazing with sublime luster. All
of you shall—about that I have no doubts—slaughter all the kings
led by Duryodhana in battle, Kṛṣṇa. Nakula, Sahadeva, and the great
warrior Sātyaki, decked with pure bracelets and necklaces, wearing
white garlands and robes, tigerlike man, had mounted on men, the
three stately men wearing white umbrellas and robes. In the
Dhārtarāṣṭra's armies too I saw three white-turbaned men, Janārdana
Keśava—know who they are: Aśvatthāman, Kṛpa, and Kṛtavarman
40 Sātvata. All other kings wore red turbans, Mādhava. Mounted on a
camel cart, O strong-armed Janārdana, Bhīṣma and Droṇa
accompanied by me and the Dhārtarāṣṭra traveled to the region ruled
by Agastya, Lord Janārdana: soon we shall reach the dwelling of
Yama; I and the other kings and the circle of barons shall doubtless
enter the fire of Gāṇḍīva.

Kṛṣṇa said:

Of a certainty, the destruction of the earth is now near, for my
words do not reach your heart, Karṇa. When the destruction of all
creatures is at hand, bad policy disguised as good does not stir from
the heart, my friend.

Karṇa said:

45 Perhaps we shall see you again, strong-armed Kṛṣṇa, if we escape
alive from the great battle, the carnage of heroes. Or surely we shall
meet in heaven, Kṛṣṇa—yes, there we shall meet again next, prince
sans blame.

Saṃjaya said:

Speaking thus, Karṇa clasped the Mādhava tightly; then, dismissed
by Keśava, he came down from the pit of the chariot. Riding his own
gold-adorned chariot, Rādheya dejectedly returned with us. Keśava
rode off with Sātyaki at a fast pace, again and again urging his
charioteer, "Go! Go!"

Vaiśaṃpāyana said:

142.1 When Kṛṣṇa's diplomacy had failed and he had departed from the

Kurus for the Pāṇḍavas, the Steward went to Pṛthā and spoke softly
in sorrow, "You know, mother of living sons, that my heart always
inclines to kindliness. I may shout, but Suyodhana does not take my
advice. Yonder, King Yudhiṣṭhira, armed with the Cedis, Pāñcālas,
and Kekayas, with Bhīma and Arjuna, Kṛṣṇa, Yuyudhāna, and the
twins, and encamped at Upaplavya, still only wishes for Law out of
5 love for his kinsmen, like a weak man although he is strong. King
Dhṛtarāṣṭra here, on the other hand, while old in years does not
make peace. Infected by the madness of his son, he walks the path of
lawlessness. Because of the bad judgment of Jayadratha, Karṇa,
Duḥśāsana, and Saubala the breach goes on. But the Law and its
consequences will overtake those who lawlessly stole that most law-
loving kingdom. Who would not run a fever when the Kurus steal the
Law by force? When Keśava comes back without peace, the Pāṇḍavas
shall arm for battle, and the bad policy of the Kurus will become the
assassin of heroes. I worry and worry, and find no sleep by day or
night."

10 Listening to his words, which were spoken by one who meant well,
Kuntī, sick with grief herself, sighed aloud and reflected in her mind,
"Accursed be this wealth for the sake of which there will be great
carnage in the slaughter of kinsmen, for there will only be defeat in
this family war. If the Pāṇḍavas, Cedis, Pāñcālas, and the Yādavas
together fight the Bhāratas, what could be worse than that? I do
see that there is evil in war, surely, but so is defeat in war evil. For
the dispossessed it is better to die, for there is no victory in the killing
of kin. Grandfather Śāṃtanava and the Teacher, master of warriors,
15 and Karṇa increase my fears in the cause of the Dhārtarāṣṭra. Droṇa
the Teacher would never willingly fight with his pupils for personal
gain, and why would Grandfather not have good feelings toward the
Pāṇḍavas? It is only *he* who perversely follows the folly of the evil-
hearted Dhārtarāṣṭra, who always has hated the Pāṇḍavas wickedly.
Karṇa is obdurate in a great cause, and always strong enough to visit
disaster on the Pāṇḍavas; and that burns me now. Today I hope to
soften Karṇa's heart toward the Pāṇḍavas, when I approach him
and show him the truth.

"When the blessed Durvāsas was satisfied and granted me the boon
of conjuring up Gods, while I lived honorably in father Kuntibhoja's
20 house, I thought in many ways with beating heart, right there in the
king's women's quarters, about the strength and weakness of spells
and the power of a brahmin's word. I thought and thought, being
both a woman and a child, protected by my trusted nurse and
surrounded by my friends, shunning mistakes and guarding my
father's good name, "How can I do something good for myself and
yet not sin?" thinking of the brahmin and bowing to him. Then, on
having attained the boon that enabled such a course I, out of

curiosity and childishness, being just a girl, made God the Sun come
25 to me. Why should he whom I carried as a girl, not obey my word,
which is proper and good for his brothers, when he has been received
back as my son?"

When Kuntī had taken this ultimate decision, she embarked upon
her task and went to the river Bhāgīrathī. On the bank of the Ganges
Pṛthā heard the sound of her compassionate and truthful son's
recitations. She stood miserably behind her son, who faced east with
his hands raised, and waited for the recitation to end. She, wedded
wife of a Kauravya, a Princess of the Vṛṣṇis, stood in the shade of
Karṇa's upper garment like a withered garland of lotuses, hurting
from the heat of the sun. He prayed until the heat reached his back,
30 being strict in his vows; then he turned around and saw Kuntī. He
saluted her and waited for her to speak with folded hands, as was
proper, this proud and splendid man, first of the upholders of the
Law.

Karṇa said:

143.1 I, Karṇa, son of Rādhā and Adhiratha, salute you. Why has your
ladyship come? Tell me what I must do for you.

Kuntī said:

You are the son of Kuntī, not of Rādhā, nor is Adhiratha your
father. You have not been born in the line of *sūtas*, Karṇa. Learn
what I am telling you. I gave birth to you before I was married. You
are my first-born whom I carried in my womb in the palace of
Kuntibhoja. You are a *Pārtha*, my son! He, the God who makes light
and spreads heat, he Virocana begot you on me, Karṇa, to be the
5 greatest of swordsmen. The child of a God, with inborn earrings and
armor, you were borne by me in my father's house, covered with
glory, invincible son. It is not at all right for you, son, innocently
to serve the Dhārtarāṣṭras without knowing your real brothers. In
the decisions of Law *that* is reckoned the fruit of the Law of men that
as parents—and also as a one-eyed mother—they rest content with
their son. Cut yourself off from the Dhārtarāṣṭras and enjoy
Yudhiṣṭhira's fortune, the fortune once won by Arjuna and then
greedily stolen by scoundrels. Let the Kurus today witness the
10 meeting of Karṇa and Arjuna in a spirit of brotherhood. Let Karṇa
and Arjuna be like Rāma and Janārdana. When the two of you are
united in spirit, what could you not achieve in the world! Surrounded
by your five brothers, you shall surely shine forth, Karṇa, like
Brahmā surrounded by the Vedas and their Branches. Endowed with
virtues, the eldest and the best among relations who are the best,
your title will no longer be that of the son of a *sūta*; you shall be
a heroic *Pārtha*!

Vaiśaṃpāyana said:

144.1 Thereupon Karṇa heard a voice that issued from the sun,
affectionate and not to be gainsaid, which the sun uttered like a
father: "Pṛthā has spoken the truth, Karṇa, obey your mother's
word. The greatest good will befall you, tiger among men, if you do
as she says." And thus addressed by his mother, and by his father
the Sun himself, Karṇa's mind did not falter, for he stood fast by the
truth.

Karṇa said:

It is not that I do not believe the words you have spoken, *ksatriya*
lady, or deny that for me the gateway to the Law is to carry out your
5 behest. But the irreparable wrong you have done me by casting me
out has destroyed the name and fame I could have had. Born a
kṣatriya, I have yet not received the respect due a baron. What enemy
could have done me greater harm than you have? When there was
time to act you did not show me your present compassion. And
now you have laid orders on me, the son to whom you denied the
sacraments. You have never acted in my interest like a mother, and
now, here you are, enlightening me solely in your own interest.

Who would not tremble before a Dhanaṃjaya aided by a Kṛṣṇa?
10 Who would not call me a coward, if I now joined the Pārthas? I who
never had been known as their brother now stand revealed as one,
at the hour of battle. If I now go to the Pāṇḍavas, what will the
baronage call me? The Dhārtarāṣṭras have let me share in all their
comforts and have honored me much at all times: how could I, *I*
betray them now? Now that they are embroiled in a feud with the
others, they attend to me at all times and honor me as much as the
Vasus honor Vāsava. How could I shatter their hopes now, if they
think that with my prowess they can engage their enemies? How
could I desert them now when they see in me the boat they need to
cross over this impassable battle and find the farther shore of this
15 shoreless ocean? Now the hour has struck for all the men who have
lived off the Dhārtarāṣṭra, and I have to discharge my duty heedless
of my life. Those evil men who, after having been well supported to
their heart's content, pay no heed to what has been done for them and
fecklessly undo past benefactions when the time of duty arrives,
wicked despoilers of their kings and thieves of their masters' riceball,
gain neither this world nor the next.

Yes, I shall fight your sons in the cause of Dhṛtarāṣṭra's son with
all my power and strength—I will *not* lie to you. While trying to
persevere in the humane conduct that becomes a decent man, I will
not carry out your word, beneficial though it may be. Yet, your effort
20 with me shall not lack fruit. I shall not kill your sons in the battle,
though I can withstand and slay them—that is, your sons Yudhiṣṭhira,

Bhīma and the twins, excepting Arjuna. Arjuna I shall fight in
Yudhiṣṭhira's army. In killing Arjuna on the battlefield I shall find
my reward, or reap fame if the Left-handed Archer kills me. So never
shall your sons number less than five, glorious woman: either without
Arjuna but with Karṇa, or with Arjuna, if I am killed.

Vaiśaṃpāyana said:

Having heard Karṇa's answer, Kuntī shuddered from sorrow; and
embracing her son, she said to Karṇa, who was unfaltering in his
fortitude, "So it must be then—the Kauravas will go to their
perdition, as you have said, Karṇa. Fate is all-powerful. But promise
25 me, enemy-plougher: the safety you have granted your four brothers,
of that pledge you will acquit yourself! Good health and good luck,"
said Pṛthā to Karṇa. Pleased, Karṇa saluted her. Then both went
their separate ways.

Vaiśaṃpāyana said:

145.1 Returning to Upaplavya from Hāstinapura, enemy-tamer Keśava
reported everything to the Pāṇḍavas. After they had discussed it for
a long time and consulted again and again, Śauri went to his own
camp to rest. The five Pāṇḍava brothers dismissed all the kings,
headed by Virāṭa. When the sun set, they worshiped the twilight.
Then their thoughts went to Kṛṣṇa, and they had the Dāśārha fetched
and deliberated again.

Yudhiṣṭhira said:

5 What did you tell the son of Dhṛtarāṣṭra in the assembly hall,
lotus-eyed one, when you had gone to the City of the Elephant?
Please repeat it to me.

Vāsudeva said:

What I told the son of Dhṛtarāṣṭra in the assembly hall, when I
had gone to the City of the Elephant, was true, salutary, and
beneficial. But the scoundrel did not accept it.

Yudhiṣṭhira said:

When that man had gone off the right path, Hṛṣīkeśa, what did
grandfather, the elder of the Kurus, have to say to the truculent
Duryodhana? And what did our Teacher, the strong-armed
Bhāradvāja, and our junior father the Steward, the first of the
upholders of Law, tell the son of Dhṛtarāṣṭra in sorrow over his sons?
What, too, did all the kings who sat together in the hall have to say?
10 Tell what happened, Janārdana. You did report what the two chief
Kurus said to that fool who thinks he is clever, overcome by lust and
greed. But unpleasant matters do not stick in my mind, Keśava. I
want to hear what they said, Lord Govinda. Act, friend, the time is
passing by; for you are our recourse, you our protector, you our guru.

Vāsudeva said:
Hear then, king, what King Suyodhana was told amidst the Kurus,
O Indra among kings, in the assembly hall. Listen to me.
After I had made my address, Dhṛtarāṣṭra's son laughed, whereupon
15 an outraged Bhīṣma said to him, "Duryodhana, listen to what I have
to say for the good of the family; and when you have heard it, tiger
among kings, do what is in the interest of your own family.
"My father was the world-renowned Śaṃtanu, king, and I was his
only son, the best of all who have sons, my son. The thought
occurred to him, 'How may I have a second son? The wise say that
having one son is having none. How may the family continue to
exist and spread its fame?' Knowing his desire I brought him Kālī,
who was to be my mother. For the sake of my father and family I
swore a difficult oath, as you well know, to be neither king nor father.
20 And here I live confidently, keeping my promise. From her the law-
spirited Vicitravīrya was born, strong-armed, illustrious scion of the
House of Kuru, my younger brother.
"When father had gone to heaven, I installed Vicitravīrya in my
kingdom as the king, while I myself became his retainer below him.
You have often heard how I brought him suitable brides in marriage
after vanquishing a whole gathering of princes. Later I became
embroiled in a duel with Rāma—he was banished by his townsmen
out of fear for Rāma. Being too greatly attached to his wives, he
succumbed to exhaustion.
"When Indra no longer rained on the kingless kingdom, the
subjects hastened to me, driven by hunger and fear.
The subjects said:
25 " 'All the subjects are dwindling! You be our king and revive
us! Be blessed, drive away the plagues, increaser of Śaṃtanu's house.
All your subjects are suffering from most terrible diseases and but few
remain, son of the Ganges. Pray rescue us! Dispel the sicknesses, hero,
and rule the subjects by the Law, lest the kingdom fall in ruins while
you are alive.' "
Bhīṣma said:
"The wailing of the subjects failed to shake my mind, and recalling
the code of the strict, I kept my promise. The townspeople, my good
mother, Kālī, retainers, house priests, and learned brahmins, great
30 king, all kept urging me in great distress, 'Be our king! The kingdom
that was ruled by Pratīpa is going to perish now that it has fallen to
you. For the sake of our well-being be you our king, O sage!' At
their words I folded my hands, greatly distressed and unhappy, and
told them again and again the promise I had made out of deference
to my father, son, that I would remain a celibate and not be king

for the good of the lineage. With folded hands I again and again
placated my mother, king, saying, 'Mother, though born from
Śaṃtanu and carrying on the lineage of Kuru, I cannot belie my oath,
withal for your own sake. Do not lay the yoke on me. I am your
servant and slave, son-loving mother!'

"Having thus placated my mother and the people, I solicited the
great hermit Vyāsa for my brother's wives. Together with my mother,
great king, I propitiated the seer and solicited him for offspring;
35 and he bestowed his grace and begot three sons then, best of the
Bharatas. Being blind and thus lacking the faculty of sight, your
father could not be king, and Pāṇḍu, great-spirited and world-
renowned, became king. He was the king and his sons are their
father's heirs. Do not quarrel, son, give them half the kingdom. What
man can rule the kingdom as long as I am alive? Do not ignore my
words, for I always have your peace at heart. I do not discriminate,
son, between you and them, king. This is also the opinion of your
40 father, of Gāndhārī and of Vidura. If the elders are to be heard, do
not disobey my words, lest you destroy everybody, yourself and the
earth."

Vāsudeva said:

146.1 When Bhīṣma had spoken, eloquent Droṇa addressed Duryodhana
in the midst of the kings, blessings upon thee. "Just as Pratīpa's son
Śaṃtanu," he said, "rose in the cause of his lineage, son, so
Devavrata Bhīṣma has stood for the interests of the family. Thereafter
Pāṇḍu, lord of men, true to his word, master of his senses, became
the king of the Kurus, law-spirited, of good vows, and devoted. Later
he, who increased the dynasty of Kuru, gave the realm to the wise
5 Dhṛtarāṣṭra, his elder, and to Vidura, his junior. Then, after having
placed him firmly on the lion throne, king, the Kauravya went to the
forest with his two wives, prince sans blame.

"Vidura stood below him like a humble servant, and the tigerlike
man waited on him, holding up the tail-hair fan. All the subjects
properly accepted Dhṛtarāṣṭra as the lord of the realm, just as they
had King Pāṇḍu, my son. After entrusting the kingdom to Dhṛtarāṣṭra
and Vidura, Pāṇḍu, the conqueror of enemy cities, roamed all of
earth. Vidura, true to his word, was in charge of generating revenue,
10 gifts, the supervision of the servants, and the upkeep of all. Mighty
Bhīṣma, conqueror of enemy cities, was in charge of war and peace
and oversaw the personal care of the king. Strong-armed King
Dhṛtarāṣṭra sat on the lion throne, always attended by the great-
spirited Vidura.

"Why do you, though born in this family, resolve to break up the

family? Enjoy your comforts in unison with your brethren, lord of the
people! I am not saying this out of either lack of nerve or hope of
personal gain: I eat what Bhīṣma gives me, not you, best of kings.
I do not want my livelihood from you, lord of the people. Where
Bhīṣma goes goes Droṇa. Do what Bhīṣma says. Give the sons of
15 Pāṇḍu half the kingdom, plougher of enemies. I have always served
both you and them equally as teacher, son. The man of the white
horses means as much to me as Aśvatthāman. Why use many
words? Victory lies where Law lies."

When Droṇa had thus spoken, great king, true-spoken and Law-
wise Vidura lifted his voice, turning to his father and looking him in
the face, "Devavrata, listen to what I have to say. This dynasty of
Kuru was lost and you rescued it—now you pay no heed to my
complaints. Who is this defiler of his family, this Duryodhana, that
you follow the judgment of this man who is possessed with greed,
20 ignoble, ungrateful, his mind diseased with avarice, disobedient to the
commandments of his father, who sees Law and Profit? The Kurus
are doomed because of Duryodhana: act, great king, so that they need
not perish. After you had created me and the lustrous King
Dhṛtarāṣṭra as a painter creates a painting, do not destroy us now.
Do not, strong-armed hero, look away at the sight of the destruction
of the Kurus, like a Prajāpati who creates the creatures to destroy
them. Or if your wits fail you, now that destruction impends, go to
the forest with me and Dhṛtarāṣṭra, and the kingdom shall be safely
25 ruled by the Pāṇḍavas. Have mercy, tiger among kings, we face a
holocaust of Pāṇḍavas and Kurus and boundlessly august kings!"

Having spoken Vidura fell silent, with sorrow in his heart, lost in
his thoughts and sighing again and again.

Thereupon King Subala's daughter herself,
Afeared of the death of the family, spoke
Irately in front of the kings to her son,
Mean-hearted, cruel Duryodhana.

"Let the kings who have entered this hall of the king,
The brahmin seers and others in council
Pay heed: before them I state the guilt
Of you and your councilors' band who are evil!

"The realm of the Kurus is ruled by succession:
That's the family Law come down to us.
You, wicked of mind and most cruel of deed,
Kill the realm of the Kurus by means that are crooked.

30 "The wise Dhṛtarāṣṭra now stands in the realm
And by him stands farsighted Vidura.

Overreaching them both, how dare you aspire
In your folly to kingship, Duryodhana?

"The King and the Steward of mighty prowess
Are subject to Bhīṣma as long as he stands;
But the son of the river, great-spirited, does not
Aspire to the realm since he knows the Law.

"This kingdom was Pāṇḍu's inalienably,
And his sons now rank, and nobody else;
This kingdom entire is the Pāṇḍavas' own,
Ancestral, bequeathed to their sons and theirs.

"What the great-souled chief of the Kurus has said,
Devavrata the sage, whose promise is true,
We must accept it all as Law undiminished,
If we are to guard the Law of our own.

"With this man of great vows' consent let the king
In like manner speak, and Vidura also,
And let it be done at their charge by our friends,
Keeping Law in the front for a long time to come.

35 "Yudhiṣṭhira, son of the Law, shall rule
This realm of the Kurus, to which he succeeded,
Exhorted by King Dhṛtarāṣṭra himself,
And placed at the head by Śaṃtanu's son!"

Vāsudeva said:

147.1 When Gāndhārī had spoken, King Dhṛarāṣṭra addressed
Duryodhana in the midst of the princes, O king, "Duryodhana, liste
to what I shall have to say to you, my son, and carry it out, and b
blessed, if you respect your father.

"Soma Prajāpati founded the dynasty of the Kurus in the beginn
and Nahuṣa's son Yayāti was the sixth from Soma. He had five son
all most eminent royal seers, and the eldest of them was the mighty
5 Lord Yadu. The youngest, Pūru, who increased our dynasty, was
born from Śarmiṣṭhā, the daughter of Vṛṣaparvan. Yadu, O best of t
Bharatas, was the son of Devayānī, and on her side the grandson o
Śukra Kāvya of immense splendor. The founder of the Yādavas, str
and esteemed for his bravery, despised the baronage, being full of
pride and slow of wit. Befuddled by his pride in his strength, he did
not abide by his father's command—this unvanquished prince
despised his father and brothers. Yadu grew mighty on four-corner
earth and after subjugating the kings dwelled in the City of the
10 Elephant. His father, Yayāti Nāhuṣa, in fury cursed his son, O

Gāndhāri, and cast him from the kingdom. Yayāti in his rage also cursed those sons of his who had followed their brother, so proud of his strength. That best of kings thereupon installed his youngest son Pūru, who took his orders obediently, in the kingdom.

"Thus even an eldest son is not born to kingship, if he is prideful, while the youngest are born to be kings by their deference to their elders. Likewise my father's grandfather, Pratīpa, who knew all the Laws, a king famed in the three worlds: to this lion among kings, who ruled the kingdom under Law, three famous Godlike sons were born. Devāpi was the eldest, Bāhlīka came after him, and steadfast Śaṃtanu, my grandfather, son, was the third. But Devāpi of great splendor and the best of kings, law-abiding, veracious, and obedient to his father, had a skin disease. Devāpi was loved by the townfolk and country people, esteemed by the good, and dear to the hearts of young and old. Wise, true to his promises, intent on the interests of all creatures, abiding by the commands of his father and the brahmins, he was a beloved brother to Bāhlīka and the great-spirited Śaṃtanu—indeed the brotherliness of these great-spirited men was exemplary.

"In the course of time his father, best among kings, had the necessaries fetched for the Royal Consecration according to precept, and the overlord had all the auspicious formalities performed. Then the brahmins and elders, supported by town and country folk, forbade the consecration of Devāpi. When the king heard about the interdiction of the consecration, his throat was choked with tears and he grieved over his son.

"Thus this generous, Law-wise, true-spoken prince, beloved by the subjects, was yet flawed by his skin disease. The Gods do not approve of a king who is lacking in limbs, and with this in mind the bulls of the twiceborn stopped their good king. Thereupon, with sorrowing spirit and grieving over his son, Pratīpa died; and seeing him dead Devāpi took shelter in the forest. Bāhlīka had left the realm and established himself in the family of his maternal uncle. He abandoned his father and brothers and acquired a wealthy town. With Bāhlīka's leave, world-famous Śaṃtanu upon his father's death ruled the kingdom as king, O king.

"Likewise I myself, the eldest, was upon much thought barred from the kingdom by the sagacious Pāṇḍu for being 'lacking in limbs,' Bhārata, and Pāṇḍu, though the younger, succeeded to the kingdom as king. Upon his demise the kingdom became his sons', enemy-tamer. If I could not inherit the realm, how can you seek it?

"Great-souled Yudhiṣṭhira is the Heir;
This realm has lawfully fallen to him.
The master is he of the Kaurava people,
For him to rule in majesty.

"He is true to his promises, never distracted,
Upright and prepared to obey his kin,
Beloved of the subjects, kind to his friends,
In control of his senses, support of the good.

"Forgiveness, forbearance, uprightness, control,
Avowedness to truth, great learning and zeal,
Compassion as well as authority—
Yudhiṣṭhira has all the virtues of kings.

"Not the son of a king and ignoble in conduct,
Avaricious, ill-intentioned to kin,
How can you, a lout, pretend to seize
This realm that others are lawfully heir to?

35 "Cast off your delusion and render them half
Of the realm and requisite mounts and retainers;
Only then, lord of men, may you and your brothers
Still have the rest of your lives to live!"

Vāsudeva said:

148.1 When Bhīṣma had thus spoken, and Droṇa, Vidura, Gāndhārī, and
Dhṛtarāṣṭra, the fool paid no heed. Shrugging them off he rose irately,
his eyes bloodshot with rage; and the kings hurried after him, laying
down their lives. He ordered those kings, whose minds were warped,
"March out to the field of the Kurus! Today it is Puṣya," again and
again. Thereupon the kings departed with their troops, after making
5 Bhīṣma supreme commander, exultant and urged on by Time. Eleven
armies of kings had massed, and at their head shone Bhīṣma with his
palm-tree standard.

Therefore, lord of your people, dispose what is meet and proper.
I have reported all that befell in the assembly of the Kurus, all that
was said in my presence by Bhīṣma, Droṇa, Vidura, Gāndhārī, and
Dhṛtarāṣṭra, King Bhārata. First I used a conciliatory approach,
hoping for a sense of brotherliness to prevail, to prevent a breach in
the dynasty of Kuru, and to further the well-being of the subjects.
When conciliatoriness failed, I tried alienation and recited your feats,
human and divine. When Suyodhana ignored my conciliatory speech,
10 I convened all the kings and attempted to sow discord. I displayed
dreadful and terrifying miracles and superhuman exploits, Lord
Bhārata. I threatened the kings, denigrated Suyodhana, and
intimidated Rādheya and Saubala time and again. Again and again
I pointed to the meanness of the Dhārtarāṣṭras and heaped blame on
them, trying to alienate those kings over and over again with words
and advice. Once more conciliatory, I mentioned gifts, in order to

prevent a breach in the dynasty of Kuru and accomplish my mission, saying, "Those boys, those Pāṇḍavas, will shed their pride and submit to Dhṛtarāṣṭra, Bhīṣma, and Vidura. Let them proffer you the kingdom and themselves remain no more masters. Let it be as the king and Gāngeya and Vidura have stated. Let the whole realm be yours, let go of just five villages. Surely your father can afford to support them, greatest of kings!" Yet at such words the evil man did not change his mind.

Now I see no other course open but the fourth—punishment. The kings are marching to Kurukṣetra to their doom! I have told all that befell in the assembly of the Kurus: they will *not* give you the kingdom without war, Pāṇḍava. Driven to destroy, they now face death.

5(56) The Marching Out

5.149–52 (B. 151–55; C. 5097–277)
149 (151–52; 5097). Yudhiṣṭhira orders his armies marshaled. He asks Sahadeva who should be marshal of all seven armies. He proposes Virāṭa (1–20). Nakula names Drupada (1–15), Arjuna chooses Dhṛṣṭadyumna (15–25), Bhīma opts for Śikhaṇḍin (25–30), while Yudhiṣṭhira leaves the choice to Kṛṣṇa (30–35). Kṛṣṇa reviews their situation, which he considers to be in their favor; the kings applaud him (35–45). The armies start moving; Draupadī remains in Upaplavya (45–55). The kings are reviewed (55–65). Yudhiṣṭhira sets up camp by the river Hiraṇvatī in Kurukṣetra (65–80).
150 (153; 5188). Duryodhana prepares for war (1–25).
151 (154; 5216). Yudhiṣṭhira again asks for Duryodhana's exact words (1–5). Kṛṣṇa emphatically declares that only war is left open, and Yudhiṣṭhira orders the Yoke (5–15). Yudhiṣṭhira remains reluctant, but Arjuna supports Kṛṣṇa (20–25).
152 (155; 5243). Duryodhana arrays his eleven armies, which are described in detail (1–30).

Vaiśaṃpāyana said:

149.1 Yudhiṣṭhira, that law-spirited King Dharma, upon hearing Janārdana's words, spoke to his brothers while Keśava watched, "You have heard what happened in the hall at the assembly of the Kurus, and you have reflected on Keśava's entire report. Therefore, marshal my armies now, best of men! Seven armies have massed together for victory, and I have seven famous generals to lead them. Hear their names: Drupada, Virāṭa, Dhṛṣṭadyumna, Śikhaṇḍin, Sātyaki, Cekitāna, and the mighty Bhīmasena. All these army commanders are heroes who lay down their lives, all are champions wise in the Veda, all observe their vows faithfully. All are modest, proficient in politics, skilled in warfare; they are experts on arrows and missiles and masters of all arms. Now, Sahadeva, scion of Kuru, you tell first which expert in army formations should be the marshal of all seven armies, who can withstand Bhīṣma on the battlefield, a fire with flames of arrows. Speak your mind, tiger among men: who is fit to be our marshal?

Sahadeva said:

Our ally who shared our sorrow, the powerful and Law-wise king to whom we resorted in order to claim our own portion—Virāṭa the Matsya, mighty armsman, fierce in battle, will outlast Bhīṣma and those great warriors on the battlefield.

Vaiśaṃpāyana said:

When the eloquent Sahadeva had said this, Nakula immediately spoke up, "Standing out in years, learning, fortitude, family, and birth, a modest man of high rank, illustrious expert on all weapons who learned archery from Bharadvāja, unassailable, true to his word, who has always rivaled Droṇa and mighty Bhīṣma, estimable army commander in the forefront of the flocks of kings, surrounded by sons and grandsons like a tree with a hundred branches, the king who, in anger, with his wife performed awesome austerities for the destruction of Droṇa, the hero who shines in battle, the bull among rulers who like a father has always cherished us—our father-in-law Drupada must lead the vanguard of the army. It is my view that he can withstand the onslaught of Bhīṣma and Droṇa, for this king, this friend of Angiras* knows the celestial weapons."

When the two sons of Mādrī had voiced their opinions, Vāsava's Indra-like son, the scion of Kuru, the Left-handed Archer, lifted his voice, "He who, through the power of asceticism and the gratification of the seer, sprang forth from the fire hearth, a divine person of great power with the color of flames, carrying bow, armor, and sword, bristling atop a chariot that was yoked with celestial horses, roaring like a huge cloud with the thunder of his chariot, a hero with the muscles of a lion, the valor of a lion, the chest of a lion, strong-armed, powerful, roaring like a lion, a hero resplendent with the shoulders of a lion, of fine brow, teeth, chin, arms, and face, husky, with a strong neck, wide eyes, good feet, and fine stance, impervious to all weapons like a rutting elephant, who was born for the destruction of Droṇa,

* = Bharadvāja.

25 true-spoken and master of his senses—Dhṛṣṭadyumna, I think, will
stand up to Bhīṣma's arrows, which have the impact of a thunderbolt,
like snakes with flaming maws, swift like the messengers of Yama,
like fire when they strike, which Rāma himself once withstood in
battle, dreaded like the stroke of lightning. I do not see a man who
could withstand that champion of the great vow, except
Dhṛṣṭadyumna, king; that is my conviction. Swift of hand, a paragon
of warriors, majestic, with an impenetrable armor, he is my choice
of a marshal, like an elephant that leads his herd!"

Bhīma said:

My choice is Śikhaṇḍin, Drupada's son, who, as the Siddhas and
gathered seers say, was born for the killing of Bhīṣma. O Indra among
30 kings, upon whose shape, as he deploys his celestial missile in the
center of every battle, the men will gaze as though it were the great-
spirited Rāma's! I do not see the man who could pierce Śikhaṇḍin in
battle with his weapon, king, when he stands girt on his chariot.
No one can withstand Bhīṣma of the great vow but Śikhaṇḍin the
hero. I think he is our marshal.

Yudhiṣṭhira said:

Brothers, the substance and lack of substance, the strength and the
weakness of all the world in past and future—the law-spirited Keśava
knows it all. Let him be the marshal of our armies whom Kṛṣṇa of
Dāśārha calls, whether he be an experienced warrior or not, whether
35 old or young. He is our root in triumph, friends, as well as in
misfortune. On him rest our lives, kingship, being, and nonbeing,
happiness and misery. He is the Placer and Ordainer, on him rests
firmly our success. He whom Kṛṣṇa of Dāśārha calls fit shall be the
marshal of our armies.

Let the greatest of speakers speak—the night is running out. Then
after creating him marshal under Kṛṣṇa's authority, we shall, when
the remainder of the night has passed, march out to the battlefield,
with our weapons anointed with perfumes, and with the ceremonies
performed.

Vaiśaṃpāyana said:

Having heard the words of the sagacious King Dharma, the Lotus-
eyed One, glancing at Dhanaṃjaya, said: "To me, too, great king,
all the valiant warriors and champions whom all of you have
proposed as fit to be the marshal of your army, appear capable indeed
40 to crush the enemy. They'd strike fear in Indra himself in a war, let
alone in those greedy and evil Dhārtarāṣṭras. Also, of course, strong-
armed enemy-tamer, I have made a great effort, as a favor to you, to
bring about peace, Bhārata. We stand acquitted of our debt to the
Law: we cannot be blamed by those who might wish to do so. That
addlebrained fool Dhārtarāṣṭra thinks he has had his way, the sick

man thinks that he has the strength needed. All right, yoke that
army: I think they can only be persuaded by death. The Dhārtarāṣṭras
won't be able to hold out, when they see Dhanaṃjaya, an enraged
Bhīmasena, the Yama-like twins, the wroth Dhṛṣṭadyumna seconded
45 by Yuyudhāna, Abhimanyu, the Draupadeyas, Virāṭa, Drupada, and
the other army commanders, kings of proven valor. Our mettlesome
forces, unassailable and irresistible, shall trounce the Dhārtarāṣṭra
forces in battle, no doubt of that!"

When Kṛṣṇa had thus spoken, the kings were infused with joy,
and a loud roar rose from the exultant men: "The Yoke!" While the
troops hurried and milled about, there were the sounds of horses and
elephants, the rattle of wheels all around, and the tumultuous clangor
of conches and drums everywhere. When the Pāṇḍavas were about
to march out with their troops on all sides, the army appeared as
relentless as the Ganges in spate.

In the vanguard rode Bhīmasena and the two sons of Mādrī in
50 armor, Saubhadra, the Draupadeyas, and Dhṛṣṭadyumna Pārṣata,
with the Prabhadrakas and Pāñcālas behind Bhīmasena. There rose
a roar as of the ocean at full moon and the racket of the excited
marchers seemed to strike the heavens. The fully armed fighters,
ready to rend the enemy ranks, exulted; and in their midst went
Kuntī's son Yudhiṣṭhira. Carts, vending vehicles, brothel tents, wagon
trains, treasure coffers, war contraptions, arsenals, physicians and
surgeons, and whatever there were of low-rated, thin, and weak
troops, and also the camp followers—having organized them all, the
king marched out.

55 Faithful Draupadī Pāñcālī remained behind in Upaplavya with the
ladies, surrounded by slave girls and slaves. The sons of Pāṇḍu began
their march only after taking basic precautions with stationary guards
and mobile patrols in a deep defense area. They marched, dispensing
cattle and gold to brahmins who crowded and lauded them, king,
on their gem-encrusted chariots.

The Kekayas, Dhṛṣṭaketu, the princely son of the king of Kāśis,
Śreṇimat, Vasudāna, undefeated Śikhaṇḍin happily and contentedly
followed King Yudhiṣṭhira in their armor and ornaments, surrounding
60 him with their swords. In the rear were Virāṭa, Yajñasena, Somaki,
Sudharman, Kuntibhoja, and the sons of Dhṛṣṭadyumna—forty
thousand chariots, five times more horses, ten times more foot
soldiers, and sixty thousand riders. Anādhṛṣṭi, Cekitāna, the king of
Cedi, and Sātyaki all marched around Vāsudeva and Dhanaṃjaya.
Upon reaching the Field of the Kurus in full battle order, the warrior
Pāṇḍavas looked like bellowing bulls. They plunged into Kurukṣetra,
the enemy-tamers, sounding their conches, and Vāsudeva and
65 Dhanaṃjaya likewise sounded theirs. When they heard the

reverberating call of Pāñcajanya, like the crackling of lightning, all
the troops were exultant. The lion roars of the impetuous men
commingling with the conches and drums resounded through earth,
sky, and oceans.

Thereupon King Yudhiṣṭhira had the army set up camp on level
and pleasant terrain with plentiful grass and kindling, avoiding
burning grounds, sanctuaries, hermitages of great seers, and holy
places. The king of the land, Kuntī's son Yudhiṣṭhira, encamped on
70 agreeable and non-saline grounds, safe and auspicious; then, when
the animals had rested, he struck camp again and joyfully marched
on, surrounded by hundreds and thousands of kings. Keśava and the
Pārtha circled the area entirely, putting to flight hundreds of patrols
of the Dhārtarāṣṭra. Dhṛṣṭadyumna Pārṣata and the majestic chariot
warrior Yuyudhāna Sātyaki measured out the cantonment, as far as
the holy river Hiraṇvatī in Kurukṣetra, which provided easy fords,
and water that was pure and clear of pebbles and mud. There Keśava
had a moat dug, Bhārata, where he posted and briefed a troop for
75 defense. Keśava also had tents set up for the other kings along the
same lines as those of the great-spirited Pāṇḍavas, with plenty of
water and firewood, quite inaccessible to enemies, provisioned with
food and victuals, hundreds and thousands of them. The magnificent
tents of the kings distributed over the cantonment were like celestial
chariots descended to the surface of the earth, Indra among kings!

There were hundreds of skilled artificers who were paid wages, and
very able physicians equipped with all their supplies. King Yudhiṣṭhira
distributed to every tent bows, bow strings, shields, and swords, as
80 well as honey, butter, hill-sized mounds of tree resin and sand, much
water and fine fodder, with chaff and charcoal, engines, iron arrows,
javelins, spears, battle axes, bows; cuirasses and the like decked the
men's chests. One saw elephants with spiked harnesses, covered with
iron-studded shields, mountainous, able to fight with hundreds and
thousands of enemies.

Upon learning that the Pāṇḍavas had pitched camp, Bhārata, their
allies flocked to their stations with their troops and mounts. The kings
of the earth, who had vowed continence, drunk the Soma, and
dispensed vast stipends, now assembled for the triumph of the sons
of Pāṇḍu.

Janamejaya said:

150.1 When King Duryodhana heard that Yudhiṣṭhira was marching
with his army to give battle, had pitched camp in Kurukṣetra, was
protected by Vāsudeva, followed by Virāṭa and Drupada and their sons,
surrounded by the Kekayas, Vṛṣṇis, and other kings in their hundreds,
like great Indra guarded by the warlike Ādityas, how did he react?

This I wish to hear in detail, ascetic, what went on in the frightening
5 confusion in the Jungle of the Kurus. Even the army of the Gods would have trembled in battle before the Pāṇḍavas, Vāsudeva, Virāṭa, Drupada, Dhṛṣṭadyumna Pāñcālya, the great warrior Śikhaṇḍin, and gallant Yuyudhāna, unapproachable even to Gods. This I wish to hear in detail, ascetic, the exploits of the Kurus and Pāṇḍavas.

Vaiśaṃpāyana said:

When the Dāśārha had gone back, King Duryodhana said to Karṇa, Duḥśāsana and Śakuni, "Adhokṣaja has returned to the Pārthas
10 unsuccessful and is certain to speak to them with anger. For Vāsudeva wants war between the Pāṇḍavas and me, Bhīmasena and Arjuna abide by his views, while Ajātaśatru is influenced by Bhīma and Arjuna. I have offended him and his brothers in the past, and Virāṭa and Drupada have feuded with me; those two army commanders follow Vāsudeva's lead. There shall be war, horrendous and hair-raising. Therefore let all preparations for war be made without delay. Let the kings all set up their tents in Kurukṣetra, spaced in such a
15 way that the enemies cannot raid them, with water and firewood close by, in their hundreds and thousands, with unbreachable supply lines and coffers of treasure, filled with all kinds of weaponry, and streaming with banners and pennants. Let the roads leading out of the city be leveled, and let at once the proclamation be made that tomorrow we march!"

"We shall!" they promised, and on the morrow they acted, great-spirited and joyful, for the destruction of the kings. Thereupon all the kings, on hearing the king's orders, rose belligerently from their costly thrones, slowly touching their bludgeonlike arms, which shone with golden upper-arm bracelets and were anointed with sandalwood and
20 aloe. They tied on their turbans with lotuslike hands, their upper and lower garments, and all their jewelry. Their best charioteers, horse experts all, readied the chariots and horses, and those steeped in elephant lore their tuskers. Then they readied their many colorful and gold-studded cuirasses and all their various weapons. The foot soldiers in countless numbers girt their bodies with all kinds of gold-sparking arms.

The vast city of the Dhārtarāṣṭra was in festive confusion, crawling with excited men. It looked like the ocean at moonrise, Bhārata,
25 with whirlpools of milling crowds, the fish of chariots, elephants, and horses, the roar of conches and drums, the pearls of piles of treasure, the waves of colorful ornaments, the foam of spotless weapons, surrounded by the coastal mountains of garlands of palaces, with backwaters of roads and bazaars, the rising moon of warriors, the billows of Kuru kings, O king.

Vaiśaṃpāyana said:

151.1 Recalling Vāsudeva's words, Yudhiṣṭhira once more questioned the
Vārṣṇeya, "How did the fool speak? Now that the time is upon us,
what is best for us, Acyuta? How should we act so as not to stray
from the Law? You, Vāsudeva, know the minds of Duryodhana,
Karṇa, Śakuni Saubala, and of me and my brothers. You have heard
the words of both Vidura and Bhīṣma, and you have listened to the
5 entire wisdom of Kuntī, man of ample wisdom. Ignore all that, and
ponder again and again on what is best for us, strong-armed man,
and say it without hesitation."

Hearing King Dharma's words informed with Law and Profit, Kṛṣṇa
replied in a voice that thundered like cloud and drum, "I said what
was beneficial and in conformity to Law and Profit, but it did not
reach the deceitfully cunning Kauravya. That evil mind does not
listen to anything that Bhīṣma or Vidura or I have to say; he ignores
it all. That man does not want law, he does not want fame, that evil
10 spirit thinks he has won it all by relying on Karṇa. Suyodhana even
ordered me jailed, but there that code-trampling villain did not get his
wish! Neither Bhīṣma nor Droṇa used the right words; they all
comply with him except Vidura, Acyuta. Śakuni Saubala, Karṇa, and
Duḥśāsana foolishly told the resentful fool lies about you. What is
the use for me to repeat to you what the Kauravas said? To sum it
up: that rogue is wronging you. Not between all the kings who make
up your ranks is there as much evil, such total lack of decency, as
15 there is in him. We ourselves, we do not want peace with the
Kauravas at the price of the total surrender of our claims. War is
the only course left."

When they heard Vāsudeva's response, all the kings remained
silent, they all watched the king's face, Bhārata. And Yudhiṣṭhira
divined the intentions of the kings and, with Bhīma, Arjuna, and the
twins, ordered the Yoke. When the Yoke was ordered, the army of the
Pāṇḍava cheered and the troops were transported with joy. Foreseeing
the killing of men who ought not to be killed, Yudhiṣṭhira the King
20 Dharma sighed and said to Bhīmasena and Vijaya, "The ultimate
disaster for which I dwelled in the forest and suffered much is upon
us in spite of all our striving. As though we had not tried at all, great
discord has fallen to our lot. For how can war be waged with men we
may not kill? How can we win if we must kill our gurus and elders?"

Hearing King Dharma, the enemy-burning Left-handed Archer*
repeated what Vāsudeva had said, "Devakī's son has conveyed the
words of Kuntī and Vidura, and you have understood them completely.

* = Arjuna.

25 It is my unshakable conviction that they would not speak Unlaw!
Nor is it right to retreat now without fighting."

Vāsudeva too, who had listened to the Left-handed Archer, smilingly told the Pārtha, "That is the way it is." Thereupon the Pāṇḍaveyas, having resolved upon war, great king, passed the night comfortably with their troops.

Vaiśaṃpāyana said:

152.1 When day broke, King Duryodhana arrayed his eleven armies,
Bhārata; he assigned his men, elephants, chariots, and horses to all
the various battle formations according to their quality as superior,
average, and weak troops. With spare axle trees, quivers, bumper
bars, javelins, arrow holders, spears, arrow cases, siege rocks, banners,
5 pennants, bows and javelins, various kinds of ropes, nooses, rugs, hair-
gripping poles, oil, molasses, sand, pots with poisonous snakes, tree
resin, dirt, wooden shields with bells, axes and choppers, covers of
tiger hide, leopard skins, *vastis*, horn, various kinds of projectiles, hoes,
spades, sesame oil, linseed oil, butter—with all this the handsome,
colorful armies blazed like fires. Champions in armor, who were
trained in weaponry, wellborn, and experts in the niceties of horse
lore, were assigned as charioteers. All the chariots, to which herbs
were tied to ward off evil, and circles of bells and flags and pennants,
10 and which were yoked with teams of four excited horses, were loaded
with weaponry and hundreds of bows. One was in charge of the two
yoke horses, one each of the two side horses; there were two more
fine chariot warriors and the charioteer who was the horse expert.
There were altogether thousands of golden-garlanded chariots, like
fortified towns, uncapturable by the enemy.

Like the chariots, the elephants too were hung with bells and
decorated like mineral-bearing mountains. There were likewise seven
men on each: two held the goads, two were excellent archers, two
15 fine swordsmen, O king, while one held spear and flag. The Kauravya's
entire force teemed with thousands of crazed elephants loaded with
weapons. There were tens of thousands of horses clad in colorful
armor, well ornamented and with pennants flying, each with its rider,
well-controlled, quite content, in gold-studded harness—many
hundreds of thousands of them in the complete control of their
horsemen.

Then there were the foot soldiers, in various shapes and guises,
with all manner of armor and weapons, wearing garlands of gold.
To one chariot there were ten elephants, to one elephant ten horses,
and to one horse ten foot soldiers, protecting their legs on all sides.
20 Fifty elephants were held in reserve to one chariot, to fill up breaches,
a hundred horses to one elephant, seven men to one horse. An army

of the *senā* type has five hundred elephants and as many chariots; a *pṛtanā* has ten *senās*, a *vāhinī* ten *pṛtanās*. But *vāhinī*, *pṛtanā*, *senā*, *dhvājinī*, *sādinī*, *camū*, *akṣauhiṇī*, and *varūthinī* are also used synonymously.

Thus were the armies arrayed by the sagacious Kaurava, eleven grand-armies totally, while the Pāṇḍavas were seven armies strong. A *patti* is declared to comprise five times fifty men. Three such *pattis* make up a *senāmukha* or *gulma*. Ten *gulmas* form a *gaṇa*, and there were tens of thousands of *gaṇas* in Duryodhana's armies, of warriors eager to fight. Strong-armed King Duryodhana examined a number of astute champions and made them his army commanders. He had the commanders of the grand-armies brought in individually with ceremony, eminent kings all of them, and consecrated them: Kṛpa, Droṇa, Śalya, the great warrior from Sindhu, Sudakṣiṇa of Kamboja, Kṛtavarman, Droṇa's son, Karṇa, Bhūriśravas, Śakuni Saubala, and the great warrior Bāhlīka. Day after day, at all hours, he gave them in person all kinds of instructions, Bhārata. Thus regulated, all the men at arms and their followers became pleased to do what the king desired.

5(57) The Consecration of Bhīṣma

5.153–56 (B. 156–59; C. 5278–406)
153 (156; 5278). Duryodhana sees the need for a marshal and invites Bhīṣma to take the position (1–15). Bhīṣma accepts, under the condition that either Karṇa or he himself be the first to fight (15–20). Karṇa swears that he will not fight as long as Bhīṣma lives (25). Bhīṣma is consecrated amidst many portents (25–30). Duryodhana marches out and sets up camp (30–35).
154 (157; 5314). Yudhiṣṭhira, on hearing of Bhīṣma's marshalcy, assembles his allies and appoints Dhṛṣṭadyumna (1–10). Balarāma appears with the Vṛṣṇis and is welcomed (15–20). He will not fight but instead go on a pilgrimage (20–30).
155 (158; 5350). King Rukmin arrives and offers his services to Yudhiṣṭhira, slighting Arjuna while doing so (1–20). Arjuna responds with sarcasm, and Rukmin withdraws (20–35).
156 (159; 5391). Dhṛtarāṣṭra asks Saṃjaya to report to him on the war (1–5). Saṃjaya agrees (5–15).

Vaiśaṃpāyana said:
153.1 Thereupon the son of Dhṛtarāṣṭra folded his hands and addressed
Bhīṣma Śāṃtanava in the company of all the kings, "Without a single
marshal even a great army is rent asunder in war like a nest of ants.
Never do two generals share the same opinion, and commanders
compete with one another in derring-do. It is told, O sage, that once
the brahmins attacked the boundlessly august Haihayas with their
5 pennants of *kuśa* grass raised. The commoners and serfs followed
them, grandfather, so on one side stood the three classes, on the
other the bulls of the barons. The three classes were routed time and
again, while the barons alone defeated that vast force. The good
brahmins questioned the barons, and those Law-wise men told them
how it came about, grandfather: 'In war we listen to the wisdom of
one man, but all of you pursue your own plans separately.' Then the
brahmins made one brahmin, brave and adept at plotting strategy,
10 their marshal, and they defeated the barons. Thus those who select
as their marshal a capable champion, unimpeachable and intent on
their well-being, defeat their enemies. You are the peer of Uśanas,
you always wish me well, you are incorruptible and stand by the
Law. Be you our marshal—a sun among luminaries, a moon to the
herbs, Kubera among Yakṣas, Vāsava among Maruts, Meru among
mountains, Suparṇa among birds, Kumāra among ghosts, the
oblation-carrying fire among Vasus. For when we are guided by you
as the celestials are by Śakra, we shall surely become invincible, even
15 to the Thirty. March at our head, sir, as Pāvaki at the head of the
Gods, and we shall follow your lead, as cows follow a bull!"

Bhīṣma said:
It is as you say, strong-armed Bhārata. But the Pāṇḍavas are to
me as you yourself are, and I must speak to their well-being as well.
Still, I must fight in your cause, as I have pledged. I do not see a
warrior on earth equal to myself, except that tiger among men
Dhanaṃjaya, son of Kuntī. For that strong-armed man knows all the
divine weapons. However, the Pāṇḍava will never fight me openly in
20 war. Yes, I could in an instant empty this world of men with the
might of my weapons, with Gods, Asuras, and Rākṣasas, but the
Pāṇḍava I cannot eradicate, king. Therefore I shall methodically kill
a myriad warriors a day and so finish them off, scion of Kuru, unless
they kill me first in battle.

There is one condition under which I shall willingly become your
marshal, pray hear it from me. Either Karṇa must fight first, or I,
lord of the earth, for this son of a *sūta* always seeks to rival me in
battle.

Karṇa said:
25 In no manner whatsoever shall I fight as long as this son of the

Ganges is alive! Only when Bhīṣma has been felled shall I fight with
the Gāṇḍīva bowman.

Vaiśaṃpāyana said:

Thereupon Dhṛtarāṣṭra's son ceremonially made Bhīṣma of the
generous stipends marshal of the armies, and consecrated he gloried.
On the king's orders the men zealously sounded the drums and
conches and kettledrums; and there rose to the skies the various
battle cries and the racket of the animals, and a rain of bloody sleet
fell. Hurricanes and earthquakes and the trumpeting noise of elephants
30 broke loose, causing the spirits of all warriors to fall. There were
disembodied voices, and meteors streaked through the sky. Jackals
howled ferociously, foreboding danger. Those were the dreadful
portents by the hundreds, O king, which occurred when the king
consecrated Gāngeya to the marshalcy.

After creating Bhīṣma marshal, shatterer of enemy forces, and
having eminent brahmins recite for much gold and cattle, he,
strengthened by their benedictions, marched out with his army,
placing first the son of the river, along with his brothers, and trooped
with a large army to Kurukṣetra. After reconnoitering Kurukṣetra
with Karṇa, the Kaurava measured out his camp on level terrain,
35 O king. And on pleasant, non-saline grounds with plenty of grass
and firewood the camp appeared like Hāstinapura itself.

Janamejaya said:

154.1 When King Yudhiṣṭhira heard that the great-spirited Bhīṣma, son
of the river, greatest of armsmen, grandfather of the Bhāratas,
standard-bearer of all kings, Bṛhaspati's equal in wisdom, a match
for the earth in patience, an ocean in imperturbability, steady as the
Himālayas, a Prajāpati in generosity, the like of the sun in splendor,
like great Indra trouncing the enemies with showers of arrows, was
consecrated for the tremendous, horrendous, hair-raising sacrifice of
5 war for many nights, what did the strong-armed king, acquainted
with all the Laws, say, or Bhīmasena and Arjuna? What insight did
Kṛṣṇa have?

Vaiśaṃpāyana said:

The wise Yudhiṣṭhira, experienced in the purport of the Law of emergencies, assembled all his brothers and Vāsudeva Sātvata, and that best of speakers said in a persuasive voice, "Make the rounds of the troops, stay prepared and in full armor. Our first battle will be with Grandfather. Therefore, while the troops are asleep, find me their commanders.

Vāsudeva said:

Bull of the Bharatas, you have spoken with sense, as you should now that the time has come. I agree, strong-armed man, that the next step must now be taken and the leaders of your army consecrated.

Vaiśaṃpāyana said:

Thereupon Yudhiṣṭhira had Drupada fetched, and Virāṭa, the bull of the Śinis, Dhṛṣṭadyumna Pāñcālya, King Dhṛṣṭaketu, Śikhaṇḍin Pāñcālya, Sahadeva of Magadha, these seven heroic and war-loving great archers, and consecrated them ceremonially as army commanders. He appointed Dhṛṣṭadyumna on the spot as marshal of all the armies, him who had been born from the fire to be the death of Droṇa. And he made Guḍākeśa Dhanaṃjaya the marshal's marshal of all those great-spirited men. Saṃkarṣaṇa's younger brother, the illustrious and wise Janārdana, was Arjuna's guide and driver of his horses.

Perceiving that pernicious war was close at hand, plough-armed Rāma entered the compound of King Pāṇḍava, accompanied by Akrūra and others, Gada, Sāmba, Ulmūka, and so on, Raukmiṇeya and Āhuka's sons led by Cārudeṣṇa. Guarded by these Vṛṣṇi grandees, who had come like power-proud tigers, as Vāsava by the Maruts, that strong-armed man clothed in dark-blue silk and white-complexioned as the peak of the Kailāsa, with a gait that mimed a lion's, illustrious, the corners of his eyes reddened by drunkenness, made his appearance. Upon seeing him, the King Dharma and resplendent Keśava arose with the Wolf-Belly Pārtha of terrible deeds, and the Gāṇḍiva bowman, and whichever kings were present, and they all approached and saluted Halāyudha. The Pāṇḍava took him by the hand and all welcomed him, led by Vāsudeva. Halāyudha saluted Virāṭa and Drupada, his elders, and then the enemy-tamer sat down with Yudhiṣṭhira.

Thereupon, while all the kings were seated around him, Rohiṇī's son glanced at Vāsudeva and said, "There shall be a grisly and gruesome holocaust of men. It is fated, I think, and cannot be averted. My hope is that I may yet see you again, sage and with hale bodies, survivors of this war. The baronage of the earth has gathered, ripened by Time, no doubt, and there will be a huge slaughter mired in flesh and blood. I have often told Vāsudeva between the two of us, "Act equably to all your relations, for Duryodhana is as close to us as the Pāṇḍavas: he too should be honored fittingly.

"But because of you, Madhusūdana did not follow my advice, being loyal to your cause with his whole body, looking to Dhanaṃjaya. I am convinced that the Pāṇḍavas' victory is secure, for thus is Madhusūdana determined, Bhārata. I myself cannot face the world without Kṛṣṇa, and therefore I follow the wishes of Keśava. Bhīma and Duryodhana, heroes both and skilled in club fighting, have both been my students—therefore I shall go and visit the sacred places of the river Sarasvatī, for I shall not be able to watch the destruction of the Kauravyas." After he had spoken, strong-armed Rāma took leave of the Pāṇḍavas and, leaving Madhusūdana behind, departed on his pilgrimage.

Vaiśaṃpāyana said:

155.1 At this time there came to the Pāṇḍavas the son of the great-
spirited Bhīṣmaka Hiraṇyaloman, the friend of Indra himself, the
overlord of the Āhṛtis, the very famous Bhoja who ruled the
Southland. His son was renowned in the world as Rukmin; as a
student of the lion of the Kiṃpuruṣas living on Gandhamādana, he
had mastered the entire four-part Veda of weaponry, a strong-armed
champion, who had obtained the bow of great Indra which matched
the power of Gāṇḍīva and equaled Śārnga, celestial and indestructible.
5 There are three divine bows of the celestials: Varuṇa's Gāṇḍīva, great
Indra's Vijaya, and Viṣṇu's Śārnga, they say, the last a divine,
powerful bow which Kṛṣṇa held, striking fear in enemy armies.
Arjuna obtained Gāṇḍīva from the Fire in the Khāṇḍava Forest, while
splendid Rukmin got his Vijaya from Druma. Hṛṣīkeśa got his superb
bow Śārnga after having cut the nooses of Murū, having killed Mūru
with a vengeance, having slain Naraka Bhauma, and having taken
the jeweled earrings, 16,000 women, and various gems.
10 Rukmin now, after obtaining the bow Vijaya, which sounded like a
thundercloud and seemed capable of terrifying the world, approached
the Pāṇḍavas. The hero, prideful of the strength of his arms, had
never forgiven Rukmiṇī's abduction by the cunning Vāsudeva.
Swearing that he would not return without killing Keśava, he had
given pursuit to the Vārṣṇeya, the best of armsmen. With a large,
far-shooting, four-membered army, with colorful weapon gear and
shields, like the Ganges in spate, he attacked the Vārṣṇeya, the lordly
Master of Yogas; he was outwitted, and out of shame did not return
15 to Kuṇḍiṇa, O king. On the very spot where that killer of enemy
heroes had been defeated by Kṛṣṇa he built a fine city named
Bhojakaṭa. With its large army and many horses and elephants this
city is still famed on earth by the name of Bhojakaṭa, king.
This heroic Bhoja king, riding in the midst of a large force, came
to the Pāṇḍavas with a grand-army. With armor, sword, arrows, bow,
arm guards, chariot, and a sun-colored banner, he entered the vast
army encampment. When he was announced to the Pāṇḍaveyas,
King Yudhiṣṭhira as a favor to Vāsudeva rose up to meet him and
20 greeted him. Saluted by the sons of Pāṇḍu and shown due hospitality,
he returned salutations to all and, after resting with his troops, spoke
in the midst of the heroes to Kuntī's son Dhanaṃjaya, "I shall stand
as your companion on the battlefield, if you are afraid, Pāṇḍava. I
shall give you such aid as the enemies will not endure. There is no
man on earth who equals me in bravery, Phalguna: I shall hand you
your foes when I have killed them!"
Thus addressed in the presence of the King Dharma and Keśava and

within earshot of the kings and all others, the sagacious Kaunteya
glanced at Vāsudeva and the Pāṇḍava King Dharma, laughed amiably
25 and said, "Who was my friendly companion when I fought the mighty
Gandharvas at the time of the Cattle Expedition? Who was my
companion when I gave battle in the fearful Khāṇḍava Forest that
was teeming with Gods and Dānavas? Who was my companion when
I fought the Nivātakavaca and Kālakeya Dānavas in battle? Who
was my companion, friend, in my combat with the many Kurus by
Virāṭa's city? I who confess my war debts to Rudra, Śakra,
Vaiśravaṇa, Yama, Varuṇa, the Fire, Kṛpa, Droṇa, and the Mādhava,
30 I who hold the divine Gāṇḍīva, my splendid hard bow, I who draw
on my inexhaustible arrows, supported by celestial weapons, born in
the dynasty of the Kauravas, son to boot of Pāṇḍu himself, deferring
to Droṇa as his pupil and with Vāsudeva as my companion—can a
man like me give voice to the dishonorable words 'I am afraid'? Even
to Him who wields the thunderbolt, O tiger among men? No, I am
not afraid, strong-armed man. I have no need of a companion. Go
somewhere else if you wish and it suits you, or stay!"

Rukmin then withdrew his oceanlike army and approached
35 Duryodhana in like manner, bull of the Bharatas. When he arrived
there, the king spoke in the same vein, but was also rebuffed by the
other, who thought of himself as a champion.

Two in all withdrew from the war, great king: Rauhiṇeya of the
Vṛṣṇis and King Rukmin. When Rāma had gone on his pilgrimage,
and Bhīṣmaka's son had also departed, the Pāṇḍaveyas again sat
down for a council. The assembly of the King Dharma crowded with
kings shone like the star-glittering sky presided over by the moon,
Bhārata.

Janamejaya said:

156.1 When the armies had been marshaled on the Field of the Kurus,
what did the Kurus do, urged on by Time, bull among brahmins?

Vaiśaṃpāyana said:

When the armies had thus been marshaled and stood ready, bull of
the Bharatas, Dhṛtarāṣṭra addressed Saṃjaya, great king: "Come,
Saṃjaya, tell me everything, omitting nothing, that happened in the
camps of the Kuru and Pāṇḍava armies. I think Fate reigns supreme,
and man's efforts count for nothing. While I know full well the evils
5 of war which will bring on a holocaust, yet I cannot restrain my
deceitful son who cheated at gambling, nor act in my own interest.
I do have the insight that perceives the evil, bard, but when I am
with my son, my mind is perverted. So it is, and what is to be shall
be, Saṃjaya—and true enough, to lay down one's life is the honored
Law of the baron.

Saṃjaya said:

The question you raise is rightly posed, great king, but pray do not
put all the blame on Duryodhana. I shall report to you in full, sire, so
listen. A man who comes to grief because of his own misdeeds should
10 not put the blame on Fate or Time. Mahārāja, if a man publicly
commits every detestable crime, he deserves to be killed publicly for
commiting those crimes. When the Pāṇḍavas and their councilors
had been cheated at the dicing, it was their respect for you that made
them endure their humiliation, best of men.

So, then, hear from me in full the slaughter in the war of horses,
elephants, and boundlessly august kings. And while you are hearing,
great king, what befell in the great war that brought on the
destruction of all the world, remain calm and do not be heartbroken.
For man is not the agent of his good and evil acts: he is helplessly
15 manipulated like a wooden puppet. Some people are foreordained by
God, others by chance, others by previous acts—and it is this triad
that is being pulled asunder.

5(58) The Embassy of Ulūka

5.157–60 (B. 160–63; C. 5407–701)
157 (160; 5407). Duryodhana summons Ulūka and gives him an inflammatory message for Yudhiṣṭhira and Bhīma (1–15).
158 (161; 5535). Ulūka arrives at Yudhiṣṭhira's camp and conveys the message, detailing the Kauravas' strength (1–20). He turns to Arjuna and once more speaks abusively in Duryodhana's name (20–40).
159 (162; 5578). The Pāṇḍavas, particularly Bhīma, are enraged (1). Kṛṣṇa replies to Ulūka with a message to Duryodhana, hinting that though he is pledged to be a charioteer, he may well take up arms himself (5–10).
160 (163; 5643). Arjuna adds his bellicose reply (1–20). Ulūka returns and reports to Duryodhana (20–25), who orders the Yoke (25).

Saṃjaya said:

157.1 When the great-spirited Pāṇḍavas were encamped by the river
Hiraṇvatī, great king, Duryodhana, accompanied by Karṇa, Saubala,*

* = Śakuni.

and Duḥśāsana, O king of kings, Bharata, summoned Ulūka and told
him in secret, "Ulūka, son of a gambler, go to the Pāṇḍavas and
Somakas, and give them my message within the hearing of Vāsudeva:
'The great war of the Pāṇḍavas and Kurus, awaited for many a year,
5 is now at hand, to the horror of the world. Now, Kaunteya, the time
has come to make true your grand boast, which Saṃjaya reported
to all the Kurus. Carry out what you have promised. Be a man!
Remember your rage, the rape of your kingdom, your exile in the
forest, the molestation of Draupadī, Pāṇḍava! The test for which a
kṣatriya lady gives birth to a son is upon you now. Avenge your
grudge, displaying your strength, bravery, boldness, superb handling
of arms, and manly vigor in war. Whose heart would not break if he
were ousted from power and had to live a long life in wretched
misery? Whose wrath would not flame up, if he, born in a dynasty,
10 greedy for the wealth of others, finds his kingdom cut up? Now act
and justify your great speech: the strict know him for a coward who
brags without acting. He who fights has two aims: to subjugate the
enemies and restore his kingship; so show you are a man! Either rule
this earth by defeating us, or, killed by us, go to the heaven of heroes.
Be a man, remember your banishment from the kingdom, your
hardships, your forest exile, the molestation of Kṛṣṇā, Pāṇḍava! Show
the grudge that lodges with those who, on the orders of their ill-
15 wishers, again and again wandered forth, for rancor is manhood. Be
a man, Pārtha, show off in war your anger, strength, power, cunning,
and deftness with arms.'

"Ulūka, repeat to that eunuch, that gluttonous cretin Bhīmasenaka on my behalf, 'Drink if you can the blood of Duḥśāsana, just as you impotently swore in the middle of the hall!'

"Men, the lustration of the weapons has been performed, Kurukṣetra is dry of mud, your horses are fat, your soldiers are paid up—fight tomorrow with Keśava!"

Saṃjaya said:

158.1 The son of the gambler, upon reaching the army camp of the
Pāṇḍava, met with the Pāṇḍaveyas and said to Yudhiṣṭhira, "You
know the words of messengers. Pray be not angry with me, when you
hear me pass on the message of Duryodhana."

Yudhiṣṭhira said:

Ulūka, you have nothing to fear. Tell without worry the notions of that rapacious, short-sighted Dhārtarāṣṭra.

Saṃjaya said:

Thereupon, in the midst of the illustrious, great-spirited Pāṇḍavas,
5 all the Sṛñjayas, the famous Kṛṣṇa, Drupada and his sons, Virāṭa,
and all the kings, Ulūka said, "This is what the spirited king

Dhārtarāṣṭra* has to say to you. Hear it, king, while the Kuru heroes listen.

" 'You were beaten at dice, Kṛṣṇā was dragged into the hall—it could indeed make someone who thinks he is a man quite angry! For no less than twelve years you lived in the forest, banished from your hearth, and you lodged for another year in a state of servitude to Virāṭa. Now be a man! Remember your rage, the rape of your
kingdom, your forest exile, and the molestation of Draupadī, Pāṇḍava!
10 If he can, let Bhīmasena drink Duḥśāsana's blood, as he so impotently
swore, Pāṇḍava! The lustration of the army has been performed, Kurukṣetra is dry of mud, the road is level, the soldiers are paid up—fight tomorrow alongside Keśava!

" 'How can you boast before encountering Bhīṣma on the battlefield, like a fool trying to climb Mount Gandhamādana! How can you hope for your kingdom, Pārtha, without defeating Droṇa, that greatest of warriors, the equal in battle of Śacī's Consort?** Your deluded hope to defeat in battle Droṇa, the master of the *brāhma* bow, steeped in both
the Vedas, unshakable leader in war, unfailing support of armies, is a
15 vain hope, for we have never heard of the wind uprooting Mount
Meru. Or, indeed, the wind shall carry off Meru, the sky shall fall on earth, the Eon shall turn around, if what you said to me comes true! What elephant, what horse, what man who wants to live will return home after encountering the enemy-shattering weapon of either one of them? How can any creature that walks the earth get away alive, when those two give him a thought, or their dreadful arms reach him?

" 'Or are you a frog that sits in his well
That you do not know of that army of kings,
Invincible like the host of the Gods,
Protected by kings, as heaven by Gods?

20 " 'Kings eastern and western and southern and northern,
Kāmbojas and Śakas and Khasas and Śālvas,
The Matsyas, the Central Kurus, the Mlecchas,
Pulindas, Draviḍas, Āndhras, and Kāñcyas—

" 'This swelling mass of peoples of war,
No more to be stopped than the Ganges in spate,
And me in the midst of my elephant forces—
Are you out of your mind that you hanker to fight us?' "

Ulūka, after speaking thus to Dharma's son King Yudhiṣṭhira, turned to Jiṣṇu and said, " 'Fight without boasting! Why do you boast so much? Success is the result of the turn of events; things do

* = Duryodhana.
** = Indra.

not succeed by bragging. If a deed did succeed by bragging in this world, Dhanaṃjaya, everybody would be successful. Any wretch can brag a great deal.

25 " 'I know Vāsudeva is your companion,
I know Gāṇḍīva stands tall as a palm,
I know that there is no warrior like you—
And knowing it all I took your domain!

A man does not achieve a great success by the Law of the turn of
events. The Placer alone brings beings into his power with a mere
thought. For thirteen years I have enjoyed the kingdom, while you
lamented about it. And after I have killed you and your relatives, I
shall rule it for even longer. Where was Gāṇḍīva when you were won
as a slave at the dicing? Where was the brawn of Bhīmasena then,
Phalguna? Deliverance did not come from Bhīmasena and his club,
or the Pārtha and his Gāṇḍīva: without the blameless Kṛṣṇā, there
30 would have been none! That glowing woman delivered you, when
you had fallen into slavery, yoked to subhuman chores, doing the
work of slaves. I called you barren sesame seeds, and rightly so! For
in the city of Virāṭa the Pārtha wore a braid, and Bhīmasena slaved
as a cook in Virāṭa's kitchen. That was my doing! That is the way
barons punish a baron who runs from a battle: they condemn him
to the gambler's row, to the kitchen, to the braid! No fear of either
Vāsudeva or you shall make me hand back the kingdom, Phalguna.
35 Fight alongside Keśava. No wizardry, no magic tricks, no jugglery
frightens me when I have taken up arms for battle—they make me
roar back! A thousand Vāsudevas, and hundreds of Phalgunas may
attack me, but with infallible arrows I drive them to the ten directions.
Go into battle with Bhīṣma, break a mountain with your head, swim
the plumbless ocean of men, with Śāradvata its whale, Viviṃśati its
shoal of fish, Bṛhadbala its billowing, Saumadatti its swallower of
whales.

" 'The flood is Duḥśāsana, Śalya the fish,
The sharks Suṣeṇa and Citrāyudha,
Jayadratha the mountain, Purumitra the depths,
The water Durmarṣaṇa, Śakuni the coast.

40 " 'When, your wit sweated out by the toil, you have plunged
In the swollen, exhaustless floodtide of arms
And find yourself with all relatives slain,
Then your heart will come to regret it all.

" 'Then your heart will turn from the rule of the earth,
As an unclean man's from hope of heaven;

For the realm is for you as hard to command
As heaven to reach for a loose-living man.' "

Saṃjaya said:

159.1 Again Ulūka spoke to Arjuna as he was told to do, pricking him,
an angry cobra, with the thorns of his words. The Pāṇḍavas, hearing
his words, were enraged; furious to begin with, they felt their rage
exacerbated by the gambler's son. They could not sit still on their
seats, they flailed about with their arms, and they eyed each other
like angry cobras. Dropping his head, Bhīmasena stared at Keśava
from eyes that were blood-streaked at the corners, hissing like a cobra.
5 Seeing the son of the wind* in pain, and sorely enraged, the
Dāśārha replied to the gambler's son with the ghost of a smile, "Leave
at once, son of a gambler, and tell Suyodhana that his words have
been heard, their sense understood, and that his will shall be done.
But give Suyodhana also my message: 'Now look forward to
tomorrow, and be a man, cad. If you think, fool, that Janārdana will
not fight since the Pārtha chose him as a charioteer, and therefore
you need not be afraid—there may be that ultimate time when I burn
10 down all your kings in my anger, as fire burns straw. But, at
Yudhiṣṭhira's behest, I shall act as the charioteer of the great-spirited
Phalguna, who knows what he is worth when he is fighting. If you
fly to all three worlds, if you crawl underground, you shall see
Arjuna's chariot right in front of you tomorrow! If you think that
Bhīma's roar means nothing, you can be sure that Duḥśāsana's blood
has been drunk! Neither the Pārtha,** nor King Yudhiṣṭhira, nor
Bhīmasena, nor the twins pay any heed to your wild ravings."

Saṃjaya said:

160.1 The bull of the Bharatas, having listened to Duryodhana's words,
stared at the gambler's son from his crimsoned eyes. With a glance at
Keśava, famous Guḍākeśa** gripped his sturdy arm and said to the
gambler's son, "He is a man who challenges others while relying on
his prowess and measures up fearlessly to his full power. But the
shameless baron who challenges others while relying on the bravery
of others because he himself is powerless, is the lowest of men to the
5 world. You think you have power because of the power of others, and,
while you are a coward and a fool to boot, you hope to rout others,
for you have consecrated the oldest of all the kings,*** benevolent,
master of his senses, and great in wisdom, to a certain death, and
brag! We know your purpose, villain, defiler of your family. You

* = Bhīma.
** = Arjuna.
*** = Bhīṣma.

think we Pāṇḍavas will not kill the son of the Ganges* out of compassion. But, Dhārtarāṣṭra, the one on whose power you rely to brag, him, Bhīṣma, I shall kill first of all before the wincing eyes of all archers.

"So go to the Bharatas, son of a gambler,
And say to Suyodhana Dhārtarāṣṭra:
'The left-handed Arjuna says, "All right!
There shall be carnage when night has passed!"

10 " 'If he, bringing joy, undejected of spirit,
In the midst of the Kurus said, true to his word,
"I shall slay the host of the Pāṇḍavas
And the Śālvas, this shall be my burden now,

" ' "For excepting Droṇa I can kill all the world,
You need have no fear of the Pāṇḍavas!"
And so our realm is your confident booty,
For you think that the Pāṇḍavas are lost.

" 'But puffed up with pride you fail to see
The disaster that lurks within yourself,
And therefore I shall in the first encounter
Kill, for all to see, the old man of the Kurus.

" 'When your army is yoked at sunrise, protect,
With banner and chariot, the true-spoken man:
With my arrows I'll cause your Bhīṣma, your haven,
To fall from his chariot while you look on!

" 'Tomorrow Suyodhana will know the meaning of boasts, when he
15 sees grandfather hurting from my volley of arrows! And the oath that Bhīmasena in his fury swore to that shortsighted man in the middle of the hall, to your brother Duḥśāsana, who has no inkling of the Law, always feuding, cruel of deeds and evil of wit, that oath too you shall soon see come true, Suyodhana. Of vainglory and pride, anger and offensiveness, abrasiveness and arrogance, of self-conceit, cruelty, scathing speech, loathing of Law, lawlessness and slander, disobedience to your elders, skewed vision and all malfeasance, you shall soon see the bitter fruit, Suyodhana.

20 " 'For when I, seconded by Vāsudeva, am enraged, king, how can you hope for life, fool, or for kingship? When Bhīṣma and Droṇa have been pacified and the *sūta*'s son** felled, you shall lose all hope of life, kingdom, and sons, Suyodhana. When you see the slaughter of your brothers and sons, and you yourself are struck down by Bhīmasena, you will remember your misdeeds.

* = Bhīṣma.
** = Karṇa.

" 'Keśava does not promise twice. I speak the truth, and true it shall all come.' "

Having thus been told, O king, the gambler's son committed those words to memory and upon his dismissal returned as he had come.
25 Returning home from the Pāṇḍavas, the gambler's son repaired to Dhṛtarāṣṭra's son and told him in the assembly of the Kurus everything that had been said.

After listening to the replies of Arjuna and Keśava, the bull of the Bharatas spoke to Duḥśāsana, Karṇa, and Śakuni. And he ordered the king's army and the forces of his allies to stand fully yoked and arrayed before sunrise. At Karṇa's orders messengers on chariots, camels, and mares, and others on fine swift horses, hastily made the rounds of the entire camp, ordering the kings: "The Yoke before sunrise!"

5(59) *The Count of the Warriors and Paladins*

5.161–69 (B. 164–72; C. 5702–941)
161 (164; 5702). Yudhiṣṭhira marches out with the principal warriors targeted to individual Kauravas (1–5). Dhṛṣṭadyumna leads the troops (10).
162 (165; 5714). Dhṛtarāṣṭra asks Saṃjaya how Bhīṣma as marshal proceeded. Saṃjaya reports (1–5). Bhīṣma speaks encouragingly to Duryodhana, who asks for a review of the rathas *and* atirathas *(5–15). Bhīṣma reviews Duryodhana, Duḥśāsana, etc., himself, Kṛtavarman, Śalya, Bhūriśravas, Somadatta, and Jayadratha (15–30).*
163 (166; 5748). The review continues: Sudakṣiṇa, Nīla, Vinda and Anuvinda, the Trigartas, Daṇḍadhara, Bṛhadbala, Kṛpa (1–20).
164 (167; 5770). Śakuni, Aśvatthāman (who is rated low), Droṇa, Paurava, Vṛṣaṣeṇa, Jalasaṃdha,, Bāhlīka, the Rākṣasa Alāyudha, Bhagadatta (1–35).
165 (168; 5808). Acala and Vṛṣabha, finally Karṇa, whom Bhīṣma rates only half a ratha*, with which Droṇa agrees (1–5). Karṇa protests furiously and advises Duryodhana to cast out Bhīṣma, who is really trying to be divisive (5–25). He will refuse to fight until Bhīṣma is dead (25).*
166 (168–69; 5838). Bhīṣma replies in kind (1–5).

Duryodhana placates him and asks about the Pāṇḍavas' warriors (10). Bhīṣma reviews Yudhiṣṭhira, Bhīma, the twins, and Arjuna (1–35); the Kauravas grow apprehensive (35).
167 (170; 5879). Bhīṣma continues with the Draupadeyas, Uttara, Abhimanyu, Sātyaki, Uttamaujas, Yudhāmanyu, Virāṭa, and Drupada (1–10).
168 (171; 5893). Śikhaṇḍin, Dhṛṣṭadyumna and his son, Dhṛṣṭaketu, the Pāñcālas, the Kekayas, other allies (1–25).
169 (172; 5921). Rocamāna, Kuntibhoja, and Ghaṭotkaca are reviewed (1–5). Bhīṣma concludes (5–15) and asserts that he will not fight Śikhaṇḍin, who was born a woman (20).

Saṃjaya said:
161.1 Kuntī's son Yudhiṣṭhira, after listening to Ulūka's speech, ordered
the army led by Dhṛṣṭadyumna to march out. With its footmen,
elephants, chariots, and troops of horses the four-membered army
was terrifying and unshakable as earth itself. Protected by Bhīmasena
and others and by its great warriors like Arjuna, and commanded by
Dhṛṣṭadyumna, the unbreachable force spread like the quiet ocean.
In the forefront the mighty archer of Pāñcāla, Dhṛṣṭadyumna,
berserker in war, who longed to find Droṇa, led the troops. He
assigned their targets to the chariot fighters as they rode in strength
5 and vigor: the *sūta*'s son* to Arjuna, Duryodhana to Bhīmasena,
Aśvatthāman to Nakula, Kṛtavarman to Śaibya, Saindhava** to
Yuyudhāna of Vṛṣṇi. He pitted Śikhaṇḍin against Bhīṣma in the front
rank, Sahadeva against Śakuni, Cekitāna against Śala, Dhṛṣṭaketu
against Śalya, Uttamaujas against Gautama,*** the Draupadeyas
against the five Trigartas. Saubhadra he put against Vṛṣaṣeṇa and
the remaining kings, for he considered him superior even to the
Pārtha in battle.
10 Having thus distributed the warriors, singly and together, the great,
fire-complexioned archer reserved Droṇa for himself. The mighty
bowman Dhṛṣṭadyumna, marshal of the armies, after arraying the
troops wisely and facing battle with fortitude, yoked the ranks of the
Pāṇḍavas according to their assignments and stood prepared on the
field of battle for the triumph of the sons of Pāṇḍu.

* = Karṇa.
** = Jayadratha.
*** = Kṛpa.

Dhṛtarāṣṭra said:
162.1 When Phalguna* had sworn himself to the killing of Bhīṣma, what
did my dull-witted sons Duryodhana and so forth do, Saṃjaya? For
already do I see father Gāngeya** killed in battle by the Pārtha of the
hard bow seconded by Vāsudeva. What did the great archer Bhīṣma,
first of fighters, whose wisdom is boundless, say when he heard the
Pārtha's reply? Having obtained the marshalcy, how did the yoke-
bearer of the Kauravas, Gāngeya of vast wisdom and valor, proceed
to act?
Vaiśaṃpāyana said:
5 Thereupon Saṃjaya reported to him everything that the boundlessly
splendid Bhīṣma, the elder of the Kurus, had said.
Saṃjaya said:
Sire, after attaining to the marshalcy, Bhīṣma Śaṃtanava spoke to
Duryodhana encouragingly: "With my homage to spear-brandishing
Kumāra, the marshal of the Gods, I shall now be your marshal, no
doubt of that. I am experienced in warfare and the various battle
formations, and I know how to direct soldier and nonsoldier alike to
their tasks. In the ways of marching in convoy, waging battle, and
neutralizing enemy fire I know as much, great king, as Bṛhaspati
10 himself. I know all the battle plans of Gods, Gandharvas, and men:
with those I shall confound the Pāṇḍavas—let your fears abate.
Indeed, I shall fight them according to proven principles, while
protecting your army, by the rules of scripture, king—put to rest the
fever in your mind!
Duryodhana said:
Strong-armed Gāngeya, I have no fear of all the Gods and Asuras
combined, and that is the truth, let alone now, when you stand here
indomitable as our marshal, and tigerlike Droṇa stands ready,
welcoming battle. With the two of you, chieftains of men, my victory
is assured; and surely not even the sovereignty of the Gods would be
15 out of my reach, best of Kurus! But I wish to know the total number
of warriors among the enemy and ourselves, and also the number
of paladins, Kaurava. For Grandfather is well acquainted with both us
and the others. I wish to hear them along with all these other kings
of earth.
Bhīṣma said:
Son of Gāndhārī, great king, listen to the count of the Warriors in
your own force: who are the Warriors and which ones the Paladins,
protector of the earth. There are many thousands, myriads, and
millions of Warriors in your army, but hear from me the principal
ones.

* = Arjuna.
** = Bhīṣma.

You yourself in the first place and your brothers Duḥśāsana, etc.,
20 are fine Warriors, a hundred in all, all expert armsmen who know
what can be cut and pierced, skilled in the chariot pit, on elephant
shoulder, in club fights, with sword and shield, all good drivers,
strikers, masters of arms, capable of your tasks, the pupils of Droṇa
and Kṛpa Śāradvata in archery. The spirited Dhārtarāṣṭras, wronged
by the Pāṇḍaveyas, shall kill the war-crazed Pāñcālas. I myself, best
of the Bharatas, marshal of all your armies, shall annihilate the
enemies, dumfounding the Pāṇḍavas. But I will not tell you my talents,
for you know them.
Now Kṛtavarman the Bhoja, that finest of fighters, is a Paladin,
25 who no doubt will accomplish your purpose in the war. He will kill
your enemies, as great Indra killed the Dānavas, unassailable by
archers, striking from afar, solid of weapons. The great archer King
Śalya of the Madras appears a Paladin to me, he who always has
competed with Vāsudeva in battle after battle. Forsaking his own
sister's sons,* Śalya is now your great warrior, and he will engage
discus- and club-bearing Kṛṣṇa in battle. Flooding the enemies with
fierce waves like the billowing ocean, Bhūriśravas is your soldier and
devoted friend. This great archer Saumadatti, leader of a horde of
30 warriors, will wreak great havoc among the enemy forces. The king
of Sindhu** seems to me the equal of two Warriors, great king; a
fine, gallant warrior, he will give a good fight. He was once bested
by the Pāṇḍavas at the abduction of Draupadī; remembering his
discomfiture he will fight hard killing enemy heroes. For he undertook
terrible austerities, king, and obtained the rare boon of fighting the
Pāṇḍavas on the battlefield. Remembering the old feud, this tiger
among warriors will fight the Pāṇḍavas, son, risking the life that is so
hard to forsake.

Bhīṣma said:

163.1 Sudakṣiṇa the Kāmboja is regarded as a single Warrior: he will
fight the enemies in battle out of a desire to accomplish your purpose.
The Kurus shall witness that lionlike warrior's gallantry in battle in
your cause like Indra's, O best of kings. He has a chariot train of
hard-hitting Kāmbojas like a swarm of locusts, great king. Nīla, who
dwells in Māhiṣmatī, wearing dark-blue armor, will rout the enemies
5 with his chariot train. Harboring an old feud with Sahadeva, that
king will always fight in your cause, king, first of the Kurus. Vinda
and Anuvinda of Avanti, fine Warriors, capable in war, of solid
bravery and valor, and tigers among men, will set fire to the army
of the foe with clubs, missiles, iron arrows, and javelins thrown from

* = the Pāṇḍavas.
** = Jayadratha.

the hand. Eager for battle, like two elephant leaders at play in the
middle of their herds, they will roam about like Death itself.
The five Trigarta brothers, who I think are excellent Warriors,
10 began a feud with the Pārtha by the city of Virāṭa. They will shake
up the army of the Pārthas in battle as crocodiles the billowing waves
of the Ganges. These five Warriors, who are headed by Satyaratha,
will fight with the recollection of the humiliation that the Pāṇḍaveya
of the white horses, the younger brother of Bhīmasena, brought upon
them at the time when he was conquering the world, King Bhārata.
They, yoke-bearers of the barons, will attack and slay the great
warriors of the Pārthas, the best of their archers.
Your son Lakṣmaṇa and Duḥśāsana's son are both tigerlike men
15 who do not retreat from battles. These young, delicate but impetuous
princes, knowing the fine points of warfare and leading all, are in my
view both excellent Warriors, tiger among warriors, and heroes who
will accomplish great feats, devoted to the law of the barons.
Daṇḍadhara, a bull among men, is a single Warrior, great king, who,
guarded by his own troops, will fight when he gets to the battle.
King Bṛhadbala of Kosala I rate as a preeminent Warrior, son.
20 He shall do battle to the delight of his own army. Kṛpa Śāradvata,
the great archer of awesome weapons, the leader of leaders of
warriors, devoted to the well-being of the Dhartarāṣṭras, laying down
his dear life, shall burn your enemies. Like Kārtikeya he was born
from a reed stalk, the invincible son of Śaradvat Gautama, the great
seer and teacher. Like a fire he shall range the battle field, son,
shattering the plentiful army with its various weapons and bows.

Bhīṣma said:

164.1 Your maternal uncle Śakuni, who equals one Warrior, shall fight
after bringing about this feud with the Pāṇḍavas, king, no doubt
about that. His irresistible troops, which do not retreat in war, carry
plenty of different weapons and have the force of a gale in speed.
Droṇa's son, a great archer beyond all archers, exemplary man at
arms, is a great Warrior with tough weapons. When shot from his
bow, his arrows, like those of the Gāṇḍīva bowman, are strung in a
5 continuous line. Still, I cannot count the hero as a prominent
Warrior, though, if he wished, this famous man could burn down the
three worlds. He built up his wrath and splendor with his austerities
when he was living in a hermitage, and, being of generous mind, he
was favored by Droṇa with celestial weapons. But he has one great
flaw because of which I do not rate him as a Warrior or Paladin, bull
of the Bharatas, best of kings: his life is extremely precious to him—
the brahmin always loves to live. He has no peer in either army and
could on a single chariot smite even the army of the Gods. This

handsome man could splinter mountains with a clap of his hands; he is a hero of countless talents, a fighter of dreadful effulgence. Unendurable like the staff-wielding God,* he shall roam like Time. The equal in wrath of the fire of Doomsday, lion-necked, sagacious, he shall break the back of the war, Bhārata.

His resplendent father, though old still better than his juniors, shall, I have no doubt at all, accomplish great exploits in war. A fire fanned by the wind of speeding arrows, rising from the kindling of the deadwood of armies, he shall burn down the troops of Pāṇḍu's son, holding out for victory. Leader of the herds of leaders of herds of warriors, this son of Bharadvāja,** this bull among men, shall do great damage for your benefit. This ancient guru, the teacher of all consecrated kings, will put an end to the Sṛñjayas; but Dhanaṃjaya is dear to him. This great archer would never kill the Pārtha of unsullied deeds, remembering his brilliant tutelage conquered by his talents. The gallant Bhāradvāja** has only praise for the multitude of the Pārtha's virtues and looks upon him as more than his son. On a single chariot the majestic man could slay with his celestial weapons Gods, Gandharvas, and Dānavas, even when these are joined together on the battlefield.

Paurava, your great warrior and a tiger among kings, I consider, brave king, a Warrior who breaks the chariots of enemy heroes. Setting fire with his own troops to the enemy army, he shall burn down the Pāñcālas as the black-trailed fire burns deadwood. Satyavrata the warrior prince is an eminent Warrior who, O king, will range in your enemy's army like Time. In their colorful armor and weaponry his fighters will roam on the battlefield killing your foes. Karṇa's son Vṛṣaṣeṇa, foremost of Warriors, strong among the strong, will set fire to the troops of the enemy. Jalasamdha of Magadha, killer of enemy heroes, one of your best Warriors, will lay down his life in war. Knowledgeable about elephant shoulders, or on his chariot, the strong-armed man shall do battle, decimating the enemy army. I deem that bull among men a Warrior, great king, who will lay down his life with his troops in your cause. A valiant and brilliant fighter, he shall fearlessly war on your enemies, king.

Bāhlīka I consider a Paladin, never retreating in battle, a champion the equal of Vaivasvata;* for he will in no way retreat when he reaches the battle, attacking the enemy like a gale, O king. Army commander Satyavat is a Paladin of wondrous feats in battle, a warrior who breaks the enemy's chariots. When he faces battle, he never stumbles but attacks, astounding the foes that stand in the way of his chariot. Among the enemies, that good man shall gallantly

* = Yama.
** = Droṇa.

accomplish the feats that become a good man in the holocaust of your cause.

The Rākṣasa king Alāyudha of cruel deeds and great strength shall
slay the foes, king, remembering his old feud. He is the best warrior
of all the Rākṣasa troops; a wizard and firm in his feuds, he shall
35 roam on the battlefield. Heroic and majestic Bhagadatta, king of
Prāgjyotiṣa, is both an excellent wielder of the elephant hook and a
skillful fighter on the chariot. He once battled with the Gāṇḍīva
bowman for a great many days, king, both being eager to triumph.
Later, in homage to his friend the Chastiser of Pāka,* he contracted
friendship with the great-spirited Pāṇḍava, O son of Gāndhārī. He
shall fight in the war, trained to elephant shoulders, like Vāsava
himself, king of the Gods, on Airāvata.

Bhīṣma said:

165.1 Both brothers Acala and Vṛṣaka are Warriors who shall irresistibly
exterminate your enemies. They are a strong, young, and handsome
pair of tigers, firm in their grudges, bellicose, foremost among the
Gāndhāras. Your beloved friend who, always harshly set on war,
prods you into this war with the Pāṇḍavas, king, the vile braggart
Karṇa Vaikartana, your mentor, guide, and friend, a most arrogant
5 self-admirer, is neither a full Warrior nor a Paladin, king. Witlessly
he lost the armor he was born with, and meekly his divine earrings.
Because of Rāma's curse, the brahmin's speech, and the loss of his
tools, I rate him half a Warrior. When he meets Phalguna,** he will
not escape alive!

Saṃjaya said:

Thereupon the strong-armed Droṇa, best of the bearers of arms,
said, "It is as you say and not a lie at all! In battle after battle he
has been seen retreating. Karṇa is meek and forgetful, therefore I
rate him half a Warrior."

When Rādheya*** heard this, his eyes popped in anger, and he said
10 to Bhīṣma, great king, lashing him with whiplike words, "Grandfather,
I am innocent, but all the time, at every step, you cut me angrily
down with words like arrows at your whim, and I suffer it all for
Duryodhana's sake. Now you rate me as impotent as a coward! I
rate *you* half a Warrior, no doubt of that. You always wish ill to all
the world and the Kurus, Gāngeya! I do not lie, but the king does
not realize it. Who else but you would unnerve these kings, who are
equal in their noble feats, by belittling them while describing their
merits, thus trying to sow discord on the battlefield! Neither years
nor gray hair, nor wealth nor relatives can make a baron be counted

* = Indra.
** = Arjuna.
*** = Karṇa.

15 a great Warrior, Kaurava. The baronage is known to excel through
strength, the brahmin through counsel, the commoner through
wealth, the serfs through age. Guided by likes and dislikes you
ignorantly set up 'Warriors' and 'Paladins' according to completely
capricious personal preferences.

"Strong-armed Duryodhana, look at it properly. Cast out this ill-
intentioned Bhīṣma, who does you mischief. For an army that is split
is hard to put together again, king, even if it is homogeneous, let
alone when it is as multifarious as ours, tiger among men! Now
discord has arisen between the fighters in this war, Bhārata. Before
20 our very eyes he is demoralizing us in the worst way. What knowledge
of 'Warriors' does this addlebrained Bhīṣma have? I myself shall beat
off the army of the Pāṇḍavas. When they encounter me with my
infallible arrows, the Pāṇḍavas and Pāñcālas will scatter to the ten
horizons like bullocks before a tiger! Where is the hurly-burly of
battle, wise counsel, and good advice, and where is senile, dull-witted
Bhīṣma, befuddled by Time? For he always and forever contends with
all the world, and with his false eyes regards no man as good enough.
The scriptures exhort us to listen to the old, but not to the senile, who
25 are considered infantile. I shall fight the Pāṇḍavas alone, no doubt of
that, in a good fight, tiger among kings—but the fame for it shall go
to Bhīṣma: you have made Bhīṣma marshal of the army, king, and
all merit goes to the marshal, never to his soldiers. I refuse to fight
in any way as long as Gāngeya is alive. But as soon as Bhīṣma is dead,
I'll fight with all the great warriors!"

Bhīṣma said:

166.1 I have taken up in this war of the Dhārtarāṣṭra the very heavy,
oceanwide burden that had been contemplated for many a year. Now
that the miserable and horrendous hour has struck I must not cause
dissension, and that is what saves your life, son of a *sūta*! Otherwise,
child, I would not hesitate to destroy your faith in war and life, old
as I am, son of a *sūta*. Rāma Jāmadagnya himself caused me not a
shudder when he hurled his huge missiles at me, so what could you
5 do to me? True, the strict do not admire the glorification of one's
own power, still I am exasperated enough to tell you about mine, vile
defiler of your family! The entire royal baronage gathered at the
Bridegroom Choice of the king of the Kāśis, and on one chariot I
defeated them all and abducted the girls quickly. Thousands and again
thousands of such superior men and their troops I whisked away on
that field of battle. Disaster has overtaken the Kurus ever since they
encountered you, a man of feuds. Strive for distinction, be a man!
Fight the Pārtha whom you seek to emulate—I shall watch you
escape from *that* fight, vicious scum!

Saṃjaya said:

King Dhārtarāṣṭra* of deep mind then said to Bhīṣma, "Look at me, Gāngeya, for a mighty task is at hand. Above all, keep in mind what is best for me. Both of you will do great deeds for me.

"I wish to hear further about the best Warriors of the other party, their Paladins, and their herd-leaders of Warriors. I want to hear about the strength and weakness of the enemies: when morning has dawned there will be war."

Bhīṣma said:

I have enumerated your Warriors and Paladins, as well as the Half-Warriors, king. Now hear the count of the Warriors of the Paṇḍavas, if you are curious about the strength of the Pāṇḍavas, strong-armed prince, along with the rulers of earth.

The king himself, son of Pāṇḍu, joy of Kuntī, is an excellent Warrior, who will undoubtedly move in the battle like fire, my son. Bhīmasena is a Warrior worth eight, Indra of kings, with the might of a myriad elephants, haughty and more than human in his fiery energy. The twin sons of Mādrī, bulls among men, are both chariot Warriors, endowed with the beauty and splendor of the Aśvins. Remembering their hardships, they will in the vanguard of the army roam around like Rudra, I have no doubt of that. All of these great-spirited men stand tall like *śāla* trunks, and in stature they are a span taller than other men. Solid like lions, all the powerful sons of Pāṇḍu have observed celibacy, and they are all practiced in extreme austerities. While modest, all these tigerlike men are proud of their strength like tigers, and superhuman in speed, striking power, and combativeness. In their conquest of the world they all defeated kings, bull of the Bharatas. No men can master their weapons, clubs, and arrows, or even string their bows, Kaurava, lift their heavy clubs, or nock their arrows. Even as children they all bested you in running, carrying off the target, gorging themselves, and wrestling in the sand. When they attack your army, proud of their strength like tigers, they will trounce it in battle. Do not try to counter them. One by one they can kill all the kings of earth in battle. You have with your own eyes seen what happened at the Royal Consecration. Remembering Draupadī's molestation and the insults at the dicing, they will roam on the battlefield like Time itself.

As to red-eyed Guḍākeśa seconded by Nārāyaṇa, in neither army is there a Warrior like him, heroic king. Among neither Gods nor Dānavas nor Snakes nor Rākṣasas nor Yakṣas, let alone among men, have I ever heard of such a once and future Warrior as accomplished as the sagacious Pārtha, great king. Vāsudeva is the driver, Dhanaṃjaya the fighter, divine Gāṇḍīva the bow, the horses swift as

* = Duryodhana.

the wind, his celestial armor impenetrable, the grand quivers inexhaustible. His arsenal is the weaponry of great Indra, Rudra, Kubera, Yama, and Varuṇa; his clubs are dreadful of aspect; and his varied armory of striking weapons, the thunderbolt and so forth, is the very best. On a single chariot he slew in battle thousands of
35 Dānavas inhabiting Hiraṇyapura—what Warrior is his peer? Wrathful, powerful, his valor vested in his word, the strong-armed champion can kill off your army while protecting his own. I can stand up to Dhanaṃjaya, so can the Teacher, but no third man in either army, Indra of kings. Raining showers of arrows, that chariot warrior will rise like the cloud at the end of the hot season driven by a mighty gale. The accomplished Kaunteya, seconded by Vāsudeva, is young and skilled; both of us are old and decrepit.

Saṃjaya said:

When the kings had heard Bhīṣma, their sturdy, golden-braceleted, sandalwood-anointed arms hung down limply, as they remembered with anxious hearts the legendary prowess of the Pāṇḍaveyas clearly before their eyes.

Bhīṣma said:

167.1 All five Draupadeyas are great Warriors, king, and I rate Virāṭa's son Uttara also a great Warrior. Abhimanyu is a leader of leaders of Warriors, great king, who will prove the equal of the Pārtha and Vāsudeva in battle. Deft with missiles, a brilliant fighter, cunning and of solid gallantry, he will display his valor, remembering his father's hardships. Sātyaki Mādhava is a champion leader of leaders of Warriors, most truculent of the Vṛṣṇi heroes, and without a trace of
5 fear. I consider Uttamaujas a great Warrior, king, and bull-like courageous Yudhāmanyu is an excellent one. They have many thousands of chariots, elephants, and horses, and they* will fight with contempt for their lives to please Kuntī's son, alongside the Pāṇḍavas, against your armies, King Bhārata, like fire and wind calling out to each other.

The two old men, Virāṭa and Drupada, are invincible in battle; I regard those two fine bull-like men as great Warriors of great prowess. Though old in years, these two, utterly devoted to the Law of the baronage, shall strive with all their might on the path walked by
10 heroes. Through marital bonds and the heritage of power and strength, those two noblemen, great archers both, are tied with the noose of affection, Indra of kings. Depending on their cause, all strong-armed men turn hero or coward, bull among men. Bound on the same course, stolidly loyal to the Pārtha, they will act with all their might regardless of their lives. With a grand-army each, both of

* = the Vṛṣṇis.

them, relentless in the covenant of war, will, guarding their relationship, achieve great exploits. Heroes of the world, great archers, laying down their lives, both of them will achieve great feats while guarding their conviction, Bhārata.

Bhīṣma said:

168.1 Śikhaṇḍin, the son of the king of Pāñcāla, conqueror of enemy
strongholds, appears to me a preeminent Warrior, on the Pārtha's
side, Bhārata. He shall fight in the war destroying the old
establishment, spreading his great fame in your armies, Bhārata. He
has many troops, Pāñcālas and Prabhadrakas, and with his chariot
train he will accomplish great feats. Dhṛṣṭadyumna, marshal of all
the armies, a pupil of Droṇa, I consider a Paladin and great Warrior,
5 King Bhārata. He shall fight in this war slaughtering the enemies like
the wrathful Lord of Pināka at the end of the Eon. War-lovers tell of
his army of chariots vast as the ocean like the hosts of the Gods.
Dhṛṣṭadyumna's son Kṣatradharman, being young in years and not
yet too well trained, I rate as half a Warrior, Indra of kings. Śiśupāla's
son Dhṛṣṭaketu, king of Cedi, and related by marriage to the Pāṇḍava,
is a great Warrior. This lord of Cedi, a champion, shall with his son
achieve great exploits as are not easy even for a great Warrior.
10 Kṣatradeva, avowed to baronial law and a conqueror of enemy
strongholds, I judge an excellent Warrior for the Pāṇḍavas, Indra
of kings. Jayanta, Amitaujas, and belligerent Satyajit, eminent and
great-spirited Pāñcālas all, are great Warriors, who will fight in the
battle like raging elephants, son. Aja and Bhoja, gallant Warriors
for the Pāṇḍavas, will exert themselves to the utmost to support the
Pāṇḍavas, fast with their missiles, brilliant in combat, skillful, of
firm gallantry.
The five Kekaya brothers, berserkers in war, are all outstanding
15 Warriors, flying their blood-red flag. Kāśika, Sukumāra, Nīla, King
Sūryadatta, Śankha, and Madirāśva are all fine Warriors proven in
battle; I rate them all as great-spirited experts on all weapons. I regard
Vārdhakṣemi as a great Warrior, king, and King Citrāyudha a very
fine one, for he shines in battle and is loyal to the Diademed One.*
Cekitāna and Satyadhṛti are great Warriors of the Pāṇḍavas: both
these tigerlike men I judge to be noble Warriors. Vyāghradatta and
Candrasena are in my opinion noble Warriors of the Pāṇḍavas, King
Bhārata, no doubt about it. Senābindu, surnamed Krodhahantar, a
king who is the equal of Vāsudeva and Bhīmasena, O Indra among
20 kings, will valiantly fight your troops in the war. You should judge
him, a fine Warrior who is celebrated for his battling, as highly as
myself, Droṇa, and Kṛpa. The king of the Kāśis, extremely fast with

* = Arjuna.

his missiles, is an excellent Warrior, a fame-deserving conqueror of
enemy cities, whom I rate a single Warrior.
Drupada's son, young Satyajit, a gallant in war and famous for his
battles, equals eight Warriors, for he has become a Paladin of the
measure of Dhṛṣṭadyumna: eager for renown he shall achieve great
25 deeds for the Pāṇḍavas. The mighty King Pāṇḍya, yoke bearer of the
Pāṇḍavas, a loyal champion, is another great Warrior. The mighty
archer Dṛḍhadhanvan is a superb Warrior for the Pāṇḍavas, and
Śreṇimat, O best of the Kauravas, and King Vasudāna are in my view
both Paladins, enemy-burner.

Bhīṣma said:

169.1 Bhārata, great king, the Pāṇḍavas' great Warrior Rocamāna shall
fight your troops in the war like an Immortal. Purujit Kuntibhoja,
a mighty bowman, Bhīmasena's maternal uncle, I judge to be a
Paladin. I consider him a heroic archer, accomplished and experienced,
a brilliant fighter and a potent bull among warriors. He will fight
valiantly as Maghavat* fights the Dānavas, and his troops are all
5 famous and skilled in battle. For the sake of his sister's sons that brave
king shall achieve great exploits in the war, bent upon the well-being
of the Pāṇḍus. Bhīmasena's and Hiḍimbā's son,** the lord of the
Rākṣasas, I consider a leader of leaders of Warriors with many wizard
tricks, who will lustily fight on the battlefield with wizardry, son, and
so will the Rākṣasas, champions and councilors under his command.
These and many other rulers from different countries have, headed
by Vāsudeva, foregathered in the Pāṇḍava's cause. These are the
principal ones rated Warriors, Paladins, and Half-Warriors of the
10 great-spirited Pāṇḍava, king. They shall lead Yudhiṣṭhira's terrible
army, protected by the Diademed Hero as by great Indra himself, O
king of men. It is with them, now marching against you in search of
triumph, that I shall do battle, hoping for either victory or death on
the battlefield. I shall encounter the Pārtha and Vāsudeva, wielding
discus and Gāṇḍīva, superior men, like sun and moon in conjunction
at twilight. I will march in the front line against the noble warrior
soldiers of the son of Pāṇḍu and their troops.

I have herewith, king, recited to you
The Paladins, Warriors and some Half-Warriors,
Selecting the principal ones, of yours
As well as of them, O lord of the Kurus.

15 Arjuna, Vāsudeva and the other kings there I shall all beat back
as soon as I see them, Bhārata, but I shall not, strong-armed king,

* = Indra.
** = Ghaṭotkaca.

kill Śikhaṇḍin of Pāñcāla, when I see him march against me on the battlefield with arrows at the ready. The world knows that in order to please my father, I relinquished the kingship that was mine, and kept the vow of celibacy. I consecrated Citrāngada as king of the Kauravas and the child Vicitravīrya as Young King. Having proclaimed my title of Devavrata among all kings on earth, I shall *not* kill a woman, or one who was a woman before. For you may have heard that Śikhaṇḍin was once a woman, king. Born a girl, he later became a man. I shall not fight him. All the other kings I shall kill, bull of the Bharatas, whomever I encounter in battle, except the sons of Kuntī, king.

5(60) Ambā

5.170–97 (B. 173–96; C. 5942–7657)
170 (173; 5942). At Duryodhana's question why Bhīṣma will not kill Śikhaṇḍin, he relates the story (1). After Śaṃtanu's death Bhīṣma installs Citrāngada and later Vicitravīrya; then he abducts Ambā, Ambikā, and Ambālikā at their svayaṃvara, *fighting off all other kings (1–20).*
171 (174; 5966). He presents the girls to Satyavatī and sets the date for their wedding to Vicitravīrya (1–5). Ambā tells him that she had chosen King Śālva (5–10).
172 (175; 5976). Bhīṣma lets Ambā go and she hastens to Śālva, who rejects her because Bhīṣma had won her (1–5). Ambā protests that she was taken by force and that she is still Śālva's (5–15). Śālva remains adamant and she departs (15–20).
173 (175; 6001). She blames Bhīṣma and vows revenge (1–5). In a hermitage she asks Śaikhāvatya to instruct her in tapas *(5–15).*
174 (176; 6022). The ascetics advise her to return to her father (1–10). She refuses: she will be mocked (10). Her maternal uncle Hotravāhana happens by, who advises her to appeal to Rāma (10–25).
175 (176; 6053). Rāma's friend Akṛtavraṇa happens by and converses with Hotravāhana, who repeats Ambā's story (1–25). Ambā says she will appeal to Rāma (25–30).
176 (177; 6083). Akṛtavraṇa agrees that Bhīṣma is to*

* In the Calcutta edition the consecutive numbering of the *ślokas* jumps from 6099 to 7000, leaving a gap of 900.

blame. Ambā wants him killed (1–10). Rāma arrives and converses with Hotravāhana (10–20). Ambā tells her story (20–30). Rāma promises to intervene with Bhīṣma or Śālva (30). Ambā insists he deal with Bhīṣma (35–40).
177 (178; 7025). Rāma is reluctant to fight; Ambā insists and is supported by Akṛtavraṇa, who reminds Rāma of several pledges (1–15). Rāma agrees to take Ambā to Bhīṣma (15–20).
178 (178; 7050). Rāma sends word to Bhīṣma, who pays him homage (1–5). Rāma tells him to take Ambā back; Bhīṣma declines (5–20). Bhīṣma is prepared to fight Rāma, though he is a brahmin, and challenges him (25–35).
179 (178; 7092). Rāma accepts the challenge and goes to Kurukṣetra (1–5). Bhīṣma rides out from Hāstinapura and faces Rāma (10–20). The Ganges vainly tries to dissuade first Bhīṣma, then Rāma (20–30).
180 (179; 7124). On a divine chariot driven by Akṛtavraṇa, Rāma challenges Bhīṣma to attack (1–10). Bhīṣma first propitiates Rāma, who acknowledges his homage (10–15). After further amenities, Bhīṣma begins the fight. Rāma is wounded and Bhīṣma is remorseful. The day ends (15–35).
181 (180; 7163). The next day the duel resumes; Bhīṣma is wounded, so is Rāma, who faints but recovers and fights on (1–35).
182 (181; 7201). The duel continues (1–15).
183 (182; 7217). The duel continues; Bhīṣma's charioteer is killed, and he himself falls (1–10). He is caught by eight brahmins; upon recovering he sees his mother Gangā, who had taken the reins (10–15). When the battle continues, Rāma falls; there are many portents (15–25).
184 (183; 7248). The same eight brahmins appear to Bhīṣma in a dream and encourage him (1–10). They remind him of a weapon that will make Rāma fall asleep (10–15).
185 (184; 7267). The duel continues and Bhīṣma is wounded; he in turn hits Rāma (1–10). Rāma and Bhīṣma employ on each other Brahmā missiles which cancel each other out (15–20). Bhīṣma is about to launch his Sleepmaker weapon (20).
186 (185; 7290). Nārada reports that the Gods are

warning Bhīṣma against using the weapon; the eight brahmins support Nārada. Bhīṣma withdraws the weapon (1–5). Rāma's ancestors appear and tell him to cease fighting Bhīṣma, who is a Vasu (5–20). Rāma says he cannot withdraw. The ancestors approach Bhīṣma, who also declines (20–25). More pressure on Rāma, who is forced to lay down his arms (25–30). At the eight brahmins' urging Bhīṣma approaches Rāma, who dismisses him in a comradely manner (30–35).

187 (186; 7328). Rāma confesses himself powerless to Ambā, who refuses to go back to Bhīṣma. Rāma returns to Mt. Mahendra (1–10). Bhīṣma returns to his city and assigns spies to Ambā; he is deeply troubled (10–15). Ambā performs tapas *by the Yamunā, in Vatsabhūmi, and elsewhere (15–25). The Ganges appears to her and curses her to become an ugly little river (25–30). Because of her* tapas *Ambā remains human in one half (40).*

188 (187; 7370). While Ambā persists in tapas*, Rudra appears and grants her a boon: she asks Bhīṣma's death. Rudra says that she will become a man in her next life (1–15). Ambā enters the fire (15).*

189 (188; 7389). Drupada, sonless, placates Rudra, who promises him a boy who is a girl (1–5). Drupada's wife duly becomes pregnant and gives birth to a girl, Śikhaṇḍin. Her sex is concealed and she is treated as a boy (10–15).

190 (189; 7409). When she is nubile, Drupada and his wife become concerned to find a wife for their supposed son. They choose the daughter of King Hiraṇyavarman of Daśārṇa (1–10). The bride discovers Śikhaṇḍin's secret, which is reported to Hiraṇyavarman; he is furious (10–15) and sends an envoy to Drupada with threats (15–20).

191 (190; 7434). Hiraṇyavarman calls on his allies, who agree to depose Drupada if Śikhaṇḍin is indeed a woman (1–5). Drupada is terrified, consults with his wife and publicly pretends that he has been deceived himself (5–20).

192 (191; 7456). Drupada consults his councilors and fortifies his city; he also prays much (1–5), but his wife prods him to action (10–15). Śikhaṇḍin, seeing her parents' distress, decides to kill herself in the forest. The Yakṣa Sthūṇākarṇa has his dwelling there (15–20), and

he grants her a boon: she chooses to be a man (20–30).
193 (192; 7487). The Yakṣa agrees to exchange sexes with Śikhaṇḍin for a brief time (1–5). Drupada is overjoyed; meanwhile Hiraṇyavarman dispatches a brahmin to Drupada with a declaration of war (5–15). Drupada sends back a brahmin with the message that Śikhaṇḍin is a man. Women sent by Hiraṇyavarman confirm this (15–25). The two kings make up (25). The God Kubera happens by the Yakṣa's dwelling; when the Yakṣa does not present himself, the king's companions explain that he is ashamed because he is now a woman (30–35). Kubera orders the Yakṣa fetched and curses him to remain a woman forever, then mitigates his curse: at least for Śikhaṇḍin's life span (35–45). When Śikhaṇḍin returns to the Yakṣa to give him back his sex, he is told what has happened and he departs happily. Droṇa teaches Śikhaṇḍin, who becomes a great warrior (45–55). Thus, since Śikhaṇḍin is Ambā reborn and has been a woman, Bhīṣma cannot fight him (55–65).
194 (193; 7558). Duryodhana asks how soon Bhīṣma can wipe out the Pāṇḍavas' troops: in one month (1–10). Droṇa also is able to do so in a month, and Kṛpa in two. Karṇa boasts he needs only five days, and Bhīṣma mocks him (15–20).
195 (194; 7581). Yudhiṣṭhira asks the same question of his brothers. Arjuna declares that he can annihilate the Kauravas in a day (1–20).
196 (195; 7603). The Kauravas march out against the Pāṇḍavas (1–10). Duryodhana sets up camp (10–15).
197 (196; 7622). The Pāṇḍava troops also march in their thousands (1–20).

Duryodhana said:

170.1 What is the reason, best of the Bharatas, that you will not kill Śikhaṇḍin when you see him approach murderously on the battlefield with his arrows at the ready, after you had first said that you would kill the Pāṇḍavas and the Somakas, strong-armed son of the Ganges? Tell me that, grandfather.

Bhīṣma said:

Listen, Duryodhana, you and these kings of earth, why I will not kill Śikhaṇḍin when I see him on the battlefield.

5 My father, Mahārāja Śaṃtanu, the law-spirited bull of the Bharatas, in time reached his appointed end, bull among men. Thereupon I,

keeping my promise, consecrated my brother Citrāngada to be king. When he died, I ceremonially consecrated Vicitravīrya king at the wishes of Satyavatī. Although still young, Vicitravīrya was consecrated by me under Law, and being law-spirited he looked to me for advice. Then, son, wishing to arrange his marriage, I became concerned to fetch him a bride from a suitable family. I heard that all three daughters of the king of the Kāśis, peerless in beauty, were up at a Bridegroom Choice, strong-armed bull of the Bharatas, to wit Ambā, Ambikā, and Ambālikā, and all the kings on earth had been invited.
10 Ambā was the eldest, Ambikā the middlemost, and Ambālikā the
youngest of the princesses, Indra among kings. So I went to the city of the Kāśi king on a single chariot and saw the three well-decked girls, strong-armed lord of the earth, as well as the kings who had collected there. Challenging all those kings, who stood in the arena, I lifted the girls on my chariot, bull of the Bharatas. Knowing that their bride price was an act of bravery, I lifted them on to my chariot and told all the kings gathered there, "Bhīṣma, son of Śaṃtanu, is taking these girls!" and repeated my challenge, "Try your best to set them free, all ye kings! I am taking them by force before your very eyes, kings!"
15 All the kings thereupon leapt up with their weapons out, angrily
ordering their charioteers, "The yoke! The yoke!" On their thunderous chariots, the elephant fighters on their elephants, other kings on their riding horses, they leapt up with their weapons out. Then all the kings encircled me on all sides with a mighty mass of chariots, lord of your people, but with a strong rain of arrows I beat off and vanquished all those princes, as the king of the Gods vanquished the Dānavas. While they were attacking me, I shot to the ground, with one arrow each,
20 their colorful, gold-adorned banners. Laughing out aloud, I felled their
horses, elephants, and charioteers in that contest with blazing arrows, bull among men. Seeing my deftness, they broke and retreated, and after beating the kings, I returned to Hāstinapura. There I conveyed to Satyavatī both the story of my feat and the girls for my brother.

Bhīṣma said:

171.1 Approaching my mother, the daughter of a fisherman and the
mother of heroes, and embracing her feet, best of the Bharatas, I said to her, "I have won these daughters of the Kāśi king for Vicitravīrya at the bride price of bravery by defeating the kings." Satyavatī kissed me on the head, king, and with eyes filled with tears, and said joyfully, "Good fortune that you have won, my son!"
5 When, with Satyavatī's consent, the marriage date was
approaching, the eldest daughter of the Kāśi king said bashfully, "Bhīṣma, you are wise in the Law and learned in all the scriptures.

Pray listen and act toward me in a lawful fashion. In my heart I had chosen the king of Śālva as my bridegroom, and he too had chosen me secretly, unbeknownst to my father. How can you, who have learned the scriptures, force me to dwell in this house, when I am in love with someone else, Prince Bhīṣma, you being a Kaurava to boot? Now that you know, decide in your mind, strong-armed bull of the Bharatas, and do what is proper. The king of Śālva is clearly waiting for me, lord of your people. Take pity on me, strong-armed upholder of the Law, for you, so we have heard, are known on earth for being true to your vows."

Bhīṣma said:

172.1 I informed Satyavatī Kālī then as well as councilors, brahmins, and
priests, and allowed the eldest maiden Ambā to leave, king. With my
leave the girl went to the city of the king of Śālva under the protection
of aged brahmins and accompanied by her nurse. Completing the
journey, she went up to King Śālva and said, "I have come for you,
strong-armed illustrious lord!" With the semblance of a smile the
king replied, O lord of your people, "I do not want you as my wife:
5 you have been another man's before, fair woman. Go back to the
Bhārata, my dear. I do not desire you after Bhīṣma's forcible abduction
of you. Bhīṣma won you and you were carried off happily, after he
tried and beat the kings in a grand battle. I do not want you as my
wife, for you have been another man's, fair one. How can a king like
me, who has learned his lessons and preaches the Law, allow into his
house a woman who has been another man's? Go where you please,
dear, don't let the time go by."

Ambā, smarting with the arrows of the Bodiless God, said to him,
O king, "Do not speak like that, king, for it is not that way at all!
I was not happily abducted by Bhīṣma, enemy-plougher. He abducted
10 me by force, in tears, after putting the kings to flight. Love me who
love you, an innocent girl, King Śālva, for the abandonment of loving
people is not praised in the Laws. I have consulted the son of the
Ganges,* who never retreats in battle, and with *his* leave I have come
to *your* house. Strong-armed Bhīṣma does not want me, lord of your
people. I have heard that Bhīṣma's undertaking was intended for his
brother. The son of the Ganges has given my sisters Ambikā and
Ambālikā, whom he also abducted, to his younger brother
Vicitravīrya. I swear by my head that I have never dreamed of anyone
at all but you, King Śālva, tiger among men! It is not as another
man's previous woman that I have come to you. I speak the truth,
15 Śālva, I swear by my head it is the truth! Love me, a girl come to you
on her own, wide-eyed Indra of kings, not as another man's woman,
hoping for your grace!"

* = Bhīṣma.

But although she pleaded in this way, Śālva rejected the daughter
of the Kāśi king as a snake casts off its worn-out skin. Though she
begged him with various words, prince sans blame, King Śālva did
not believe the girl, bull of the Bharatas. With tears in her eyes she
20 said, overcome with anger, in a sob-choked voice, "May the strict be
my shelter, wherever I go, rejected by you: it is true what I have
said."

So she spoke, but King Śālva cruelly rejected the piteously wailing
woman, Kauravya, repeating to her "Go, now go! I fear Bhīṣma,
fair-hipped woman, and you are Bhīṣma's chattel." At these words of
this not too farsighted Śālva she departed from the city wretchedly,
screeching like an osprey.

Bhīṣma said:

173.1 Departing from the city she thought to herself, Bhārata, "There is
not a young woman on earth more miserable than I, deprived of my
relatives and rejected by Śālva. I cannot go back to the City of the
Elephant, I was let go by Bhīṣma for the sole reason of joining Śālva.
Am I to blame myself, or indomitable Bhīṣma, or my foolish father
who arranged the Bridegroom Choice? It is really my own fault, that
I did not jump off that chariot and run for Śālva while that carnage
went on. And this is the result I have to face like the fool I am.
5 A curse on Bhīṣma, a curse on my dull-witted mindless father, who
dangled me like a harlot for the bride price of some derring-do. A
curse on myself, a curse on King Śālva, a curse on the Placer. Thanks
to the folly of all of them I have now come to this sorry pass. Man
always gets what his fate has in store. But Bhīṣma Śāṃtanava was
the beginning of my misfortune. I see now that I have to revenge
myself on Bhīṣma, by austerities or battle, for I consider him the cause
of my misery. But what king can beat Bhīṣma in battle?"

With this resolve she went outside the city to the hermitage of
great-spirited ascetics of holy habits. Surrounded by the ascetics she
10 spent the night and told them all that had happened to her, strong-
armed Bhārata, that sweet-smiling woman, in all detail, her abduction,
her release, and her rejection by Śālva. There was a great brahmin
there of sharp vows, Śaikhāvatya, wizened in austerities and a guru in
scripture and *āraṇyaka*. The great ascetic and hermit Śaikhavatya
spoke to the suffering young woman, who was sighing, immersed in
the despair of grief. "What," he asked, "can ascetics do in these
circumstances, good woman, lordly and great-spirited hermitage
dwellers deep into austerities?" She said to him, O king, "You can do
me a favor: I want to wander forth. I shall practice severe asceticism.
15 Surely there must have been evil deeds that I foolishly committed in
previous bodies, and this as surely is their fruit. I cannot go back to
my own people, ascetics, disowned, disconsolate, discarded by Śālva.

I want you to instruct me in asceticism. Godlike men, innocent of evil, have mercy on me!"

He comforted the girl with examples, quotations and arguments, calmed her and, along with the other brahmins, promised they would do so.

Bhīṣma said:

174.1 Thereupon all the ascetics busied themselves with their tasks, those
men of Law, worrying about the girl: "What are we to do?" Some
ascetics said, "She should be taken back to her father's house." Other
brahmins thought that I myself should be reprimanded. Others opined
that they should go to King Śālva and enjoin him. "No," said others,
"for he has repudiated her." Again, all those ascetics of sharp vows
5 said, "What can sages do in these circumstances, good woman? No
wandering forth now, dear girl. Listen to our good advice. Go hence
to your father's house, be blessed. Your father the king shall know
what to do next. There you shall dwell, beautiful woman, comforted
and favored in every way. You have no other recourse than your
father, my dear. Either the husband or the father is a woman's
recourse, fair maiden. The husband is her recourse when things go
smoothly, the father when things are rough. Wandering forth is quite
difficult, especially for a delicate woman like you, a princess by nature
dainty, radiant maiden. Dear, there are many discomforts when you
live in a hermitage, which there will not be in your father's house,
10 fair one." Then the brahmins added to the distraught girl, "When
they see you living alone in the empty and dense woods, kings will
proposition you, therefore do not set your mind on this."

Ambā said:

I cannot go back to the city of the Kāśis, to my father's house: my relatives are sure to despise me! It was different when I lived in my father's house as a child, ascetics. I shall not go near my father, be blessed. I wish to practice austerities under the protection of ascetics, best of brahmins, so that in the world hereafter I do not suffer such a sorrow, such misfortune.

Bhīṣma said:

While those brahmins were thus considering back and forth, there
15 arrived in their forest the royal seer and ascetic Hotravāhana. All the
ascetics received the king with honor, offering him the welcome and
so forth, a seat and water. When he was seated and rested and
attentive, the forest dwellers again began talking about the girl. When
he heard the story of Ambā and the king of the Kāśis, O Bhārata,
Hotravāhana, who was her mother's father, rose trembling, lifted the
maiden on his lap and comforted her, king. He asked her about the
source of her troubles in detail from the beginning, and she recounted

to him everything that had happened. The royal seer was grief-
stricken, and that very great ascetic addressed his thoughts to what
20 now was to be done. Tremulously and sorrowfully he said to the
suffering girl, "Do not go to your father's house, my dear. I am your
mother's father and I shall cut away your grief; you must rely on
me, little daughter. The desire that desiccates you is fulfilled. Go at
my bidding to Rāma Jāmadagnya the ascetic: Rāma shall dispel your
great grief and sorrow. He shall kill Bhīṣma in battle, if he does not
obey his word. Go to that best of the Bhārgavas, whose splendor is
like the fire of Doomsday. The great ascetic shall put you back on an
even path."

While sobbing tearfully all the while, she saluted Hotravahana, her
25 mother's father, with her head and said, "I shall go as you say. But
shall I get to see that noble man, who is world-renowned? How will
the Bhārgava dispel my bitter grief? This I want to hear, then I shall
go there.

Hotravāhana said:

175.1 You will see Rāma Jāmadgagnya in the great wilderness, my calf,
engaged in severe austerities, true to his promises, powerful. The seers,
the scholars of the Veda, the Gandharvas, and Apsarās used to
worship him on that finest of mountains, Mahendra. Go there, bless
you, and, after saluting that ancient sage of hard vows with your
head, tell him what I have said. And tell him once more what you
want done, my dear. When you mention my name, Rāma will do
5 anything for you. Rāma is my friend, my calf, a very affectionate
friend, this son of Jamadagni, a hero and finest of all who bear
arms."

While King Hotravāhana was thus speaking to the girl, Akṛtavraṇa
appeared, Rāma's favorite companion. All the hermits rose up in their
thousands, and so did the aged Sṛñjaya King Hotravāhana. The two
forest-dwellers asked about each other's health, as was fitting, and
all sat down around him, best of the Bharatas. Thereafter they spun
all kinds of charming stories, beloved and celestial ones, in a spirit of
affection, joy, and delight.

10 Then, at the end of their conversations, the great-spirited royal seer
Hotravāhana queried Akṛtavraṇa concerning that greatest of seers,
Rāma, "Where may the majestic son of Jamadagni at present be
found, Akṛtavraṇa, that finest of Vedic scholars?"

Akṛtavraṇa said:

Rāma is always talking about you, my lord: "The royal seer
Sṛñjaya is my dear friend," he says. I think that Rāma will be here on
the morrow. You will see him when he comes with a desire to visit
you. But this girl now, royal seer, why has she come to the forest?

Whose is she and what is she to you? I should like to know.
Hotravāhana said:
15 She is my daughter's daughter, sir, the lovely child of the king of
the Kāśis. The eldest, she stood with her two sisters at a Bridegroom
Choice, lord sans blame. Her name is Ambā, the eldest daughter of
the king of the Kāśis, the younger ones being Ambikā and Ambālikā,
ascetic. The royal baronage gathered in the city of the Kāśis for the
sake of the girls, brahmin seer, and there was a grand festival. Then
it happened that the heroic and resplendent Bhīṣma Śāṃtanava,
contemptuous of the other kings, carried off the three damsels; and
after vanquishing the kings, the pure-spirited Bhīṣma returned to the
20 City of the Elephant with the girls. The lord turned them over to
Satyavatī and ordered at once the marriage of his brother Vicitravīrya.
Thereupon, on seeing the arrangements for the wedding being
made, this girl, O bull among brahmins, said to the son of the Ganges
amidst his councilors, "I have chosen the king of Śālva for my
husband in my heart. Pray, man of Law, do not marry me off while
my heart is set on another man!" When he had heard her words,
Bhīṣma consulted his councilors, made his decision and, with
Satyavatī's leave, let her go. Dismissed by Bhīṣma this maiden happily
journeyed to Śālva lord of Saubha, brahmin, and on arriving said to
25 him, "I have been released by Bhīṣma: teach me the Law. I had
chosen you in my heart, bull among kings."
Śālva rejected her, being suspicious of her conduct; and she came
to this forest of austerities greatly set upon asceticism. I recognized
her from her mention of her lineage. Now she thinks that Bhīṣma
alone is the cause of her sorrows.
Ambā said:
My lord, it is as King Hotravāhana Sṛñjaya, the begetter of my
mother's body, has said. I cannot return to my own city, ascetic, for
fear of contemptuous treatment and because I am ashamed, great
30 hermit. I am convinced, reverend lord, that my most pressing task is
to do what Lord Rāma will tell me, good brahmin.

Akṛtavraṇa said:
176.1 Here there are two grievances, my dear: which one do you seek to
redress, woman? Tell me exactly, my calf. If the lord of Saubha is to
be enjoined, dear, then I am sure the great-spirited Rāma shall put the
injunction upon him as a favor to you. Or if you wish to see the
river's son Bhīṣma worsted in battle by the sage, Bhārgava will do
that too. We shall consider right now what is to be done next, after
hearing both Sṛñjaya and you, sweet-smiling girl.
Ambā said:
5 Bhīṣma acted in ignorance when he abducted me, reverend lord,

for he did not know that my heart was set on Śālva. That you should take into consideration, sir, and pass judgment justly and dispose accordingly. Take appropriate measures in the case of either the Kuru tiger Bhīṣma, or King Śālva, or both, brahmin. I have told you the source of my grief precisely as it is, pray take measures about it as reason dictates, reverend lord.

Akṛtavraṇa said:

What you say concerning the Law is correct, fair woman. Now
10 listen to what I have to say, my dear. If the son of the river had not taken you to the City of the Elephant, Śālva, at Rāma's urging, would now have carried you on his head, timid girl. But since you have in fact been won and abducted, dear glowing maiden with the pretty waist, King Śālva has reason to doubt you. So Bhīṣma is the one, a self-styled hero flushed with the glow of victory, and hence it is proper that you avenge yourself on him.

Ambā said:

This is the fierce desire of my heart, brahmin: if only I could have Bhīṣma killed in battle! Whether it be on Bhīṣma or on King Śālva that you put the blame, punish the one because of whom I have come to grief, strong-armed one!

Bhīṣma said:

15 While they were thus talking, the day went by, best of the Bharatas, and night fell with a pleasantly mild breeze. Thereupon Rāma appeared, as though ablaze with splendor, surrounded by his disciples, O king, a bark-clad hermit with matted hair. Bow in hand, carrying sword and battle-axe, in cheerful spirits and untouched by dust, he approached King Sṛñjaya, O tiger among kings. When they saw him, the ascetics as well as the ascetic king and the wretched girl all rose with folded hands. They zealously honored the Bhārgava with the
20 honey-dish, and duly welcomed he sat down with them. Jāmadagnya and King Sṛñjaya talked about the old days, Bhārata, and when they had finished, the royal seer spoke to the mighty chief of the Bhṛgus in due time these kindly and meaningful words, "Rāma, this is my daughter's daughter, the child of the king of the Kāśis, my lord. Listen to what task she wants performed just so, you who are experienced in tasks." "Very well," Rāma replied to her, "tell me!"

Thereupon she drew close to Rāma, who blazed like fire. The beautiful woman saluted Rāma's feet with her head, touched them
25 with hands soft like lotus petals, and stood up before him. Her eyes filling with tears, she wept piteously and took refuge with the scion of Bhṛgu, shelter of all.

Rāma said:

Princess, you are to me as you are to Sṛñjaya. Tell us what grieves your heart. I shall do what you ask.

Ambā said:
Reverend lord of mighty vows, save me from the dread mud-sea
of my sorrow, I throw myself at your mercy, reverend lord!
Bhīṣma said:
Studying her shape and fresh bloom and very delicate features,
Rāma was sunk in thought. Thinking, "What is she going to say?"
the best of Bhṛgus, Rāma, mused for a long time, flooded with
30 compassion. "Tell me," Rāma repeated, and the sweet-smiling girl
told the Bhārgava everything that had happened. When he had heard
the princess out, Jāmadagnya made his decision and said to the fine-
hipped woman, "I shall send word to Bhīṣma, chief of the Kurus,
glowing maiden. When he has heard my law-informed word, the
prince will obey it. If not, I shall burn the son of the Jāhnavī* and his
councilors in battle with the might of my weapons, my dear. Or if
your mind turns that way, princess, I shall first yoke brave King
Śālva to his task."
Ambā said:
35 As soon as Bhīṣma heard that my heart had longingly gone out to
King Śālva, he let me go, scion of Bhṛgu. I went to the king of Saubha
and spoke my difficult words, and he did not accept me, suspecting
my behavior. Pray think on what should be done to remedy matters,
after reflecting on all this in your own mind, scion of Bhṛgu. Bhīṣma
of the mighty vows is the root of my distress, since he overpowered
and carried me off forcibly. Kill Bhīṣma, strong-armed tiger of the
Bhṛgus, because of whom I have fallen in such grief and wander in
40 utter misery! For he is greedy, arrogant and flushed with victory,
Bhārgava: therefore it is just that you avenge me on him, lord sans
blame. When the Bhārata was abducting me, I conceived in my heart
the plan to have that man of great vows killed, my lord. Therefore,
strong-armed, blameless Lord Rāma, fulfil my desire: kill Bhīṣma as
the Sacker of Cities slew Vṛtra!

Bhīṣma said:
177.1 Having thus been told to kill Bhīṣma, O king, Rāma spoke to the
weeping maiden, who kept urging him, "Woman of the Kāśis, I do not
willingly take up weapons other than in the cause of scholars of the
brahman. What else can I do for you, fair one? Both Bhīṣma and Śālva
will obey my word, princess of flawless limbs. That I can do. Do not
grieve. But I will not take up arms in any way, glowing woman,
except at the behest of the brahmins: that is my covenant."
Ambā said:
5 Somehow dispel the grief that Bhīṣma had visited on me, reverend
lord. Kill him at once, master!

* = Ganges.

Rāma said:

Daughter of Kāśi, say the word and Bhīṣma, however deserving of honor, will touch your feet with his head at my orders!

Ambā said:

Kill Bhīṣma in battle, Rāma, if you want to give me pleasure! Pray make true what you have promised!

Bhīṣma said:

While the two were arguing, Rāma and Ambā, Akṛtavraṇa said to
Jāmadagnya, O king, "Strong-armed Rāma, do not abandon this girl
10 who seeks refuge. Kill Bhīṣma, who roars like an Asura! If Bhīṣma is
challenged by you to a duel, Rāma, great hermit, he will either say,
'I stand defeated!' or obey your word. Then the task of this girl will
be done, scion of Bhṛgu, and your word made true, gallant lord.

"One time you made this pledge, Rāma, great hermit. After you had
defeated all barons, you pledged to the brahmins, Bhārgava: 'If ever a
brahmin, baron, commoner, or serf becomes a hater of brahmins, I
shall kill him in battle. A shelter for those who seek refuge in fear of
their lives, I shall not be able to abandon anyone ever, while I am
15 alive. If ever one shall defeat the entire collected baronage, I shall kill
that prideful man.' Rāma, Bhīṣma, the scion in the line of the Kurus,
is triumphant. Meet him and fight him in battle, joy of the Bhṛgus!"

Rāma said:

I remember the promise I made, best of seers. I shall do what can
be accomplished with conciliation. It is a grave matter on which this
Kāśi girl has set her heart, brahmin. I shall take the girl and go myself
wherever Bhīṣma is. If battle-famed Bhīṣma does not as I tell him,
20 I shall kill the swaggerer, I have decided. For the arrows I shoot do
not lodge in the bodies of men: that you found out in the battle of
the barons!

Bhīṣma said:

Having thus spoken, Rāma set his mind on departure, and the spirited man rose up with the *brahman*-scholars. After staying the night the ascetics offered into the fire, said their prayers, and departed, seeking to kill me. Rāma went forth to the Field of the Kurus with the bulls of the brahmins and the maiden, King Bhārata. Reaching the river Sarasvatī they set up camp, the great-spirited ascetics headed by the best of the Bhṛgus.

Bhīṣma said:

178.1 On the third day after he had established himself on even terrain,
that man of mighty vows sent word to me, O king: "I have arrived."
On learning that the mighty lord, an ocean of splendors, had come to
the border of the realm, I quickly went to him in happy spirits, placing
ahead Law and surrounded by brahmins, godlike sacrificial priests,

and house priests, Indra among kings. Majestic Jāmadagnya, seeing me arrive, accepted the homage and said to me, "Bhīṣma, what thoughts prompted you first to abduct the daughter of the king of the Kāśis against her will, and then again to let her go? You have caused her to fall from the higher and lower merit of Law: for who can approach this woman whom you have touched? Now, because you abducted her she has been rejected by Śālva, Bhārata. Therefore take her back on my orders. Bhārata, tiger among men, let the princess regain her own Law. It is unseemly for you, a king, to treat her with contempt, prince sans blame!"

Perceiving him to be not too irate, I said, "Brahmin, there is no way I can give her now to my brother. She told me, Bhārgava, 'I am Śālva's woman!' I let her go, and she went to the city of Saubha. I will not abandon the Law of the baronage for either fear or compassion, greed or self-interest: that is the vow by which I live."

Rāma replied with eyes rolling in anger, "If you refuse to do as I say, bull of the Kurus, I shall kill you today with your councilors!" Again and again Rāma repeated this in a rage, his eyes rolling in anger. I pleaded with the enemy-tamer every time with appealing words, but the tiger of the Bhṛgus did not calm down. Then I bowed my head to that best of brahmins and said: "What is the reason that you want to fight with me? You yourself have taught me as a child the four kinds of weaponry. I am your pupil, strong-armed Bhārgava!"

Rāma then said to me, his eyes bloodshot from anger, "You know that I am your guru, and still you do not take back this daughter of the Kāśi king to indulge my pleasure, King Kauravya! I will not make my peace with you otherwise, scion of Kuru. Take that girl, strong-armed man, and save your family, for since you have lowered her she will find no husband." I replied to Rāma, conqueror of enemy cities, when he spoke in this vein, "This will never come to pass, brahmin seer! What is the use of troubling yourself? Looking to you as my guru of old, Jāmadagnya, I implore you, my lord, for I have relinquished this woman. What man who knows the perilous flaws of women would ever allow a woman in love with another man to lodge in his house like a snake? Not even the fear of Vāsava will make me forsake the Law, illustrious lord. Show me your grace, or do to me swiftly what you want. This verse, pure-spirited sage, is heard in the ancient lore as chanted by the great spirited Marutta:

'A guru's will must be done
Be he ever so arrogant,
Or ignorant of right and wrong,
Or astray from the righteous path.'

"Out of affection, because you are my guru, I have always honored

you greatly, but you do not act like a guru, and therefore I shall fight
with you. I cannot kill a guru in battle, let alone one who is a
brahmin, let alone one who is steeped in asceticism. I am at peace
with you. But there is this judgment in the Laws: that he who in
anger kills a brahmin who has raised his weapon and fights without
fleeing does not incur brahmin murder. I am a baron, ascetic, who
stands by baronial Law. A man commits no lawlessness when he
reacts to a man according to the other's acts; rather he finds well-
being. A man who, while conversant with Law and Profit and
knowing place and time, is struck with doubt whether something is
to his profit, is better off when his doubt is removed. Since you
proceed in a doubtful matter as though it were settled, I shall fight
30 with you in a great duel, Rāma. Behold the might of my arms and
my superhuman bravery. Whatever I can do in the circumstances,
scion of Bhṛgu, that I shall do! Brahmin, I shall fight you in the Field
of the Kurus. Rāma, great hermit, prepare yourself for the duel.
Struck down there by me on a pile of hundreds of arrows, you will
attain to the worlds you have won, hallowed by my weapons in a
great battle!

"So go and return to the Field of the Kurus, you who love war:
I shall meet you there for battle, strong-armed ascetic. I shall sanctify
you by killing you in the same place where you once sanctified your
35 father, Bhārgava. Hasten there, Rāma, berserker in war; I shall dispel
your legendary pride, self-styled brahmin. You often boast in
assemblies, Rāma, that you by yourself wiped out all the barons in
the world. But listen: at that time no Bhīṣma had been born or a
baron like me who would have destroyed your pride of war and love
for war. But now I have been born, strong-armed Rāma, I, Bhīṣma,
the conqueror of enemy strongholds, and I shall take away your
pride of war, have no doubt!"

Bhīṣma said:

179.1 Then Rāma started laughing and said to me, Bhārata, "What good
fortune that you want to do battle with me, Bhīṣma! I am going with
you to the Field of the Kurus, Kauravya. I shall follow your advice;
you go there too, enemy-burner. Let your mother the Jāhnavī watch
me kill you on a pile of hundreds of arrows, fodder for vultures,
cranes, and crows. Let the Goddess, cherished by Siddhas and Cāraṇas,
5 see you miserably killed by me today, and weep, king! The river,
stately daughter of Bhagīratha, does not deserve the spectacle, she
who gave birth to you, a fool, a lover of war, a sick man. Come, go
with me, Bhīṣma, and let there be a battle this very day. Take chariot
and all, Kauravya, bull of the Bharatas!" I bowed my head to Rāma,
conqueror of enemy cities, who spoke thus, king, and said, "So be it."

After those words Rāma went to the Field of the Kurus, eager to fight, and I went into the city and told Satyavatī. Then, with the rites for godspeed performed, with my mother's benediction, and after having the brahmins perform the Blessing of the Day and the Good Fortune, illustrious prince, I mounted my chariot, bright and silver, well-appointed, well-constructed, covered with tiger skins, equipped with all great weapons and all tools, drawn by white horses, yoked by an experienced charioteer of a *sūta* family, a brave man, expert in horse lore, who had often witnessed my feats; and I started out, armored in a handsome white cuirass and carrying a white bow, best of the Bharatas, while the white umbrella was held over my head and I was fanned with white yak tails, O king. Dressed and turbaned in white, all my adornment white, I departed from the City of the Elephant, lauded with benedictions for victory, and repaired to the Field of the Kurus, the field of battle, bull of the Bharatas.

Goaded by the charioteer my horses, swift as thought and wind, carried me lustily to the battlefield, O king. Arriving at the Field of the Kurus, I and the majestic Rāma displayed our prowess to each other with zest for the coming battle. I stood in the full sight of the great ascetic Rāma. I took my superb conch and began to blow it. Thereupon the brahmins and forest-dwelling ascetics, the Gods and the throngs of seers came to watch the divine battle, king. Again and again celestial garlands appeared, celestial instruments sounded, and masses of clouds rumbled. All the ascetics in the Bhārgava's retinue became spectators around the battle arena.

Then my mother, the Goddess who wishes all creatures well, appeared in person and said to me, "What are you attempting to do? I shall go to Jāmadagnya and plead with him again and again, scion of Kuru, saying, 'Do not fight with Bhīṣma, your student!' And you, prince, do not show such obstinacy toward a brahmin, wanting to do battle with Jāmadagnya!" she scolded me; "Do you not know the slayer of barons, Rāma, equal in prowess to Hara himself, that you want to fight him?"

I saluted the Goddess with folded hands and told her all that had happened at the Bridegroom Choice, best of the Bharatas, how I had tried to placate Rāma, O Indra among kings, and about the old love of the daughter of the king of the Kāśis. Thereupon my mother, the great River Goddess, went to Rāma and tried to appease the Bhārgava seer on my behalf. "Do not fight with Bhīṣma," she said, "he is your student!" He answered to her pleas, "It is Bhīṣma you should stop, for he does not do what I want. Therefore I attack him."

Saṃjaya said:

Thereupon the Ganges returned to Bhīṣma out of love for her son, but, his eyes rolling in anger, he did not obey her word. Then the

law-spirited ascetic appeared, the chief of the Bhṛgus, and the
eminent brahmin challenged him again to a duel.

Bhīṣma said:

180.1 Smiling I said to him, who stood ready for battle, "I cannot fight
you from my chariot, while you are on the ground. Mount a chariot,
strong-armed hero, bind on a cuirass, Rāma, if you want to fight
with me!" Rāma replied to me smilingly in the arena, "The earth is
my chariot, Bhīṣma, the Vedas are my horses like fine steeds, the
wind is my charioteer, the mothers of the Veda are my armor: well-
5 covered by them I shall give battle, scion of Kuru!" Still speaking,
Rāma, whose valor is his truth, encompassed me on all sides with a
large net of arrows, son of Gāndhārī.

Thereupon I saw Jāmadagnya standing on a celestial chariot,
carrying all manner of weaponry, luminous, of miraculous aspect.
Created by his mind, it was holy and vast as a city, yoked with
divine horses, ready for action, adorned with gold and a banner that
was emblazoned with a moon. Akṛtavraṇa, the bellicose Bhārgava's
good and Veda-wise friend, acted as his charioteer, carrying bow and
10 quiver, with wrist and finger guards tied on. Challenging me to battle,
the Bhārgava cheered my heart as he kept shouting, "Attack!" And
this powerful killer of the barons, invincible like the rising sun, this
lone Rāma I attacked alone.

At the distance of three arrow shots I reined in my horses, leapt
down, laid down my bow, and approached on foot that best of seers,
Rāma, in order to pay worship to that greatest of brahmins. I saluted
him ceremonially and spoke these good words, "I shall fight with you,
Rāma, my better and my superior, my law-accustomed guru. Wish
me victory, my lord!"

Rāma said:

15 So should he behave who wants prosperity, strong-armed chief of
the Kurus, for this is the Law of those who fight with their betters.
I would have cursed you, if you had not approached me like this,
lord of your people. Summon up all your fortitude and battle me
watchfully, Kaurava. But I will not wish you victory, for here I stand
to defeat you. Go and fight by the Law—I am pleased with your
conduct.

Bhīṣma said:

I bowed to him, quickly mounted the chariot, and once more blew
my gold-covered conch for battle. Thus began the battle between
him and me, Bhārata, which lasted a good many days as we sought
20 to defeat each other. He was the first to hit me in the duel with
nine hundred and sixty crane-fletched fiery arrows. My four horses
and charioteer were checked, but I stood fast in my armor.

I bowed to the Gods and the brahmins, Bhārata, and I smilingly
said to him where he stood on the battlefield, "I have honored you as
my teacher, even though you overstepped the bounds. Hear once
more from me, brahmin, what leads to advantage in the acquisition
of Law. I shall not strike you in the Vedas that are in your body,
your grand brahminhood, and the ascetic power you have
25 accumulated. I strike you in the Law of the baronage which you have
adopted, for by taking up arms a brahmin becomes a baron. Behold
the might of my bow, behold the strength of my arms; I'll split in
two your bows and arrows, hero!" I shot at him a sharp bear arrow,
bull of the Bharatas, and the end of his bow was cut through and fell
to the ground. I shot at Jāmadagnya nine hundred straight-shafted
spotted arrows fletched with crane feathers. Aimed at his body and
30 sped by the wind, the arrows flew spitting blood like snakes. His whole
body wet with wounds, and pouring blood from them, Rāma
appeared somewhat like Mount Meru pouring forth its minerals, O
king, or the *aśoka* tree at the end of winter adorned with red blossoms,
or like a *kiṃśuka* tree.

Rāma, enraged, took another bow and rained very sharp golden-
nocked arrows. The terrible shafts, piercing weak spots, hit me with
great impact, like the fiery poison of snakes, and shook me. Propping
myself up in that encounter I angrily splattered Rāma with hundreds
35 of arrows. Rāma, smarting from the fire and sunlike sharp arrows, as
so many poisonous snakes, seemed to lose consciousness. Pierced with
pity I blamed myself, bull of the Bharatas, saying, "A curse, a curse
on battle and baronage!" Flooded with a tide of sorrow I said time
and again, "Woe! Great evil have I done by acting as a baron, so
that my guru, a law-spirited brahmin, is hurt by my arrows!" I did
not strike Jāmadagnya anymore, Bhārata.

Then the thousand-rayed sun, after having warmed the earth, at
the end of the day went to its setting, and our fighting ended.

Bhīṣma said:

181.1 My charioteer, who was esteemed for his competence, removed the
shafts from himself, the horses, and me, lord of your people. With
the horses washed, rolled, watered, and refreshed, the battle continued
when the sun rose in the morning. Seeing me quickly approach on my
chariot in full armor, majestic Rāma made his chariot fully ready.
When I saw Rāma draw near eager for battle, I let go of my fine bow
5 and jumped from my chariot. I saluted him as before, remounted the
chariot, Bhārata, and fearlessly drew up before Jāmadagnya, ready to
fight. He sprinkled me with a heavy rain of arrows and I showered
him in return. Angrily Jāmadagnya shot at me feathered shafts like
fiery-mouthed snakes, O king. Again and again I vehemently cut

through them with honed bear arrows in the sky by the hundreds and thousands.

Thereupon majestic Jāmadagnya unleashed at me celestial missiles, and I warded them off, trying to gain the upper hand with my own, strong-armed prince, and there was a mighty din in the sky all around. Then I employed against Jāmadagnya the *vāyavya* weapon, and Rāma countered it with his *guhyaka* missile. I enchanted and shot the *āgneya* weapon, and Lord Rāma warded it off with the *vāruṇa*. Likewise I warded off Rāma's celestial missiles, and Rāma mine, that resplendent enemy-tamer, wise in the ways of divine weapons. Then, maneuvering from the left, the great brahmin, powerful Rāma Jāmadagnya, irately hit me in the chest. I sank down in my fine chariot, best of the Bharatas, and my charioteer, seeing my dejection, quickly carried me off to the distance of a cow's bellow, smarting from Rāma's arrow. When they saw me carried away sorely wounded and unconscious, all the followers of Rāma cheered happily, led by Akṛtavraṇa, and so did the maiden of Kāśi, Bhārata.

When I regained consciousness and became aware, I said to the charioteer, "Get to Rāma, charioteer; my pain is gone and I am ready." My charioteer took me back, Kauravya, the beautifully decked horses dancing and equaling the speed of the wind. On reaching Rāma I angrily covered the angry man with a mass of arrows in an attempt to defeat him. But Rāma quickly cut through my straight-flying shafts in the duel with his own arrows, each with three of his own. All my very sharp arrows were broken and cut into two by Rāma's by the hundreds on the battlefield. Then I shot one fiery, very shiny arrow, like Time itself, at Rāma Jāmadagnya to kill him. Struck deeply, Rāma fainted from the pain of the arrow cut and fell heavily to the ground.

All the people, alarmed, wailed over Rāma lying on the ground, Bhārata, as though at the falling of the sun. Terribly upset, all the ascetics and the girl from Kāśi ran to the scion of Bhṛgu. They embraced him and comforted him gently with hands cooled in water and with benedictions for victory, Kaurava. Confused, Rāma rose and, nocking an arrow to his bow, said to me, "Stand, Bhīṣma, you are dead!" The swift arrow he shot struck me in the left side, as the battle went on, and hurt me badly like a gnarled tree. After killing my horses with a fast bolt in that grand battle, Rāma pelted me confidently with hair-fletched arrows. I too shot a fast bolt that could not be fended off, strong-armed prince. Rāma's arrows and mine stayed in the air, quickly covering the skies. Obfuscated by masses of arrows, the sun cooled, and the wind whistled through them as though barred by clouds. By the friction of the wind and the heat of the sun's rays a fire broke out spontaneously in the sky. Burning with the flickering fire that sparked from themselves, the arrows fell to the ground in ashes, king.

Hundreds and thousands and myriads and millions and billions of
35 shafts Rāma let angrily and nimbly loose at me, Kaurava, but I cut
them up with my snakelike arrows and made them fall down like
serpents on the battlefield.

Thus did the battle go on, best of the Bharatas; and when twilight had passed, my guru withdrew.

Bhīṣma said:

182.1 The next day when I encountered Rāma, there was again a grisly
and horrifying battle, best of the Bharatas. Day after day the law-
spirited lord, the champion, wise in the lore of celestial missiles, nocked
a multitude of such missiles. But with such bolts as could counter
them, I blew them away in that frightening fight, risking the life that
is so hard to relinquish. With his many missiles destroyed time after
time, the mighty-splendored Bhārgava grew wroth and careless of his
life in the fighting.

5 Great-spirited Jāmadagnya, besieged
By my bolts, now hurled a terrible spear,
Like a meteor blazing released by Time
Illumining space with the fire of its tip.

When it came at me like the suns of Doomsday,
I cut it in three with my own blazing shafts
And caused it to fall to the ground, whereupon
A breeze blew up with a beautiful fragrance.

With that great spear shattered and blazing with wrath,
Twelve terrible javelins Rāma unleashed:
Their shapes are impossible, Bhārata, to paint
Because of their luminousness and their speed.

But I watched them alarmed in their various shapes,
Like meteors all that came burning from space,
Their points afire with luminescence
As the twelve suns at the end of the world.

As soon as I saw that lattice of spears
Spread out, I caught it in a net of bolts.
I too hurled off twelve spears in that battle
And blew those terrible javelins away.

10 Great-spirited Jāmadagnya again
Threw three horrible spears with golden shafts,
That sparkled with colors, trailing gold cloth,
Like giant comets trailing fire.

I warded those too off with shield and sword,
So they hit the dust of the battlefield, king;
With celestial arrows I showered in battle
Rāma's horses divine and his charioteer.

On seeing his gold-glitter spears cut down,
In shape like snakes that dart from their sloughs,
The great-spirited bane of the Haihaya king*
Irately displayed a celestial missile.

Then, fearsome like streaking swarms of locusts,
The fire fell of streaks of featherless shafts,
And it massively, hurtfully piled on the body,
The horses, the chariot, and driver of mine.

My chariot was covered all over with arrows
And so were the charioteer and the horses, O king.
The chariot's yoke, its pole and its wheels
And the axle as well were cut by the shafts.

When that shower of arrows abated at last
I blew back at my guru a floodtide of bolts;
And that treasure of brahmin wounded by arrows
Kept shedding his copious blood from his limbs.

As Rāma was hurt by my nets of arrows,
So I was smarting from many deep cuts,
And the fighting stopped in the late afternoon
When the sun sought out the hill of its setting.

Bhīṣma said:

183.1 When in the morning the spotless sun arose, Indra of kings, the Bhārgava's battle with me started all over again. Rāma, greatest of fighters, standing on his dashing chariot, rained showers of arrows on me as Śakra on a mountain. My charioteer and friend was hit by that rain of shafts and fell into the pit of the chariot, to my despair. He dropped into a deep swoon and as a result of the arrow strikes fell unconscious on the ground. Severely wounded by Rāma's arrows, he gave up the ghost.

For a while, Indra among kings, fear possessed me then after my charioteer was slain. While I myself was shooting distractedly, Rāma pelted me with deadly arrows. Then the Bhārgava drew his mighty bow and hit me deep with his arrow, while I was still in shock at the death of my charioteer. The blood-gorging bolt hit me through the collar bone, and when I fell, it fell next to me on the ground, Indra among kings. Rāma, thinking me dead, bull of the Bharatas, again and again roared with the thunder of a cloud and exulted. And while

* = Kārtavīrya.

I lay felled, Rāma, filled with joy, bellowed forth a mighty roar with his followers, O king. The Kauravas, who stood on my side, and the people who had come to watch the duel, were totally overcome when I was felled.

Though fallen, I, lion of kings, espied
Eight brahmins like sun and the offering fires;
They crowded around me on every side
And held me in their arms on the battlefield.

Held by those brahmins I did not touch the ground, but the brahmins kept me in the air, as though they were kinsmen. I was as it were asleep in the sky, and they sprinkled me with drops of water. The brahmins who were holding me said to me in chorus several times, "Have no fear, may you fare well!" Nourished by their words I suddenly rose up and saw my mother, greatest of rivers, stand on my chariot.

Indeed the great river herself had driven
My steeds in the combat, Kaurava king.
I bowed to the feet of my mother as well
As to Ārṣṭiṣeṇa and climbed on my cart.

She had guarded my chariot, horses, and tools. Folding my hands I now bade her go. I thereupon myself took control of the wind-fast steeds, Bhārata, and battled Jāmadagnya until the day passed. I then shot a swift, powerful, heart-piercing arrow at Rāma in the course of the duel, best of Bharatas, and struck by the impact of the bolt, Rāma, stunned, let go of his bow and fell to the ground on his knees. When Rāma, donor of many thousands, had fallen, clouds covered the vault of heaven, raining blood, and meteors fell by the hundreds, accompanied by hurricanes and earthquakes. Svarbhānu suḍdenly covered the blazing sun, scathing winds blew, and earth shook. Vultures, crows, and cranes circled gloatingly about, and on the burning horizon a jackal kept howling balefully. Unstruck drums resounded with great noise.

These dread portents befell, bull of the Bharatas, when great-spirited Rāma fell unconscious to the ground.

In a softened halo of rays the sun
Now went to its setting and plunged in the dust,
And night fell cooled by a pleasant breeze,
And the two of us now withdrew from the fight.

There was thus a truce for the night, O king;
When it dawned the battle resumed, horrendous.
And daybreak on daybreak it started again
For twenty days and three days more.

Bhīṣma said:

184.1 That night, O Indra among kings, after bowing my head to the
brahmin, the Ancestors, all the Gods, and the creatures that stalk in
the night, and to Night herself, lord of your people, I went to my bed
and in my privacy thought to myself, "This very ghastly and most
perilous battle between me and Jāmadagnya has now been going on
for a good many days. I cannot defeat the powerful and puissant
5 brahmin Rāma Jāmadagnya in a pitched fight. Let the deities
graciously show me tonight whether I can ever defeat the majestic
Jāmadagnya."
Then I fell asleep in the night, sore from the arrows, on my right
side as though it were morning. Now, those same eminent brahmins
who had lifted me up when I had fallen from my chariot, and had
held me and comforted me with, "Have no fear!" appeared to me in
a dream, O great king, and standing around me said, listen, scion of
Kuru: "Arise, fear not, Gāngeya! You are in no danger: we are
10 protecting you, tiger among men, for you are our own body. Rāma
Jāmadagnya shall never defeat you in battle, but you shall defeat
Rāma, bull of the Bharatas. You will recognize this favorite weapon,
for you knew it when you wore an earlier body. It is the weapon of
Prajāpati, created by Viśvakarman, called Sleepmaker, Bhārata. Even
Rāma does not know it, nor any other man on earth. Call it to mind,
strong-armed king of men, and employ it with vigor. Rāma will not
die from this weapon, and you will incur no guilt whatsoever, giver
of honor. When Jāmadagnya is hit with the force of your arrow, he
15 will fall asleep. Then, when you have thus defeated him, you shall
make him rise again on the battlefield with your beloved Awakening
weapon, Bhīṣma. Act in this manner tomorrow, Kauravya, when you
stand on your chariot. We consider a sleeping man and a dead man
the same. Rāma can never die, king; therefore employ this
Sleepmaker, when it comes back to your memory." Having spoken,
those eminent brahmins disappeared, all eight of them bearing the
same form, all like the sun embodied.

Bhīṣma said:

185.1 When the night had passed, I woke up, Bhārata, and thinking of
my dream, I found the greatest happiness. Then the battle between
him and me started again, Bhārata, and our fighting was hair-raising
and wondrous to all creatures. The Bhārgava rained a shower of
arrows upon me, and I warded them off with a net of shafts, Bhārata.
Totally enraged with yesterday's fury, the great ascetic hurled at me a
5 javelin as hard to the touch as Indra's thunderbolt, with the glow of
Yama's staff, blazing like fire, licking all around the battlefield. Then,
tiger of the Bharatas, like an airborne fire altar it struck me with
great speed in the shoulder; and like minerals washing down a

mountain, frightful blood poured from the wound struck by Rāma,
strong-armed prince with blood-red eyes. Filled with great anger I
shot at Jāmadagnya a bolt like death itself, like the poison of snakes.
That heroic great brahmin, struck in his forehead, shone like a
10 mountain with a peak on top, great king! He turned on me in a rage
and drawing his bow powerfully he aimed at me a terrifying, enemy-
destroying arrow that was like Time and Death. Hissing like a snake,
the awesome shaft hit me in the chest, and I went to the ground
covered with blood, O king. Regaining consciousness I hurled at the
sagacious Jāmadagnya a spotless spear streaking like lightning. It
struck the great brahmin between the arms, and he was stunned,
king, and a tremor shook him. His friend, the great ascetic and
brahmin Akṛtavraṇa, embraced him and comforted him time and
15 again with beautiful words. Restored, Rāma of the great vows,
seething with anger, thereupon manifested the ultimate Brahmā
weapon. To counter it I too employed the same great Brahmā
missile, and it blazed as though to display the end of the Eon. The
two Brahmā missiles clashed in mid-air without reaching either Rāma
or me, best of the Bharatas. The sky became one vast fire and all
creatures were undone. Overwhelmed by the power of the weapons,
20 Bhārata, Gods, seers, and Gandharvas suffered greatly. Earth with her
mountains, wildernesses and trees trembled and the tormented
creatures fell into the deepest despair. The sky was on fire, king, the
ten horizons smoked, and the creatures of the sky were unable to
remain in their domain. While the world with Gods, Asuras, and
Rākṣasas groaned, I saw my chance and was ready to launch my
favorite Sleepmaker weapon at the behest of the scholars of the
brahman, Bhārata. And no sooner did I think of the weapon than it
came to mind.

Bhīṣma said:

186.1 Thereupon there was a big tumult in the sky, king: "Bhīṣma, do
not release the Sleepmaker, joy of the Kauravas!" I aimed the weapon
at the scion of Bhṛgu, and while I was aiming the Sleepmaker, Nārada
raised his voice, "Kauravya, the throngs of the Gods are standing in
the sky. They are stopping you: do not employ the Sleepmaker.
5 Rāma is a brahminic ascetic, a brahmin, and your own guru. Do not
show him contempt in any way, Kauravya!" Then I saw standing in
the sky those eight scholars of the *brahman*; and they smiled at me,
Indra of kings, and softly said, "Do as Nārada says, best of the
Bharatas, for that is best for the worlds, bull of the Bharatas." Then
I withdrew that Sleepmaker weapon from the battle and lit the
Brahmā missile ceremonially on the battlefield.

When the furious Rāma, O son of a king,
Observed that the weapon had been withdrawn,

He suddenly lifted his voice and cried,
"I've been beaten by Bhīṣma, the more fool I!"

Then Jāmadagnya espied his father,
And the father of him, and *his* father too,
And they stood in a circle around his person
And said to him there in a soothing voice:

"Do never again act so foolhardily, calf, as attacking a baron like Bhīṣma. It is the baron's Law that he fight, scion of Bhṛgu, while the greatest wealth of the brahmin is Veda study and the observation of vows. On some occasion we persuaded you to take up arms, and you performed a most horrible feat. Calf, let this battle with Bhīṣma suffice: this is your final defeat, strong-armed one; withdraw from the battle. Be blessed, let this be the end of your wielding the bow. Let go of it, invincible Bhargava, and practice austerities. Bhīṣma Śaṃtanava is being stopped by all the Gods and repeatedly urged to withdraw from the battle himself. 'Do not fight Rāma,' they are urging, 'for it is not right for you to defeat Rāma in battle, scion of the Kurus. Show the brahmin honor on the field of battle, son of the Ganges. We are your gurus, and therefore we are stopping you!' Bhīṣma is one of the Vasus: it is fortunate that you are still alive, little son. The son of Śaṃtanu and the Ganges is a famous Vasu: how can he be defeated by you, Rāma? Withdraw! Arjuna, first of the Pāṇḍavas, the mighty son of the Sacker of Cities, the heroic Nara Prajāpati, the ancient primeval God, full of puissance, renowned in the three worlds as the Left-handed Archer, has been ordained to be the death of Bhīṣma in due time."

Thus addressed by his Fathers, Rāma replied to his Fathers, "I cannot retreat in battle—that is the vow I have always observed. Never before have I retreated from a pitched fight! Let the son of the river withdraw from this encounter, grandfathers! In no way shall I retreat from this fight."

Thereupon the hermits, led by Ṛcīka and accompanied by Nārada, gathered, O king, and said to me, "Withdraw from the battle, son, pay honor to the good brahmins." "No," I said out of respect for the baronial Law, "I have vowed before the world that I would never turn away and retreat from battle and be hit in the back by arrows! Neither greed nor cowardice, fear nor self-interest can make me abandon the sempiternal Law: my mind is set!"

Then all the hermits, headed by Nārada, and my mother Bhāgīrathī, repaired to the center of the battlefield, but I held my ground, with arrow nocked to my bow as before, firmly resolved to fight. Then they once more spoke in unison to Rāma, scion of Bhṛgu, "The heart of brahmins is like butter: make peace, Bhārgava! Rāma, Rāma, withdraw from this battle, greatest of brahmins! For Bhīṣma is invincible to you, and you to Bhīṣma, Bhārgava." Speaking thus, they all obstructed the battlefield, and his Fathers forced the scion of Bhṛgu to lay down his weapons.

Hereupon I again beheld those eight scholars of the *brahman*,
blazing like eight planets ascending. Gently they spoke to me where
I was standing on the battlefield, "Go forward to Rāma, your guru,
strong-armed one, and do what is best for the world!" Seeing that
Rāma had withdrawn at the counsel of his friends, I took the counsel
of mine to benefit the worlds. I went up to Rāma and, sorely
wounded, I greeted him. Rāma the ascetic said to me smiling with
35 affection, "There is no baron like you walking the earth. Go, Bhīṣma,
I have been greatly gratified by you in this battle!"

Before my eyes he summoned the maiden and said to her in a sad voice amidst the ascetics—

Rāma said:

187.1 Radiant woman, in full view of all these people I have exhibited great manly prowess to the utmost of my power. But I am not able to surpass in battle that foremost of armsmen, Bhīṣma, although I fully displayed my superb weapons. This is the limit of my power; this is the limit of my strength. Go now, good woman, wherever you wish. Or is there anything else I can do for you? Throw yourself on Bhīṣma's mercy, there is no other course for you to take. For Bhīṣma, shooting his great weapons, has defeated me.

Bhīṣma said:

5 Having thus spoken, the spirited Rāma sighed and fell silent. The maiden then said to the scion of Bhṛgu, "Blessed lord, it is as you say. This Bhīṣma of generous mind is invincible in battle even to the Gods. To the extent of your power and energy you have done for me what had to be done, without stinting your prowess in battle or your many weapons. And in the end he could not be surpassed in the fight. But I shall on no condition whatever go back to Bhīṣma again. Rather I shall go there where I myself can bring Bhīṣma down in battle, ascetic, scion of Bhṛgu!"

10 Thus the maiden spoke, her eyes rolling in anger, and she set her mind on austerities, brooding on my death. Thereupon Rāma, chief of the Bhṛgus, went with the hermits to Mt. Mahendra whence he had come, after bidding me farewell, Bhārata. I myself ascended my chariot, and, lauded by the brahmins, entered my city and conveyed to mother Satyavatī all that had happened, great king, and she congratulated me.

I assigned sagacious men to the doings of the maiden, and everyday they reported to me diligently her goings, words, and behavior, keeping my interests at heart. From the very day that the maiden departed for the forest set on austerities, I became troubled, wretched, and well-nigh lost my wits. For no baron can defeat me in battle with his prowess, son, except one who knows the *brahman* and whose vows have been honed by austerity. In my terror I conveyed all this to Nārada too, king, and to Vyāsa, and both said to me, "Do not despair over that daughter of Kāśi. Who can endeavor to avert by his own effort what is fated?"

The maiden herself entered a settlement of hermitages, great king, and on the bank of the river Yamunā gave herself up to superhuman self-mortification. Going without food, emaciated, coarsened, with matted hair, caked with dirt, she lived for six months on air, a stockstill ascetic. Repairing to the bank of the Yamunā she wore through another year standing in the water, without food, glowering. Another year she spent in subsisting on one withered leaf, ferocious in her wrath, while standing on tiptoe. For fourteen years she set heaven and earth aglow, and though dissuaded by her relatives, she was not to be stopped.

She went to Vatsabhūmi, frequented by Siddhas and Cāraṇas, the hermitage of great-spirited ascetics of holy habits. There, bathing her body at sacred fords day and night, the daughter of Kāśi roamed about, ranging at will—at the hermitage of Nanda, great king, the holy hermitage of Ulūka, the hermitage of Cyavana, the Site of Brahmā, and Prayāga, the sacrificial terrain of the Gods; in the Forests of the Gods as well as Bhogavatī the hermitage of Kauśika, king, the hermitage of Māṇḍavya, the hermitage of Dilīpa, the Pond of Rama, O King Kauravya, and the hermitage of Pailagārgya. At all those fords the maiden bathed her limbs, lord of your people, and performed severe austerities.

My mother, rising from the water, said to her, Kauraveya, "Good woman, why do you inflict pain on yourself? Tell me the truth!" The blameless woman folded her hands, king, and replied, "Beautiful-eyed One, Bhīṣma was not defeated by Rāma, so who else would try to vanquish that lord of the earth with ready arrows? I myself shall undertake the most gruesome self-mortifications for the destruction of Bhīṣma. I roam the earth, Goddess, so that I may kill the king. May this be the fruit of my vow in another body!"

Then the ocean-going river said, "Radiant woman, your course is crooked! This desire of yours is impossible to fulfil, woman of flawless limbs. If you observe a vow for the destruction of Bhīṣma, and if you indeed shed your body while fulfilling that vow, beautiful maiden of Kāśi, you shall become a crooked river, flowing only in the rainy season, with miserable fords, unrecognizable! A mere monsoon stream, dry for eight months of the year, filled with horrible crocodiles, dreadful and terrifying to all creatures!" Saying this with a seeming smile, O king, my stately, glowing mother tried to stop her.

The fair-complexioned maiden took no food, nor even water,
sometimes for eight months, sometimes for ten. In her greed for more
sacred fords, Kauravya, the daughter of the Kāśi king, on her
wanderings hither and yon, again fell into Vatsabhūmi. She became
a river in Vatsabhūmi, known as the river Ambā, Bhārata, a mere
monsoon stream, teeming with crocodiles, and with miserable fords,
40 and crooked. By the grace of her austerities she became that river in
Vatsa with only half her body, and with one half remained that
maiden.

Bhīṣma said:

188.1 The ascetics, seeing her set on austerities, tried to stop her and
said, "What do you seek to achieve?" The maiden replied to the
seers, who had grown old in austerities, "I have been rejected by
Bhīṣma and cannot abide by the Law I owe a husband. I am
consecrated to his death, not to a higher world, ascetics! I have
resolved that only by killing Bhīṣma I shall find peace. I shall not
desist, brahmins, until I have slain Gaṅgā's son in battle, him because
of whom I have found this everlasting life of misery, deprived of the
5 world of a husband, neither a woman nor a man! That resolve is
lodged in my heart, and for that I have undertaken this vow. I am
totally disgusted with being a woman and I have resolved to become
a man: I want to pay Bhīṣma back, and I am not to be diverted,"
she repeated.

The God who wields the Trident, the Consort of Umā, appeared in
his own form to the maiden in the midst of the great seers. He
gratified her with a boon and she chose my defeat. The God replied
to the spirited girl, "Thou shalt smite him." The maiden said again
to Rudra, "How can it be that I, a woman, will triumph in battle, for
since I am a woman, my heart is meek to its core, Consort of Umā.
10 Yet, Lord of Ghosts, thou hast promised Bhīṣma's defeat, therefore act
so that his defeat come true, bull-bannered God, that I may encounter
Bhīṣma Śāṃtanava and slay him in battle!"

The Great God, whose emblem is the bull, said to the maiden, so it
is reported, "My voice speaks no lies, good woman—it shall come true.
Thou shalt attain manhood and slay Bhīṣma in battle. And thou shalt
remember everything when thou hast gone to a new body. Thou
shalt be born a great warrior in the House of Drupada; thou shalt
become a nimble armsman and a much honored exemplary warrior.
All this shall befall as foretold, beautiful damsel. Thou shalt become a
15 man after the lapse of some time." Having thus spoken, lustrous bull-
bannered Kapardin disappeared then and there before the eyes of the
brahmins.

Thereupon, while the great seers were looking on, the blameless, fair-complexioned maiden gathered firewood from that forest, made a very high pyre, and set fire to it. When the fire was blazing, great king, she spoke with her heart on fire with wrath, "For Bhīṣma's death!" and entered the fire, did the eldest daughter of Kāśi by the bank of the Yamunā, king.

Duryodhana said:
189.1 How, son of Gangā, did Śikhaṇḍin become a man, after having
been born a proper maiden? Tell me that, grandfather, foremost in
war.
Bhīṣma said:
King Drupada's wife, his beloved queen, had had no sons, Indra
among kings, lord of your people. During this time King Drupada
placated Śaṃkara for the sake of offspring, great king, while
undertaking grim austerities, determined upon our death. He obtained
5 a daughter from the God, though he prayed for a son: "Blessed Lord,
I wish for a son to wreak revenge on Bhīṣma!" The God of Gods said
to him, "You shall have a man child who is a woman. Return, king,
it shall never be otherwise."
He went back to his city and said to his wife, "I have made a great
effort for a son, my queen, by means of austerities, and Śaṃbhu said
to me, "He shall be a man after having been a maiden." Again and
again I pleaded with him but Śiva said, "It is fated, it shall not be
otherwise, for so it is destined to be." Then King Drupada's spirited
wife purified herself when her season had come and cohabited with
10 Drupada. In due time she became with child by Pārṣata because it
was destined, O king, as Nārada told me. The lotus-eyed queen bore
her child, while strong-armed King Drupada happily attended to his
dear wife in fond hopes for a son, scion of Kuru. The glorious queen
gave birth to a most beautiful daughter for King Drupada, who was
sonless, O king, and proclaimed, "I have borne a son!" King Drupada
then had all the rites pertaining to a son performed for the concealed
15 daughter as though she were a son. Drupada's queen kept her counsel
with all her efforts, saying it was a son, and no one in the city but
Pārṣata knew about the girl. For trusting the words of the God of
wondrous splendor, the king concealed the girl and said, "It is a
boy!" The king had all the birth rites performed which go with the
injunction concerning a man child, and people knew him as
Śikhaṇḍin. I alone, through a spy and from Nārada's report, by the
words of the God and the austerities of Ambā, knew.

Bhīṣma said:
190.1 Drupada spent great efforts on his entire family. Śikhaṇḍinī became
very skilled in painting and so forth, and in the crafts, and was a

pupil of Droṇa in archery, O Indra of kings. The child's fair-complexioned mother urged the king to find a wife for the girl, as though she were a son. Seeing that his daughter had reached maturity and knowing that she was a woman, Pārṣata began to worry with his wife.

Drupada said:

My daughter has become a woman, adding to my worries. I have
5 kept her concealed at the behest of the Trident-Wielder. It can in no
way turn out to be false, my queen, for how could the Maker of the
three worlds lie?

His wife said:

Listen to what I have to say, if it pleases you, king, and having listened you should carry out your task, son of Pṛṣata. Let our child take a wife ceremonially: I am convinced that the God's word will come true.

Bhīṣma said:

Having reached a decision in this matter, the couple chose as bride the daughter of the king of Daśārṇa.

> Then Drupada, lionlike king, inquired
> About all kings' purity of descent,
> And chose for Śikhaṇḍin, to be his bride,
> The daughter of King Dāśārṇaka.

10 The Dāśārṇaka king was called Hiraṇyavarman, and this ruler of
the land gave his daughter to Śikhaṇḍin. Hiraṇyavarman was a
mighty king in Daśārṇa country, high-minded and invincible
commander of a large army. After the marriage was performed, best
of kings, the bride reached maturity, as had the maiden Śikhaṇḍinī.
Having taken a wife, Śikhaṇḍin returned to Kāmpilya, and for some
time the bride did not know that Śikhaṇḍinī was in fact a woman.
When later Hiraṇyavarman's daughter did realize it, she shamefacedly
told her nurses and companions that the daughter of the king of
15 Pāñcāla, Śikhaṇḍinī, was a girl. The nurses from Daśārṇa were
terribly aggrieved and sent word back, tiger among kings.

The messengers reported to the king of Daśārṇa the entire deception
as it had happened, and the king waxed wroth. Śikhaṇḍin meanwhile
happily disported himself like a man in the royal palace, great king,
dissembling his womanhood. When a few days later Hiraṇyavarman
learned about the matter, bull of the Bharatas, Indra among kings, he
became exceedingly angry. The Daśārṇa king, in the grip of fierce
20 anger, dispatched a messenger to the house of Drupada.
Hiraṇyavarman's messenger approached Drupada, took him aside,
and in secret spoke these words, "Sire, the king of Daśārṇa has been
deceived by you and is enraged at the humiliation, prince sans blame.
He tells you as follows: 'Surely I have been badly advised by you!

You have insulted me by foolishly asking me my daughter for your own girl. Now reap the reward of your deception, ruffian! I shall exterminate you with family and councilors. Stand firm!' "

Bhīṣma said:

191.1 At these words of the messenger, king, not a word came out of
Drupada, who was like a thief caught in the act. He made an earnest
effort through conciliatory relatives and honey-tongued messengers,
signaling it was not so. The king, after once more ascertaining that
she was in fact a girl, marched out forthwith.
He sent messengers to his immensely powerful allies about the
deception played on his daughter, as reported by his appointed nurses.
5 Thereupon the good king levied troops and was determined to attack
Drupada, O Bhārata. King Hiraṇyavarman consulted his allies about
King Pāñcālya, O Indra of kings. The great-spirited kings decided: "If
it is true that Śikhaṇḍinī is a girl, then we shall capture King
Pāñcālya and take him home. We shall install another prince as king
of Pāñcāla and kill King Drupada and Śikhaṇḍin." Learning of the
verdict the king sent his steward as envoy to Pārṣata, saying, "I am
going to kill you; stand firm!"
10 Being timid by nature and guilty to boot, King Drupada was seized
by a terrible fear. After dispatching another embassy to the Dāśārṇa,
King Drupada, grief-stricken, met his wife in private and, with panic
in his heart and sick with worry, the king said to the beloved mother
of Śikhaṇḍin, "My powerful relation, King Hiraṇyavarman, is going
to attack me in his fury, leading a large army. What am I, fool that
I am, to do now about this girl? It is suspected that your son
Śikhaṇḍin is in fact a girl. Having decided that that is the truth,
Hiraṇyavarman intends, with allies, troops and followers, to
15 exterminate me, no less, thinking he has been deceived. What is true,
what is false, fair-hipped, lovely woman? Tell me. When I have heard
what you have to say, my dear, I shall do just so. For I am in danger,
so is the girl Śikhaṇḍinī, and you too, fair-complexioned queen."
Though the king had known all the time, he spoke (in public) to
convince the enemy: "I am asking, tell me the truth to save us all.
I shall do what I have to do, fair-hipped, sweet-smiling woman. Do
not worry about Śikhaṇḍin. I shall act according to the facts. I myself
was misled by the actual rites into believing that he was a son, and
20 in turn deceived the king of Daśārṇa. Tell me, my lady, I shall act
for our good."
And on his urging the queen replied to the king—

Bhīṣma said:

192.1 Now Śikhaṇḍin's mother (publicly) told her husband the truth,
great-armed king, about the girl Śikhaṇḍinī. "Sire," she said, "being

without sons myself, I gave out, in fear of my co-wives, that Śikhaṇḍin was a son, though she was born a girl. And you, best of men, indulged me out of love, and a son's rites were performed for a daughter, bull among kings. Then you married her to the daughter of the king of Daśārṇa. You had been told before, while discussing the purport of the statement of a God, that the girl that was born would be a man, and so you overlooked it."

Upon hearing this Drupada Yajñasena
Conveyed the whole truth to his councilors;
And the king, O king, took counsel with them,
Whatever was right to protect his subjects.

Convinced that there still was a marital bond,
O Indra of kings, with the king of Daśārṇa,
Though he himself had played a deception,
He, intent on his counsel, now came to decide.

While the city was naturally protected for a time of emergency, O Bhārata, Indra of kings, he fortified it even more and strengthened it all around. The king and his wife were much depressed by their dispute with the king of Daśārṇa, bull of the Bharatas. Thinking worriedly, "How can I have a big war with a relation?" Drupada worshiped the deities in his thoughts. The queen, on seeing him absorbed in the Gods and offering worship, spoke to her husband, king: "Recourse to the Gods is always true and esteemed by the good, and it is the more so for us who are worshiping in a sea of sorrow. Let all the deities be worshiped with rites of rich stipends and let offerings be made into the fire, so that the Dāśārṇa may be warded off. Think with your mind, my lord, on how to make him desist without waging war. By the grace of the Gods it will all turn out well. Wide-eyed king, carry out what you have decided in counseling with your councilors, so that the city may not perish. Divine influence assisted by human effort brings much success, king, while neither succeeds when the two are in conflict. Take therefore appropriate measures for the city with your ministers; *then* worship the deities as much as you please, lord of your people!"

When the spirited maiden Śikhaṇḍinī saw her parents talk together in obvious grief, she became ashamed. "It is because of me," she thought, "that both of them are suffering," and she resolved to kill herself. Having made her decision in great torment of grief, she left her house and went into deep unpeopled forest. It happened to be the domain of a rich Yakṣa, Sthūṇākarṇa, O king, and out of fear of him people avoided that forest. Sthūṇa had a white-plastered brick dwelling there, rich with the smoke of fried rice-cakes, with a tall wall and gateway.

Śikhaṇḍī, Drupada's daughter, entered that forest, king, and by
fasting for many a day dried out her body. The honey-eyed Yakṣa
Sthūṇa appeared to her: "What do you seek to achieve? Speak, I shall
do it at once!" She repeated to the Yakṣa, "It is an impossible thing!"
25 The Guhyaka rejoined, "I shall do it! I am a boon-granting companion
of the Lord of Riches, princess. I shall give it even if it cannot be
given. Speak what you wish to say!" Thereupon Śikhaṇḍin told that
Yakṣa chief Sthūṇākarṇa everything completely, Bhārata: "Yakṣa, my
father is in trouble and will soon perish, for the king of the Daśārṇas
is marching on him in fury. Hiraṇyavarman is a king of mighty
puissance and vigor: save me therefore, Yakṣa, and my father and
mother. You have promised to relieve my sorrow: so let me be a man
30 without blame by your grace! Show me your grace, great Yakṣa,
before the king attacks my city, Guhyaka!"

Bhīṣma said:

193.1 When the Yakṣa heard Śikhaṇḍin's words, bull of the Bharatas, he
paused for thought, then declared under the press of destiny—for
indeed it was fated thus to my grief, Kaurava—"Good woman, I shall
fulfil your desire, but listen, there is one condition. I shall give you
this, my own male organ, for a limited time; after that you must
come back, I swear to you! I am a master whose will comes true, an
aerial spirit that changes at will. Save your city and all your relatives
by my grace. I shall wear your female organ, princess. Promise me
truly and I shall do you this favor."

Śikhaṇḍin said:

5 I shall return this your organ to you, blessed lord. You will bear
my womanhood only for a limited time. When King Hiraṇyavarman
of Daśārṇa has turned back, I shall be a maiden again, and you shall
be a man.

Bhīṣma said:

Having said this both made a covenant not to betray each other,
king, and exchanged their organs. The Yakṣa Sthūṇa wore the female
organ, king, and Śikhaṇḍin obtained the Yakṣa's blazing form.
Śikhaṇḍin, now *prince* of Pāñcāla, joyously returned to the city upon
attaining manhood, king, approached his father Drupada, and told
10 him all that had happened. When Drupada heard this from him he
was overjoyed, and with his wife reminisced about the Great God's
prediction. Then he sent word to the king of Daśārṇa, my lord: "My
son is a man: you must believe me!"

Meanwhile the king of Daśārṇa, troubled by grief and ire, belligerently marched on King Drupada of Pāñcāla. When he reached Kāmpilya, he sent off an eminent scholar of the *brahman* as his envoy with proper ceremony, "Envoy, tell on my orders that vile king of

Pāñcāla this: 'Today, and let there be no doubt about it, you shall
witness the consequences of your insolence, ruffian, of choosing my
15 daughter to marry your daughter!' " With this charge, best of kings,
that brahmin envoy started for the city under the orders of the
Daśārṇa king.

The royal chaplain approached Drupada in the city, and the king of Pāñcāla and Śikhaṇḍin offered the well-received envoy the cow and guest gift. He refused the honors and said, "Thus speaks the heroic King Hiraṇyavarman, 'Ruffian, you shall reap the reward of the wicked deception you played on me for the sake of your daughter, churl! Give me battle, king and in a pitched fight I shall eradicate you today with councilors, sons, and relatives!' "

20 King Drupada, forced in the midst of his ministers to listen to these abusive words of the chaplain envoy of the Daśārṇa king, bowed courteously, best of the Bharatas, and said, "Brahmin, my own envoy shall carry my reply to the statement which you have made on the orders of my brother-in-law." Drupada then sent a Veda-steeped brahmin as his envoy to the great-spirited Hiraṇyavarman. The envoy met with the king of Daśārṇa and gave him the message as voiced by Drupada, O king: "Let an inquiry be made. My son is clearly a male. Someone has lied: the former account is not to be credited."

25 Upon hearing Drupada's message, the king
Reflectively sent some fine young women
Of gorgeous beauty in order to learn
If Śikhaṇḍin was female or a man.

The women he sent found out the truth
And fondly reported it all to the king,
That Śikhaṇḍin was male, O Kaurava prince,
Of potency puissant, to the king of Daśārṇa.

When he learned this news, the king was overjoyed. He met with his brother-in-law and lodged with him happily. The lord of men cheerfully gave Śikhaṇḍin riches—elephants, horses, cows, and many hundreds of slave women. Then, after indeed reconducting his daughter, he returned home with full honors. When King Hiraṇyavarman of Daśārṇa had gone back in happy spirits, his offence removed, Śikhaṇḍinī was greatly relieved.

30 A short time afterward Kubera, whose mount is a man, came to Sthūṇa's dwelling while on a tour of the world.

The protector of Riches, hovering over
His dwelling place, inspected it closely,
Learning this was the house of the Yakṣa Sthūṇa.
Well-adorned, with colorful garland strings,

With rice-cakes, fragrances, canopies,
It gloried and bathed in incense smoke,
With banners and pennants decorated,
With raw meats, foodstuffs, and liquors pouring.

When he saw his dwelling, which was well-adorned on every side,
the king of the Yakṣas said to the Yakṣas who were in his train, "This
house of Sthūṇa is beautifully decorated, O boundlessly mighty
35 Yakṣas. But why doesn't that blockhead instantly present himself?
Since that big fool fails to appear, though he knows I am here, I
think that he deserves a severe punishment.

The Yakṣas said:

Sire, King Drupada has a daughter called Śikhaṇḍinī, and for some
reason Sthūṇa has given her his manhood. He took over her
womanhood, and since he is now a woman he stays at home. That
is why he failed to appear, out of shame for having the shape of a
woman. This is the reason why Sthūṇa has not come to see you
today. Now that you have heard, do what is proper. Let the chariot
stop here.

Bhīṣma said:

"Fetch Sthūṇa!" said the king of the Yakṣas and repeated several
40 times, "I shall punish him!" Summoned, Sthūṇa appeared before the
king of the Yakṣas and stood there shamefacedly in his female form,
great king. Most wrathfully the Giver of Wealth cursed him, O scion
of Kuru, "Let the evil-doer remain a woman forever, Guhyakas!"

Quoth the great-spirited king of the Yakṣas
"Forasmuch as you have insulted the Yakṣas,
And given Śikhaṇḍin your manhood, churl,
And taken the sex of a woman, scoundrel—

forasmuch as you have perpetrated a deed never done before, most
foul of spirit, therefore you shall henceforth be a woman and she a
man!"

Thereupon the Yakṣas pleaded with Vaiśravaṇa* for Sthūṇa's sake,
45 it is said, again and again, to put a term to his curse; and the great-
spirited Indra of Yakṣas replied to his retinue, all the throngs of
Yakṣas, in a desire to put a limit to his curse, son, "Sthūṇa the Yakṣa
will regain his own form when Śikhaṇḍin has been killed in battle.
Let the spirited Sthūṇa rest assured!" Having spoken, the blessed Lord
who is worshiped by Yakṣas and Rākṣasas departed with all his
retinue, who flew in the blink of an eye.

Sthūṇa meanwhile, having incurred his curse, dwelled there and
at the appointed time Śikhaṇḍin came to the Stalker of the Night.
Approaching him he said, "I have arrived, my lord." Sthūṇa said

* = Kubera.

50 repeatedly that he was pleased. Seeing Prince Śikhaṇḍin, who had
come as honesty dictated, he told him all that had happened.

The Yakṣa said:

Son of a king, Vaiśravaṇa has cursed me because of you. Go now, as you please, and walk the world as your fancy takes you. This has been fated of old, I think, and cannot be averted, your coming here and the visit of Paulastya.

Bhīṣma said:

At these words of the Yakṣa Sthūṇa, Śikhaṇḍin returned to the
city, Bhārata, filled with great joy. With manifold garlands and
perfumes and much wealth he paid worship to brahmins, deities,
55 sanctuaries, and crossroads. Drupada of Pāñcāla and his relatives
found supreme joy in his son Śikhaṇḍin, who had achieved his goal.
He gave Śikhaṇḍin to Droṇa as his student, great king, bull of the
Kurus, this son who had been a woman before. Prince Śikhaṇḍin
and Dhṛṣṭadyumna Pārṣata learned the four-part science of weaponry,
along with all of you. Spies, disguised as simpletons, and as blind and
deaf men, whom I had assigned to Drupada, reported to me what
went on.

Thus then, great king, Śikhaṇḍin, the illustrious male–female child
60 of Drupada, became a great warrior, best of the Kauravas. The eldest
daughter of the king of the Kāśis, famed as Ambā, was born in
Drupada's lineage as Śikhaṇḍin, bull of the Bharatas. When he
encounters me with bow in hand eager to fight, I shall not look at
him even for a moment, and I shall refuse to hit him. This my vow
has always been renowned in the whole world: that I shall shoot no
arrows at a woman, a former woman, one with the name of a
woman, and an apparent woman, joy of the Kauravas, and for this
65 reason I shall not kill him when he ambushes me in battle. Were a
Bhīṣma to kill a woman he would kill himself; therefore I shall not
kill him, though I may see him on the field of battle.

Saṃjaya said:

Having heard this, King Duryodhana Kauravya pondered awhile, and concluded that this was worthy of a Bhīṣma.

Saṃjaya said:

194.1 When the starry night had made room for dawn, your son queried
grandfather in the middle of the whole army, "Son of the Ganges, this
mighty army of the Pāṇḍaveya, with its multitudes of men, elephants,
and horses, and teeming with great warriors protected, as though by
the World Guardians themselves, by great and strong archers, Bhīma,
Arjuna, etc., headed by Dhṛṣṭadyumna, unassailable, unstoppable like
5 a churning sea, this oceanlike army unshakable in battle even by the
Gods—in how much time would you, lustrous Gāngeya, be able to

annihilate it, or that great archer the Teacher,* or the very strong
Kṛpa? Or Karṇa, famed in war, or the eminent son of Droṇa? For
all of you in my army are experts with divine missiles. This I wish to
hear, for I am always very curious in my heart, strong-armed hero.
Pray tell me.

Bhīṣma said:

It is becoming to you, best of the Kurus, lord of the land, that you
should ask about the strengths and weaknesses of the enemies and
your own.

Hear, king, what the limits of my power are in battle, the limit of
10 the prowess of my arms with missiles, strong-armed prince. An
ordinary man should be fought with honesty, a wizard with magic
tricks—that is the decision of the Law. Strong-armed prince, if I fill
my forenoon portion every day, making one portion ten thousand
fighters and a thousand chariot warriors—which I think is my
measure—I can, when girt and always at the ready, slay the great
army of the Pāṇḍavas in this manner over a period of time, Bhārata.
If I shoot my mighty missiles, which kill hundreds and thousands each,
while standing on the battlefield, I can kill it off in a month.

Saṃjaya said:

15 Having heard Bhīṣma's reply, King Duryodhana questioned Droṇa,
O Indra of kings, the first of the Angirases, "Teacher, in how much
time can you slay the troops of the son of Pāṇḍu?" With a laugh
Droṇa replied, "I am an old man, best of Kurus, my breath and
energy are short. I think that with the fire of my missiles I could burn
down the army of the Pāṇḍavas in a month's time, like Bhīṣma
Śāṃtanava. That is the limit of my power and strength." "In two
months," said Kṛpa Śāradvata, and Drauṇi** promised the destruction
of the troops in ten days.

But Karṇa, expert with great missiles, promised: "In five days."
20 When the son of the river heard that reply of the *sūta*'s son, he
laughed out loud and said, "As long as you do not encounter on the
battlefield the arrow-, sword-, and bow-wielding Pārtha seconded by
Vāsudeva, rising invincibly on his chariot, so long you may think so,
Rādheya. But you can say anything you want!"

Vaiśaṃpāyana said:

195.1 Having heard this reported, the Kaunteya*** summoned all his
brothers secretly, O best of the Bharatas, and said to them, "Spies of
mine among the troops of the Dhārtarāṣṭra brought me these tidings
this morning. Duryodhana, they say, questioned the son of the river of
great vows, 'In how much time can you kill off the army, lord?' 'In

* = Droṇa.
** = Aśvatthāman.
*** = Yudhiṣṭhira.

a month,' he replied to the evil-minded Dhārtarāṣṭra. Droṇa
5 acknowledged the same length of time. Gautama said in twice that
time, and we hear that Drauṇi, expert with great missiles, pledged ten
days. Karṇa, expert with divine missiles, when he was asked the
same in the assembly of the Kurus, promised to slay the army in
five days.

"Therefore I now also wish to hear your reply, Arjuna. In how
much time can you annihilate the enemies in battle?"

At these words of the king, Guḍākeśa Dhanaṃjaya glanced at
Vāsudeva and replied, "They are all great-spirited armsmen and
10 excellent fighters, who, no doubt, will slay your army, great king. But
have no worries on your mind, I speak the truth. On one chariot I,
seconded by Vāsudeva, can annihilate the three worlds with
Immortals, moving and standing creatures, past and present and
future, in the blink of an eye. I possess that great, gruesome missile
which Paśupati gave me at the time of the duel with the mountain
man. I possess the missile that Paśupati employs at the end of the
Eon to destroy all creatures. Gāngeya does not know that weapon,
neither do Droṇa, Gautama, and Droṇa's son, king, let alone the son
15 of the *sūta*. But it is not proper to kill ordinary men in battle with
divine weapons: we shall fight the enemies honorably. These tigerlike
men are your companions, king, all expert with divine missiles, all
welcoming war. They are all invincible, having made their final
ablutions in the Vedānta; they would destroy even the army of the
Gods in battle, Pāṇḍava: Śikhaṇḍin Yuyudhāna, Dhṛṣṭadyumna
Pārṣata, Bhīmasena, the twins, Yudhāmanyu, Uttamaujas, Virāṭa,
and Drupada, who both equal Bhīṣma and Droṇa in battle, and you
20 yourself, capable of eradicating even the three worlds. He upon whom
you, Indra's equal in luster, look in anger will surely soon cease to
be—I know it well, Kaurava.

Vaiśaṃpāyana said:

196.1 The next morning, under a clear sky, the kings, at Duryodhana
Dhārtarāṣṭra's orders, marched out against the Pāṇḍavas. They all had
bathed and purified themselves, wore garlands and white robes, held
swords and banners, and had offered into the fire and had had the
svasti pronounced. All were Veda-wise champions, all had observed
good vows, all were performers of rites, all were battle-scarred,
powerful men who hoped to conquer better worlds hereafter in
5 battles, all had concentrated minds and trusted one another. Vinda
and Anuvinda of Avanti, the Kekayas and Bāhlīkas, all marched out
led by Bhāradvāja. Aśvatthāman, Śāṃtanava, Jayadratha of Sindhu,
the southerners, westerners, and the mountain warriors, the Gāndhāra
prince Śakuni, all the easterners and northerners, Śakas, Yavanas,

Śibis, Vasātis, with their own troops surrounding their great warriors, all these warriors marched out in the second army. Kṛtavarman with his force, the mighty Trigartas and King Duryodhana surrounded by
10 his brothers, and Śala, Bhūriśravas, Śalya, Bṛhadbala of Kosala
followed in the rear led by the Dhārtarāṣṭra.
They marched, these warriors about to give battle, over even roads, and, in full armor, they took up positions in the western part of the Field of the Kurus. Duryodhana had a camp set up there, Bhārata, that was decorated like Hāstinapura—experienced men who lived in the city saw no difference between the city and the camp, Indra among kings. The Kauravya king had similar fortresses built for the
15 other kings as well, by the hundreds and thousands. The army
bivouacs in hundreds of groupings stretched a distance of five leagues into the circular battle arena, O king. The rulers of earth, according to their vigor and strength, entered their thousands of opulent camps quickly. King Duryodhana portioned out superb foods to the great-spirited princes and their troops as well as noncombatants. Elephants, horses, men, artisans, other camp followers, bards, songsters and minstrels, merchants, courtesans, harlots, and spectators—King Kaurava looked after them all in proper fashion.

Vaiśaṃpāyana said:

197.1 Likewise King Yudhiṣṭhira Kaunteya, son of Dharma, urged on his
heroes led by Dhṛṣṭadyumna, O Bhārata. He gave orders to the steadfastly brave leader of Cedis, Kāśis, and Karūṣas, the enemy-killing Dhṛṣṭaketu, to Virāṭa, Drupada, Yuyudhāna, Śikhaṇḍin, the two archers of Pāñcāla: Yudhāmanyu and Uttamaujas. The champions, wearing colorful armor and earrings of pure gold, blazed like fires on sacrificial hearths sprinkled with butter; those archers shone like luminous planets.
5 The king, a bull among men, paid honor to the army, division by
division, and ordered the troops to the march. Pāṇḍu's son first sent off Abhimanyu, Bṛhanta, and all the Draupadeyas who were led by Dhṛṣṭadyumna. In the second formation Yudhiṣṭhira sent Bhīma, Yuyudhāna and Dhanaṃjaya Pāṇḍava. The noise of the happy warriors hoisting on harnesses, milling about, running around, seemed to touch heaven. The king himself, with Virāṭa, Drupada, and other princes, marched in the rear.
10 That army of the fearful bows led by Dhṛṣṭadyumna appeared as
the Ganges in spate, stagnating, then flowing. Then the sagacious king again regrouped his ranks in order to fool the torrential wits of the sons of Dhṛtarāṣṭra. The Pāṇḍava ordered the Draupadeya archers, Abhimanyu, Nakula, Sahadeva and all the Prabhadrakas, ten thousand horses, two thousand elephants, ten thousand foot, and five

thousand chariots, and the invincible Bhīmasena to the vanguard. In the center he placed Virāṭa, Jayatsena of Magadha, the two Pāñcāla warriors Yudhāmanyu and Uttamaujas, both heroic and great-spirited wielders of clubs and bows, while Vāsudeva and Arjuna also followed in the center.

There were berserk men there, clutching their weapons—twenty thousand standards commanded by champions. There were five thousand elephants, all the chariot trains, footmen, and commanders, carrying bows and swords and clubs by the thousands in front and by the thousands in back. The other kings were largely stationed in this sea of troops where Yudhiṣṭhira himself was, with thousands of elephants, tens of thousands of horses, thousands of chariots and foot soldiers, relying on which he marched to attack Suyodhana Dhārtarāṣṭra. Behind followed hundreds of thousands and myriads of men, marching and shouting in thousands of formations. And in their thousands and tens of thousands the happy warriors sounded their thousands of drums and their tens of thousands of conches.

Notes

The Book of Virāṭa

4(45) Virāṭa

1.5. *The boon granted by Dharma*: cf. 3.298 (II, 804).*
20. *Royal Dicing Master*: *rajñaḥ sabhāstaraḥ*: lit., "he who spreads the rug in the hall," sc., the dicing carpet; here it is clearly intended as an official position of note. ***luminiscent nuts*: *phalair jyotīrasaiḥ*, sc., the *vibhītaka* nuts used at dicing, here artificial and apparently carved from precious stones.

2.1. *Curries*: *sūpān*: lit., "flavored sauces."
5. *Cook*: *ārālika*: the semantics of this word is uncertain, since it also means "deceitful"; perhaps cooks were notorious for padding bills, or making off with food.
10. *Dhṛtarāṣṭra*: cf. 1.1.142 (I, 51); 1.31.5 (I, 91).
15. *Five years*: cf. 3.45.5 (II, 310). ***Twelfth Rudra*, etc.: officially there are eleven Rudras and twelve Ādityas.
25. *Much to say about*: I take *bahu* with *vadan*: Draupadī's intention is sarcastic: she will have many comments to make about prosperity resulting from action—which her husbands have failed to take for the last twelve years. ***Artificial way*: *vidhinā kṛtakena*: by disguising himself.

3.15. *Maid servants*: *sairaṃdhrī*: cf. Introduction, p. 6 ff.

4.1. *The agnihotras*: i.e., the sacred fire and the paraphernalia for fire worship; Dhaumya will continue the Pāṇḍavas' fire rites *in absentia*.
20. *Increased prosperity*: *kiṃcit pravṛddham api*: i.e., one should, in all prudence, not remind the king of the financial rewards his favor has bestowed.

5.10. *Śāmī tree*: *prosopis spicigera*: a sacred tree, from which King Purūravas was the first mortal to drill fire.
20. *Yellow swords*: does this imply they were actually copper or brass, or is it simply an old epithet that has stuck?
25. *The rain would not enter*: I construe: *yāni tasyāvakāśāni . . . yatra . . . tirovarṣāṇi varṣati tatra tāni paryabandhata*, lit., "which open spaces of her (sc., the *śāmī* tree) there were, and where they were out of the rain when it rained." Correct cr. ed. *tiro varṣāṇi* accordingly. *Tasyāva*° has double sandhi of *tasyāḥ* and *ava*, hence Vulgate *tasyā vakāśani*.

* The cross-references are, first, to the book and chapter number of the text and, then, in parentheses, to the volume and page number of this translation.

I further take *varṣati* as loc. abs. ***Who questioned them*: I construe: *iti samāsajjānā vṛkṣe 'smin te paraṃtapāḥ [sarveṣām] ā gopālāvipālebhya ācakṣāṇāḥ*; for the idiom "down to cowherds and shepherds," cf. 2.137.35.
30. *Promises made*: sc., the covenant at the dicing.

6.1. *Curious king: varayan*: lit., "being ready to choose [him]."

8.10. *Deep in the three: Nīlakaṇṭha*: deep of speech, spirit, and navel. ***Six*: nose, eyes, ears, nails, breasts, neck. ***Five*: foot-soles, hand-palms, eye corners, lips and tongue, and nails.
15. *Garland girl: mālinī*: also the name of an Apsarā.
25. *For her own destruction*: I find no folklore on the belief that the crab dies in giving birth.

9.10. *Divided by colors: varṇasya varṇasya suniścitā guṇaiḥ, varṇa*: standing practically for "class," even "herd."

10.6. *But wrongly attired: paridhāya cānyathā*: "having put on [clothes] in a way not befitting [his character]."
8. *Uttarā*, name of the eldest daughter of Virāṭa, not to be confused with Uttara, name of his son.
9. *As son and daughter*: they will not accept him either as son, because he is too effeminate, or as daughter, because he is too masculine.
11. *He was not a man*: these accomplishments were apparently considered typically feminine.

11.11. *As pleasing to me as Yudhiṣṭhira's: Yudhiṣṭhirasyeva . . . darśanena me samaṃ tavedaṃ darśanam*: it is possible to construe: "as pleasing to me as [it was once] to Yudhiṣṭhira."

12.1. *Birds tied to a string*: cf. *Nala* (II, 332), where the wayward dice turn into birds that fly away with his clothing; the intention here is that the dice were always under control. Yudhiṣṭhira "knew the heart [secret] of the dice," a gift bestowed by Bṛhadaśva in *Nala* (II, 364); this passage clearly presupposes *Nala*.
20. *Sixty-year-old elephants*: i.e., at the height of their strength.

4(46) The Slaying of Kicaka

13.19. *Impassable*: there is no sense in the emendation *aśakyarūpaiḥ*; read *aśakyarūpam* (sc., *adhvānam*) with the MSS.

14.5. *Holiday: parviṇi.*
7. *Well-strained: suparisrutam* (emendation for °*śrutam*): so? It must be a particular sort of liquor, soon forgotten, to judge by the variants.

15.5. *Well-drained: parisrutam* (neuter): apparently also an emendation, though not so signaled.
15. *Men who give and do not beg*: sc., *kṣatriyas*. ***Tied in the noose of the Law*: viz., by the covenant of the dicing game.

16.5. *Gāndhārī note: Nīlakaṇṭha: svaraviśeṣa*: Monier-Williams lists it as a *rāgiṇī*.
10–15. Bhīma's reaction indicates that he was not aware of Draupadī's latest molestation, though he is presumed to have been a witness of it (see above, 15.10).

17.2. *An usher dragged me in the hall: prātikāmin*: the incident is described in 2.60 (II, 139 ff.) where, however, the *prātikāmin* (who implicitly called her a slave—2.60.4) in the end is afraid to bring Draupadī (2.60.17), and Duḥśāsana does it.
4. *The wicked Saindhava*: the story in 3.248 ff. (II, 705 ff.).
10. *Niṣka*: a golden breastplate, also used at times in the sense of a gold coin.

18.5. *Kaikeya woman*: apparently her mistress, Sudeṣṇā.
20. *The Lady does not know: āryā* refers to Kuntī.
25. *You must watch over him*: cf. Kuntī's request 2.70.5 (II, 164).

30. *Dāmagranthi*: the fuller name of Nakula as Granthika; it means "fastener of the [horse's] girth strap."

19.5. *Where there has been water before*: in rivers that are dry in summer and fill up in the rainy season.
13. *Disfavor: prasādāt*: used sarcastically: "thanks to him."

20.1. *Hands that once were red*: namely, by the application of a red dye to the palms as a sign of elegance and opulence.
5. *Sukanyā*: the story in 3.121 ff. (II, 456 ff.).

21.7. *In order to appease her: Cyavanaṃ śāmyantam*: lit., "Cyavana who [in consequence] grew at peace": reference is to his anger when Sukanyā pricked his eyes when he was overgrown by an anthill.
9. *Nāḍāyanī*: daughter of Naḍa = Nala; cf. 3.57.20 (II, 331), and Introduction II, 185.
10. *Followed no one but Rāma*: sc., definitely not Rāvaṇa. ***Lopāmudrā*: cf. 3.95 (II, 413)
13. *Don't grieve*: I interpret *mā* absolutely (cf. *maivam*), for it cannot be taken with *kṣama*.
30. *Jaṭāsura*: the story in 3.154 (II, 514 f.). ***Jayadratha*: the story in 3.248 ff. (II, 705 ff.). ***Hiḍimba*: the story in 1.139 ff. (II, 294 ff.).

22.10. *Jaya*, etc.: the secret names of the Pāṇḍavas.
17. *Advāreṇa nirjagāma*: lit., "he went out without using the door": bursting out through window or wall.

23.4. *Fond propensity to copulation: iṣṭaś ca viṣayo maithunāya*: the meaning is that Draupadī will attract other would-be lovers.
15. *In secret language: saṃjñābhiḥ*: lit., "with signs," but the adverb *śanakaiḥ*, "softly," indicates that words were used.
25. *Thirteen days more*: but above (20.13) Bhīma urged Draupadī to hold out for one and a half months (*māsam adhyardhasaṃmitam*). Possibly the "thirteen" here is symbolic of the thirteen years of exile.

4(47) The Cattle Robbery

28.25. *Concealed under his disguise: channaṃ satreṇa*: the semantics of this *satra/sattra*, "disguise," where the word commonly means "sacrificial session of a certain type" is insufficiently explained. One might speculate that here, at least, there is a notion of a sort of ritual separation from the rest of the world, hence the usage.
19.3. *tīrthaiḥ*: which may have the meaning of either "sacred ford" or "holy men."

29.25. *Warm fortnight*: sc., of waning moon.

30.9. *Well worth the honor: sūpasevyāni*: I presume this implies some lustration of the weapons.
23. *Showing their loyalty: rājabhaktipuraskṛtāḥ*: note this meaning of *bhakti*, which is the normal one in nonreligious usage and which in religious contexts remains central to other connotations.

31.5. *As though by fireflies*: viz., by burning arrows.

32.6. *With fine copper blades: supītadhāraiḥ*.
13. *Acquit us of our sojourn: tasya vāsasya niṣkṛtiḥ*: that is to say, "repay him for lodging us."
44. *Vaiyāghrapadya*: apparently this is the brahmin *gotra* name that Yudhiṣṭhira has affected in his role as the brahmin Kanka.

34.10–15. *Khāṇḍava forest*: the story, of course, without Bṛhannaḍā, in 1.214 ff. (II, 412 ff.).

36.4. *Close by a burning field: śmaśānam abhitaḥ*: this burning field, an open-air crematorium, may also be understood as a metaphor for the army of Kurus in which the prince was sure to find his death.

37.6. *The burning quarter: dīptāyāṃ diśi*: this is a normal aspect of the portent of howling jackals; whether it is supposed to refer to any specific quarter, e.g., the south, or simply to "the burning horizon" is hard to say.

38.30. *With a frog: śilīpṛṣṭhah śilīmukhah.*
50. *Subjugated the entire West*: the story in 2.29 (II, 85).

39.10. *Dhanaṃjaya*: lit., "winner of booty." ***Vijaya*: "conquest, conqueror." ***Phalguna*: the "glittering, white" one; he may well have been named after the stars Phālgunī (the double constellation δ and ϑ Leonis, and β and 93 Leonis), which, according to *Śatapatha Brāhmaṇa* 2.1.2.11, are also called Ārjunī, and are presided over by Indra, whose "secret name" is Arjuna.
15. *The Terrifier: Bībhatsu*: lit., "loathsome"; this obvious meaning is intentionally reversed. ***Arjuna*: "white."
20. *Jiṣṇu*: "in the habit of conquering," also an epithet of Indra. ***That little boy: kṛṣṇāvadātasya sataḥ priyatvād bālakasya vai*, a rare reference to the boyhood of Kṛṣṇa so celebrated in later texts.
23. The resonances with the *Bhagavadgītā*, also a text in which a charioteer admonishes a faint-hearted prince, are striking; cf. *BhG.* 11.41 f.; 18. 72.

40.15–20. *Sainya*, etc.: these are the names of Kṛṣṇa's horses; normally he drives two horses: Sainya and Sugrīva.
23. *Fences*: so I think should *valayāni* be understood here.
41.5. *Ordered his creatures to the flag*: or "exhorted his creatures in the flag": *dhvaje bhutāny acodayat.* The creatures are the terrifying, practically alive beasts that are in Arjuna's flag beside the monkey.
21. *The birds flying toward the left: śakunāś cāpasavyāḥ.*

42.10. *From fear they sought refuge with us: teṣām bhayābhipannānām*: I understand here that the Trigartas at Duryodhana's court who suggested the cattle robbery (above 4.29.1) were there as refugees from an earlier defeat at the hands of the Matsyas.

43.6. *Full of attention: samāhitāḥ*: perhaps it should be rendered more strongly: "totally absorbed [viz., in the coming revenge]"; cf. samādhi.
10. *Repay . . . the debt . . . which I promised him of old*: this translates literally *ṛṇam akṣayyaṃ purā vācā pratiśrutam . . . dāsyāmi.* Karṇa acknowledges that he owes Duryodhana a debt of undying loyalty, which he at one time (*purā*) had verbally (*vācā*) pledged, namely, in exchange for Duryodhana's support and that he will now repay him; cf. 1.126 (I, 279); 5.139.15 ff. below.
15. *Like serpents to an anthill*: during the summer snakes seek shelter from the heat in anthills.

44.4. *For the wise do not judge*, etc.: *bhāraṃ hi rathakārasya na vyavasyanti paṇḍitāḥ.* N. interprets: "On this he quotes a proverb: just as the wise do not decide, viz. to fight, by giving weight to, i.e. relying on, a cartwright's word that 'this chariot I have made is divine and sturdy; with it you shall defeat even Gods entirely,' without considering suitability to time and place." I should prefer an ellipsis: *(rathasya) bhāraṃ rathakārasya (śrutvā)* or *(vacaḥ śrutvā) na vyavasyanti paṇḍitāḥ.*
6. *Lived in the aura of the brahman: brahmacaryam adhārayat*: I think reference is here to Arjuna's five-year sojourn in heaven, hence my somewhat forced translation; cf. 3.45 (II, 310). Possibly it refers to Arjuna's *tapas* before meeting Indra, but no precise amount of time is specified there (cf. 3.39), and five years seem excessive.
7. *Learned from Śakra*: cf. 3.45 (II, 310). ***Sāṃyaminī*: a demoness or a city? Nothing further known.
8. *Citrasena*: cf. 3.234 (II, 684 f.).
9. *Nivātakavacas*: 3.165 ff. ((II, 544 ff.). ***Kālakhañjas (= Kālakeyas)*: 3.170 (II, 569 ff.).
22. *As the Dānavas fight Vāsava*: i.e., without hope of success.

45.5. *Sacrifice for himself and for others*: i.e., performing rituals whose fruits accrue to himself, and officiating at the rituals of others.
10. *Like a sandal tree*: i.e., instead of the tree being allowed to grow and yearly profits being made from its cuttings, it has been cut down once and for all for a quick profit but no more future prospects. ***What did Vidura have to say*: cf. 2.61.55 ff.; 63.15.

20. *This uncle of yours*: this makes explicit what was evident already: that Aśvatthāman is not berating Karṇa but Duryodhana; although below (46.5), Bhīṣma states the opposite.

46.5. *The two combined*: Droṇa and Aśvatthāman are brahmins. ***The weapon of the brahman: brahmastram*: another case where it is impossible to make out whether *astra* means "weapon" or "spell."
15. *With Duryodhana engaged*: I read *Duryodhane yatte* for cr. ed. *'yatte*; it is also possible that *'yatte* (if there is indeed MS evidence for the *avagraha*) stands for *āyatte*.

47.1. Cf. Introduction, p. 3.
5. *At that very time*: viz., soon after their departure for the forest, when their allies rallied to them; cf. 3.48 (II, 314 ff.).
15. *I shall not give the kingdom*: the real *casus belli*, much adumbrated in Book 5.

48.1. *His monkey that is screeching*: viz., in his flag.
10. *Meatless: nirāmiśam*: the intention appears to be that there will be great carnage—*āmiśa* means "raw meat."
20. *Their private thoughts*, etc.: the cr. ed. has: *teṣāṃ nātmanino yuddhe nāpayāne 'bhavan matiḥ*, where *ātmanino* should be *atmaninī* if it is to agree with *matiḥ*; this seems to be not just a misprint, as it is repeated in the apparatus. I translate *atmaninī*.

49.11. *Tortoise-nail: kūrmanakha*: apparently some kind of arrow (tip).
18. *Driver of red steeds: śoṇāśvavāha*: I take this as appositional to (or another name of) Saṃgrāmajit; normally it is an epithet of Droṇa.

50.5. *Water gourd: kamaṇḍalu*: used as a pitcher, which is also the meaning *droṇa*.
10. *An elephant on a field of gold*: probably because Duryodhana rules the "City of the Elephant."
15. *Over there is . . . Karṇa*: in contradiction with the *triṣṭubh* verses (above, 49.23), where he has fled.
20. *A golden helmet: jātarūpaśirastrāṇa*: the occurrence of a helmet is quite rare; Bhīṣma is normally depicted as "white-turbaned." One may wonder if a golden helmet would afford much protection from the Indian sun.

51.5. *Likewise King Vasumanas*, etc.: legendary kings.
15. *The red and reddish umbrellas: raktārakta*: I analyze this as *rakta* + *arakta*, with prefix *ā-* in the sense of "slightly"; the normal analysis would be *rakta* + *arakta*, "red and nonred" (= white?).

52.27. *Executing a double circle: yamakaṃ maṇḍalaṃ kṛtva*: probably a figure eight.

53.5. *Friend: māriṣa*: a rather late and elsewhere in the *MBh*. rare form of address.
36. *Many creatures: bahuśaḥ prajāḥ*; the śloka is hard to understand: *śarāṇām . . . viyati dṛśyante bahuśaḥ prajāḥ* may on the face of it mean: "offspring of the arrows appears plentifully in the sky," which does not make much sense either.
50. *Flowering* kiṃśuka *trees*: they have red blossoms.

54.14. *Arjuna had the upper hand*: because his quivers were inexhaustible.

55.15. *Arrows like fire crests . . . a mighty shower of shafts like a raining cloud*: it is interesting to note the reversal of imagery: Arjuna, the son of the rain god, shoots fire; Karṇa, the son of the sun god, shoots water; cf. 1.126.20 ff. (I, 280).

56.1. *The golden palm*: emblem of Bhīṣma.
10. *Across the ocean: pāre samudrasya, pāra* being normally the "shore across." The story in 3.170 (II, 549 ff.) gives no location for the "airborne city"; the parallel version of *Saubha* (3.15 ff. [II, 254 ff.]) places it "by the ocean" (ibid., 21).

60.5. *Both Ājamīḍhas*: i.e., descendants of Ajamīḍha, a title like Kaurava and Bhārata, but largely confined to the *triṣṭubh* verses.
18. *You have no more Duryodhana in you: na hīha Duryodhanatā tavāsti*: Duryodhana, "he who is hard to fight."
19. *One to defend Duryodhana*: I read *Duryodhanarakṣitāram*.

61.6. *Like a goose to a cloud that is suddenly looming: haṃso yathā megham ivāpatantam*: *haṃsas* are supposed to migrate to the mountains at the onset of the monsoon.

21. *Putting your faith in peace: śāntiṃ parāśvasya*: if *parā-śvas* does indeed mean "to confide in," I take it to mean that Duryodhana was so confident of being left in peace by Arjuna that he threw his weapons away.

4(48) The Wedding

63.25. *My bell-ringer: ghaṇṭāpaṇavakaḥ.*
32. *You won't save me*: Virāṭa means that he is so happy that he would gladly give away all his goods, even without gambling.

64.5. *If that blood had fallen on the ground*: that would have made it a battlefield.
27. *Father: māriṣa*: here equivalent to *tāta.*
36. *The Kaunteya had secretly worked out with Uttara*: I do not quite understand the intention. *Itikartavyatā* is a technical Mīmāṃsa term for "ritual procedure," which N. paraphrases as "the ritual, desired to be done first (*agre kartum iṣṭām . . . kriyām*), of seating the king on a fine seat, etc. (read *bhadrāsanena*)." Does it simply mean that Arjuna enlisted Uttara to set up the thrones, below 65.1 ff.?

65.15. *Eighty-thousand* snātaka *brahmins*: a refrain since 2.48.35 (II, 119).

66.1. *Demons on Mount Gandhamādana*: the story in 3.157 ff. (II, 525 ff.).
10. *Infants in the womb*: this suggests that the last year was also an incubation period for the Pāṇḍavas to be reborn.

67.5. *I see no suspicion attached,* etc.: *snuṣāyā duhitur vāpi putre cātmani vā punaḥ / atra śankām na paśyāmi.* While Arjuna's life together with Uttarā was an indecent event on the face of it, any possible opprobrium would be obviated if Uttarā married Arjuna's son: Arjuna would not have permitted his son to marry a girl who had been polluted (by himself, to boot), hence the marriage would establish, (1) the girl's purity with respect to Arjuna's son (*putre*), as Arjuna's daughter-in-law (*snuṣā*), and (2) her purity with regard to Virāṭa himself (*ātmani*), as his daughter (*duhitṛ*). However, this interpretation forces me to take *ātmani* as reflexive to Virāṭa instead of Arjuna, which is against idiom.
14. *Went and settled in Virāṭa's city Upaplavya: Upaplavye Virāṭasya samapadyante*: the use of *sam-pad* indicates that movement is involved.
15. *Grand-army* will translate *akṣauhiṇī,* the largest military unit mentioned in the *MBh.*
20. *Plough-armed Rāma*: he will, however, absent himself from the war, below 5.7.20. ***Kṛtavarman*: he will choose for Duryodhana, below 5.7.25.

The Book of the Effort

5(49) The Effort

2.3. *For obtaining half*: lit., "obtaining the kingdom [*rājyam*]," but this refers to the half kingdom of 2.2.
8. *Approached like a friend: priyābhyupetasya,* which may also be interpreted as "Yudhiṣṭhira had agreed [to the dicing] in a friendly fashion." In either case the meaning is clear: according to Rāma, Yudhiṣṭhira came willingly enough to the dicing game and has only himself to blame if he lost.
9. *Warned by his friends, the Kaurava heroes*: not really; it was Yudhiṣṭhira himself who had misgivings, with which Vidura agreed, 2.52.10 f. (II, 125 f.). ***He knew of no dicing: ayam apy atajjñaḥ,* which is what Śakuni said (and not as warning to Yudhiṣṭhira but as encouragement to Duryodhana), 2.44.15 (II, 111 f.). ***Yet he challenged*: on the contrary, he was challenged by Śakuni, 2.52.13; 53.1 ff. (II, 126 ff.).
11. *Śakuni is not to blame*: then Rāma does not believe that Yudhiṣṭhira was cheated;

and whether he was cannot really be deduced from the letter of the text of the *Sabhā*, where no doubt *nikṛtyā* is used (2.54 ff.) but most likely in a game-technical sense, though *nikṛti* surely at the same time had the overtone of deception like everything about gaming; my translation "tricked" is deliberately ambiguous. In his account of the dicing match Rāma clearly follows the party line of Duryodhana, for which he is berated by Sātyaki below.

3.5. *If they had come to his house*: Sātyaki here makes an interesting distinction: if the Kauravas had joined Yudhiṣṭhira in a true family game (*suhṛddyūta*), freely engaged in at his own house, there would have been no trouble with *dharma*; the *adharma* comes in by their challenging Yudhiṣṭhira, who was *kṣatradharmarata* (8) and therefore in no position to decline, and then by winning through *nikṛti*, here clearly "deceit." ***Could they indeed have acted more handsomely: kiṃ nu teṣāṃ paraṃ śubham*: *param* has many variants, probably because the sarcasm was not understood.
10. *Bhīṣma pleaded with them*: but this will happen much later.
15. *A furious Yuyudhāna*: that is to say, Sātyaki, the speaker himself.
20. *And anoint the Pāṇḍava*: this is to be taken figuratively ("make him king de facto") for Yudhiṣṭhira has already been consecrated. ***The kingdom Dhṛtarāṣṭra relinquished to them*: i.e., half the kingdom at Indraprastha ceded to the Pāṇḍavas by partition, 1.195 ff. (I, 382 ff.).

4.1. *Bhīṣma and Droṇa from poverty*: the assumption throughout the *MBh.* is that the sympathies of Bhīṣma and Droṇa are with the Pāṇḍavas, but that they are obligated to the Kauravas who have maintained them all these years.
3. *For that should have been done*, etc.: *etad dhi puruṣeṇāgre kāryaṃ samayam icchatā.* Drupada means to say that Rāma spoke out of turn: the warnings he mentioned or implied should have been given "at first," namely, before the dicing, at which time, however, no one except Vidura spoke up.
5. *Śalya*: the king of the Madras; *Dhṛṣṭaketu*: the king of Cedi; *Jayatsena*: the king of Magadha.
9. *Who have been loyal: pūrvābhipannāḥ*: "previously allied," if we may take the participle in an active sense; or "first gotten to," if we take it as passive. Nilakantha takes the latter meaning: *pūrvaṃ sāhāyyārthaṃ vṛtāḥ.*
14. *The great warrior Paurava*: sc., the Panjab king known to the Greeks as Poros, cf. Introduction, p. 154 ff.
15. *The Dusty Domain*: Pāṃsurāṣṭra in the Sindh desert.

5.3. *The same loyalty: tulyaṃ saṃbandhakam*: lit., "the same alliance." The "we" here stands for the Vṛṣṇis in general, including Kṛṣṇa.
5. *Friendly with . . . Droṇa*: hardly, if we go by the accounts of 1.122 and 128.
8. *Brotherly feeling: saubhrātra.*

6.1. *Intelligent: buddhijīvin.* ***Has achieved understanding: kṛtabuddhi.* ***Śakra and Āngirasa*: sc., Uśanas Kāvya, adviser to the Asuras, and Bṛhaspati, adviser to the Devas.
15. *At the conjunction of Puṣya*: i.e., when the moon stands in the *nakṣatra* Puṣya. ***The hour of Jaya*: name of the *muhūrta* (hour of forty-eight minutes = one-thirtieth of the natural day). These are favorable times, Puṣya indicating prosperity and Jaya victory.

7.11. *The strict who take precedence*: the line *pūrvaṃ cābhigataṃ* [vv. °*gatān*, °*gatāḥ*] *santo bhajante pūrvasāriṇaḥ* is parallel to 4.9cd *pūrvābhipannāḥ santaś ca bhajante pūrvacodanam.*
20. *Saying again and again*: Rāma must refer here to his speech above in 5.2, where, however, he follows Duryodhana's line.

8.10. *Duryodhana showed himself to his maternal uncle*: this illustrates how broadly relations were extended: Śalya is Duryodhana's maternal uncle only in so far as he is a "brother" (in our terms: cousin) to the Pāṇḍavas, the youngest two of whom were sons of Mādrī, Śalya's sister. This relationship is stressed here no doubt because a maternal uncle stands in a special benefactor relation to the sons of his sister, a position Duryodhana now claims. The situation also shows the validity of the rule: first asked, first ally.

27. *Obscure the splendor: tejovadhaś ca te kāryaḥ*; *tejas* is a particularly hard concept to render: it is the sunlike fiery power in a person which gives him energy, prestige, and a nimbus of splendor. It is specially appropriate to Karṇa, the son of the sun, hence the translation.
30. *The insults*: e.g., 2.61.25 ff. (II, 145 f.). ***Jaṭāsura*: 3.154 (II, 514 ff.). ***Kīcaka*: 4.13 ff. above.

5(49a) Indra's Victory

For general, as well as some detailed, comments, see Introduction, p. 159.

9.35. *There issued from Triśiras*: *triśirās* is to be taken as ablative of *triśiras*, cf. Whitney's *Sanskrit Grammar*, §414a on formation. ***Heathcocks*, etc.: cf. Introduction, p. 159 ff.

10.5. *Thou hast fetched the Elixir*: viz., when it was appropriated by the Asuras after the churning of the ocean: 1.16.30 (I, 74). ***Having smitten Bali*: a feat normally ascribed by the *MBh.* to Indra.
15. *Like sun and moon*: the text suggests that *sūryacandramasau yathā* be construed with *grasantam iva*, but that would make an unlikely simile.
23. *For the strict to meet*: the construction is not less awkward in Skt.: *sakṛt satāṃ saṃgataṃ lipsitavyam*: "a *saṃgata* of strict men is to be desired to be obtained once." In this context, *saṃgata*, 'getting together," has practically the meaning of "pact" as translated in c, where it is implied that such a *saṃgata* can be transgressed (*ati-kram-*). The *triṣṭubh* is clearly formulaic: it is paralleled (not noticed by the editor) in 3.281.29 (*Sāvitrī*), where *pāda a* reads: *satāṃ sakṛt saṃgatam īpsitaṃ param* (likewise 5.10.23a has the well-supported variant *īpsitam* for *lipsitavyam*). The general meaning of this *pāda* is that for strict men only one pact is required for it to stand forever; hence 3.281.29 continues in *b*: *tatah paraṃ mitram iti pracakṣate*: "Henceforth they call it an alliance" (which I translated II, 770: "and friendship—they say—with them is higher still," a possible translation which, however, needs revision if my present construction is correct), and 5.10.24a, *dṛḍhaṃ satāṃ saṃgataṃ cāpi nityam.*
24c. *To meet with a strict man is to great profit: mahārthavat satpuruṣeṇa saṃgatam*, which corresponds to 3.281.29c: *na cāphalaṃ satpuruṣeṇa saṃgatam*. Note that *satpuruṣeṇa saṃgatam* must have been part of the pact formulation: in all three related occurrences (3. 281.29; 5.10.23c, and 24c) it makes the *triṣṭubh pāda* hypermetrical. In the context the verses are no doubt intentionally ambiguous: neither Vṛtra nor Indra may be enough of a *satpuruṣa* for this pact to stand eternally, and the "wise man" may well wish to kill the "strict one."
25. *The abode of those who are great-spirited: nivāsa*: probably a paraphrasis of part of the pact formulation which in 3.281.29 survives as *tataḥ satāṃ saṃnivaset samāgame.*
30. *The hour that is parlous*: at dusk dangerous spirits are abroad.
40. *The earth looked ravaged*: with the disappearance of Indra the monsoon, of course, failed.

11.10. *Viśvāvasu, Nārada*: note Nārada's occasional role as Gandharva.
15. *Brahmā*: it is impossible to be sure whether *brahman* is to be taken as Brahmā or brahmin; in any case Bṛhaspati is Brahmā and brahmin.

12.15. *Brahmin*: see preceding note. ***Especially being a brahmin*: here the text has *brāhmaṇa*. ***What Brahmā sang*: is Brahmā also different from Bṛhaspati?

13.15. *He distributed the brahmin murder over the trees*, etc.: this becomes intelligible from *Taittirya Saṃhitā* 2.5.1.2–5: when Indra has killed Viśvarūpa, he carries the guilt for a year, with creatures calling him a brahmin murderer. He asks Earth to take a third of the guilt; she agrees if she henceforth will not suffer from digging; indeed in a year she shall be grown out again. Then Indra appeals to the trees, which accept if they will not henceforth suffer from pruning; indeed, pruning now helps the trees to bear shoots. Then he appeals to the women, who accept if they may bear children after their menses. The connecting link is that earth/trees/women are "cut into," as Viśvarūpa was, but it is to their advantage, and they take on the guilt of the cutting up of Viśvarūpa and expiate it by sublimating it.

13.20. *The oracular Whisper: upaśruti*, which is Rumor personified.

15.10. *Palanquin: śibikā*.
27. *Assumed a womanly form: strīveṣaṃ kṛtvā*, an intriguing detail.
30. *Their power vanishes before their sources*: they are powerless against that which produced them.

16.1. *Concealed as their witness*: viz., as the *vaiśvānara* fire within each body. ***Triple*: the three fires of the *śrauta* sacrifice.
5. *Everyone loves his mother: svayoniṃ bhajate sarvaḥ*: Water is the yoni of fire, for it springs from the drilling wood block that contains tree sap, hence fire is *apāṃ napāt*.
30. On the sacrificial shares of the Gods, cf. Introduction, p. 161; we may also quote *Taittirīya Saṃhitā* 2.5.2.3.
31. *The lord of the waters*: Varuṇa. ***With this person himself: sahaiva tena*, i.e., Indra himself, all four *lokapālas* now being accounted for.
32. *One share for Indra-and-Fire: aindrāgno bhāgaḥ*, sc., the offerings made simultaneously to Indra and Agni.

17.5. The *mantras* for the Sprinkling-of-the-Cows: according to Nīlakaṇṭha, this refers to the sprinkling, fetching, and immolating of sacrificial animals, and he quotes the mantras: *devāṃś ca yābhir yajate ca . . . gāvaḥ somasya prathamasya bhakṣaḥ*. These are found *RV*. 6.28. 3cd and following, hence their authenticity cannot be in question. They occur in *Taittirīya Brāhmaṇa* 2.8.8 as occurring in connection with special animal sacrifices which in *Taittirīya Saṃhitā* are found in 2.1–4, where, however, these mantras are not cited. If Nīlakaṇṭha's citation of the *RV*. lines is correct, and I have no doubt it is, I suggest that the question concerns this: are these mantras, which are found in the *Brāhmaṇa* but not in the *Saṃhitā*, nevertheless authentic to these rituals? Nahuṣa, to his grief, answers in the negative.
10. *Despoiled the pure brahman*: viz., by denying the authenticity of the above mantras.
15. *You shall regain heaven*: for the story of Nahuṣa's deliverance, see 3.175 ff. (II, 560 ff.).

18.5. *In this Veda*: this appears to mean that in citing the *Atharvaveda* one quotes it as *Atharvāṅgirasah*, which is in fact the way the *Upaniṣads* refer to it: *Chāndogya* 3.4.1 f.; *Bṛhadāraṇyaka* 2.4.10; *Taittirīya* 2.3.1. These texts refer to it as a plural: *atharvāṅgirasa eva madhukṛtaḥ/ete 'tharvāṅgirasaḥ etad itihāsapurāṇam* (*ChUp*. 3.4.1 f.). S. K. De was probably ill-advised to read it as a singular masculine against overwhelming MSS evidence. ***You shall receive a share*: i.e., the *AthV*. would henceforth participate in *śrauta*, ritual. The question remains why Angiras is so suddenly brought on the scene.

5(49) The Effort *(continued)*

19.1. *Slingshot: bhiṇḍipāla*: also *bhindi°*.
15. *Shone as a forest*, etc.: the image suggests yellow-complexioned peoples.
20. *Both kings of Avanti*: sc., Vinda and Anuvinda.
25. *Kekayas, five brother kings*: this is an error: the "Five Kekayas" are firmly on the Pāṇḍava side, while the Kekayas as a nation are on Duryodhana's; cf. below 5.22.19.
30. *The Yāmuna hills: Yāmunaś ca parvataḥ*: reference to the mountain where the river springs?

20.10. *Like men who had undergone another birth*: complete with new identities and names; cf. my remarks, Introduction, pp. 5–10.

21.10. *Without heeding the covenant*: the contention is that the Pāṇḍavas came out of hiding too early. ***As much as a foot of land: padam antataḥ*.
15. *Defeated six chariot warriors*: reference is to Arjuna's *aristeia* in *Virāṭa*.

5(50) The Coming of Saṃjaya

22.6. *Long usage*, etc.: *na saṃvasāj jīryati maitram eṣam*. ***Ājamīḍha's party*: the Kauravas. *Ājamīḍha* is a favorite patronymic with the *triṣṭubh* authors.
18. *Śālvas: Śālveyas*: an error corrected in numerous MSS: Virāṭa is king of the Matsyas.
26. *Of whom the Karūṣaka chieftains extolled the fame*: the Karūṣas were allied with Śiśupāla, who was king of Cedi, but split at Śiśupāla's death.
28. *He hoped to win in a chariot duel: aśaṃsamāno dvairathe*: this confirms my hypothesis that the challenge by, and the killing of, Siśupāla at Yudhiṣṭhira's *rājasūya* parallel the ceremony of the "chariot drive" in the Vedic prototype, cf. Introduction, II, 23 f.
30. *Two Kṛṣṇas*: Arjuna and Kṛṣṇa.

23.10. *Yuyutsu*: the bastard son of Dhṛtarāṣṭra, cf. 1.107.35 (I, 245).
17. *It's the high bright light*: in the context this is the glory of supporting and deferring to brahmins.
23. *Sahadeva defeated*: reference clearly to his conquest of the south; the Kalingas are mentioned in passing, 2.28.45.
24. *Nakula brought the West*: 2.29.
25. *The Defeat in the Dvaita forest*: the *Cattle Expedition*, 3.224 ff. (II, 669 ff.).

24.1. *This is what you are capable of*: i.e., this punctilious courtesy.
3. *As one harming the harmless: adrugdheṣu drugdhavat*, where both participles should be taken as active; *druh* = "harm treacherously."

26.19. *He thinks that my wealth is all too close: atyāsannaṃ madgataṃ manyate 'rtham*. The meaning is this: if the Kauravas hope to win a great kingdom or kingship (*mahārājyam*), they cannot afford to let go of Yudhiṣṭhira's "wealth," i.e., kingdom, which is right next door, in which case peace cannot be had, since the Pāṇḍavas will fight for it.
20. *Not an island*: *dvīpa* is regularly used in the sense of "haven, shelter": the Kauravas have not in the past been able to rely on Karṇa.
27. How difficult the following discourse by Saṃjaya was considered to be is shown by the very large number of variants to virtually every verse. In this discourse Saṃjaya seeks to deflect Yudhiṣṭhira from the war which he has just promised if his Indraprastha kingdom is not returned. As the translation is of necessity as elliptic, even obscure, as the text, I give here a paraphrasis as I understand the matter.

1. The contrast is between *dharme nityā viceṣṭā*, "activity eternally, invariably, based on *dharma*," and *jīvitaṃ anityam*, "transient life." While Yudhiṣṭhira's action is rightly found (*dṛśyate*) renowned (*śrutā*) among people (*loke*), he should look upon (*saṃpaśya*) life as so transient and "torrential" (as I interpret *mahā-āsrava, bahuvrihi*, with connotations of "helpless suffering") that he must not add destruction to it (*vinīnaśaḥ*).

2. If the Kurus do not hand over (*prayacchante*) his patrimonial share (*bhāgam*), namely, the kingdom, without war, it would in Saṃjaya's opinion still be better to lead a mendicant life (*bhaiksacaryām*) in the kingdom of the Andhaka-Vṛṣṇis, where they could live off the generosity of a friendly Kṛṣṇa, than to have kingship (*rājyam*) by waging war.

3. The life that is allotted to men (*yad manuṣye*) is of little reward (*alpaphalam*); it is torrential, perpetually miserable (*nityaduḥkham*) and fugitive (*calam*), and it by no means (*bhūyaś ca na*) conforms (*anurūpam*) to one's zest for life (*vayasaḥ*); therefore Yudhiṣṭhira must not proceed to (perhaps) stretch out (*prasārṣīḥ*) the evil thereof, or follow an evil course of his own, by waging war.

4. Desires, such as that for kingship, attach themselves to a man (note the inversion: normally it is a man who gets attached to *kāmas*); these desires are thus the root of all obstacles (*vighnamūlam*) to *dharma*. By thwarting them (*vinighnan*, play on *vighna*) from the first (*pūrvam*), a persevering man earns blameless repute among people.

5. Thirst for property (*arthatṛṣṇā*) is shackling (*nibandhanī*) here on earth (*iha*), so that the very *dharma* (*dharma eva*) of the man who hastens, sc., to quench it (*tām eṣataḥ*) is imperiled (*bādhyate*). He who opts for (*pravṛṇīte*) *dharma* instead of property, is enlightened (*buddhaḥ*) (note the Buddhist-sounding terminology), while one greedy for the object of his desire (*kāme gṛddhaḥ*) is diminished by chasing after property (*arthānurodhāt*) instead

of *dharma*. Here *dharma, artha,* and *kama* are contradistinguished: *kama,* in order to be gratified, needs *artha* at the expense of *dharma*.

6. If he, on the contrary, makes *dharma* the guide (*mukhyam*) of his actions, he shines like the effulgent sun; while by the diminution of his *dharma* (*hānena,* paralleling *hīyate*) he sinks (*sīdati*), being evil-intentioned (*pāpabuddhiḥ*) even though he may have won the entire earth.

7. *Yudhiṣṭhira has learned the Veda,* practiced *brahmacarya* as a student, subsequently, as householder, offered sacrifices and made gifts to the brahmins; yet, while knowing the ultimate estate or goal (*paraṃ sthānam*), that is to say, the selfless pursuit of *dharma,* he has given himself up (*ātmā dattaḥ*) to pleasures that are the reward of his virtue, for too many years (*varṣapūgam*), viz., before his exile.

8. However, a man who, while cultivating comfort and pleasure beyond measure (*ativelam*), does not perform acts while practicing *yoga* that is, the *karmayoga* of acting without hope of reward is deprived of happiness beyond measure by the attrition of his wealth (*vittakṣaye*) and lies about miserably (*duḥkhaṃ śete*), for he is still prodded on by the rush of desire (*kāmavegapraṇunnah*).

9. Thus the man who, addicted to the pursuit of property (*arthacaryāprasaktaḥ*) and therefore giving up *dharma,* consequently sets as his goal (*prakaroti*) *adharma,* and moreover foolishly gives no credence to what the next life will have in store for him (*aśraddadhat paralokāya*), will, like the dimwit he is, burn with remorse hereafter when he has died (*hitvā dehaṃ pretya*).

10. In the afterlife (*amutra*) there is no disappearance of the *karman* of one's acts, whether good or bad: the good or bad *karman* of the doer precedes him and he himself follows it.

11. Yudhiṣṭhira's acts so far are renowned (*vikhyāyate*) as being of the same kind as (*tathārūpaṃ yad*) food which is given according to ritual rules (*nyāyopetam*) to brahmins, purified by faith (*śraddhāpūtam*), fragrant and tasty, at *śrāddhas* for which the *dakṣiṇās* paid out are the best (*anvāhāryeṣūttamadakṣineṣu*).

12. All acts (*kāryam*) are done here in this life (*iha*) in this body-field (*kṣetra*), and absolutely nothing can be done about it, viz., *karman,* after death (*pretya*). What acts Yudhiṣṭhira has done survive in the afterlife (*pāralokyam*), and they happen to be good, great, and applauded by strict people.

13. With such good *karman* a person, i.e., in the world hereafter, is rid of death, old age, and other perils (*bhayam*); there is no hunger or thirst, nothing displeasing to the heart (*manasaś cāpriyāṇi*), and he finds nothing else to do there but what pleases his senses (*anyatra vai indriyaprīṇanārthāt*).

14. Such then is the fruit of acts that spring from either anger (hatred) or joy (love), i.e., all acts done with *saṅga*. Yudhiṣṭhira should not fall short (*mā prahāsīḥ*) for a long time to come (*cirāya*) in both worlds (*lokāv ubhau,* viz., this life and the afterlife), just for a short-lived (*mātrāvatā*) pleasuring of his heart (*hṛdayasya priyeṇa*), namely, his desire for ephemeral kingship. The best, indeed the only, sense is had by construing the verse as *pāda* 1 followed by 3, and 2 followed by 4, since *krodhajam* and *harṣajam* clearly modify *karmaphalam,* and *mātrāvatā* contrasts with *cirāya*. In that case *sa* (for *sa tvam*) is really misplaced; the variant *saṃkrodhajam* commends itself but is poorly supported.

15. Now that Yudhiṣṭhira has reached the end, namely, the culmination of his (good) acts, which have brought him praise, virtue, and the reward of sacrifices, he must not now go to the other extreme of bad acts, viz., by waging war.

16. *Prima facie*: If the Pārthas now in this fashion are going to do evil (wage war) by following custom, they should dwell miserably for many years in the forest for the sake of *dharma*.—This verse is difficult. *Deśarūpeṇa* is puzzling; S. K. De glosses "with propriety," which is unlikely since Saṃjaya is warning the Pāṇḍavas of the evil that is war; my rendering is a guess. *Kariṣyadhvam* can be defended as a mixed form, with an imperative ending on a future felt to be imperative (cf. *BhG.* 3.10, *prasaviṣyadhvam*) but *nivasadhvam* can only be an imperative. If we compare vs. 20, *niruṣya kasmāt varṣapūgān vaneṣu*

yuyutsase hīnakālam, as being similar in sense, we may perhaps interpret *nivasadhvam* as an imperative of the past and understand the inversion of the verb as indicating a question: "If you are now going to fight, must you have lived for that all those years in the forest to preserve the dharma?"

17–18. In that case, you could, without departing for the forest, first have readied for war the army which you then had and was at your command, and all the kings would have supported you (*saṃśrayeyuḥ*), and you would have wiped out Duryodhana's pride by killing the finest foes in the arena. Then, why do you want to fight *now*, at the wrong time (*hīnakālam*), why now, after enabling the army of your enemy to become strong, after causing your allies to dwindle, after having lived many years in the forest?—The verbs all have to be taken as conditionals in sense, with *haniṣyan* as a conditional participle.

28.3. *When applied to one's livelihood: vrttinityam*: the meaning is that a *vṛtti* which is *adharma* under normal conditions can be *dharma* in emergencies. ***The first alternative*: viz., that *adharma* appears as *dharma*.
4. They both are open to blame, viz., the one who under abnormal conditions (*luptāyāṃ prakṛtau*) does acts which otherwise would be forbidden, and the one who does not do so and thus cannot act. The one is open to blame for doing *adharma* (misaction), the other for not doing *dharma* (inaction).
6. *Non-brahmin and non-Vedic folk*: I am not sure I understand the qualification: are brahmins and *vaidikas* not subject to the rules of vocation?
7. *Things are not in the end what they seem, I think: nāstyantato nāsti nāstīti manye* is puzzling; if we take the three *nāstis* literally, there are three negations; and since this concludes Yudhiṣṭhira's discourse on *adharma* and *dharma*, I take it that this negates the question raised in vs. 3: under special conditions (1) *adharma* is not *adharma* but *dharma*, (2) *dharma* is not *dharma* but *adharma*, (3) *adharma* is not *dharma*.
9. *rājanya*: a ruler of proper *kṣatriya* rank; *bhoja*: a ruler who is not a *kṣatriya*.
12. *Take their pleasure: bhogavantaḥ*, i.e., as a result of Kṛṣṇa's sound advice.

29.5. *some . . . some . . .* : the ritualists and renouncers respectively. ***It is known*: this looks like a witticism that puts down the renouncers.
14: *The Hermits*: I understand these are the Seven Seers.
29. *inherited share*: it is more praiseworthy to fight to regain one's patrimony than to conquer another king's kingdom.
35. *This difficult thing*: the question about Yudhiṣṭhira's right to stake her, 2.62 ff. (II, 148 ff.).
36. *The sūta's son spoke*: cf. 2.63.1 ff. (II, 150 ff.).
38. *Barren seeds*: 2.68.1 ff. (II, 151 f.).
39. *You lost Nakula*: but this is hardly the sequence, as Draupadī was staked after Yudhiṣṭhira had lost himself.
46–47. Repeated from 1.1.65 f.

30.7. *Schoolmen: caraṇopapannān*: belonging to a Vedic school.
18. *Cutting: nikartana*: if that is the meaning, or is it rather synonymous with *nikṛti*?
32. *The women you know for our wives: bhāryāḥ*: or just "dependent women"?

31.5. *Give five villages*: this is the first instance of this curious concession, of which it is difficult to say whether it was proposed seriously or just as a ploy to show up Duryodhana's greed. Of the four mentioned only Vāraṇāvata has significance: it was the town of their semi-exile and the house of lac, 1.124 ff. (I, 274 ff.).

32.20. *All hell has burst loose: nirayo vyapādi.*
22. *Was it beyond the domain of the Gods: kim anyatra viṣayād īśvarāṇām*, which could be as much as to say: "where else but in the domain of the Gods," but this would conflict with the sequel. The intention is probably: "it was only with the consent of the Gods."
24. *When the Thirst is quenched*: viz., by sensual indulgence.
25. *Act takes on form*: i.e., an act takes on a life of its own.
28. *Behold the result: extinction is all: nānyac chamāt paśya vipākam asya. Asya* should refer to *dyūta* in *dyūtakāle*; since *vipāka* is masculine, it reads literally, "look at its result: nothing but extinction." I take *śama* in the older sense of "extinguishing fire"; the normal meaning in the *MBh.* is "peace, appeasement," which hardly fits here.

5(51) Dhṛtarāṣṭra's Vigil

33.91. *Does not act hostile: na prātibhāvyam karoti*: I follow Nīlakaṇṭha who derives the word from *pratibhāva* "a contrary mood," thus "recalcitrance, hostility."
103. *The five Indra-like sons*: lit., "the five who resembled five Indras," which may or may not be a reference to the story of the *Five Indras* 1.189 (I, 369 ff.).

34.45. *Defeats the shared meal: samāśā*: so? Does this simply mean that when a man has cows enough (= rich enough), he does not have to share the meals of others?

35.21. *Were offered me for the road*: a polite way of saying that he declines taking food from Prahrāda, another sign of superiority.
22. *Like another son*: the only sense I can make (if that) of this line is by taking *vā* in the old sense of *iva*.
25. *He kills five*: sc., family members.
42. From here on in this Book I translate the *triṣṭubhs* mostly in prose.

36.23. Read *tapo* for *tamo*.
30. *Syandana tree*: the central meaning of *syandana* is "chariot, cart," which, of course, "supports a weight"; the wheels were made of the wood of a certain tree (MW identifies this as *Dalbergia Ougeinensis*) which is therefore called the "syandana" tree; even though small, it can in the form of cartwheels support a load other trees cannot. The metaphor is extended by calling men of great families "yoked," i.e., "capable," as a cart is yoked.
65. *Stop Duryodhana, I said*: cf. 2.55 ff. (II, 131 ff.).

37.3. *Who fails to guard his women: striyaś ca yo 'rakṣati*: we have no choice but to treat *arakṣati* as a finite verbal form with the privative *a-*: "he who non-guards his women" (*striyaḥ* for *strīn* is quite common).
9. *Rapacity: ativivitsā*, which I take as desiderative noun from *vid-*, *vindati* (cf. *vitta*), which seems to fit the context a bit better than *vid-*, *vetti*, which gives "over-inquisitiveness."
21. *Housemates: amatyaḥ*.
35. *And acquitted them of debts*: one would expect: "and thus has acquitted himself of the debt [owed to the ancestors, viz., begetting sons]," but the reading is widely supported; the meaning would be: "not saddling his sons with his own debts."

38.1. A saw also known to Manu (2.120) and Patañjali, *Mahābhāṣya* (6.1.84); the idea is that, upon a visit of a senior person, his junior has "his heart in his throat" and relocates it by quickly rising in courtesy.
5. *Not to be sold*: viz., by a brahmin, cf. Manu 10.85 ff., Yājñavalkya 3.36 ff.
34. *Retinue: parivāraṇam*: cf. the meaning of *parivārita*, so also S. K. De; it practically means "though poor, he has always a crowd around him."
39. *Reckless people: prathamotpatiteṣu*: Devabodha glosses *tatksaṇenāḍhyatām gateṣu*, "people who have just now become rich, nouveau-riche"; I assume: "jumping up at the first occasion, foolhardy."

39.3. *Power of spells and herbs*: I read *mantramūlabalena*, for cr. ed. *mantraṃ mūla°*, which S. K. De defends by taking *mantram* "as appositional to *anyaḥ*," which yields no sense. ***He who is loved is loved*, sc., for whatever reason.
37. *Faithful*: the text has *atyāgi*, which is strange, since *tyāgin*, "self-sacrificing," is a very positive term as expected here; the many and widely spread variants show it is an old crux. Perhaps we must assume a hiatus that was excised: *mitraṃ ca tyāgi iṣyate*.
44. *At the cessation of misery: dukhanāśe*, which makes little sense. I suspect (if there was a *dukhanāśe* at all; the authority is not clear) that it came from *duhkhanāśasukhasya*: "the root of good fortune, of the cessation of misery, and of happiness," and "corrected" because that should have been a dual.
57. *The other proceeds from desire: kāmād anyaḥ pravartate*: Nīlakaṇṭha glosses *anyaḥ* with *adharmaḥ*, no doubt correctly.

40.9. *Iron, copper*: Nīlakaṇṭha glosses *viṣam* (normally "poison") with *loham*, on the authority of the *Sarvajña* lexicon, and *audumbara* (normally: "made of udumbara wood") with copper, on the authority of the *Viśva*.
12. *For contentment is the greatest good: toṣaparo hi lābhaḥ*: Nīlakaṇṭha takes *toṣapara* as

a *bahuvrīhi*: "Gain is that in which the principal is contentment."
19. *The eternal water is the water: nityam ambho 'mbhaḥ*: since the soul is likened to a river, I take it that this water (apparently distinct from the water in *satyodadaka*) equals the primordial waters, but I am doubtful about the reading.

41.11. *Intoxication and power: madobhavam*: not a very common meaning for *udbhava*; perhaps the compound should be taken as qualifying *bhayāmarṣau*: "arising from befuddlement."

5(52) Sanatsujāta

42. On the interpretation of 42.1–19, see Introduction, p. 182.
16. The meter is helped if we read *ubhayam eva tatropabhujyate/phalaṃ dharmasya caivetarasya ca.*
24. *It is because of such conduct*: the translation is quite uncertain; text: *tasmād dhi kiṃcit kṣatriya brahmāvasati paśyati.*
27. *Whosoever knows*: translation very uncertain, for the text is elliptic. The meaning I get is this: anyone who has the certainty that all the gods have been properly worshiped (*sv-iṣṭa-kṛtāḥ*) because he has zealously seen to that, is not the equal of a true brahmin (who apparently does not need to be so zealous), (because this is a matter) in which he has to exert himself.

43.5. *These worlds are achieved: ime lokā saṃyatāḥ*: where I take *saṃyata* in the sense of "held together, controlled, achieved"; "these worlds" should refer to the present life and afterlives. ***Prosperous: ṛddha*, may seem an odd translation, but *tapas* is often considered an ascetic's "wealth" in a very real sense, a kind of power capital that he may spend or conserve.
6. *Either prosperous or not so*: text: *samṛddham apy ṛddhaṃ tapo . . . kevalam*, which may mean "quite prosperous or only just prosperous," but I prefer the well-supported variant *asamṛddham*, which makes the *pāda* hypermetric. The question does not really get answered (at least not until 28ef), so the context does not help.
7. *The one is that which*: *yasya*, which may refer to the *tapas* or the ascetic, or for that matter to anyone.
11. *Pride of cunning: medhamānaḥ*: so? I take *medha* as equivalent to *medhā*, perhaps by metrical shortening.
23. *With Story as fifth: ākhyānapañcamaiḥ*: elsewhere *itihāsapurāṇa* occurs in this place, with which *ākhyāna* should be synonymous.
25. *The Great One: mahati*: probably equals *mahān ātmā.*
28. Cf. my "The speculations on the Name Satyam," *Festschrift Emeneau, Indian Linguistics* (1968).
28ef. Here seems to be resumed the discourse of 43.6.
32. *With his doubts removed: chinnavicikitṣaḥ*: that is to say: who narrates (= recites) the Vedas with all their problems (about the One) as though there were no problems at all (because he does not see them).
36. *One is called a grammarian*: this looks like a marginal note on the previous verse, which derives *mauna* from *muni.*
37. *By following the Vedas in succession: vedānām cānupūrvyeṇa*: and then, presumably, going beyond them.

44. I render the *triṣṭubhs* in prose.
4. *Firm in sattva: sattvasaṃsthāḥ*: on the range of *sattva*, cf. my "Studies in Samkhya III: *sattva*," *JAOS* 77 (1957): 2.
5. *The birth instructed by the teacher*: viz., in the initiation.
7. *Fill with truth: āvṛnoty avitathena.*
15. *Of yore: ahnāya.*
16. *Who lies down: āśayet*: active for middle.
20. *Rathantara*, etc.: types of *ṣāmans.*
24. *Sages hold that they are the products of speech: vāco vikārān kavayo vadanti*: this probably refers to the Vedas of 21, which do not contain the One, because they are mere speech products.

45.1. *Seed*: *śukram*, which may also mean "luminous."
3. *The centripetal, etc.*: *sa sadhrīcīḥ sa viṣūcīr vasānā*; while it cannot be decided what feminine nouns the two adjectives qualify (possibly *śākhā*?), it is clear that the double *sa* refers to the two deities and that *vasānā* should be interpreted as a dual.
7. *Twelvefold river*: *dvādaśapūgāṃ saritam*: i.e., the year.
14. *The swan*: based on *AthV.* 11.4.21; *satatam ṛtvijam* is doubtless corrupt.
18. These "mortals" appear to be brahmins who have not by insight attained to immortality and still hide in the thicket of *saṃsāra*.
21. *The lightness of brahman*: *brāhmīṃ laghutām*: i.e., swiftness bestowed by the insight into *brahman*.
23. *As much use*: cf. *BhG.* 2.46.
25. *I am I*: this is the supreme speaking through the one who has reached it.

5(53) The Suing for Peace

In the title *yānasaṃdhi*, *yāna* is most likely to be taken in the sense of "embassy," as in *Saṃjayayāna* and *Bhagavadyāna*, and *saṃdhi* as "the connecting link" between them. My "suing for peace" is just a convenient rendering, indicating that between the two embassies peace deliberations continue.

47.4. *Sandal water*: *paramavāri*.
12. *Dhṛtarāṣṭra's son shall rue*: note *anvatapsyat*, which in the refrain throughout is used for the future; perhaps the intention is something like "will have rued," perhaps it is *metri causa*; elsewhere, in reverse, the future does duty for the conditional.
16. *Counters*: *pratiyāt*, which must be *metri causa* for pratīyāt; it can hardly be an augmentless aorist.
21. *Resistless*: *gatodvāham*: Nīlakaṇṭha: *apagatodvṛttagatim anukūlagatim ity arthaḥ*.
39. *Against us*: for the senseless *tam* of the cr. ed. I read *naḥ*, correlating with *yeṣām*.
68. *Rukmiṇī of the Bhojas*: *Rukmiṇīm . . . Bhojyām*.
73. *The sky-going Saubha*: 3.15 ff. (II, 253 ff.).
77. We must read *Mūru* for cr. ed. *Mūra*, cf. *Mauravas* in the same context in 3.13.26 (II, 247). ***Rākṣasa host*: *augharākṣasam*: with *upanipāta*.
80. *Lavished boons*: *varān adadan*: note this irregular third plural imperfect of *dā*, not built on the present stem *dadā*, but on *dad-*.
92. *Spellers of years*: *sāṃvatsarāḥ*: i.e., experts on the divisions of the year.
93. *Of the Kurus and the Sṛñjayas*: the Sṛñjayas = Pāñcālas are firmly on the Pāṇḍavas' side, but their ultimate disaster is predicted.

48.10 ff. *Nara slew the enemies*: story in 3.165 ff. (II, 543 ff.), where it is told of Arjuna.
15. *Sated Jātavedas*: at the burning of the Khāṇḍava Forest, 1.214 ff. (II, 412 ff.).

49.23. Read *nāgāyutam* for *nāmā°*.
30. *The daughter of the king of the Kāśis*: story below in *Ambā*.

50.23. Read *mama* for *mamā*.
24. *When it swings out*: *niṣkīrṇām*: so?
48. *That leads to Indra*: *aindram*.

51.4. *There will be no victory for me*: *na tv asti vijayo mama*: with a pun on Vijaya: "I have no Arjuna."

52.16. *If we sue for peace*: *śikṣamāṇānām*: MW records a meaning "befriend" (but for the *Ṛgveda*); S. K. De: "wishing to serve, suppliant."

53.1 ff. *Mahārāja*: the repeated use of this title is, I think, ironic, for Dhṛtarāṣṭra has effectively forfeited his authority; hence I retain the Sanskrit.
18. *For wronging these men*: *vikarmaṇā* apparently has verbal government on *anarhān*.

54.5. *Their neighbor*: I treat *prativāsitam* as *prativāsinam*, but on second thought it might be better to take it in the sense of "exiled," though *prati* in that sense is odd.
15. *Your sons have blocked the enemies*: *kṛtaṃ hi tava putraiś ca pareṣām avarodhanam*: *tava* is probably to be taken as referring to Dhṛtarāṣṭra, though he supposedly was not

present at the council Duryodhana recounts.
53. *When Duryodhana*, etc.: *tasya śaktyopagūḍhasya kasmāj jīved Dhanaṃjayaḥ*: I take *tasya °gūrḍhasya* as an absolute genitive.
61. *Both of them*: it is not clear to whom *ubhau* refers.

56.3. *With a count: pṛthag akṣauhiṇībhyāṃ tau samākhyātau*: they each count for one army.
17. *The Kekaya brothers took the Kekayas*: they are out of power and seek to regain it by fighting the present powers who have joined Duryodhana.

57.1. *Chaste: brahmacārin.*

60.3. *Sentiments: bhavānām*: so? But in 7 clearly "affairs."

61.2. *Apratibhāsyati*: once again we must accept an anomalous privative *a-* with a finite form.

62.23. *Not bees' honey: amakṣikam.*
25. This story is obviously behind Vidura's more cryptic reference in 2.55.4 (II, 131).

67.12. *The old one and the new: purāṇaṃ yac ca* [for *yaṃ ca*?] *navam.*
15. *A great man does not attach himself: mahāṃs tatra na sajjate*: it is not clear to me what *tatra* refers to.

68.3. *Vāsudeva* is explained with a pseudo-etymology from *vas-* "to clothe," *vasu*, "wealth," and *devayoni*. ***Viṣṇu*: because of similarity to the noun *vṛṣan*.
4. *Mādhava*: i.e., *mā-dha-va*, from *mauna*, *dhyana*, and *yoga*; *yogāc ca*, I cannot connect; perhaps: "and by etymological derivation"? ***Madhu*: "honey = creation, all beings."
5. *Kṛṣṇa*: out of kṛṣ- and *na*, probably from *nand-*.
6. *Janārdana*: lit., "scourge of people."
7. *Sātvata*: out of *sattva*.
8. *Dāmodara*: out of *dam-*; the literal meaning, of course, is "belly-belted."
9. *Hṛṣīkeśa*: out of *hṛṣ-* and *īśa*.
10. *Adhokṣaja*: out of *adhas* and *kṣi-*; the literal meaning: "born below a cart axle." ***Nārāyaṇa*: out of *nara* and *ayana*. ***Puruṣa*: out of *pṛ-* and *sad-*.
13. *Viṣṇu*: now out of *vi-kram-*. ***Jiṣṇu*: out of *ji-*. ***Govinda*: out of *go* and *vid-*, either "knowing" or "finding."

5(54) The Coming of the Lord

70.10. *We have not broken*: *nāhāsma*: *ahāsma* is a curious hybrid aorist form: a root aorist with sigmatic ending.
15. *The Dhārtarāṣṭra did not allow us that much*: but the matter has not yet come up.
29. *A lovely fortune*: *bhadrāṃ śriyam.*
42. *We and they may enjoy our fortune*: read *tām* (sc., *śriyam*) for cr. ed. *tān*: "this [our] fortune."
49. *Force merely extends policy: balam nītimātrāya.* ***Chance*: I take *haṭha* in the sense of "chance," as it has in 3.33.10 f. (II, 284).
64. *There is no way*, etc.: *ato 'nyathā nāsti śāntir nityam antaram antataḥ/antaraṃ lipsamānānām ayaṃ doṣo nirantaraḥ*: the difficulty of the line comes in with the obvious play on the meanings of *antara*: "Hence there is no peace any other way—in the end there always remains vulnerability [*antaram*]; it is the impervious [*nirantara*] flaw of those who seek their opportunity [*antara*]."
67. *But peace through renunciation*, etc.: another difficult verse: "But which peace (is effected) by renunciation [*yā tu tyāgena śāntiḥ syād*], that peace [*saḥ* is in gender dictated by *vadhaḥ*] is death without it [*tadṛte*, I take *tad* as referring to *rājyam*], and also on account of the risk [*saṃśayāc ca*] from the eradication of enemies and self." My understanding: Relinquishing the kingdom is no solution for peace, for such a peace without a kingdom is tantamount to death (for the above reason: poverty is death), and also because the final elimination of either enemies or self remains to be feared (for the above reason: feuds never die).

70. *A mess of dogs*: *gopāda* has many variants, but is clearly equivalent to *goṣpada* "a cow's footprint," which in wet soil immediately is filled with water and becomes messy; by extension, any messy situation; cf. 1.27.9, where the Vālakhilyas come to grief in such a "cow's step."
89. *Godspeed: svasti.*
90. *Viṣvaksena*: the first time this name is used for Kṛṣṇa.

71.10. *When they left you in your loin cloth*: lit., "they did not regret [that] only a loin cloth [*kaupīnaṃ tāvat*] was [left] on you." Reference is to the way in which he was robbed of everything.
12. *Sleight of hand: upadhi.*
30. *No Unlaw*: we must read *nādharmam* for *na dharmam.*
33. *War effort: pravṛttiṃ yuddhādhikārikām.*

72.9. *Indra's elders: Indrajyeṣṭhāḥ*: or "[the gods] led by Indra."

74.3. *You are getting at me: māṃ tvam samarchasi*, from *sam-ā-ṛcchati.*

75.5. *The outcome of a doubtful Law: dharmasya saṃdigdhasya paryāyam*: here *dharma* has the unusual meaning of a "norm" by which to judge, not morality, but worldly affairs open to rational investigation, practically = *pramāṇa*; the verse becomes clearer when we take *dharmasya saṃdigdhasya* as an absolute genitive and paraphrase: "if one wants to know the outcome, when the criterion [*dharma*] for judging what is fate and what human effort is itself dubious, one does not reach a decision." ***Countervails against fate*: while cold and heat, etc., are "acts of God," one can do something about them.
14. *If luck changes*: I take *tathā bhavati paryāye* as an absolute locative: "when such is the turn of events," sc., against you.
20. *Saying, "Don't act like a eunuch": aklībayā vācā.*

76.5. Reads: *kiṃ caitan manyase kṛcchram asmākaṃ pāpam aditaḥ/kurvanti teṣām karmāṇi yeṣām nāsti phalodayaḥ*: ab.: "moreover, you think that our distress [*kṛcchram*] [has been our] trouble [*pāpam*] from the beginning"; cd is puzzling; *teṣām* and *yeṣām* obviously correlate and together stand in contrast to *asmākam*; now, *kurvanti teṣām karmāṇi* makes no sense. Hence, surely, Nīlakaṇṭha interprets *kurvanti* as *kṛṇvanti*, not from *kṛ-* but a root *kṝ-* "to injure," explaining the use of the *tan* (8th) present class (*kurvanti*) for the *su* (5th) class (*kṛṇvanti*) as either *ārṣa* or a scribal error. But *kṝ-* of the *Dhātupāṭha* has no lexical existence. My suggestion is to accept *teṣām* as attracted by *yeṣām* and *asmākam*, and really to stand for *te*; the (unusual) attraction was probably caused by strong emotion: "*they* have been doing deeds for which there has been no success." I render accordingly.

77.1. *The two kinds of action*: sc., *daivam* and *mānuṣyam.*
5. *I am unable to take care of fate: daivam na mayā śakyaṃ karma kartum*: lit., "I am unable to do the act of fate," i.e., act as fate.
17. *The divine secret: paramaṃ divyam*: viz., that they are Nara and Nārāyaṇa reborn.
19. *Did he talk of wanting such shelter: kathaṃ bruyād icchañ śarma tathāvidham*: in *Virāṭa* 3.47.15 Duryodhana refuses to return the kingdom, after having stated that it was his duty to fight Arjuna (3.42.10); thus he did indeed not talk of seeking shelter with Arjuna. However, I see no context in which Bhīṣma asked him to do so.

79.4. Should we not read *dharmikāḥ*, since it is the predicate for a plural subject?

80.20. *Who by Law are to you as Abhimanyu himself*: Kṛṣṇa, brother of Subhadrā, who is the mother of Abhimanyu, is the maternal uncle of the latter and by extension also of his half-brothers, the sons of Draupadī.
25. *"Choose a boon!"*: 2.63.25.

81.5. *Kaumuda*: the month Kārttika, October–November.
20. *Garuḍa standard*: the bird of Viṣṇu.
42. *Deceptions*: *nikāra*, which I take as synonymous with *nikṛti.*
44. *When we went forth*: *pravrajanto* for *pravrajato.*
46. *Looked after by the Ānartas* (Kṛṣṇa's people): yet she is staying in Hāstinapura.
66. *Honorable*: *mānayantaḥ*, which seems to stand for *mānitāḥ.*

82.17. *Enemy circles: paracakrāṇām*: i.e., surrounding hostile kingdoms.

88.61. *Who paid me out to Kuntibhoja: yenāhaṃ Kuntibhojāya dhanam arpitā*. In 1.104 (I, 240) it is related that Śūra, the grandfather of Kṛṣṇa, had promised his firstborn to his cousin Kuntibhoja; when Pṛthā was born, he stuck to the letter of his promise and passed his daughter on to Kuntibhoja; ever since she has also been named Kuntī. It is not made clear what the occasion of the promise was; this text implies that if the firstborn had been a son, he would have been similarly passed on, which makes it an incredible promise. Here Kuntī calls herself *dhana* "prize, booty, wealth" transferred, or paid out (*arpitā*), as is done by *dhūrtas* ("rogue," often "gambler"): did Śūra pay off an old gambling debt to Kuntibhoja?
65. *In a war between peoples*: *grāmajanye*, sc., *yuddhe*.
75. *You'll end up with cruelty*: viz., to herself.
79. *Walk the path of Draupadī*: sc., of vengefulness.
87. *I and my sons have you as protector*: here Kuntī appeals to her consanguineous Vṛṣṇi relations.

89.16. *Grasped his sturdy arm: pragṛhya vipulaṃ bhujam*: that is to say, grasped his right arm with his left hand in a challenging gesture. Nīlakaṇṭha, however, glosses *udyamya* for *pragṛhya*.
19. *It is not right to act improperly*: sc., by refusing to accept food.

5(54a) Dambhodbhava

94.1. *Rāma Jāmadagnya*: here in his role as seer.
35. *Nīlakaṇṭha* explains these weapons as follows: *kākudīya* ("related to humps"): lulling horses, elephants, etc. to sleep; *śuka* ("parrot"): bewildering; *nāka* ("heaven"): maddening; *akṣisaṃtarjana* ("hurting the eye"): terrifying; *saṃtāna* ("continuity"): continuously shooting; *nartaka* ("causing to dance"): ghoulish; *ghora* ("dreadful"): demoniac; *ājyamodaka* ("buttered titbits"): relating to Yama. The text's own explanation, he adds, should be fitted in accordingly.

5(54b) Mātali

95.6. *Die within the hour: muhurtamaraṇās*: i.e., ephemeral.
10. *Lord of the cows*: normally a title of the sun. ***The daughter of Soma*: i.e., the moon.
13. *It is said that he*, etc.: an obscure line: *he* should refer to Puṣkara, who, since *puṣkara* is also the name of a cloud, may be said to be the son of a cow (= cloud), and who was adopted by Āditya (= sun), who is also *gopati*.
14. *Vāruṇī* is also the name of an inebriating drink, which equals *surā*, through which the gods became *suras*.
17. *Defeated by the previous Gods: purvadaivatanirjitāḥ*: cr. ed. °*nirmitāḥ* is hard to explain, if it refers to Rākṣasas and Bhūtas; the previous Gods are normally Asuras.
18. *A brilliant fire*: the submarine fire.
19. *Gāṇḍīva*: derived from *gaṇḍa* "rhinoceros and its horn"; since a rhinoceros horn is not horn, the description is figurative for the toughest bow imaginable.
22. *Invigorated*: I read *bhāvitam* for the meaningless *bhāṣitam*, "mentioned."

97.6. *Forms in which water appears: jalamūrtayaḥ*. ***Rain down: patanti*: from which the word *Pātāla* is derived.
10. *The liquid of the elixir*: embroidering the old idea that the moon contains *soma*, which became understood as *amṛta*. ***He is said to observe*: clearly a gloss on the preceding verse.
15. *Here is this egg*: an intriguing vestige of the cosmic egg, here understood as destructive instead of creative.

98.1. This is the Hiraṇyapura which Arjuna destroyed with its inhabitants, 3.170 (II, 549 ff.).

99.5. Śrīvatsa whorl: a curl of chest hair, usually the attribute of Kṛṣṇa. ***Their* *kinsmen*: the snakes which, as sons of Kadrū, the sister of Vinatā, are the cousins of the Garuḍas. ***Viṣṇu* has the Garuḍa as his emblem.

100.10. *Named after Ilavila's son*: sc., Kubera, who also "yields all objects of desire," and is the regent of the north.

101.1. *Carries a thousand*: a thousand of what, is not indicated.
5–10. Cf. the list of snakes 1.31 (I, 91 f.).
15. *Kaśyapa's sons*: viz., by Kadrū.

103.1. *After giving me a boon*: the boon of feeding on snakes, cf. 1.30.10 ff. (I, 90).
5. *Another's servant*: viz., Viṣṇu's, cf. 1.29.10 (I, 89). ***Viṣṇu is not the cause of my servitude*: but Indra as king of the universe.
10. *Your younger brother's*: sc., Viṣṇu's.
18. *Carries the chariot wheel*: *rathacakradhṛt*: an interesting explanation of Viṣṇu's *cakra*.

5(54c) Gālava

104.5. *One of the Seven Seers*: viz., Vasiṣṭha.
10. *Caru dish*: a dish of rice, barley, and beans cooked with butter and milk in a pot called *caru*.
13. *Holding it with his hands*: cr. ed. *tad bāhūbhyām pārśvato 'gamat*; *agamat* makes no sense, since the point is that the seer remains stockstill (*sthāṇur iva*); I adopt *avahat*.

105.1. *Vāsava's younger brother*: Viṣṇu.
4. *The first thought was born*: *pūrvaṃ matir jātā*.
5. *Through whose mouths*: *yatomukhaiḥ*: viz., the three fires.
9. *The First Quarter*: pun on *pūrva* "eastern" and "previous."
12. *Partake of their own source*: *svām yonim upabhuñjate*: viz., liquid oblations, since fire is thought to spring from water.
14. *Ten times ten times*: *daśatir daśa*: or: ten times a hundred. ***Havirdhāna barn*: the area immediately west of the main fire altar, where the utensils are kept and the *soma* is pressed.

107.1. *Uṣmapa Gods*: those *pitars* who live off the heat of the sacrificial fire. ***The same portions*: viz., as the *pitars*.
4. *Time here is reckoned by instants and moments*: this must refer to the moments of death at which the dead become *pitars*.
8. *Who sinks in himself*: *ātmāvasādinaḥ*: or: sinks into the self, that is to say, dies.
15. *I obtained an elephant and a tortoise*: the story in 1.25 (I, 82). ***Kapila who consumed the sons of Sagara*: the story in 3.104 ff. (II, 424 ff.).

108. *The Late Quarter*: play on *paścima*: "western" and "later."
5. *The mountain called Asta*, sc., the mountain on which the sun sets (*astaṃ gam-*). ***Whereof sprang the band of the Maruts*: for the story see Vāmana Purāṇa (Kashiraj edition) 45.18–43, where it is related that Diti did *tapas* to beget a son who would defeat Indra; Indra apprenticed himself to Diti, and when she was impure entered her belly and aborted the son, who was cut up into pieces which became the Maruts.
10. *Svarbhānu*: i.e., Rāhu: his head was sliced off by Viṣṇu's discus when he had drunk the Elixir, cf. 1.17 (I, 75); the immortal head devours sun and moon, the dead trunk is deposited in the ocean.
14. *The course of the sun is askew*: *sūryasya tiryag āvartate gatiḥ*: that is to say, the sun turns northward (*uttarāyaṇa*) at the winter solstice.

109.1. *Inasmuch as one is saved*: play on *uttara*, "north," and *uttārayati*, "to rescue."
2. *The road to the field of the northern gold*: Nīlakaṇṭha interprets this as *svargamārga*.
5. *The moon was consecrated*: i.e., the moon as *soma*, which is regularly called King Soma.
9. *Mandākinī*: a tributary to the Ganges in the Himālayas.
13. *Svāti*: the star Arcturus. ***Here is fixed*: *dhruvaṃ sthātā pitāmahaḥ*, lit., "the grandfather will stand immovably," i.e., the Polar Star.
15. *Orbits*: *parivarta*.
17. *Except Jiṣṇu*: perhaps when Arjuna penetrated as far as the Northern Kurus: 2.52 (II, 79).

24. *Famed as the best*: play on *uttara*: "northern" and "superior."

110.1. *Two eyes of the Law*: sun and moon, which determine the times of rituals.
12. *Like two noble gems*: I take *maṇīva* as *maṇī (pragṛhya) iva.*

111.8. *This sorceress: imāṃ siddhām.*

112.1. *Purified*: I do not know what to do with cr. ed. *vaidhitam* and translate Nīlakaṇṭha's *śodhitam.* ***Consists in hira: hiraṇmaya.*
2. *It puts and keeps man: dhatte dhārayate ca*: play on *dhana.*
3. *Foot of the Stool* (dual): *proṣṭhapada*, name of a double *nakṣatra*; Śukra is the planet Venus.

114.17. *Richer than the Vasus: vasubhyo vasumattaraḥ*: all plays on *vasu*: "wealth" and "a group of Gods."

117.1. *A quarter of the task undone*: he still lacked two hundred horses. ***Ṛcīka*: the story in 3.115 (II, 444 f.).

5(54) The Coming of the Lord *(continued)*

125.6. *Lie on a bed of arrows: śaratalpagatāḥ.*

126.6. *A game joyless and destructive of the strict: satāṃ aratināśana*: I take the compound as a dvandva of two adjectives.

127.46. *Be it enough now: alam ahnā*: or *ahnā* = *ahnāya* "previously".

129.34. *His father's sister*: note the form *pitṛṣvasām.*

130.22. *Enjoyment of strength: balabhoja*: so?

5(54d) The Instruction of Vidurā's Son

131.2. *Benefit and well-being: śreyaś ca bhūyaś ca.*
5. *Hanging on to a low branch: upaśākhīya*: or: "hiding underneath branches."
9. *Are you going to die*: cr. ed. *apyarerārujandaṃstrāmāśveva.* First, I accept tmesis, *ā śvā vraja* for *śvā āvraja*, and take initial *api* as indicating a question: "Must you go to your death?" For *arer* I accept *aher*, which is well supported; I think that *apyarer* is attracted by the same words in the next verse. Finally I emend *ārujan* to *arujan.*
13. *The fugitive life of a crow: kākaraṅkhāḥ* presupposes the hapax *raṅkhas*, which I take as a by-form of *raṅghas*, or a parallel formation on the (Dhātupāṭha) root *raṅkh-*; either noun would have the connotation of haste. The compound is a bahuvrihi: "having the [fugitive] haste of a crow."
14. *A birth of a man-child as meek as a she-mule: janī* (for *janiḥ*) *kharīmṛduḥ*, lit., "a birth as gentle as a she-mule."
15. *Na prāṇāṃām dhanāyate*: denominative from *dhana* "wealth": "he does not make of his life his [only] wealth."
23. *The vile living of the begging bowl: jālmīṃ kāpālīm vṛttim.*
25. *The look-what-I-got kind: aho-lābha-karam*: "saying [*kara*], O wonder, I got something!"
27. *A Kali*: a person fomenting discord.
33. *Puruṣa*: a play on *pura* and *sah-*.
37. *Of those who wail, "What now?": kimadyakānām.*

132.7. *A Saṃjaya in name only*: S. means "conqueror."
14. *I went from one pond to another*: frequent expression for a woman of good family marrying into another such.
24. *Great Indra's soma cup: māhendraṃ graham.*
28. *Do not spare an enemy at hand*: I can do nothing with cr. ed. *pralabdhasya* that would make sense and translate *na labdhasya*; the idiom is *śeṣaṃ na kurvanti* "they leave no survivors."
38. *Rather break in the middle than bend: aparvaṇi bhajyeta na named*, which I take to

mean: one should be broken not on the knot (of cane, but between the knots).

133.9. *In a son or a grandson: putranaptṛṇā*: note formation for *naptrā*. Or should we simply read *putranaptṛṇoḥ*, which is regular?
13. *Puruṣeṇa . . . śatrūn pratijigīṣayā* is an anacolouthon, to which we may supply, e.g., *bhavitavyam*; the lines cr. ed. 512* and 513*, which occur after 14ab, are likely to be displaced attempts to complete vs. 13.
15. *He . . . will only become trifling*: *tasya* is, I think, attracted by *yasya* and replaces a *sa alpam* (with hiatus) or *sa svalpam*, which is expected here.
18. *You who need scolding*: text *codyaṃ*, while I translate as if *codyo*; either that, or interpret *codyaṃ yan māṃ codayasi*: "It is worth scolding that. . . ."
26. *Pushes away growth and success to his own disadvantage: nuded vrddhisamṛddhī sa pratikūle*: "[so that they become] disadvantageous."
37. *It is inconceivable*: text *ataḥ saṃbhāvyam*, "hence it is conceivable," which makes no sense; I accept *sa na saṃbhāvyam*, where *sa* was "corrected" because it was wrongly construed with *saṃbhāvyam* instead of *prāpnuyāt*.

134.6. *I have spoken to embolden you*: a difficult construction which changes syntax: *mayā . . . ullapantyā samāśvāsam*: "By me . . . who am speaking encouragement, as a strong person to a weak one."

137.1. *A curse on the baron's life*: but Droṇa is a brahmin!

5(55) The Temptation of Karṇa

The word I translate as "temptation" is *upanivada*, which can be interpreted as a secret (*upa-*) invitation, *nivāda* like *nimantraṇa*.

139. *Subrahmaṇyā* is the name of a loud invocation at the *soma* sacrifice, which is clearly intended here, while *subramanya*, masc., in the text is the Subrahmaṇya priest, which is less appropriate.
46. *Re-piling: punaściti.*

141. *In retrograde position: kṛtvā vakram*: so? ***As though pleading for the peace of friendship: maitram saṃśamayann iva.*
21. *Gandharva city*: a hallucinatory apparition.
22. *A single jackal: eka sṛg*, a hapax for *sṛgāla*.

142.10. *Sighed aloud*: cr. ed. has *aniṣṭanantī*, with many variants pointing to "sighing." *Ni-ṣṭan-* means "to breathe one's last in a death rattle, expire"; *aniṣṭananti* could possibly be explained as "[barely] without expiring, close to death."

143. *One-eyed mother: mātā . . . ekadarśinī*: Nīlakaṇṭha: "having eyes only for her son," but I suspect an idiom here: a mother without her husband, the son's father.

145.23. *I became embroiled with Rāma*: for the story, cf. *Ambā* below. ***He was banished*: this must refer to Vicitravīrya; the story is further unknown; apparently the citizens evacuated their king during the hostilities. ***Exhaustion: yakṣman.*

146.33. *We must accept it all as Law undiminished: sarvam . . . ahatya dharmam*: i.e., without opposing or offending it, cf. variant *ahīna*.

147.1 ff. *Yayāti*: story in 1.70 ff. (I, 173 ff.).
15. *Pratīpa*: this extends the brief remarks of 1.89.45 (I, 212) and 1.90.45 (I, 214), and my note.

5(56) The Marching Out

149. *This friend of Angiras*: according to Nīlakaṇṭha, this is Droṇa Bhāradvāja; Drupada was Droṇa's fellow student, cf. 1.121.5–10 (I, 267); Agniveśya taught them the *āgneya* weapon.
37. *Our weapons anointed with perfume*: this must refer to the ceremony of lustrating the weapons, cf. below, p. 463.

56. *Basic precautions: mūlapratikāra.* **A large headquarters: skandhāvāra.*

150.19. *Slowly touching their arms*: in challenge.

152. The best, indeed only, treatment of ancient Indian weapons is found in E. Washburn Hopkins, "The Social and Military Position of the Ruling Caste in Ancient India," *JAOS* 13: 293 ff., which might be updated by a study of the *MBh.* commentaries collected for the cr. ed.

5(57) The Consecration of Bhīṣma

153.1–5. *The brahmins attacked the Haihayas*: this appears still another version of the conflict of the Bhṛgu brahmins and the Haihaya Kārtavīryas, cf. Introduction, p. 146 ff.
12. *A moon to the herbs*: once more we must take *candramās* as synonymous with *soma*, often called the king of the herbs.

155.10. *Rukmiṇī's abduction by Vāsudeva*: Kṛṣṇa's wife Rukmiṇī was a sister of Rukmin and promised to Śiśupāla, cf. 2.42.
25. *I who confess my war debts*: the personages mentioned provided him with weapons and with training or guidance.
35. *Was also rebuffed*: the rejection of Rukmin by both parties appears to be the consequence of his feud with Kṛṣṇa.

156. *Dhṛtarāṣṭra addressed Saṃjaya*: this is the first appearance of Saṃjaya as war reporter to Dhṛtarāṣṭra, which he becomes "officially" only in 6.2.8 ff. I intend to take up the issues raised by the shift of narrator from Vaiśaṃpāyana to Saṃjaya in my Introduction to the *Bhīṣmaparvan.*
15. *Some people are fore-ordained,* etc.: this summarizes the three factors in action, cf. 3.33.35 (II, 285) in Draupadī's discourses in 3.31 and 33, viz., *daiva* "fate" (*īśvaranirdiṣṭa*), *haṭha* "chance" (*yadṛcchayā*), and *karman* (*pūrvakarma*). **This triad is pulled asunder: trividham etad vikṛṣyate*: I do not understand *vikṛṣyate*, and would much prefer the readings with *dṛśyate* "is witnessed."

5(58) The Embassy of Ulūka

157.3. *Son of a gambler: kaitavya*: the gambler apparently is Śakuni.
14. *Again and again wandered forth*: to their semi-exile in Vāraṇāvata, their exile after the Lacquer House episode, the twelve years in the forest, and their incognito year.
16. *That eunuch: tūbaraka*: the meaning of *tūpara* and *tūbara* ("hornless goat," "hornless bull, "beardless man") all indicate that signs of manhood are lacking.
15. *Lustration: lohābhihāra*: Devabodha: "invocation of the deity with the mantras over the irons, or the lustration (*nirājana*) of the kings."

158.23. *Success is a result of the turn of events: paryāyāt*: so? But in vs. 26 this seems to be contradicted.
31. *Barren sesame seeds*: e.g., 2.68.13 (II, 160).
33. *They condemn him*: I follow Devabodha in this interpretation.

5(59) The Count of Warriors and Paladins

161. I translate *ratha* as "Warrior," *atiratha* as "Paladin" for contrast.
3. *Like the quiet ocean*: *sāgarastimitopamam*, with *upanipāta.*
20. *The arrows do not lodge*: they go straight through.

162.8. *Soldier and nonsoldier alike: bhṛtān . . . abhṛtān*, i.e., those who receive soldier's pay and those who do not.
22. *Wronged by the Pāṇḍavas: kṛtakilbiṣāḥ*: perhaps "on whom the blame has been placed."

30. *The abduction of Draupadī*: in 3.248 ff. (II, 706 ff.).

163.5 *An old feud with Sahadeva*: who had defeated him, 2.28 (II, 83 ff.).
9. *The five Trigarta brothers began a feud*: they were defeated at the cattle robbery.

164.5. *The brahmin bows to him*: sc., Droṇa.
30. *Remembering his old feud*: viz., because of Bhīma's slaying of the Rākṣasas Hiḍimba, Baka, and Kirmīra.
35. *He once battled*: cf. 2.23.15–20 (II, 78).

165.5. *Rāma's curse*: this incident is unknown to me; at any rate this is probably Bala-Rāma. ***The loss of his tools*, cf. 3.287 ff. (II, 779 ff.).

166.1. *Rāma Jāmadagnya himself*: viz., in his duel in *Ambā*.

167.10. *Through marital bonds*: they are related through the Pāṇḍavas, Drupada being the Pāṇḍavas' father-in-law, and Virāṭa Abhimanyu's father-in-law.
12. *Stolidly loyal*: *dṛḍhabhaktikam*.

168.2. *The old establishment*: viz., by killing Bhīṣma.
8. *Related by marriage*: Dhṛṣṭaketu's sister Kareṇumatī is Nakula's wife.
16. *Loyal*: *bhakta*.

169.2. *Purujit, Bhīma's uncle*: Purujit is the son of the Kuntibhoja who adopted Pṛthā as Kuntī, thus is Bhīma's mother's brother and Bhīma's maternal uncle.

5(60) Ambā

173.5. *Who dangled me*: *praveritā*.

176.15. *Mild*: *śitoṣṇa*.

177.15. *If ever one shall defeat the entire baronage*: as Bhīṣma had figuratively done at the abduction of the three Ambās.

178.9. *Not too irate*: *nātimanasam*, which I take as *nātimanyum*.
34. *Sanctified your father*: *kṛtaṃ śaucam*: i.e., revenged him and offered up oblations with the blood of the *kṣatriyas* at Samantapañcaka in Kurukṣetra, cf. 1.2.1 ff. (I, 32).
35. *Self-styled brahmin*: *brāhmaṇabruva*: because he, though a born brahmin, behaves like a *kṣatriya*.

180.4. *The mothers of the Veda*: the meters; Nīlakaṇṭha: Gāyatrī, Sāvitrī, and Sarasvatī.
8. *Emblazoned with a moon*: or with *soma*, reminding us that Rāma is a brahmin.

183.16. *Ārṣṭiṣeṇa*: I am at a loss to explain the presence of this seer; perhaps Ārṣṭiṣeṇa is to be taken as a patronymic of Rāma.

184.6. *As though it were morning*: *prabhātasamaya iva*: how to explain this (doubtful) *iva*?
12. *Created by Viśvakarman*: so I take *viśvakṛtam*.

186.12. *We persuaded you to take up arms*: viz., when his father Jamadagni has been killed by Kārtavīrya(s).
23. *Ṛcīka*: Rāma's grandfather.

187.27. *The Pond of Rāma*: probably Samantapañcaka.
35. *Dry for eight months*: *nāṣṭamāsikī*: "not there for eight months."

189.4. *Determined upon my death*: *asmadvadhārtham niścitya*: as there is no particular reason for Drupada to hate Bhīṣma, this is probably borrowed from Drupada's effort to beget a son to kill Droṇa: 1.155 (I, 316 ff.).
5. *A man-child who is a woman*: *strīpumān*.

191.13. *My powerful relation*: *sambandhin*: in other words, Drupada still thinks of Hiraṇyavarman as his brother-in-law.
15. *He spoke [in public]*, etc.: the *ślokas* have to be punctuated as follows: in 13–17 Drupada speaks in private to his wife (cf. vs. 11 *rahite*). In 18–19 he speaks in public as stated in vs. 20.

192.10. *Offering worship*: one of the rare times that a personage in the *MBh.* is engaged in theistic worship.
22. *Śikhaṇḍī*: *Śikhaṇḍī sā*, to be taken as a feminine.

193.28. *Reconducting his daughter: nivartya tanayām*, i.e., into the marital state.

194.10. *An ordinary man: itaro janaḥ.*

195.15. *Ordinary men: pṛthagjanam.*

197.10. *Stagnating: stimitā*: so?
11. *Torrential wits: buddhinisravam.*

Concordance of Critical Edition and Bombay Edition

The concordance is of the chapters only. It is based on the marginal references marked B in the critical edition, and has been cross-checked with the *Concordanz* in Jacobi (1903). Since its purpose is principally to facilitate comparison with Sörensen, the "Roy" and Dutt translations, and other reference books that quote chapters by their number in B., the verse numbers of the Calcutta edition have not been collated: these numbers and their concordance with the verse numbers of the critical edition are only retrievable from the marginal figures marked C. in the critical edition, and, mostly, from the C. figures in my summaries.

Be it noted that the concordance, where it shows deletions [indicated by ( ), e.g., (22)], only shows deletions of chapters; it does not show the very numerous deletions of verses. For information on verse deletions the only recourse is the *apparatus* of the critical edition.

Critical Edition	Bombay
4. 1–5	1–5
	(6)
6–31	7–32
32	33 (..)–34 (..)
33–37	35–39
38	40–43
39–62	44–67
63–64	68
64	69
65–67	70–72
5. 1–44	1–44
	(45)
45–61	46–62

Critical Edition	Bombay
62	63–64
63–148	65–150
149	151–52
150–56	153–59
157	160 (..)
	160 (..)
158–64	161–67
165	168
166	168–69
167–71	170–74
172–73	175
174–75	176
177–79	178
180–97	179–96

Index of Proper Names*

*Only the proper names occurring in the text of the translation are indexed; those occurring in the introductions, summaries, and notes are not.